COMPUTATIONAL FLUID DYNAMICS - BASIC INSTRUMENTS AND APPLICATIONS IN SCIENCE

Edited by **Adela Ionescu**

Computational Fluid Dynamics - Basic Instruments and Applications in Science
http://dx.doi.org/10.5772/intechopen.68688
Edited by Adela Ionescu

Contributors
Muhammad Aziz, Arif Darmawan, Dwika Budianto, Koji Tokimatsu, Jorge Flores-Velazquez, Abraham Jesus Arzeta-Rios, Waldo Ojeda Bustamante, Teodoro Espinosa-Solares, Sham Rane, Ahmed Kovacevic, Nikola Stosic, Ian Smith, Luis Zárate, Mario Edgar Cordero Sánchez, Sebastián Uribe, Reyna Natividad, Ever Peralta Reyes, Alejandro Regalado-Méndez, Blanca Bermúdez, Alejandro Rangel-Huerta, W. Fermín Guerrero Sánchez, José David Alanís Urquieta, Ramasamy Marappa Gounder, Sampath Emani, Andrej Prošek, Matjaž Leskovar, Boštjan Končar, Omar M. Basha, Badie I. Morsi, Bruno Carpentieri, Carlos Borrego, Vera Rodrigues, Sandra Rafael, Bruno Vicente, Sandra Sorte, Joana Leitão, Myriam Lopes, Ana Isabel Miranda, Giacomo Viccione, Altomare Corrado, Bonaventura Tagliafierro, Vittorio Bovolin, José Manuel Domínguez, Alejandro Jacobo Cabrera Crespo, Jong-Taek Oh, Chien Ba Nguyen, Aamir Shahzad, Muzamal Hussain, Nawaz Naeem, Maogang He, Guillaume Houzeaux, Marta Garcia-Gasulla, Ricard Borrell, Elie Hachem, Mariano Vázquez, Youssef Mesri, Dipl.-Ing. Jens Henrik Göbbert, Yvan Fournier, Vassili Karanassios, Hamid Badiei, Gordon Stubley, Ryan L Fitzgerald, Malanie Saddler

Published by InTech
Janeza Trdine 9, 51000 Rijeka, Croatia

Publishing Process Manager Martina Usljebrka
Technical Editor SPi Global
Cover InTech Design team

First published February, 2018
Printed in Croatia
Legal deposit, Croatia: National and University Library in Zagreb

Additional hard copies can be obtained from orders@intechopen.com

Computational Fluid Dynamics - Basic Instruments and Applications in Science, Edited by Adela Ionescu
p. cm.
Print ISBN 978-953-51-3790-0
Online ISBN 978-953-51-3791-7

For EU product safety concerns:
IN TECH d.o.o., Prolaz Marije Krucifikse Kozulić 3, 51000 Rijeka, Croatia,
info@intechopen.com or visit our website at intechopen.com.

Meet the editor

Dr. Adela Ionescu is a lecturer at the University of Craiova, Romania. She received her PhD degree from the Polytechnic University of Bucharest, Romania. Her research focuses on development and implementation of new methods in the qualitative and computational analysis of differential equations and their applications. This includes constructing adequate models for approaching the study of different industrial phenomena from a dynamical system standpoint and also from a computational fluid dynamics standpoint. By its optimizing techniques, the aim of the modeling is to facilitate the high understanding of the experimental phenomena and to implement new methods, techniques, and processes. Currently, Dr. Ionescu is working in developing new analytical techniques for linearizing nonlinear dynamical systems, with subsequent applications in experimental cases. She has published six monographs and few scientific papers in high-impact journals. She is also a member of few scientific international associations and has attended more than 45 international conferences.

Contents

Preface

Computational fluid dynamics (CFD) is a much more challenging interdisciplinary field. It provides a qualitative (and sometimes even quantitative) prediction of fluid flows by means of mathematical modeling (by differential and partial differential equations), numerical methods (by specific discretization and solution techniques), and software tools (by solvers and pre and postprocessing appliances). The modern techniques allow the scientists to perform "numerical experiments," which mean computer simulations, in a "virtual flow laboratory."

The use of CFD on a large scale in all applied domains is rapidly justified if we look at the context "experiments vs. simulations." CFD gives an insight into flow patterns that are difficult, expensive, or impossible to study using traditional (experimental) techniques. In experiments, we are talking about a *quantitative description* of flow phenomena using experiments, and in simulations, we are talking about *quantitative predictions* of flow phenomena using CFD software. As a rule, CFD does not replace the measurements completely, but the amount of experimentation and the overall cost can be significantly reduced. CFD software is portable and easy to use and modify.

This book is the result of a careful selection of contributors in the field of CFD. It is divided into three sections according to the purpose and approaches used in the development of the contributions. The first section describes the "high-performance computing" (HPC) tools and their impact on CFD modeling. The discretization process for a model implies three basic stages: the mesh generation (decomposition into cells/elements), space discretization (approximation of spatial derivatives of the mathematical model), and time discretization (approximation of temporal derivatives). The five chapters of the first section draw attention to an up-to-date presentation of this context: high-order vs. low-order approximation and local time stepping vs. adaptive time stepping control. From preprocess (meshing) to postprocess (visualization), through the simulation itself (assembly and iterative solvers), the section brings the reader to the world of recent solution techniques in what we call "iterative solution strategy."

The second section is dedicated to "CFD models for local and large-scale industrial phenomena." Two types of approaches are basically contained here: one concerns the adaptation from global to local scale, —e.g., the applications of CFD to study the climate changes and the adaptations to local scale. The second approach, very challenging, is the multiscale analysis. The eight chapters of this section draw attention to some approaches for different industrial "local-scale and multiscale models."

This type of analysis, where the same phenomenon is analyzed at different scales, can lead to better understanding of the phenomenon, and the analysis can be further used in optimization and to provide adequate scale-up methodologies. In fact, in this section, there are approaches to solve the "coupled problems," which imply a lot of mathematical and physical/ experimental problems. That is why the CFD simulations depend on few features: the choice of numerical algorithms and data structure, linear algebra tools (stopping criteria for iterative solvers), discretization parameters, and programming language.

In this section, an important class of models, the *mathematical models of multiphase flow processes*, is also exhibited. These are nonlinear models, coupled with partial differential equations. Analytical solutions are possible only for some simple cases. For most flow processes, which are of interest to a chemical engineer, the governing equations need to be solved numerically by means of computational fluid dynamics (CFD) enabling one to model and estimate the hydrodynamics of multiphase flow in process equipment. In these situations, CFD is the science of solving and analyzing momentum, mass and heat transfer, turbulence, chemical reactions, and associated phenomena using computational methods of conservation equations (mass, momentum, heat, and species mass).

The postprocessing analysis will depend on few aspects in these special cases of "coupled models": calculation of derived quantities (e.g., streamfunction and vorticity); calculation of integral parameters (lift, drag, and total mass); and visualization of 2D data (streamlines and color diagrams) and 3D data (isosurfaces and isovolumes). Finally, the systematic data analysis by means of statistic tools emphasizes the advantage of the methods and could provide adequate scale-up methodologies.

The third section is devoted to "CFD in numerical modeling approach for experimental cases." It contains four chapters, which emphasize on the numerical approach of the mathematical models associated to few experimental (industrial) cases. Here, the impact of the mathematical modeling in CFD is focused on comparing different numerical methods for solving a basic mathematical model in fluid dynamics (Navier-Stokes equations) is outlined. Second, the *influence of uncertainty* on CFD models is well exposed in a chapter dedicated to optimal statistical estimator (OSE) model for turbulent mixing flows. Turbulence modeling is a classical example in which *uncertainty* acts as a potential deficiency due to the lack of knowledge. Whether or not the results of a CFD simulation can be trusted depends on the degree of uncertainty and on the cumulative effect of various errors. *Errors* are defined as recognizable deficiencies due to some reasons. The chapter suggests that in the case when thousands of complex computer code runs are needed for the Monte Carlo statistical analysis, the OSE model can be used to replace the numerous CFD code simulations.

The other two chapters of the third section exhibit the utility of the mathematical models in constructing and validating CFD models. The application of CFD simulations in a high understanding of the crude oil fouling process on heat transfer surfaces is a good example. These chapters exhibit in a professional manner two basic stages in CFD: simplifying the governing equations of the mathematical model in order to reduce the computational effort and validation of CFD model, with its important parts—verifying the code to make sure that the numerical solutions are correct; comparing the results with available experimental data to check if the reality is represented accurately enough; performing sensitivity analysis and parametric study to assess the inherent uncertainty due to incomplete understanding of physical process; using different alternate models, geometries, and initial/boundary conditions; and reporting the findings, model limitations, and parameter settings.

It is expected that the collection of these chapters will enrich the state of the art in the CFD domain and its applications in a lot of fields. This collection provesthat CFD is a highly interdisciplinary research area, which lies at the interface of physics, engineering, applied mathematics, and computer science. All the main components of a CFD design cycle are presented here: the *human being* (analyst) who states the problem to be solved; *scientific knowledge* (models and methods) expressed mathematically; the *computercode* (software) that embodies this knowledge and provides detailed instructions (algorithms) for the *computer hardware* that performs the actual calculations; and the *human being* who inspects and interprets the simulation results.

Adela Ionescu
University of Craiova,
Romania

Section 1

The High Performance Computing and Impact on CFD Modeling

Chapter 1

High-Performance Computing: Dos and Don'ts

Guillaume Houzeaux, Ricard Borrell, Yvan Fournier,
Marta Garcia-Gasulla, Jens Henrik Göbbert,
Elie Hachem, Vishal Mehta, Youssef Mesri,
Herbert Owen and Mariano Vázquez

Additional information is available at the end of the chapter

http://dx.doi.org/10.5772/intechopen.72042

Abstract

Computational fluid dynamics (CFD) is the main field of computational mechanics that has historically benefited from advances in high-performance computing. High-performance computing involves several techniques to make a simulation efficient and fast, such as distributed memory parallelism, shared memory parallelism, vectorization, memory access optimizations, etc. As an introduction, we present the anatomy of supercomputers, with special emphasis on HPC aspects relevant to CFD. Then, we develop some of the HPC concepts and numerical techniques applied to the complete CFD simulation framework: from preprocess (meshing) to postprocess (visualization) through the simulation itself (assembly and iterative solvers).

Keywords: parallelization, high-performance computing, assembly, supercomputing, meshing, adaptivity, algebraic solvers, parallel I/O, visualization

1. Introduction to high-performance computing

1.1. Anatomy of a supercomputer

Computational fluid dynamics (CFD) simulations aim at solving more complex, more real, more detailed, and bigger problems. To achieve this, they must rely on high-performance computing (HPC) systems as it is the only environment where these kinds of simulations can be performed [1].

At the same time, HPC systems are becoming more and more complex and the hardware is exposing massive parallelism at all levels, making a challenge exploiting the resources.

In order to understand the concepts that are explained in the following sections, we explain briefly the different levels of parallelism available in a supercomputer. We do not aim at giving a full description or state of the art of the different architectures available in supercomputers, but a general overview of the most common approaches and concepts. First, we depict the different levels of hardware that form a supercomputer.

1.1.1. Hardware

Core/Central Processing Unit: We could consider a core as the first unit of computation, and a core is able to decode instructions and execute them. Here, within the core, we find the first and most low level of parallelism: the instruction-level parallelism. This kind of parallelism is offered by superscalar processors, and its main characteristic is that they can execute more than one instruction during a clock cycle. There are several developments that allow instruction-level parallelism such as pipelining, out-of-order execution, or multiple execution units. These techniques are the ones that allow to obtain instructions per cycle (IPC) higher than one. The exploitation of this parallelism relies mainly on the compiler and on the hardware units itself. Reordering of instructions, branch prediction, renaming or memory access optimization are some of the techniques that help to achieve a high level of instruction parallelism.

At this level, complementary to instruction-level parallelism, we can find data-level parallelism offered by vectorization. Vectorization allows to apply the same operation to multiple pieces of data in the context of a single instruction. The performance obtained by this kind of processors depends highly on the type of code that it is executing. Scientific applications or numerical simulations are often codes that can benefit from this kind of processors as the kind of computation they must perform usually consists in applying the same operation to large pieces of independent data. We briefly see how this technique can accelerate the assembly process in Section 4.4.

Socket/Chip: Coupling of several cores in the same integrated circuit is a common approach and is usually referred as multicore or many-core processors (depending on the amount of cores it aggregates, one name or the other is used). One of the main advantages is that the different cores share some levels of cache. The shared caches can improve the reuse of data by different threads running on cores in the same socket, with the added advantage of the cores being close on the same die (higher clock rates, less signal degradation, less power).

Having several cores in the same socket allows to have thread-level parallelism, as each different core can run a different sequence of instructions in parallel but having access to the same data. Section 4.2 studies this parallelism through the use of OpenMP programming interface.

Accelerators/GPUs: Accelerators are a specialized hardware that includes hundreds of computing units that can work in parallel to solve specific calculations over wide pieces of data. They include its own memory. Accelerators need a central processing unit (CPU) to process the main code and off-load the specific kernels to them. To exploit the massive parallelism available within the GPUs, the application kernels must be rewritten. The dominant programming language is OpenCL that is cross-platform, while other alternatives are vendor dependent (e.g., CUDA [2]).

http://dx.doi.org/10.5772/intechopen.72042

Node: A computational node can include one or several sockets and accelerators along with main memory and I/O. A computational node is, therefore, the minimum autonomous computation unit as it includes cores to compute, memory to store data, and network interface to communicate. The main classification of shared memory nodes is based on the kind of memory access they have: uniform memory access (UMA) or [3] nonuniform memory access (NUMA). In UMA systems, the memory system is common to all the processors and this means that there is just one memory controller that can only serve one petition at the same time; when having several cores issuing memory requests, this becomes a bottleneck. On the other hand, NUMA nodes partition the memory among the different processors; although the main memory is seen as a whole, the access time depends on the memory location relative to the processor issuing the request.

Within the node, also thread-level parallelism can be exploited as the memory is shared among the different cores inside the node.

Cluster/Supercomputer: A supercomputer is an aggregation of nodes connected through a high-speed network with a specialized topology. We can find different network topologies (i.e., how the nodes are connected), such as 2D or 3D Torus or Hypercube. The kind of network topology will determine the number of hoops that a message will need to reach its destination or communication bottlenecks. A supercomputer usually includes a distributed file system to offer a unified view of the cluster from the user point of view.

The parallelism that can be used at the supercomputer level is a distributed memory approach. In this case, different processes can run in different nodes of the cluster and communicate through the interconnect network when necessary. We go through the main techniques of such parallelism applied to the assembly and iterative solvers in Sections 4.1 and 5.2, respectively.

Figure 1 shows the different levels of hardware of a supercomputer presented previously, together with the associated memory latency and size, as well as the type of parallelism to

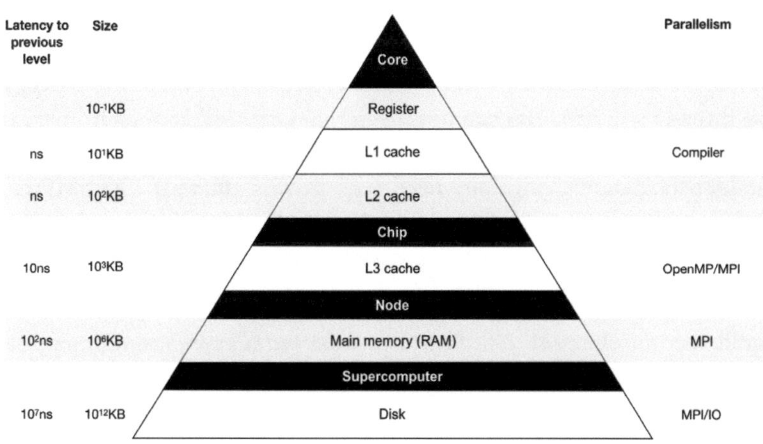

Figure 1. Anatomy of a supercomputer. Memory latency and size (left) and parallelism (right) to exploit the different levels of hardware (middle).

exploit them. The numbers are expressed in terms of orders of magnitude and pretend to be only orientative as they are system dependent.

We have seen all the computational elements that form a supercomputer from a hierarchical point of view. All these levels that have been explained also include different levels of storage that are organized in a hierarchy too. Starting from the core, we can find the registers where the operands of the instructions that will be executed are stored. Usually included also in the core or CPU, we can find the first level of cache and this is the smallest and fastest one; it is common that it is divided in two parts: one to store instructions (L1i) and another one to store data (L1d). The second level of cache (L2) is bigger, still fast, and placed close to the core too. A common configuration is that the third level of cache (L3) is shared at the socket and L1 and L2 private to the core, but any combination is possible.

The main memory can be of several gigabytes (GB) and much slower than the caches. It is shared among the different processors of the node, but as we have explained before it can have a nonuniform memory access (NUMA), meaning that it is divided in pieces among the different sockets. At the supercomputer level, we find the disk that can store petabytes of data.

1.1.2. *Software*

We have seen an overview of the hardware available within a supercomputer and the different levels of parallelism that it exposes. The different levels of the HPC software stack are designed to help applications exploit the resources of a supercomputer (i.e., operating system, compiler, runtime libraries, and job scheduler). We focus on the parallel programming models because they are close to the application and specifically on OpenMP and MPI because they are the standard "de facto" at the moment in HPC environments.

OpenMP: It is a parallel programming model that supports C, C++, and Fortran [4]. It is based on compiler directives that are added to the code to enable shared memory parallelism. These directives are translated by the compiler supporting OpenMP into calls to the corresponding parallel runtime library. OpenMP is based on a fork-join model, meaning that just one thread will be executing the code until it reaches a parallel region; at this point, the additional threads will be created (*fork*) to compute in parallel and at the end of the parallel region all the threads will *join*. The communication in OpenMP is done implicit through the shared memory between the different threads, and the user must annotate for the different variables the kind of data sharing they need (i.e., private, shared). OpenMP is a standard defined by a nonprofit organization: OpenMP Architecture Review Board (ARB). Based on this definition, different commercial or open source compilers and runtime libraries offer their own implementation of the standard.

The loop parallelism in OpenMP had been the most popular in scientific applications. The main reason is that it fits perfectly the kind of code structure in these applications: loops. And this allows a very easy and straightforward parallelization of the majority of codes.

Since OpenMP 4.0, the standard also includes task parallelism which together with dependences offers a more flexible and powerful way of expressing parallelism. But these advantages have a cost: the ease of programming. Scientific programmers still have difficulties in expressing parallelism with tasks because they are used at seeing the code as a single flow with some parallel regions in it.

In Section 4.2, we describe how loop and task parallelism can be applied to the algebraic system assembly.

MPI: The message passing interface (MPI) is a parallel programming model based on an API for explicit communication [5]. It can be used in distributed memory systems and shared memory environments. The standard is defined by the MPI Forum, and different implementations of this standard can be found. In the execution model of MPI, all the processes will run the *main()* function in parallel. In general, MPI follows a single program multiple data (SPMD) approach although it allows to run different binaries under the same MPI environment (multicode coupling [6]).

1.2. HPC concepts

The principal metrics used in HPC are the second (sec) for time measurements, the floating point operation (flop) for counting arithmetic operations, and the binary term (byte) to quantify memory. A broad range of unit prefixes are required; for example, the time spent on individual operations is generally expressed in terms of nanoseconds (ns), the computing power of a high-end supercomputer is expressed in terms of petaflops (10^{15} flop/sec), and the main memory of a computing node is quantified in terms of gigabytes (GB). There are also more specific metrics, for example, *cache misses* are used to count the data fetched from the main memory to the cache, and the IPC index refers to the instructions per clock cycle carried out by a CPU.

The principal measurements used to quantify the parallel performance are the load balance, the strong speedup, and the weak speedup. The load balance measures the quality of the workload distribution among the computing resources engaged for a computational task. If $time_i$ denotes the time spent by process i, out of n_p processes, on the execution of such parallel task, the load balance can be expressed as the average time, $ave_i(time_i)$, divided by the maximum time, $\max_i(time_i)$. This value represents also the ratio between the resources effectively used with respect to the resources engaged to carry out the task. In other words, the load balance $\in [0, 1]$ is equivalent to the efficiency achieved on the usage of the resources:

$$\text{efficiency} := \frac{\sum_i time}{n_{core}\ \max_i(time_i)} = \frac{\text{ave}_i(time_i)}{\max_i(time_i)} =: \text{load balance.}$$

Another common measurement is the strong speedup that measures the relative acceleration achieved at increasing the computing resources used to execute a specific task. If $T(p)$ is the time achieved to carry out the task under consideration using p parallel processes, the strong speedup achieved at increasing the number of processes from p_1 to p_2 $(p_1 < p_2)$ is

$$\text{strong speedup} := \frac{T(p_1)}{T(P_2)},$$

the ideal one being $p2/p1$. The parallel efficiency is defined as:

$$\text{parallel efficiency} := \frac{T(p_1)p_2}{T(p_2)p_1}.$$

Finally, the weak speedup measures the relative variation on the computing time when the workload and the computing resources are increased proportionally. If $T(n,p)$ represents the time spent on the resolution of a problem of size n with p parallel processes, the weak speedup at increasing the number of parallel processes from p_1 to p_2 (and thus multiplying the problem size by $\frac{p_2}{p_1}$) is defined as:

$$\text{weak speedup} := \frac{T\left(n\frac{p_1}{p_2}\right)p_2}{T(p_2)p_1}.$$

In the CFD context, the weak speedup is measured at increasing proportionally the mesh size and the computational resources engaged on the simulation. The ideal result for the speedup would be 1; however, this is hardly possible because the complexity of some parts of the problem, such as the solution of the linear system, increases above the linearity (see Section 5.4 on domain decomposition (DD) preconditioners). A second degradation factor is the communication costs, necessary to transfer data between parallel processes in a distributed memory context. This is especially relevant for the strong speedup tests: the overall workload is kept constant, and therefore, the workload per parallel process reduces at increasing the computing resources; consequently, while the computing time reduces, the overhead produced by the communications grows.

While the strong and weak speedups measure the relative performance of a piece of code by varying the number of processes, the load balance is a measure of the proper exploitation of a particular amount of resources. An unbalanced computation can be perfectly scalable if the dominant part is properly distributed on the successive partitions. This situation can be observed in **Figure 9** from Section 4. It shows the strong scalability and the timings for two different parallel methods for matrix assembly. The faster method is not the one that shows better strong scaling, and in this case, it is the one that guarantees a better load balance between the different parallel processes.

Nonetheless, a balanced and scalable code does not mean yet an optimal code in terms of performance. The aforementioned measurements account for the use of parallel resources but do not say anything about how fast the code is at performing a task. In particular, if we consider a sequential code to be parallelized, the more efficient it is, the harder it will be to achieve good scalability since the communication overheads will be more relevant. Indeed, "*the easiest way of making software scalable is to make it sequentially inefficient*" [7].

CFD is considered a memory-bounded application, and this means that sequential performance is limited by the cost of fetching data from the main to the cache memory, rather than by the cost of performing the computations on the CPU registers. The reason is that the sparse operations, which dominate CFD computations, have a low arithmetic intensity (flops/byte), that is, few operations are performed for each byte moved from the main memory to the cache memory.

http://dx.doi.org/10.5772/intechopen.72042

Therefore, the sequential performance of CFD codes is mostly determined by the management of the memory transfers. A strategy to reduce data transfers is to maximize the data locality. This means to maximize the reuse of the data uploaded to the cache by: (1) using the maximum percentage of the bytes contained in each block (referred as *cache line*) uploaded to the cache, known as spatial locality, or (2) reuse data that have been previously used and kept into the cache, known as temporal locality. An example illustrates data locality in Section 4.4.

1.2.1. Challenges

Moore's law says: *The number of transistors in a dense integrated circuit doubles approximately every two years*. This law formulated in 1965 not only proved to be true, but it also translated in doubling the computing capacity of the cores every 24 months. This was possible not only by increasing the number of transistors but by increasing the frequency at which they worked. But, in the last years, it has come what computer scientists call *The End of Free Lunch*. This refers to the fact that the performance of a single core is not being increased at the same pace. There are three main issues that explain this:

The memory wall: It refers to the gap in performance that exists between processor and memory [8] (CPU speed improved at an annual rate of 55% up to 2000, while memory speed only improved at 10%). The main method for bridging the gap has been to use caches between the processor and the main memory, increasing the sizes of these caches and adding more levels of caching. But memory bandwidth is still a problem that has not been solved.

The ILP wall: Increasing the number of transistors in a chip as Moore's law says is used in some cases to increase the number of functional units, allowing a higher level of instruction-level parallelism (ILP) because there are more specialized units or several units of the same kind (i.e., two floating point units that can process two floating point operations in parallel). But finding enough parallelism in a single instruction stream to keep a high-performance single-core processor busy is becoming more and more complex. One of the techniques to overcome this has been hyper-threading. This consists in a single physical core to appear as two (or more) to the operating system. Running two threads will allow to exploit the instruction-level parallelism.

The power wall: As we said, not only the number of transistors was increasing but also the frequency was increasing. But there exists a technological limit to surface power density, and for this reason, clock frequency cannot scale up freely any more. Not only the amount of power that must be supplied would not be assumable, but the chip would not be able to dissipate the amount of heat generated. To address this issue, the trend is to develop more simple and specialized hardware and aggregate more of them (i.e., Xeon Phi, GPUs).

Nevertheless, computer scientists still want to achieve the Exascale machine, but they cannot rely on increasing the performance of a single core as they used to. The turnaround is that the number of cores per chip and per node is growing quite fast in the last years, along with the number of nodes in a cluster. This is pushing the research into more complex memory hierarchies and networks topologies.

Once the Exascale machines are available, the challenge is to have applications that can make an efficient use and scale there. The increase in complexity of the hardware is a challenge for scientific application developers because their codes must be efficient in more complex hardware and address a high level of parallelism at both shared and distributed memory levels. Moreover, rewriting and restructuring existing codes is not always feasible; in some cases, the amount of lines of code is hundreds of thousands and, in others, the original authors of those codes are not around anymore.

At this point, only a unified effort and a codesign approach will enable Exascale applications. Scientists in charge of HPC applications need to trust in the parallel middleware and runtimes available to help them exploit the parallel resources. The complexity and variety of the hardware will not allow anymore the manual tuning of the codes for each different architecture.

1.3. Anatomy of a CFD simulation

A CFD simulation can be divided into four main phases: (1) mesh generation, (2) setup, (3) solution, and (4) analysis and visualization. Ideally, these phases would be carried out consecutively, but, in practice, they are interleaved until a satisfactory solution is achieved. For example, on the solution analysis, the user may realize that the integration time was not enough or that the quality of the mesh was too poor to capture the physical phenomena being tackled. This would force to return to the solution or to the mesh generation phase, respectively. Indeed, supported by the continued increase of the computing resources available, CFD simulation frameworks have evolved toward a runtime adaptation of the numerical and computational strategies in accordance with the ongoing simulation results. This dynamicity includes mesh adaptivity, in situ analysis and visualization, and runtime strategies to optimize the parallel performance. These mechanisms make simulation frameworks more robust and efficient.

The following sections of this chapter outline the numerical methods and computational aspects related with the aforementioned phases. Section 2 is focused on meshing and adaptivity, and Section 3 on the partitioning required for the parallelization. Sections 4 and 5 focus on the two main parts of the solution phase, that is, the assembly and the solution of the algebraic system. Finally, Section 6 is focused on the I/O and visualization issues.

2. Meshing and adaptivity

Mesh adaptation is one of the key technologies to reduce both the computational cost and the approximation errors of PDE-based numerical simulations. It consists in introducing local modifications into the computational mesh in such a way that the calculation effort to reach a certain level of error is minimized. In other words, adaptation strategies maximize the accuracy of the obtained solution for a given computational budget. Three main components constitute the mesh adaptation process: error estimators to derive and make decisions where and when mesh adaptation is required and remeshing mechanics to change the density and orientation of mesh entities. Last but not least, dynamic load balancing is to ensure efficient computations on parallel systems. We develop the main ideas behind the first two concepts in the following subsections, and mesh partitioning and dynamic load balance are considered in Section 3.

2.1. Error estimators and adaptivity

The discretization of a continuous problem leads to an approximate solution more or less representative of the exact solution according to the care given to the numerical approximation and mesh resolution. Therefore, in order to be able to certify the quality of a given calculation, it is necessary to be able to estimate the discretization error—between this approximated solution, resulting for example from the application of the finite element (FE) or volume methods, and the exact (often unknown) solution of the continuous problem. This field of research has been the subject of much investigation since the mid-1970s. The first efforts focused on the a priori convergence properties of finite element methods to upper-bound the gap between the two solutions. Since a priori error estimate methods are often insufficient to ensure reliable estimation of the discretization error, new estimation methods called a posteriori are rather quickly preferred. Once the approximate solution has been obtained, it is then necessary to study and quantify its deviation from the exact solution. The error estimators of this kind provide information overall the computational domain, as well as a map of local contributions which is useful to obtain a solution satisfying a given precision by means of adaptive procedures. One of the most popular methods of this family is the error estimation based on averaging techniques, as those proposed in [9]. The popularity of these methods is mainly due to their versatile use in anisotropic mesh adaptation tools as a metric specifying the optimal mesh size and orientation with respect to the error estimation. An adapted mesh is then obtained by means of *local mesh modifications* to fit the prescribed metric specifications. This approach can lead to elements with large angles that are not suitable for finite element computations as reported in the general standard error analysis for which some regularity assumption on the mesh and on the exact solution should be satisfied. However, if the mesh is adapted to the solution, it is possible to circumvent this condition [10].

We focus now on anisotropic mesh adaptation driven by directional error estimators. The latter are based on the recovery of the Hessian of the finite element solution. The purpose is to achieve an optimal mesh minimizing the directional error estimator for a constant number of mesh elements. It allows, as shown in **Figure 2**, to refine/coarsen the mesh, stretch and orient the elements in such a way that, along the adaptation process, the mesh becomes aligned with the fine scales of the solution whose locations are unknown a priori. As a result of this, highly accurate solutions are obtained with a much lower number of elements.

More recently, estimation techniques have also been developed to evaluate the error committed on quantities of interest (e.g., drag, lift, shear, and heat flux) to the engineer. On this point, the current trend is to develop upper and lower bounds to delimit the observed physical quantity [11].

2.2. Parallel meshing and remeshing

The parallelization of mesh adaptation methods goes back to the end of the 1990s. The SPMD MPI-based paradigm has been adopted by the pioneering works [12–14]. The effectiveness of

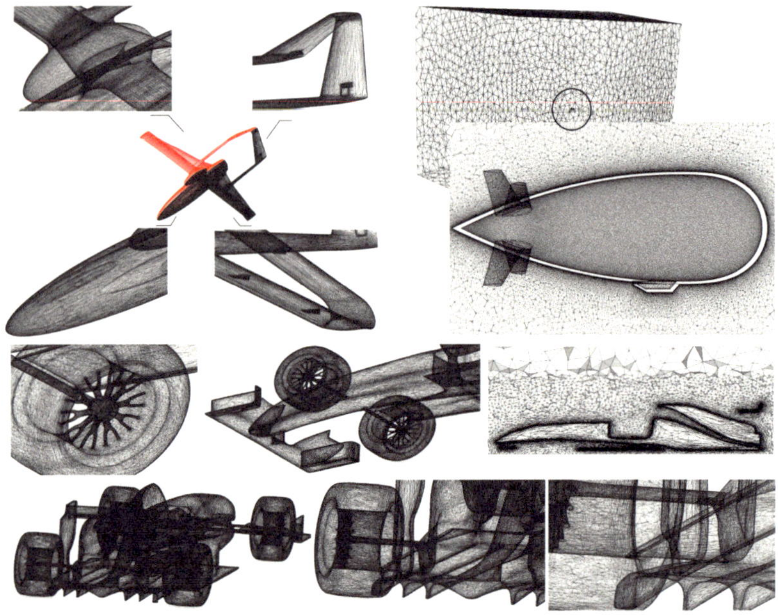

Figure 2. Meshing and remeshing of 3D complex geometries for CFD applications: Airship (top left), drone (top right) and F1 vehicle (bottom).

these methods depends on the repartitioning algorithms used and on how the interfaces between subdomains are managed. Indeed, mesh repartitioning is the key process for most of today's parallel mesh adaptation methods [15]. Starting from a partitioned mesh into multiple subdomains, remeshing operations are performed using a sequential mesh adaptator on each subdomain with an extra treatment of the interfaces. Two main approaches are considered in the literature: (1) It is an iterative one. At the first iteration, remeshing is performed concurrently on each processor, while the interfaces between subdomains are locked to avoid any modification in the sequential remeshing kernel. Then, a new partitioning is calculated to move the interfaces and remesh them at the next iteration. The algorithm iterates until all items have been remeshed (**Figure 3**). (2) The second approach consists in handling the interfaces by considering a complementary data structure to manage remeshing on remote mesh entities.

The first approach is preferred because of its high efficiency and full code-reusing capability for sequential remeshing kernels. However, hardware architectures go to be more dense (more cores per compute node) than before to fit the energy constraints fixed as a *sine qua none* condition to target Exascale supercomputers. Indeed, it is assumed that the nodes of a future Exascale system will contain thousands of cores per node. Therefore, it is important to rethink meshing algorithms in this new context of high levels of parallelism and using fine-grain parallel programming models that exploit the memory hierarchy. However, unstructured data-based applications are hard to parallelize effectively on shared-memory architectures for reasons described in [16].

It is clear that one of the main challenges to meet is the efficiency of anisotropic adaptive mesh methods on the modern architectures. New scalable techniques, such as asynchronous, hierarchical

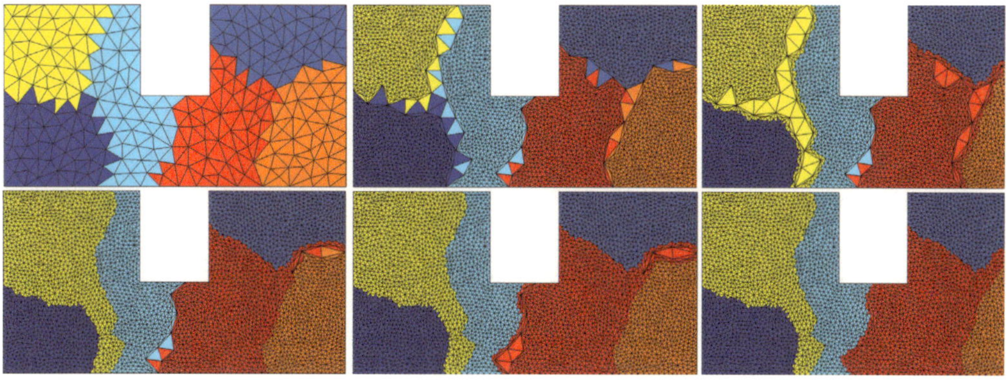

Figure 3. Iterative parallel remeshing steps on a 2D distributed mesh.

and communication avoiding algorithms, are recognized today to bring more efficiency to linear algebra kernels and explicit solvers. Investigating the application of such algorithms to mesh adaptation is a promising path to target modern architectures. Before going further on algorithmic aspects, another challenge arises when considering the efficiency and scalability analysis of mesh adaptation algorithms. Indeed, the unstructured and dynamic nature of mesh adaptation algorithms leads to imbalance the initial workload. Unfortunately, the standard metrics to measure the scalability of parallel algorithms are based on either a fixed mesh size for strong scalability analysis or a fixed mesh size by CPU for weak scalability.

2.3. Dynamic load balancing

In the finite element point of view, the problem to solve is subdivided into subproblems and the computational domain into subdomains. To adapt the mesh, an error estimator [17] is computed for each subdomain. According to the derived error estimator, and under the constraint of a given number of desired elements in the new adapted mesh, an optimal mesh is generated.

The constraint could be considered as local to each subdomain. In this case, solving the error estimate problem is straightforward. Indeed, all computations are local and no need to exchange data between processors. Another advantage to consider a local constraint is the possibility to generate a new mesh with the same number of elements per processor. This allows avoiding heavy load balancing cost after each mesh adaptation. However, this approach tends toward an overestimate of the mesh density on subdomains where flow activity is almost neglected. From a scaling point of view, this approach leads to a weak scalability model for which the problem size grows linearly with respect to the number of processors.

To derive a strong scalability model, which refers in general to parallel performance for fixed problem size, the constraint on the number of elements for the new generated mesh should be global. The global number of elements over the entire domain is distributed with respect to the mesh density prescribed by the error estimator. This is a good hard scalability model that leads to a quite performance analysis. However, reload balancing is needed after each mesh adaptation stage. The parallel behavior of the mesh adaptation is very close to the serial one and the error analysis still the same. For these reasons, this model is more relevant than the former one; nevertheless, we should investigate new efficient load balancing algorithms (see Section 3) able to take into account the error estimator prescription that will be derived.

3. Partitioning

The common strategy for the parallelization of CFD applications, to run on distributed memory systems, consists of a domain decomposition: the mesh that discretizes the simulation domain is partitioned into disjoint subsets of elements/cells, or disjoint sets of nodes, referred to as subdomains, as illustrated by **Figure 4**.

Then, each subdomain is assigned to a parallel process which carries out all the geometrical and algebraic operations corresponding to that part of the domain and the associated components of the defined fields (velocity, pressure, etc.). Therefore, both the algebraic and geometric partitions are aligned. For example, the matrices expressing the linear couplings are distributed in such a way that each parallel process holds the entries associated with the couplings generated on its subdomain. As shown in Section 4.1, there are different options to carry out this partition, which depend on how the subdomains are coupled at their interfaces.

Some operations, like the sparse matrix vector product (SpMV) or the norms, require communications between parallel processes. In the first case, these are related to couplings at the subdomain interfaces, so are point-to-point communications between processes corresponding to neighboring subdomains. Indeed, a mesh partition requires the subsequent generation of communication scheme to carry out operations like the SpMV. On the other hand, for other parallel operations like the norm, a unique value is calculated by adding contributions from all the parallel processes; these are solved by means of a collective reduction operations and do not require a communication scheme.

Two properties are desired for a mesh partition, good balance of the resulting workload distribution and minimal communication requirements. However, in a CFD code, different types of operations coexist, acting on fields of different mesh dimensions like elements, faces or nodes. This situation hinders the definition of a unique partition suitable for all of them, thus damaging the load balance of the whole code. For example, in the finite element (FE) method,

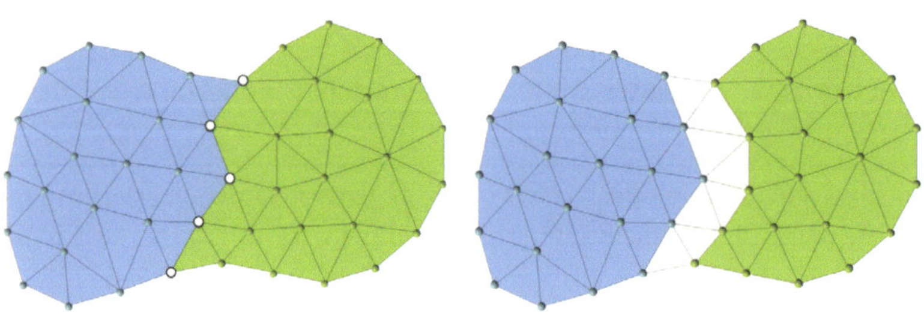

Figure 4. Partitioning into: (left) disjoint sets of elements. In white, interface nodes; and (right) disjoint sets of nodes. In white, halo elements.

the matrix assembly requires a good balance of the mesh elements, while the solution of the linear system requires a good distribution of the mesh nodes. In Section 4.3, we present a strategy to solve this trade-off by applying a runtime dynamic load balance for the assembly. Also, when dealing with hybrid meshes, the target balance should take into account the relative weights of the elements, which can in practice be difficult to estimate. Regarding the communication costs, these are proportional to the size of the subdomain interfaces, and therefore, we target partitions minimizing them.

The two main options for mesh partitioning are the *topological approach*, based on partitioning the graph representing the adjacency relations between mesh elements, and the *geometrical approach*, which defines the partition from the location of the elements on the domain.

Mesh partitioning is traditionally addressed by means of graph partitioning, which is a well-studied NP-complete problem generally addressed by means of multilevel heuristics composed of three phases: coarsening, partitioning, and uncoarsening. Different variants of them have been implemented in publicly available libraries including parallel versions like METIS [18], ZOLTAN [19] or SCOTCH [20]. These topological approaches not only balance the number of elements across the subdomains but also minimize subdomains' interfaces. However, they present limitations on the parallel performance and on the quality of the solution at growing the number of parallel processes performing the partition. This lack of scalability makes graph-based partitioning a potential bottleneck for large-scale simulations.

Geometric partitioning techniques obviate the topological interaction between mesh elements and perform its partition according to their spatial distribution; typically, space filling curve (SFC) is used for this purpose. A SFC is a continuous function used to map a multidimensional space into a one-dimensional space with good locality properties, that is, it tries to preserve the proximity of elements in both spaces. The idea of geometric partitioning using SFC is to map the mesh elements into a 1D space and then easily divide the resulting segment into equally weighted subsegments. A significant advantage of the SFC partitioning is that it can be computed very fast and does not present bottlenecks for its parallelization [21]. While the load balance of the resulting partitions can be guaranteed, the data transfer between the resulting subdomains, measured by means of edge cuts in the graph partitioning approach, cannot be explicitly measured and thus neither minimized.

Adaptive Mesh Refinement algorithms (see Section 2) can generate imbalance on the parallelization. This can be mitigated by migrating elements between neighboring subdomains [15]. However, at some point, it may be more efficient to evaluate a new partition and migrate the simulation results to it. In order to minimize the cost of this migration, we aim to maximize the intersection between the old and new subdomain for each parallel process, and this can be better controlled with geometric partitioning approaches.

4. Assembly

In the finite element method, the assembly consists of a loop over the elements of the mesh, while it consists of a loop over cells or faces in the case of the finite volume method. We study the parallelization of such assembly process for distributed and shared memory parallelism, based on MPI and OpenMP programming models, respectively. Then, we briefly introduce some HPC optimizations. In the following, to respect tradition, we refer to elements in the FE context and to cells in the FV context.

4.1. Distributed memory parallelization using MPI

According to the partitioning described in the previous section, there exist three main ways of assembling the local matrices $\mathbf{A}^{(i)}$ of each subdomain Ω_i, as illustrated in **Figure 5**. The choice for one or another depends on the discretization method used, on the parallel data structures required by the algebraic solvers (Section 5.2), but also sometimes on mysterious personal or historical choices. Let us consider the example of **Figure 5**.

Partial row matrix. Local matrices can be made of partial rows (square matrices) or full rows (rectangular matrices). The first option is natural in the finite element context, where partitioning consists in dividing the mesh into disjoint element sets for each MPI process, and where only interface nodes are duplicated. In this case, the matrix rows of the interface nodes of neighboring subdomains are only partial, as its coefficients come from element integrations, as illustrated in **Figure 5** (1) by matrices $A_{33}^{(1)}$ and $A_{33}^{(2)}$. In next section, we show how one can take advantage of this format to perform the main operation of iterative solvers, namely the sparse matrix vector product (SpMV).

Full row matrix. The full row matrix consists in assigning rows exclusively to one MPI process. In order to obtain the complete coefficients of the rows of interface nodes, two options are

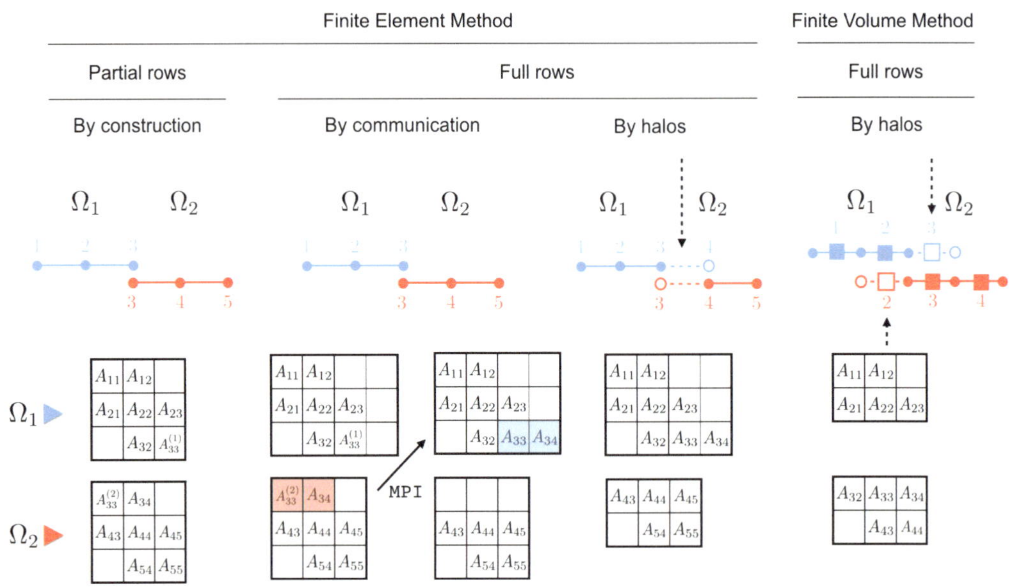

Figure 5. Finite element and cell-centered finite volume matrix assembly techniques. From left to right: (1) FE: Partial rows, (2) FE: Full rows using communications, (3) FE: Full rows using halo elements, and (4) FV: Full rows using halo cells.

available in the FE context, as illustrated by the middle examples of **Figure 5**: (1) by communicating the missing contributions of the coefficients between neighboring subdomains through MPI messages and (2) by introducing halo elements. The first option involves additional communications, while the second option duplicates the element integration on halo elements.

In the first case, referring to the example of **Figure 5** (2), the full row of node 3 is obtained by communicating coefficients $A_{33}^{(2)}$ from subdomain Ω_2 to Ω_1. If the full row is obtained through the introduction of halo elements, a halo element is necessary to fully assemble the row of node 3 in subdomain 1 and the row of node 4 in subdomain 2, as illustrated in **Figure 5** (3).

The relative performance of partial and full row matrices depends on the size of the halos, involving more memory and extra computation, compared to the cost of additional MPI communications. Note that open-source algebraic solvers (e.g., MAPHYS [22], PETSC [23]) admit the first, second or both options and perform the communications internally if required.

In cell-centered FV methods, the unknowns are located in the cells. Therefore, halo cells are also necessary to fully assemble the matrix coefficients, as illustrated by **Figure 5** (4). This is the option selected in practice in FV codes, although a communication could be used to obtain the full row format without introducing halos on both sides (only one side would be enough). In fact, let us imagine that subdomain 1 does not hold the halo cell 3. To obtain the full row for cell 2, a communication could be used to pass coefficient A_{23} from subdomain 2 to subdomain 1.

Partial vs. full row matrix:

Load balance. As far as load balance is concerned, the partial row method is the one which a priori enables one to control the load balance of the assembly, as elements are not duplicated. On the other hand, in the full row method, the number of halo elements depends greatly upon the partition. In addition, the work on these elements is duplicated and thus limits the scalability of the assembly: for a given mesh, the relative number of halo elements with respect to interior elements increases with the number of subdomains.

Hybrid meshes. In the FE context, should the work load per element be perfectly predicted, the load balance would only depend on the partitioner efficiency (see Section 3). However, to obtain such a prediction of the work load, one should know the exact relative cost of assembling each and every type of element of the hybrid mesh (hexahedra, pyramids, prisms, and tetrahedra). This is a priori impossible, as this cost not only depends on the number of operations, but also on the memory access patterns, which are unpredictable.

High-order methods. When considering high-order approximations, the situations of the FE and FV methods differ. In the first case, the additional degrees of freedom (DOF) appearing in the matrix are confined to the elements. Thus, only the number of interface nodes increases with respect to the same number of elements with a first-order approximation. In the case of the FV method, high-order methods are generally obtained by introducing successive layer of halos, thus reducing the scalability of the method.

Sparse matrix vector product. As mentioned earlier, the main operation of Krylov-based iterative solvers is the SpMV. We see in next section that the partial row and full row matrices lead to different communication orders and patterns.

4.2. Shared memory parallelization using OpenMP

The following is explained in the FE context but can be translated straightforwardly to the FV context. Finite element assembly consists in computing element matrices and right-hand sides ($\mathbf{A}^e$ and $\mathbf{b}^e$) for each element e, and assembling them into the local matrices and RHS of each MPI process i, namely $\mathbf{A}^{(i)}$ and $\mathbf{b}^{(i)}$. From the point of view of each MPI process, the assembly can thus be idealized as in Algorithm 1.

Algorithm 1 Matrix Assembly in each MPI partition i.

1: **for** elements e **do**

2: Gather: copy global arrays to element arrays.

3: Computation: element matrix and RHS $\mathbf{A}^e$, $\mathbf{b}^e$.

4: Scatter: assemble $\mathbf{A}^e$, $\mathbf{b}^e$ into $\mathbf{A}^{(i)}$, $\mathbf{b}^{(i)}$.

5: **end for**

OpenMP pragmas can be used to parallelize Algorithm 1 quite straightforwardly, as we will see in a moment. So why this shared memory parallelism has been having little success in CFD codes?

Amdahl's law states that the scalability of a parallel algorithm is limited by the sequential kernels of a code. When using MPI, most of the computational kernels are parallel by construction, as they consist of loops over local meshes entities such as elements, nodes, and faces, even though scalability is obviously limited by communications. One example of possible sequential kernel is the coarse grain solver described in Section 5.4. On the other hand, parallelization with OpenMP is incremental and explicit, making remaining sequential kernels a limiting factor for the scalability as stated by Amdahl's law. This explains, in part, the reluctance of CFD code developers to rely on the loop parallelism offered by OpenMP. There exists another reason, which lies in the difficulty in maintaining large codes using this parallel programming, as any new loop introduced in a code should be parallelized to circumvent the so-true Amdahl's law. As an example, Alya code [24] has more than 1000 element loops.

However, the situation is changing, for two main reasons. First, nowadays, supercomputers offer a great variety of architectures, with many cores on nodes (e.g., Xeon Phi). Thus, shared memory parallelism is gaining more and more attention as OpenMP offers more flexibility to parallel programming. In fact, sequential kernels can be parallelized at the shared memory level using OpenMP: one example is once more the coarse solve of iterative solvers; another example is the possibility of using dynamic load balance on shared memory nodes, as explained in [25] and introduced in Section 4.3.

As mentioned earlier, the parallelization of the assembly has traditionally been based on loop parallelism using OpenMP. Two main characteristics of this loop have led to different algorithms in the literature. On the one hand, there exists a *race condition*. The race conditions comes from the fact that different OpenMP threads can access the same degree of freedom coefficient when performing the scatter of element matrix and RHS, in step 4 of Algorithm 1. On the other hand, spatial locality must be taken care of in order to obtain an efficient algorithm. The main techniques are illustrated in **Figure 6** and are now commented.

Loop parallelism using ATOMIC pragma. The first method to avoid the race condition consists in using the OpenMP ATOMIC pragmas to protect the shared variables $\mathbf{A}^{(i)}$ and $\mathbf{b}^{(i)}$ (**Figure 6** (1)). The cost of the ATOMIC comes from the fact that we do not know a priori when conflicts occur and thus this pragma must be used at each loop iteration. This lowers the IPC (defined in Section 1.2) that therefore limits the performance of the assembly.

Loop parallelism using element coloring. The second method consists in coloring [26] the elements of the mesh such that elements of the same color do not share nodes [27], or such that cells of the same color do not share faces in the FV context. The loop parallelism is thus applied for elements of the same color, as illustrated in **Figure 6** (2). The advantage of this technique is that one gets rid of the ATOMIC pragma and its inherent cost. The main drawback is that spatial locality is lessened by construction of the coloring. In [28], a comprehensive comparison of this technique and the previous one is presented.

Loop parallelism using element partitioning. In order to preserve spatial locality while disposing of the ATOMIC pragma, another technique consists in partitioning the local mesh of each MPI process into disjoint sets of elements (e.g., using METIS [18]) to control spatial locality inside each subdomain. Then, one defines *separators* as the layers of elements which connect neighboring subdomains. By doing this, elements of different subdomains do not share nodes. Obviously, the

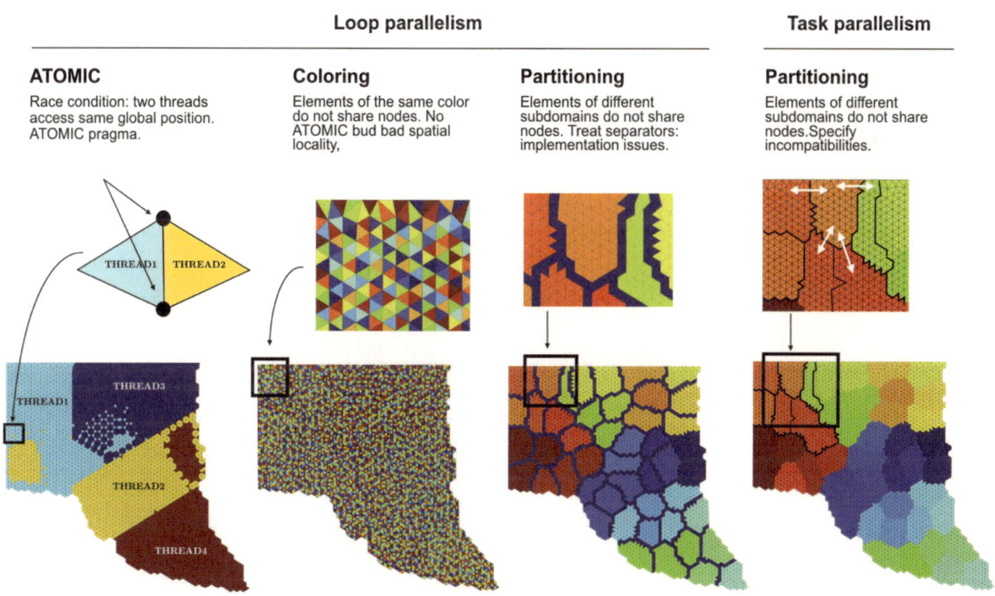

Figure 6. Shared memory parallelism techniques using OpenMP. (1) Loop parallelism using ATOMIC pragma. (2) Loop parallelism using element coloring. (3) Loop parallelism using element partitioning. (4) Task parallelism using partitioning and multidependences.

elements of the separators should be assembled separately [29, 30], which breaks the classical element loop syntax and requires additional programming (**Figure 6** (3)).

Task parallelism using multidependences. Task parallelism could be used instead of loop parallelism, but the three algorithmics presented previously would not change [30–32]. There are two new features implemented in OmpSs (a forerunner for OpenMP) that are not yet included in the standard that can help: multidependences and commutative. These would allow us to express incompatibilities between subdomains. The mesh of each MPI process is partitioned into disjoint sets of elements, and by prescribing the neighboring information in the OpenMP pragma, the runtime will take care of not executing neighboring subdomains at the same time [33]. This method presents good spatial locality and circumvents the use of ATOMIC pragma.

4.3. Load balance

As explained in Section 1.2, efficiency measures the level of usage of the available computational resources. Let us take a look at a typical unbalanced situation illustrated in the trace shown in **Figure 7**. The x-axis is time, while the y-axis is the MPI process number, and the dark grey color represents the element loop assembly (Algorithm 1). After the assembly, the next operation is a reduction operation involving MPI, the initial residual norm of the iterative solver (quite common in practice). Therefore, this is a synchronization point where MPI processes are stuck until all have reached this point. We can observe in the figure that one of the cores is taking almost the double time to perform this operation, resulting in a load imbalance.

Load imbalance has many causes: mesh adaptation as described in Section 2.3, erroneous element weight prediction in the case of hybrid meshes (Section 3), hardware heterogeneity, software or hardware variabilities, and so on. The example presented in the figure is due to wrong element weights given to METIS partitioner for the partition of a hybrid mesh [28].

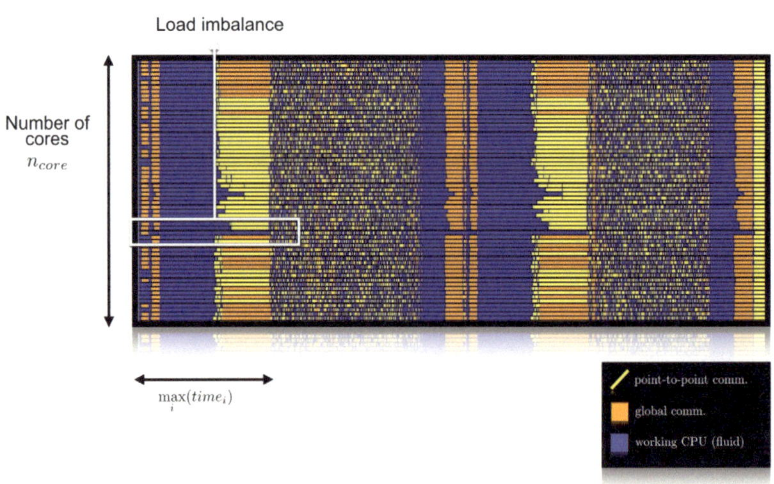

Figure 7. Trace of an unbalanced element assembly.

There are several works in the literature that deal with load imbalance at runtime. We can classify them into two main groups, the ones implemented by the application (may be using external tools) and the ones provided by runtime libraries and transparent to the application code.

In the first group, one approach would be to perform local element redistribution from neighbors to neighbors. Thus, only limited point-to-point communications are necessary, but this technique provides also a limited control on the global load balance. Another option consists in repartitioning the mesh, to achieve a better load distribution. In order for this to be efficient, a parallel partitioner (e.g., using the space filling curve-based partitioning presented in Section 3) is necessary in order to circumvent Amdahl's law. In addition, this method is an expensive process so that imbalance should be high to be an interesting option.

In the second group, several parallel runtime libraries offer support to solve load imbalance at the MPI level, Charm++ [34], StarPU [35], or Adaptive MPI (AMPI). In general, these libraries will detect the load imbalance and migrate objects or specific data structures between processes. They usually require to use a concrete programming language, programming model, or data structures, thus requiring high levels of code rewriting in the application.

Finally, the approach that has been used by the authors is called DLB [25] and has been extensively studied in [28, 33, 36] in the CFD context. The mechanism enables to lend resources from MPI idle processes to working ones, as illustrated in **Figure 8**, by using a hybrid approach MPI + OpenMP and standard mechanisms of these programming models.

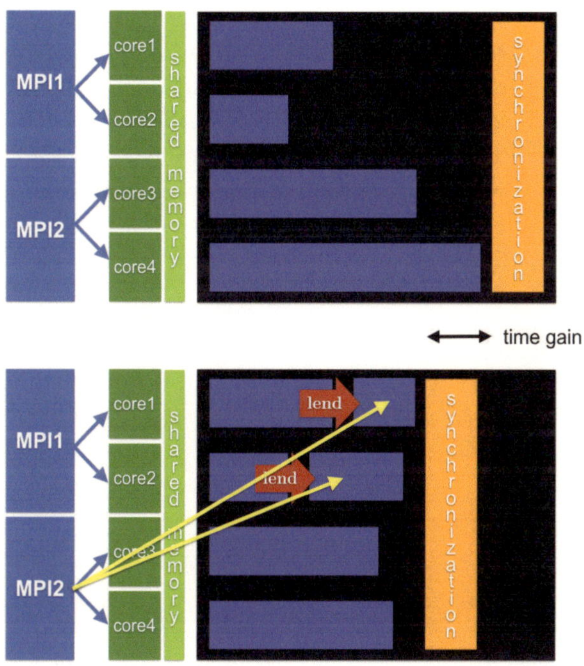

Figure 8. Principles of dynamic load balance with DLB [25], via resources sharing at the shared memory level. (Top) Without DLB and (bottom) with DLB.

In this illustrative example, two MPI processes launch two OpenMP threads on a shared memory node. Threads running on cores 3 and 4 are clearly responsible for the load imbalance. When using DLB, threads running in core 1 and core 2 lend their resources as soon as they enter the synchronization point, for example, an MPI reduction represented by the orange bar. Then, MPI process 2 can now use four threads to finish its element assembly.

Let us take a look at the performance of two assembly methods: MPI + OpenMP with loop parallelism and MPI + OpenMP with task parallelism and dynamic load balance. **Figure 9** shows the strong scaling and timings of these two methods. The example corresponds to the assembly of 140 million element meshes, with highly unbalanced partitions [33], as illustrated by the trace shown in **Figure 7**. As already noted in Section 1.2, although the strong scaling of the MPI + OpenMP with loop parallelism method is better than the other one, the timing is around three times higher. This is due to the combination of: substituting loop parallelism using coloring by task parallelism, thus giving a higher IPC; using the dynamic load balance library DLB to improve the load balance at the shared memory level.

4.4. More HPC optimizations

Let us close this section with some basic HPC optimizations to take advantage of some hardware characteristics presented in Section 1.1.1.

Spatial and temporal locality The main memory access bottleneck of the assembly depicted in Algorithm 1 is the gather and scatter operations. **Figure 10** illustrates the concept. On the top figure, we illustrate the action of node renumbering [37, 38] to achieve a better data locality: nodes are "grouped" according their global numbering [37, 38]. For example, when assembling element 3945, the gather is more efficient after renumbering (top right part of the figure) as nodal array positions are closer in memory. Data locality is thus enhanced. However, the assembly loop accesses elements successively. Therefore, when going from element 1 to 2, there is no data locality, as element 1 accesses positions 1,2,3,4 and element 2 positions 6838,

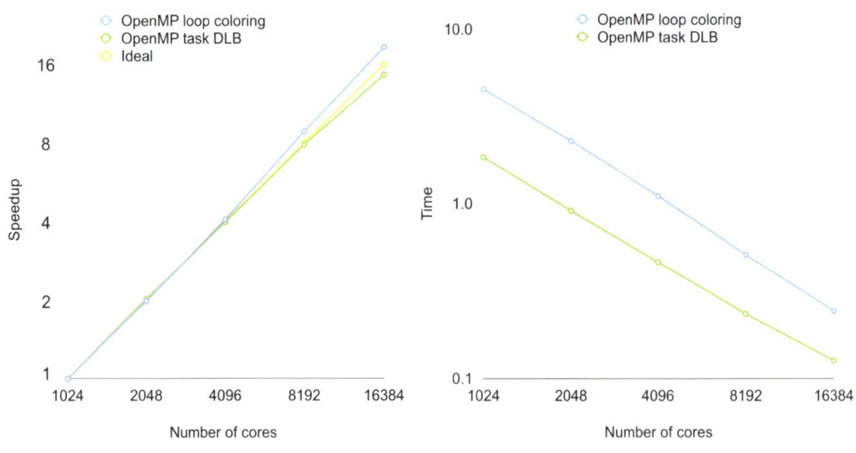

Figure 9. Strong speedup and timings of two hybrid methods: MPI + OpenMP with loop parallelism and MPI + OpenMP with task parallelism and DLB, on 1024 to 16,384 cores.

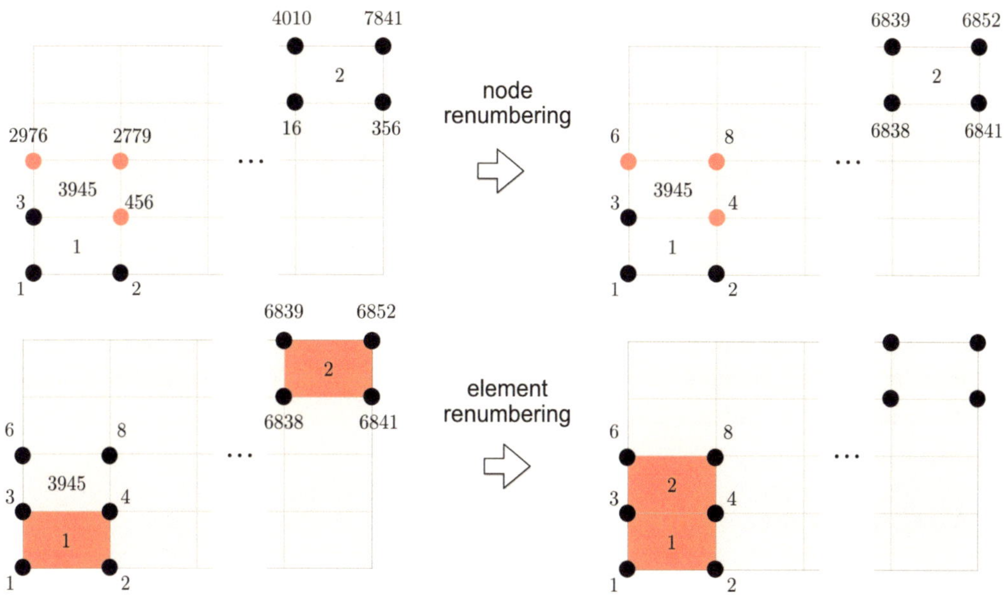

Figure 10. Optimization of memory access by renumbering nodes and elements. (1) Top: satial locality. (2) Bottom: temporal locality.

6841, 6852, 6839. Therefore, renumbering the elements according to the node numbering enables one to achieve temporal locality, as shown in the bottom right part of the figure. Data already present in cache can be reused (data of nodes 3 and 4).

Vectorization. According to the available hardware, vectorization may be activated as a data-level parallelism. However, the vectorization will be efficient if the compiler is able to vectorize the appropriate loops. In order to help the compiler, one can do some "not-so-dirty" tricks at the assembly level. Let us consider a typical element matrix assembly. Let us denote `nnode` and `ngaus` as the number of nodes and Gauss integration points of this element; `Ae`, `Jac`, and `N` are the element matrix, the weighted Jacobian, and the shape function, respectively. In Fortran, the computation of an element mass matrix reads:

```
do ig = 1,ngaus
   do jn = 1,nnode
      do in = 1,nnode
        Ae(in,jn) = Ae(in,jn) + Jac(ig) * N(in,ig) * N(jn,ig)
      end do
   end do
end do
```

This loop, part of step 3 of Algorithm 1, will be carried out on each element of the mesh. Now, let us define Ne, a parameter defined in compilation time. In order to help vectorization, last loop can be substituted by the following.

```
do ig = 1,ngaus
   do jn = 1,nnode
     do in = 1,nnode
       Ae(1:Ne,in,jn) = Ae(1:Ne,in,jn) + Jac(1:Ne,ig) * N(1:Ne,in,ig) * N(1:
Ne,jn,ig)
      end do
   end do
end do
```

thus assembling Ne elements at the same time. To have an idea of how powerful this technique can be, in [39], a speedup of 7 has been obtained in an incompressible Navier–Stokes assembly with Ne = 32. Finally, note that this formalism can be relatively easily applied to port the assembly to GPU architectures [39].

5. Algebraic system solution

5.1. Introduction

This section is devoted to the parallel solution of the algebraic system

$$\mathbf{Ax} = \mathbf{b}, \tag{1}$$

coming from the Navier–Stokes equation assembly described in last section. The matrix and the right-hand side are distributed over the MPI processes, the matrix having a partial row or full row format.

As explained in last section, the assembly process is embarrassingly parallel, as it does not require any communication (except the case illustrated in **Figure 5** (b)). The algebraic solvers are mainly responsible for the limitation of the strong and weak scalabilities of a code (see Section 1.2). Thus, adapting the solver to a particular algebraic system is fundamental. This is a particularly difficult task for large distributed systems, where scalability and load balance enter into play, in addition to the usual convergence and timing criteria.

In this section, we do not derive any algebraic solver, for which we refer to Saad's book [40] or [41] for parallelization aspects, but rather discuss their behaviors in a massively parallel context. The section does not intend to be exhaustive, but rather to expose the experience of the authors on the topic.

The main techniques to solve Eq. (1) are categorized as explicit, semi-implicit and implicit. The explicit method can be viewed as the simplest iterative solver to solve Eq. (1), namely a preconditioned Richardson iteration:

$$\begin{aligned} \mathbf{x}^{k+1} &= \mathbf{x}^k + \delta t \mathbf{M}^{-1}\left(\mathbf{b} - \mathbf{Ax}^k\right), \\ &= \mathbf{x}^k + \delta t \mathbf{M}^{-1}\mathbf{r}^k, \end{aligned} \tag{2}$$

where $\mathbf{M}$ is the mass matrix, δt the time step, and k the iteration/time counter. In practice, matrix $\mathbf{A}$ is not needed and only the residual $\mathbf{r}^k$ is assembled. High-order schemes have been presented in the literature such as Runge–Kutta methods, but from the parallelization point of view, all the methods require a single point-to-point communication in order to assemble the residual $\mathbf{r}^k$ or alternatively the solution $\mathbf{x}^{k+1}$ if halos are used.

Semi-implicit methods are mainly represented by fractional step techniques [42, 43]. They generally involve an explicit update of the velocity, such as Eq. (2) and an algebraic system with an SPD matrix for the pressure. Other semi-implicit methods exist, based on the splitting of the unknowns at the algebraic level. This splitting can be achieved for example by extracting the pressure Schur complement of the incompressible Navier–Stokes Eqs. [44]. The Schur complement is generally solved with iterative solvers, which solution involves the consecutive solutions of algebraic systems involving unsymmetric and symmetric matrices (SPD for the pressure). These kinds of methods have the advantage to extract better conditioned and smaller algebraic systems than the original coupled one, at the cost of introducing an additional iteration loop to converge to the monolithic (original) solution.

Finally, implicit methods deal with the coupled system (1). In general, much more complex solvers and preconditioners are required to solve this system than in the case of semi-implicit methods. So, in any case, we always end up with algebraic systems like Eq. (1).

We start with the parallelization of the operation that occupies the central place in iterative solvers, namely the sparse matrix vector product (SpMV).

5.2. Parallelization of the SpMV

Let us consider the simplest iterative solver, the so-called simple or Richardson iteration, which consists in solving the following equation for $k = 0, 1, 2\ldots$ until convergence:

$$\mathbf{x}^{k+1} = \mathbf{x}^k + \left(\mathbf{b} - \mathbf{A}\mathbf{x}^k\right). \tag{3}$$

The parallelization of this solver amounts to that of the SpMV (say $\mathbf{y} = \mathbf{A}\mathbf{x}$) and depends on whether one considers the partial row or full row format, as illustrated in **Figure 11**.

SpMV for partial row matrix with MPI. When using the partial row format, the local result of the SpMV (in each MPI process) is only partial as the matrices are also partial on the interface, as explained in Section 4. By applying the distributive property of the multiplication, the results of neighboring subdomains add up to the correct solution on the interface:

$$\begin{aligned} y_3 &= A_{32}x_2 + A_{33}x_3 + A_{34}x_4, \\ &= \left(A_{32}\,x_2 + A_{33}^{(1)}x_3\right) + \left(A_{33}^{(2)}x_3 + A_{34}x_4\right), \\ &= y_3^{(1)} + y_3^{(2)}. \end{aligned}$$

In practice, the exchanges of $y_3^{(1)}$ and $y_3^{(2)}$ between Ω_1 and Ω_2 are carried out through the MPI function MPI_Sendrecv. In the case, a node belongs to several subdomains, and all the neighbors' contributions should be exchanged. Note that with this partial row format, due to the duplicity of the interface nodes, the MPI messages are symmetric in neighborhood (a subdomain is a neighbor of its neighbors) and size of interfaces (interface of i with j involves the same degrees

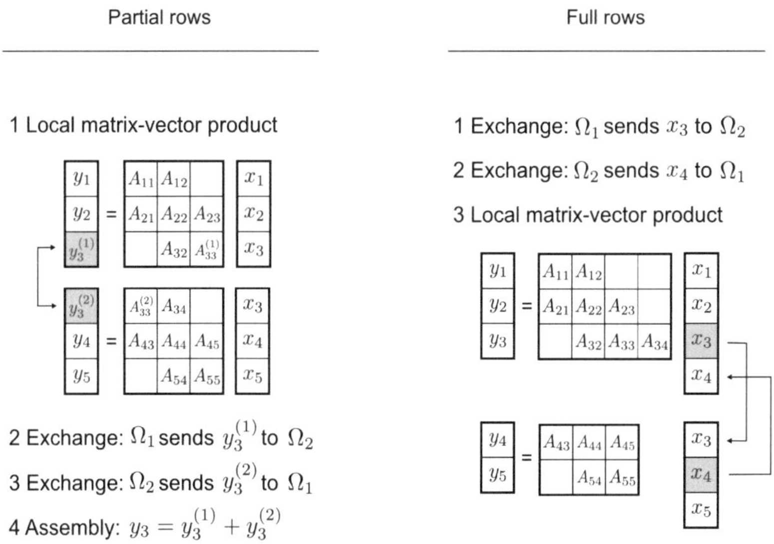

Figure 11. Synchronous parallelization of SpMV for the partial row and full row formats.

of freedom as that of j with i). Finally, let us note that the same technique is applied to compute the right-hand sides, as $b_3 = b_3^{(1)} + b_3^{(2)}$. After this matrix and RHS exchange, the solution of Eq. (3) is therefore the same as in sequential.

SpMV for full row matrix with MPI. For this format, where all local rows are fully assembled and matrices are rectangular, the exchange is carried out before the local products on the multiplicands x_3 and x_4, as shown in **Figure 11**. The exchanges are carried out using MPI_Sendrecv, which in the general case and contrary to the partial row format are no longer symmetric in size. Nothing needs to be done with the RHS as it has been fully assembled through the presence of halos.

Asynchronous SpMV with MPI. The previous two algorithms are said to be synchronous, as the MPI communication comes before or after the complete local SpMV for the partial or full row formats, respectively. The use of nonblocking MPI communications enables one to obtain asynchronous versions of the SpMV [41]. In the case of the partial row format, the procedure would consist of the following steps: (1) perform the SpMV for the interface nodes; (2) use nonblocking MPI communications (MPI_Isend and MPI_Irecv functions) to exchange the results of the SpMV on interface nodes; (3) perform the SpMV for the internal nodes; (4) synchronize the communications (MPI_Waitall); and (5) assemble the interface node contributions. This strategy permits to overlap communication (results of the SpMV for interface nodes) and work (SpMV for internal nodes).

SpMV with OpenMP. The loop parallelization with OpenMP is quite simple to implement in this case. However, care must be taken with the size of the chunks, as the overhead for creating the threads may be penalizing if the chunks are too small. Another consideration is the matrix format selected such as CSR, COO, ELL. For example, COO format requires the use of an ATOMIC pragma to protect **y**.

Load balance. In terms of load balance, FE and cell-centered FV methods behave differently in the SpMV. In the FV method, the degrees of freedom are located at the center of the elements. The partitioning into disjoint sets of elements can thus be used for both assembly and solver. In the case of the finite element, the number of degrees of freedom involved in the SpMV corresponds to the nodes and could differ quite from the number of elements involved in the assembly. So the question of partitioning a finite-element mesh into disjoint sets of nodes may be posed, depending on which operation dominates the computation. As an example, if one balances a hexahedra subdomain with a tetrahedra subdomain in terms of elements, the latter one will hold six times more elements than the last one.

5.3. Krylov subspace methods

The Richardson iteration given by Eq. (7) is only based on the SpMV operation. SpMV does not involve any global communication mechanism among the degrees of freedom (DOF), from one iteration to the next one. In fact, the result for one DOF after one single SpMV is only influenced by its first neighbors, as illustrated by **Figure 12** (1). To propagate a change from one side of the domain to the other, we thus need as many iterations as number of nodes between both sides, that is $\sim 1/h$, where h is the mesh size.

Krylov subspace methods, represented by the GMRES, BiCGSTAB, and CG methods among others, construct specific Krylov subspaces where they minimize the residual $\mathbf{r} = \mathbf{b} - \mathbf{Ax}$ of the equation. Such methods seek some *optimality*, thus providing a certain global communication mechanism. These parameters are functions of scalar products that can be computed locally on each MPI process and then assembled through reduction operations using the MPI_Allreduce function in the case of MPI, and the REDUCTION pragma using OpenMP. Nevertheless, this global communication mechanism is very limited and the convergence of such solvers degrades with the mesh size. Just like the Richardson method, Krylov methods damp high-frequency errors through the SpMV, but do not have inherent low-frequency error damping.

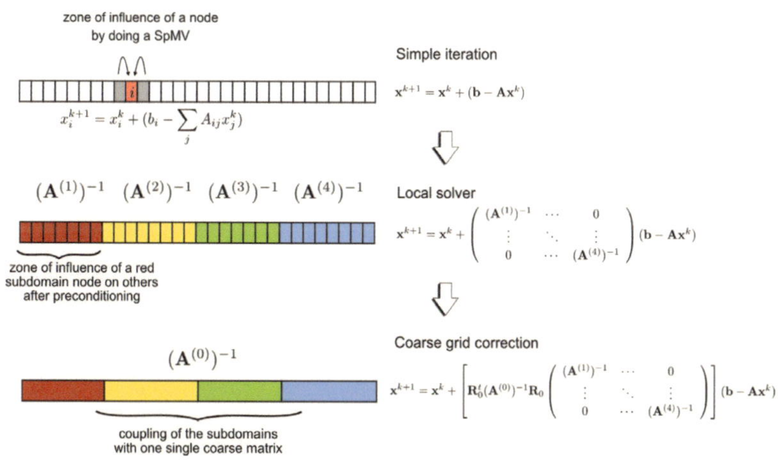

Figure 12. Accelerating iterative solvers. From top to bottom: (1) SpMV has a node-to-node influence; (2) domain decomposition (DD) solvers have a subdomain-to-subdomain influence; and (3) coarse solvers couple the subdomains.

The low-frequency damping can be achieved by introducing a DD preconditioner and/or a coarse solver, as is introduced in next subsection.

5.4. Preconditioning

The selection of the preconditioning of Eq. (1) is the key for solving the system efficiently [45, 46]. Preconditioning should provide robustness at the least price, for a given problem, and in general, robustness is expensive. Domain decomposition preconditioners provide this robustness, but can result too expensive compared to smarter methods, as we now briefly analyze.

Domain Decomposition. Erhel and Giraud summarized the attractiveness of domain decomposition (DD) methods as follows:

> *One route to the solution of large sparse linear systems in parallel scientific computing is the use of numerical methods that combine direct and iterative methods. These techniques inherit the advantages of each approach, namely the limited amount of memory and easy parallelization for the iterative component and the numerical robustness of the direct part.*

DD preconditioners are based on the exact (or almost exact) solution of the local problem to each subdomain. In brief, the local solutions provide a coupling mechanism between the subdomains of the partition, as illustrated in **Figure 12** (2) (note that the subdomain matrices $\mathbf{A}^i$ are not exactly the local matrices in this case). The different methods mainly differentiate in the way the different subdomains are coupled (interface conditions) and in terms of overlap between them, the Schwarz method being the most famous representative. On the one hand, SpMV is in charge of damping high frequencies. On the other hand, DD methods provide a communication mechanism at the level of the subdomains. The convergence of Krylov solvers using such preconditioners now depends on the number of subdomains.

Coarse solvers try to resolve this dependence, providing a global communication mechanism among the subdomains, generally one degree of freedom per subdomain. The coarse solver is a "sequential" bottleneck as it is generally solved using a direct solver on a restricted number of MPI processes. Let us mention the deflated conjugate gradient (DCG) method [47] which provides a coarse grain coupling, but which can be independent of the partition.

As we have explained, solvers involving DD preconditioners together with a coarse solver aim at making the solver convergence independent of the mesh size and the number of subdomains. In terms of CPU time, this is translated into the concept of weak scalability (Section 1.2). This can be achieved in some cases, but hard to obtain in the general case.

Multigrid solvers or preconditioners provide a similar multilevel mechanism, but using a different mathematical framework [48]. They only involve a direct solver at the coarsest level, and intermediate levels are still carried out in an iterative way, thus exhibiting good strong (based on SpMV) and weak scalabilities (multilevel). Convergence is nevertheless problem dependent [49, 50].

Physics and numerics based solvers. DD preconditioners are brute force preconditioners in the sense that they attack local problems with a direct solver, regardless of the matrix properties. Smarter approaches may provide more efficient solutions, at the expense of not being weak scalable. But do we really need weak scalability to solve a given problem on a given number of available CPUs? Well, this depends. Let us cite two physical–/numerical-based preconditioners. The linelet preconditioner is presented in [51]. In a boundary layer mesh, a typical situation in CFD, the discretization of the Laplacian operator tends to a tridiagonal matrix when anisotropy tends to infinity (depending also on the discretization technique), and the dominant coefficients are along the direction normal to the wall. The anisotropy linelets consist of a list of nodes, renumbered in the direction normal to the wall. By assembling tridiagonal matrices along each linelet, the preconditioner thus consists of a series of tridiagonal matrices, very easy to invert.

Let us also mention finally the streamwise linelet [52]. In the discretization of a hyperbolic problem, the dependence between degrees of freedom follows the streamlines. By renumbering the nodes along these streamlines, one can thus use a bidiagonal or Gauss–Seidel solver as a preconditioner. In an ideal situation where nodes align with the streamlines, the bidiagonal preconditioner makes the problem converge in one complete sweep.

These two examples show that listening to the physics and numerics of a problem, one can devise simple and cheap preconditioners, performing local operations.

Figure 13 illustrates the comments we have previously made concerning the preconditioners. In this example, we solve the Navier–Stokes equations together with a k-ϵ turbulence model to simulate a wind farm. The mesh comprises 4 M nodes, with a moderate boundary layer mesh near the ground. The figure presents the convergence history in terms of number of iterations and time for solving the pressure equation (SPD) [53], with four different solvers and preconditioners: CG for Schur complement preconditioned by an additive Schwarz method; the DCG with diagonal preconditioner; the DCG with linelet preconditioner [51]; and the DCG with a block LU (block Jacobi) preconditioner. We observe that in terms of robustness (**Figure 13** (1)) the additive Schwarz is the most performant solver, as it converges in six times less iterations than the DCG with diagonal preconditioner. However, taking a look at the CPU time, the performance is completely inverted and the best one is the DCG with linelet preconditioner. We

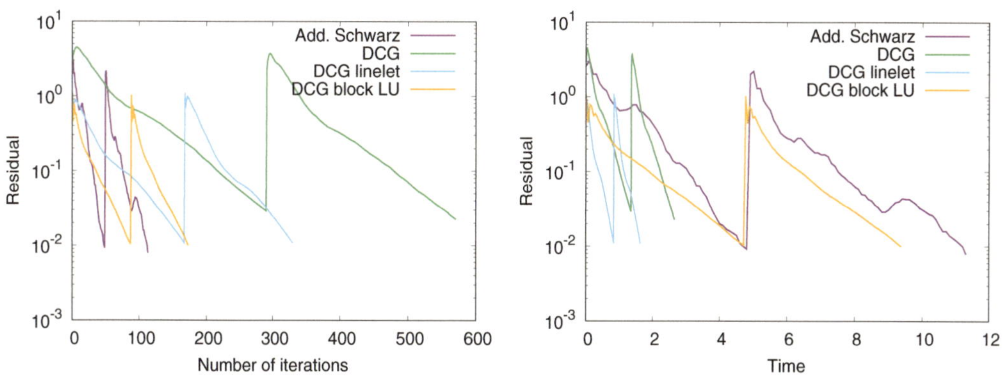

Figure 13. Convergence of pressure equation with 512 CPUs using different solvers (4 M node mesh). (1) Residual norm vs. number of iterations. (2) Residual norm vs. time.

should stress that these conclusions are problem dependent, and one should adapt to any situation. In a simulation of millions of CPU hours, a factor six in time can cost several hundred thousands of euros (see [54] for a comparison of preconditioners for the pressure equation).

5.5. Breaking synchronism

Iterative parallel computing requires a lot of global synchronizations between processes, coming from the scalar products to compute descent and orthogonalization parameters or residual norms. These synchronizations are very expensive due to the high latencies of the networks. They also imply a lot of wasted time if the workloads are not well balanced, as explained in Section 4.3 for the assembly. The heterogeneous nature of the machines makes such load balancing very hard to achieve, resulting in higher time loss, compared to homogeneous machines.

Pipelined solvers. Pipelined solvers consist of algorithmically equivalent solvers (e.g., pipelined CG wrt CG) that are devised by introducing new recurrence variables and rearranging some of the basic solver operations [55, 56]. The main advantage of pipelined versions is the possibility to overlap reduction operations with some operations, like preconditioning. This is achieved by means of the MPI3 [5] nonblocking reduction operations, MPI_IAllreduce. This enables one to hide latency, provided that the work to be overlapped is sufficient, and thus to increase the strong scaling. Although algorithmically equivalent to their classical versions, pipelined solvers introduce local rounding errors due to the addition recurrence relations, which limit their attainable accuracy [57].

Communication avoiding solvers. Asynchronous iterations provide another mechanism to overcome the synchronism limitation. In order to illustrate the method, let us take the example of the Richardson method of Eq. (3). Each subdomain $i = 1, 2, \ldots$ has now its own iteration counter k_i. Let $\tau_{ij}(k_i)$ define the iteration at which the solution of neighbor j is available to i at iteration k_i. Then, let us define $\mathbf{A}_{ij}^{(i)}$ the matrix block of subdomain i connected to subdomain j and $\mathbf{x}_i^k$ the solution in subdomain i at iteration k. The method reads:

$$\mathbf{x}_i^{k_i+1} = \left(I - \sum_j \mathbf{A}_{ij}^{(i)} \right) x_j^{\tau_{ij}(k_i)} + \mathbf{b}.$$

This means that each subdomain i updates its solution with the last available solution of its neighbors j. Note that with this notation we have of $\tau_{ii}(k_i) = k_i$. In addition, if $k_i = k \ \forall i$, then we recover the synchronous version of the Richardson iteration. The main difficulty of such methods consists in establishing a common stopping criterion among all the MPI processes, minimizing the number of synchronizations. Such asynchronous Jacobi and block Jacobi solvers have been developed since 1969 [58]. Recent developments have extended these algorithms to asynchronous substructuring method [59] and to asynchronous optimized Schwarz method [60].

6. I/O and visualization

Scientific visualization focuses on the creation of images to provide important information about underlying data and processes. In recent decades, the unprecedented growth in computing and sensor performance has led to the ability to capture the physical world in unprecedented levels of detail and to model and simulate complex physical phenomena. Visualization plays a decisive role in the extraction of knowledge from these data—as the mathematician Richard Hamming famously said, "*The purpose of computing is insight, not numbers [..].*" [61] It allows you to understand large and complex data in two, three, or more dimensions from different applications. Especially for CFD data, the visualization is of great importance, as its results can be well represented in the three-dimensional representation known to us.

Traditionally, I/O and visualization are closely related, as in most workflows, data used for visualization are written to disk and then read by a separate visualization tool. This is also called "postmortem" visualization, since the visualization may be done after the CFD solver has finished running. Other modes of interaction with visualization are becoming more common, such as "in situ" visualization (the CFD solver also directly produces visualization images, using the same nodes and partitioning), or "in-transit" visualization (the CFD solver is coupled to a visualization program, possibly running on other nodes and with a different partitioning scheme).

I/O. Output of files for postmortem visualization usually represents the highest volume of output from a CFD code, as well as some possibly separate operations, especially explicit checkpointing a restart, requiring writing and reading of large datasets. Logging or output of data subsets also requires I/O, often with a smaller volume but higher frequency.

As CFD computations can be quite costly, codes usually have a "checkpoint/restart" feature, allowing the code to output its state (whether converging for a steady computation or unsteady state reached for unsteady cases) to disk, for example, before running out of allocated computer time. This is called checkpointing. The computation may be restarted from the state reached by reading the checkpoint from a previous run. This incurs both writing and reading. Some codes use the same file format for visualization output and checkpointing, but this assumes data required are sufficiently similar and often that the code has a privileged output format. When restarting requires additional data (such as field values at locations not exactly matching those of the visualization, or multiple time steps for smooth restart of higher order time schemes), code-specific formats are used. Some libraries, such as Berkeley Lab Checkpoint/Restart (BLCR) [62], try to provide a checkpointing mechanism at the runtime level, including for parallel codes. This may require less programming on the solver side, at the expense of larger checkpoint sizes. BLCR's target is mostly making the checkpoint/restart sufficiently transparent to the code that it may be checkpointed, stopped, and then restarted based on resource manager job priorities, not I/O size and performance. In practice, BLCR does not seem to have evolved in recent years, and support in some MPI libraries has been dropped; so it seems the increasing complexity of systems has made this approach more difficult.

As datasets used by CFD tools are often large, it is recommended to use mostly binary representations rather than text representations. This has multiple advantages when done well:

1. avoid need for string to binary conversions, which can be quite costly;
2. avoid loss of precision when outputting floating point values;
3. reduced data size: 4 or 8 bytes for a single- or double-precision floating point value, while text often requires more characters even with reduced precision;
4. fixed size (which is more difficult to ensure with text formats), allowing easier indexing for parallel I/O;

As binary data are not easily human-readable, additional precautions are necessary, such as providing sufficient metadata for the file to be portable. This can be as simple as providing a fixed-size string with the relevant information, and associating a fixed-size description with name, type, and size for each array, or much more advanced depending on the needs. Many users with experience with older fields tend to feel more comfortable with text files, so this advice may seem counterintuitive, but issues which plagued older binary representations have disappeared, while text files are not as simple as they used to be, today with many possible character encodings. Twenty years ago, some systems such as Cray used proprietary floating-point types, while many already used the IEEE-754 standard for single-, double-, and extended-precision floating point values. Today, all known systems in HPC use the IEEE-754 standard, so it is not an issue anymore.[1] Other proponents of text files sometimes cite the impossibility of "repairing" slightly damaged binary files or the possibility of understanding undocumented text files, but this is not applicable to large files anyways. Be careful if you are using Fortran: by default, "unformatted" files do not just contain the "raw" binary data that are written, but small sections before and after each record, indicating at least the record's size (allowing moving forward and backward from one record to another as mandated by the Fortran standard). Though vendors have improved compatibility over the years, Fortran binary files are not portable by default. To use raw data in Fortran as would be done in C, the additional access = 'stream' option must be passed to the open statement.

Some libraries, such as HDF5 [63] and NetCFD [64], handle binary portability, such as big endian/little endian issues or floating point-type conversions, and provide a model for simple, low-level data such as sets of arrays. They also allow for parallel I/O based on MPI I/O. Use of HDF5 has become very common on HPC systems, as many other models build on it.

As data represented by CFD tools is often structured in similar ways, some libraries such as CFD General Notation System (CGNS) [65], Model for Exchange of Data (MED) [66], Exodus II, or XDMF offer a data model so as to handle I/O on a more abstract level (i.e., coordinates, element connectivity, field values rather than raw data). MED and CGNS use HDF5 as a low-level layer.[2] Exodus II uses NetCDF as a lower-level layer, while XDMF stores arrays in HDF5 files and metadata in XML files. In CFD, CGNS is probably the most used of these standards.

Parallel I/O. As shown in **Figure 1**, the access to disk has from far the highest latency in the memory hierarchy.

There are several ways of handling I/O for parallel codes. The most simple solution is to read or write a separate file for each MPI task. On some file systems, this may be the fastest method, but

[1] Some alternative representations exist, but they are not the "native" representations on most systems.

[2] CGNS can also use and older internal library named ADF, but not for parallel I/O.

it leads to the generation of many files on large systems, and requires external tools to reassemble data for visualization, unless using libraries which can assemble data when reading it (such as VTK using its own format). Reassembling data for visualization (or partitioning on disk) require additional I/O, so it is best to avoid them if possible. Another approach is to use "shared" or "flat" files, which are read and written collectively by all tasks. MPI I/O provides functions for this (for example MPI_File_write_at_all using MPI), so the low-level aspects are quite simple, but the calling code must provide the logic by which data are transformed from a flat, partition-independent representation in the file to partition-dependent portions in memory. This approach provides the benefit of allowing checkpointing and restarting on different numbers of nodes and making parallelism more transparent for the user, though it requires additional work for the developers. Parallel I/O features of libraries such as HDF5 and NetCFD seek to make this easier (and libraries build on them such as CGNS and MED can exploit those too).

Performance of parallel I/O is often highly dependent on the combination of approach used by a code and the underlying file system. Even on machines with similar systems but different file system tuning parameters, performance may vary. In any case, for good performance on parallel file systems (which should be all shared file systems on modern clusters), it is recommended to avoid funneling all data through a single node except possibly as a fail-safe mode. In any case, keeping data fully distributed extending to the I/O level is a key to handling very large datasets which do not fit in the memory of a single node. Given the difficulty of obtaining portable I/O performance, some libraries like adaptable I/O system (ADIOS) [67] seek to provide an adaptable approach, allowing hybrid approaches between flat or separate files, with groups of file for process subsets, based on easily tunable XML metadata. ADIOS also provides other features, such as staging in memory (possible also with HDF5), at the cost of another library layer.

Visualization pipeline. The "visualization pipeline" is a common method for describing the visualization process. When the pipeline is run through, an image is calculated from the data using the individual steps $\text{Filtering} \rightarrow \text{Mapping} \rightarrow \text{Rendering}$. The pipeline filter step includes raw data processing and image processing algorithm operations. The subsequent "mapping" generates geometric primitives from the preprocessed data together with additional visual attributes such as color and transparency. Rendering uses computer graphics methods to generate the final image from the geometric primitives of the mapping process.

While the selection of different visualization applications is considerable, the visualization techniques in science are generally used in the following areas of the dimensionality of the data fields. A distinction is made between scalar fields (temperature, density, pressure, etc.), vector fields (speed, electric field, magnetic field, etc.), and tensor fields (diffusion, electrical and thermal conductivity, stress and strain tensor, etc.).

Regardless of the dimensionality of the data fields, any visualization of the whole three-dimensional volume can easily flood the user with too much information, especially on a two-dimensional display or piece of paper. Hence, one of the basic techniques in visualization is the reduction/transformation of data. The most common technique is slicing the volume data with cut planes, which reduces three-dimensional data to two dimensions.

Color information is often mapped onto these cut planes using another basic well-known technique called color mapping. Color mapping is a one-dimensional visualization technique.

It maps scalar value into a color specification. The scalar mapping is done by indexing into a color reference table—the lookup table. The scalar values serve as indexes in this lookup table including local transparency. A more general form of the lookup table is the transfer function. A transfer function is any expression that maps scalars or multidimensional values to a color specification.

Color mapping is not limited to 2D objects like cut planes, but it is also often used for 3D objects like isosurfaces. Isosurfaces belong to the general visualization technique of data fields, which we focus on in the following.

Visualization of scalar fields. For the visualization of three-dimensional scalar fields, there are two basic visualization techniques: isosurface extraction and volume rendering (**Figure 14**).

Isosurface extraction is a powerful tool for the investigation of volumetric scalar fields. An isosurface in a scalar volume is a surface in which the data value is constant, separating areas of higher and lower value. Given the physical or biological significance of the scalar data value, the position of an isosurface and its relationship to other adjacent isosurfaces can provide a sufficient structure of the scalar field.

The second fundamental visualization technique for scalar fields is volume rendering. Volume rendering is a method of rendering three-dimensional volumetric scalar data in two-dimensional images without the need to calculate intermediate geometries. The individual values in the dataset are made visible by selecting a transfer function that maps the data to optical properties such as color and opacity. These are then projected and blended together to form an image. For a meaningful visualization, the correct transfer function must be found that highlights interesting regions and characteristics of the data. Finding a good transfer function is crucial for creating an informative image. Multidimensional transfer functions enable more precise delimitation from the important to the unimportant. Therefore, they are widely used in volume rendering for medical imaging and the scientific visualization of complex three-dimensional scalar fields (**Figure 14**).

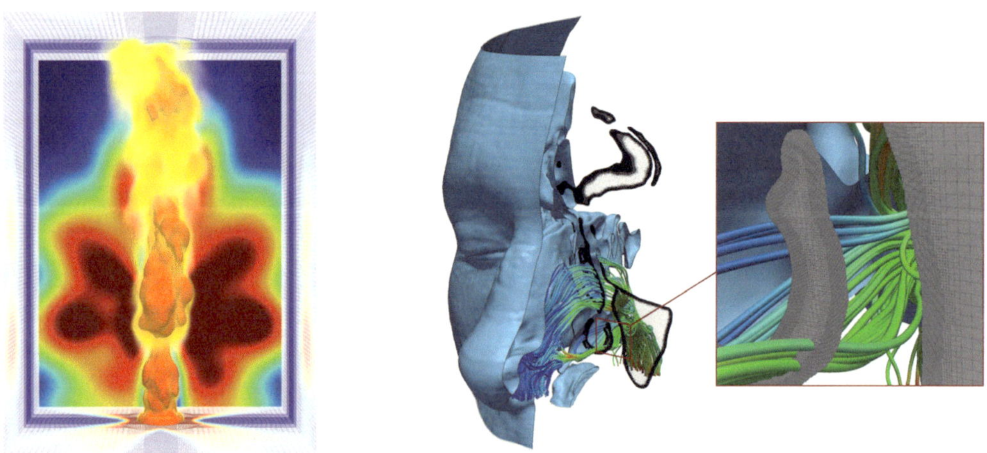

Figure 14. Visualization of flame simulation results (left) using slicing and color mapping in the background, and isosurface extraction and volume rendering for the flame structure. Visualization of an inspiratory flow in the human nasal cavity (right) using streamlines colored by the velocity magnitude [68].

http://dx.doi.org/10.5772/intechopen.72042

Visualization of vector fields. The visualization of vector field data is challenging because no existing natural representation can convey a visually large amount of three-dimensional directional information. Visualization methods for three-dimensional vector fields must therefore bring together the opposing goals of an informative and clear representation of a large number of directional information. The techniques relevant for the visual analysis of vector fields can be categorized as follows.

The simplest representations of the discrete vector information are oriented glyphs. Glyphs are graphical symbols that range from simple arrows to complex graphical icons, directional information, and additional derived variables such as rotation.

Streamlines provide a natural way to follow a vector dataset. With a user-selected starting position, the numerical integration results in a curve that can be made easily visible by continuously displaying the vector field. Streamlines can be calculated quickly and provide an intuitive representation of the local flow behavior. Since streamlines are not able to fill space without visual disorder, the task of selecting a suitable set of starting points is crucial for effective visualization. A limitation of flow visualizations based on streamlines concerns the difficult interpretation of the depth and relative position of the curves in a three-dimensional space. One solution is to create artificial light effects that accentuate the curvature and support the user in depth perception.

Stream surfaces represent a significant improvement over individual streamlines for the exploration of three-dimensional vector fields, as they provide a better understanding of depth and spatial relationships. Conceptually, they correspond to the surface that is spanned by any starting curve, which is absorbed along the flow. The standard method for stream surface integration is Hultquist's advancing front algorithm [69]. A special type of stream surface is based on the finite-time Lyapunov exponent (FTLE) [70]. FTLE enables the visualization of significant coherent structures in the flow.

Texture-based flow visualization methods are unique means to address the limitations of representations based on a limited set of streamlines. They effectively convey the essential patterns of a vector field without lengthy interpretation of streamlines. Its main application is the visualization of flow structures defined on a plane or a curved surface. The best known of these methods is the line integral convolution (LIC) proposed by Cabral and Leedom [71]. This work has inspired a number of other methods. In particular, improvements have been proposed, such as texture-based visualization of time-dependent flows or flows defined via arbitrary surfaces. Some attempts were made to extend the method to three-dimensional flows.

Furthermore, vector fields can be visualized using topological approaches. Topological approaches have established themselves as a reference method for the characterization and visualization of flow structures. Topology offers an abstract representation of the current and its global structure, for example, sinks, sources, and saddle points. A prominent example is the Morse-Smale complex that is constructed based on the gradient of a given scalar field [72].

Visualization of tensor fields. Compared to the visualization of vector fields, the state of the art in the visualization of tensor fields is less advanced. It is an active area of research. Simple techniques for tensor visualization draw the three eigenvectors by color, vectors, streamlines, or glyphs.

In situ visualization. According to the currently most common processing paradigm for analyzing and visualizing data on supercomputers, the simulation results are stored on the hard disk and reloaded and analyzed/visualized after the simulation. However, with each generation of supercomputers, memory and CPU performance grows faster than the access and capacity of hard disks. As a result, I/O performance is continuously reduced compared to the rest of the supercomputer. This trend hinders the traditional processing paradigm.

One solution is the coupling of simulations with real-time analysis/visualization—called in situ visualization. In situ visualizing is visualization that necessarily starts before the data producer finishes. The key aspect of real-time processing is that data are used for visualization/analysis while still in memory. This type of visualization/analysis can extract and preserve important information from the simulation that would be lost as a result of aggressive data reduction.

Various interfaces for the coupling of simulation and analysis tools have been developed in recent years—for the scientific visualization of CFD data, ParaView/Catalyst [73] and VisIt/libSim [74] are to be mentioned in particular. These interfaces allow a fixed coupling between the simulation and the visualization and integrate large parts of the visualization libraries into the program code of the simulation. Recent developments [75, 76] favor methods for loose coupling as tight coupling proves to be inflexible and susceptible to faults. Here, the simulation program and visualization are independent applications that only exchange certain data among each other via clearly defined interfaces. This enables independent development of simulation code and visualization/analysis code.

Acknowledgements

Part of the research developments and results presented in this chapter were funded by: the European Union's Horizon 2020 Programme (2014–2020) and from Brazilian Ministry of Science, Technology and Innovation through Rede Nacional de Pesquisa (RNP) under the HPC4E Project, grant agreement 689772; EoCoE, a project funded by the European Union Contract H2020-EINFRA-2015-1-676629; PRACE Type C and Type A projects.

Author details

Guillaume Houzeaux[1]*, Ricard Borrell[1], Yvan Fournier[3], Marta Garcia-Gasulla[1], Jens Henrik Göbbert[4], Elie Hachem[2], Vishal Mehta[1], Youssef Mesri[2], Herbert Owen[1] and Mariano Vázquez[1]

*Address all correspondence to: guillaume.houzeaux@bsc.es

1 Barcelona Supercomputing Center, Spain

2 Mines Paristech, France

3 Electricité de France, France

4 Jülich Supercomputing Centre, Germany

References

[1] Afzal A, Ansari Z, Faizabadi AR, Ramis MK. Parallelization strategies for computational fluid dynamics software: State of the art review. Archives of Computational Methods in Engineering. 2017;**24**(2):337-363

[2] NVIDIA, CUDA Toolkit Documentation (2017). http://docs.nvidia.com/cuda/cuda-c-programming-guide/index.html

[3] Blagodurov S, Fedorova A, Zhuravlev S, Kamali A. A case for numa-aware contention management on multicore systems, In: 2010 19th International Conference on Parallel Architectures and Compilation Techniques (PACT). 2010. pp. 557-558

[4] O. A. R. Board, OpenMP Application Program Interface Version 2.5 (may 2005). http://www.openmp.org/mp-documents/spec25.pdf

[5] M. P. I. Forum, Mpi: A Message-Passing Interface Standard Version 3.0, Tech. rep. 2012. http://mpi-forum.org/docs/mpi-3.0/mpi30-report.pdf

[6] Cajas J, Houzeaux G, Zavala M, Vázquez M, Uekermann B, Gatzhammer B, Mehl M, Fournier Y, Moulinec C. Multi-physics multi-code coupling on supercomputers. In: 1st International Workshop on Software Solutions for ICME, Aachen (Germany); 2014

[7] Henderson M, Anderson C, Lyons S eds. Object Oriented Methods for Interoperable Scientific and Engineering Computing, SIAM; 1999

[8] Wulf W, McKee S. Hitting the memory wall: Implications of the obvious. SIGARCH Computer Architecture News. 1995;**23**(1):20-24

[9] Zienkiewicz O, Zhu J. A simple error estimator and adaptive procedure for practical engineerng analysis. International Journal of Numerical Methods in Engineering. 1987;**24**(2):337-357

[10] Mesri Y, Khalloufi M, Hachem E. On optimal simplicial 3d meshes for minimizing the hessian-based errors. Applied Numerical Mathematics. 2016;**109**:235-249

[11] Venditti D, Darmofal D. Anisotropic grid adaptation for functional outputs: Application to two-dimensional viscous flows. Journal of Computational Physics. 2005;**187**(1):22-46

[12] Coupez T, Digonnet H, Ducloux R. Parallel meshing and remeshing. Applied Mathematical Modelling. 2000;**25**(2):153-175

[13] Said R, Weatherill N, MorgaN K, Verhoeven N. Distributed parallel delaunay mesh generation. Computer Methods in Applied Mechanics and Engineering. 1999;**177**(7):109-125

[14] Cougny HD, Shephard M. Parallel refinement and coarsening of tetrahedral meshes. International Journal of Numerical Methods in Engineering. 1999;**46**(7):1101-1125

[15] Mesri Y, Digonnet H, Guillard H. Mesh partitioning for parallel computational fluid dynamics applications on a grid. In: Finite Vol. Complex App. 2005. pp. 631-642

[16] Lumsdaine A, Gregor D, Hendrickson B, Berry J. Challenges in parallel graph processing. Parallel Processing Letters. 2007;**17**(01):5-20

[17] Mesri Y, Zerguine W, Digonnet H, Silva L, Coupez T. Dynamic parallel adaption for three dimensional unstructured meshes: Application to interface tracking. In: Int. Meshing Roundtable. 2008. pp. 195-212

[18] K. Lab, Metis - Serial Graph Partitioning and Fill-Reducing Matrix Ordering. http://glaros.dtc.umn.edu/gkhome/metis/metis/overview

[19] S. N. Laboratories, Zoltan: Parallel Partitioning, Load Balancing and Data-Management Services. http://www.cs.sandia.gov/zoltan

[20] Sud-Ouest IB. Scotch & pt_scotch: Software Package and Libraries for Sequential and Parallel Graph Partitioning, Static Mapping and Clustering, Sequential Mesh and Hypergraph Partitioning, and Sequential and Parallel Sparse Matrix Block Ordering. https://www.labri.fr/perso/pelegrin/scotch

[21] Borrell R, Cajas J, Houzeaux G, Vazquez M, Enabling Space Filling Curves Parallel Mesh Partitioning in Alya, Tech. rep., PRACE white paper (2017). http://www.prace-ri.eu/IMG/pdf/WP223.pdf

[22] INRIA, Maphys: The Massively Parallel Hybrid Solver (Maphys) Aims at Solving Large Sparse Linear Systems Using Hybrid Direct/Iterative Methods (2017). https://gitlab.inria.fr/solverstack/maphys

[23] A. N. Laboratory, Portable, Extensible Toolkit for Scientific Computation (2017). https://www.mcs.anl.gov/petsc

[24] Vázquez M, Houzeaux G, Koric S, Artigues A, Aguado-Sierra J, Arís R, Mira D, Calmet H, Cucchietti F, Owen H, Taha A, Burness ED, Cela JM, Valero M. Alya: Multiphysics engineering simulation towards exascale. Journal of Computer Science. 2016;**14**:15-27

[25] Garcia-Gasulla M, Corbalan J, Labarta J, LeWI: A runtime balancing algorithm for nested parallelism, in: Proceedings of the International Conference on Parallel Processing (ICPP09), 2009

[26] Misra J, Gries D. A constructive proof of vizing's theorem. Information Processing Letters. 1992;**41**(3):131-133

[27] Farhat C, Crivelli L. A general approach to nonlinear fe computations on shared-memory multiprocessors. Computer Methods in Applied Mechanics and Engineering. 1989;**72**(2):153-171

[28] Garcia-Gasulla M, Houzeaux G, Artigues A, Labarta J, Vázquez M. Load balancing of an mpi parallel unstructured cfd code using dlb and openmp. Submitted to International Journal of HPC Applications

[29] Aubry R, Houzeaux G, Vázquez M, Cela JM. Some useful strategies for unstructured edge-based solvers on shared memory machines. International Journal of Numerical Methods in Engineering. 2011;**85**(5):537-561

[30] Thébault L, Petit E, Tchiboukdjian M, Dinh Q, Jalby W. Divide and conquer parallelization of finite element method assembly. In: International Conference on Parallel Computing - ParCo2013, Vol. 25 of Advances in Parallel Computing, Muncih (Germany); 2013. pp. 753-762

[31] Thébault L. Scalable and efficient algorithms for unstructured mesh computations, Ph.D. thesis. Université de Versailles; 2016

[32] Carpayea JC, Roman J, Brenner P. Design and analysis of a task-based parallelization over a runtime system of an explicit finite-volume CFD code with adaptive time stepping. Journal of Computer Science. In press

[33] Garcia-Gasulla M, Houzeaux G, Ferrer R, Artigues A, López V, Labarta J, Vázquez M. Mpi+x: task-based parallelization and dynamic load balance of finite element assembly

[34] Kale LV, Krishnan S. Charm++: Parallel programming with message-driven objects. In: Parallel Programming Using C++. 1996. pp. 175-213

[35] Augonnet C, Aumage O, Furmento N, Namyst R, Thibault S. StarPU-MPI: Task Programming over Clusters of Machines Enhanced with Accelerators. Berlin, Heidelberg: Springer Berlin Heidelberg; 2012. pp. 298-299

[36] Houzeaux G, Garcia-Gasulla M, Cajas J, Artigues A, Olivares E, Labarta J, Vázquez M. Dynamic load balance applied to particle transport in fluids, Int. J. Comp. Fluid Dynamics. 2016:408-418

[37] Cuthill E, McKee J. Reducing the Bandwidth of Sparse Symmetric Matrices, in: 24th National Conference (ACM 69). New York (USA): ACM; 1969. p. 157172

[38] Lange M, Mitchell L, Knepley M, Gorman G. Efficient mesh management in firedrake using PETSC DMPLEX. SIAM Journal on Scientific Computing. 2016;**38**(5):S143S155

[39] Owen H, Houzeaux G. Porting of Alya, a High Performance Computational Mechanics Code, to Accelerators: KNL and GPU, in: Scientific Applications towards Exascale, Montpellier (France). 2017

[40] Saad Y. Iterative Methods for Sparse Linear Systems. SIAM; 2003

[41] Magoulès F, Roux F, Houzeaux G. Parallel Scientific Computing, Computer Engineering Series. ISTE-John Wiley & Sons; 2016

[42] Quarteroni A, Saleri F, Veneziani A. Factorization methods for the numerical approximation of navierstokes equations. Computational Methods in Applied Mechanics and Engineering. 2000;**188**:505-526

[43] Codina R. Pressure stability in fractional step finite element methods for incompressible flows. Journal of Computational Physics. 2001;**170**:112-140

[44] Houzeaux G, Aubry R, Vázquez M. Extension of fractional step techniques for incompressible flows: The preconditioned orthomin(1) for the pressure schur complement. Computers and Fluids. 2011;**44**:297-313

[45] Giraud L. On the numerical solution of partial differential equations: Iterative solvers for parallel computers. Tech. Rep. TH/PA/00/64, CERFACS; 2000

[46] Benzi M. Preconditioning techniques for large linear systems: A survey. Journal of Computational Physics. 2002;**182**:418477

[47] Löhner R, Mut F, Cebral J, Aubry R, Houzeaux G. Deflated preconditioned conjugate gradient solvers for the pressure-poisson equation: Extensions and improvements. International Journal of Numerical Methods in Engineering. 2011;**87**:2-14

[48] Trottenberg U, Oosterlee C, Schuller A. Multigrid. Elsevier Science. 2000

[49] Notay Y, Napov A. A massively parallel solver for discrete poisson-like problems. Journal of Computational Physics

[50] Notay Y. A new algebraic multigrid approach for stokes problems. Numerische Mathematik

[51] Soto O, Löhner R, Camelli F. A linelet preconditioner for incompressible flow solvers. International Journal of Numerical Methods Heat Fluid Flow. 2003;**13**(1):133-147

[52] Córdoba P, Houzeaux G, Caja JC. Streamwise numbering for gauss-seidel and bi-diagonal preconditioners in convection dominated flows. In: 9th International Workshop on Parallel Matrix Algorithms and Applications, Bordeaux (France); 2016

[53] Houzeaux G, Khun M, Córdoba P, Guillamet G. Maphys performance in alya. In: 7th JLESC Workshop - National Center for Supercomputing Applications (NCSA), Urbana (USA); 2017

[54] Singh K, Avital E, Williams J, Ji C, Bai X, Munjiza A. On parallel pre-conditioners for pressure poisson equation in les of complex geometry flows. International Journal of Numerical Methods Fluids. 2017;**83**(5):446-464

[55] Ghysels P, Vanroose W. Hiding global synchronization latency in the preconditioned conjugate gradient algorithm. Parallel Computing. 2014;**40**:224238

[56] Sanan P, Schnepp S, May D, Pipelined, flexible krylov subspace methods, arXiv.org (arXiv:1511.07226). https://arxiv.org/pdf/1511.07226.pdf

[57] Cools S, Yetkin E, Agullo E, Giraud L, Vanroose W. Analyzing the effect of local rounding error propagation on the maximal attainable accuracy of the pipelined conjugate gradients method, arXiv.org (arXiv:1601.07068). https://arxiv.org/pdf/1601.07068.pdf

[58] Bertsekas DP, Tsitsiklis JN. Parallel and Distributed Computation: Numerical Methods. Upper Saddle River, NJ, USA: Prentice-Hall, Inc.; 1989

[59] Magoulès F, Venet C. Asynchronous iterative sub-structuring methods. Mathematics and Computers in Simulation

[60] Magoulès F, Szyld D, Venet C. Asynchronous optimized Schwarz methods with and without overlap. Numerische Mathematik. 2017;**137**:199-227

[61] Hamming RW. Numerical Methods for Scientists and Engineers, International Series in Pure and Applied Mathematics. New York: McGraw-Hill; 1962

[62] Hargrove P, Duell J. Berkeley lab checkpoint/restart (blcr) for linux clusters. Journal of Physics: Conference Series. 2006;**46**(1):494

[63] HDF5 (2017). https://support.hdfgroup.org/HDF5/

[64] Network Common Data Form (NetCDF) (2017). http://doi.org/10.5065/D6H70CW6

[65] CFD General Notation System, an AIAA Recommended Practice. https://cgns.github.io/index.html

[66] MED file format (2017). http://www.salome-platform.org/user-section/about/med/

[67] ORNL, ADIOS, easy to use, fast, and portable IO. https://www.olcf.ornl.gov/center-projects/adios/

[68] Lintermann A, Göbbert JH, Vogt K, Koch W, Hetzel A, Rhinodiagnost - Morphological and functional precision diagnostics of nasal cavities, InSiDE, Innovatives Supercomputing in Deutschland 15 (2)

[69] Hultquist JP. Constructing stream surfaces in steady 3d vector fields. In: Proceedings of the 3rd conference on Visualization'92, IEEE Computer Society Press; 1992, pp. 171-178

[70] Barreira L, Pesin YB. Lyapunov exponents and smooth ergodic theory, Vol. 23, American Mathematical Soc., 2002

[71] Cabral B, Leedom LC. Imaging vector fields using line integral convolution. In: Proceedings of the 20th annual conference on Computer graphics and interactive techniques. ACM. 1993. pp. 263-270

[72] Gyulassy A, Bremer P, Hamann B, Pascucci V. A practical approach to morse-smale complex computation: Scalability and generality. IEEE Transactions on Visualization and Computer Graphics. 2008;**14**(6):1619-1626

[73] Ayachit U, Bauer A, Geveci B, O'Leary P, Moreland K, Fabian N, Mauldin J. Paraview catalyst: Enabling in situ data analysis and visualization, in: Proceedings of the First Workshop on In Situ Infrastructures for Enabling Extreme-Scale Analysis and Visualization, ACM, 2015, pp. 25-29

[74] Whitlock B, Favre JM, Meredith JS. Parallel in situ coupling of a simulation with a fully featured visualization system. Eurographics Symposium on Parallel Graphics and Visualization. 2011:101-109

[75] Ayachit U, Bauer A, Duque EP, Eisenhauer G, Ferrier N, Gu J, Jansen KE, Loring B, Lukic Z, Menon S, et al. Performance analysis, design considerations, and applications of extreme-scale in situ infrastructures, in: High performance computing, networking, storage and analysis, SC16: International conference for supercomputing. IEEE. 2016:921-932

[76] Dorier M, Sisneros R, Peterka T, Antoniu G, Semeraro D. Damaris/viz: A nonintrusive, adaptable and user-friendly in situ visualization framework, in: Large-scale data analysis and visualization (LDAV), 2013 IEEE symposium on. IEEE. 2013:67-75

Chapter 2

Multilevel Variable-Block Schur-Complement-Based Preconditioning for the Implicit Solution of the Reynolds-Averaged Navier-Stokes Equations Using Unstructured Grids

Bruno Carpentieri and Aldo Bonfiglioli

Additional information is available at the end of the chapter

http://dx.doi.org/10.5772/intechopen.72043

Abstract

Implicit methods based on the Newton's rootfinding algorithm are receiving an increasing attention for the solution of complex Computational Fluid Dynamics (CFD) applications due to their potential to converge in a very small number of iterations. This approach requires fast convergence acceleration techniques in order to compete with other conventional solvers, such as those based on artificial dissipation or upwind schemes, in terms of CPU time. In this chapter, we describe a multilevel variable-block Schur-complement-based preconditioning for the implicit solution of the Reynolds-averaged Navier-Stokes equations using unstructured grids on distributed-memory parallel computers. The proposed solver detects automatically exact or approximate dense structures in the linear system arising from the discretization, and exploits this information to enhance the robustness and improve the scalability of the block factorization. A complete study of the numerical and parallel performance of the solver is presented for the analysis of turbulent Navier-Stokes equations on a suite of three-dimensional test cases.

Keywords: computational fluid dynamics, Reynolds-averaged Navier-Stokes equations, Newton-Krylov methods, linear systems, sparse matrices, algebraic preconditioners, incomplete LU factorization, multilevel methods

1. Introduction

A considerable number of modern high-fidelity Computational Fluid Dynamics (CFD) solvers and codes still adopt either one-dimensional physical models based on the Riemann problem using higher order shape functions, such as higher order Finite Volume (FV) and Discontinuous Galerkin Finite Element (FE) methods for the discrete data representation, or truly multi-dimensional physical models using linear shape functions, like Fluctuation Splitting (FS) schemes. Both of these approaches require fast convergence acceleration techniques in order to compete with conventional solvers based on artificial dissipation or upwind schemes in terms of CPU time. Implicit methods based on the Newton's rootfinding algorithm are receiving an increasing attention in this context for the solution of complex real-world CFD applications, for example in the analyses of turbulent flows past three-dimensional wings, due to their potential to converge in a very small number of iterations [1, 2]. In this chapter, we consider convergence acceleration strategies for the implicit solution of the Reynolds-averaged Navier-Stokes (RANS) equations based on the FS space discretization using a preconditioned Newton-Krylov algorithm for the integration. The use of a Newton solver requires the inversion of a large nonsymmetric system of equations at each step of the non-linear solution process. Choice of linear solver and preconditioner is crucial for efficiency especially when the mean flow and the turbulence transport equation are solved in fully coupled form. In this study, we use the restarted Generalized Minimal Residuals (GMRES) [3] algorithm for the inner linear solver, preconditioned by a block multilevel incomplete lower-upper (LU) factorization. We present the development lines of the multilevel preconditioning strategy that is efficient to reduce the number of iterations of Krylov subspace methods at moderate memory cost, and shows good parallel performance on three-dimensional turbulent flow simulations.

The chapter is structured as follows. The governing conservation equations for both compressible and incompressible flows are reviewed in Section 2. Section 3 briefly describes the fluctuation splitting space discretization, the time discretization and the Newton-Krylov method used to solve the space- and time-discretized set of governing partial differential equations (PDEs). In Section 4, we present the development of the multilevel preconditioning strategies for the inner linear solver. We illustrate the numerical and parallel performance of the preconditioner for the analysis of turbulent incompressible flows past a three-dimensional wing in Section 5. Some concluding remarks arising from the study are presented in Section 6.

2. Governing equations

In the case of inviscid and laminar flows, given a control volume C_i, fixed in space and bounded by the control surface ∂C_i with inward normal $\mathbf{n}$, the governing equations of fluid dynamics are obtained by considering the conservation of mass, momentum and energy. In the case of viscous turbulent flows, one approach to consider the effects of turbulence is to average the unsteady Navier-Stokes (NS) equations on the turbulence time scale. Such averaging procedure results in a new set of steady equations (the RANS equations) that differ from the steady NS equations for the presence of the Reynolds' stress tensor, representing the effects of turbulence on the averaged flow field. The appearance of this tensor yields a closure problem, which is often solved by adopting an algebraic or a differential turbulence model. In the present work, we use the Spalart-Allmaras [4] one-equation model for the turbulent viscosity. Thus the integral form of the conservation law of mass, momentum, energy and turbulence transport equations has the form

$$\int_{C_i} \frac{\partial U_i}{\partial t} dV = \oint_{\partial C_i} \mathbf{n} \cdot F dS - \oint_{\partial C_i} \mathbf{n} \cdot G dS + \int_{C_i} S dV \quad (1)$$

where U is the vector of conserved variables. For compressible flows, we have $U = \left(\rho, \rho e^0, \rho\mathbf{u}, \tilde{\nu}\right)^T$, and for incompressible, constant density flows, $U = (p, \mathbf{u}, \tilde{\nu})^T$. The operators F and G represent the inviscid and viscous fluxes, respectively; for compressible flows, we have

$$F = \begin{pmatrix} \rho\mathbf{u} \\ \rho\mathbf{u}h^0 \\ \rho\mathbf{u}\mathbf{u} + pI \\ \tilde{\nu}\mathbf{u} \end{pmatrix}, \quad G = \frac{1}{Re_\infty} \begin{pmatrix} 0 \\ \mathbf{u} \cdot \underline{\underline{\tau}} + \mathbf{q} \\ \underline{\underline{\tau}} \\ \frac{1}{\mathrm{Pr}_T}[(\nu + \tilde{\nu})\nabla\tilde{\nu}] \end{pmatrix}, \quad (2)$$

and for incompressible, constant density flows,

$$F = \begin{pmatrix} a^2\mathbf{u} \\ \mathbf{u}\mathbf{u} + pI \\ \tilde{\nu}\mathbf{u} \end{pmatrix}, \quad G = \frac{1}{Re_\infty} \begin{pmatrix} 0 \\ \underline{\underline{\tau}} \\ \frac{1}{\mathrm{Pr}_T}[(\nu + \tilde{\nu})\nabla\tilde{\nu}] \end{pmatrix}. \quad (3)$$

Finally, the source term S has a non-zero entry only in the row corresponding to the turbulence transport equation; its expression is not reported here for brevity, but can be found in [4]. Note that the standard NS equations are retrieved from (1) by removing the source term S and the differential equation associated with the turbulence variable, and setting the effective viscosity and thermal conductivity to their laminar values. The Euler equations are instead recovered by additionally removing the flux vector G.

3. Solution techniques

The model used in this study for the discrete data representation is based on the coupling of an hybrid class of methods for the space discretization, called Fluctuation Splitting (or residual distribution) schemes [5], and a fully coupled Newton algorithm. By "fully coupled" we mean that the mass, momentum and energy conservation equations on one hand, and the turbulent equation on the other, are solved simultaneously rather than in a decoupled or staggered fashion. We discuss in the following subsections, separately, the space and time discretization, the numerical integration of the set of equations resulting from the discretization, and the solution of the large linear system at each Newton's step.

3.1. Space discretisation

The Fluctuation Splitting approach has features common to both Finite Element (FE) and Finite Volume (FV) methods. Like in standard FE methods, the dependent variables are stored at the vertices of the computational mesh made up of triangles in the two-dimensional (2D) space, and tetrahedra in three-dimensional (2D), and are assumed to vary linearly and continuously in space. Denoting Z_i as the nodal value of the dependent variable at the grid point i and N_i as the FE linear shape function, this dependence can be written as

$$Z(\mathbf{x}, t) = \sum_i Z_i(t) N_i(\mathbf{x}). \tag{4}$$

Note that, although the summation in Eq. (4) extends over all grid nodes, the computational molecule of each node is actually limited only to the set of its nearest neighbors due to the compact support of the linear shape functions. In the compressible case, Roe's parameter vector

$$Z = \left(\sqrt{\rho}, \sqrt{\rho} h^0, \sqrt{\rho}\mathbf{u}, \tilde{\nu}\right)^T \tag{5}$$

is chosen as the dependent variable to ensure discrete conservation [6]. In the incompressible case, discrete conservation is obtained by simply setting the dependent variable Z equal to the vector of conserved variables U. In our code, we group the dependent variables per gridpoint. The first m entries of the array Z are filled with the m flow variables of gridpoint 1, and these are followed by those of gridpoint 2, and so on. Blocking the flow variables in this way, also referred to as "field interlacing" in the literature, is acknowledged [7–9] to result in better performances than grouping variables per aerodynamic quantity.

The integral Eq. (1) is discretized over each control volume C_i using a FV-type approach. In two dimensions, the control volumes C_i are drawn around each gridpoint by joining the centroids of gravity of the surrounding cells with the midpoints of all the edges that connect that gridpoint with its nearest neighbors. An example of polygonal-shaped control volumes (so-called median dual cells) is shown by green lines in **Figure 1(a)**. With FS schemes, rather than calculating the inviscid fluxes by numerical quadrature along the boundary ∂C_i of the median dual cell, as would be done with conventional FV schemes, the net inviscid flux $\Phi^{e,\,inv}$ over each triangular/tetrahedral element

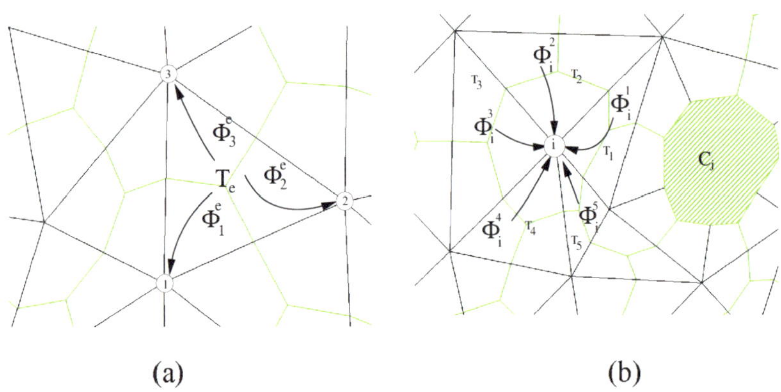

Figure 1. Residual distribution concept. (a) The flux balance of cell T is scattered among its vertices. (b) Gridpoint i gathers the fractions of cell residuals from the surrounding cells.

$$\Phi^{e,\,inv} = \oint_{\partial T_e} \mathbf{n} \cdot F dS \tag{6}$$

is evaluated by means of a conservative linearization based on the parameter vector [6], and scattered to the element vertices using elemental distribution matrices B_i^e [5]. The inviscid contribution to the nodal residual $(R_\Phi)_i$ is then assembled by collecting fractions $\Phi_i^{e,\,inv}$ of the net inviscid fluxes $\Phi^{e,\,inv}$ associated with all the elements by which the node i is surrounded. This is schematically shown in **Figure 1(b)**. Concerning the viscous terms, the corresponding flux balance is evaluated by surface integration along the boundaries of the median dual cell: node i receives a contribution $\Phi_i^{e,\,vis}$ from cell e which accounts for the viscous flux through the portion of ∂C_i that belongs to that cell. This approach can be shown to be equivalent to a Galerkin FE discretization.

Summing up the inviscid and viscous contributions to the nodal residual of gridpoint i one obtains

$$(R_\Phi)_i = \sum_{e \ni i} \left(\Phi_i^{e,\,inv} + \Phi_i^{e,\,vis} \right) = \sum_{e \ni i} \left(B_i^e \Phi^{e,\,inv} + \Phi_i^{e,\,vis} \right). \tag{7}$$

In Eq. (7), the summation ranges over all the elements e that meet in meshpoint i, as shown in **Figure 1(b)**. The construction of the distribution matrices B_i^e involves the solution of $d+1$ small (of order m) dense linear systems for each triangular/tetrahedral element of the mesh thus making FS schemes somewhat more expensive than state-of-the-art FV schemes based upon either central differencing with artificial dissipation or upwind discretizations. The relatively high computational cost of FS discretizations has to be accounted for when deciding whether the Jacobian matrix should be stored in memory or a Jacobian-free method be used instead.

3.2. Time discretisation

One route to achieve second-order time accuracy with FS schemes is to use mass matrices that couple the time derivatives of neighboring grid points. This leads to implicit schemes, even if the spatial residual were treated explicitly. Although a more general framework for the derivation of the mass matrices can be devised [10], the approach adopted in our study consists of formulating the FS scheme as a Petrov-Galerkin FE method with elemental weighting function given by

$$\Omega_i^e = \left(N_i - \frac{1}{d+1} \right) I_{m \times m} - B_i^e. \tag{8}$$

The contribution of element e to the weighted residual equation for grid point i reads

$$\int_{T_e} \left(\Omega_i^e \frac{\partial U}{\partial t} \right) dV = \int_{T_e} \left(\Omega_i^e \frac{\partial U}{\partial Z} \frac{\partial Z}{\partial t} \right) dV, \tag{9}$$

where the chain rule is used to make the dependent variable Z appear. Since the conservative variables U are quadratic functions of the parameter vector Z, the transformation matrix

$\partial U/\partial Z$ is linear in Z and can thus be expanded using the linear shape functions N_j, just as in Eq. (4). A similar expansion applies to the time-derivative $\partial Z/\partial t$. Replacing both expansions in the RHS of Eq. (9), the discrete counterpart of the time derivative of Eq. (9) is given by the contribution of all elements sharing the node i:

$$\int_{C_i} \frac{\partial U_i}{\partial t} dV = \sum_e \int_{T_e} \left(\Omega_i^e \frac{\partial U}{\partial t} \right) dV = \sum_{e \ni i} \sum_{j \in e} M_{ij}^e \left(\frac{\partial Z}{\partial t} \right)_j . \tag{10}$$

In Eq. (10) the index j spans the vertices of the element e and the nodal values $(\partial Z/\partial t)_j$ are approximated by the three-level Finite Difference (FD) formula

$$\left(\frac{\partial Z}{\partial t} \right)_j = \frac{3Z_j^{n+1} - 4Z_j^n + Z_j^{n-1}}{2\Delta t} . \tag{11}$$

The matrix M_{ij}^e in Eq. (10) is the contribution of element e to the entry in the ith row and j^{th} column of the global mass matrix $[M]$. Similarly to what is done in the assembly of the inviscid and viscous flux balance, Eq. (7), the discretization of the unsteady term, Eq. (10), is obtained by collecting elemental contributions from all the elements that surround the node i. Second-order space and time accuracy of the scheme described above has been demonstrated for inviscid flow problems by Campobasso et al. [11] using an exact solution of the Euler equations.

3.3. Numerical integration

Writing down the space- and time-discretized form of Eq. (1) for all gridpoints of the mesh, one obtains the following large, sparse system of non-linear algebraic equations

$$R_g(U(Z)) = R_\Phi(U(Z)) - [M] \frac{1}{\Delta t} \left(\frac{3}{2} Z^{n+1} - 2Z^n + \frac{1}{2} Z^{n-1} \right) = 0 \tag{12}$$

to be solved at time level $n+1$ to obtain the unknown solution vector U^{n+1}. The solution of Eq. (12) is obtained by means of an implicit approach based on the use of a fictitious time-derivative (Jameson's dual time-stepping [12]) that amounts to solve the following evolutionary problem

$$\frac{dU}{d\tau} [V_M] = R_g(U) \tag{13}$$

in pseudo-time τ until steady state is reached. Since accuracy in pseudo-time is obviously irrelevant, the mass matrix has been lumped into the diagonal matrix $[V_M]$ and a first-order accurate, two-time levels FD formula

$$\frac{dU}{d\tau} \approx \frac{U^{n+1,k+1} - U^{n+1,k}}{\Delta \tau} \tag{14}$$

is used to approximate the pseudo-time derivative in the LHS of Eq. (13). The outer iterations counter k has been introduced in Eq. (14) to label the pseudo-time levels.

Upon replacing Eq. (14) in Eq. (13), an implicit scheme is obtained if the residual R_g is evaluated at the unknown pseudo-time level $k+1$. Taylor expanding R_g about time level k, one obtains the following sparse system of linear equations

$$\left(\frac{1}{\Delta\tau_k}[V_M] - [J]\right)\Delta U = R_g\left(U^{n+1,k}\right) \qquad [J] = \frac{\partial R_g}{\partial U} \tag{15}$$

to be solved at each outer iteration until the required convergence of R_g is obtained. Steady RANS simulations are accommodated within the presented integration scheme by dropping the physical time-derivative term in Eq. (12). In the limit $\Delta\tau_k \to \infty$, Eq. (15) recovers Newton's rootfinding algorithm, which is known to yield quadratic convergence when the initial guess $U^{n+1,0} = U^n$ is sufficiently close to the sought solution U^{n+1}. This is likely to occur when dealing with unsteady flow problems because the solution of the flow field at a given physical time starts from the converged solution at the preceding time, and this latter constitutes a very convenient initial state. In fact, it is sufficiently close to the sought new solution to allow the use of the exact Newton's method (i.e. $\Delta\tau_k = \infty$ in Eq. (15)) since the first solution step.

The situation is different when dealing with steady flow problems. Newton's method is only locally convergent, meaning that it is guaranteed to converge to a solution when the initial approximation is already close enough to the sought solution. This is generally not the case when dealing with steady flows, and a "globalization strategy" needs to be used in order to avoid stall or divergence of the outer iterations. The choice commonly adopted by various authors [13, 14], and in this study as well, is a pseudo-transient continuation, which amounts to retain the pseudo-transient term in Eq. (15). At the early stages of the iterative process, the pseudo-time step length $\Delta\tau_k$ in Eq. (15) is kept small. The advantage is twofold: on one hand, it helps preventing stall or divergence of the outer iterations; on the other hand, it makes the linear system (15) easier to solve by means of an iterative solver since for moderate values of $\Delta\tau_k$ the term $[V_m]/\Delta\tau_k$ increases the diagonal dominance of the matrix. Once the solution has come close to the steady state, which can be monitored by looking at the norm of the nodal residual R_Φ, we let $\Delta\tau_k$ grow unboundedly so that Newton's method is eventually recovered during the last steps of the iterative process. The time step length $\Delta\tau_k$ is selected according to the Switched Evolution Relaxation (SER) strategy proposed by Mulder and van Leer [15], as follows:

$$\Delta\tau_k = \Delta\tau \min\left(C_{\max}, C_0 \frac{\left\|R_g\left(U^{n+1,0}\right)\right\|_2}{\left\|R_g\left(U^{n+1,k}\right)\right\|_2}\right), \tag{16}$$

where $\Delta\tau$ is the pseudo-time step based upon the stability criterion of the explicit time integration scheme, and C_0 and $C_{\max}$ are user-defined constants controlling the initial and maximum pseudo-time steps used in the actual calculations.

In the early stages of the iterative process, the turbulent transport equation and the mean flow equations are solved in tandem (or in a loosely coupled manner, following the nomenclature used by Zingg et al. [16]): the mean flow solution is advanced over a single pseudo-time step using an analytically computed, but approximate Jacobian while keeping turbulent viscosity frozen, then the turbulent variable is advanced over one or more pseudo-time steps using a FD Jacobian with frozen mean flow variables. Due to the uncoupling between the mean flow and turbulent transport equations, this procedure will eventually converge to steady state, but never yields quadratic convergence. Close to steady state, when a true Newton strategy preceded by a "short" pseudo-transient continuation phase can be adopted, the mean flow and the turbulence transport equation are solved in fully coupled form, and the Jacobian is computed by FD. For the sake of completeness, we give further details of each of these two steps in the following two paragraphs.

3.3.1. *Tandem solution strategy with (approximate) Picard linearization*

Consider re-writing the steady nodal residual R_Φ, see [17] for full details, as

$$R_\Phi(U) = ([C] - [D])U, \tag{17}$$

where $[C]$ and $[D]$ are (sparse) matrices that account for the convective and diffusive contributions to the nodal residual vector R_Φ. Matrix $[D]$ is constant for isothermal, incompressible flows whereas it depends upon the flow variables through molecular viscosity in the case of compressible flows. Matrix $[C]$ depends upon U for both compressible and incompressible flows. Both matrices can be computed analytically as described in [17]. What we refer to as a Picard linearization consists in the following approximation

$$J \approx [C] - [D], \tag{18}$$

which amounts to neglect the dependence of matrices $[C]$ and $[D]$ upon U when differentiating the residual, written as in Eq. (17).

Once the mean flow solution has been advanced over a single pseudo-time step using the approximate Picard linearization, keeping the turbulent viscosity frozen, the turbulent variable is advanced over one or more (typically ten) pseudo-time steps using a FD Jacobian approximation (described in Section 3.3.2) with frozen mean flow variables. Blanco and Zingg [18] adopt a similar strategy, but keep iterating the turbulence transport equation until its residual has become lower than that of the mean flow equations. The loosely coupled solution strategy is a choice often made as it "allows for the easy interchange of new turbulence models" [19] and also reduces the storage [18], compared to a fully coupled approach. However, due to the uncoupling between the mean flow and the turbulent transport equations, the tandem solution strategy never yields quadratic convergence nor it is always able to drive the nodal residual to machine zero. The last statement cannot be generalized, since Blanco and Zingg [16, 20] report convergence to machine zero for their loosely coupled approach on two-dimensional unstructured grids. However, even if convergence to machine zero is difficult to achieve, the nodal residual is always sufficiently converged for any practical "engineering" purpose and close enough to "true" steady-state solution to be a good initial guess for Newton's method.

3.3.2. *Fully coupled solution strategy with FD Newton linearization*

Once the tandem solution strategy has provided a good approximation to the steady flow, or when dealing with unsteady flows, in which case the solution at a given time level is generally a good approximation to the one sought at the next time level, it becomes very attractive to take advantage of the quadratic convergence of Newton's method. In order to do so, however, the mean flow and the turbulence transport equations must be solved fully coupled and the Jacobian matrix $[J]$ must be accurate. We take advantage of the compactness of the computational stencil required by FS schemes to compute a close approximation to the true Jacobian matrix even for second-order accurate discretizations. The analytical evaluation of the Jacobian matrix, though not impossible [5, 21], is rather cumbersome and thus this approach is not pursued here.

When the equations are fully coupled, the structure of the Jacobian matrix $[J]$ is naturally organized into small dense blocks of order m. This has implications both in terms of storage, since it is possible to reduce the length of the integer pointers that define the Compressed Sparse Row (CSR) data structure of the sparse matrix, and also in the design of the preconditioner for solving the large linear system at each Newton step, where division operations can be efficiently replaced by block matrix factorizations. We will address these issues in detail in the next section. Two neighboring gridpoints, i and j, in the mesh will contribute two block entries, J_{ij} and J_{ji}, to the global Jacobian matrix $[J]$. Each of these two block entries (say J_{ij}, for instance) will be computed by assembling elemental contributions coming from all the cells that share vertex i, as follows

$$J_{ij} = \sum_{e \ni i} J^e_{ij}. \tag{19}$$

Eq. (19) follows by applying the sum rule of differentiation and by observing that the nodal residual itself is a sum of contributions from the elements that share vertex i, see **Figure 1(b)**. Specifically, element J^e_{ij} accounts for the contribution of cell e to the residual change at gridpoint i, due to a change in the state vector of a neighboring gridpoint j that belongs to the same element e. The contribution of cell e to the element (p, q) of the block J_{ij} is computed from the following one-sided FD formula

$$\left(J^e_{i,j}\right)_{p,q} = \frac{\left(R^e_g\right)^p_i \left(U_i, \widehat{U}^q_j, \dots\right) - \left(R^e_g\right)\left(U_i, U_j, \dots\right)}{\varepsilon} \quad 1 \le p, q \le m; \; i, j \in e, \tag{20}$$

where $\left(R^e_g\right)^p_i$ is the pth component of the contribution of cell e to the nodal residual of gridpoint i. In Eq. (20) we have emphasized that $\left(R^e_g\right)_i$ only depends upon the flow state of the $d + 1$ vertices of cell e, which include both i and j. The first partial derivative, $\left(R^e_g\right)^p_i \left(U_i, \widehat{U}^q_j, \dots\right)$ is computed by perturbing the qth component of the conserved variables vector at gridpoint j as follows

$$\widehat{U}^q_j = \left(u^1_j, u^2_j, \dots, u^q_j + \varepsilon\left(u^q_j\right), \dots, u^m_j\right), \tag{21}$$

where ε is a "small" quantity. Due to the use of a one-sided FD formula, the FD approximation (20) of the Jacobian entry is affected by a truncation error which is proportional to the first power of ε. Small values of ε keep the truncation error small, but too small values may lead to round-off errors. Following [21], ε is computed as

$$\varepsilon(x) = \sqrt{\varepsilon_{mc}}\max(|x|, 1) \ \ \mathrm{sgn}\,(x). \tag{22}$$

From a coding viewpoint, the same loop over all cells used to build the nodal residual R_g is also used to assemble matrix $[J]$. The operations to be performed within each cell are the following: *i*) perturb each of the m components of the conserved variables vector of the $d+1$ vertices of cell e; *ii*) evaluate the residual contribution to each of the vertices; *iii*) calculate the Jacobian entries according to Eq. (20). While looping over cell e, this contributes $(d+1)^2$ block entries to the global matrix $[J]$. Moreover, it follows that the cost of a Jacobian evaluation is equal to $m \times (d+1)$ residual evaluations, which can be quite a large number. For instance, for a 3D compressible RANS calculation using a one-equation turbulence model, $m \times (d+1) = 24$. In this study, it was decided to store the Jacobian matrix in memory rather than using a Jacobian-free (JFNK), as the Jacobian matrix is relatively sparse even for a second-order accurate discretization due to the compactness of the stencil. The JFNK approach avoids assembling and, more important, storing the Jacobian matrix. However, the matrix-vector product is replaced with the Jacobian matrix by FD formulae which requires extra costly FS residual evaluations. Note that the JFNK method still requires the construction of a preconditioner to be used by the iterative linear solver, often an Incomplete Lower Upper factorization, which is typically constructed using a lower order approximation of the residual vector. Matrix-free preconditioners might also be used [22], saving a huge storage at the expense of extra CPU cost. These latter are referred to as MFNK methods. Although JFNK or MFNK approaches should certainly be favored from the viewpoint of memory occupation, it cannot always be "assumed that the Jacobian-free matrix-vector products are inherently advantageous in terms of computing time" [13].

The compactness of the FS stencil, which never extends beyond the set of distance-1 neighbors even for a second-order-accurate space-time discretization, offers two advantages. On one hand, apart from the truncation and round-off errors involved in the FD derivatives, the numerical Jacobian matrix is a close approximation of the analytical Jacobian, even for a second-order-accurate discretization. This feature is crucial for retaining the quadratic convergence properties of Newton's algorithm. On the other hand, it is considerably sparser than that obtained using more traditional FV discretizations, which typically extend up to distance-2 [1] or even distance-3 neighbors [8]. In these latter cases, contributions from the outermost gridpoints in the stencil have to be neglected [1], or at least lumped [8], when constructing the Jacobian approximation upon which the ILU(ℓ) preconditioner is built. These approximations are a potential source of performance degradation as reported in [8]. The memory occupation required to store the Jacobian matrix still remains remarkable. Moreover, not only the Jacobian matrix, but also its preconditioner needs to be stored in the computer memory. It is therefore clear that a key ingredient that would help reducing memory occupation is an effective preconditioner having a relatively small number of non-zero entries, as close as possible to that of the Jacobian matrix. This demanding problem is addressed in the next section.

4. Linear solve and preconditioning

The previous discussions have pointed that the solution of the large nonsymmetric sparse linear system (15) at each pseudo-time step is a major computational task of the whole flow simulation, especially when the mean flow and the turbulence transport equations are solved in fully coupled form, the Jacobian is computed *exactly* by means of FD, and the size of the time-step is rapidly increased to recover Newton's algorithm. For convenience, we write system (15) in compact form as

$$Ax = b, \tag{23}$$

where $A = [a_{ij}]$ is the large and sparse coefficient matrix of, say, size n, and b is the right-hand side vector. It is well established that, when A is highly nonsymmetric and/or indefinite, iterative methods need the assistance of preconditioning to transform system (23) into an equivalent one that is more amenable to an iterative solver. The transformed *preconditioned system* writes in the form $M^{-1}Ax = M^{-1}b$ when preconditioning is applied from the left, or $AM^{-1}y = b$ with $x = M^{-1}y$ when preconditioning is applied from the right. The matrix M is a nonsingular approximation to A called the *preconditioner matrix*. In the coming sections, we describe the development of an effective algebraic preconditioner for the RANS model.

4.1. Multi-elimination ILU factorization preconditioner

Incomplete LU factorization methods (ILUs) are an effective, yet simple, class of preconditioning techniques for solving large linear systems. They write in the form $M = \overline{L}\,\overline{U}$, where $\overline{L}$ and $\overline{U}$ are approximations of the L and U factors of the standard triangular LU decomposition of A. The incomplete factorization may be computed directly from the Gaussian Elimination (GE) algorithm, by discarding some entries in the L and U factors according to various strategies, see [3]. A stable ILU factorization is proved to exist for arbitrary choices of the sparsity pattern of $\overline{L}$ and $\overline{U}$ only for particular classes of matrices, such as M-matrices [23] and H-matrices with positive diagonal entries [24]. However, many techniques can help improve the quality of the preconditioner on more general problems, such as reordering, scaling, diagonal shifting, pivoting and condition estimators [25–28]. As a result of this recent development, in the past decade successful experience have been reported using ILU preconditioners in areas that were of exclusive domain of direct solution methods like, in circuits simulation, power system networks, chemical engineering plants modeling, graphs and other problems not governed by PDEs, or in areas where direct methods have been traditionally preferred, such as structural analysis, semiconductor device modeling, computational fluid dynamics (see [29–33]).

Multi-elimination ILU factorization is a powerful class of ILU preconditioners, which combines the simplicity of ILU techniques with the robustness and high degree of parallelism of domain decomposition methods [34]. It is developed on the idea that, due to sparsity, many unknowns of a linear system are not coupled by an equation (i.e. they are *independent*) and thus they can be eliminated simultaneously at a given stage of GE. If the, say m, independent unknowns are numbered first, and the other $n - m$ unknowns last, the coefficient matrix of the system is permuted in a 2×2 block structure of the form

$$PAP^T = \begin{pmatrix} D & F \\ E & C \end{pmatrix}, \tag{24}$$

where D is a diagonal matrix of dimension m and C is a square matrix of dimension $n - m$. In multi-elimination methods, a reduced system is recursively constructed from (24) by computing a block LU factorization of PAP^T of the form

$$\begin{pmatrix} D & F \\ E & C \end{pmatrix} = \begin{pmatrix} L & 0 \\ G & I_{n-m} \end{pmatrix} \times \begin{pmatrix} U & W \\ 0 & A_1 \end{pmatrix}, \tag{25}$$

where L and U are the triangular factors of the LU factorization of D, $A_1 = C - ED^{-1}F$ is the Schur complement with respect to C, I_{n-m} is the identity matrix of dimension $n - m$, and we denote $G = EU^{-1}$ and $W = L^{-1}F$. The reduction process can be applied another time to the reduced system with A_1, and recursively to each consecutively reduced system until the Schur complement is small enough to be solved with a standard method such as a dense LAPACK solver [35]. Multi-elimination ILU factorization preconditioners may be obtained from the decomposition (25) by performing the reduction process inexactly, by dropping small entries in the Schur complement matrix and/or factorizing D approximately at each reduction step. These preconditioners exhibit better parallelism than conventional ILU algorithms, due to the recursive factorization. Additionally, for comparable memory usage, they may be significantly more robust especially for solving large problems as the reduced system is typically small and better conditioned compared to the full system.

The factorization (25) defines a general framework which may accommodate for many different methods. An important distinction between various methods is rooted in the choice of the algorithm used to discover sets of independent unknowns. Many of these algorithms are borrowed from graph theory, where such sets are referred to as *independent sets*. Denoting as $G = (V, E)$ the adjacency graph of A, where $V = \{v_1, v_2, \ldots, v_n\}$ is the set of vertices and E the set of edges, a *vertex independent set* S is defined as a subset of V such that

$$\forall v_i \in S, \forall v_j \in S : (v_i, v_j) \notin E. \tag{26}$$

The set S is maximal if there is no other independent set containing S strictly [36]. Independent sets in a graph may be computed by simple greedy algorithms which traverse the vertices in the natural order $1, 2, \ldots, n$, mark each visited vertex v and all of its nearest neighbors connected to v by an edge, and add v and each visited node that is not already marked to the independent set [37]. As an alternative to the greedy algorithm, the nested dissection ordering [38], mesh partitioning, or further information from the set of nested finite element grids of the underlying problem can be used [39–41].

The multilevel preconditioner considered in our study is the Algebraic Recursive Multilevel Solvers (ARMS) introduced in [25], which uses block independent sets computed by the simple greedy algorithm. Block independent sets are characterized by the property that unknowns of two different sets have no coupling, while unknowns within the same set may be coupled. In this case, the matrix D appearing in (24) is block diagonal, and may typically consist of large-sized diagonal blocks that are factorized by an ILU factorization with threshold (ILUT [42]) for memory efficiency. In the ARMS implementation described in [25], first the incomplete triangular factors $\overline{L}$, $\overline{U}$ of D are computed by one sweep of ILUT, and an approximation $\overline{W}$ to $\overline{L}^{-1}F$ is also computed. In a second loop, an approximation $\overline{G}$ to $E\overline{U}^{-1}$ and an approximate Schur complement matrix $\overline{A}_1$ are derived. This holds at each reduction level. At the last level, another sweep of ILUT is applied to the (last) reduced system. The blocks $\overline{W}$ and $\overline{G}$ are stored temporarily, and then discarded from the data structure after the Schur complement matrix is computed. Only the incomplete factors of D at each level, those of the last level Schur matrix, and the permutation arrays are needed for the solving phase. By this implementation, dropping can be performed separately in the matrices $\overline{L}$, $\overline{U}$, $\overline{W}$, $\overline{G}$, $\overline{A}_1$. This in turns allows to factor D accurately without incurring additional costs in $\overline{G}$ and $\overline{W}$, achieving high computational and memory efficiency. Implementation details and careful selection of the parameters are always critical aspects to consider in the design of sparse matrix algorithms. Next, we show how to combine the ARMS method with matrix compression techniques to exploit the block structure of A for better efficiency.

4.2. The variable-block ARMS factorization

The discretization of the Navier-Stokes equations for turbulent compressible flows assigns five distinct variables to each grid point (density, scaled energy, two components of the scaled velocity, and turbulence transport variable); these reduce to four for incompressible, constant density flows, and to three if additionally the flow is laminar. If the, say ℓ, distinct variables associated with the same node are numbered consecutively, the permuted matrix has a sparse block structure with non-zero blocks of size $\ell \times \ell$. The blocks are usually fully dense, as variables at the same node are mutually coupled. Exploiting any available block structure in the preconditioner design may bring several benefits [43], some of them are explained below:

1. *Memory.* A clear advantage is to store the matrix as a collection of blocks using the variable-block compressed sparse row (VBCSR) format, saving column indices and pointers for the block entries.

2. *Stability.* On indefinite problems, computing with blocks instead of single elements enables a better control of pivot breakdowns, near singularities, and other possible sources of numerical instabilities. Block ILU solvers may be used instead of pointwise ILU methods.

3. *Complexity.* Grouping variables in clusters, the Schur complement is smaller and hopefully the last reduced system is better conditioned and easier to solve.

4. *Efficiency.* A full block implementation, based on higher level optimized BLAS as computational kernels, may be designed leading to better flops to memory ratios on modern cache-based computer architectures.

5. *Cache effects.* Better cache reuse is possible for block algorithms.

It has been demonstrated that block iterative methods often exhibit faster convergence rate than their pointwise analogues for the solution of many classes of two- and three-dimensional partial differential equations (PDEs) [44–46]. For this reason, in the case of the simple Poisson's equation with Dirichlet boundary conditions on a rectangle $(0, \ell_1) \times (0, \ell_2)$ discretized uniformly by using $n_1 + 2$ points in the interval $(0, \ell_1)$ and $n_2 + 2$ points in $(0, \ell_2)$, it is often convenient to number the interior points by lines from the bottom up in the natural ordering, so that one obtains a $n_2 \times n_2$ block tridiagonal matrix with square blocks of size $n_1 \times n_1$; the diagonal blocks are tridiagonal matrices and the off-diagonal blocks are diagonal matrices. For large finite element discretizations, it is common to use substructuring, where each substructure of the physical mesh corresponds to one sparse block of the system. If the domain is highly irregular or the matrix does not correspond to a differential equation, finding the best block partitioning is much less obvious. In this case, graph reordering techniques are worth considering.

The PArameterized BLock Ordering (PABLO) method proposed by O'Neil and Szyld is one of the first block reordering algorithms for sparse matrices [47]. The algorithm selects groups of nodes in the adjacency graph of the coefficient matrix such that the corresponding diagonal blocks are either full or very dense. It has been shown that classical block stationary iterative methods such as block Gauss-Seidel and SOR methods combined with the PABLO ordering require fewer operations than their point analogues for the finite element discretization of a Dirichlet problem on a graded L-shaped region, as well as on the 9-point discretization of the Laplacian operator on a square grid. The complexity of the PABLO algorithm is proportional to the number of nodes and edges in both time and space.

Another useful approach to compute dense blocks in the sparsity pattern of a matrix A is the method proposed by Ashcraft in [48]. The algorithm searches for sets of rows or columns having the exact same pattern. From a graph viewpoint, it looks for vertices of the adjacency graph (V, E) of A having the same adjacency list. These are also called *indistinguishable nodes* or *cliques*. The algorithm assigns a *checksum* quantity to each vertex, using the function

$$chk(u) = \sum_{(u,w) \in E} w, \tag{27}$$

and then sorts the vertices by their checksums. This operation takes $|E| + |V| \log |V|$ time. If u and v are indistinguishable, then $chk(u) = chk(v)$. Therefore, the algorithm examines nodes having the same checksum to see if they are indistinguishable. The ideal checksum function would assign a different value for each different row pattern that occurs but it is not practical because it may quickly lead to huge numbers that may not even be machine-representable. Since the time cost required by Ashcraft's method is generally negligible relative to the time it takes to solve the system, simple checksum functions such as (27) are used in practice [48].

On the other hand, sparse unstructured matrices may sometimes exhibit *approximate dense blocks* consisting mostly of non-zero entries, except for a few zeros inside the blocks. By treating these few zeros as non-zero elements, with a little sacrifice of memory, a block ordering may be generated for an iterative solver. Approximate dense blocks in a matrix may be computed by numbering consecutively rows and columns having a similar non-zero structure. However, this would require a new checksum function that preserves the proximity of patterns, in the sense that close patterns would result in close checksum values. Unfortunately, this property does not hold true for Ashcraft's algorithm in its original form. In [49], Saad proposed to compare angles of rows (or columns) to compute approximate dense structures in a matrix A. Let C be the pattern matrix of A, which by definition has the same pattern as A and the non-zero values are equal to 1. The method proposed by Saad computes the upper triangular part of CC^T. Entry (i,j) is the inner product (the cosine value) between row i and row j of C for $j > i$. A parameter τ is used to gauge the proximity of row patterns. If the cosine of the angle between rows i and j is smaller than τ, row j is added to the group of row i. For $\tau = 1$ the method will compute perfectly dense blocks, while for $\tau < 1$ it may compute larger blocks where some zero entries are padded in the pattern. To speed up the search, it may be convenient to run a first pass with the checksum algorithm to detect rows having an identical pattern, and group them together; then, in a second pass, each non-assigned row is scanned again to determine whether it can be added to an existing group. Two important performance measures to gauge the quality of the block ordering computed are the *average block density* (*av_bd*) value, defined as the amount of non-zeros in the matrix divided by the amount of elements in the non-zero blocks, and the *average block size* (*av_bs*) value, which is the ratio between the sum of dimensions of the square diagonal blocks divided by the number of diagonal blocks. The cost of Saad's method is closer to that of checksum-based methods for cases in which a good blocking already exists, and in most cases it remains inferior to the cost of the least expensive block LU factorization, i.e. block ILU(0).

Our recently developed variable-block variant of the ARMS method (VBARMS) incorporates an angle-based compression technique during the factorization to detect fine-grained dense structures in the linear system automatically, without any users knowledge of the underlying problem, and exploits them to improve the overall robustness and throughput of the basic multilevel algorithm [50]. It is simpler to describe VBARMS from a graph point of view. Suppose to permute A in block form as

$$\tilde{A} \approx P_B A P_B^T = \begin{bmatrix} \tilde{A}_{11} & \tilde{A}_{12} & \cdots & \tilde{A}_{1p} \\ \tilde{A}_{21} & \tilde{A}_{22} & \cdots & \tilde{A}_{2p} \\ \vdots & \vdots & \ddots & \vdots \\ \tilde{A}_{p1} & \tilde{A}_{p2} & \cdots & \tilde{A}_{pp} \end{bmatrix}, \tag{28}$$

where the diagonal blocks $\tilde{A}_{ii}$, $i = 1, \ldots, p$ are $n_i \times n_i$ and the off-diagonal blocks $\tilde{A}_{ij}$ are $n_i \times n_j$. We use upper case letters to denote matrix sub-blocks and lower case letters for individual matrix entries. We may represent the adjacency graph of $\tilde{A}$ by the quotient graph of $A + A^T$ [36]. Calling $\mathcal{B}$ the partition into blocks given by (28), we denote as $\mathcal{G}/\mathcal{B} = \{V_\mathcal{B}, E_\mathcal{B}\}$ the quotient graph obtained by coalescing the vertices assigned to the block $\tilde{A}_{ii}$ (for $i = 1, \ldots, p$) into a supervertex Y_i. In other words, the entry in position (i,j) of $\tilde{A}$ is a block of dimension $|Y_i| \times |Y_j|$, where $|X|$ is the cardinality of the set X. With this notation, the quotient graph $\mathcal{G}/\mathcal{B} = \{V_\mathcal{B}, E_\mathcal{B}\}$ is defined as

$$V_\mathcal{B} = \{Y_1, \ldots, Y_p\}, E_\mathcal{B} = \{(Y_i, Y_j) \mid \exists v \in Y_i, w \in Y_j \text{ s.t.} (v, w) \in E\}. \tag{29}$$

An edge connects two supervertices Y_i and Y_j if there exists an edge from a vertex in A_{ii} to a vertex in A_{jj} in the graph $\{V, E\}$ of $A + A^T$.

The complete pre-processing and factorization process of VBARMS consists of the following steps.

Step 1. Find the block ordering P_B of A such that, upon permutation, the matrix $P_B A P_B^T$ has fairly dense non-zero blocks. We use the angle-based graph compression algorithm proposed by Saad and described earlier to compute exact or approximate block structures in A.

Step 2. Scale the matrix at Step 1 in the form $S_1 P_B A P_B^T S_2$ using two diagonal matrices S_1 and S_2, so that the 1-norm of the largest entry in each row and column is smaller or equal than 1.

Step 3. Find the block independent sets ordering P_I of the quotient graph $\mathcal{G}/\mathcal{B} = \{V_\mathcal{B}, E_\mathcal{B}\}$. Apply the permutation to the matrix obtained at Step 2 as

$$P_I S_1 P_B A P_B^T S_2 P_I^T = \begin{pmatrix} D & F \\ E & C \end{pmatrix}. \tag{30}$$

We use a simple form of weighted greedy algorithm for computing the ordering P_I. The algorithm is the same as the one used in ARMS, and described in [25]. It consists of traversing the vertices $\mathcal{G}/\mathcal{B}$ in the natural order $1, 2, \ldots, n$, marking each visited vertex v and all of its nearest neighbors connected to v by an edge and adding v and each visited node that is not already marked to the independent set. We assign the weight $\|Y\|_F$ to each supervertex Y.

In the 2×2 partitioning (30), the upper left-most matrix D is block diagonal like in ARMS. However, due to the block permutation, the diagonal blocks of D are additionally block sparse matrices, as opposed to simply sparse matrices in ARMS and in other forms of multilevel incomplete LU factorizations, see [51, 52]. The matrices F, E, C are also block sparse because of the same reason.

Step 4. Factorize the matrix (30) in the form

$$\begin{pmatrix} D & F \\ E & C \end{pmatrix} = \begin{pmatrix} L & 0 \\ EU^{-1} & I \end{pmatrix} \times \begin{pmatrix} U & L^{-1}F \\ 0 & A_1 \end{pmatrix}, \tag{31}$$

where I is the identity matrix of appropriate size, and form the reduced system with the Schur complement

$$A_1 = C - ED^{-1}F. \tag{32}$$

The Schur complement is also block sparse and has the same block partitioning of C.

Steps 2–4 can be repeated on the reduced system a few times until the Schur complement is small enough. After one additional level, we obtain

$$P_I^{(1)} S_1^{(1)} A_1 S_2^{(1)} (P_I^{(1)})^T = \left[\begin{array}{cc|c} D & F_1 & F_2 \\ E_1 & C_{11} & C_{12} \\ \hline E_2 & C_{21} & C_{22} \end{array}\right], \tag{33}$$

that can be factored as

$$\left[\begin{array}{cc|c} L_D & 0 & 0 \\ L_{E_1} & I & 0 \\ \hline L_{E_2} & L_{C_{21}} & I \end{array}\right]\left[\begin{array}{cc|c} D & 0 & 0 \\ 0 & D_{C_{11}} & 0 \\ \hline 0 & 0 & A_2 \end{array}\right]\left[\begin{array}{cc|c} U_D & U_{F_1} & U_{F_2} \\ 0 & I & U_{C_{12}} \\ \hline 0 & 0 & I \end{array}\right]. \tag{34}$$

Denote as A_ℓ the reduced Schur complement matrix at level ℓ, for $\ell > 1$. After scaling and preordering A_ℓ, a system with the matrix

$$P_I^{(\ell)} D_1^{(\ell)} A_\ell D_2^{(\ell)} \left(P_I^{(\ell)}\right)^T = \begin{pmatrix} D_\ell & F_\ell \\ E_\ell & C_\ell \end{pmatrix} = \begin{pmatrix} L_\ell & 0 \\ E_\ell U_\ell^{-1} & I \end{pmatrix} \times \begin{pmatrix} U_\ell & L_\ell^{-1} F_\ell \\ 0 & A_{\ell+1} \end{pmatrix} \tag{35}$$

needs to be solved, with

$$A_{\ell+1} = C_\ell - E_\ell D_\ell^{-1} F_\ell. \tag{36}$$

Calling

$$x_\ell = \begin{pmatrix} y_\ell \\ z_\ell \end{pmatrix}, \ b_\ell = \begin{pmatrix} f_\ell \\ g_\ell \end{pmatrix} \tag{37}$$

the unknown solution vector and the right-hand side vector of system (35), the solution process with the above multilevel VBARMS factorization consists of level-by-level forward elimination followed by an exact solution on the last reduced system and suitable inverse permutation. The solving phase is sketched in Algorithm 1.

In VBARMS, we perform the factorization approximately, for memory efficiency. We use block ILU factorization with threshold to invert inexactly both the upper leftmost matrix $D_\ell \approx \overline{L}_\ell \overline{U}_\ell$ at each level ℓ, and the last level Schur complement matrix $A_{\ell_{max}} \approx \overline{L}_S \overline{U}_S$. The block ILU method used in VBARMS is a straightforward block variant of the one-level pointwise ILUT algorithm. We drop small blocks $B \in R^{m_B \times n_B}$ in $\overline{L}_\ell$, $\overline{U}_\ell$, $\overline{L}_S$, $\overline{U}_S$ whenever $\frac{\|B\|_F}{m_B \cdot n_B} < t$, for a given user-defined threshold t. The block pivots in block ILU are inverted exactly by using GE with partial pivoting. In assembling the Schur complement matrix $A_{\ell+1}$ at level ℓ, we take advantage of the finest block structure of D_ℓ, F_ℓ, E_ℓ, C_ℓ, imposed by the block ordering P_B on the small (usually dense) blocks in the diagonal blocks of D_ℓ and the corresponding small off-diagonal blocks in E_ℓ and F_ℓ; we call optimized level-3 BLAS routines [53] for computing $A_{\ell+1}$ in Eq. (36). We do not drop entries in the Schur complement, except at the last level. The same threshold is applied in all these operations.

The VBARMS code is developed in the C language and is adapted from the existing ARMS code available in the ITSOL package [54]. The compressed sparse storage format of ARMS is modified to store block vectors and block matrices of variable size as a collection of contiguous non-zero dense blocks (we refer to this data storage format as VBCSR). First, we compute the factors $\overline{L}_\ell$, $\overline{U}_\ell$ and $\overline{L}_\ell^{-1} F_\ell$ by performing a variant of the IKJ version of the Gaussian Elimination algorithm, where index I runs from 2 to m_ℓ, index K from 1 to $(I-1)$ and index J from $(K+1)$ to n_ℓ. This loop applies implicitly $\overline{L}_\ell^{-1}$ to the block row $[D_\ell, F_\ell]$ to produce $\left[U_\ell, \overline{L}_\ell^{-1} F_\ell\right]$. In the second loop, Gaussian Elimination is performed on the block row $[E_\ell, C_\ell]$ using the multipliers computed in the first loop to give $E_\ell \overline{U}_\ell^{-1}$ and an approximation of the Schur complement $A_{\ell+1}$. Then, after Step 1, we permute explicitly the matrix at the first level as well as the matrices involved in the factorization at each new reordering step. For extensive performance assessment results of the VBARMS method, we point the reader to [50].

Algorithm 1 `VBARMS_Solve`$(A_{\ell+1}, b_\ell)$. The solving phase with the VBARMS method.

Require: $\ell \in \mathbb{N}^*$, $\ell_{max} \in \mathbb{N}^*$, $b_\ell = (f_\ell, g_\ell)^T$

1: Solve $L_\ell y = f_\ell$

2: Compute $g'_\ell = g_\ell - E_\ell U_\ell^{-1} y$

3: **if** $\ell = \ell_{max}$ **then**

4: Solve $A_{\ell+1} z_\ell = g'_\ell$

5: else

6: Call `VBARMS_Solve`$(A_{\ell+1}, g'_\ell)$

7: **end if**

8: Solve $U_\ell y_\ell = \left[y - L_\ell^{-1} F_\ell z_\ell\right]$

---

5. Numerical experiments

In this section, we illustrate the performance of the VBARMS method for solving a suite of block structured linear systems arising from an implicit Newton-Krylov formulation of the RANS equations in the turbulent incompressible flow analysis past a three-dimensional wing. On multicore machines, the quotient graph $\mathcal{G}/\mathcal{B}$ is split into distinct subdomains, and each of them is assigned to a different core. Following the parallel framework described in [55], we separate the nodes assigned to the ith subdomain into *interior nodes*, that are those coupled by the equations only with the local variables, and *interface nodes*, those that may be coupled with the local variables stored on processor i as well as with remote variables stored on other processors (see Figure below).

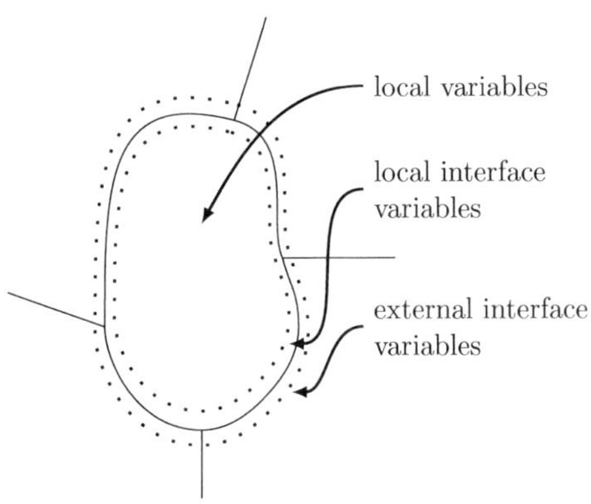

The vector of the local unknowns x_i and the local right-hand side b_i are split accordingly in two separate components: the subvector corresponding to the internal nodes followed by the subvector of the local interface variables

$$x_i = \begin{pmatrix} u_i \\ y_i \end{pmatrix}, \quad b_i = \begin{pmatrix} f_i \\ g_i \end{pmatrix}. \tag{38}$$

The rows of A indexed by the nodes of the ith subdomain are assigned to the ith processor. These are naturally separated into a local matrix A_i acting on the local variables $x_i = (u_i, y_i)^T$, and an interface matrix U_i acting on the remotely stored subvectors of the external interface variables $y_{i,\text{ext}}$. Hence, we can write the local equations on processor i as

$$A_i x_i + U_{i,\text{ext}} y_{i,\text{ext}} = b_i \tag{39}$$

or, in expanded form, as

$$\begin{pmatrix} B_i & F_i \\ E_i & C_i \end{pmatrix} \begin{pmatrix} u_i \\ y_i \end{pmatrix} + \begin{pmatrix} 0 \\ \sum_{j \in N_i} E_{ij} y_j \end{pmatrix} = \begin{pmatrix} f_i \\ g_i \end{pmatrix}, \tag{40}$$

where N_i is the set of subdomains that are neighbors to subdomain i and the submatrix $E_{ij}y_j$ accounts for the contribution to the local equation from the jth neighboring subdomain. Note that matrices B_i, C_i, E_i, and F_i still preserve the fine block structure imposed by the block ordering P_B. From a code viewpoint, the quotient graph is initially distributed amongst the available processors; then, the built-in parallel hypergraph partitioner available in the Zoltan package [56] is applied on the distributed data structure to compute an optimal partitioning of the quotient graph that can minimize the amount of communications.

At this stage, the VBARMS method described in Section 4.2 can be used as a local solver for different types of global preconditioners. In the simplest parallel implementation, the so-called block-Jacobi preconditioner, the sequential VBARMS method can be applied to invert approximately each local matrix A_i. The standard Jacobi iteration for solving $Ax = b$ is defined as

$$x_{n+1} = x_n + D^{-1}(b - Ax_n) = D^{-1}(Nx_n + b), \tag{41}$$

where D is the diagonal of A, $N = D - A$ and x_0 is some initial approximation. In cases we have a graph partitioned matrix, the matrix D is block diagonal and the diagonal blocks of D are the local matrices A_i. The interest to consider the block Jacobi preconditioner is its inherent parallelism, since the solves with the matrices A_i are performed independently on all the processors and no communication is required.

If the diagonal blocks of the matrix D are enlarged in the block-Jacobi method so that they overlap slightly, the resulting preconditioner is called Schwarz preconditioner. Consider again a graph partitioned matrix with N nonoverlapping sets W_i^0, $i = 1, \ldots, N$ and $W_0 = \cup_{i=1}^N W_0^i$. We define a δ-overlap partition

$$W^{\delta} = \bigcup_{i=1}^{N} W_i^{\delta} \tag{42}$$

where $W_i^{\delta} = adj(W_i^{\delta-1})$ and $\delta > 0$ is the level of overlap with the neighboring domains. For each subdomain, we define a restriction operator R_i^{δ}, which is an $n \times n$ matrix with the (j, j)th element equal to 1 if $j \in W_i^{\delta}$, and zero elsewhere. We then denote

$$A_i = R_i^{\delta} A R_i^{\delta}. \tag{43}$$

The global preconditioning matrix M_{RAS} is defined as

$$M_{RAS}^{-1} = \sum_{i=1}^{s} R_i^T A_i^{-1} R_i \tag{44}$$

and named as the Restricted Additive Schwarz (RAS) preconditioner [3, 57]. Note that the preconditioning step still offers a good scope par parallelism, as the different components of the error update are formed independently. However, due to overlapping some communication is required in the final update, as the components are added up from each subdomain. In our experiments, the overlap used for RAS was the level 1 neighbors of the local nodes in the quotient graph.

A third global preconditioner that we consider in this study is based on the Schur complement approach. In Eq. (40), we can eliminate the vector of interior unknowns u_i from the first equations to compute the local Schur complement system

$$S_i y_i + \sum_{j \in N_i} E_{ij} y_j = g_i - E_i B_i^{-1} f_i \equiv g_i', \tag{45}$$

where S_i denotes the local Schur complement matrix

$$S_i = C_i - E_i B_i^{-1} F_i. \tag{46}$$

The local Schur complement equations considered altogether write as the global Schur complement system

$$\begin{pmatrix} S_1 & E_{12} & \dots & E_{1p} \\ E_{21} & S_2 & \dots & E_{2p} \\ \vdots & & \ddots & \vdots \\ E_{p1} & E_{p-1,2} & \dots & S_p \end{pmatrix} \begin{pmatrix} y_1 \\ y_2 \\ \vdots \\ y_p \end{pmatrix} = \begin{pmatrix} g_1' \\ g_2' \\ \vdots \\ g_p' \end{pmatrix}, \tag{47}$$

where the off-diagonal matrices E_{ij} are available from the parallel distribution of the linear system. One preconditioning step with the Schur complement preconditioner consists in solving approximately the global system (47), and then recovering the u_i variables from the local equations as

$$u_i = B_i^{-1}\left[f_i - F_i y_i\right] \tag{48}$$

at the cost of one local solve. We solve the global system (47) by running a few steps of the GMRES method preconditioned by a block diagonal matrix, where the diagonal blocks are the local Schur complements S_i. The factorization

$$S_i = L_{S_i} U_{S_i} \tag{49}$$

is obtained as by-product of the LU factorization of the local matrix A_i,

$$A_i = \begin{pmatrix} L_{B_i} & 0 \\ E_i U_{B_i}^{-1} & L_{S_i} \end{pmatrix} \begin{pmatrix} U_{B_i} & L_{B_i}^{-1} F_i \\ 0 & U_{S_i} \end{pmatrix} \tag{50}$$

which is by the way required to compute the u_i variables in Eq. (48).

5.1. Results

The parallel experiments were run on the large-memory nodes (32 cores/node and 1 TB of memory) of the TACC Stampede system located at the University of Texas at Austin. TACC Stampede is a 10 PFLOPS (PF) Dell Linux Cluster based on 6400+ Dell PowerEdge server nodes, each outfitted with 2 Intel Xeon E5 (Sandy Bridge) processors and an Intel Xeon Phi Coprocessor (MIC Architecture). We linked the default vendor BLAS library, which is MKL. Although MKL is multi-threaded by default, in our runs we used it in a single-thread mode since our MPI-based parallelisation employed one MPI process per core (communicating via the shared memory for the same-node cores). We used the Flexible GMRES (FGMRES) method [58] as Krylov subspace method, a tolerance of $1.0e-6$ in the stopping criterion and a

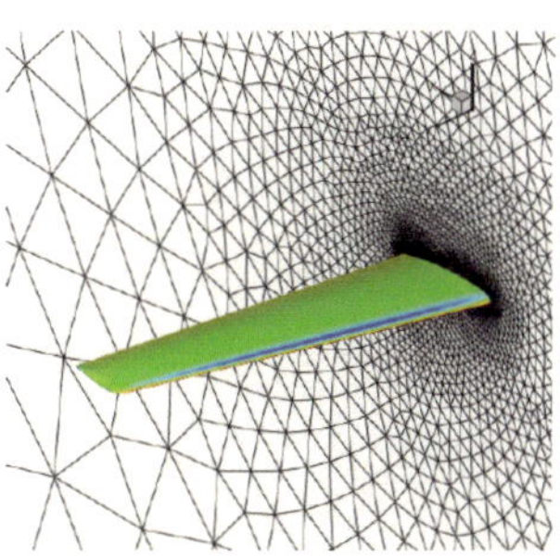

Ref. Area,	S = 290322 mm^2	= 450 in^2
Ref. Chord,	c = 197.556 mm	= 7.778 in
Ref. Span,	b = 1524 mm	= 60 in

RANS1 :	$n =$ 4918165	$nnz =$ 318370485
RANS2 :	$n =$ 4918165	$nnz =$ 318370485
RANS3 :	$n =$ 9032110	$nnz =$ 670075950
RANS4 :	$n =$ 12085410	$nnz =$ 893964000
RANS5 :	$n =$ 22384845	$nnz =$ 1659721325

Figure 2. Geometry and mesh characteristics of the DPW3 Wing-1 problem proposed in the 3rd AIAA drag prediction workshop. Note that problems RANS1 and RANS2 correspond to the same mesh, and are generated at two different Newton steps.

maximum number of iteration equal to 1000. Memory costs were calculated as the ratio between the sum of the number of non-zeros in the local preconditioners and the sum of the number of non-zeros in the local matrices A_i.

In our experiments, we analyzed the turbulent incompressible flow past a three-dimensional wing illustrated in **Figure 2** using the *EulFS* code developed by the second author [59]. The geometry, called DPW3 Wing-1, was proposed in the 3rd AIAA Drag Prediction Workshop [35]. Flow conditions are 0.5° angle of attack and Reynolds number based on the reference chord equal to $5 \cdot 10^6$. The freestream turbulent viscosity is set to 10% of its laminar value. In

Matrix	Method	Graph time (s)	Factorization time (s)	Solving time (s)	Total time (s)	Its	Mem
	BJ + VBARMS	17.3	8.58	41.54	50.13	34	2.98
RANS1	RAS + VBARMS	17.4	10.08	42.28	52.37	19	3.06
	SCHUR + VBARMS	17.6	11.94	55.99	67.93	35	2.57
	BJ + VBARMS	17.0	16.72	70.14	86.86	47	4.35
RANS2	RAS + VBARMS	16.8	21.65	80.24	101.89	39	4.49
	SCHUR + VBARMS	17.5	168.85	173.54	342.39	24	6.47
	BJ + VBARMS	27.2	99.41	187.95	287.36	154	4.40
RANS3	RAS + VBARMS	25.2	119.32	90.47	209.79	71	4.48
	SCHUR + VBARMS	22.0	52.65	721.67	774.31	140	4.39

Table 1. Experiments on the DPW3 Wing-1 problem. The RANS1, RANS2 and RANS3 test cases are solved on 32 processors. We ran one MPI process per core, so in these experiments we used shared memory on a single node.

Matrix	Method	Graph time (s)	Factorization time (s)	Solving time (s)	Total time (s)	Its	Mem
	BJ + VBARMS	51.5	12.05	105.89	117.94	223	3.91
RANS4	RAS + VBARMS	43.9	14.05	91.53	105.58	143	4.12
	SCHUR + VBARMS	39.3	15.14	289.89	305.03	179	3.76
RANS5	RAS + VBARMS	1203.94 (1)	16.80	274.62	291.42	235	4.05

Table 2. Experiments on the DPW3 Wing-1 problem. The RANS4 and RANS5 test cases are solved on 128 processors. Note (1): due to a persistent problem with the Zoltan library on this run, we report on the result of our experiment with the metis (sequential) graph partitioner [60].

Solver	Number of processors	Graph time (s)	Total time (s)	Its	Mem
	8	38.9	388.37	27	5.70
	16	28.0	219.48	35	5.22
RAS + VBARMS	32	17.0	101.49	39	4.49
	64	16.0	54.19	47	3.91
	128	18.2	28.59	55	3.39

Table 3. Strong scalability study on the RANS2 problem using parallel graph partitioning.

Matrix	Method	Factorization time (s)	Solving time (s)	Total time (s)	Its	Mem
	pARMS	–	–	–	–	6.63
RANS3	BJ + VBARMS	99.41	187.95	287.36	154	4.40
	BJ + VBILUT	20.45	8997.82	9018.27	979	13.81
	pARMS	–	–	–	–	5.38
RANS4	BJ + VBARMS	12.05	105.89	117.94	223	3.91
	BJ + VBILUT	1.16	295.20	296.35	472	5.26

Table 4. Experiments on the DPW3 Wing-1 problem. The RANS3 test case is solved on 32 processors and the RANS4 problem on 128 processors. The dash symbol – in the table means that in the GMRES iteration the residual norm is very large and the program is aborted.

Tables 1 and **2** we show experiments with the parallel VBARMS solver on the five meshes of the DPW3 Wing-1 problem. On the largest mesh we report on only one experiment, in **Table 2**, as this is a resource demanding problem. In **Table 3** we report on a strong scalability study on the problem denoted as RANS2 by increasing the number of processors. Finally, in **Table 4** we show comparative results with parallel VBARMS against other popular solvers; the method denoted as pARMS is the solver described in [55] using default parameters while the method VBILUT is a variable-block incomplete lower-upper factorization with threshold from the ITSOL package [54]. The results of our experiments show that the proposed preconditioner is effective to reduce the number of iterations especially in combination with the Restricted Additive Schwarz method, and exhibits good parallel scalability. A truly parallel implementation of the VBARMS method that may offer better numerical scalability will be considered as the next step of this research.

6. Conclusions

The applicability of Newton's method in steady flow simulations is often limited by the difficulty to compute a good initial solution, namely, one lying in a reasonably small neighborhood of the sought solution. This problem can now be overcome by introducing some approximations in the first stages of the solution procedure. In the case of unsteady flow problems, on the other hand, the use of Newton's method in conjunction with a dual-time stepping procedure is even more effective since the flow field computed at the preceding physical time level is likely to be sufficiently close to the sought solution at the next time level to allow the use of Newton's algorithm right from the beginning of the sub-iterations in pseudo-time. On the downside of Newton-Krylov methods is the need for efficiently preconditioned iterative algorithms to solve the sparse linear system arising at each inner iteration (Newton step). The stiffness of the linear systems to be solved increases when the Jacobian is computed "exactly" and the turbulence transport equations are solved fully coupled with the mean flow equations.

In this chapter, we have presented a block multilevel incomplete factorization preconditioner for solving sparse systems of linear equations arising from the implicit RANS formulation. The method detects automatically any existing block structure in the matrix, without any user's prior knowledge of the underlying problem, and exploits it to maximize computational efficiency. The results of this chapter show that, by taking advantage of this block structure, the solver can be more robust and efficient. Other recent studies on block ILU preconditioners have drawn similar conclusions on the importance of exposing dense blocks during the construction of the incomplete LU factorization for better performance, in the design of incomplete multifrontal LU-factorization preconditioners [61] and adaptive blocking approaches for blocked incomplete Cholesky factorization [62]. We believe that the proposed VBARMS method can be useful for solving linear systems also in other areas, such as in Electromagnetics applications [63–65].

Acknowledgements

The authors acknowledge the Texas Advanced Computing Center (TACC) at the University of Texas at Austin for providing HPC resources that have contributed to the research results reported in this chapter. URL: http://www.tacc.utexas.edu. The authors are grateful to Prof. Masha Sosonkina at the Department of Modeling Simulation & Visualization Engineering, Old Dominion University for help and insightful comments.

Nomenclature

Roman symbols

a	artificial sound speed
d	dimension of the space, $d = 2, 3$
e^0	specific total energy
h^0	specific total enthalpy
ℓ	level of fill in incomplete lower upper factorizations
m	number of degrees of freedom within a gridpoint
n	order of a matrix
nnz	number of non-zero entries in a sparse matrix
$\mathbf{n}$	unit inward normal to the control surface
p	static pressure
$\mathbf{q}$	flux vector due to heat conduction
t	time
$\mathbf{u}$	velocity vector
$\mathbf{x}$	vector of the d Cartesian coordinates

C_i	median dual cell (control volume)
∂C_i	boundary of the median dual cell (control surface)
E	edges of a graph
$\mathbf{G}(A)$	graph of matrix A
M	global mass matrix
M_L	left preconditioning matrix
Ma	mach number
I	identity matrix
N_i	shape function
P	permutation matrix
Pr_T	turbulent Prandtl number
R_Φ	spatial residual vector
Re	Reynolds' number
T	triangle or tetrahedron
$\mathbf{U}$	conserved variables vector
V	vertices of a graph
V_M	lumped mass matrix
z	parameter vector

Greek symbols

α	angle of attack
Δt	physical time step
$\Delta \tau$	pseudo-time step
ΔU	$= U^{n+1,k+1} - U^{n+1,k}$
ε_{mc}	machine zero
ρ	density
ν	kinematic viscosity
$\tilde{\nu}$	working variable in the turbulence transport equation
τ	pseudo-time variable
$\underline{\underline{\tau}}$	Newtonian stress tensor

Φ	flux balance
Ω_i^e	Petrov Galerkin weighting function
Subscript	
i	nodal index or row index of a matrix
j	nodal index or column index of a matrix
e	cell index
∞	Free-stream condition
Superscript	
inv	inviscid
k	inner iterations counter
n	physical time step counter
T	transpose
vis	viscous

Author details

Bruno Carpentieri[1]* and Aldo Bonfiglioli[2]

*Address all correspondence to: bcarpentieri@gmail.com

1 Free University of Bolzano-Bozen, Faculty of Computer Science, Italy

2 Scuola di Ingegneria, University of Basilicata, Potenza, Italy

References

[1] Wong P, Zingg DW. Three-dimensional aerodynamic computations on unstructured grids using a Newton-Krylov approach. Computers & Fluids. 2008;**37**(2):107-120

[2] Bonfiglioli A, Campobasso S, Carpentieri B. Parallel unstructured three-dimensional turbulent flow analyses using efficiently preconditioned Newton-Krylov solvers. In: Proceedings of the 19th AIAA Computational Fluid Dynamics Conference 2009, San Antonio, Texas; 2009

[3] Saad Y. Iterative Methods for Sparse Linear Systems. 2nd edition. Philadelphia: SIAM; 2003

[4] Spalart PR, Allmaras SR. A one-equation turbulence model for aerodynamic flows. LaRecherche-Aerospatiale. 1994;**1**:5-21

[5] van der Weide E, Deconinck H, Issman E, Degrez G. A parallel, implicit, multi-dimensional upwind, residual distribution method for the Navier-Stokes equations on unstructured grids. Computational Mechanics. 1999;**23**:199-208

[6] Deconinck H, Roe PL, Struijs R. A multi-dimensional generalization of Roe's flux difference splitter for the Euler equations. Journal of Computers and Fluids. 1993;**22**(2/3):215-222

[7] Gropp WD, Kaushik DK, Keyes DE, Smith BF. High-performance parallel implicit cfd. Parallel Computing. 2001;**27**(4):337-362

[8] Lucas P, Bijl H, van Zuijlen AH. Efficient unsteady high Reynolds number flow computations on unstructured grids. Computers & Fluids. 2010;**39**(2):271-282

[9] Lucas P, van Zuijlen AH, Bijl H. Fast unsteady flow computations with a Jacobian-free Newton-Krylov algorithm. Journal of Computational Physics. 2010;**229**(24):9201-9215

[10] De Palma P, Pascazio, Rossiello G, Napolitano M. A second-order-accurate monotone implicit fluctuation splitting scheme for unsteady problems. Journal of Computational Physics. 2005;**208**(1):1-33

[11] Campobasso MS, Bonfiglioli A, Baba-Ahmadi M. Development of efficient and accurate CFD technologies for wind turbine unsteady aerodynamics. In CMFF'09 Conference on Modelling fluid flow; 2009

[12] Jameson A. Time-dependent calculations using multigrid with applications to unsteady flows past airfoils and wings. AIAA Paper. 1991;**91-1596**

[13] Chisholm TT, Zingg DW. A Jacobian-free Newton-Krylov algorithm for compressible turbulent fluid flows. Journal of Computational Physics. 2009;**228**(9):3490-3507

[14] Geuzaine P. Newton-Krylov strategy for compressible turbulent flows on unstructured meshes. AIAA Journal. October 2001;**39**(3):528-531

[15] Mulder W, van Leer B. Experiments with an implicit upwind method for the Euler equations. Journal of Computational Physics. 1985;**59**:232-246

[16] Blanco M, Zingg DW. A Newton-Krylov Algorithm with a loosely-coupled turbulence model for aerodynamic flows. 44th AIAA Aerospace Sciences Meeting and Exhibit, 9–12 Jan. Reno: Nevada Paper 2006–691; 2006

[17] Bonfiglioli A. Fluctuation splitting schemes for the compressible and incompressible Euler and Navier-Stokes equations. IJCFD. 2000;**14**:21-39

[18] Blanco M, Zingg DW. Newton-Krylov algorithm with a loosely coupled turbulence model for aerodynamic flows. AIAA Journal. 2007;**45**(5):980

[19] Anderson WK, Bonhaus DL. An implicit upwind algorithm for computing turbulent flows on unstructured grids. Journal of Computers and Fluids. 1994;**23**(1):1-21

[20] Nichols JC, Zingg DW. A Three-Dimensional Multi-Block Newton-Krylov Flow Solver for the Euler Equations. 2005. AIAA Paper 2005–5230

[21] Issman E. Implicit Solution Strategies for Compressible Flow Equations on Unstructured Meshes. [PhD thesis]. Bruxelles: Université Libre de Bruxelles; 1997

[22] Qin N, Ludlow DK, Shaw ST. A matrix-free preconditioned Newton/GMRES method for unsteady Navier-Stokes solutions. International Journal for Numerical Methods in Fluids. 2000;**33**(2):223-248

[23] Meijerink JA, van der Vorst HA. An iterative solution method for linear systems of which the coeffcient matrix is a symmetric M-matrix. Mathematics of Computation. 1977;**31**: 148-162

[24] Varga RS, Saff EB, Mehrmann V. Incomplete factorizations of matrices and connections with H-matrices. SIAM Journal on Numerical Analysis. 1980;**17**:787-793

[25] Saad Y, Suchomel B. ARMS: An algebraic recursive multilevel solver for general sparse linear systems. Numerical Linear Algebra with Applications. 2002;**9**(5):359-378

[26] Bollhöfer M, Saad Y. Multilevel preconditioners constructed from inverse–based ILUs. SIAM Journal on Scientific Computing. 2006;**27**(5):1627-1650

[27] Duff IS, Koster J. The design and use of algorithms for permuting large entries to the diagonal of sparse matrices. SIAM Journal on Matrix Analysis and Applications. 1999;**20**(4): 889-901

[28] Magolu monga Made M, Beauwens R, Warzee G. Preconditioning of discrete Helmholtz operators perturbed by a diagonal complex matrix. Communications in Numerical Methods in Engineering. 2000;**11**:801-817

[29] Benzi M. Preconditioning techniques for large linear systems: A survey. Journal of Computational Physics. 2002;**182**:418-477

[30] Bollhöfer M. A robust and efficient ILU that incorporates the growth of the inverse triangular factors. SIAM Journal on Scientific Computing. January 2003;**25**(1):86-103

[31] Manguoglu M. A domain-decomposing parallel sparse linear system solver. Journal of Computational and Applied Mathematics. 2011;**236**(3):319-325

[32] Saad Y. Multilevel ILU with reorderings for diagonal dominance. SIAM Journal on Scientific Computing. 2005;**27**:1032-1057

[33] Saad Y, Soulaimani A, Touihri R. Variations on algebraic recursive multilevel solvers (ARMS) for the solution of CFD problems. Applied Numerical Mathematics. 2004;**51**:305-327

[34] Saad Y. ILUM: A multi-elimination ILU preconditioner for general sparse matrices. SIAM Journal on Scientific Computing. 1996;**17**(4):830-847

[35] Drag Prediction Workshop. URL: http://aaac.larc.nasa.gov/tsab/cfdlarc/aiaa-dpw/Workshop3/workshop3.html

[36] George A, Liu JW. Computer Solution of Large Sparse Positive Definite Systems. Englewood Cliffs, New Jersey: Prentice-Hall; 1981

[37] Saad Y. ILUM: A multi-elimination ILU preconditioner for general sparse matrices. SIAM Journal on Scientific Computing. 1996;**17**(4):830-847

[38] George J. Nested dissection of a regular finite element mesh. SIAM Journal on Numerical Analysis. 1973;**10**:345-363

[39] Axelsson O, Vassilevski PS. Algebraic multilevel preconditioning methods, I. Numerische Mathematik. 1989;**56**:157-177

[40] Axelsson O, Vassilevski PS. Algebraic multilevel preconditioning methods. II. SIAM Journal on Numerical Analysis. 1990;**27**:1569-1590

[41] Botta EFF, van der Ploeg A, Wubs FW. Nested grids ILU-decomposition (NGILU). Journal of Computational and Applied Mathematics. 1996;**66**:515-526

[42] Saad Y. ILUT: A dual threshold incomplete LU factorization. Numerical Linear Algebra with Applications. 1994;**1**:387-402

[43] Chapman A, Saad Y, Wigton L. High-order ILU preconditioners for CFD problems. International Journal for Numerical Methods in Fluids. 2000;**33**(6):767-788

[44] Concus P, Golub GH, Meurant G. Block preconditioning for the conjugate gradient method. SIAM Journal on Scientific and Statistical Computing. 1985;**6**:220-252

[45] Meurant GA. Computer Solution of Large Linear Systems, Volume 28 of Studies in Mathematics and Its Applications. Amsterdam: North-Holland;1999

[46] Magolu monga Made M, Polman B. Experimental comparison of three-dimensional point and line modified incomplete factorizations. Numerical Algorithms, **23**(1):51-70, 2000

[47] O'Neil J, Szyld DB. A block ordering method for sparse matrices. SIAM Journal on Scientific and Statistical Computing. 1990;**11**(5):811-823

[48] Ashcraft C. Compressed graphs and the minimum degree algorithm. SIAM Journal on Scientific Computing. 1995;**16**(6):1404-1411

[49] Saad Y. Finding exact and approximate block structures for ilu preconditioning. SIAM Journal on Scientific Computing. 2002;**24**(4):1107-1123

[50] Carpentieri B, Liao J, Sosonkina M. VBARMS: A variable block algebraic recursive multilevel solver for sparse linear systems. Journal of Computational and Applied Mathematics. 2014;**259**(A):164-173

[51] Saad Y, Zhang J. BILUM: Block versions of multielimination and multilevel ILU preconditioner for general sparse linear systems. SIAM Journal on Scientific Computing. 1999;**20**:2103-2121

[52] Saad Y, Zhang J. BILUTM: A domain-based multilevel block ILUT preconditioner for general sparse matrices. SIAM Journal on Matrix Analysis and Applications. 1999;**21**(1):279-299

[53] Dongarra JJ, Du Croz J, Duff IS, Hammarling S. A set of level 3 basic linear algebra subprograms. ACM Transactions on Mathematical Software. 1990;**16**:1-17

[54] Na L, Suchomel B, Osei-Kuffuor D, Saad Y. ITSOL: Iterative Solvers Package. https://www-users.cs.umn.edu/~saad/software/ITSOL/

[55] Li Z, Saad Y, Sosonkina M. pARMS: A parallel version of the algebraic recursive multilevel solver. Numerical Linear Algebra with Applications. 2003;**10**:485-509

[56] Boman E, Devine K, Fisk LA, Heaphy R, Hendrickson B, Leung V, Vaughan V, Catalyurek U, Bozdag D, Mitchell W. Zoltan home page. http://www.cs.sandia.gov/Zoltan, 1999

[57] Quarteroni A, Valli A. Domain Decomposition Methods for Partial Differential Equations. Oxford: Clarendon Press Oxford; 1999

[58] Saad Y. A flexible inner-outer preconditioned GMRES algorithm. SIAM Journal on Scientific and Statistical Computing. 1993;**14**:461-469

[59] Bonfiglioli A, Carpentieri B, Sosonkina M. EulFS: a parallel CFD code for the simulation of Euler and Navier-Stokes problems on unstructured grids. In: Kågström B, Elmroth E, Dongarra J, Waśniewski J, editors. Applied Parallel Computing. State of the Art in Scientific Computing., volume 4699 of Lecture Notes in Computer Science. Springer-Verlag; 2007. pages 676-685

[60] Karypis G, Kumar V. Metis: A software package for partitioning unstructured graphs, partitioning meshes, and computing fill-reducing orderings of sparse matrices version 4.0. http://glaros.dtc.umn.edu/gkhome/views/metis. University of Minnesota, Department of Computer Science/Army HPC Research Center Minneapolis, MN 55455

[61] Gupta A, George T. Adaptive techniques for improving the performance of incomplete factorization preconditioning. SIAM Journal on Scientific Computing. 2010;**32**(1):84-110

[62] Vannieuwenhoven N, Meerbergen K. IMF: An incomplete multifrontal LU-factorization for element-structured sparse linear systems. SIAM Journal on Scientific Computing. 2013;**35**(1):A270-A293

[63] Carpentieri B, Liao J, Sosonkina M. Parallel Processing and Applied Mathematics, volume 8385 of Lecture Notes in Computer Science, chapter Variable block multilevel iterative solution of general sparse linear systems. In: Wyrzykowski R, Dongarra J, Karczewski K, Wasniewski J, editors. 11th International Conference, PPAM 2015. Krakow: Springer-Verlag. 2014. pp. 520-530

[64] Anderson E, Bai Z, Bischof C, Blackford S, Demmel J, Dongarra JJ, Du Croz J, Greenbaum A, Hammarling S, McKenney A, Sorensen D. LAPACK Users' Guide. third ed. Philadelphia, PA: Society for Industrial and Applied Mathematics; 1999

[65] Li X. An overview of SuperLU: Algorithms, implementation, and user interface. ACM Transactions on Mathematical Software. September 2005;**31**(3):302-325

Chapter 3

Free-Surface Flow Simulations with Smoothed Particle Hydrodynamics Method using High-Performance Computing

Corrado Altomare, Giacomo Viccione,
Bonaventura Tagliafierro, Vittorio Bovolin,
José Manuel Domínguez and
Alejandro Jacobo Cabrera Crespo

Additional information is available at the end of the chapter

http://dx.doi.org/10.5772/intechopen.71362

Abstract

Today, the use of modern high-performance computing (HPC) systems, such as clusters equipped with graphics processing units (GPUs), allows solving problems with resolutions unthinkable only a decade ago. The demand for high computational power is certainly an issue when simulating free-surface flows. However, taking the advantage of GPU's parallel computing techniques, simulations involving up to 10^9 particles can be achieved. In this framework, this chapter shows some numerical results of typical coastal engineering problems obtained by means of the GPU-based computing servers maintained at the Environmental Physics Laboratory (EPhysLab) from Vigo University in Ourense (Spain) and the Tier-1 Galileo cluster of the Italian computing centre CINECA. The DualSPHysics free package based on smoothed particle hydrodynamics (SPH) technique was used for the purpose. SPH is a meshless particle method based on Lagrangian formulation by which the fluid domain is discretized as a collection of computing fluid particles. Speedup and efficiency of calculations are studied in terms of the initial interparticle distance and by coupling DualSPHysics with a NLSW wave propagation model. Water free-surface elevation, orbital velocities and wave forces are compared with results from experimental campaigns and theoretical solutions.

Keywords: SPH, HPC, free-surface flows, Navier-Stokes equations, Lagrangian techniques

1. Introduction

The non-stopping growing of computing power allowed increasing more and more spatial and temporal discretization when simulating engineering problems. The use of modern high-performance computing (HPC) systems, such as clusters equipped with graphics processing units (GPUs) or central processing units (CPUs) structured into a multi-node framework, let academics and professionals solve free-surface flow problems with resolutions unthinkable just a decade ago. Different spatial and temporal scales are often involved when simulating such kinds of phenomena, which may comprise wave generation, propagation, transformation and interaction with coastal or inland defences.

Among the others, smoothed particle hydrodynamics (SPH) method is a promising meshless technique for modelling fluid flows through the use of particles as it is capable to deal with large deformations, complex geometries and inlet wave shapes. Its original frame was developed in 1977 for astrophysical applications [1, 2]. Since then, it has been used in several research areas, e.g. coastal engineering [3–7], flooding forecast [8–11], solid body transport [12–15], soil mechanics [16–20], sediment erosion or entrainment processes [21–24], fast-moving non-Newtonian flows [25–33], flows in porous media [34–36], solute transport [37–39], turbulent flows [40–42] and multiphase flows [43–47], not to mention manifold industrial applications (see, for instance [48–51]). The main feature of SPH is that local quantities are evaluated by weighting information carried by neighbouring particles enclosed within a compact support, i.e. by performing short-range interactions among particles. Since the related neighbourhood definition takes most of the computing time, fast neighbour search algorithms have been developed so far [52–55, 64, 79].

Since a decade or so, SPH has been coded in the massive high-performance computing (HPC) context, making use of the Message Passing Interface (MPI) [56, 57] and the OpenMP library [58, 59], the standards for distributed and shared memory programming, respectively. Several applications involving multicore processors [60, 61] and graphics processing units (GPUs) [62–67] have been proposed so far. Joselli and co-workers [68] showed in 2015 that performing neighbour search on GPUs yields up to 100 times speedup against CPU implementations, therefore proving the benefits on exploiting the high floating-point arithmetic performance of GPUs for general purpose calculations. The same conclusion was drawn earlier in Ref. [69]. The first versions of SPH running on GPUs were presented in Ref. [70] and then in Ref. [69]. Non-Newtonian fluid flow simulations have been carried as well. Bilotta and co-workers, for instance, applied their GPUSPH model to lava flows [71]. In 2013, Wu and co-workers run GPUSPH to model dam-break flood through complex city layouts [72, 73]. Rustico et al. [74] measured the overall efficiency of the GPUSPH parallelization by applying the Karp-Flatt metric [75]. In Ref. [76], massive simulations of free-surface flow phenomena were carried on single and multi-GPU clusters. They used the sorting radix algorithm for inter-GPU particle swapping and subdomain 'halo' building to allow SPH particles of different subdomains interacting. In 2015, Cercos-Pita proposed the software AQUAgpusph [77] based on the use of the freely available Open Computing Language (OpenCL) framework instead of using the Compute Unified Device Architecture (CUDA) platform. In Ref. [78], Gonnet proposed scalable algorithms based on hierarchical cell decompositions and sorted interactions executed on hybrid shared/distributed memory parallel architectures. In Ref. [79], a general rigid body dynamics and an absolute nodal coordinate formulation (ANCF) were implemented to model rigid and flexible objects interacting with a moving fluid. In 2012, Cherfils and co-workers released JOSEPHINE [80], a parallel weakly compressible SPH code written in Fortran 90, intended for free-surface flows. Incompressible SPH (ISPH) algorithms, running on GPUs, have been developed as well [81–83].

This chapter shows some numerical SPH results of typical coastal engineering problems obtained by means of two different supercomputers: the GPU-based machine maintained at the EPhysLab from Vigo University in Ourense (Spain), mounting 14 NVIDIA Kepler-based cards, with a total of 39168 CUDA cores and the Tier-1 Galileo cluster, introduced on January 2015 by the Italian computing centre CINECA, a non-profit consortium, made up of 70 Italian universities, 6 Italian research institutions and the Italian Ministry of Education, University and Research (MIUR). Galileo is equipped with 516 nodes, each mounting 2 8-cores Intel Haswell 2.40 GHz for a total of 8256 cores, up-to-date Intel Phi 7120p (2 per node on 384 nodes) and NVIDIA Tesla K80 accelerators (2 per node on 40 nodes). Comparison with theoretical and experimental results is also included.

2. SPH fundamentals

Recent comprehensive reviews and related applications of the SPH method are given in [84–89]. Governing equations describing the motion of fluids are usually given as a set of partial differential equations (PDEs). These are discretized by replacing the derivative operators with equivalent integral operators (the so-called integral representation or kernel approximation) that are in turn approximated on the particle location (particle approximation). Next, Section 2.1 gives further details about these two steps, with reference to a generic field $f(\vec{x})$ depending on the location point $\vec{x} \in \Re^{n_d}$, whereas Section 2.2 provides more specific details concerning the treatment of Navier-Stokes equations.

2.1. Approximation of a field f(x) and its spatial gradients

Following the concept of integral representation, any generic continuous function $f\left(\vec{x}\right)$ can be obtained using the Dirac delta functional δ, centred at the point $\vec{x}$ (**Figure 1**) as

$$f\left(\vec{x}\right) = \int_{\Omega} f\left(\vec{y}\right)\delta\left(\vec{x} - \vec{y}\right)d\Omega_y \tag{1}$$

where Ω_y represents the domain of definition of f and $\vec{x},\ \vec{y} \in \Omega$. Replacing δ with a smoothing function $W\left(\vec{x} - \vec{y}, h\right)$, Eq. (1) can be approximated as

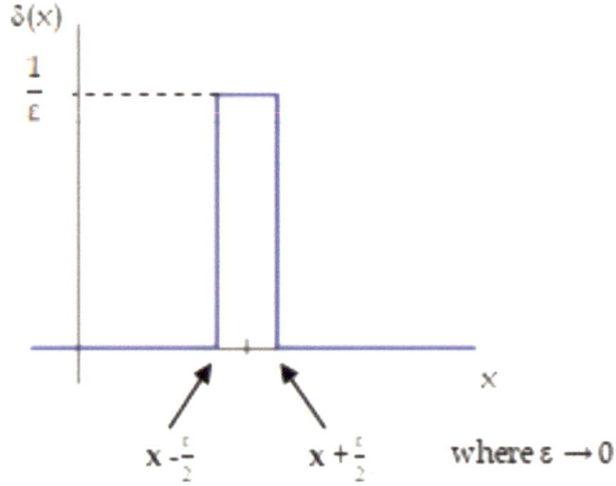

Figure 1. Dirac delta function centred at the point **x**.

$$f_I(\vec{x}) = \int_\Omega f(\vec{y}) W(\vec{x} - \vec{y}, h) \, d\Omega_y \tag{2}$$

W is the so-called smoothing kernel function or simply kernel and h, acting as spatial scale, is the smoothing length defining the influence area where W is not zero. While Eq. (1) yields an exact formulation for the function $f(\vec{x})$, Eq. (2) is an approximation. The definition of W is a key point in the SPH method since it establishes the accuracy of the approximating function $f(\vec{x})$ as well as the efficiency of the calculation. Note that the kernel approximation operator is marked by the index I.

The kernel function W has to satisfy some properties (see, for instance, [90, 91]). The following condition

$$\int_\Omega W(\vec{x} - \vec{y}, h) \, d\Omega_y = 1 \tag{3}$$

is known as partition of unity (or the zero-order consistency) as the integration of the smoothing function must yield the unity. Since W has to mimic the delta function, Eq. (3) can be rewritten as a limit condition in which the smoothing length tends to zero:

$$\lim_{h \to 0} W(\vec{x} - \vec{y}, h) \to \delta(\vec{x}). \tag{4}$$

Still, W has to be defined even, positive and radial symmetric on the compact support:

$$W(\vec{x} - \vec{y}, h) = W(\vec{y} - \vec{x}, h) = W(|\vec{x} - \vec{y}|, h) > 0 \quad |\vec{x} - \vec{y}| < \varphi \cdot h \tag{5a}$$

$$W(|\vec{x} - \vec{y}|, h) = 0 \quad \text{otherwhise} \tag{5b}$$

where φ is a positive quantity defining the extent of the compact support. A large number of kernel functions are proposed in literature. Among the others, a computational-efficient and high accurate kernel is proposed by Wendland [92], defined as.

$$W\left(\vec{x}-\vec{y},h\right)=A(n_d)\left(1-\frac{q}{2}\right)^4(2q+1), 0\leq q\leq 2, \text{ i.e. } \varphi=2 \tag{6}$$

where $A(n_d)$, depending on the number of dimensions n_d, denotes a scaling factor that ensures the consistency of Eq. (3), whereas q denotes the dimensionless distance $\left|\vec{x}-\vec{y}\right|/h$.

The integral representation given by Eq. (2) can be converted into a discretized summation over all particle N within the compact support (**Figure 2**), yielding the particle approximation:

$$f_a\left(\vec{x}\right)=\sum_{k=1}^{N}\frac{m_k}{\rho_k}f\left(\vec{x}_k\right)W\left(\vec{x}-\vec{x}_k,h\right). \tag{7}$$

where the index k refers to particles within the compact support (see bold ones in **Figure 2**), with mass m_k and density ρ_k being carried. Note that in this case the particle approximation is marked by the 'a' pedix. The subscript will be avoided from now on. Eq. (7) can be rewritten with reference to particle 'i' as

$$f_i=f\left(\vec{x}_i\right)=\sum_{k=1}^{N}\frac{m_k}{\rho_k}f_k W_{ik}. \tag{8}$$

Particle approximation of spatial derivatives of a field function, such as divergence and gradient, is expressed using the gradient of the kernel function rather than the derivatives of the function itself:

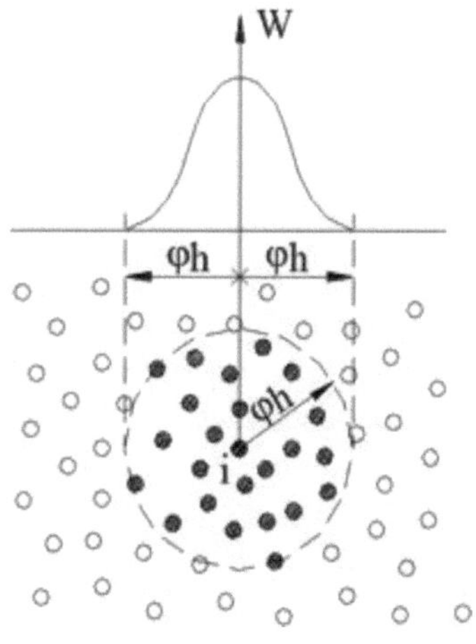

Figure 2. A kernel function defined at the particle 'i' and its support of radius φh. Local neighbourhood corresponds to the bold particles.

$$\vec{\nabla}\cdot\vec{f}_{\mathrm{i}} = \sum_{k=1}^{N} \frac{m_{\mathrm{k}}}{\rho_{\mathrm{k}}} \vec{f}_{\mathbf{k}}\cdot\vec{\nabla}_{\mathrm{i}} W_{\mathrm{ik}} \tag{9}$$

$$\vec{\nabla} f_{\mathrm{i}} = \sum_{k=1}^{N} \frac{m_k}{\rho_k} f_{\mathrm{k}} \vec{\nabla}_{\mathrm{i}} W_{\mathrm{ik}} \tag{10}$$

where the nabla operator $\vec{\nabla}$ is referred to the location of particle 'i'. The symbol '·' denotes the dot product. Eqs. (9) and (10) offer the great advantage of estimating their left-hand side in terms of the kernel gradient, i.e. allowing no special hypotheses on the particular field function. A different formulation of the gradient field can be derived by introducing the following identity [87]

$$\vec{\nabla}\cdot\vec{f}\left(\vec{x}\right) = \frac{1}{\rho}\left\{\vec{\nabla}\cdot\left[\rho\vec{f}\left(\vec{x}\right)\right] - \vec{f}\left(\vec{x}\right)\cdot\vec{\nabla}\rho\right\} \tag{11}$$

inside the integral in Eq. (2), yielding in this case

$$\vec{\nabla}\cdot\vec{f}_{\mathrm{i}} = \frac{1}{\rho_{\mathrm{i}}} \sum_{k=1}^{N} m_{\mathrm{k}} \left(\vec{f}_k - \vec{f}_i\right)\cdot\vec{\nabla}_{\mathrm{i}} W_{\mathrm{ik}} \tag{12}$$

Likewise, the divergence, another particle approximation of the gradient, can be derived, taking into account the following equation:

$$\vec{\nabla} f\left(\vec{x}\right) = \rho\left\{\vec{\nabla}\frac{f\left(\vec{x}\right)}{\rho} + \frac{f\left(\vec{x}\right)}{\rho^2}\vec{\nabla}\rho\right\} \tag{13}$$

yielding

$$\vec{\nabla} f_{\mathrm{i}} = \rho_{\mathrm{i}} \sum_{k=1}^{N} m_{\mathrm{j}} \left(\frac{f_{\mathrm{k}}}{\rho_{\mathrm{k}}^2} + \frac{f_{\mathrm{i}}}{\rho_{\mathrm{i}}^2}\right) \vec{\nabla}_{\mathrm{i}} W_{\mathrm{ik}} \tag{14}$$

Eqs. (12)–(14) are conveniently employed in fluid dynamics as they preserve the conservation of linear and angular momentum.

2.2. SPH form of governing equations

The mostly used governing laws ruling fluid motion are the Navier-Stokes equations, which specify that mass and linear momentum are preserved. Conservation laws in Lagrangian form are as follows:

$$\frac{\mathrm{d}\rho}{\mathrm{d}t} + \rho\vec{\nabla}\cdot\vec{v} = 0 \tag{15a}$$

$$\frac{\mathrm{d}\vec{v}}{\mathrm{d}t} = -\frac{\vec{\nabla} p}{\rho} + \nu\Delta\vec{v} + \vec{f} \tag{15b}$$

in which ρ and $\vec{v}$ are, respectively, the density and velocity field, p is the isotropic pressure, ν is the laminar kinematic viscosity, $\Delta = \vec{\nabla}\cdot\vec{\nabla}$ is the Laplacian operator and $\vec{f}$ the external force. Different approaches [93–95] are available to derive the density particle approximation of the continuity, Eq. (15a), and momentum, Eq. (15b). For instance, referring to Eq. (12), the density rate at particle 'i' can be approximated as follows:

$$\frac{d\rho_i}{dt} = -\sum_{k=1}^{N} m_k \left(\vec{v}_k - \vec{v}_i\right)\cdot\vec{\nabla}_i W_{ik}. \quad (16)$$

The material derivative of the velocity field can be deduced from Eq. (14) for the case of inviscid fluids, that is, $\nu = 0$:

$$\frac{d\vec{v}_i}{dt} = -\sum_{k=1}^{N} m_k \left(\frac{p_k}{\rho_k^2} + \frac{p_i}{\rho_i^2}\right) \vec{\nabla}_i W_{ik} + \vec{f}\ . \quad (17)$$

Numerical diffusion in terms of an artificial viscosity, e.g. proposed in Ref. [96], can be added in Eq. (17), allowing shock waves to be properly simulated:

$$\frac{d\vec{v}_i}{dt} = -\sum_{k=1}^{N} m_k \left(\frac{p_k}{\rho_k^2} + \frac{p_i}{\rho_i^2} + \Pi_{ik}\right) \vec{\nabla}_i W_{ik} + \vec{f} \quad (18)$$

The dissipative term Π_{ik} introduced above is the most general viscosity used in SPH computations, since it provides good results when modelling shock fronts. It is here defined as

$$\Pi_{ik} = \frac{-\alpha\,\bar{c}_{ik}\,\vartheta_{ik}}{\bar{\rho}_{ik}} \text{ when } \vec{v}_{ik}\cdot\vec{x}_{ik} < 0$$
$$\Pi_{ik} = 0 \qquad \text{otherwise} \quad (19)$$

where

$$\vartheta_{ik} = \frac{-h\,\vec{v}_{ik}\cdot\vec{x}_{ik}}{\vec{x}_{ik}^{\,2} + \eta^2} \quad (20)$$

The notation $\bar{a}_{ik} = (a_i + a_k)/2$, $b_{ik} = b_i - b_k$ is introduced above. The term c refers to the speed of sound which magnitude has conveniently to be at least 10 times greater than the maximum estimate of the scalar velocity field [94], $\eta = 0.1$ h is employed to prevent numerical divergences when two particles are approaching and α is a coefficient that needs to be tuned in order to introduce the proper dissipation. A value of $\alpha = 0.01$ is suggested in Ref. [5] for wave propagation and wave-structure interaction studies.

Problem closure is achieved by combining conservation equations in discrete form (16) and (18) with an equation of state, when the weakly compressible scheme is adopted. A relationship between pressure and density is given in Ref. [97]:

$$p_i = \frac{c_0^2 \rho_0}{\gamma}\left[\left(\frac{\rho_i}{\rho_0}\right)^{\gamma} - 1\right] \tag{21}$$

where c_0 is the reference speed of sound, large enough to guarantee Mach numbers lower than 0.1–0.01, $\gamma = 7$, $\rho_0 = 1000\ \text{kg/m}^3$, when the liquid is water. c_0 is numerically computed like at least 10 times the expected maximum velocity.

3. The DualSPHysics code

DualSPHysics [98–100] is an open-source code developed by the University of Vigo (Spain) and the University of Manchester (UK) in collaboration with experts from all around the globe that can be freely downloaded from www.dual.sphysics.org. The code, written in two languages, namely, C++ and CUDA, is capable of using the parallel processing power of either CPUs or GPUs making the study of real engineering problems possible. Graphics processing units (GPUs) are massive floating-point stream processors adopted in computer game industry and image processing. Recently, they have been used in scientific computing thanks to the widespread of tools such as CUDA and OpenCL. Using CUDA as the programming framework for SPH leads to possible confusion with the word 'kernel'. An SPH kernel is the weighting function used in the SPH interpolation process in particle approximation of ruling equations, e.g. Eqs. (16) and (18). A CUDA kernel, however, is defined as a CUDA function that is set up and executed *N* times in parallel by *N* different CUDA threads. Herein, to avoid confusion, we use the term function to describe the CUDA kernels. DualSPHysics makes full use of the function hierarchy present within the CUDA framework. A function executed and called by the CPU is declared as a host function, whereas a global function is called by the CPU but executed in parallel by the GPU. A device function, on the other hand, is only called and executed within the GPU by a global or another device function. This hierarchy is used for the computation of the interparticle forces. The simulations in DualSPHysics consist of three main steps: (i) creation of the particle neighbour list (NL), (ii) force computation (FC) for the particle interaction and (iii) the system update (SU) at the end of the time step.

Due to the Lagrangian nature of SPH, the particle interaction results to be the most time-consuming part of the whole algorithm. Each particle, as already stated, only interacts with its neighbour particles. Therefore, the construction of the neighbour list must be optimised. The cell-linked list described in Ref. [54] is implemented in DualSPHysics. This approach is preferred to the traditional approach, named Verlet list [101] that implies higher memory requirements than the cell-linked list. Besides, [54] proposed an innovative searching procedure based on a dynamic updating of the Verlet list and analyzed the efficiency of all the algorithms in terms of computational time and memory requirements.

DualSPHysics has proven its performance, reaching limits like being able to simulate more than 10^9 particles using 128 GPUs with an efficiency close to 100% [67].

3.1. Boundary conditions

Extensive research has been conducted over the last few years to develop accurate and efficient boundary conditions (BCs) in SPH method. Several approaches are proposed in the literature, such as boundary repulsive forces, fluid extensions to the solid boundary and boundary integral representing the term preservation. In DualSPHysics, boundaries (walls, bottom, coastal structures, wave generators, vessels, floating devices, etc.) are described using a discrete set of boundary particles that exert a repulsive force on the fluid particles when they approach. The so-called dynamic boundary condition [102] is used in DualSPHysics, where the boundary particles satisfy the same equations as the fluid particles; however, they do not move according to the forces exerted on them. Instead, they remain fixed (fixed boundary) or move according to some externally imposed movement (gates, flaps, etc.). Using this boundary condition, when a fluid particle approaches a boundary particle and the distance between them decreases beyond the kernel range, the density of the boundary particles increases giving rise to an increase of the pressure. This results in a repulsive force being exerted on the fluid particle due to the pressure term in the momentum equation. This dynamic boundary condition implemented in DualSPHysics does not include a specific value to define wall friction. However, this has been achieved in different validations by specifying a different viscosity value in the momentum equation when the fluid particles interact with the boundary ones.

3.2. Extra functionalities

3.2.1. Long-crested wave generation

The waves are generated in DualSPHysics by means of moving boundaries that aim to mimic the movement of a piston-type and flap-type wavemakers as in physical facilities. Only long-crested wave can be generated at this stage. The implementation of first-order and second-order wave generation theories is fully described in Ref. [3]. For monochromatic waves, this means to include super-harmonics. For random waves, subharmonic components are considered to suppress spurious long waves. Two standard wave spectra are implemented and used to generate random waves: JONSWAP and Pierson-Moskowitz spectra. The generation system allows having different random time series with the same significant wave height (H_{m0}) and the same peak period (T_p), just defining different phase seeds.

3.2.2. Wave reflection compensation

Wave reflection compensation is used in physical facilities to absorb the reflected waves at the wavemaker in order to avoid that they will be reflected back into the domain. In this way, the introduction into the system of extra spurious energy that will bias the results is prevented. The so-called active wave absorption system (AWAS) is implemented in DualSPHysics. The water surface elevation η at the wavemaker position is used and transformed by an appropriate time-domain filter to obtain a control signal that corrects the wave paddle displacement in order to absorb the reflected waves every time step. Hence, the target wavemaker position is corrected to avoid reflection at the wavemaker. The position in real time of the wavemaker is obtained through the velocity correction of its motion. Further details on AWAS in DualSPHysics are reported in Ref. [3].

3.2.3. Hybridization with SWASH model

The hybridization technique between DualSPHysics model and SWASH model (http://swash.sourceforge.net/) is fully described in Ref. [5]. This technique aims to use each model for a specific purpose that best matches with its own capabilities, reducing the total computational cost and increasing the model accuracy. The advantages of using a hybridization technique between SWASH and DualSPHysics can be summarised as follows:

- Fast computations with large domains can be performed with SWASH, avoiding simulating large domains with DualSPHysics that requires huge computation times even using hardware acceleration.
- SWASH is suitable for calculation where statistical analysis is necessary such as computing wave height and good accuracy is obtained for wave propagation.
- SWASH is not suitable for calculation of wave impacts, while DualSPHysics can easily compute wave impacts, pressure load and exerted force onto coastal structures.
- Complex geometries cannot be represented with SWASH, and computation stability problems may appear when applied to rapidly changing bathymetry. Using DualSPHysics, any complex geometry or varying bathymetry can be simulated.

The hybridization between DualSPHysics and SWASH has been obtained through a one-way hybridization at this stage. The basic idea is to run SWASH for the biggest part of the physical domain to impose some boundary conditions on a fictitious wall placed between both media. This fictitious wall acts as a nonconventional wave generator in DualSPHysics: each boundary particle that forms the wall (hereafter called moving boundary or MB) will experience a different movement to mimic the effect of the incoming waves. SWASH provides values of velocity in different levels of depth. These values are used to move the MB particles. The displacement of each particle can be calculated using a lineal interpolation of velocity in the vertical position of the particle. Therefore, the MB is a set of boundary particles whose displacement is imposed by the wave propagated by SWASH and only exists for DualSPHysics. A multilayer approach can be used in SWASH. The SWASH velocity measured at each layer is therefore interpolated and converted into displacement time series for DualSPHysics.

4. Hardware features

4.1. The EPhysLab cluster

The GPU cluster maintained at the Environmental Physics Laboratory (EPhysLab) of Vigo University comprises four computing servers, whose details are as follows:

- Supermicro 7047: 4× NVIDIA GeForce GTX Titan Black, 2880 × 4 = 11,520 CUDA cores, 2× Intel Xeon E5–2640 at 2 GHz (16 cores), RAM 64 GB, storage 16 TB, estimated performance 6800 GFLOPS

- Supermicro 7047: 4× NVIDIA GeForce GTX Titan 2688 × 4 = 10,752 CUDA cores, 2× Intel Xeon E5-2640 at 2 GHz (16 cores), RAM 64 GB, storage 20 TB, estimated performance 6000 GFLOPS
- Supermicro 7046: 4× NVIDIA GeForce GTX Titan Black, 2880 × 4 = 11,520 CUDA cores, 2× Intel Xeon E5620 at 2.4 GHz (8 cores), RAM 64 GB, storage 9 TB, estimated performance 6800 GFLOPS
- Supermicro 6016GT-TF-TM2: 1× NVIDIA Tesla K40 2880 CUDA cores + 1× NVIDIA Tesla K20 2496 CUDA cores, 2× Intel X5550 at 2.66 GHz (8 cores), RAM 64 GB, storage 1.7 TB, estimated performance 2855 GFLOPS

4.2. The Galileo supercomputer

Galileo is a Tier-1 supercomputer among the fastest available to Italian industrial and public researchers. Introduced in the Italian computing centre CINECA on January 2015, this IBM NeXtScale model is equipped with up-to-date Intel accelerators (Intel Phi 7120p), NVIDIA accelerators (NVIDIA Tesla K80), as well as a top-level programming environment and a number of application tools. It is characterised by:

- 516 computing nodes with Intel Haswell 2.40 GHz processors, 2 × 8 core each (8256 cores in total)
- 128 GB of RAM per computing node, 8 GB per core, 66 TB of total RAM
- Internal network: InfiniBand with 4× QDR switches (≈40 Gb/s)
- Two Intel accelerators Phi 7120p per node on 384 nodes (768 in total)
- Two NVIDIA accelerators K80 per node on 40 nodes (80 in total, 20 available for scientific research)
- Eight nodes devoted to login/visualisation
- Theoretical peak performance 1.2 PFlops
- ≈480 GFLOPS single-node LINPACK (only CPU) sustained performance
- Disc space: ≈2 PB of local scratch
- Operating system: Linux CentOS 7.0

On June 2017, Galileo was ranked in 281st position on the top 500 supercomputer list (https://www.top500.org/lists/).

5. Test cases

Aiming to prove the capability of DualSPHysics model to reproduce accurately waves and wave-structure interaction phenomena, three different test cases have been selected and are here reported, namely:

1. Wave generation and propagation of random wave train in 2D.
2. Wave run-up on a cubic block breakwater in 3D.
3. Coupling of DualSPHysics with SWASH model and application to wave forces on coastal structures in shallow water conditions (2D).

5.1. Test case N. 1

The first test case comprises the generation and absorption of random waves in DualSPHysics. The 150 s time series to be generated is calculated starting from a JONSWAP spectrum. The target wave conditions are H_{m0} = 0.06 m and T_p = 1.3 s. The water depth is 0.36 m. The wavelength is 2.09 m. Second-order wave generation has been used (i.e. bound long waves). The wave conditions correspond to a second-order Stokes wave. The geometrical layout of the case is depicted in **Figure 3**: an 8.4-m long wave tank is modelled. A damping zone (passive absorption) is defined at the end of the tank. The water surface elevation and orbital velocities are measured using a 5-wave gauge array where the central wave gauge is at 2 L from the generator. The numerical results are compared with theoretical solutions.

A sensitivity analysis on the initial interparticle distance, *dp*, has been carried out. Four different values of *dp* have been selected in a range of *H*/*dp* between 6 (coarsest resolution) and 20 (finest resolution). For each case, the number of fluid particles and the computational runtime are reported in **Table 1**.

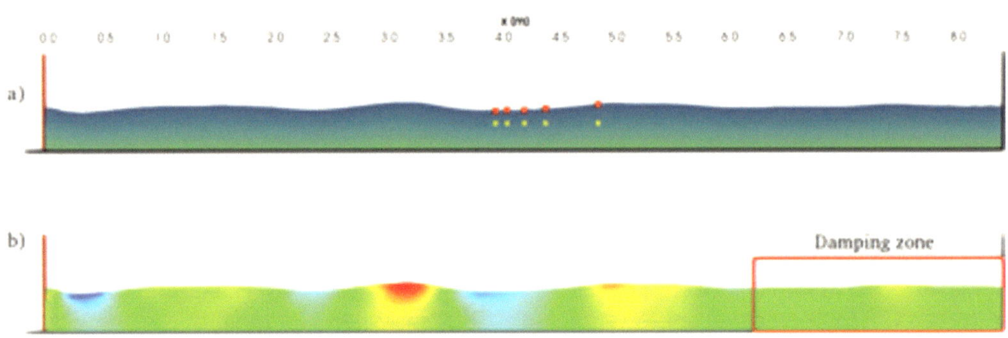

Figure 3. Layout of test case N.1: (a) position of the wave gauges (dots on the free surface) and velocity measurements (inner dots) and (b) horizontal velocity field and indication of the damping zone in the fluid domain.

H/*dp*	No. of fluid particles	Runtime [h]
6	29,365	0.9
10	82,541	2.9
12	119,209	4.5
20	333,081	16.6

Table 1. Runtimes and the number of fluid particles for each model resolution of test case N. 1.

The case with $H/dp = 10$ has been simulated also on Galileo supercomputer, specifically using one node in order to compare the computing capabilities between Galileo and one GPU from the EPhysLab cluster. The comparison is expressed in terms of the number of calculation steps per second of computational time. For each node in Galileo, 23.9 step/s can be simulated, whereas with a Tesla K20, 156.3 step/s are achieved. These results refer to 2D simulations, and they are expected to be different for 3D modelling.

The numerical results for $H/dp = 10$ have been plotted against the theoretical ones for each sensor position. They are all depicted in **Figures 4–6**. The model accuracy has been estimated in terms of spectral values of wave height and period. The numerical error, together with the calculated values for H_{m0} and $T_{m-1,0}$, is reported in **Table 2** for WG3 ($x = 4.18$ m). For $H/dp = 6$, the wave height is underestimated about 4%; meanwhile, starting from $H/dp = 10$, the errors for both wave height and period are in the order of 1–2%. Similar results are attained for the other four wave gauges. The orbital velocities show same degree of accuracy.

5.2. Test case N. 2

The second test case consists of a 3D case where the wave run-up on an armour breakwater has been simulated. Cubic blocks are displaced forming two layers with regular pattern on the seaward face of the breakwater, which has an angle of 28.3° with the horizontal. The side of each

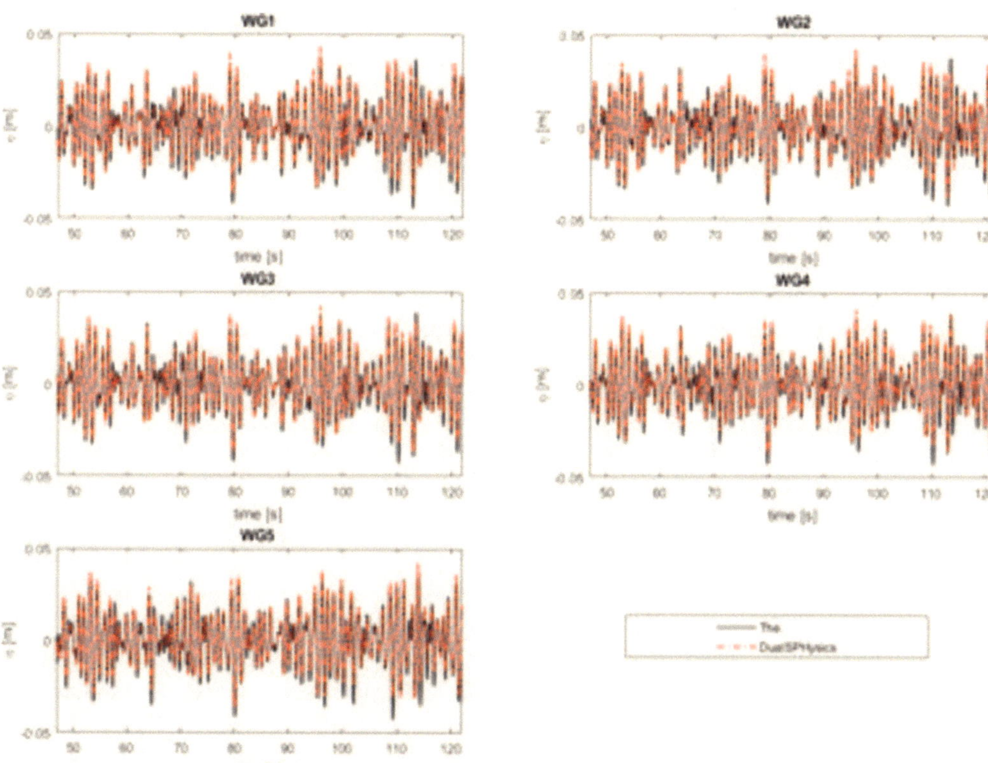

Figure 4. Comparison between the numerical and theoretical free-surface elevation at the 5-wave gauge positions.

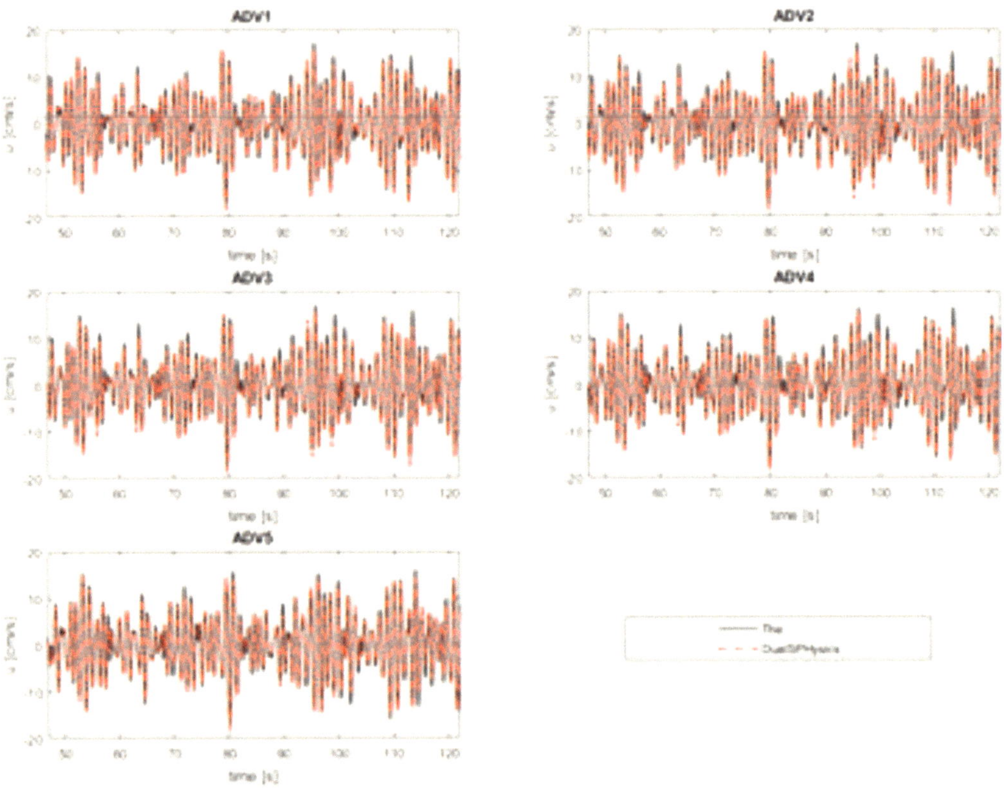

Figure 5. Comparison between the numerical and theoretical horizontal orbital velocity.

block measures 0.058 m. The case resembles an experimental one carried out in the small-scale wave flume CIEMito at the Technical University of Barcelona, Spain. The flume width is 0.38 m. Monochromatic waves have been simulated. The simulated wave height is 0.10 m, with mean period equal to 0.97 s. In total, 15 s of physical time has been simulated. The initial interparticle distance was 0.012 m, about one-eighth of the target wave height, resulting in 1,039,775 fluid particles. The simulation took 8.7 h using the Tesla K20 from the EPhysLab cluster.

Four wave gauges are located to measure the water surface elevation along the flume. The first wave gauge is at 3.10 m from the wavemaker; the last one is at 4.23 m. The distance between the toe of the breakwater and the wavemaker is 5.95 m. Moving boundaries mimicking a piston-type wavemaker are used in DualSPHysics to generate waves. To measure the run-up, the water surface elevation has been measured at 4160 locations across the breakwater. The results, post-processed in Matlab, have given the time series of wave run-up. A three-dimensional view of the numerical model is depicted in **Figure 7**. Using post-processing tools of DualSPHysics, an isosurface of the fluid has been extracted and plotted in ParaView software (www.paraview.org): this is coloured in blue in **Figure 7**. The two layers of cubic blocks are coloured in grey. The four yellow dots on the free surface indicate where the water surface elevation has been measured. The coloured area (from yellow to white) indicates all locations where the run-up has been measured.

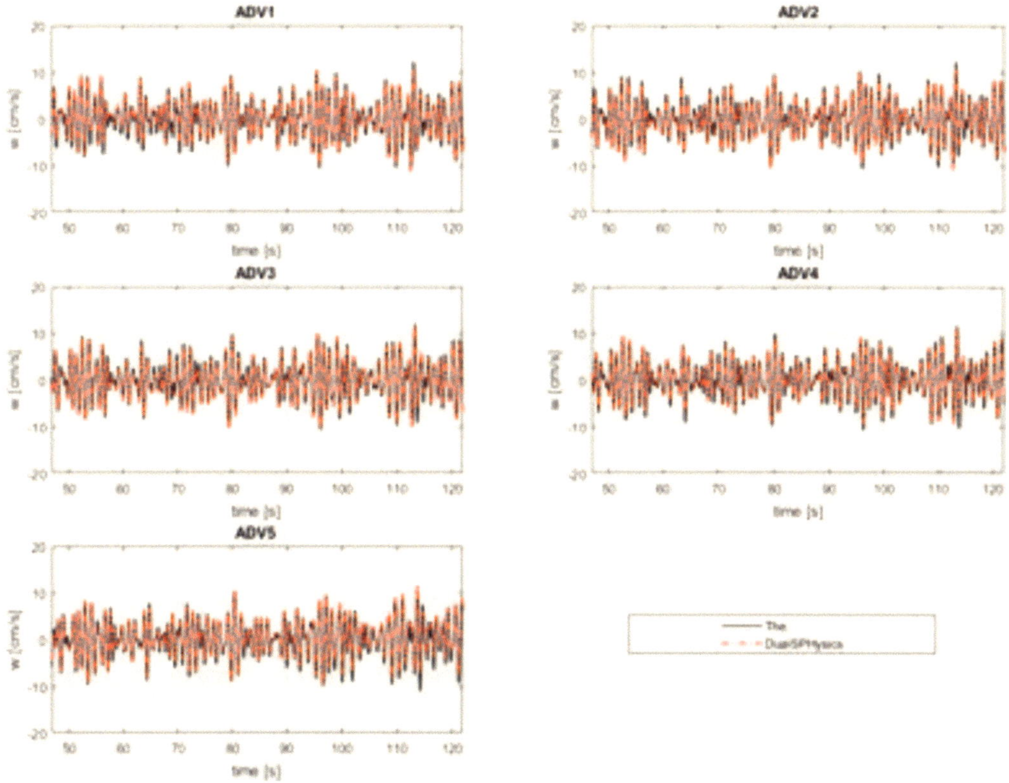

Figure 6. Comparison between the numerical and theoretical vertical orbital velocity.

H/*dp*	$H_{m0\text{-}THE}$ [m]	$T_{m-1,0\text{-}THE}$ [s]	$H_{m0\text{-}SPH}$ [m]	$T_{m-1,0\text{-}SPH}$ [s]	ε_H [%]	ε_T [%]
6	0.061	1.214	0.058	1.250	−4.52	+3.00
10			0.060	1.233	−1.00	+1.54
12			0.061	1.231	−0.12	+1.43
20			0.062	1.234	+1.70	+1.67

Table 2. Model accuracy at WG3 for different values of *H*/*dp*.

Figure 8 shows four different instants of time that make an entire run-up/run-down cycle over the breakwater. The colours indicate the fluid velocity field, i.e. horizontal orbital velocity. Red indicates high positive velocities (directed shorewards), whereas blue indicates negative velocities (directed seawards).

The water surface elevation measured in the numerical tank is depicted in **Figure 9** for each wave gauge location. The wave run-up has been calculated for 26 cross sections along the width of the flume: the averaged time series is shown in **Figure 10**.

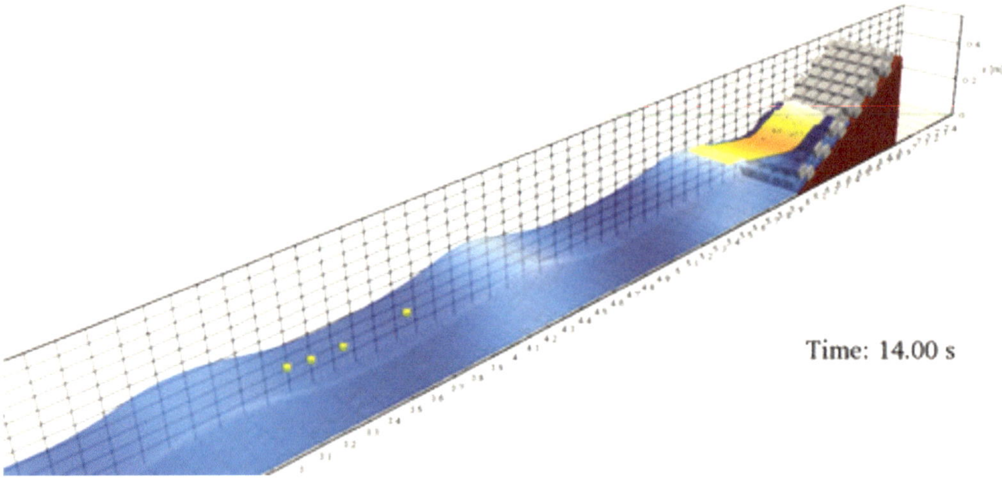

Figure 7. 3D view of the run-up simulation.

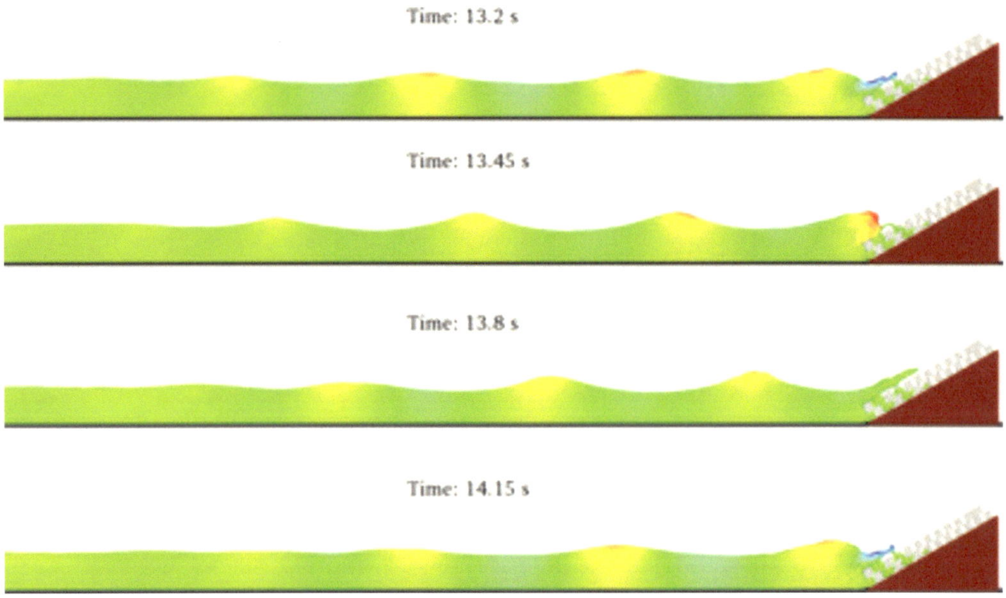

Figure 8. Snapshots of the wave run-up simulation during one run-up cycle.

5.3. Test case N. 3

The third test case comprises the validation of the hybridization technique between DualSPHysics model and SWASH model to study the impact of overtopping flows on multifunctional sea dikes with shallow foreshore. The main aim is to prove that overtopping flow characteristics and wave forces are modelled correctly and that the hybridization can represent a reliable solution that can be used as complementary or alternative to physical

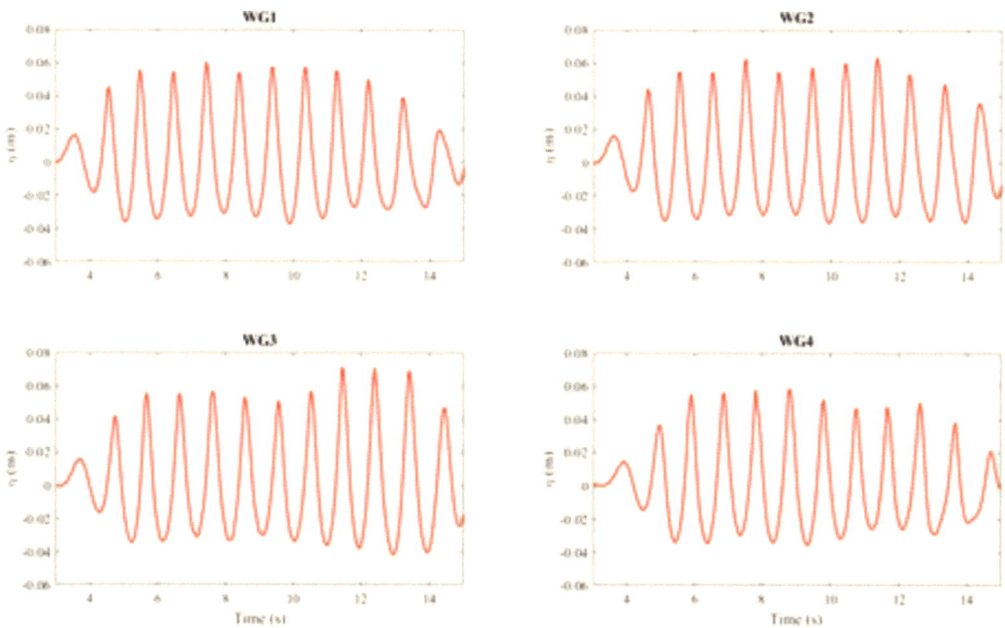

Figure 9. Water surface elevation along the numerical wave tank.

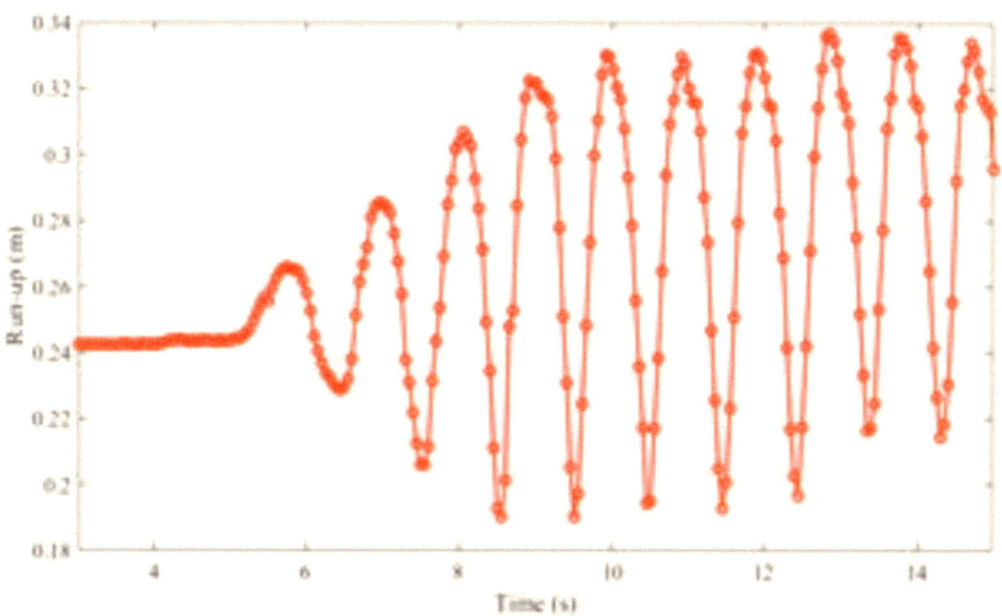

Figure 10. Time series of wave run-up: average along the width of the numerical tank.

modelling. The case of study is a typical case from the Belgian and Dutch coastline, where a building is constructed on the top of the dike. Physical model tests were carried out in a 4.0 m wide, 1.4 m deep and 70.0 m long wave flume at Flanders Hydraulics Research, Antwerp

(Belgium) to measure forces on the vertical wall (i.e. building), the layer thickness and velocities of the overtopping flows [103]. The geometrical layout is depicted in **Figure 11**: the foreshore slope was 1:35 and dike height 0.1 m. The dike slope was 1:3. Here, we refer to only regular wave cases.

SWASH has been previously validated against the physical model results: wave propagation, transformation and breaking have been accurately modelled, and the conditions at the toe of the dike are reproduced as in the physical model test. Then, SWASH has been implemented together with DualSPHysics to model the wave impact. Eight layers have been used in SWASH simulation. A hybridization point along the physical domain has been defined, and it is located at x = 30.24 m from the physical wavemaker in its neutral position (**Figure 11**), far enough from the location where the waves start to break (≈35.5 m). SWASH provides the boundary conditions for DualSPHysics at that location. DualSPHysics is used to model the part of domain between the coupling point and the dike. The quantities that have been measured and compared with the experimental results are (a) free-surface elevation after the coupling point, (b) overtopping flow thickness in three different locations along the dike crest and (c) wave forces on the vertical wall (measured in the physical model by means of two-load cells of model series Tedea-Huntleigh 614). Both free-surface elevation and layer thickness were measured in the physical model by means of resistive wave gauges.

An initial interparticle distance, dp, of 0.003 m has been used leading to 494,388 fluid particles in DualSPHysics model. Fifty seconds of physical time has been simulated in the TITAN X graphic card, taking 10.8 h. A case with the whole physical domain modelled in DualSPHysics has been also modelled: in such case, the moving boundary is represented by the physical

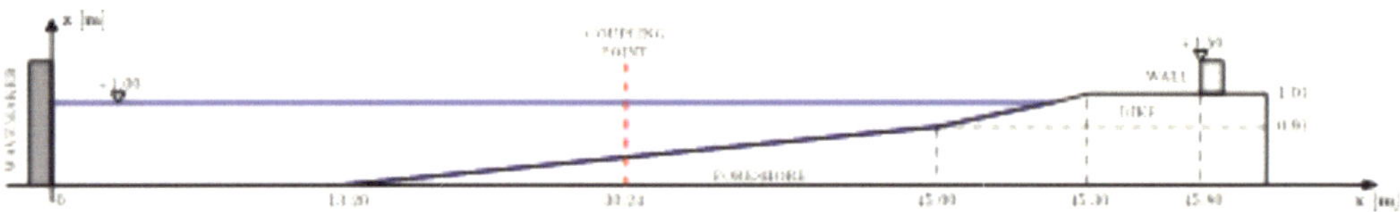

Figure 11. Layout of the flume at FHR and indication of the coupling point location for the SWASH-DualSPHysics model.

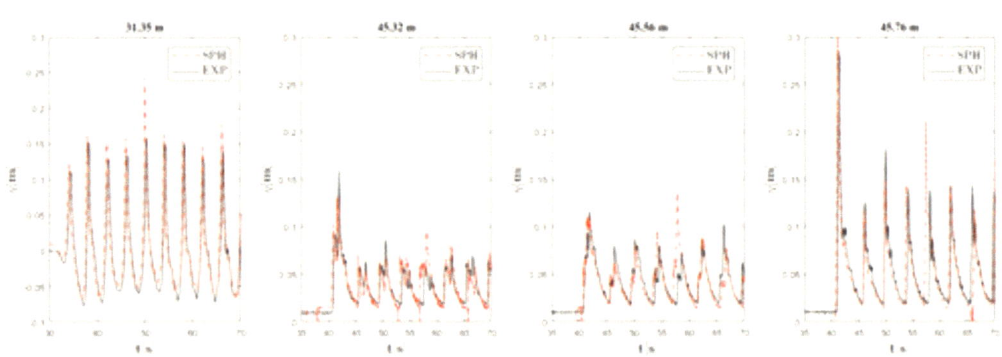

Figure 12. Results of free-surface elevation (left image) and overtopping layer thickness: numerical (red dash-dot line) vs. experimental (black solid line).

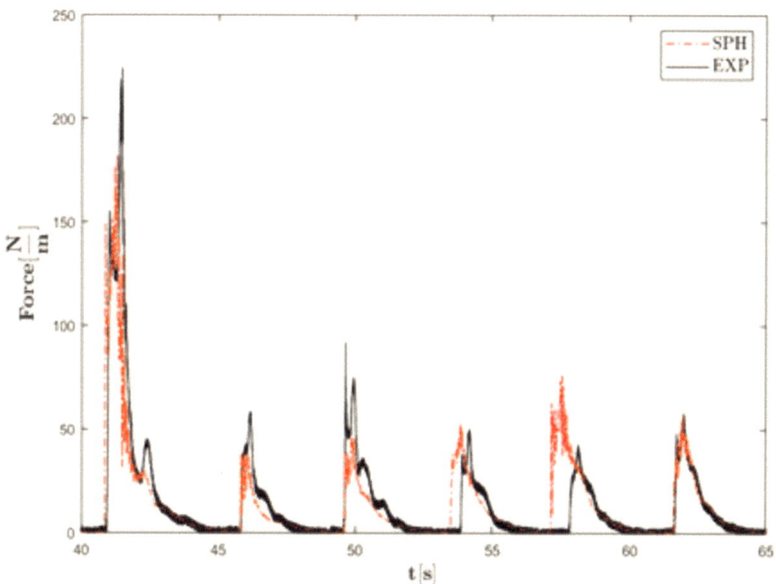

Figure 13. Results of overtopping wave forces on the wall: numerical (red dash-dot line) vs. experimental (black solid line).

wave generator, and its location is then at x = 0.00 m. This stand-alone DualSPHysics model took 95.6 h using the same TITAN X to simulate 3,389,266 fluid particles, about 10 times slower than the hybridised model.

The numerical and experimental free-surface elevation and layer thickness are plotted in **Figure 12**, showing that the numerical solution resembles the experimental accurately. The forces on the wall are represented in **Figure 13**. The differences between numerical and experimental results might be explained because of the highly turbulent and stochastic nature of the overtopping wave impact in this case, which makes the experimental test not repeatable (see [3] for further discussion on model inaccuracy for wave impacts).

6. Conclusions

The chapter offers a panoramic on the application of the SPH-based DualSPHysics code on supercomputers maintained at the EPhysLab from Vigo University in Ourense (Spain) and the Italian computing centre CINECA. Three test cases were selected in the general context of the coastal engineering: (1) wave generation and propagation of random wave train in 2D, (2) wave run-up on a cubic block breakwater in 3D and (3) coupling of DualSPHysics with SWASH model and application to wave forces on coastal structures in shallow water conditions (2D). Scalability is discussed by varying the spatial resolution, and efficiency is proved in the case of the hybridization. Comparison with theoretical free-surface elevation and orbital velocities for test case N. 1 and measured overtopping layer thickness and forces on vertical walls for test case N. 3 was satisfactory.

Acknowledgements

We acknowledge the CINECA award under the ISCRA initiative, for the availability of high-performance computing resources and support. Part of the computations was carried within the high-performance computing for Environmental Fluid Mechanics (HPCEFM17) project.

Author details

Corrado Altomare[1], Giacomo Viccione[2*], Bonaventura Tagliafierro[2], Vittorio Bovolin[3], José Manuel Domínguez[4] and Alejandro Jacobo Cabrera Crespo[4]

*Address all correspondence to: gviccion@unisa.it

1 Flanders Hydraulics Research, Antwerp, Belgium

2 Department of Civil Engineering, University of Salerno, Italy

3 University Centre for the Prediction and Prevention of Great Hazards (C.U.G.Ri.), Italy

4 Environmental Physics Laboratory (EPhysLab), Universidade de Vigo, Spain

References

[1] Gingold RA, Monaghan JJ. Smoothed particle hydrodynamics: Theory and application to non-spherical stars. Monthly Notices of the Royal Astronomical Society. 1977;**181**:375-389

[2] Lucy LB. A numerical approach to the testing of the fission hypothesis. Astronomical Journal. 1977;**82**:1013-1024

[3] Altomare C, Domínguez JM, Crespo AJC, González-Cao J, Suzuki T, Gómez-Gesteira M, et al. Long-crested wave generation and absorption for SPH-based DualSPHysics model. Coastal Engineering. 2017;**127**:37-54. DOI: 10.1016/j.coastaleng.2017.06.004

[4] Crespo AJC, Altomare C, Domínguez JM, González-Cao J, Gómez-Gesteira M. Towards simulating floating offshore oscillating water column converters with smoothed particle hydrodynamics. Coastal Engineering. 2017;**126**:11-26. DOI: 10.1016/j.coastaleng.2017.05.001

[5] Altomare C, Crespo AJC, Domínguez JM, Gómez-Gesteira M, Suzuki T, Verwaest T. Applicability of smoothed particle hydrodynamics for estimation of sea wave impact on coastal structures. Coastal Engineering. 2015;**96**:1-12. DOI: 10.1016/j.coastaleng.2014.11.001

[6] Meringolo DD, Aristodemo F, Veltri P. SPH numerical modeling of wave-perforated breakwater interaction. Coastal Engineering. 2015;**101**:48-68. DOI: 10.1016/j.coastaleng.2015.04.004

[7] Barreiro A, Crespo AJC, Domínguez JM, Gómez-Gesteira M. Smoothed particle hydrodynamics for coastal engineering problems. Computers and Structures. 2013;**120**:96-106. DOI: 10.1016/j.compstruc.2013.02.010

[8] Prakash M, Rothauge K, Cleary PW. Modelling the impact of dam failure scenarios on flood inundation using SPH. Applied Mathematical Modelling. 2014;**38**(23):5515-5534. DOI: 10.1016/j.apm.2014.03.011

[9] Vacondio R, Rogers BD, Stansby PK, Mignosa P. Shallow water SPH for flooding with dynamic particle coalescing and splitting. Advances in Water Resources. 2013;**58**:10-23. DOI: 10.1016/j.advwatres.2013.04.007

[10] Vacondio R, Mignosa P, Pagani S. 3D SPH numerical simulation of the wave generated by the Vajont rockslide. Advances in Water Resources. 2013;**59**:146-156. DOI: 10.1016/j.advwatres.2013.06.009

[11] Kao H-M, Chang T-J. Numerical modeling of dambreak-induced flood and inundation using smoothed particle hydrodynamics. Journal of Hydrology. 2012;**448-449**:232-244

[12] Canelas RB, Domínguez JM, Crespo AJC, Gómez-Gesteira M, Ferreira RML. Resolved simulation of a granular-fluid flow with a coupled SPH-DCDEM model. Journal of Hydraulic Engineering. 2017;**143**(9):06017012. DOI: 10.1061/(ASCE)HY.1943-7900.0001331

[13] Canelas RB, Crespo AJC, Domínguez JM, Ferreira RML, Gómez-Gesteira M. SPH-DCDEM model for arbitrary geometries in free surface solid-fluid flows. Computer Physics Communications. 2016;**202**:131-140. DOI: 10.1016/j.cpc.2016.01.006

[14] Canelas RB, Domínguez JM, Crespo AJC, Gómez-Gesteira M, Ferreira RML. A smooth particle hydrodynamics discretization for the modelling of free surface flows and rigid body dynamics. International Journal for Numerical Methods in Fluids. 2015;**78**:581-593. DOI: 10.1002/fld.4031

[15] Amicarelli A, Albano R, Mirauda D, Agate G, Sole A, Guandalini R. A smoothed particle hydrodynamics model for 3D solid body transport in free surface flows. Computers and Fluids. 2015;**116**:205-228. DOI: 10.1016/j.compfluid.2015.04.018

[16] Goodin C, Priddy JD. Comparison of SPH simulations and cone index tests for cohesive soils. Journal of Terramechanics. 2016;**66**:49-57. DOI: 10.1016/j.jterra.2015.09.002

[17] Niroumand H, Mehrizi MEM, Saaly M. Application of mesh-free smoothed particle hydrodynamics (SPH) for study of soil behaviour. Geomechanics and Engineering. 2016;**11**(1):1-39. DOI: 10.12989/gae.2016.11.1.001

[18] Nonoyama H, Moriguchi S, Sawada K, Yashima A. Slope stability analysis using smoothed particle hydrodynamics (SPH) method. Soils and Foundations. 2015;**55**(2): 458-470. DOI: 10.1016/j.sandf.2015.02.019

[19] Wu Q, An Y, Liu QQ. A smoothed particle hydrodynamics method for modelling soil-water interaction. Procedia Engineering. 2015;**126**:579-583. DOI: 10.1016/j.proeng.2015.11.298

[20] Grabe J, Stefanova B. Numerical modeling of saturated soils, based on smoothed particle hydrodynamics (SPH): Part 1: Seepage analysis. Geotechnik. 2014;**37**(3):191-197. DOI: 10.1002/gete.201300024

[21] Braun A, Wang X, Petrosino S, Cuomo S. SPH propagation back-analysis of Baishuihe landslide in south-western China. Geoenvironmental. Disasters. 2017;**4**:1-10. DOI: 10.1186/s40677-016-0067-4

[22] Khanpour M, Zarrati AR, Kolahdoozan M, Shakibaeinia A, Amirshahi SM. Mesh-free SPH modeling of sediment scouring and flushing. Computers & Fluids. 2016;**129**:67-78

[23] Ran Q, Tong J, Shao S, Fu X, Xu Y. Incompressible SPH scour model for movable bed dam break flows. Advances in Water Resources. 2015;**82**:39-50. DOI: 10.1016/j.compfluid.2016.02.005

[24] Razavitoosi SL, Ayyoubzadeh SA, Valizadeh A. Two-phase SPH modelling of waves caused by dam break over a movable bed. International Journal of Sediment Research. 2014;**29**(3):344-356. DOI: 10.1016/S1001-6279(14)60049-4

[25] Farhadi A, Emdad H, Rad EG. Incompressible SPH simulation of landslide impulse-generated water waves. Natural Hazards. 2016;**82**(3):1779-1802. DOI: 10.1007/s11069-016-2270-8

[26] Calvo L, Haddad B, Pastor M, Palacios D. Runout and deposit morphology of Bingham fluid as a function of initial volume: Implication for debris flow modelling. Natural Hazards. 2015;**75**(1):489-513. DOI: 10.1007/s11069-014-1334-x

[27] Deng L, Wang W. Smoothed particle hydrodynamics for coarse-grained modeling of rapid granular flow. Particuology. 2015;**21**:173-178. DOI: 10.1016/j.partic.2014.08.012

[28] Xenakis AM, Lind SJ, Stansby PK, Rogers BD. An incompressible SPH scheme with improved pressure predictions for free-surface generalised Newtonian flows. Journal of Non-Newtonian Fluid Mechanics. 2015;**218**:1-15. DOI: 10.1016/j.jnnfm.2015.01.006

[29] Cascini L, Cuomo S, Pastor M, Sorbino G, Piciullo L. SPH run-out modelling of channelised landslides of the flow type. Geomorphology. 2014;**214**:502-513. DOI: 10.1016/j.geomorph.2014.02.031

[30] Cuomo S, Pastor M, Cascini L, Castorino GC. Interplay of rheology and entrainment in debris avalanches: A numerical study. Canadian Geotechnical Journal. 2014;**51**(11):1318-1330. DOI: 10.1139/cgj-2013-0387

[31] Lemiale V, Karantgis L, Broadbrige P. Smoothed particle hydrodynamics applied to the modelling of landslides. Applied Mechanics and Materials. 2014;**553**:519-524. DOI: 10.4028/www.scientific.net/AMM.553.519

[32] Xu X, Ouyang J, Yang B, Liu Z. SPH simulations of three-dimensional non-Newtonian free surface flows. Computer Methods in Applied Mechanics and Engineering. 2013;**256**:101-116. DOI: 10.1016/j.cma.2012.12.017

[33] Viccione G, Bovolin V. Simulating triggering and evolution of debris-flows with smoothed particle hydrodynamics (SPH). In: International Conference on Debris-Flow Hazards Mitigation: Mechanics, Prediction, and Assessment, Proceedings. 2011. pp. 523-532

[34] Peng C, Xu G, Wu W, Yu H-S, Wang C. Multiphase SPH modeling of free surface flow in porous media with variable porosity. Computers and Geotechnics. 2017;**81**:239-248. DOI: 10.1016/j.compgeo.2016.08.022

[35] Ren B, Wen H, Dong P, Wang Y. Numerical simulation of wave interaction with porous structures using an improved smoothed particle hydrodynamic method. Coastal Engineering. 2014;**88**:88-100. DOI: 10.1016/j.coastaleng.2014.02.006

[36] Aly AM, Asai M. Three-dimensional incompressible smoothed particle hydrodynamics for simulating fluid flows through porous structures. Transport in Porous Media. 2015;**110**(3):483-502. DOI: 10.1007/s11242-015-0568-8

[37] Mayoral-Villa E, Alvarado-Rodríguez CE, Klapp J, Gómez-Gesteira M, Di G, Sigalotti L. Smoothed particle hydrodynamics: Applications to migration of radionuclides in confined aqueous systems. Journal of Contaminant Hydrology. 2016;**187**:65-78

[38] Boso F, Bellin A, Dumbser M. Numerical simulations of solute transport in highly heterogeneous formations: A comparison of alternative numerical schemes. Advances in Water Resources. 2013;**52**:178-189

[39] Herrera PA, Massabó M, Beckie RD. A meshless method to simulate solute transport in heterogeneous porous media. Advances in Water Resources. 2009;**32**(3):413-429

[40] Hu XY, Adams NA. A SPH model for incompressible turbulence. Procedia IUTAM. 2015;**18**:66-75

[41] Ren B, Wen H, Dong P, Wang Y, Improved SPH. Simulation of wave motions and turbulent flows through porous media. Coastal Engineering. 2016;**107**:14-27. DOI: 10.1016/j.jconhyd.2016.01.008

[42] Violeau D, Issa R. Numerical modelling of complex turbulent free-surface flows with the SPH method: An overview. International Journal for Numerical Methods in Fluids. 2007;**53**:277-304. DOI: 10.1002/fld.1292

[43] Mokos A, Rogers BD, Stansby PK. A multi-phase particle shifting algorithm for SPH simulations of violent hydrodynamics with a large number of particles. Journal of Hydraulic Research. 2017;**55**(2):143-162. DOI: 10.1080/00221686.2016.1212944

[44] Gong K, Shao S, Liu H, Wang B, Tan SK. Two-phase SPH simulation of fluid-structure interactions. Journal of Fluids and Structures. 2016;**65**:155-179. DOI: 10.1016/j.jfluidstructs.2016.05.012

[45] Zhou L, Cai ZW, Zong Z, Chen Z. An SPH pressure correction algorithm for multiphase flows with large density ratio. International Journal of Computational Methods. 2016;**81**(12):765-788. DOI: 10.1002/fld.4207

[46] Chen Z, Zong Z, Liu MB, Zou L, Li HT, Shu C. An SPH model for multiphase flows with complex interfaces and large density differences. Journal of Computational Physics. 2015;**283**:169-188. DOI: 10.1016/j.jcp.2014.11.037

[47] Aristodemo F, Federico I, Veltri P, Panizzo A. Two-phase SPH modelling of advective diffusion processes. Environmental Fluid Mechanics. 2010;**10**(4):451-470. DOI: 10.1007/s10652-010-9166-z

[48] Cleary PW, Hilton JE, Sinnott MD. Modelling of industrial particle and multiphase flows. Powder Technology. 2017;**314**:232-252. DOI: 10.1016/j.powtec.2016.10.072

[49] Shadloo MS, Oger G, Le Touzé D. Smoothed particle hydrodynamics method for fluid flows, towards industrial applications: Motivations, current state, and challenges. Computers and Fluids. 2016;**136**:11-34. DOI: 10.1016/j.compfluid.2016.05.029

[50] Wieth L, Kelemen K, Braun S, Koch R, Bauer H-J, Schuchmann HP. Smoothed particle hydrodynamics (SPH) simulation of a high-pressure homogenization process. Microfluidics and Nanofluidics. 2016;**20**(2):1-18. DOI: 10.1007/s10404-016-1705-6

[51] Harrison SM, Cleary PW, Eyres G, Sinnott M, Lundin L. Challenges in computational modelling of food breakdown and flavour release. Food and Function. 2014;**5**(11):2792-2805. DOI: 10.1039/C4FO00786G

[52] Wang D, Zhou Y, Shao S. Efficient implementation of smoothed particle hydrodynamics (SPH) with plane sweep algorithm. Communications in Computational Physics. 2016;**19**:770-800. DOI: 10.4208/cicp.010415.110915a

[53] Gan BS, Nguyen DK, Han A, Alisjahbana SW. Proposal for fast calculation of particle interactions in SPH simulations. Computers and Fluids. 2014;**104**:20-29. DOI: 10.1016/j.compfluid.2014.08.004

[54] Domínguez JM, Crespo AJC, Gómez-Gesteira M, Marongiu JC. Neighbour lists in smoothed particle hydrodynamics. International Journal for Numerical Methods in Fluids. 2011;**67**:2026-2042. DOI: 10.1002/fld.2481

[55] Viccione G, Bovolin V, Pugliese Carratelli E. Defining and optimizing algorithms for neighbouring particle identification in SPH fluid simulations. International Journal for Numerical Methods in Fluids. 2008;**58**:625-638. DOI: 10.1002/fld.1761

[56] Yeylaghi S, Moa B, Oshkai P, Buckham B, Crawford C. ISPH modelling for hydrodynamic applications using a new MPI-based parallel approach. Journal of Ocean Engineering and Marine Energy. 2017;**3**:3-35. DOI: 10.1007/s40722-016-0070-6

[57] Oger G, Le Touzé D, Guibert D, De Leffe M, Biddiscombe J, Soumagne J, et al. On distributed memory MPI-based parallelization of SPH codes in massive HPC context. Computer Physics Communications. 2016;**200**:1-14. DOI: 10.1016/j.cpc.2015.08.021

[58] Nishiura D, Furuichi M, Sakaguchi H. Computational performance of a smoothed particle hydrodynamics simulation for shared-memory parallel computing. Computer Physics Communications. 2015;**194**:18-32. DOI: 10.1016/j.cpc.2015.04.006

[59] Winkler D, Meister M, Rezavand M, Rauch W. gpuSPHASE—A shared memory caching implementation for 2D SPH using CUDA. Computer Physics Communications. 2017; **213**:165-180. DOI: 10.1016/j.cpc.2016.11.011

[60] Domínguez JM, Barreiro A, Crespo AJC, García-Feal O, Gómez-Gesteira M. Parallel CPU/GPU computing for smoothed particle hydrodynamics models. In: Klapp J, Sigalotti L Di G, Medina A, Gerardo Ruiz-Chavarría AL,editors. Recent Advances in Fluid Dynamics with Environmental Applications. 2016. pp. 477–491. DOI: 10.1007/978-3-319-27965-7_34

[61] Domínguez JM, Crespo AJC, Gómez-Gesteira M. Optimization strategies for CPU and GPU implementations of a smoothed particle hydrodynamics method. Computer Physics Communications. 2013;**184**(3):617-627. DOI: 10.1016/j.cpc.2012.10.015

[62] Alvarado-Rodríguez CE, Klapp J, Mayoral E, Domínguez JM. GPU simulations of fluid and composition dispersion in a porous media with smoothed particle hydrodynamics. In: Gitler I, Klapp J, editors. High Performance Computer Applications. ISUM 2015. Communications in Computer and Information Science. Vol. 595. Cham: Springer; 2016. pp. 485-494. DOI: 10.1007/978-3-319-32243-8_34

[63] Ji Z, Xu F, Takahashi A, Sun Y. Large scale water entry simulation with smoothed particle hydrodynamics on single- and multi-GPU systems. Computer Physics Communications. 2016;**209**:1-12. DOI: 10.1016/j.cpc.2016.05.016

[64] Xia X, Liang Q. A GPU-accelerated smoothed particle hydrodynamics (SPH) model for the shallow water equations. Environmental Modelling and Software. 2016;**75**:28-43. DOI: 10.1016/j.envsoft.2015.10.002

[65] Liang Q, Xia X, Hou J. Efficient urban flood simulation using a GPU-accelerated SPH model. Environmental Earth Sciences. 2015;**74**(11):7285-7294. DOI: 10.1007/s12665-015-4753-4

[66] Mokos A, Rogers BD, Stansby PK, Domínguez JM. Multi-phase SPH modelling of violent hydrodynamics on GPUs. Computer Physics Communications. 2015;**196**:304-316. DOI: 10.1016/j.cpc.2015.06.020

[67] Domínguez JM, Crespo AJC, Valdez-Banderas D, Rogers BD, Gómez-Gesteira M. New multi-GPU implementation for smoothed particle hydrodynamics on heterogeneous clusters. Computer Physics Communications. 2013;**184**(8):1848-1860. DOI: 10.1016/j.cpc.2013.03.008

[68] Joselli M, Junior d SJR, Clua EW, Montenegro A, Lage M, Pagliosa P. Neighborhood grid: A novel data structure for fluids animation with GPU computing. Journal of Parallel and Distributed Computing. 2015;**75**:20-28. DOI: 10.1016/j.jpdc.2014.10.009

[69] Hérault A, Bilotta G, Dalrymple RA. SPH on GPU with CUDA. Journal of Hydraulic Research. 2010;**48**(Suppl. 1):74-79. DOI: 10.1080/00221686.2010.9641247

[70] Harada T, Koshizuka S, Kawaguchi Y. Smoothed particle hydrodynamics on GPUs. In: Computer Graphics International Conference, Petròpolis, Brazil. 2007;63–70

[71] Bilotta G, Hérault A, Cappello A, Ganci G, Del Negro C. GPUSPH: A smoothed particle hydrodynamics model for the thermal and rheological evolution of lava flows. Geological Society Special Publication. 2016;**426**(1):387-408. DOI: 10.1144/SP426.24

[72] Wu J-S, Zhang H, Dalrymple RA. Simulating dam-break flooding with floating objects through intricate city layouts using GPU-based SPH method. Lecture Notes in Engineering and Computer Science. 2013;**3**:1755-1760

[73] Wu J-s, Zhang H, Yang R, Dalrymple RA, Hérault A. Numerical modeling of dam-break flood through intricate city layouts including underground spaces using GPU-based SPH method. Journal of Hydrodynamics. 2013;**25**(6):818-828. DOI: 10.1016/S1001-6058 (13)60429-1

[74] Rustico E, Bilotta G, Hérault A, Del Negro C, Gallo G. Advances in multi-GPU smoothed particle hydrodynamics simulations. IEEE Transactions on Parallel and Distributed Systems. 2014;**25**(1):43-52. DOI: 10.1109/TPDS.2012.340

[75] Karp AH, Flatt HP. Measuring parallel processor performance. Communications of the ACM. 1990;**33**:539-543. DOI: 10.1145/78607.78614

[76] Valdez-Balderas D, Domínguez JM, Rogers BD, Crespo AJC. Towards accelerating smoothed particle hydrodynamics simulations for free-surface flows on multi-GPU clusters. Journal of Parallel and Distributed Computing. 2013;**73**:1483-1493. DOI: 10.1016/j.jpdc.2012.07.010

[77] Cercos-Pita JL. AQUAgpusph, a new free 3D SPH solver accelerated with OpenCL. Computer Physics Communications. 2015;**192**:295-312. DOI: 10.1016/j.cpc.2015.01.026

[78] Gonnet P. Efficient and scalable algorithms for smoothed particle hydrodynamics on hybrid shared/distributed-memory architectures. SIAM Journal on Scientific Computing. 2015;**37**(1):C95-C121. DOI: 10.1137/140964266

[79] Pazouki A, Serban R, Negrut D. A high performance computing approach to the simulation of fluid-solid interaction problems with rigid and flexible components. Archive of Mechanical Engineering. 2014;**61**(2):227-251. DOI: 10.2478/meceng-2014-0014

[80] Cherfils JM, Pinon G, Rivoalen E. JOSEPHINE: A parallel SPH code for free-surface flows. Computer Physics Communications. 2012;**183**(7):1468-1480. DOI: 10.1016/j.cpc.2012.02.007

[81] Chow AD, Rogers BD, Lind SJ, Stansby PK. Implementing an optimized ISPH solver accelerated on the GPU. 12th International SPHERIC Workshop, Ourense, 2017

[82] Nie X, Chen L, Xiang T. Real-time incompressible fluid simulation on the GPU. International Journal of Computer Games Technology. 2015;12 pages. DOI: 10.1155/2015/417417

[83] Qiu LC. OpenCL-based GPU acceleration of ISPH simulation for incompressible flows. Applied Mechanics and Materials. 2014;**444-445**:380-384. DOI: 10.4028/www.scientific.net/AMM.444-445.380

[84] Monaghan JJ. Smoothed particle hydrodynamics and its diverse applications. Annual Review of Fluid Mechanics. 2012;**44**:323-346. DOI: 10.1146/annurev-fluid-120710-101220

[85] Violeau D. Fluid Mechanics and the SPH Method: Theory and Applications. Oxford University Press; 2012

[86] Viccione G, Bovolin V, Pugliese Carratelli E. Simulating Flows with SPH: Recent Developments and Applications. Intech Hydrodynamics—Optimizing Methods and Tools. 2011;69-84. DOI: 10.5772/26132

[87] Liu MB, Liu GR. Smoothed particle hydrodynamics (SPH): An overview and recent developments. Archives Computation Methods Engineering. 2010;**17**(1):25-76. DOI: 10.1007/s11831-010-9040-7

[88] Gómez-Gesteira M, Rogers BD, Dalrymple RA, Crespo AJC. State-of-the-art of classical SPH for free-surface flows. Journal of Hydraulic Research. 2010;**48**(sup1):6-27. DOI: 10.1080/00221686.2010.9641242

[89] Monaghan JJ. Smoothed particle hydrodynamics. Reports on Progress in Physics. 2005;**68**(8):1703-1759. DOI: 10.1088/0034-4885/68/8/R01

[90] Monaghan JJ. Introduction to SPH. Computer Physics Communication. 1988;**48**:89-96

[91] Vila JP. On particle weighted methods and smooth particle hydrodynamics. Mathematical Models and Methods in Applied Sciences. 1999;**9**(2):191-209

[92] Wendland H. Piecewise polynomial, positive definite and compactly supported radial functions of minimal degree. Advances in Computational Mathematics. 1995, 1995;**4**(1): 389-396. DOI: 10.1007/BF02123482

[93] Oger G, Doring M, Alessandrini B, Ferrant P. An improved SPH method: Towards higher order convergence. Journal of Computational Physics. 2007;**225**(2):1472-1492. DOI: 10.1016/j.jcp.2007.01.039

[94] Monaghan JJ. Smoothed particle hydrodynamics. Annual Review of Astronomy and Astrophysics. 1992;**30**:543-574. DOI: 10.1146/annurev.aa.30.090192.002551

[95] Viccione G, Bovolin V, Pugliese Carratelli E. Simulating fluid-structure interaction with SPH. AIP Conference Proceedings. 2012;**1479**(1):209-212. DOI: 10.1063/1.4756099

[96] Monaghan JJ, Lattanzio JC. A refined particle method for astrophysical problems. Astronomy and Astrophysics. 1985;**149**:135-143

[97] Dymond JH, Malhotra R. The Tait equation: 100 years on. International Journal of Thermophysics. 1988;**9**(6):941-951. DOI: 10.1007/BF01133262

[98] Crespo AJC, Domínguez JM, Rogers BD, Gómez-Gesteira M, Longshaw S, Canelas R, et al. DualSPHysics: Open-source parallel CFD solver based on smoothed particle hydrodynamics (SPH). Computer Physics Communications. 2015;**187**:204-216. DOI: 10.1016/j.cpc.2014.10.004

[99] Gómez-Gesteira M, Rogers BD, Crespo AJC, Dalrymple RA, Narayanaswamy M, Domínguez JM. SPHysics—Development of a free-surface fluid solver—Part 1: Theory and formulations. Computers & Geosciences. 2012;**48**:289-299. DOI: 10.1016/j.cageo.2012.02.029

[100] Gómez-Gesteira M, Crespo AJC, Rogers BD, Dalrymple RA, Domínguez JM, Barreiro A. SPHysics—Development of a free-surface fluid solver—Part 2: Efficiency and test cases. Computers & Geosciences. 2012;**48**:300-307. DOI: 10.1016/j.cageo.2012.02.028

[101] Verlet L. Computer "experiments" on classical fluids. I. Thermodynamical properties of Lennard-Jones molecules. Physical Review. 1967;**159**(1):98-103

[102] Crespo AJC, Gomez-Gesteira M, Dalrymple RA. Boundary conditions generated by dynamic particles in SPH methods. CMC: Computers, Materials, & Continua. 2007;**5**(3): 173-184. DOI: 10.3970/cmc.2007.005.173

[103] Chen X. Impacts of Overtopping Waves on Buildings on Coastal Dikes. Enschede, The Netherlands: Gildeprint; 2016

Chapter 4

Highly Deforming Computational Meshes for CFD Analysis of Twin-Screw Positive Displacement Machines

Sham Rane, Ahmed Kovačević, Nikola Stošić and
Ian Smith

Additional information is available at the end of the chapter

http://dx.doi.org/10.5772/intechopen.71885

Abstract

Commercial flow solvers can be used to obtain flow solutions in applications with deforming domains, but, in general, are not suitable for screw machine flow calculations. This is due to the large magnitude of deformation of the domain and the geometrical complexity of helical rotors. In this chapter, the governing equations for deforming domains and three methods of obtaining mesh movement, commonly used by FVM solvers, have been analysed. A comparative study of customised methods of grid generation for screw machines, using algebraic and differential approaches, is shown to help in the selection of techniques that can improve grid quality, robustness and speed of grid generation. The analysis of an oil-injected twin-screw compressor is included as a test case to demonstrate the application of SCORG, a deforming grid generator, as a means of predicting performance.

Keywords: finite volume method, deforming grid generation, arbitrary Lagrangian-Eulerian mesh motion, positive displacement machines, twin-screw compressors, twin-screw expanders

1. Introduction

Rotary screw compressors and expanders are positive displacement machines with two meshing rotors in the form of helical lobed screws. The working principle of these machines is simple. The male rotor engages with the female rotor forming a closed space with the housing, which forms the working chamber within a casing and its formation, and volumetric change, with rotation, is shown in **Figure 1**.

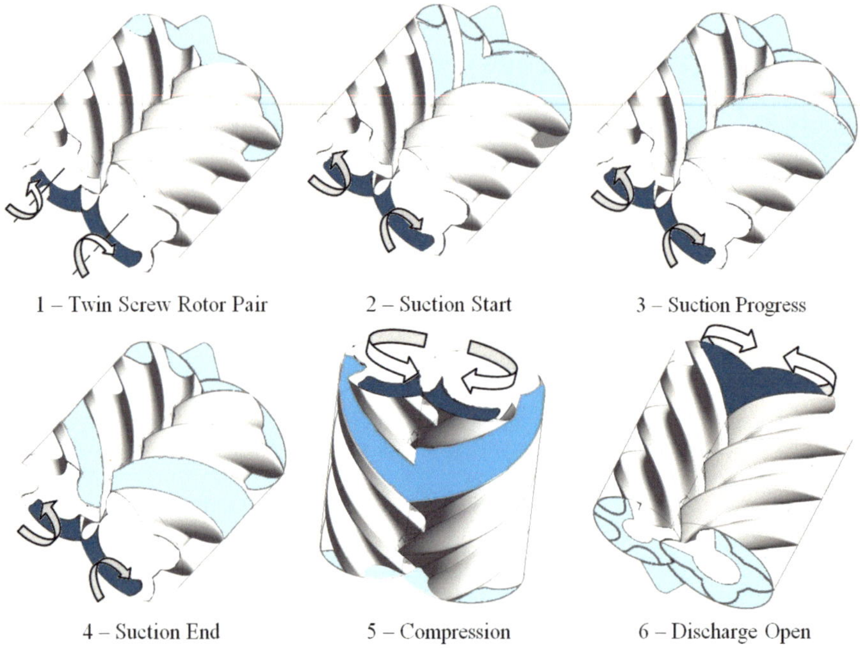

Figure 1. Operating stages in a twin-screw compressor.

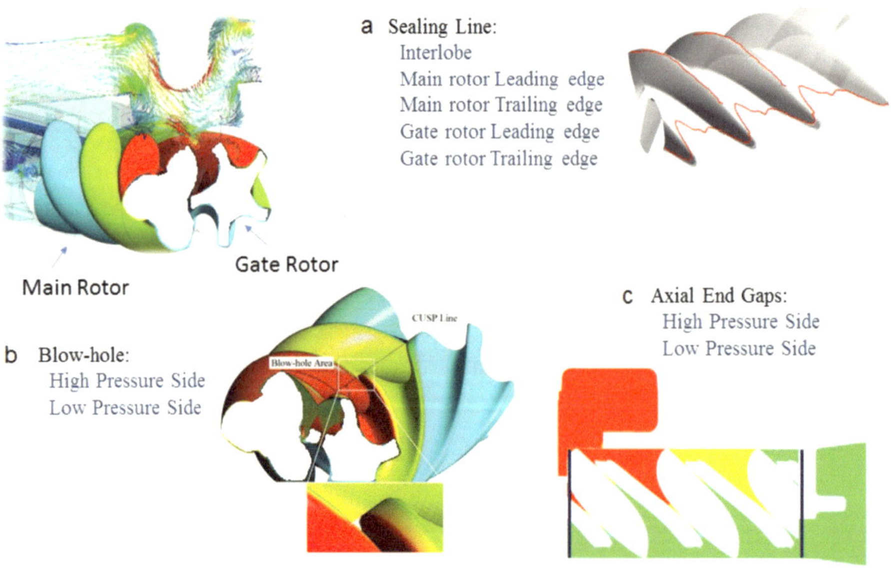

Figure 2. Leakages in a twin-screw compressor to be captured by computation mesh.

The compression process takes place between positions 4 and 6, and its analysis, by means of computational fluid dynamics (CFD), is challenging due to the existence of very small fluid leakage paths within the working chamber, associated with the volume change, the coexistence of both the working fluid and its lubricant, or coolant, as well as fluid injection and, most importantly, the lack of methodologies available to generate meshes required for full three-dimensional transient simulations.

Figure 2(a–c) shows the various leakage gap flows that are required to be accurately predicted by the flow solver [6]. An essential requirement for the computational mesh is to capture these gaps accurately. In the core region of the compression chamber, the size is of the order of 1000× as compared to the gaps, and all these regions are dynamically deforming.

Hence, only numerical solvers, operating with customised grid generators, have been used successfully to analyse the processes within these machines. Accordingly, in the next section, the governing equations for deforming domains and methods to analyse mesh movement that handle large mesh deformations with high-solution accuracy are reviewed, and a **user-defined nodal displacement** procedure, using external grids, derived from them is given in detail.

2. CFD calculations using arbitrary Lagrangian-Eulerian formulation with FVM for deforming control volumes

For a general variable ϕ, which can be a scalar or vector quantity, the integral form of the conservation equation, as given by Ferziger and Perić [10], can be represented by the general transport in Eq. (1):

$$\underbrace{\frac{\partial}{\partial t}\int_{\Omega}\rho\phi d\Omega}_{transient} + \underbrace{\int_{S}\rho\phi \boldsymbol{v}\,.\,\boldsymbol{n}dS}_{convec\ tion} = \underbrace{\int_{S}\Gamma\, grad\,\phi\,.\,\boldsymbol{n}dS}_{diffusio\ n} + \underbrace{\int_{\Omega}q_{\phi}\,d\Omega}_{source} \tag{1}$$

When the control volume is deforming, or not fixed in space, the Ω domain changes with time, due to movement of the boundaries. This movement is defined either as a function of time or as dependent on the current solution field. The convective fluxes such as the mass flux are calculated in such cases, using relative velocity components at the cell faces. If the coordinate system remains fixed and Cartesian velocity components are used, the only change in the conservation equations is the appearance of the relative velocity $(v - v_b)$ in all convective terms, where v_b is the velocity vector at the cell's face.

The application of Leibnitz's rule, given in Eq. (2), to differentiate the integral transient term of Eq. (1), results in Eq. (3) that gives the integral form of a general conservation equation in **arbitrary Lagrangian-Eulerian (ALE)** formulation:

$$\frac{\partial}{\partial t}\int_{\Omega}\rho\phi d\Omega = \frac{d}{dt}\int_{\Omega}\rho\phi d\Omega - \int_{S}\rho\phi\, \boldsymbol{v}_b\,.\,\boldsymbol{n}dS \tag{2}$$

$$\underbrace{\frac{d}{dt}\int_{\Omega}\rho\phi d\Omega}_{transient} + \underbrace{\int_{S}\rho\phi(\boldsymbol{v} - \boldsymbol{v}_b)\,.\,\boldsymbol{n}dS}_{convection} = \underbrace{\int_{S}\Gamma\, grad\,\phi\,.\,\boldsymbol{n}dS}_{diffusion} + \underbrace{\int_{\Omega}q_{\phi}\,d\Omega}_{source} \tag{3}$$

This is arbitrary, because the grid velocity v_b and grid motion are independent on the fluid motion. However, when the cell faces move, the conservation of mass and other conserved quantities are not necessarily ensured if the grid velocities are calculated explicitly and, in turn, are used to calculate the convective fluxes. To ensure that these equations are completely conserved, the space conservation law needs to be satisfied. This is given by

$$\frac{d}{dt}\int_{\Omega} d\Omega + \int_{S} \boldsymbol{v}_b \,.\, \boldsymbol{n} dS = 0 \tag{4}$$

Space conservation can be regarded as mass conservation with zero fluid velocity. The unsteady terms involving integrating the control volume Ω, in the governing equation, which is now changing with time, need to be treated to satisfy the space conservation equation with a deforming and/or moving grid. If the implicit first-order Euler scheme is used for temporal discretisation, the transient term can be discretised as

$$\frac{d}{dt}\int_{\Omega} \rho\phi d\Omega = \frac{(\rho\phi\Omega)^{n+1} - (\rho\phi\Omega)^{n}}{\Delta t} \tag{5}$$

where n and $n+1$ represent the current and next time levels, respectively. The $n+1$ volume Ω^{n+1} is computed from

$$\Omega^{n+1} = \Omega^{n} + \frac{d\Omega}{dt}\Delta t \tag{6}$$

where $d\Omega/dt$ is the rate of change of volume of the CV. In order to satisfy Eq. (4), this is calculated as

$$\frac{d\Omega}{dt} = \int_{S} \boldsymbol{v}_b \,.\, \boldsymbol{n} dS = \sum_{j}^{n_f} \boldsymbol{v}_{b,j} \cdot S_j \tag{7}$$

where n_f is the number of faces on the control volume and S_j is the jth face area vector.

The dot product $v_{b,j} \cdot S_j$ on each control volume face is calculated as $\partial\Omega_j/\Delta t$, from the volume swept out $-\partial\Omega_j$by that face over the time step Δt. Therefore, the mass flux $\dot{m}_j$ can be calculated using $\partial\Omega_j/\Delta t$ instead of being explicitly calculated from the grid velocity $v_{b,j}$:

$$\dot{m}_j = \int_{S_j} \rho(\boldsymbol{v} - \boldsymbol{v}_{b,j}) \,.\, \boldsymbol{n} d S_j \approx \rho_j (\boldsymbol{v} \,.\, \boldsymbol{n})_j S_j - \frac{\rho_j \partial\Omega_j}{\Delta t} \tag{8}$$

The requirement for space conservation in flow equations at moving integration points was introduced by Trulio and Trigger [11] when applied to a finite difference calculation framework. If the volume change and mass fluxes are calculated as given in Eq. (8), then this is ensured. Thomas and Lombard [12] presented the implementation of space conservation for a density-based finite difference scheme on structured meshes. Gosman [13] presented applications of this to reciprocating in-cylinder problems with moving boundaries.

When FVM is applied to solve for flows in screw machines, it faces a major challenge in the grids required for transient simulations. These grids have to capture the complex geometry formed by the fluid enveloping the screw rotors, and at the same time, they need to change their shape by large orders of magnitude. These domains are treated as highly deforming grids.

2.1. Solution of governing equations

Figure 3 represents a flow chart of the solution process for a FVM with deforming domains. The solver used in this analysis is a pressure-based coupled solver, ANSYS CFX. For compressible flows, where the density varies, an equation of state is used to obtain the relationship

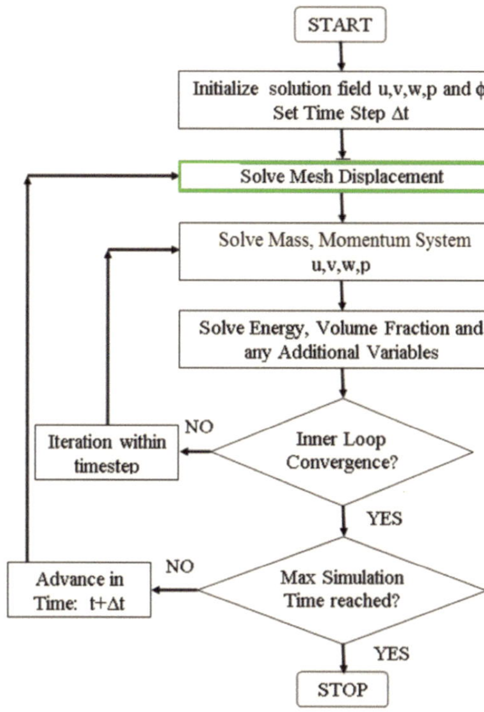

Figure 3. Flow chart of solution process with deforming domains.

between density and pressure, and the mass conservation equation is linearised in terms of pressure. Hence, a coupled system of equations, involving three Cartesian velocity components and pressure, is solved for every iteration in a time step.

The integration process and the solution of the governing equations ensure that the space conservation is retained at the new time instance. The highlighted block, named 'Solve Mesh Displacement' in **Figure 3**, should allow for the movement of the initial grid, in time, to the new position, during which the control volume deforms. The mesh should retain the same number of nodes, cells and topology, while the cell deformation should be defined by the movement of its nodes. The node displacement in ALE approach can be solved using different strategies, for example, (a) spring smoothing, (b) diffusion equation smoothing, (c) user-defined nodal displacements through external subroutines or (d) key-frame re-meshing.

2.1.1. Diffusion equation-based mesh smoothing

In the diffusion equation-based mesh smoothing, the specified displacement on the boundary nodes is propagated to the interior nodes by solving Eq. (9) internally in the solver:

$$\nabla \cdot \left(\Gamma_{disp} \nabla \delta\right) = 0 \tag{9}$$

Here, Γ_{disp} is the mesh stiffness that depends on the local cell volumes and the distance of the nodes from their deforming boundaries. This method is presented in **Figure 4**.

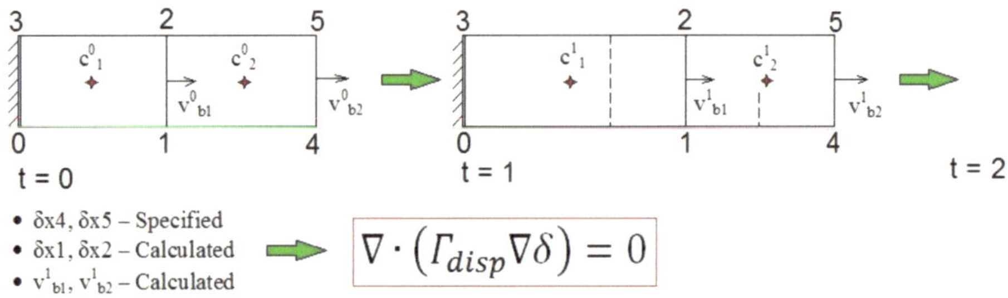

Figure 4. Grid deformation using diffusion equation mesh smoothing.

The number of cells, and their connectivity, remains constant for the duration of the calculation, with the grid being deformed at the beginning of each time step. A mesh smoothing method is not suitable for large boundary displacements because it produces cells with high skewness and there are chances of element failure due to negative volumes being formed after high nodal displacements. This limitation is dependent on the types of cell; the grid size, relative to the magnitude of the boundary displacement; the relative orientation of the cells; the boundary displacement; the position of the nondeforming boundaries, etc. For example, for tetrahedral types of cell, the skewness quality degrades faster with the boundary displacements, compared to hexahedral cells. Hence, for cases with simple geometries like a piston-cylinder combination, this method can be used, even with large displacements with hexahedral grids, but it fails for complex geometries, as in the case of screw compressors.

2.1.2. User-defined nodal displacement

Customised grid generators can be used to generate a set of grids representing nodal locations for every time step externally, prior to the numerical solution of flow in the calculation domain. The numerical grid is replaced at the beginning of each time step by the use of appropriate user subroutines, often called 'junction boxes'. This method is called user-defined nodal displacement and is shown graphically in **Figure 5**.

In the principle, it achieves the same result as the diffusion equation mesh smoothing, but it is suitable for large boundary displacements because the nodal positions are controlled externally.

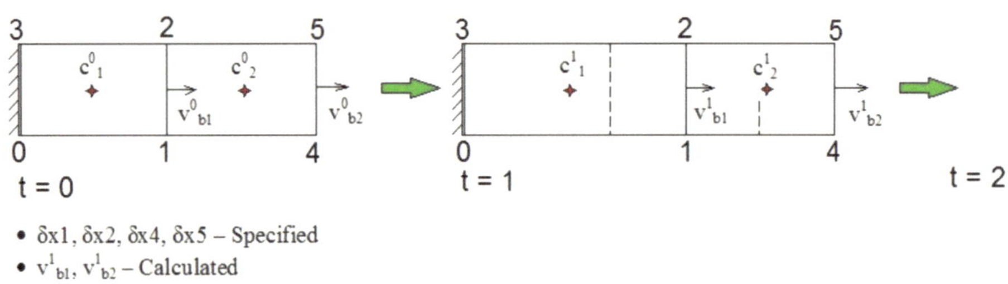

Figure 5. Grid deformation using user-defined nodal displacement.

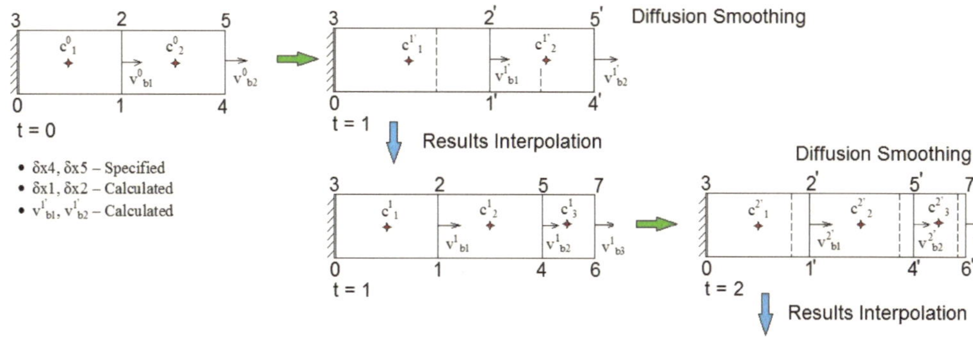

Figure 6. Grid deformation using key-frame grid re-meshing.

2.1.3. *Key-frame grid re-meshing*

Figure 6 shows another strategy suitable for high grid deformations which uses general-purpose grid generators.

After every time step, diffusion smoothing is performed to obtain the new geometry. A check is then performed to determine whether the control volume cells can absorb further deformation without generating negative volume elements. Upon the discovery of irregular cells, groups of cells are selectively re-meshed locally, retaining the boundary geometry but with a change in the number of cells and their connectivity. This process is called key-frame re-meshing. Re-meshing is followed by the next time step calculations, similar to those described in Section 2.1.1, but an intermediate interpolation of the solution is required after the previous time step, because, generally, all the cells will have changed connectivity.

In Section 2.2, a comparison of the solutions, derived from the methods of grid deformation described, has been presented, to study the accuracy of calculations, when applied to positive displacement flow applications.

2.2. Investigation of mesh deformation techniques

A case study is presented here to assess the applicability of the key-frame re-meshing method to the calculation of flow in positive displacement machines. A reversible adiabatic compression process in a piston cylinder was solved by the use of three grid deformation techniques, namely diffusion smoothing, user-defined nodal displacements and key-frame grid re-meshing. Such a simplistic geometry and thermodynamic process was chosen because it forms the fundamental mechanism for calculating performance by CFD in positive displacement machines and analytically derived results are available for error estimation. The isentropic compression-expansion process in a reciprocating piston cylinder can be modelled by a polytropic process equation relating the gas pressure and volume. Since the process is both adiabatic and reversible, there will be no energy losses or gains in the control volume, and the gas will return to its initial state given by Eq. (10):

$$\left(\frac{p_2}{p_1}\right) = \left(\frac{V_1}{V_2}\right)^{\gamma} = \left(\frac{T_2}{T_1}\right)^{\frac{\gamma}{(\gamma-1)}} \tag{10}$$

Consider a hypothetical piston cylinder arrangement with a sinusoidal displacement given to the piston. For this trial, a cylinder with diameter 100 mm and length 100 mm was considered. The initial position of the piston was for a maximum volume of 7.854×10^{-4} mm^3. The piston displacement was 70 mm, varying sinusoidally with a frequency of 50 Hz. The final minimum cylinder volume was 2.356×10^{-4} mm^3. This gave a fixed volume ratio of 3.333 for the system. Based on Eq. (10), for an initial absolute pressure in the cylinder of 2.013 bar, the expected peak pressure is 10.86 bar. Similarly, for an initial temperature of 298 K, the expected peak temperature is 482.35 K. In order to make the CFD model isentropic, all boundaries were defined as adiabatic, and the calculation of the viscous dissipation term, in the conservation equation of total energy, was turned off. This took reversibility, due to the turbulent viscosity dissipation factor, into account. Molecular viscosity and no-slip conditions at the walls were retained, for the formulation to be close to physical conditions.

The most suitable configuration for diffusion smoothing is a hexahedral mesh since the cell quality does not deteriorate much when boundaries deform. **Figure 7** shows the hexahedral mesh generated by diffusion smoothing at three different time steps. The hexahedral meshes generated by diffusion smoothing were identified as SH. The mesh shown in **Figure 7** is coarse, consisting of 22,752 cells identified as SH1. Two refined meshes were generated by the same method and named SH2 consisting of 49,962 cells and SH3 consisting of 74,720 cells (**Table 1**). For the key-frame-based re-meshing, a tetrahedral mesh was selected, as shown in **Figure 8**. Three different cases were generated, namely coarse KR1, medium KR2 and fine KR3 consisting of an equal number of cells and nodes, as shown in **Table 1**. For the user-defined nodal displacement, a hexahedral mesh was selected, and three grid sizes were generated to correspond to sizes of the diffusion smoothing. These were named UH1, UH2 and UH3, respectively, as listed in **Table 1**.

The time step was 2.8571×10^{-4} s, while each cycle contained 70 time steps which corresponded to 50 cycles per second. Mesh deformation was applied after each time step. The implicit second-order backward Euler discretisation was used within the pressure-based coupled solver. The advection scheme was high resolution, and the turbulence model was κ-ε. An rms residual target of 1.0×10^{-4} was maintained for all the equations. The fluid was air, assumed to be an ideal gas, with a molar mass of 28.96 kg kmol^{-1}, specific heat capacity of 1004.4 J kg^{-1} K^{-1}, dynamic viscosity of 1.831×10^{-5} kg m^{-1} s^{-1} and thermal conductivity of 2.61×10^{-2} W m^{-1} K^{-1}.

Figure 9 shows the variation of the piston displacement with time for the same volume ratio in cases SH1 and KR1. **Figure 10** shows the change of pressure with time in cases SH1 and KR1.

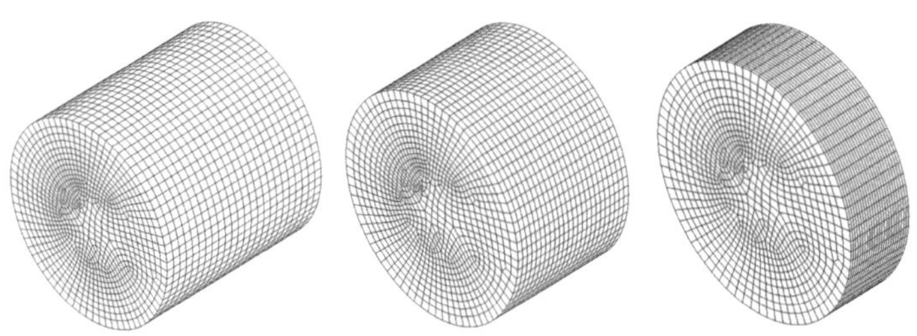

Figure 7. Hexahedral mesh using diffusion smoothing (SH1).

	Cycle	SH1	SH2	SH3	KR1	KR2	KR3	UH1	UH2	UH3
Number of cells		22,752	49,962	74,720	42,098	118,749	211,418	22,752	49,962	74,720
Number of nodes		24,650	53,244	79,171	11,849	31,514	53,148	24,650	53,244	79,171
Error in pressure [%]	I	−0.44	−0.44	−0.44	1.17	1.34	1.11	−0.44	−0.44	−0.44
	II	−0.42	−0.42	−0.42	6.23	7.26	7.41	−0.42	−0.42	−0.42
	III	−0.41	−0.41	−0.41	10.55	12.95	14.41	−0.41	−0.41	−0.41
Error in temperature [%]	I	−0.08	−0.08	−0.08	0.05	0.32	0.25	−0.08	−0.08	−0.08
	II	−0.07	−0.07	−0.07	3.44	4.18	3.74	−0.07	−0.07	−0.07
	III	−0.05	−0.05	−0.05	8.56	9.80	10.24	−0.05	−0.05	−0.05
Error in mass [%]	I	−0.38	−0.32	−0.30	1.78	1.91	2.27	−0.38	−0.32	−0.30
	II	−0.38	−0.32	−0.30	2.91	3.21	3.88	−0.38	−0.32	−0.30
	III	−0.38	−0.32	−0.30	2.15	3.29	4.43	−0.38	−0.32	−0.30

Table 1. Error in pressure, temperature and gas mass.

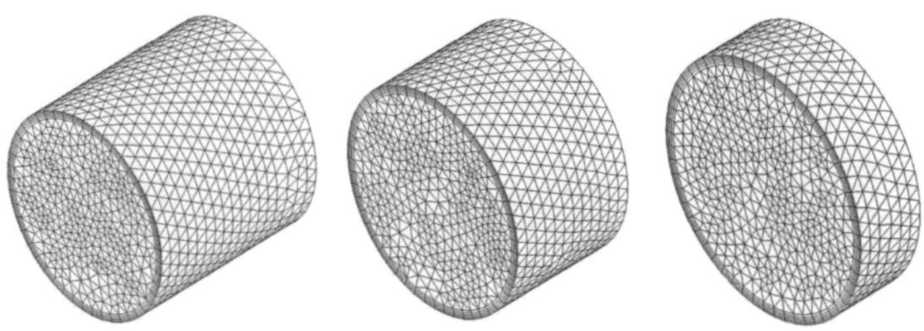

Figure 8. Tetrahedral mesh used in key-frame re-meshing (KR1).

The results obtained with user-defined nodal displacement UH1 were identical to that of SH and hence are not plotted. All cases, grid details and results are presented in **Table 1**. Although both diffusion smoothing (SH1) and key-frame re-meshing (KR1) follow the same change of volume during compression and expansion, the calculated peak pressures are not equal. In the case of diffusion smoothing, the pressure in the first cycle achieved the theoretical peak of 10.86 bar and consistently repeated itself in the following cycles. But in the case of key-frame re-meshing, the maximum pressure in the first cycle was higher than the theoretical value, and it continued to increase in the following cycles. Similarly, the initial state of pressure at the end of expansion did not return to its base value as it did in the case of diffusion smoothing.

Figure 11 shows the temperature change with time in the cylinder for both cases SH1 and KR1. The peak temperatures are not equal in the two. In the case of diffusion smoothing, the temperature in the first cycle rises to the theoretical peak of 482.35 K and repeats itself in the following cycles consistently. In the case of key-frame re-meshing, the peak temperature in the first cycle is similar to the theoretical value, but it continues to increase in the following

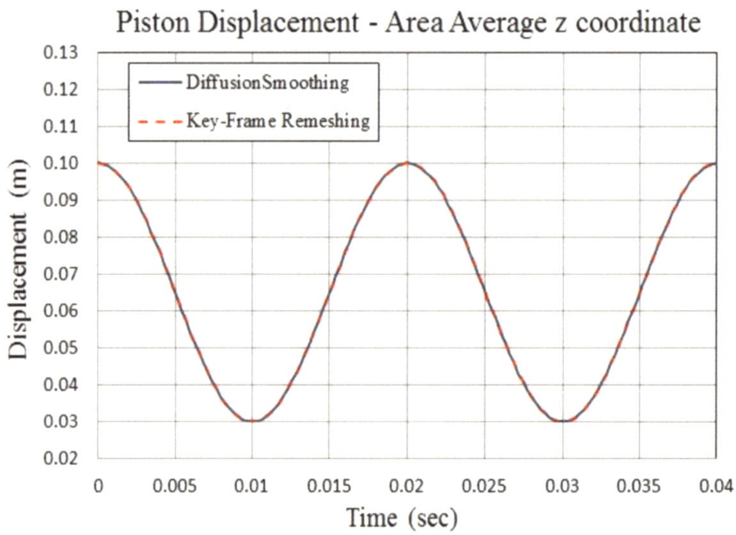

Figure 9. Piston displacement plot.

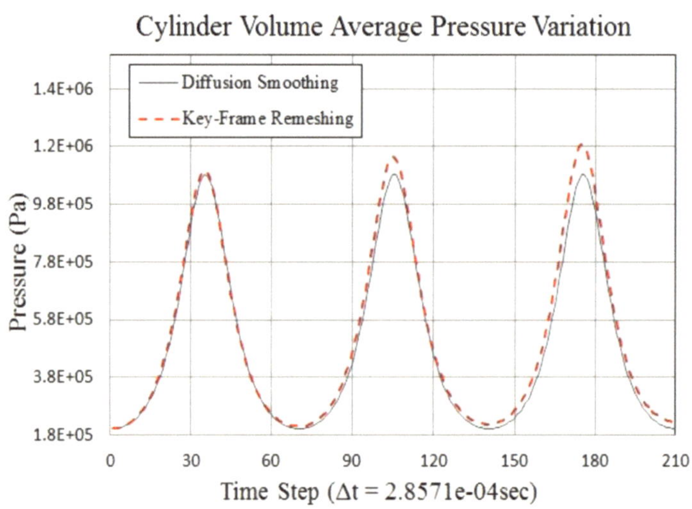

Figure 10. Cyclic temperature history.

cycles. Similarly, the initial state of temperature, at the end of expansion, does not return to its base level of 298 K as it does in the case of diffusion smoothing. **Table 1** shows the error in the prediction of pressure and temperature obtained from the three different grid deformation strategies with three different grid sizes and over multiple consecutive compression cycles.

The error in the pressure predictions over three consecutive compression cycles for the various grid deformation strategies is shown in **Figure 12**. The results show that the diffusion smoothing (SH)-based method of grid displacement and the user-defined nodal displacement (UH)-based method of grid displacement produce the same, highly accurate predictions which

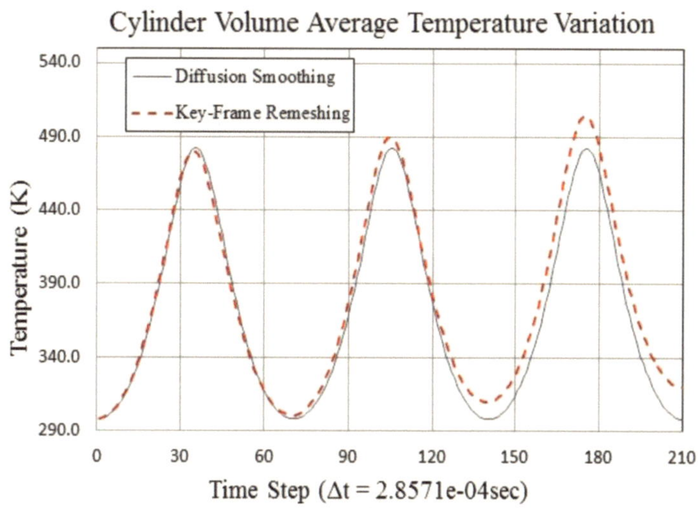

Figure 11. Cyclic pressure history.

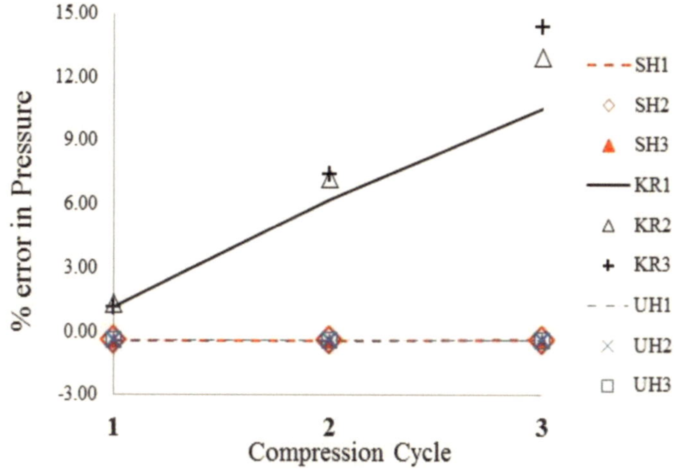

Figure 12. Error in pressure predictions of consecutive adiabatic cycles.

conform with the theoretical results for this highly deforming boundary formulation. However, errors in the pressure and temperature prediction exist when the key-frame re-meshing-based method of grid deformation is used. For the key-frame re-meshing method, the error increases with the grid refinement. Since the mesh is replaced for each time step, it is quite possible that it induces an increase in calculation error. As pointed out by Ferziger and Perić [10], this can lead to artificial mass source errors in the continuity equation that can also accumulate with flow time. **Table 1** shows the error in mass over multiple consecutive compression cycles for the three different grid deformation strategies. Limiting the mesh, to be replaced, only when the cell quality is severely reduced, should help to reduce the error, but in the case of complex topologies, as in screw machines, this is very difficult. In conclusion, the key-frame re-meshing method gave inconsistent results with increasing error in pressure and temperature predictions in successive compression cycles. Grid refinement also did not improve the accuracy of key-frame re-meshing, while reducing the time step made excessive demands on preprocessing. However, diffusion smoothing and user-defined nodal displacement produced identical results with accurate estimates of pressure and temperature and hence are the preferred approaches to deal with highly deforming domains such as twin-screw machines.

2.3. Algebraic grid generation of highly deforming screw rotor grids for user-defined nodal displacement

Figure 13 shows the main stages of the procedure developed by Kovačević et al. [5, 6]. The domain of the working chamber is first decomposed into the low-pressure port, the rotor domain and the high-pressure port. The rotor domain, which deforms with time, consists of a hexahedral grid, and a set of grids representing the entire compression cycle are required to be supplied to the solver for continuous simulation. The low-pressure and high-pressure ports can be meshed using general-purpose grid generators, and it is easier to have a tetrahedral grid with fine prism layers covering the boundaries. These tetrahedral grids interface with a structured grid, built on the rotor domain via nonconformal conservative interfaces. An algebraic grid generation method employing multiparameter one-dimensional adaptation and transfinite interpolation is used to construct the hexahedral grid in the rotor domain. A block-structured numerical mesh is desired in the rotor domain. In order to construct an O grid, it is necessary to subdivide the topology of the male rotor, the female rotor and the casing together into two.

One O grid is constructed on the male side and the other on the female side. It is most convenient to do this splitting in 2D cross section of the rotors, and the envelope method of gearing is used to construct a rack curve between the male and the female rotor profiles to split into two O grid primitives as shown in **Figure 13**. Consecutive 2D cross sections are calculated individually, as shown by Kovačević [5]. This procedure is the most important function of the framework and provides flexibility to extend it to more complex rotor designs like variable pitch or variable profiles. A detailed description of the algebraic approach for variable screw rotors is given by Rane [4].

2.4. Differential approach for generation of highly deforming screw rotor grids for user-defined nodal displacement

Differential equation-based decomposition is a generic method that can be applied to a variety of twin rotor machines like tooth compressors, screw compressors, etc. The working chamber is again split into the deforming domain of the rotors and the static domains of the low-pressure and high-pressure ports. The compression chamber is defined using the rotor profile and the casing, and a block structure grid is generated by the stages shown in **Figure 14** [3]. An FVM can be used to solve a Laplace equation system in the 2D domain, so formed. Since the rotor profiles have close tolerances, the region formed between the casing, and the two profiles have a very complex boundary. Hence, discretisation, using unstructured triangular cells, is the most appropriate. The gaps can be highly refined to capture, accurately, the iso-potential lines conforming with the boundary. **Figure 14** shows a triangular mesh generated using the commercial

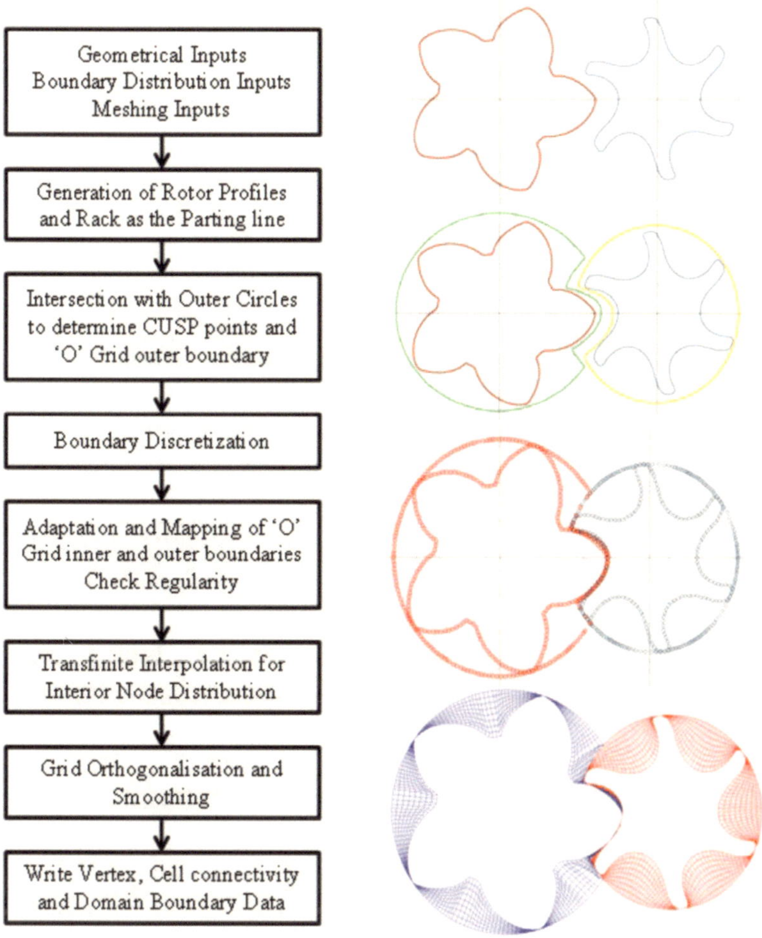

Figure 13. Simplified block diagram: algebraic rotor grid generation.

grid generator ANSYS. In practice, 10–15 times higher refinement is necessary. Vande Voorde et al. [3] used a customised Delaunay triangulation program, as given by Riemslagh et al. [14], for this initial triangular grid construction. Further details of this approach are given in [3].

The beneficial properties of the differential solution are well known and were first utilised by Crowley and Winslow [9] for generating a triangular 2D mesh in the numerical solution of PDEs for static magnetic fields. With the differential approach, the grid for the main flow calculations is, in turn, generated from the solution of an elliptic PDE like the Laplace equation $\nabla^2 \varnothing = 0$. Hence, the first task, after representing the compression chamber, is to slice it into a number of 2D cross sections. Depending on the lead of the helical rotor, each 2D section spacing is such that it corresponds to a unit degree of rotation of the main rotor. This allows for smooth representation of the rotor lead as well as physical rotation of the rotors during simulation. **Figure 14** shows the splitting curve or division line obtained in a 2D cross section of the compression chamber.

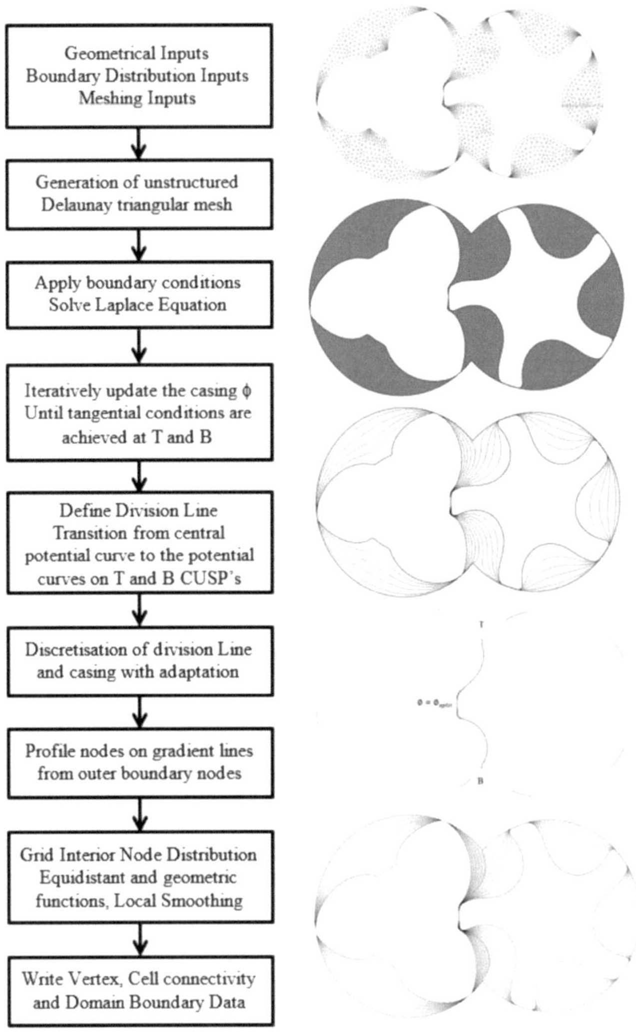

Figure 14. Simplified block diagram: differential rotor grid generation.

2.5. Comparison of the algebraic and differential approaches

Table 2 presents a comparison between the algebraic and the differential approaches applied to screw rotor grid generation. Each approach has its own advantages and limitations.

From the description of the techniques in the algebraic and differential approaches and the comparison of the two, it can be said that a good choice of theories is currently available for extending the grid generation to improve the quality, robustness and speed.

2.6. Combination of algebraic and differential grid generation approach

Algebraic methods are favourable for their speed of grid generation. In order to improve the resulting grid quality, the generated algebraic mesh can be used, and the partial differential

http://dx.doi.org/10.5772/intechopen.71885

	Criteria	Algebraic approach [6]	Hybrid differential approach [3]
1	Rotor domain decomposition	Analytical rack or numerical rack Rack-based decomposition is very fast	Differential division line Differential division line decomposition is generic in nature
2	Boundary distribution	Profile discretisation according to selected adaptation Rotor projection used with regularity checks for outer boundary Rotor ⇒ outer boundary With rotor ⇒ outer boundary, the O blocks rotate with the rotor. Grid deformation occurs at the rack interface	Casing plus division line distributed first using equidistance and radius of curvature factors. Profile nodes projected of gradient line Outer boundary ⇒ rotor With outer boundary ⇒ rotor, the O blocks do not rotate but deform as rotor surface turns
3	Interface between the two O blocks	Nonconformal Nonconformal interface is handled by flux balance in the solver and gives more flexibility for adaptation	Conformal Conformal interface is desirable for higher-solution accuracy Demanded by some CFD solvers
4	Control on grid size	Circumferential and radial divisions and rotor angular positions Fixed number of angular positions constraint the solver time step size for the given speed	Circumferential and radial divisions and rotor angles at every degree position Intermittent rotor positions obtained by linear interpolation
5	Control functions	Two variable unidirectional adaptations on the rotor, TFI with tension spline factor, orthogonalisation and smoothing factors Rotor profile adaptation captures the 3D surface more accurately	Division line to CUSP transition, local smoothing and geometric spacing in radial direction
6	Time required for grid generation	For 50 rotor positions, on an i3 processor, it takes about 5 s for boundary distribution and 30 s for 2D mesh generation Full set with 750 grids takes about 1 h	A representative mesh took about 900 s for one position on DS20 processor. Full set took about 15 h Solution to the initial PDE is iterative and consumes time to get tangential conditions at the CUSPs
7	Cell structure	In order to retain the CUSP line in 3D, some pyramid or prism cells are introduced by merging nodes at the CUSP	All cells are purely hexahedral. Near tip of the gate rotors some face Warpage occurs due to grid line alignments
8	Cell jump	Generally, near the CUSP region between the two O blocks	Generally, in the transition region from central division line to casing
9	Adaptation to variable lead rotors	Directly possible with 3D grid rearrangement [8]	Directly possible with 3D grid rearrangement
10	Adaptation to variable profile rotors	Possible with modification in the algorithm to execute 2D generation on each profile and with 3D grid rearrangement [8]	Practically, challenging due to the requirement of potential solution in 3D or on multiple 2D profiles for each position
11	Advantages	Fast and good control over the node distribution Rotor profile smoothly captured in the grid Grid refinement is relatively easy to be achieved	Very smooth cells Fully hexahedral Conformal interface between O blocks makes the grid suitable for a variety of solvers and complexities like multiphase flows
12	Difficulties	Due to nonconformal interface, some solvers do not function with the helical rotor grids	No functional difficulties except for the computationally expensive generation procedure

Table 2. Comparison of algebraic and differential approach for screw rotor grids.

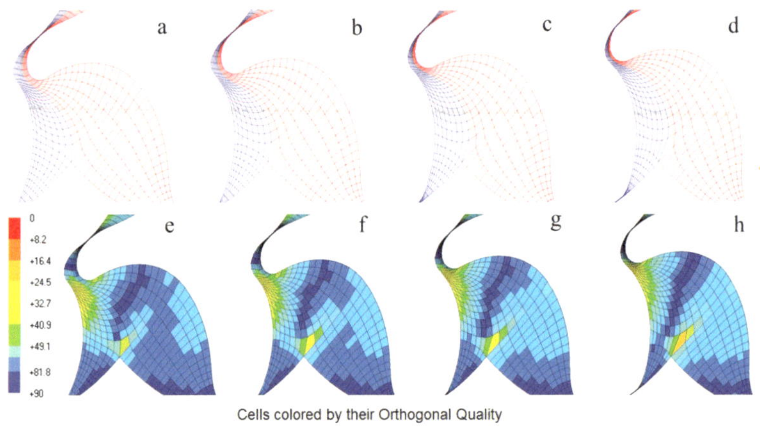

Figure 15. Improved grid transition and cell quality achieved by a combination of algebraic and differential approach.

equation (PDE) system can be solved over this grid. Rane et al. [1, 2] describe the procedure to produce an algebraic grid that consists of a single domain enclosing both the main and gate rotors. In such a domain, a further PDE system of the Poisson form is solved. The improvement in mesh transition and cell orthogonality quality, obtained by implementing a combined algebraic and differential grid generation, is shown in **Figure 15**. This algorithm is currently available in the SCORG grid generation tool and a test case to demonstrate its application to oil-injected screw compressor calculation presented in the next section [7].

3. Analysis of an oil-injected twin-screw compressor

Flow in an oil-flooded twin-screw compressor with a combined axial and radial suction and an axial discharge port was calculated with a PDE grid, as shown in **Figure 15**. The CFD model setup in CFX solver is shown in **Figure 16**. The compressor with 'N' profile rotors has four male lobes and five female lobes. The nominal interlobe and radial and axial leakage gaps are 60 μm. The operating speed of the machine is between 3000 and 6000 rpm, while discharge pressure can vary between 4.0 and 12.0 bar. A complete description of the model's numerical setup is given by Rane et al. [7]. Only discussion of the important results is presented here.

The quality of generated rotor mesh had a minimum orthogonal angle of 6.5°, a maximum expansion factor of 857 and a maximum aspect ratio 906 in less than 1% of the cells. The rotor grid node count was 467,992, while the total model's node count was 713,911. This includes the suction, discharge and oil injection ports.

3.1. Pressure distribution

The variation of pressure in the compression chamber with abscissa as the main rotor rotation angle is shown in **Figure 17**. From the pressure angle plots, it can be observed that in all three cases the pressure during the compression part of the process aligns closely. At 3000 rpm when the discharge port opens, the flow pulsations in the port are low as compared to that at 6000 rpm. These increase with the increase in discharge pressure. Still for 3000 rpm, the

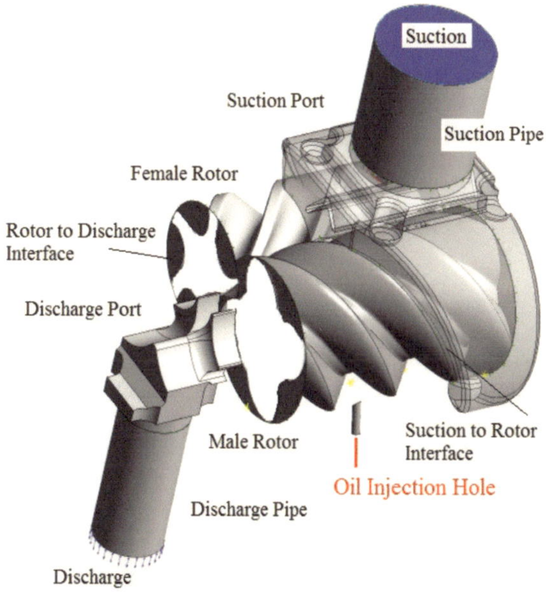

Figure 16. CFD model of an oil-injected twin-screw compressor in ANSYS CFX solver.

pulsations and the maximum pressure are both lower that at the higher speed. At 8.0 bar discharge pressure and 6000 rpm, the peak pressure reaches 10.0 bar. For the built-in volume ratio of 3.6, the 8.0 bar discharge pressure is an under-compression condition, also visible in the pressure curve. The peak over-compression at higher speed is due to throttling in the port.

A comparison of the performance predicted by CFD model with measured data is shown in **Figure 18**. Here, measurements at 6.0 bar and 3000 rpm have been used for normalisation. A close prediction of flow is seen at 6000 rpm. At 3000 rpm, the CFD model is under predicting flow at both 6.0 and 8.0 bar discharge pressures by about 10%. This could be due to the amount of injected oil in the CFD model, not being equal to that in the tests. By assuming a mechanical efficiency of 77%, the derived input power deviates from the measured values by less than 2% at both speeds and pressures.

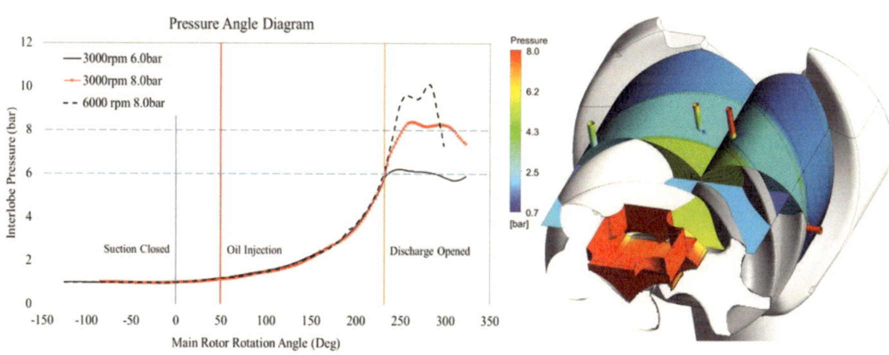

Figure 17. Pressure diagram for three cases and distribution at 6000 rpm (8.0 bar discharge).

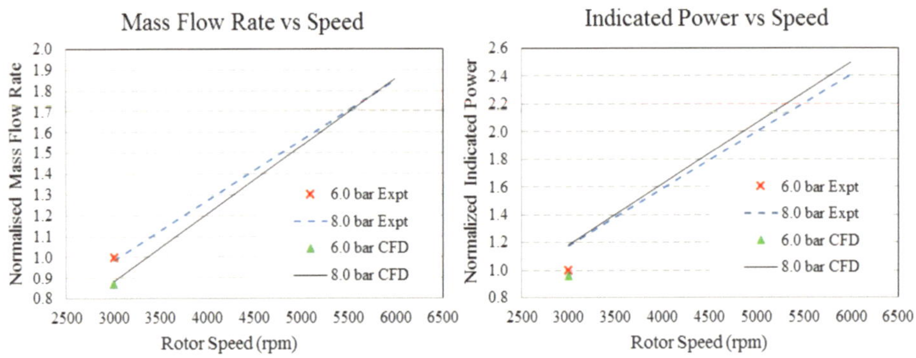

Figure 18. Performance comparison as normalised air flow and indicated power.

3.2. Oil distribution inside the compression chamber

The close interaction of the injected oil with the gate rotor lobes over one complete interlobe rotation is shown in **Figure 19(a–h)**. At position 'a', the formation of the oil spray begins when the injection hole is just exposed to the compression chamber. Its direction is influenced by the passing leading gate rotor lobe. The velocity of oil depends on the injection pressure. At 'c' oil film forms in the root of the rotor. At positions 'd', 'e' and 'f', the film spreads, the spray continues and, finally, intersection with the trailing lobe starts. At 'g' the hole is completely blocked by the trailing lobe width, and it follows, from the oil velocity vectors, that an oil flow pulse is formed. At 'h' the position of injection coincides with that at 'a', and the cycle repeats itself. A large vortex remains in the trailing working chamber.

The pulsating nature of the oil injection can also be seen in **Figure 20**. The quantity of oil injected at 8.0 bar is the same at both 3000 and 6000 rpm. In the analysis, the system pressure loss from separator vessel to the injection hole is assumed to be 0.5 bar in all the three cases.

For a more accurate model, an injection pressure measurement would be required that can be specified as a boundary condition. The oil flow rate at 6.0 bar is lower than that at 8.0 bar discharge pressure. The distribution of oil on gate rotor surface and its interaction in the discharge

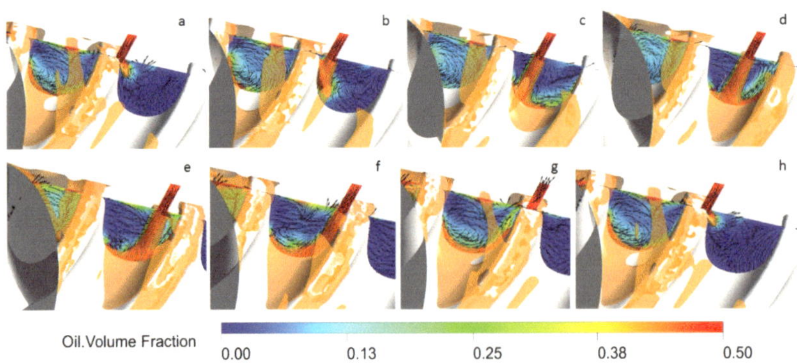

Figure 19. Oil injection interaction with the gate rotor lobes during one cycle.

http://dx.doi.org/10.5772/intechopen.71885

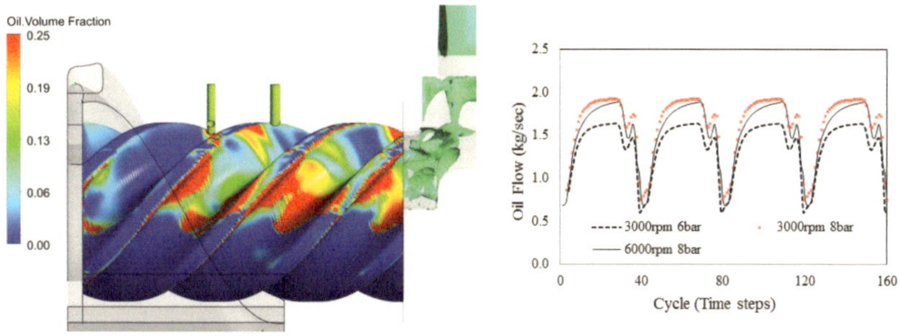

Figure 20. Oil flow distribution near the discharge port and flow cycles for three cases.

port can also be seen in **Figure 20**. Oil accumulates in the interlobe gaps and is transported by the rotors. The oil distribution in the discharge port is unsteady but cyclically repeating.

3.3. Gas temperature distribution

The cyclic variation of the discharge air temperature in the three cases is shown in **Figure 21**. With a built-in volume ratio of 3.6, the adiabatic discharge temperature without oil injection would be about 500 K, but due to leakage and recompression effects, the temperature rise would be much higher. Due the oil being injected at 323 K, the gas temperature is substantially lowered and does not exceed 340 K. At 3000 rpm and 8 bar discharge pressure, the peak temperature is about 10° lower than that at 6000 rpm. This is because the amount of oil injected at the same discharge pressure and different rotational speeds is almost the same, as shown in **Figure 20**. This, when combined with the lower residence time of the oil at higher speed, there is less heat transfer from gas to oil, and this results in a higher discharge temperature. Similarly, there is only a small difference in the gas temperature at the same speed and different discharge pressures because the quantity of oil injected at higher pressure increases, as shown in **Figure 20**. This higher amount of oil lowers the gas temperature which remains close to the injection temperature of 323 K. The distribution of gas temperature at 8.0 bar discharge pressure and 6000 rpm is shown in **Figure 21**. It can be seen that the local maximum temperature reaches 340 K. Also, the gas temperature is not uniformly distributed. This non-uniformity is due to the non-homogeneous distribution of oil in the compression chamber.

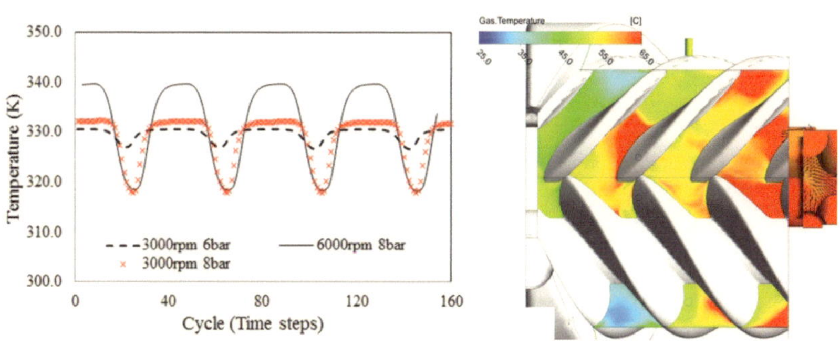

Figure 21. Discharge gas temperature cycles for three cases and distribution at 6000 rpm (8.0 bar pressure).

4. Summary

In this chapter, the governing equations and strategies of mesh deformation have been reviewed for their applicability to twin-screw machine flow calculations. For the simplistic case of adiabatic compression and expansion by a piston in a cylinder type of system, the key-frame re-meshing method gave inconsistent results, with increasing error in pressure and temperature predictions in successive compression cycles, whereas the methods of diffusion smoothing and user-defined nodal displacement produced identical results with accurate estimates of pressure and temperature. Thus, it is necessary to extend the customised grid generation techniques and use a strategy such as user-defined nodal displacement, during the ALE calculations. A comparative study between the algebraic and differential approaches has helped in the selection of techniques that can offer feasibility for implementing grids for a deforming rotor domain and also for improving the grid quality. In the combined algebraic and differential approach, a special procedure has been introduced that completely smooths the transition of the algebraically generated splitting rack curve between the two rotors, thus smoothing the grid node movement in time and space. These grid features have improved the robustness of the solution in CFD solvers.

The results from the simulation of the compression process in an oil-injected twin-screw compressor provided an exceptional visualisation of the interaction of gas and oil inside the compression chamber. The interaction of the phases, the oil distribution and heat transfer between the gas and the oil and also the effects of high oil concentration in the leakage gaps on the sealing were well captured. The developments presented in this chapter together with the case study will be useful for flow analysts practising CFD in screw machines as well as computational solver developers considering such highly deforming grids in these classes of flow machines.

Nomenclature

x, y, z	Cartesian coordinates
$q_{\phi s}$	Flux source
grad	Gradient operator
div	Divergence operator
$\mathbf{v}$	Fluid velocity
p	Pressure
V	Cell volume
Δt	Time step
ϕ	Conserved variable in transport equations
γ	Adiabatic index

http://dx.doi.org/10.5772/intechopen.71885

SCORG	Screw Compressor Rotor Grid Generator
ALE	Arbitrary Lagrangian-Eulerian
$\boldsymbol{n}$	Cell face normal vector
$q_{\varnothing V}$	Volume source
S	Cell surface
δ	Displacement
t	Time
T	Temperature
$\mathbf{v}_b$	Surface velocity
Ω	Control volume
Γ	Diffusion coefficient
ρ	Density
μ	Viscosity
rms	Root-mean-square value

Acknowledgements

A major portion of the chapter is derived from the thesis 'Grid Generation and CFD Analysis of Variable Geometry Screw Machines' [4].

Author details

Sham Rane*, Ahmed Kovačević, Nikola Stošić and Ian Smith

*Address all correspondence to: sham.rane@city.ac.uk

School of Mathematics, Computer Science and Engineering, City, University of London, London, UK

References

[1] Rane S, Kovačević A. Algebraic generation of single domain computational grid for twin screw machines. Part I. Implementation. Advances in Engineering Software. 2017;**107**:38-50. DOI: https://doi.org/10.1016/j.advengsoft.2017.02.003

[2] Kovačević A, Rane S. Algebraic generation of single domain computational grid for twin screw machines part II – Validation. Advances in Engineering Software. 2017;**109**:31-43. DOI: https://doi.org/10.1016/j.advengsoft.2017.03.001

[3] Voorde VJ, Vierendeels J. A grid manipulation algorithm for ALE calculations in screw compressors. In: 17th AIAA Computational Fluid Dynamics Conference; Canada. Canada: AIAA; 2005. pp. 2005-4701

[4] Rane S. Grid Generation and CFD Analysis of Variable Geometry Screw Machines [Thesis]. London: City, University of London; 2015. 350 p. Available from: http://openaccess.city.ac.uk/id/eprint/15129

[5] Kovačević A. Three-Dimensional Numerical Analysis for Flow Prediction in Positive Displacement Screw Machines [Thesis]. London: City, University of London; 2002. 350 p

[6] Kovačević A, Stošić N, Smith IK. Screw Compressors – Three Dimensional Computational Fluid Dynamics and Solid Fluid Interaction. 1st ed. New York: Springer-Verlag; 2007. 200 p. ISBN 3-540-36302-5

[7] Rane S, Kovačević A, Stošić N. CFD analysis of oil flooded twin screw compressors. In: International Compressor Engineering Conference at Purdue; July; Purdue, USA. Purdue: 2016. p. 2392. DOI: http://docs.lib.purdue.edu/icec/2392

[8] Rane S, Kovačević A, Stošić N, Kethidi M. Deforming grid generation and CFD analysis of variable geometry screw compressors. Computers and Fluids. 2014;**99**:124-141. DOI: https://doi.org/10.1016/j.compfluid.2014.04.024

[9] Winslow A. Numerical solution of the quasilinear poisson equation in a nonuniform triangle mesh. Journal of Computational Physics. 1966;**1**(2):149-172. DOI: https://doi.org/10.1016/0021-9991(66)90001-5

[10] Ferziger JH, Perić M. Computational Methods for Fluid Dynamics. Berlin: Springer; 1996. ISBN 978-3-540-42074-3

[11] Trulio GJ, Trigger RK. Numerical solution of the one-dimensional hydrodynamic equations in an arbitrary time-dependent coordinate system. University of California Lawrence Radiation Laboratory Report. 1961;UCLR-6522

[12] Thomas P, Lombard C. Geometric conservation law and its application to flow computations on moving grids. AIAA Journal. 1979;**17**:1030-1037

[13] Gosman DA. Prediction of in-cylinder processes in reciprocating internal combustion engines. Computing Methods in Applied Science and Engineering. 1984. Glowinski and Lions edition. pp. 604-629

[14] Riemslagh K, Vierendeels J, Dick E. An arbitrary Lagrangian-Eulerian finite-volume method for the simulation of rotary displacement pump flow. Applied Numerical Mathematics. 2000;**32**:419-433

Chapter 5

Optimization Design by Coupling Computational Fluid Dynamics and Genetic Algorithm

Jong-Taek Oh and Nguyen Ba Chien

Additional information is available at the end of the chapter

http://dx.doi.org/10.5772/intechopen.72316

Abstract

Nowadays, optimal design of equipment is one of the most practical issues in modem industry. Due to the requirements of deploying time, reliability, and design cost, better approaches than the conventional ones like experimental procedures are required. Moreover, the rapid development of computing power in recent decades opens a chance for researchers to employ calculation tools in complex configurations. In this chapter, we demonstrate a kind of modern optimization method by coupling computational fluid dynamics (CFD) and genetic algorithms (GAs). The brief introduction of GAs and CFD package OpenFOAM will be performed. The advantage of this approach as well as the difficulty that we must tackle will be analyzed. In addition, this chapter performs a study case in which an automated procedure to optimize the flow distribution in a manifold is established. The design point is accomplished by balancing the liquid-phase flow rate at each outlet, and the controlled parameter is a dimension of baffle between each channel. Using this methodology, we finally find a set of results improving the distribution of flow.

Keywords: computational fluid dynamics, VOF, optimization, OpenFOAM, genetic algorithm, open sourced

1. Introduction

Computational fluid dynamics (CFD)-based optimization approach has been growing rapidly in the past decades. The demand of optimizing the product designs with high reliability and the time constraints have promoted engineers and researchers to develop the frameworks tackling the problems, in which CFD simulation becomes one of the key roles. In addition, the computing power has raised the performance over 10,000 times in comparison with the point in the mid-1980s. Thus, the computing tasks now could adapt in much complex and bigger models. In other words, the computing century has changed the way engineers finding the solutions, and traditional approaches like experimental ones now are moving apart to modeling approaches.

In fact, the capability of CFD-based optimization has been early deployed in aerospace field to generate the wing profiles, which could reduce the drag force [1]. Jameson [2–4] firstly proposed a shape optimization method for aerodynamic design using the control theory. In this methodology, the authors used adjoint equations. The design space could be extended to the number of coordinate transformations or cost functions. It is also called as nonparametric method. Following that, several studies on shape optimization in this field have been published [5–7]. The other methodology, so-called the parametric method, was also successfully applied in this field such as the research of Eero Immonen [8], which investigated the CFD-based optimization framework for the NACA airfoil using response surface method (RSM).

In the branch of thermal design, CFD-based optimization is applied in various objects such as the optimization of chemical reactor [9], steam turbine blade cascade [10], or plate-fin heat exchanger [11]. Also, several CFD-based optimization studies on other fields were published in literature including ship hull [12], car [13, 14], vascular [15], or engine [16].

However, in this chapter, instead of describing all the above techniques, we introduce a parametric approach of CFD-based optimization that couples CFD and evolution algorithms since this approach could be applied in more complex systems of equations as well as the complex physical models. Although evolution algorithm tree has several branches, we are going to focus only on the popular type, genetic algorithm (GA). A general concept is illustrated to help readers to follow easily. Finally, a study case that uses CFD and single-objective genetic algorithm (SOGA) to optimize the uniformity of flow in the manifold is investigated.

2. A brief introduction about GAs

2.1. Definition of gas

Genetic algorithms are first proposed by John Holland in the 1960s and were continuously developed together with his students during the 70th decade. The idea of the generic algorithm is inspired by the natural selection and the famous Darwin's law, survival of the fittest.

The characteristics of GAs show some advantages in comparison with the classical optimization method, especially when coupling them with CFD simulation. At first, GAs can generate the individuals (or chromosomes) of populations independently. In the complex systems, CFD solver may cost much time to reach to convergence. The simultaneous running takes advantage of modern computing power. Each job will be solved separately and then synchronized when GAs do their operators. Moreover, we could restart the work at interrupt point if there is any corruption, whereas this may be difficult when an individual is produced iteratively like the way gradient-based methods operate. Second, since the cost function in GAs is constant, GAs may overcome the numerical noise, which normally occurs in a CFD problem due to the limit of grid resolution or residual.

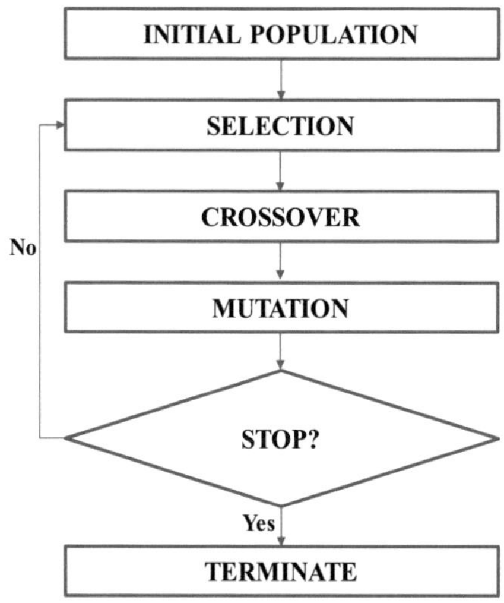

Figure 1. Flow chart of the general GAs.

2.2. The genetic operators

In GAs, the population is generated toward the best solution by improving the quality of individuals. During the evaluation process, a population is generated through the three main generic operators including selection, crossover, and mutation. An individual could be alive, reproduced, or removed from population depending on its fitness value and the probability of randomly modifying itself, called mutation. The evaluation process of GAs is operated as follows:

- **Initializing the population**—At the starting point, GAs will randomly produce a number of individuals.
- **Selection operator**—In this step, the individuals are evaluated by a fitness function. The fitness value is the best answer according to the specific problem. The individuals then are sorted based on their fitness value. The purpose of selection operator is to determine the candidates to pass their characteristics to the next generation.
- **Crossover operator**—This operator works in two selected individuals to generate two new individuals or offspring. The numbers of characteristics of an individual will be swapped to the other with the corresponding length. The new offspring created in this step will be put into the next generation of the population. By this way, the populations move toward the better solution.
- **Mutation operator**—This is an important operator of GAs, which keeps the results of GAs away from local optima. A small probability of individual's characteristics is modified randomly.
- **Stop condition**—The selection, crossover, and mutation are looping in a number of evaluations. The quality of population is improved after each iteration, but there is no way to be

sure that the present results are the best solutions. Thus, we need a strategy to stop GAs in the constraint of time of project or when population reaches to an approximation in which the result is placed around the best-known space.

The flow chart of the general GAs is shown in **Figure 1**.

3. CFD coupled GAs for shape optimization

In the present case, the procedure is deployed relying on the open-source software OpenFOAM in CFD block, the DAKOTA in algorithm block, and the interface script to connect two blocks. All programs run on Linux system. The flow chart of coupling GAs and CFD simulation is shown in **Figure 2**.

The working flow of coupled procedure could be mainly described by the following five steps:

1. Template declaration
2. Geometry and grid generation
3. Simulation
4. Post-processing
5. Genetic operator

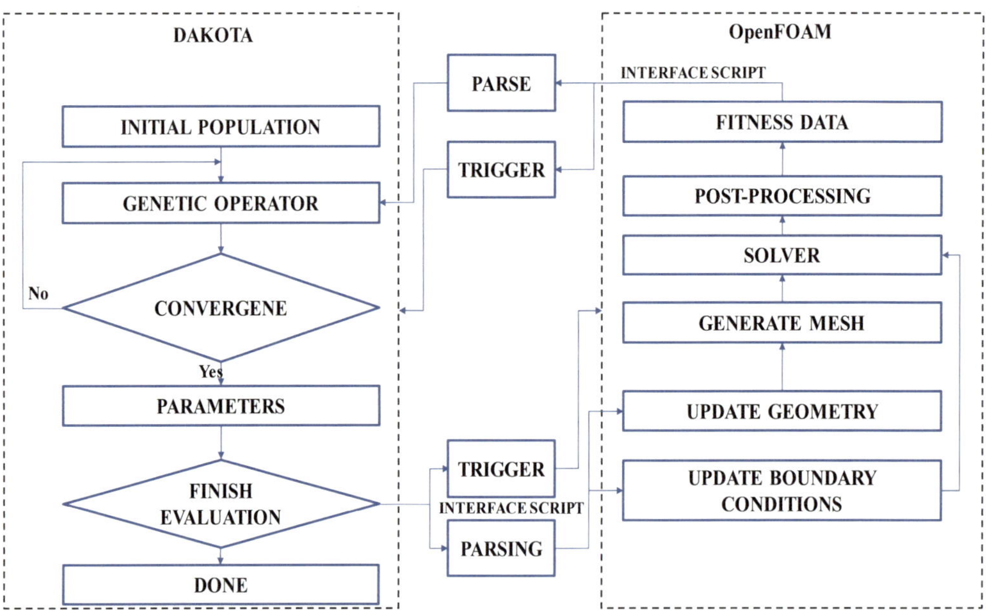

Figure 2. Flow chart of coupled optimization framework.

http://dx.doi.org/10.5772/intechopen.72316

3.1. Template declaration

Before running the coupled procedure, all the template files must be implemented. In CFD block, we create a geometry, a mesh file, boundary types, a solver, and a sampling template. The design parameters are declared in the templates as variables and can be changed during the evaluation of GA block. By this way, the evaluation can run in parallel. The simulation script copies the CFD templates for each separated job, inserts the values, and starts the solver. As mentioned before, since all individuals can be evaluated independently in each generation, this approach can adjust to adapt the scale of computing power. As a result, it can save the running time on the specific hardware. Moreover, there is no limit of license running on stations, so this structure shows the economy when deploying on the multi-node cluster.

3.2. Geometry and grid generation

In this step, the CFD block will generate geometry and grid. In the first cycle, GA block initializes the population and then triggers and parses control parameters to CFD block. The control parameters are selected depending on the objectives of problem. We can adjust boundary, geometry, and solver to adapt the purpose of simulation.

The geometry can be created by OpenSCAD or Salome, both are open-source software. In some cases, if the geometry is not so complex, OpenFOAM supports block-mesh and snappy-hex-mesh utilities, which can be used to generate the geometry and grid. For complex geometry, some commercial meshing programs such as Pointwise or ICEM CFD show their advantages. We may also consider other open-source meshing programs like cfMesh or Salome.

3.3. CFD simulation

After generating the grid, CFD solver will be triggered by batch command. Various solver types are implemented in OpenFOAM, and we need to choose an appropriate one for our problem. OpenFOAM also supports a simple way to create our boundary type or modifying solver for the specific models. However, we need to validate them with the experimental data, and then the configuration can be used as template.

3.4. Post-processing

For steady-state simulation, after convergence, the post-processing will export the selected raw data. A python script is then implemented to calculate the results. This approach is flexible in preparing the clean data. In the case of transient simulation, it is most important to choose the right collecting periods to warrant the correctness as of physical model.

3.5. Generic operator

When the post-processing completes, interface script will trigger and parse the data to GA block. GA block then does its operator as demonstrated. When GA block is completed, in turn, interface script triggers and parses data back to CFD block. The coupled procedure will stop if it finishes the predefined evaluation step. The best results and running history are finally archived. All steps are automatically driven by an interface script.

4. Optimization of the maldistribution of flow in a manifold

4.1. Introduction

In designing air-cooled heat exchanger, nonuniformity of flow in manifolds is one of the common issues. The maldistribution of flow could significantly affect to the performance and efficiency of heat exchanger. Thus, analyzing the behavior of flow in manifolds or header is necessary to improve the design.

In practical design, flow maldistribution in manifolds can be induced by the geometry and operating conditions [17]. Jiao et al. [18] investigated experimentally the effect of various geometry parameters including the inlet pipe diameter, the first header's diameter, and the second header's diameter. The authors reported that the flow distribution can be significantly improved by optimum design of header configuration. The study of Wen and Li [19] showed a serious flow maldistribution problem in heat exchanger using conventional header. They recommended to install a baffle with small-sized holes to improve the uniform of flow. Wang et al. [20] presented five modified inlet headers to enhance the uniform of liquid flow distribution in the compact heat exchangers.

Besides of using experiments, various studies used modeling approaches to analyze the flow distribution. Tonomura et al. [21] demonstrated a CFD approach to discover the effect of design header on the uniform of flow. The results in this study showed that the shape of manifolds, the length and location of inside fins, and the inlet flow rate significantly affected the flow uniformity. The authors also proposed a CFD-based optimization method to find the optimal design of plate-fine microdevices. Wang et al. [22] proposed a different computational approach. The authors presented a Lattice Boltzmann method for shape optimization of distributor. Recently, Facão [23] developed a correlation model to improve the uniform of flow in solar collector. The model was then validated by the CFD simulation.

In this chapter, we demonstrated another approach to optimize the flow distribution by coupling the CFD simulation and a genetic algorithm. It comes from the fact that the uniform of flow could depend on various parameters and has no general form for specific applications. Hence, combination of GA and CFD would be a good solution to save time and design cost.

4.2. Numerical model

4.2.1. Mathematical model

In this study, two-phase flow of refrigerant is simulated using OpenFOAM software. The working fluid is R134a. Since the experimental test was taken under the adiabatic condition, the simulation will only solve the continuity and momentum equations. VOF method, therefore, has been implemented. VOF solver in OpenFOAM calculates one momentum and one continuity equation for both liquid and gas phases of R134a. The physical properties of one phase are determined based on the volume fraction, α, of two phases in a cell. The continuity equation is defined as follows:

$$\nabla \bullet U = 0 \tag{1}$$

http://dx.doi.org/10.5772/intechopen.72316

The momentum equation is determined as follows:

$$\frac{\partial \rho U}{\partial t} + \nabla \cdot (\rho U U) - \nabla \cdot \mu \nabla U - \rho g = -\nabla p - F_s \tag{2}$$

where F_s is the surface tension force at free surfaces and is defined as

$$F_s = \sigma \kappa(x) n \tag{3}$$

where κ is the curvature of the interface and n is a unit vector normal to the interface. κ and n are calculated as follows:

$$\kappa(x) = \nabla \cdot n \tag{4}$$

and

$$n = \frac{\nabla \alpha}{|\nabla \alpha|} \tag{5}$$

Volume fraction, α, in a cell is 0 if it is completely filled by vapor phase, and, on the contrary, volume fraction equals 1 if a cell is completely filled by liquid phase. Volume fraction is calculated by a transport equation as follows:

$$\frac{\partial \alpha}{\partial t} + \nabla \cdot (\alpha U) = 0 \tag{6}$$

The compression of the surface in OpenFOAM is defined as follows:

$$\frac{\partial \alpha}{\partial t} + \nabla \cdot (\alpha U) + \nabla \left(\alpha (1 - \alpha) U_r \right) = 0 \tag{7}$$

where U_r is a suitable velocity field to compress the interface.

The properties of two-phase flow of R134a are obtained in REFPROP 8 and are listed in **Table 1**.

4.2.2. Geometry and grid

The dimensions of manifold are referred from a report of Fei and Hrnjak [24]. In the first phase, we set up a model to validate with the experiment. A three-dimensional model was then created. To reduce the computational cost as well as enhance the accuracy and stability of simulation, the grid was manually generated with hexahedral meshes. In addition, to validate the independence of grid, three types of mesh with the total elements of 377,540, 415,644, and 453,748 were also made, and the last mesh was chosen for the simulation in this study. The detailed dimension of manifold is illustrated in **Table 2**. The sample of grid is shown in **Figure 3**.

Inlet length (mm)	Inlet diameter (mm)	Body length (mm)	Body height (mm)	Outlet dimension (mm)
120	9.5	305	25.4	8.8

Table 1. Dimension of genetic manifold.

Saturation temp. (°C)	Pressure (kPa)	Density of liquid (kg/m³)	Density of vapor (kg/m³)	Viscosity of liquid (Pa.s)	Viscosity of vapor (Pa.s)
24.473	665	1208.7	31.841	1.96E−4	1.17E−5

Table 2. Properties of R134a.

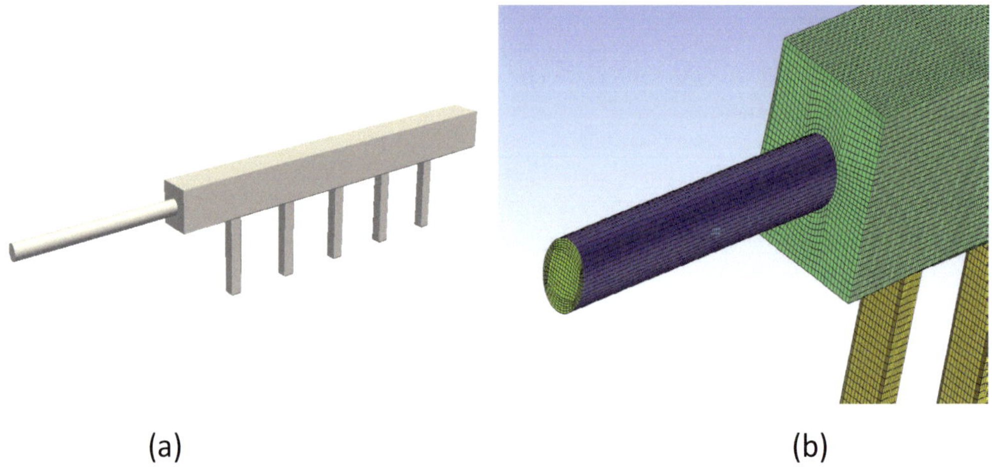

Figure 3. The 3D model: (a) geometry and (b) sample of grid.

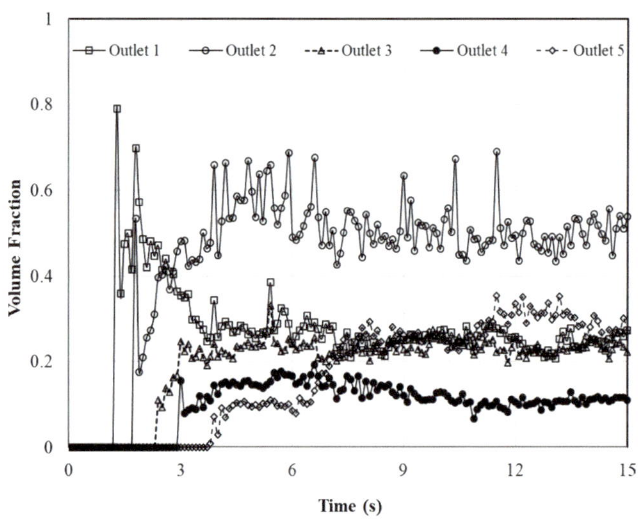

Figure 4. Liquid fraction at the outlets.

Figure 4 shows a time history of the simulation for volume fraction at the outlets. In this case, the total mass flow rate of two-phase is 10 g/s, and the vapor quality is 0.2. The trend shows that volume fraction in the first outlet firstly raises and quickly drops when the pattern of flow is formed. The liquid phase is then accumulated in the second outlet. The volume fraction in the fifth outlet increases steeply from the sixth to ninth second since the flow bouncing back from the ending wall almost returns to this channel. The fourth outlet, in consequent, has the lowest volume fraction. It turns out that the mass flow rate and the body shape of header are strongly influent to the uniform of flow. The contour of liquid fraction is illustrated in detail in **Figure 5**.

The result demonstrates that the maldistribution is difficult to avoid within the conventional design of manifold. This problem could be overcome by modifying the inlet type, changing the body shape of manifolds or adding the baffles. In this work, we modified the inside of the conventional manifold by generating the baffles between each outlet channel. The ideal is that

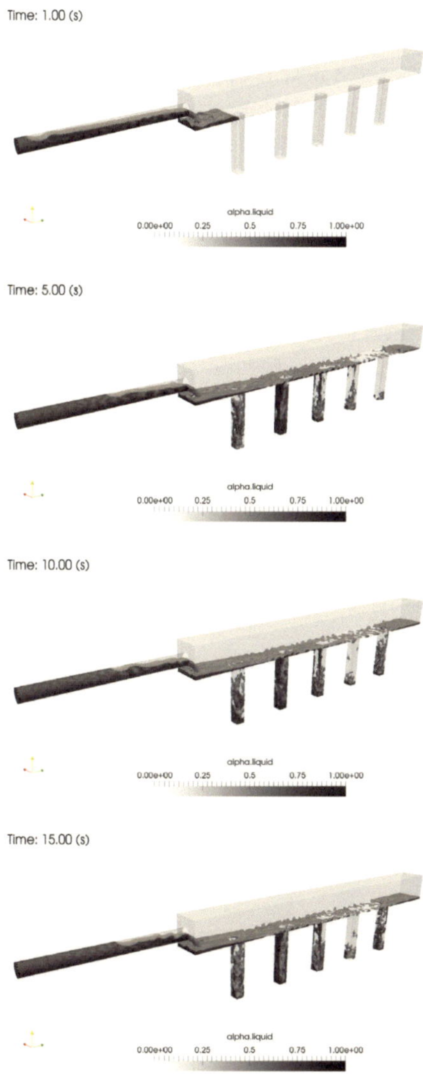

Figure 5. Contour of liquid fraction.

supplied fluid is enough for all outlets, and the flow would be uniform. Hence, we created five subsections inside the manifold. Each subsection works as a liquid pool to accumulate and to distribute liquid. However, the baffle height needs to be designed carefully to archive the purpose of optimization. The work can be tackled by using GA in which the design space is the height of baffles, and the object is the average mean difference of liquid flow rate at the outlet. The cost function, therefore, can be determined as follows:

$$J = \frac{\sum_{i=1}^{k}\left(\dot{m}_{f,i} - \overline{\dot{m}}_{f}\right)}{k} \tag{8}$$

where $\dot{m}_f$ is the mass flow rate (kg/s) of liquid phase and k is the number of outlet.

4.2.3. Optimization

In the second phase, we proposed a new geometry with the baffles between each outlet channel. Since the baffles divide the header to subsections, the geometry now can be reduced to 2D problem. A geometry and grid now are generated using C code. The schematic of proposed header and sample of grid are shown in **Figure 6**.

In this study, a single-objective genetic algorithm (SOGA) was implemented. The purpose of algorithm is to minimize the mean difference between the flow rate in each outlet and the average mass flow rate of liquid phase. The fitness type was set as the domination count. The crossover was 80%, the mutation scale was 10%, and the number of evaluation was set as 500. SOGA script automatically generates baffle dimension and updates the boundary conditions as described in the previous part. In addition, another script drives the CFD code run and exports the results for the next evaluation in SOGA.

Figure 7 illustrates the variation of baffle height and the mean difference of flow rate during the evaluation of GA. The height of baffle is ranged from 0.1 to 7.9 mm, and 16 populations were created. The optimal point is found at evaluation 372nd with the baffle height of 7.52 mm.

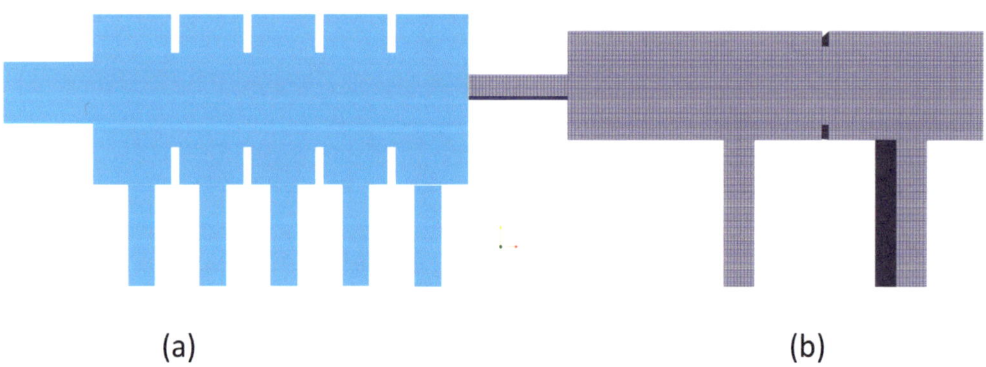

Figure 6. Schematic of proposed model: (a) geometry and (b) sample of grid.

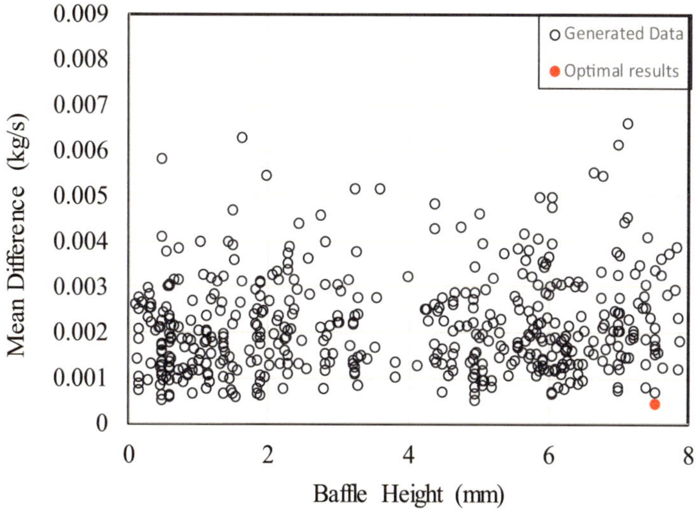

Figure 7. Evaluation history.

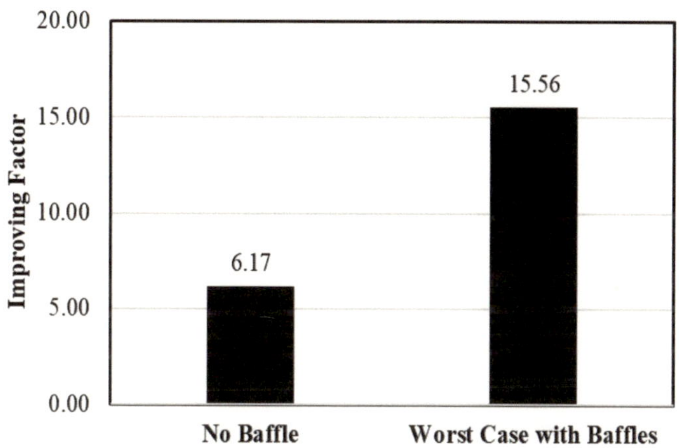

Figure 8. Improvement of optimal design.

The improvement factor is shown in **Figure 8**. The results show that the optimal design improves the mean difference of liquid flow rate about 6 and 15 times in comparison with the general manifold without baffle and the worst case of manifold with baffles, respectively.

5. Conclusions

In this chapter, we demonstrated a CFD-based optimization framework that couples a CFD block and a GA block. In addition, a CFD simulation and the optimization of two-phase flow distribution of R134a in a manifold were also investigated. The optimal design shows much improvement in comparison with the general case. Although only single object is produced, this framework can easily expand to multi-objects.

Acknowledgements

This research was supported by the Basic Science Research Program through the National Research Foundation of Korea (NRF) funded by the Ministry of Education, Science and Technology (NRF-2016R1D1A1A09919697).

Author details

Jong-Taek Oh* and Nguyen Ba Chien

*Address all correspondence to: ohjt@chonnam.ac.kr

Department of Refrigeration and Air-Conditioning Engineering, Chonnam National University, South Korea

References

[1] Mohammadi B, Pironneau O. Applied shape optimization for fluids. Oxford University Press, 2009

[2] Jameson. Aerodynamic design via control theory. Journal of Scientific Computing. 1988; **3**:233-260

[3] Jameson A. Automatic design of transonic airfoils to reduce the shock induced pressure drag. 31st Israel Annual Conference on Aviation and Aeronautics, Tel Aviv, February 21-22, 1990

[4] Jameson. Optimum aerodynamic design via boundary control. In: AGARD-VKI Lecture Series, Optimum Design Methods in Aerodynamics. von Karman Institute for Fluid Dynamics; 1994

[5] Jameson A. Re-engineering the design process through computation. Journal of Aircraft. 1999;**36**(1):36-50

[6] Reuther J, Jameson A, Alonso JJ, Remlinger MJ, Saunders D. Constrained multipoint aerodynamic shape optimisation using and adjoint formulation and parallel computers, Part 1. Journal of Aircraft. 1999;**36**(1):51-60

[7] Reuther J, Jameson A, Alonso JJ, Remlinger MJ, Saunders D. Constrained multipoint aerodynamic shape optimisation using and adjoint formulation and parallel computers, Part 2. Journal of Aircraft. 1999;**36**(1):61-74

[8] Sun H, Lee S. Response surface approach to aerodynamic optimization design of helicopter rotor blade. International Journal for Numerical Methods in Engineering. 2005; **64**:125-142

[9] Ortega-Casanova J. Application of CFD on the optimization by response surface methodology of a micromixing unit and its use as a chemical microreactor. Chemical Engineering and Processing: Process Intensification. 2017;**117**:18-26. ISSN: 0255-2701

[10] Noori Rahim Abadi SMA, Ahmadpour A, Abadi SMNR, Meyer JP. CFD-based shape optimization of steam turbine blade cascade in transonic two phase flows. Applied Thermal Engineering. 2017;**112**:1575-1589. ISSN: 1359-4311

[11] Liu C, Weiyang B, Dong X. Multi-objective shape optimization of a plate-fin heat exchanger using CFD and multi-objective genetic algorithm. International Journal of Heat and Mass Transfer. 2017;**111**:65-82. ISSN: 0017-9310

[12] Kim H, Yang C. A new surface modification approach for cfd-based hull form optimization. Journal of Hydrodynamics, Series B. 2010;**22**(5):520-525

[13] Papoutsis-Kiachagias E, Magoulas JMN, Othmer C, Giannakoglou K. Noise reduction in car aerodynamics using a surrogate objective function and the continuous adjoint method with wall functions. Computers and Fluids. 2015;**122**:223-232

[14] Gilkeson CA, Toropov VV, Thompson HM, Wilson MCT, Foxley NA, Gaskell PH. Dealing with numerical noise in CFD-based design optimization. Computers & Fluids. 2014; **94**:84-97. ISSN: 0045-7930

[15] Javid Mahmoudzadeh Akherat SM, Cassel K, Boghosian M, Hammes M, Coe F. A predictive framework to elucidate venous stenosis: CFD & shape optimization. Computer Methods in Applied Mechanics and Engineering. 2017;**321**:46-69. ISSN: 0045-7825

[16] Jafari M, Parhizkar MJ, Amani E, Naderan H. Inclusion of entropy generation minimization in multi-objective CFD optimization of diesel engines. Energy. 2016;**114**:526-541. ISSN: 0360-5442

[17] Shah RK, Sekuli DP. Fundamentals of heat exchanger design, John Wiley & Sons, Inc., Hoboken, NJ, USA, 2003

[18] Jiao A, Zhang R, Jeong S. Experimental investigation of header configuration on flow maldistribution in plate-fin heat exchanger. Applied Thermal Engineering. 2003;**23**:1235-1246

[19] Wen J, Li Y. Study of flow distribution and its improvement on the header of plate-fin heat exchanger. Cryogenics (Guildf). 2004;**44**:823-831

[20] Wang CC, Yang KS, Tsai JS, Chen IY. Characteristics of flow distribution in compact parallel flow heat exchangers, part II: Modified inlet header. Applied Thermal Engineering. 2011;**31**:3235-3242

[21] Tonomura O, Tanaka S, Noda M, Kano M, Hasebe S, Hashimoto I. CFD-based optimal design of manifold in plate-fin microdevices. Chemical Engineering Journal. 2004;**101**: 397-402

[22] Wang L, Fan Y, Luo L. Lattice Boltzmann method for shape optimization of fluid distributor. Computers and Fluids. 2014;**94**:49-57

[23] Facão J. Optimization of flow distribution in flat plate solar thermal collectors with riser and header arrangements. Solar Energy. 2016;**120**:104-112

[24] Fei P, Hrnjak PS. Adiabatic developing two-phase refrigerant flow in manifolds of heat exchangers, ACRC Technical Report 225, University of Illinois at Urbana-Champaign. 2004

Section 2

CFD Models for Local and Large Scale Industrial Phenomena

Chapter 6

Applications of CFD for Process Safety

Luis G. Zárate, Sebastián Uribe and Mario E. Cordero

Additional information is available at the end of the chapter

http://dx.doi.org/10.5772/intechopen.70563

Abstract

Nowadays, the statistical studies have revealed that major accidents (MA) are frequent in diverse industries, which has originated the development of strategies and normative focussed in foreseeing and preventing these. Thus, the process safety is in continuous improvement. The experimental studies in this field result in situations of high risks and are usually expensive. Therefore, the implementation of developments as the computational fluid dynamics (CFD) techniques is now applied, and has proven to be advantageous. In this work, CFD models for pool and jet fires are presented, as these kinds of fires are usually involved in major accidents. The results of the CFD models show orders of magnitude and behaviors in good agreement with experimental observations found in literature. The outputs of the simulations showed values of around 500 and 1400 K for the pool fires; while the jet fires predictions were of temperatures around 500 and 1050 K. Furthermore, the information obtained by these models can be used in order to develop safety plans to diminish risks in the facilities designs, safe zones and emergency exit routes.

Keywords: CFD multiphysics, mathematical modeling, safety, major accident, process safety

1. Introduction

The development of the chemical industries, as well as emerging fields of nanotechnology, energy generation, biotechnology and pharmaceutical, among others, as well as the storing, handling, transport and transformation of their products, has resulted in an increasing need of handling and storing flammable and explosive substances. Consequently, the risks in chemical plants have increased dramatically and major accidents (MA) have taken place more frequently [1]. It has been recorded that these kinds of accidents represent great losses in terms of lives, environmental impact and destruction of equipment and buildings. In fact, only in 2015 the National Fire Protection Association (NFPA) reported that there were 1,345,500 fires in the USA, that caused the death of 3280 civilians and injured 15,700 more, and represented $14.3 billion dollars in property damage [2].

Statistical studies of MA, such as those shown in **Table 1**, show how these events have been constantly present throughout history and throughout the civilized worldwide. And therefore, further efforts must be carried out in researching on the process safety.

This has conducted to the development of a scientific discipline: The Process Safety [7]. This concept must be now part of our daily life in order to ensure the sustainable development of the planet [4], to ensure the safety of the people and to reduce the economical impact. Furthermore, the risk analysis is yet in continuous development. Large multi-sector efforts for identifying hazards to ensure the safe design and operation of a system in process plants and other facilities [8] are being developed, with the challenge of dealing with real-time support for decision-making, in the multiple scenarios with unpredictable conditions [7].

Regarding the study of MA in the process safety, three kinds of accidents can be distinguished: breaching, explosions and fires [5]. All of which have been widely studied, mostly through experimental methods, that have led to the generation of a great number of semi-empirical correlations [9, 10]. These have been used like tools or guidelines as assistance for the Inspection Management in Chemical Plants, and for the calculation of consequences by simplified procedures [11].

Authors, year	Description
Girgin and Krausmann [3]	Incidents at US onshore hazardous liquid pipeline systems were analyzed with an emphasis on natural hazards (natechs). The analysis covered about 7000 incidents in 1986–2012. Natechs resulted in 317,700 bbl of hazardous substance release and 597 million USD economic damage.
Kannan Pranav et al. [4]	A collection of 96 incidents of process safety from across de world is categorized and analyzed to identify proximate causes and deficiencies in the safety management. Emphasis is placed in that these are not statistically representative due to the lack of a universal database of incidents.
Mannan [5]	In Chapter 2, incidents and loss statistics are discussed, with information from proper sources. The arrangements for the control of major hazards in the European Community and in the United States are briefly reviewed. Chapter 26 shows important things to be learned from the incident about case histories and information from some recognized databases in the world.
Chen Yinting et al. [1]	From 1951 to 2012, 318 domino accidents were collected and analyzed. Flammable substances are the most common material involved in Domino effects. Of all 318 samples, 237 cases associated with flammable substances. 71.1% domino accidents occurred in developed countries, while only 28.9% occurred in developing countries. It can be explained by the massive presence of large-scale chemical plants with giant facilities which contain large quantities of flammable substances and toxic materials. Besides, the accidents reporting mechanisms in developed countries allow getting information easier.
Vílchez et al. [6]	A survey of accidents involving hazardous materials has been performed. A total of 5325 accidents taken from the database MHIDAS, covering from the beginning of twentieth century up to July 1992. The data show the distribution of percentages of accidents in various areas.

Table 1. Selection of statistical and historical studies of MA.

However, despite the extensive efforts and development in the study of fires in MA, the unpredictability of the phenomena and the difference in the length scales that these take place, as well as the influence and limitations given by the experimental conditions in the reported works, have motivated the development of mathematical models that allow the prediction of fires and their consequences. It is noteworthy that the implementation of these models implies further complications in the evaluation of parameters and variables that are frequently unknown, such as the heat transfer coefficient (*h*), emissivity, radiation models, transmissivity, reflectance, among others, leading to a great gamut of approaches. For example, the hybrid models, where the semi-empirical correlations are coupled with the mathematical models in order to find valid solutions to the transport equations; and also, in recent years, with the development of computers and numerical methods, the computational fluid dynamics (CFD) applied in these topics have shown to be advantageous. Principally, due to that these techniques and models provide not only accurate hazard assessments such as thermal energy flux level, overpressure contour and distribution of toxic cloud, but also detailed information about the spatial and temporal evolution of accidental events [7], allowing detailed three-dimensional analysis in the presence of obstacles, bunds and congested industrial layouts [12]. Thereby, several specialized CFD software in the study of fires have been developed, as well as applications for general purpose CFD software. A selection of general purpose and specialized CFD software can be seen in **Table 2.**

This approach, through CFD simulations, has been of great advantage compared with experimental methods, as experiments are usually expensive, dangerous and practically impossible

Software	Characteristics	Developer/ License	Platform
COMSOL Multiphysics	General-purpose CFD software, based on FEM, specialized in the modeling of coupled multiphysics phenomena, such as non-isothermal flows with mass transfer and chemical reactions	COMSOL/ Paid	Windows Mac OS X Linux
Ansys CFX	CFD software, part of the ANSYS family of products of Fluid Dynamics. Allows to simulate chemical reactions and combustions as well as fluid flow	ANSYS/ Paid	Windows, Linux
FLAIR	Special-purpose CFD software for HVAC systems, smoke movement and fire spreading	CHAM/ Paid	Windows, Linux
Fire dynamic simulator and smoke view (FDS – SMV)	FDS is a special-purpose CFD model for fire-driven fluid flow. SMW is the visualization software for the FDS simulations results	NIST/Free	Windows, Mac OS X, Linux
SmartFire	Special-purpose CFD software for fires simulation and analysis, as well as evacuation analysis	FSEG/Paid	Windows
Kobra-3D	Special-purpose CFD software for smokes simulation and heat transfer in buildings. Includes mass transfer with generation equations	IST GmbH/ Paid	Windows
Solvent	Special-purpose CFD software for the simulation of fluid flows, heat transfer and smoke transport in tunnels	Solvent/ Paid	Windows

Table 2. Commercial CFD software with application for process safety and fires analysis.

to perform at very low scales, such as microscales [13], or very large scales of hundreds of meters. Thus, there are still lots of unsolved issues in the process safety engineering. Many of those issues related to the domino effect usually presented in MA [3, 6, 14].

It is common to find turbulent flows when studying the MA, and thus this has been a great motivation for their study and modeling, besides the motivation due to the costs reduction, as the need to build and test prototypes is avoided [15]. The main approaches through CFD in order to model the turbulent flows in MA leading to acceptable results are the implementation of Reynolds-Averaged Navier-Stokes (RANS) models, large eddy simulations (LES), direct numerical simulation (DNS) and hybrid LES/RANS techniques. However, computational costs may exceed the computing capacities if the detailed characteristics of reactive turbulent flows are intended to be observed, such as eddies, velocity patterns, high-vorticity regions, large structures that stretch and engulf, etc. And thus, generally the standard $\kappa-\varepsilon$ turbulence models provide good results; although sometimes, certain modifications need to be taken into account.

The procedure to approach the solution of problems through CFD techniques is depicted in **Figure 1**. In general, the process consists of three important steps: preprocessing, processing and postprocessing. It is also of great importance the validation of the outputs of the CFD models results against experimental data. Special attention should be drawn to the preprocessing step, as in this step the understanding of the phenomena will be developed; and a correct understanding of the phenomena will allow to take into account the proper considerations and simplifications. As seen in the diagram, when there is a bad agreement between the models results and the experimental observations, sometimes the problem lays in the definition of the problem itself, this means, in the preprocessing steps. In this chapter, following the CFD modeling process

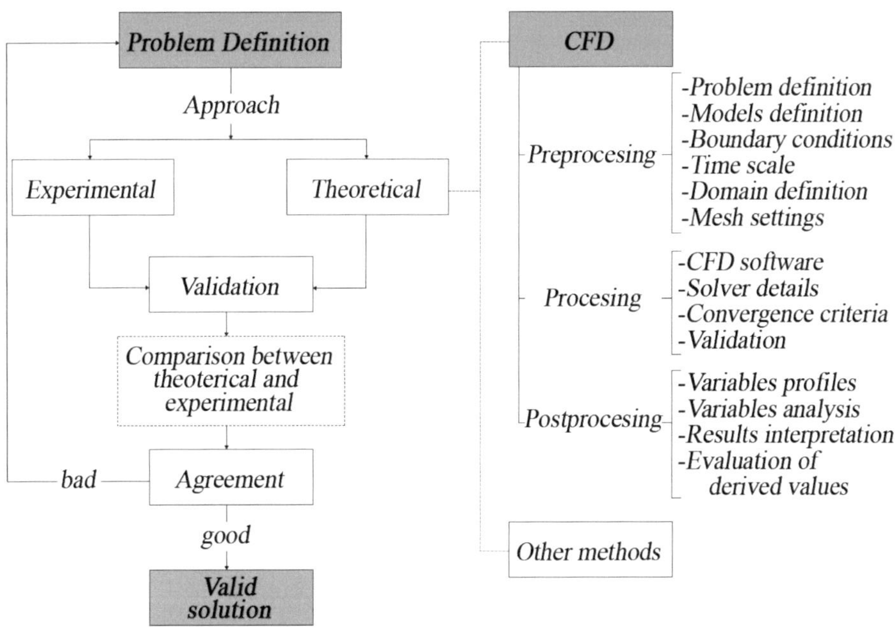

Figure 1. Proposed CFD modeling process considering comparison against experimental approaches.

http://dx.doi.org/10.5772/intechopen.70563

aforementioned, two characteristic kinds of fires in MA are presented. Sections 2 and 3 present the preprocessing steps; the processing step is also depicted in Section 3; and lastly Section 4 presents the postprocessing steps. The models for these fires are developed though COMSOL Multiphysics CFD simulations, coupling momentum, mass and heat transfer, considering radiation, for pool and jet fires. The models also consider the turbulence flows through Reynolds-Averaged Navier-Stokes (RANS) equations, using the $\kappa-\varepsilon$ model. The predictions obtained with the models properly predict the behavior of experimental observations reported in literature.

2. Fire modeling

The fire consists of a process where complex physical and chemical phenomena occurs simultaneously producing heat. In order to study fires, there are several classifications according to the materials involved, the source or the place in which they are presented. These are of great importance in order to understand how to control the fires, which kind of fire extinguisher should be selected, the consequences of the fire and the radius of impact of these. Two of the main classifications are the following

i. By the material: Fires involving solid, liquid or gases, which gives rise to the following classification or class. For each class, there is a suggested kind of fire extinguisher.
   a. Combustible materials: wood, paper, textiles, rubber
   b. Flammable liquids and gases: gasoline, solvents, hydrocarbons
   c. Electrical fires
   d. Flammable metals: sodium, potassium, magnesium, titanium, zirconium and other metals
   e. Cooking oils and fats

ii. By the source or the place where they are presented.
   a. Wildfire or forest fires: sub classified in other three types: crown fires, surface fires and ground fires
   b. Industrial process fires: vapor clouds fires, fireballs, jet flames, pool fires, running liquid fires, fires of solid materials, dust fires, warehouse fires, sea fires, fires in oil spills in the ocean
   c. Building fires: Structures of diverse dimensions, from small houses to large buildings

Regarding MA, these take place in uncontrolled places and times, which is actually what defines, up to a great extent, the characteristics and dynamics of the fire. Thus, in order to properly model the fire, the behavior of each kind of fire must be understood, as this will allow the adequate establishment of the differential equations and their most convenient boundary conditions. Due to the aforementioned, a further discussion of the phenomena in jet and pool fires is presented in the subsequent pages.

2.1. Pool fire

Pool fires occur when a flammable liquid spills or is poured in the ground and ignites. The shape and dynamics of these fires depend on many variables, such as obstacles, barriers found, whether the leaking is continuous or of a brief duration, as well as the surroundings meteorological and environmental conditions. This prior is highly important as MA usually takes place in open areas, and thus there is a remarkable effect of the wind over the geometry of the flame, the oxygen inflow and the heat transfer mechanisms. These kinds of incidents represent a major complexity as great quantity of phenomena take place simultaneously. **Figure 2** depicts a simplified representation of the phenomena involved in pool fires.

The volatile flammable compounds feed the combustion zone in gas phase under the proper conditions. The drag of the air can be impelled by the wind force or the free convection, depending on the conditions surrounding the fire. The combustion can consist of up to thousands of elementary reactions with intermediate steps that may include hundreds of more chemical species (this great amount of species is commonly observed in MA involving hydrocarbons, as fuels and diesel). Also, generally fires produce smokes with solid particles. Depending on the nature of the combustible, the smoke may contain high concentrations of finely dispersed particles, commonly known as soot, and somniferous gases, as carbon monoxide, as well as other commonly produced products of combustions. Due to these complexities, it can be understood why this is yet an issue of research.

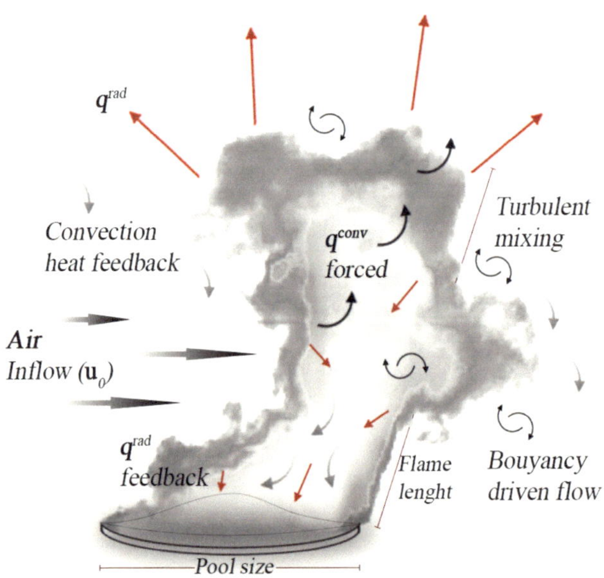

Figure 2. Typical pool fire in presence of wind.

For many years and with diverse approaches, pool fires have been widely studied. Experimental approaches that have led to correlations to predict the fire characteristics are noteworthy, such as burning rate [16], flame tilt angle [17], flame length [18], surface emissive power [19], soot production and radiation [20]. However, it is important to point out that major efforts in the amount of experiments over diverse scenarios, large scales and wind influence, are yet required [21]. The theoretical proposal, that consist in the resolution of the transport equations coupled with the kinetics for the diverse reactions taking place in the phenomena, will be discussed in the upcoming section.

Despite the great advances in the study of pool fires, there is still no model that accurately predicts the proper behavior of fires at the diverse length-scales, and describes all the relevant variables satisfactorily [22]. This is by reason of that most of these have been developed in small scales, and due to the complexity and variability of fires. Furthermore, in theoretical studies turbulence models are still being developed [15], and the multiphysic-multiscale nature is still a challenge to overcome [23]. Moreover, there are also restrictions in theoretical approaches due to the high computational costs.

2.2. Jet fire

Jet fires are characterized by the presence of stationary turbulent diffusion of flames that can reach great lengths and short amplitudes. This kind of fires can be present in closed or open areas. This can be whether generated or accidental, without having notable differences. The source of generated jet fires are usually valves, and can reach supersonic velocities; while accidental jet fires are usually due to holes caused by breakings in pipelines or flanges, and thus the outlet velocities are usually lower, reaching at most (most cases) sonic velocities. Jet fires can arise from gases, liquids or biphasic mixtures. **Figure 3** depicts a simplified diagram of some of the phenomena present in jet fires.

The properties of jet fires depend on the composition of the fuel, the release conditions, the amount of released mass, geometry of the outlet hole, wind direction and the surrounding conditions. These have been widely studied, and thus several models have been developed, mostly through experimental observations [24–28]. Nowadays, aside from the experimental studies [29, 30], computational methods have been implemented into the study of jet fires, allowing the inclusion and development of more complex numerical methods, in order to solve hundreds of equations simultaneously [31–33].

Jet fires are, in a great extent, of paramount importance due to their frequent presence in industrial applications. For example, in hydrocarbon process plants to eliminate undesired gases in the production of crude oil; in oil refineries and industrial processes to evacuate undesired sub-products, or released gases through security valves; or in controlled areas such as furnaces, gas turbines or industrial burners.

Regarding MA, it has been observed through historical analysis of accident, that when accidental jet fires are present, one of each two causes another greater accident. [34]; 90% of them leading to an explosion [35].

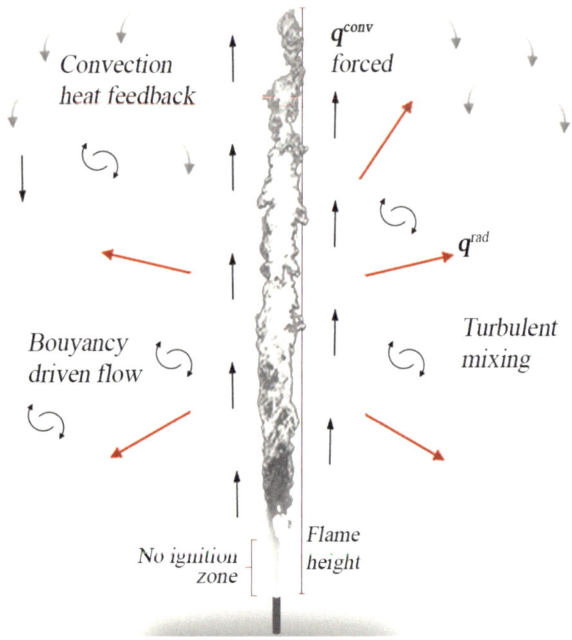

Figure 3. Typical jet fire.

3. CFD modeling

3.1. Geometry

Defining the geometrical representation of the model and the domains is part of the preprocessing. This will set the regions where the mathematical models (the partial differential equations) are valid; and defines the region where the phenomena will be studied. **Figure 4** depicts the geometrical representations of the models and the implemented mesh.

The size of the mesh in these representations is determined by the detail of the required information. It is clear that a 3D representation will require greater computational resources, and it may not provide further information than the 2D representation, depending on the required information from the model.

3.2. Mathematical models: partial differential equations and kinetics expressions

The phenomena described in the foregoing section are simulated by coupling and simultaneously solving the models described in **Table 3** [36]. Momentum balance, heat transfer and mass with combustion reaction are solved, using the hydrodynamics solution in the energy and mass balances, as well as the solution of the energy balance in the two other constitutive equations. It is important to note that the energy balance considers the generation due to the reaction, thus the energy balance is coupled with mass balance. It is important to consider that corrections to the mass and energy balance equations due to the turbulence should be added.

http://dx.doi.org/10.5772/intechopen.70563

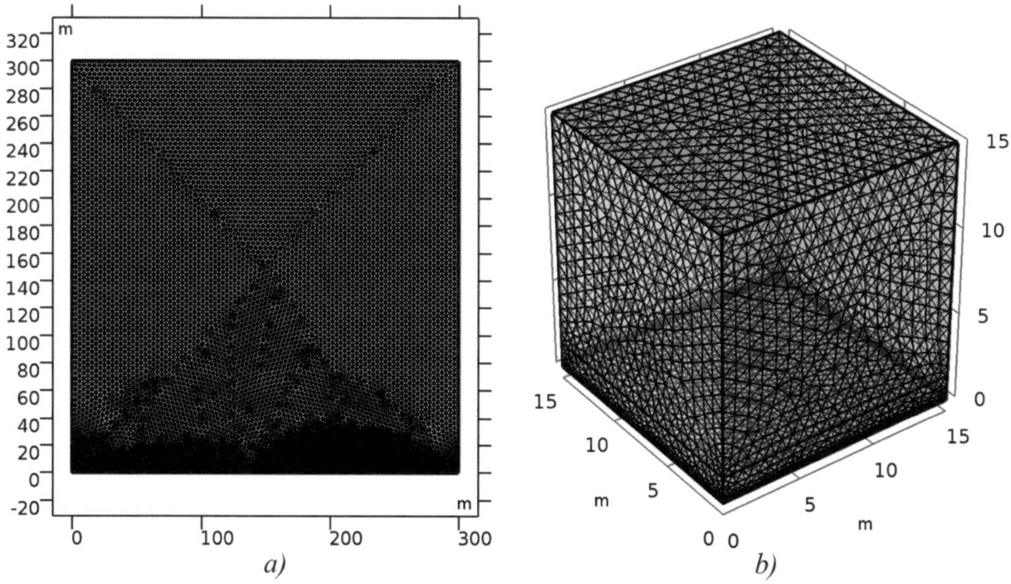

Figure 4. Geometry, domain and mesh considered for the simulations, (a) 2D domain of 300 m^2, (b) 3D domain with 15 m per side.

Momentum	$\rho\frac{\partial \mathbf{u}}{\partial t}+\rho(\mathbf{u}\cdot\nabla)=\nabla\cdot\left[-p\mathbf{I}+(\mu+\mu_T)\left(\nabla\mathbf{u}+(\nabla\mathbf{u})^T-\frac{2}{3}(\mu+\mu_T)(\nabla\mathbf{u})\mathbf{I}\right)\right]+\mathbf{F}$ $\rho\frac{\partial\mathbf{u}}{\partial t}+\nabla\cdot(\rho\mathbf{u})=0$
Turbulence	$\rho\frac{\partial\kappa}{\partial t}+\rho(\mathbf{u}\cdot\nabla)\kappa=\nabla\cdot\left[\left(\mu+\frac{\mu_T}{\sigma_\kappa}\right)\nabla\kappa\right]+P_\kappa-\rho\varepsilon$ $\rho\frac{\partial\varepsilon}{\partial t}+\rho(u\cdot\nabla)\varepsilon=\nabla\cdot\left[\left(\mu+\frac{\mu_T}{\sigma_\varepsilon}\right)\nabla\varepsilon\right]+C_{\varepsilon1}\frac{\varepsilon}{\kappa}P_\kappa-C_{\varepsilon2}\rho\frac{\varepsilon^2}{\kappa};\quad \varepsilon=ep$ $\mu_T=\rho C_\mu\frac{\kappa^2}{\varepsilon};\quad P_\kappa=\mu_T\left[\nabla\mathbf{u}:\left(\nabla\mathbf{u}+(\nabla\mathbf{u})^T\right)-\frac{2}{3}(\nabla\cdot\mathbf{u})^2\right]-\frac{2}{3}\rho\kappa\nabla\cdot\mathbf{u}$
Energy	$\rho C_P\frac{\partial T}{\partial t}+\rho C_P\mathbf{u}\cdot\nabla T+\nabla\mathbf{q}=Q_{gen}$ $\mathbf{q}=-k\nabla T;\quad Q_{gen}=-\Delta H_{rxn}R_i$
Mass	$\frac{\partial c_i}{\partial t}+\nabla\cdot(-D_i\nabla c_i)+\mathbf{u}\cdot\nabla c_i=R_i$ $\mathbf{N}_i=-D_i\nabla c_i+\mathbf{u}c_i$

Table 3. Models solved in CFD software.

However, this prior would add further non-linearities and would require greater computational resources.

The solution of these models require the proper evaluation of the thermophysics variables and parameters. Also, a fundamental task is determining the combustion reaction, which is included in the mass balances. Due to the nature of the studied fires, the inclusion of all chemical species involved is practically impossible, not only due to the great computational resources that the kinetics models would consume, but the determination of all chemical species reaction rates expressions, which are often unknown, mostly for the emerging alternative fuels that are still being developed. Despite the implementation of new methodologies to characterize and design new fuels, where molecular structures of the mixtures are studied in order to obtain a deeper and better understanding of the kinetic, physical and chemical properties that conduct the combustion in the energy conversion processes [37], it is still necessary to approach the combustion processes by simplified steps and considering only a representative mixture or selection of components (more common when fuel surrogates are involved). Regarding this last point, when studying the gasoline surrogates, several authors have proposed different representative mixtures, for example, Battin-Leclerc [38] considers a ternary mixture of iso-octane, 1-hexane and toluene; while Zhang [39] considers a mixture of 22 components.

The simplest combustion reaction for a hydrocarbon is:

$$Fuel + n_1O_2 \rightarrow n_2CO_2 + n_3H_2O \tag{1}$$

where the stoichiometric coefficients *ni* are determined by the selected fuel. And the global reaction rate must be represented by a suitable average of all reaction rates for the involved components. The simplest expression for the reaction rate can be expressed as

$$R_i = A_i T^n e^{\left(\frac{-Ea_i}{RT}\right)} [fuel]^a [O_2]^b \tag{2}$$

The general reaction rate constant depends on the temperature and is given by a modified form of the Arrhenius equation: $K_i = A_i T^n e^{\left(\frac{-Ea_i}{RT}\right)}$, where A is a collision pre-exponential factor and Ea is the activation energy. Also, the exponents a and b are experimentally determined empirical constants. Most of the cases, it is assumed that the global reaction is of first order for the fuel and the oxidant, and thus $a = b = 1$. However, it has been seen that this assumption may lead to great errors. **Table 4** shows some examples of common fuels with their kinetic parameters for the combustion kinetics expressions, which have been published in specialized literature.

3.3. Boundary conditions

In recent years, the boundary conditions have been widely investigated, as these are essential to find a valid solution, and often a misled selection of these conduces to significant errors in

Fuel	a	b	A	Ea (kcal)
Metano	−0.3	1.3	1.3×10^9	48.4
Propano	0.1	1.65	8.6×10^{11}	30
n-Heptane	0.25	1.5	4.3×10^{11}	30
n-Undecae	1	0.8	5×10^{15}	45
Kerosene	1	0.8	2.8×10^{15}	45

Table 4. Kinetic parameters for common fuels.

the results [40]. In the study of fires, as well as for other engineering fields, involving closed domains, three kinds of boundary conditions can be usually found:

1. The dependent variable derivate is specified (Neumann condition): $\mathbf{n} \cdot \nabla\varphi = f(r)$ in the surface.

2. The value for the dependent variable is specified (Dirichlet condition): $\varphi = f(r)$ in the surface.

3. A function of the normal component of the gradient and the dependent function is specified. Hence, a combination of the other two boundary conditions (Cauchy condition): $\alpha\mathbf{n} \cdot \nabla\varphi + \beta\varphi = f(r)$ in the surface.

Also, the values for the boundary values can fluctuate according to a determined behavior, as the ones shown in **Figure 5**. For example, the fuel inflow may vary following a Gaussian distribution due to the increase in the vaporization of the fuel that feeds the combustion zone. Another fluctuation commonly seen are the differences in the air inflow velocities, which have important consequences not only in the turbulences and the geometry of the flame, as seen in **Figure 2**, but also in the inflow of oxygen, which determines the reaction rate. The fluctuation of air should be taken into account properly as it will vary depending on the height that it is observed and also depending on the time. Furthermore, this air inflow is usually not symmetrical, and depending on the studied region, the surroundings conditions and the atmospheric conditions, at different times the air may be going as an inlet to the control volume through a boundary, and sometimes it may go as an outlet from the same boundary.

The proper understanding of the phenomena is of great importance in order to stablish adequate boundary conditions that may even reduce computational times and save computational resources, as symmetry conditions in the applicable cases. However, these same simplifications must be supported by scientific background. Sometimes, the lack of a scientific background for these lead to oversimplified models that do not properly describe the phenomena. **Table 5** shows the boundary conditions used in both of the models.

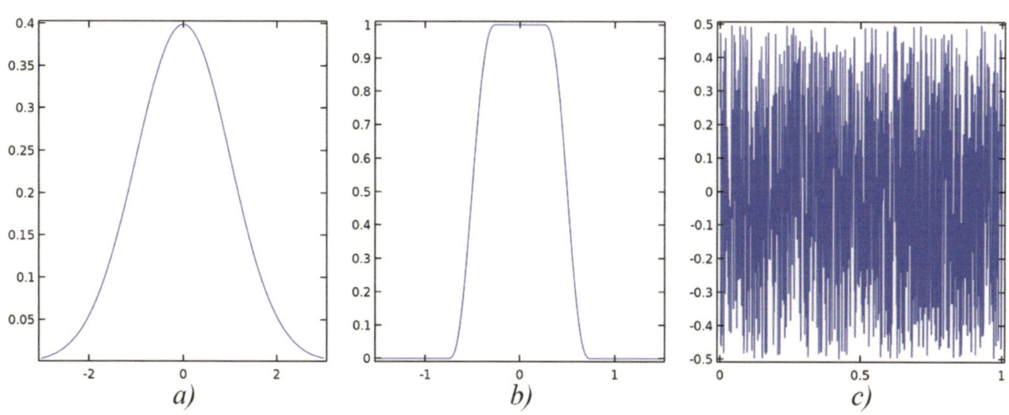

Figure 5. Variables distributions examples (a) Gaussian, (b) smooth rectangle step and (c) random.

	Pool fire		Jet fire	
Momentum	**Value**	**Boundary (m)**	**Value**	**Boundary (m)**
$\mathbf{u} = -u_{fuel}\mathbf{n}$ (*Fuel inlet*)	$u_{fuel} = 0.316[m/s]$	$\begin{pmatrix}125 \le x \le 175\\ y=0\end{pmatrix}$	$u_{fuel} = 50[m/s]$	$\begin{pmatrix}4.98 \le x \le 5.01\\ y=0\end{pmatrix}$
$\mathbf{u} = -u_{air}\mathbf{n}$ (*Air inlet*)	$u_{air} = 7.2[m/s]$	$\begin{pmatrix}x=\{0,300\}\\ 1.5 \le y \le 300\end{pmatrix}$	$u_{air} = 7.2[m/s]$	$\begin{pmatrix}x=\{0,10\}\\ 1.5 \le y \le 10\end{pmatrix}$
$\mathbf{u} = -u_{air}\mathbf{n}$ (*Air inlet*)	$u_{air} = 2.88[m/s]$	$\begin{pmatrix}x=\{0,300\}\\ 0 \le y \le 1.5\end{pmatrix}$	$u_{air} = 2.88[m/s]$	$\begin{pmatrix}x=\{0,10\}\\ 0 \le y \le 1.5\end{pmatrix}$
$[-p\mathbf{I} + a]\mathbf{n} = -p_0\mathbf{n}$ $a = (\mu + \mu_T)(\nabla\mathbf{u} + \nabla\mathbf{u}^T)$ (*Outlet pressure*)	$p_0 = 1[atm]$	$\begin{pmatrix}0 \le x \le 300\\ y=300\end{pmatrix}$	$p_0 = 1[atm]$	$\begin{pmatrix}0 \le x \le 10\\ y=10\end{pmatrix}$
$\mathbf{u} \cdot \mathbf{n} = 0$ (*Wall*)		$\begin{pmatrix}125 \ge x \ge 175\\ y=0\end{pmatrix}$		$\begin{pmatrix}4.98 \ge x \ge 5.01\\ y=0\end{pmatrix}$
Mass transport	**Value**	**Boundary (m)**	**Value**	**Boundary (m)**
$c_i = c_j^0$ (*Specie inflow*)	$c^0_{C_7H_{16}} = 12[mol/m^3]$	$\begin{pmatrix}125 \le x \le 175\\ y=0\end{pmatrix}$	$c^0_{C_7H_{16}} = 12[mol/m^3]$	$\begin{pmatrix}4.98 \le x \le 5.01\\ y=0\end{pmatrix}$
$c_i = c_j^0$ (*Specie inflow*)	$c^0_{O_2} = 8.6[mol/m^3]$	$\begin{pmatrix}x=\{0,300\}\\ 0 \le y \le 300\end{pmatrix}$	$c^0_{O_2} = 8.6[mol/m^3]$	$\begin{pmatrix}x=\{0,10\}\\ 0 \le y \le 10\end{pmatrix}$
$-\mathbf{n} \cdot D_i \nabla c_i = 0$ *if* $\mathbf{n} \cdot \mathbf{u} \ge 0$ $c_i = c_j^0$ *if* $\mathbf{n} \cdot \mathbf{u} < 0$ (*Open boundary*)	$c^0_{O_2} = 8.6[mol/m^3]$	$\begin{pmatrix}0 \le x \le 300\\ y=300\end{pmatrix}$	$c^0_{O_2} = 8.6[mol/m^3]$	$\begin{pmatrix}0 \le x \le 10\\ y=10\end{pmatrix}$
$-\mathbf{n} \cdot \mathbf{N}_i = \mathbf{0}$ (*Wall*)		$\begin{pmatrix}125 \ge x \ge 175\\ y=0\end{pmatrix}$		$\begin{pmatrix}4.98 \ge x \ge 5.01\\ y=0\end{pmatrix}$
Energy transport	**Value**	**Boundary (m)**	**Value**	**Boundary (m)**
$T = T_0$ (*Ignition temperature*)	$T_0 = 488.15[K]$	$\begin{pmatrix}125 \le x \le 175\\ y=0\end{pmatrix}$	$T_0 = 488.15[K]$	$\begin{pmatrix}4.98 \le x \le 5.01\\ y=0\end{pmatrix}$
$T = T_0$ (*Air temperature*)	$T_0 = 300[K]$	$\begin{pmatrix}x=\{0,300\}\\ 0 \le y \le 300\end{pmatrix}$	$T_0 = 300[K]$	$\begin{pmatrix}x=\{0,10\}\\ 0 \le y \le 10\end{pmatrix}$
$T = T_0$ *if* $\mathbf{n} \cdot \mathbf{u} < 0$ $-\mathbf{n} \cdot \mathbf{q} = 0$ *if* $\mathbf{n} \cdot \mathbf{u} \ge 0$ (*Open boundary*)	$T_0 = 300[K]$	$\begin{pmatrix}0 \le x \le 300\\ y=300\end{pmatrix}$	$T_0 = 300[K]$	$\begin{pmatrix}0 \le x \le 10\\ y=10\end{pmatrix}$

Table 5. Boundary conditions set to the CFD models.

4. Results

4.1. Computation

The described models were implemented in COMSOL Multiphysics 5.2a models. The simulations were carried out in the described 2D models, due to the computational resources that the 3D models required, as well as the great computing times. Then, two different domains were stablished, a 300 m^2 domain for the pool fires and a 15 m^2 for the jet fires. These were selected

http://dx.doi.org/10.5772/intechopen.70563

according to the common lengths of these kinds of fires. The mesh for the pool fire model consisted of 71,665 triangular elements; while the mesh for the jet fire model consisted of 63,821 triangular elements.

The pool fire simulation was a time dependent simulation. 20 s in steps of 0.02 s were simulated (a total of 1001 frames). It consumed 3.72 GB of RAM and 3.96 GB of virtual memory, and required a computing time of 6.72 hours.

The jet fire simulation was also a time dependent simulation. 10 s in steps of 0.02 s were simulated (a total of 501 frames). It consumed 3.4 GB of RAM and 3.95 GB of virtual memory, and required a computing time of 9.73 hours.

The simulations were carried out in a HP z600 Workstation with an Intel® Xeon® E5620 CPU (quad-core, 2.4 GHz, 12 Mb of Cache), with 24 GB of RAM.

4.2. Pool and jet fire CFD model results

Figure 6 shows a sequence of the results from the pool fire CFD model previously described at different times. This pool fire model considers the combustion of heptane (C_7H_{16}) as the main

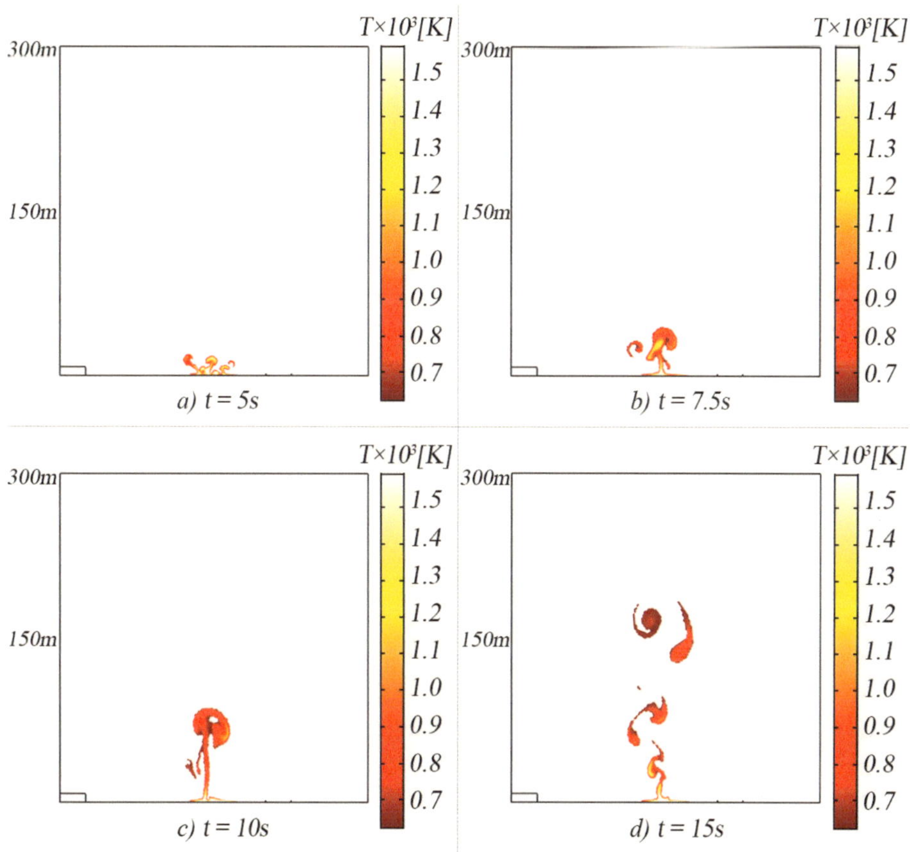

Figure 6. Results sequence from the pool fire CFD model temperature field (a) $t = 5$ s, (b) $t = 7.5$ s, (c) $t = 10$s, (d) $t = 15$ s.

combustion, a pool diameter of 50 m, a total time of 20 s, and a 300 m^2 domain. It is important to note that in these images, highly turbulent flames can be seen which tend to develop in large-size eddies, and that from the beginning moments of the pool fire, very high temperatures and flame heights can be reached.

Figure 7 shows a similar sequence of results for the jet fire CFD model. In this model, the fuel inflow was modified in order to follow a smooth rectangle distribution over the time, and thus it can be appreciated in the figures that in the beginning times the flame develops, then it reaches an almost steady behavior and afterwards it starts to diminish until it is consumed. Again, in this simulation, the main considered reaction was the combustion of heptane (C_7H_{16}). The shown images also consider a hole of 3 cm from where the jet fire arises, a total time of 10 s and a 15 m^2 domain.

The results of these models allow the analysis and evaluation of important variables in the process safety, such as the maximum and average temperatures and flame lengths. **Table 6** shows the resume of the average flame lengths in pool fires, taking as criteria the reaction rate; as well as the maximum temperature, which is evaluated in the whole domain, and thus this value might not necessary be found in a flame zone, it can be a hot zone where no

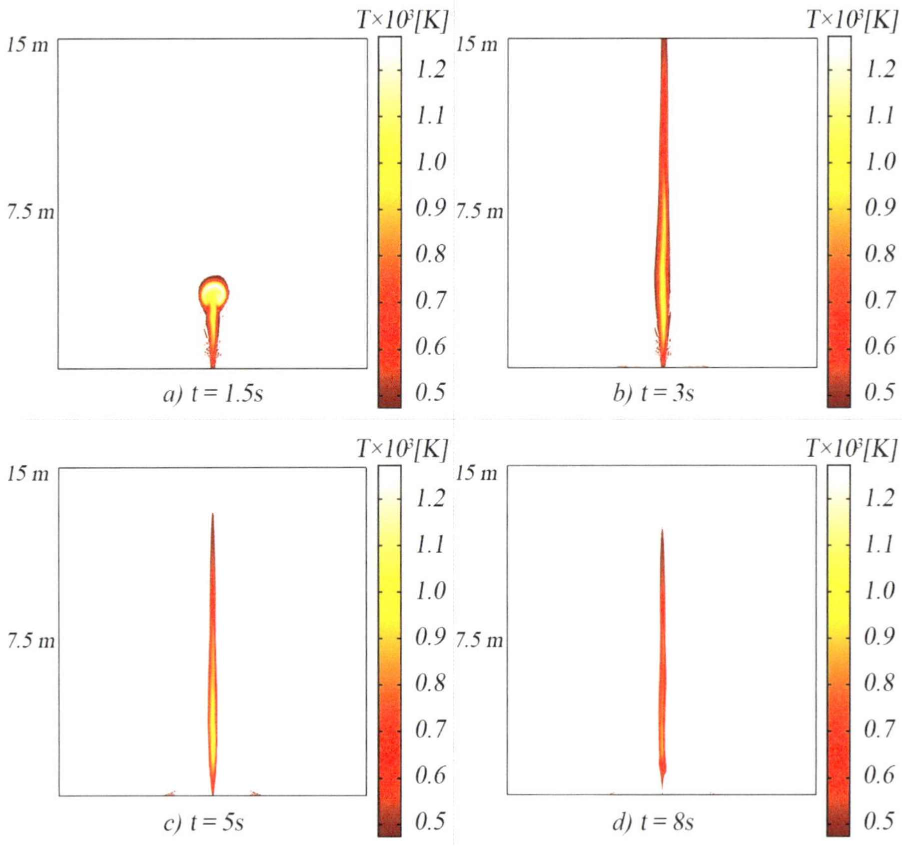

Figure 7. Results sequence from the jet fire CFD model temperature field (a) t = 1.5 s, (b) t = 3 s, (c) t = 5 s, (d) t = 8 s.

combustion reaction is taking place. Note that there is no proportional correlation between the flame height and the flame diameter, nor between the flame diameter and the temperature. Furthermore, it was observed that the highest reaction rate values did not always correspond to the highest temperatures. It can also be seen that the fire exhibits lower temperature values when starting, and these values tend to increase with time, presenting great fluctuations not only in the temperature but other parameters as the flame geometry. These observations are an expected behavior for turbulent flames. Also, several pool diameters were tested, from 3 to 60 m.

Table 7 show a similar analysis to the one in **Table 6**, but for the jet fire CFD model. Different diameters for the hole of the jet fire were tested, from 3 to 19 cm. It is noteworthy that, despite that the jet fires arise from a breach of a few centimeters, these fires can reach great magnitudes,

Diameter (m)	Time (s)	Height (m)	$T_{average}$ (K)	T_{max} (K)
3	0.2	0.5	480	362
	3.0	11.6	697	1572
	9.5	11.6	620	1371
15	0.2	1.1	540	613
	3.0	8.2	1185	1411
	9.5	40.3	538	1363
30	0.2	2.3	541	614
	3.0	4.5	1470	1973
	9.5	96.4	669	1959
60	0.2	4.6	541	616
	3.0	21	1276	>2000
	9.5	31.1	1006	>2000

Table 6. Observed flame height and temperatures average values for different pool fires diameters models.

Diameter (cm)	Time (s)	Height (m)	$T_{average}$ (K)	T_{max} (K)
3	0.2	0.7	569	755
	3.0	7.1	754	938
	4.5	15.0	657	944
9	0.2	1.6	612	770
	3.0	11.5	722	1029
	4.5	15.0	831	996.49
19	0.2	1.42	657	863.9
	3.0	15.0	1054	1352
	4.5	>15.0	1039	1309

Table 7. Observed flame height and temperatures average values for different hole diameters for jet fire models.

with average temperatures around 550 and 1100 K, and punctual maximum values that can reach over 1300 K.

For both kinds of fires models, the results were compared against experimental data, and similar behaviors were found [29, 41].

Even though the detailed study of fires is not the objective of this chapter, it is important to point out that when the CFD heat, momentum and mass transport models are solved, the information of a great number of variables are obtained as an output. A way to use this information is through the dimensionless numbers analyses [42], as the evaluation of these will allow the comparison of different phenomena presented, neglecting the length-scales. For example, by evaluating the Reynolds numbers, it can be seen when will a flame be highly distorted; and the Froude number will show small values in the region near to surface area ($Fr \leq 1$) and increases with the flame height, where the forces of momentum are dominant.

As a resume, the results of the CFD fires simulations presented here show that for pool fires can reach over 90 m in height, average temperatures fluctuating between 500 and 1400 K, and punctual temperatures between 1500 and 1900 K; while the jet fire CFD simulation results predicted flame heights of over 15 m, with average temperatures fluctuating 550 and 1050 K. These results are in good agreement with the observations in experimental studies. Due to the aforementioned, it is important to point out that, even though that as aforementioned the pool fires and jet fires are usually present in other MA, they are by their own considered as MA.

Other applications of CFD models of MA, which are recently developed and widely applied, are the prediction of consequences in a combination of possible scenarios [43]. This is done by combining the CFD models' predictions with vulnerability values, proposing intervention zones, safe distances, equipment distribution in a plant, etc. For example, in the scenario depicted in **Figure 6**, it can be seen that only a few seconds after the pool fire started, temperatures of up to 1500 K can be found, with average temperatures of around 1000 K, and heights over 200 m. With this information, as shown in **Figure 8**, it can then be proceeded to

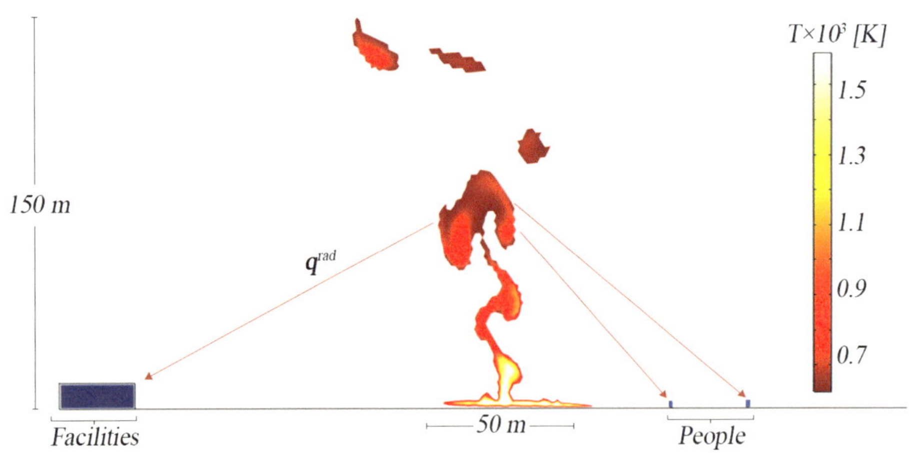

Figure 8. Possible scenario of MA considering the effect in the surroundings.

evaluate the thermal radiation that an industrial facility 150 m away from the fire and persons 50 and 75 m away would receive, considering the view factors. This can be done by applying the Stefan-Boltzmann equation:

$$q_{rad} = \varepsilon \sigma F_{1-2} \left(T_1^4 - T_2^4 \right) \tag{3}$$

where σ is the Stefan-Boltzmann constant, ε is the emissivity and $F_{1\text{-}2}$ is the view factor, defined as

$$F_{ij} = \frac{1}{A_i} \sum_{i=1}^{n} \sum_{j=1}^{m} \frac{\cos\theta_i \cdot \cos\theta_j}{\pi \cdot r^2} dA_i dA_j \tag{4}$$

Also, the determination of the thermal radiation can be coupled with the analytical equations developed for several geometries [44]. The maximum thermal radiation fluxes defined by the vulnerability factors have been widely studied, and are reported in the specialized literature. For example, Jagger [45] studied the consequences of the exposition of personal to different levels of thermal radiation, and proposes recommendations for the gas and petrol offshore industries, suggesting a review of the structural damage that may represent obstacles in emergency exit routes criteria. Raj [46] makes a review of the criteria of diverse normative regarding the exposition of people to fires. Further studies in specific cases can be found in the works of Casal [47].

When vulnerability factors are evaluated, it is important to take into account the maximum observed values, as these will represent the worst-case scenario, with the highest risks for the people and the structures. In this sense, as observed by the simulation results, taking as an example the 50 m pool fire results, the maximum temperature produces a thermal radiation of over 200 kW/m^2, which if far above the safe criteria. Taking in consideration the consequences in the reported vulnerability criteria for people and objects found in literature, it can be concluded that no one would survive that amount of thermal radiation flux; and that the steel structures would lose all their mechanical integrity. This scenario would definitely cause domino effects with greater consequences.

If the 3 m pool fire is considered, the consequences would be lower. However, due to the produced thermal radiation, the safe zone for a person would be no closer than 25 m, as a person can receive a maximum amount of thermal radiation between 4.7 and 5 kW/m^2 [46]; and for the metal structures, the safe zone would be found in a distance of 7.5 m, in order to avoid the collapse of the structure, that can receive a maximum thermal radiation of 37.5 kW/m^2. Although, exposition to this value of 37.5 kW/m^2 would lead to the death of a person, even in a short exposition period of time [46].

5. Conclusions

Process safety is of major importance due to the consequences in matter of lives, economy and wide regions affections. Thus, the prediction of the behavior of major accidents is of key importance in the better development of process safety engineering. In this context, CFD tool represent an opportunity to provide more accurate solutions in the prediction of the complex multiscale and multiphysic phenomena that MA involve (some problems that have been experimentally impossible to solve). These tools are of special necessity in the quantitative analysis of results, as the previously developed methods still have great restrictions and failures in predictions, for example, of highly turbulent flows, rapid compressions or expansions, low Reynolds number effects and chemical reactions.

Despite the development of diverse strategies for the CFD simulations that allow taking into account the turbulence present in MA (LES, DNS, RANS), the RANS equations have been widely used, as the results predicted by those have shown a good agreement compared with experimental methodologies. Also, applying other methodologies require greater computational resources, and are in many cases unpractical. On the other hand, the CFD simulations provide a great advantage to study large-scale MA, as these would be practically impossible to control and study in experimental studies (due to the high costs and the scientific and technical challenges).

Finally, it is noteworthy that the results of the CFD simulations of MA have several practical applications in diverse Process Safety fields and issues. For example, the study of safe distances, emergency exit routes and facilities design. Even though, the aforementioned manifests that there is still a strong need of developing research in these underexplored fields, which have special application in the process safety engineering.

Nomenclatures

Abbreviations

MA	Major accidents
NFPA	National Fire Protection Association
CFD	Computational fluid dynamics
RANS	Reynolds-Average Navier-Stokes
LES	Large eddy simulations
DNS	Direct numerical simulations

Symbols

h	Convective coefficient
$\mathbf{u}$ (m/s)	Velocity vector
$\mathbf{N}$ (mol/m^{2}s)	Total mass flux
D_i	Specie i diffusivity
C_P (J/mol K)	Heat capacity

http://dx.doi.org/10.5772/intechopen.70563

ΔH_{rxn} (J/mol)	Heat of reaction
R_i (mol/m^3s)	Reaction rate
A_i	Pre-exponential collision factor
Ea	Activation energy
a	Kinetics empirical constant 1
B	Kinetics empirical constant 2
n_i	Stoichiometric coefficient for specie i
K_i	Reaction rate constant
$\mathbf{n}$	Unitary vector
p (Pa)	Pressure
c_i (mol/m^3)	Specie i concentration
k (W/mK)	Thermal conductivity
$F_{1\text{-}2}$	View factor

Sub-superscripts

0	At reference conditions

Greek letters

μ (Pa s)	Dynamic viscosity
ε	Emissivity factor
σ (W/m^2K^4)	Stefan-Boltzmann constant

Author details

Luis G. Zárate*, Sebastián Uribe and Mario E. Cordero

*Address all correspondence to: luis.zarate@upaep.mx

Universidad Popular Autónoma del Estado de Puebla, Puebla, México

References

[1] Yinting C, Mingguang Z, Peijie G, Juncheng J. International symposium on safety science and technology investigation and analysis of historical domino effects statistic. Procedia Engineering. 2012;**45**:152-158. DOI: 10.1016/j.proeng.2012.08.136

[2] NFPA. Available from: http://www.nfpa.org/news-and-research/fire-statistics-and-reports/fire-statistics/fires-in-the-us [Accessed: 2017-06-28]

[3] Girgin S, Krausmann E. Historical analysis of U.S. onshore hazardous liquid pipeline accidents triggered by natural hazards. Journal of Loss Prevention in the Process Industries. 2016;**40**:578-590. DOI: 10.1016/j.jlp.2016.02.008

[4] Kannan P, Flechas T, Mendez E, Angarita L, Chaudhari P, Hong Y, Mannan MS. A web-based collection and analysis of process safety incidents. Journal of Loss Prevention in the Process Industries. 2016;**44**:171-192. DOI: 10.1016/j.jlp.2016.08.021

[5] Mannan S. Lees' Process Safety Essentials. Waltham: Elsevier-BH; 2016. p. 547 978-1-85617-776-4

[6] Vílchez JA, Sevilla S, Montiel H, Casal J. Historical analysis of accidents in chemical plants and in the transportation of hazardous materials. Journal of Loss Prevention in the Process Industries. 1995;**8**:87-97. DOI: 10.1016/0950-4230(95)00006-2

[7] Villa V, Paltrinieri N, Khan F, Cozzani V. Chapter 1 – A short overview of risk analysis background and recent developments. In: Dynamic Risk Analysis in the Chemical and Petroleum Industry. Evolution and Interaction with Parallel Disciplines in the Perspective of Industrial Application. Cambridge: Elsevier-BH; 2016. p. 3-12. DOI: 10.1016/B978-0-12-803765-2.00001-9

[8] Dunjó J, Fthenakis V, Vílchez JA, Arnaldos J. Hazard and operability (HAZOP) analysis. A literature review. Journal of Hazardous Materials. 2010;**173**:19-32. DOI: 10.1016/j.jhazmat.2009.08.076

[9] TNO. Methods for the Calculation of the Physical Effects -Due to Releases of Hazardous Materials (Liquids and Gases). The Hague: Publicatiereeks Gevaarlijke Stoffen; 2005

[10] Longhua H. A review of physics and correlations of pool fire behavior in wind and future challenges. Fire Safety Journal. 2017;**91**:41-45. DOI: 10.1016/j.firesaf.2017.05.008

[11] Vianello C, Milazzo MF, Guerrini L, Mura A, Maschio G. A risk-based tool to support the inspection management in chemical plants. Journal of Loss Prevention in the Process Industries. 2016;**41**:154-168. DOI: 10.1016/j.jlp.2016.03.005

[12] Landucci G, Pontiggia M, Paltrinieri N, Cozzani V. Chapter 9 – Dynamic consequence analysis through computational fluid dynamics modeling. In: Dynamic Risk Analysis in the Chemical and Petroleum Industry. Evolution and Interaction with Parallel Disciplines in the Perspective of Industrial Application. Cambridge: Elsevier-BH; 2016. p. 105-114

[13] Chakrabarty A, Mannan S, Cagin T. Multiscale Modeling for Process Safety Applications. Waltham: Elsevier-BH; 2016

[14] Darbra RM, Palacios A, Casal J. Domino effect in chemical accidents: Main features and accident sequences. Journal of Hazardous Materials. 2010;**183**:565

[15] Argyropoulos CD, Markatos NC. Recent advances on the numerical modelling of turbulent flows. Applied Mathematical Modelling. 2015;**39**(2, 15):693-732. DOI: 10.1016/j.apm.2014.07.001

[16] Babrauskas V. Pool fires: Burning rates and heat fluxes. In: Cote AE, Linville JM, editors. Fire Protection Handbook. Quincy, MA: National Fire Protection Association. 1986; p. 2136

[17] Sliepcevich CM, Welker JR. Bending of wind-blow flames from liquid pools. Fire Technology. 1966;**2**:127-135

[18] Thomas PH. The size of flames from natural fires. Symposium (International) on Combustion. 1963;**9**:844

[19] Mudan K. Thermal radiation hazards from hydrocarbon pool fires. Progress in Energy and Combustion Science. 1984;**10**:59-80

[20] Mulholland GW. Chapter 13. Smoke production and properties. In: SFPE Handbook of Fire Protection Engineering. Quincy, Massachusetts. 2002

[21] Longhua H. A review of physics and correlations of pool fire behavior in wind and future challenges. Fire Safety Journal. 2017. DOI: 10.1016/j.firesaf.2017.05.008

[22] Faghri M, Sundén B, Transport Phenomena in Fires. Southampton, Boston: WIT Press. 2008; p. 477; ISBN:978-1-84564-160-3

[23] Raynal L, Augier F, Bazer-Bachi F, Haroun Y, Pereira da Fonte C. CFD applied to process development in the oil and gas industry – A review. Oil & Gas Science and Technology - Revue d'IFP Energies nouvelles. 2016;**71**:42. DOI: 10.2516/ogst/2015019

[24] Ricou FP, Spalding DB. Measurements of entrainment by asymmetrical turbulent jets. Journal of Fluid Mechanics. 1961;**8**:21-32

[25] Brzustowski TA. Anew criterion for the length of a gaseous turbulent diffusion flame. Combustion Science and Technology. 1973;**6**:313-319

[26] Chamberlain GA. Developments in design methods for predicting thermal radiation from flares. Chemical Engineering Research and Design. 1987;**65**:299-309

[27] Johnson AD, Brightwell HM, Carsley AJ. A model for predicting the thermal radiation hazards from large-scale horizontally released natural gas jet fires. Hazards. 1994;**13**:123

[28] Cook DT, Fairweather M, Hammonds J. Size and radiative characteristics of natural gas flares. Chemical Engineering Research and Design. 1987;**65**:310-318

[29] Gómez MM. Jet fires experimental studies and numerical simulations [thesis]. Barcelona, Spain: Universitat Politècnica de Catalunya; 2009

[30] Palacios A. Study of jet fires geometry and radiative features [thesis]. Barcelona, Spain: Universitat Politècnica de Catalunya; 2011

[31] Health and Safety Executive, CFD calculation of impinging gas jet flames, 1999. OTO Report No. OTO 1999 011

[32] Yan Z. Chapter10 – CFD fire simulation and its recent development. In: Faghri M. and Sundén B. (Editors) Transport Phenomena in Fires. WIT Press, Boston, 2008: pp. 357 – 405. ISBN: 978-1-84564-160-3

[33] Modest M.F. Chapter 7 – Radiative heat transfer in fire modeling. In: Faghri M. and Sundén B. (Editors) Transport Phenomena in Fires. WIT Press, Boston, 2008: p. 261 – 299. ISBN: 978-1-84564-160-3

[34] Gómez MM, Zárate L, Casal J. Jet fires and the domino effect. Fire Safety Journal. 2008;**43**(8): 583-588

[35] Casal J, Gómez-Mares M, Muñoz M, Palacios A. Jet fires: A "minor" fire hazard? Chemical Engineering Transactions. 2012;**26**:13-20. DOI: 10.3303/CET1226003

[36] D.C. Wilcox, Turbulence Modeling for CFD, 2nd ed., DCW Industries, Inc., La Cañada, California. 1998. ISBN:13: 978-0963605153

[37] Dryer FL. Chemical kinetic and combustion characteristics of transportation fuels. Proceedings of the Combustion Institute. 2015;**35**(1):117-144. DOI: 10.1016/j.proci.2014.09.008

[38] Battin-Leclerc F. Detailed chemical kinetic models for the low temperature combustion of hydrocarbons with application to gasoline and diesel fuel surrogates. Progress in Energy and Combustion Science. 2008;**34**:440-498. DOI: 10.1016/j.pecs.2007.10.002

[39] Zhang HR, Eddings EG, Sarofim AF. Criteria for selection of components for surrogates of natural gas and transportation fuels. Proceedings of the Combustion Institute. 2007;**31**:401-409. DOI: 10.1016/j.proci.2006.08.001

[40] Phillips TS, Derlaga JM, Roy CJ, Borggaard J. Error transport equation boundary conditions for the Euler and Navier–Stokes equations. Journal of Computational Physics. 2017;**330**(1):46-64. DOI: 10.1016/j.jcp.2016.11.002

[41] Chatris JM. Velocitat de combustion I distribució de temperatures en incendis de bassals d'hidrocarburs [thesis]. Barcelona, Spain: Universitat Politècnica de Catalunya; 2001

[42] Ruzicka MC. On dimensionless numbers. Chemical Engineering Research and Design. 2008;**86**:835-868. DOI: 10.1016/j.cherd.2008.03.007

[43] Rajendram A, Khan F, Garaniya V. Modelling of fire risks in an offshore facility. Fire Safety Journal. 2015;**71**:79-85. DOI: 10.1016/j.firesaf.2014.11.019

[44] Howell JR, Menguc MP. Radiative transfer configuration factor catalog: A listing of relations for common geometries. Journal of Quantitative Spectroscopy & Radiative Transfer. 2011;**112**:910-912. DOI: 10.1016/j.jqsrt.2010.10.002

[45] Jagger S. Human Vulnerability to Thermal Radiation Offshore. Harpur Hill, Buxton, Derbyshire: Healt and Safety Laboratory, 2004; HSL/2004/04

[46] Raj PK. A review of the criteria for people exposure to radiant heat flux from fires. Journal of Hazardous Materials. 2008;**159**(2008):61-71. DOI: 10.1016/j.jhazmat.2007.09.120

[47] Casal J. Evaluation of the Effects and Consequences of Major Accidents in Industrial Plants. Elsevier. Oxford; 2008; ISBN: 978-0-444-53081-3

Chapter 7

Adaptation to Climate Change at Local Scale: A CFD Study in Porto Urban Area

Vera Rodrigues, Sandra Rafael, Sandra Sorte,
Sílvia Coelho, Hélder Relvas, Bruno Vicente,
Joana Leitão, Myriam Lopes,
Ana Isabel Miranda and Carlos Borrego

Additional information is available at the end of the chapter

http://dx.doi.org/10.5772/intechopen.72972

Abstract

Green infrastructures play an essential role in urban planning, namely with their potential to reduce the impact from air pollution episodes together with extreme weather events. This chapter focuses on the assessment of green infrastructures' benefits on current and future microclimate and air quality patterns in Porto's urban area (Portugal). The effects of green infrastructures on flow dynamics are evaluated for the baseline scenarios by means of numerical and physical simulations, using the computational fluid dynamics (CFD) model VADIS and the wind tunnel of the University of Aveiro. The baseline morphological (BM) scenario focuses on the current morphological characteristics of Porto's urban area, while a baseline green (BG) scenario comprises the replacement of built-up areas by green areas and parks. In addition, the benefits of green infrastructures on air quality are assessed for the baseline and under future climate scenarios. The air quality simulations focus on particulate matter, one of the most critical air pollutants with severe impacts on human health. For the BM scenario, the simulated concentrations are compared with hourly averaged PM10 concentrations measured during a weekday at the air quality station located within the study domain.

Keywords: urban areas, CFD, climate change, adaptation, green infrastructures, future climate scenarios, morphological scenarios

1. Introduction

Despite the advances over the last decades on mitigation of greenhouse gas emissions, climate change still remains a major concern, threatening ecosystems and human systems [1–3]. Currently, climate change (CC) impacts are recorded worldwide, through extreme weather events, such as heat waves, droughts, floods, cyclones and wildfires [1–3]. In addition, urban areas are facing a continuous unsustainable growth of population [4, 5], associated with extreme weather events and critical air pollution episodes, highly affected by these climate-related events, among other environmental pressures, again threatening human health and lifestyle standards [1–5].

Given the expected increase of extreme weather events, the design and implementation of countermeasures in densely populated urban areas are an important goal in adaptation of societies to climate change in coming decades. Adaptation policies and strategies have the potential to increase resilience of urban areas to climate change, i.e., to improve the ability of a city and the surroundings to readily recover from a disturbance and return to the original functions of the urban metabolism [6]. Recently, several adaptation strategies turn to innovative solutions supported by nature, the so-called nature-based solutions, such as green infrastructures and urban forests, white roofs and highly reflective facades, urban water streams and wetlands, etc. [7–14]. These nature-based solutions provide sustainable, cost-effective, multipurpose and flexible alternatives for tackling societal and environmental challenges, such as climate change, air pollution and human health protection. In particular, green infrastructures (e.g., green roofs, walls and corridors) and urban forests play an essential role in urban planning, leading to several benefits to the environment as solutions of not only resilience to climate change but also to improve air quality and thermal comfort [7–11].

An improved knowledge about the highly complex urban microclimate and consequent air pollutant dispersion patterns is therefore of utmost importance to circumvent climate change impact at local scale (e.g., at street canyon level). A better understanding of the overall urban microclimate, and all the physical- and chemical-related processes, requires not only accurate measurements but also numerical and physical modeling of the exchanges within the urban atmospheric boundary layer [15, 16]. In recent years, several studies have been performed using physical models, such as wind tunnel simulations, experimental campaigns and numerical models [17–29]. In particular, computational fluid dynamics (CFD) models have been used to compute turbulent flow dynamics and atmospheric pollutant dispersion within the urban surface layer. These models usually allow taking into account the morphological specificities of the urban environment, and consequently, they are able to simulate the flow dynamics perturbations caused by distinct urban obstacles [23–29]. Specifically, CFD models have been applied to assess the role of urban vegetation in mitigating air pollution, mainly considering the effects of trees induced by mechanical drag of trees and/or including the pollutant removal capacity of trees by deposition and filtration mechanisms [30–38]. Still, most of the numerical, physical and experimental studies have been performed over urban-like geometries, through idealized configurations and hypothetical scenarios [33]. Although the effects of green infrastructures on urban atmospheric dynamics have been widely studied, a deeper knowledge is still required regarding the overall perturbations induced by trees on turbulent flow dynamics and, consequently, air pollutant dispersion. Up to now, despite the several contributions from outdoor measurements, wind tunnel measurements, extensive database on idealized street canyons and several CFD studies, the current understanding of turbulent flow dynamics within and around vegetation is not sufficient, denoting local increases and decreases of wind speed and turbulence, depending on several parameters (e.g., characteristics of vegetation, urban morphology and meteorological conditions). Therefore, the first identified knowledge gap, which motivates this work, refers to the need to contribute to improve the knowledge of the effects of green infrastructures on turbulent flow dynamics at a local scale and, consequently, on air pollutant dispersion patterns.

Furthermore, in literature, the study of climate change impacts ranges from global scale down to the regional and urban scale [39, 40] (e.g., in [40] the authors have performed a 10-year air quality projection under climate and city-level emission changes at urban scale applying a horizontal resolution of 4 km × 4 km). Nevertheless, the full understanding of the impact on air quality at a local scale is a challenge and the effects are still unknown. Another identified knowledge gap is the lack of studies focused on local-scale effects, with an insufficient understanding and accurate predictions of the changes in urban microclimate patterns and in pollutant concentrations under climate changes. Air pollutant dispersion is mainly driven by meteorological forces, and thus it is natural that changes in future climate will strongly affect air quality patterns, resulting, potentially, in an increase of the magnitude and frequency of air pollution episodes. Therefore, several issues arise concerning how the changes on global and regional circulations will affect local-scale urban microclimate, how to use GI as an adaptation measure to increase resilience to CC at local scale, and what is the link between the impact of GI under future, past and current climate.

This chapter aims to foster urban microclimate knowledge and to assess CC effects at a local scale, evaluating strategies of adaptation to CC toward an urban sustainable development. The chapter's main objective is to evaluate the impact of distinct resilience measures on the urban microclimate and air quality, in recent past, current and future climate scenarios for Porto's urban area. These resilience measures will be based on green infrastructures.

2. Numerical modeling approach

A cascade of numerical models is applied in this work, from global scale down to local scale (e.g., street canyon and surroundings) to assess the urban microclimate and air quality patterns.

2.1. From global to urban scale

A cascade of numerical models, from global to urban scale, was applied to the Greater Porto area. The numerical model *Weather Research and Forecasting* (WRF) *Model* version 3.7.1 [41] was applied to perform regional climate simulations for Porto city and surrounding areas through dynamical downscaling. WRF setup has included four domains on line nested with increasing resolution at a downscaling ratio of three: domain 1 at 27 km resolution covering West Europe, Atlantic Ocean and North Africa; domain 2 at 9 km resolution over the Iberian Peninsula; domain 3 at 3 km resolution over Portugal; and domain 4 with 1 km resolution over North West Portugal. All these domains were used to perform a representative simulation of the recent past climate (1976–2005) that was used as the reference simulation and a representative simulation of the future medium-term climate (2041–2070). For the future simulation, the Representative Concentration Pathway Scenario RCP8.5 has been adopted, from the new generation of climate change future scenarios included in the Fifth Assessment Report of the Intergovernmental Panel on Climate Change [42]. The MPI-ESM-LR model was used to provide initial and boundary conditions to WRF model, with a spatial resolution of 1.9° and 47 hybrid sigma-pressure levels (Max Planck Institute for Meteorology Earth System Model) [43].

2.2. CFD numerical formulation

Pollutant DISpersion in the atmosphere under VAriable wind conditions (VADIS) is the CFD model applied to Porto urban area to assess local-scale flow dynamics and air quality. This CFD model was developed by the University of Aveiro to numerically simulate air pollutant dispersion in complex urban areas and under unfavorable wind conditions. VADIS consists of two distinct modules: the FLOW and DISPER.

2.2.1. Turbulent flow dynamics

FLOW is a Eulerian module able to simulate the turbulent flow dynamics under stationary conditions within the atmospheric boundary layer. This module numerically solves by means of finite differences (SIMPLE solver), over a Cartesian tridimensional grid, the Navier-Stokes (NS) equations for the wind velocity components, the turbulent viscosity, pressure and the turbulent kinetic energy, applying Reynolds averages (the so-called Reynolds-Averaged Navier-Stokes [RANS] approach). The equation of mass conservation is written as Eq. (1), while the NS equations for the momentum conservation are given by Eq. (2).

$$\frac{\partial u_i}{\partial x_i} = 0 \tag{1}$$

$$u_j \frac{\partial u_i}{\partial x_i} = -\frac{1}{\rho}\frac{\partial P}{\partial x_i} + \frac{\partial}{\partial x_j}\left(v_e \frac{\partial u_i}{\partial x_j}\right) + S_u \tag{2}$$

where ui represents each velocity component (u, v and w) and x_i the spatial coordinates (x, y and z), P denotes the pressure, ρ is the air density, v_e is the effective viscosity and S_u indicates the source and/or sink term for u_i.

The computation of the NS equations is based on the mechanics of fluid fundamental laws, simplified through a set of considerations and completed with closure formulations, namely in the turbulence simulation. The equation system closure is made through the turbulent isotropic viscosity approach, calculated from the kinetic turbulent energy transport equations and their dissipation rate. The first-order k-ε closure scheme [44] is used to model the turbulent viscosity (v_t), solving two additional equations for the turbulent kinetic energy (k), Eq. (3), and the dissipation rate (ε), Eq. (4).

$$u_j \frac{\partial k}{\partial x_j} = \frac{\partial}{\partial x_i}\left(\frac{v_t}{\sigma_k}\frac{\partial k}{\partial x_i}\right) + v_t\left(\frac{\partial u_i}{\partial x_j} + \frac{\partial u_j}{\partial x_i}\right)\frac{\partial u_i}{\partial x_j} - \varepsilon + S_k \tag{3}$$

$$u_j \frac{\partial \varepsilon}{\partial x_j} = \frac{\partial}{\partial x_i}\left(\frac{v_t}{\sigma_\varepsilon}\frac{\partial \varepsilon}{\partial x_i}\right) + c_{\varepsilon 1}\frac{\varepsilon}{k} v_t\left(\frac{\partial u_i}{\partial x_j} + \frac{\partial u_j}{\partial x_i}\right)\frac{\partial u_i}{\partial x_j} - c_{\varepsilon 2}\frac{\varepsilon^2}{k} + S_\varepsilon \tag{4}$$

where σ_k, σ_ε, $c_{\varepsilon 1}$ and $c_{\varepsilon 2}$ are closure constants set to the standard values of 1, 1.3, 1.44 and 1.92, respectively. S_k and S_ε are the additional source terms of k and ε.

VADIS model is suited for the simulation of the wind field and the turbulent viscosity affected by a set of obstacles (e.g., buildings) localized over the Cartesian grid. The CFD model VADIS was updated by [31] to consider the aerodynamic effect of urban vegetation, adding source terms to momentum (Eq. (5)), turbulent kinetic energy (Eq. (6)) and its dissipation rate (Eq. (7)) equations, calculated based on tree-airflow interactions, neglecting viscous drag relative to form (or pressure) drag [45, 46].

$$S_u = -C_d LAD|U|\, u_i \tag{5}$$

where C_d is the mechanical drag coefficient, *LAD* denotes the leaf area density and $|U|$ is the magnitude of the wind speed vector.

S_k denotes the production of turbulence by the action of vegetation elements.

$$S_k = -C_d LAD\left(\beta_p |U|^3 - \beta_d |U| k\right) \tag{6}$$

where β_p is set to 1 and indicates the fraction of the mean flow kinetic energy converted to wake-generated turbulent energy by canopy drag. β_d is set to 4 and denotes the fraction of turbulent energy dissipated by "short-circuiting" of the Kolmogorov cascade [47, 48] and $\beta_d |U| k$ points out the dissipation of the generated wakes [49]. Then, S_k represents the sum of the source and sink of turbulent kinetic energy due to the effect of vegetation elements.

The numerical formulation of S_ε is similar to the formulation of S_k.

$$S_\varepsilon = -C_d LAD\left(c_{\varepsilon 4} \beta_p |U|^3 \frac{\varepsilon}{k} - c_{\varepsilon 5} \beta_d |U| \varepsilon\right) \tag{7}$$

where $c_{\varepsilon 4}$ and $c_{\varepsilon 5}$ are both equal to 1.5.

Therefore, VADIS model is suited for the calculation of the perturbations induced by vegetation elements on the flow dynamics and dispersion patterns.

2.2.2. Pollutant dispersion over complex geometries

The DISPER module uses the data provided by the previously mentioned module, namely the wind field, and estimates the tridimensional concentration field of the air pollutant dispersion, based on the Lagrangian Stochastic approach. This methodology assumes that the pollutant spatial and temporal dispersion is conveniently represented by a large number of numerical particles randomly released in the flow. Langevin equation (Eq. (9)) computes particle displacement at each time step by the sum of the deterministic component obtained from the wind velocity (u_i), the aleatory component (u_i') related with the local turbulence and the influence of the fluctuation forces. T_L is the Lagrangian timescale.

$$d u_i = -\left(\frac{u_i}{T_L}\right) dt + du'_i \tag{8}$$

The fundamental Lagrangian equation assumes that each particle is represented by a constant mass quantity. The mean concentration of the pollutant at point *X* and time *t* due to the contribution of point X_0 is represented by the probability of occurrence (the probability $P(X_0,X,t)$ of a particle emitted at X_0 to be at point *X* and at time *t*) and the concentration at the original point. Then, the sum of the contributions of all points within the computational domain represents the mean concentration at point *X* and instant *t*. *C(s)* is written as [50]:

$$C(X) = \int P(X_0, X, t)\, C_0(X_0) dX_0 \tag{9}$$

The performance of VADIS model has been evaluated by comparison with wind tunnel data, other CFD models and in-situ measurements [31, 50–52].

3. Modeling system application

3.1. Case study

Porto urban area is located in coastal northern Portugal bounded by the Atlantic Ocean and the Douro River. Porto is the second largest city in Portugal with a population of 237,591 inhabitants and the city center of Porto metropolitan area covering 1900 km^2 with more than 1.5 million inhabitants [53]. Porto metropolitan area is characterized by a fast urban expansion with dense residential and commercial areas and a few and sparse green areas. Porto city features a temperate Atlantic climate with warm and dry summers and mild rainy winters [54]. The urban area is surrounded by two metropolitan rings, each one with important links to Porto metropolitan area, in terms of mobility, with high rates of emissions from road traffic. Porto urban area has been selected as the case study in the framework of CLICURB project—"Urban atmospheric quality, climate change and resilience." The main objective of CLICURB project was to improve the scientific knowledge about urban microclimate and to bridge the gap between global climate change trends and urban development considering the inclusion of adaptation strategies on urban planning and decision-making processes. This research project is aimed to identify a set of measures suited for the increase of urban resilience, including the quantification of their effectiveness to mitigate climate change impact. CLICURB project intended to assess the impact of future climate on urban areas at different levels, e.g., meteorology, energy fluxes and air quality. The most relevant outcome of CLICURB was the production of an urban atlas, both for present and mid-twenty-first century, consisting of a series of layers for urban climate, thermal comfort, air pollutant emissions and air quality.

3.1.1. Computational domain

The modeling system was applied following three distinct steps, in order to assess the impact of green infrastructures on flow dynamics and air quality levels, evaluating their effectiveness as green urban planning strategies, under recent past, current and future medium-term climate. The **first step** focuses on the comparison of flow dynamics between wind tunnel and CFD simulation results, for both a baseline and a green scenario. The **second step** includes the comparison of CFD simulation results with PM10 concentrations measured at the air quality station located within the computational domain, for 24th September 2010 (this specific day was selected due to the data availability of traffic counting and meteorological data). The **third step** comprises the simulation of meteorological fields, from global down to urban scale (following the procedure described in section 2.1), as well as the CFD simulation at local scale of the urban microclimate and air quality under recent past climate and future medium-term climate. **Figure 1** shows the selected study area within Porto city center. D1 points out the selected study area for **step 1**, while D2 denotes the selected study area used in **step 2** and **step 3**.

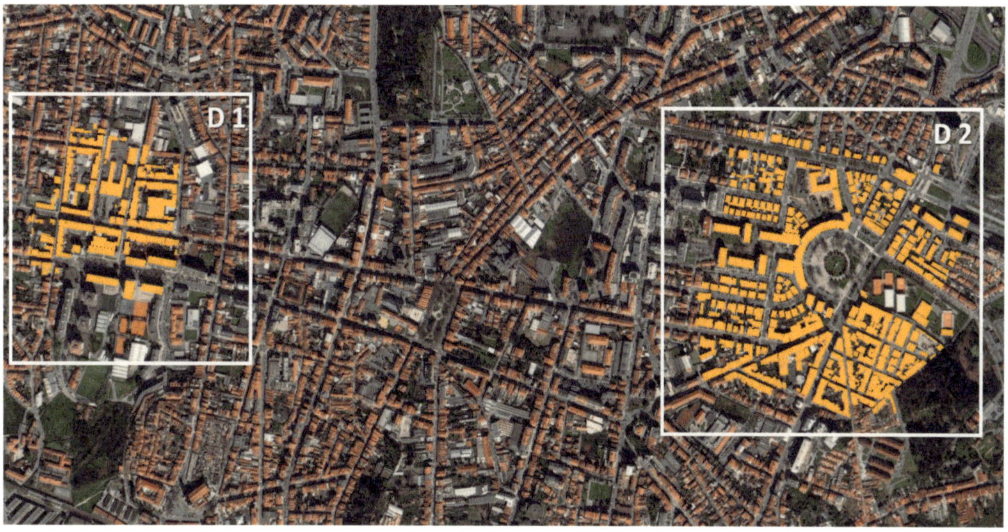

Figure 1. Selected study area in Porto city center, with the location of domains D1 and D2.

Figure 2 shows the simulation domain used in the wind tunnel and in the CFD simulations (**step 1**). The study area is centered in part of *Rua da Constituição*, a street canyon located in the city center of Porto. The baseline domain (**Figure 2a**) corresponds to the current morphological conditions of the study area, while the hypothetical green scenario (**Figure 2b**) corresponds to the replacement of two blocks of buildings for parks flanked by groups of trees.

A set of physical simulations were carried out using the wind tunnel facilities of the University of Aveiro, for the baseline and the corresponding green scenario (**Figure 2**), to assess the impact

Figure 2. Computational domain for (a) the baseline scenario and (b) the green scenario, including the wind speed measurement point location, or the corresponding computational cells in the CFD simulations. The newly implemented green areas are represented by green circles.

on local wind of replacing a built-up area by green parks. The wind tunnel experiments were performed using a scaled mock-up within the test section of the tunnel with 6.5 m × 1.5 m × 1 m. For that purpose, a 1:250 scaled interchangeable model of the urban domain D1, covering a full extension of approximately 360 m, was built for both the baseline and the green scenarios corresponding to the domain in **Figure 2a** and **b**. The atmospheric boundary layer was simulated using a specific setup of turbulence generators and floor roughness elements, located upstream the test section. The flow analysis was performed by measurements of the wind speed and turbulence, with a time resolution sampling rate of 0.5 s, using a hot-wire anemometer (TSI IFA-300).

Both the mock-up of the baseline and the green scenario were tested in the wind tunnel. The wind speed was measured at different locations, from points 1 to 8 indicated in **Figure 2b**), at a height corresponding to 1.5 m in full scale. A corresponding set of CFD simulations were performed using VADIS model. The simulated values are extracted at the cell corresponding to the location of the measurement points.

The typical meteorological conditions were established from the analysis of an historical database of climatological data for the northern Portuguese region. The prevailing conditions correspond to a wind blowing from North, West and Southeast. The wind speeds of 3 and 6 m s^{-1}, at 10 m high, were selected as prevailing conditions, while a wind speed of 9 m s^{-1} was selected as representative of strong wind speed conditions.

In **step 2**, the CFD model is applied to an area defined in the city center of Porto (computational domain of 1300 m × 1300 m × 150 m shown in **Figure 3**), which includes the air quality station Francisco Sá Carneiro-Campanhã, mainly influenced by road-traffic emissions. The CFD simulations were performed with a grid resolution of 3 m × 3 m × 3 m in a total of 9,417,800 number of cells. The baseline computational domain is presented in **Figure 3a**, including the

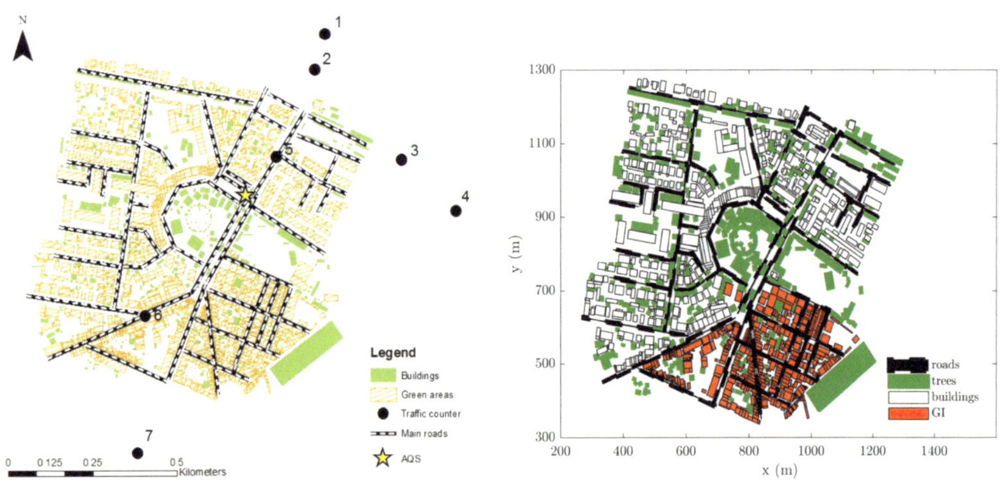

(a) (b)

Figure 3. Computational domain for (a) the baseline scenario, including the location of the traffic counter devices, as well as the air quality station; and (b) the green scenario, where the newly implemented green areas are represented by red rectangles (GI).

location of the traffic count devices (1–4 and 7), the air quality station, as well as the location of buildings, trees and roads, corresponding to the current morphological data of the study area. The green scenario is shown in **Figure 3b** and comprises the implementation of green areas in 35% of the current built-up area located in the Southeast part of the domain (pointed out by the red rectangles). Within the newly implemented green areas, the height of trees varies between 3 and 30 m. The overall roads keep the same hourly emission rate as for the baseline scenario.

In the **third step,** the CFD model is also applied to the area defined in the city center of Porto included in the computational domain D2.

3.2. Emissions from road traffic

The traffic roads are defined within the computational domain as line sources (see **Figures 3** and **4**). All these roads were considered as emission sources with an associated emission rate. Hourly averaged PM10 emission rates from on-road transport vehicles were calculated with high temporal and spatial resolution using the *Transport Emission Model for Line Sources (TREM)*. This model was developed at the University of Aveiro, based on MEET/COST319 methodology [50]. The hourly emission rates are estimated for each road segment, considering the local information on traffic counting data. Vehicle counting data was acquired using automatic devices installed in seven distinct locations (**Figure 3a**). Empirical rates expressing the relation with the traffic in the surrounding roads were applied in case of roads without available data.

In addition, the calculation of the emission rates are also based on emission factors following the European guidelines [55] and considering the fleet composition and the characteristics of the vehicles, such as age of vehicles, average speed, engine type, capacity and technology, vehicle weight and fuel consumption (e.g., diesel, gasoline or LPG). TREM algorithm applies an aggregation of vehicles by categories (e.g., passengers, light-duty vehicles, heavy-duty vehicles, busses, motorcycles and new-technology vehicles, such as hybrid and electric cars). For all vehicle categories, 350 classes were considered including EURO1 to EURO5 vehicles and depending on the characteristics of vehicles and their emission standards. Fleet data of the percentage of vehicles in each class were obtained from national databases [56, 57].

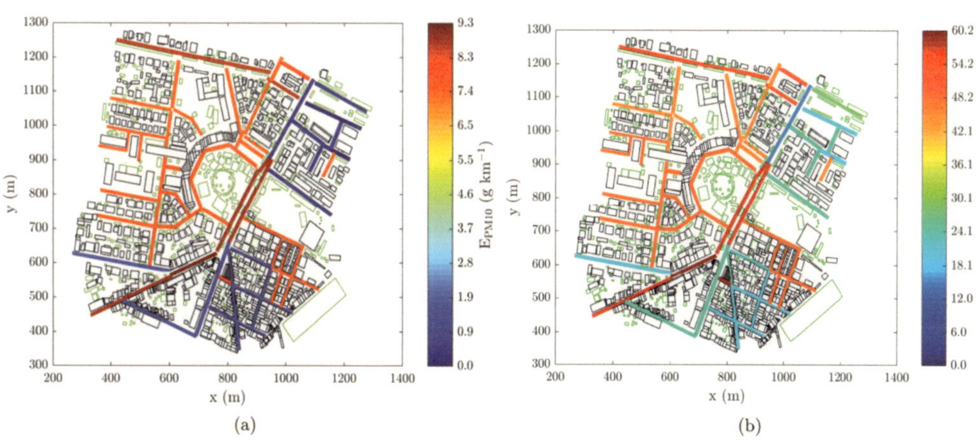

Figure 4. Hourly averaged PM10 emission rates calculated for each road segment at (a) 4 am and (b) 8 am.

Figure 4 shows the hourly averaged PM10 emission rates calculated for each road segment, in 68 segments. The figure points out the variation of PM10 emission rates depending on the road segment for two distinct hours characterized by low emission rates, at 4 am (**Figure 4a**), and high emission rates, at 8 am (**Figure 4b**). The results correspond to a weekday (Friday, 24th September 2010) typical behavior of downtown traffic flow.

The main road in the domain is *Avenida de Fernão Magalhães*, constituted by five lanes, i.e., three on the right side and two on the left, from South to North direction, separated by a central row of trees. This main avenue is divided into four road segments, for the computation of the emission rates. The two parallel road segments with high emission rates are located in the intersections with the roundabout where the Air Quality Station is located. On the contrary, the low emission rates are registered in the road segments located in the Southeast neighborhood of the computational domain.

Figure 5 presents the calculated PM10 emission rates in an hourly basis: the minimum, the maximum and the average values. The minimum values are recorded in several road segments in the Southeast part of the domain, while the maximum values are always registered in the main avenue. The average curve corresponds to the average of the hourly emission rates estimated for all the 68 road segments.

The maximum emission rates registered at 4 and 8 am are equal to 9.2 and 60.2 g km^{-1} h^{-1}, respectively, while the minimum rates are equal to 0.12 g km^{-1} h^{-1} at 4 am and to 14.9 g km^{-1} h^{-1} at 8 am. The high emission levels are registered during the morning, after 8 am, until evening, while the low emission levels are estimated during the night.

3.3. Meteorological inflow boundary conditions

Several CFD simulations were performed over the computational domain D2, in the **second step**, for 24th September 2010, for both the baseline morphological and the baseline green scenarios. The meteorological inflow conditions for these CFD simulations were obtained from mesoscale simulations using WRF model [41]. The mesoscale simulations were conducted over Continental Portugal with a horizontal grid resolution of 5 km. The meteorological data for 24th September 2010 are presented in **Figure 6**, i.e., the hourly average wind speed (**Figure 6a**) and wind direction (**Figure 6b**).

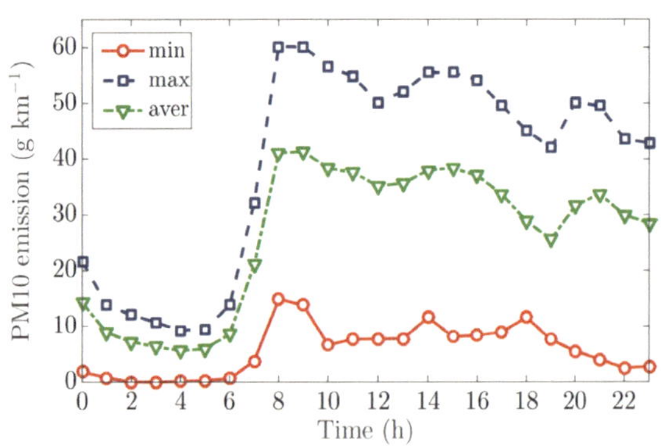

Figure 5. Hourly maximum, minimum and average values of PM10 emissions.

http://dx.doi.org/10.5772/intechopen.72972

The hourly wind speed (**Figure 6a**) ranges from low to moderate wind speed conditions, between 0.1 m s^{-1}, during the night at 5 am, and 6.5 m s^{-1}, during the afternoon at 3 pm, while the wind direction (**Figure 6b**) varies from South-Southwest to North-Northeast, blowing predominantly from the 4th quadrant. The high wind speed is registered during daylight time, between 8 am and 6 pm. In addition, the friction velocity ranges from a minimum near zero to a maximum of 1 m s^{-1}. The aerodynamic roughness length was calculated in an hourly basis from the vertical wind profile and ranges from 0.8 to 2.2 m.

3.4. Meteorological data for recent past and future medium-term climate

The meteorological results in **Figure 7** show the greatest reduction of wind speed in the first autumn months in the mid-term future climate, compared to the recent past climate. For the remaining seasons, the simulation results only show negligible variations with any clear trend. The simulation results show a slight decrease in the average number of days with moderate to strong wind speed or higher and a slight increase in the average number of days recording low wind speed conditions, in the future medium-term climate.

Temperature data show an annual average increase of about 1.1°C in the mid-term future climate. **Figure 8** shows the minimum and maximum monthly values of temperature, together with the monthly average values. Monthly maximum temperatures increase almost every month. The highest anomaly records are projected for summer and autumn, e.g., in July (one of the hottest months), the anomaly points out an increase of 5°C. The monthly minimum temperatures also increase, again with the largest anomalies occurring in the summer and autumn time.

The number of heat waves in the mid-term future climate increases about seven times compared to recent past climate. The average of duration of the heat waves also increases and the days with the maximum temperature greater than 35°C increase 4 times. The results also show an increase in the number of summer days and tropical nights. Although for the recent past climate the greatest number of heat waves occurs during spring and summer time, in the mid-term future climate, these extreme events will occur in summer and autumn time.

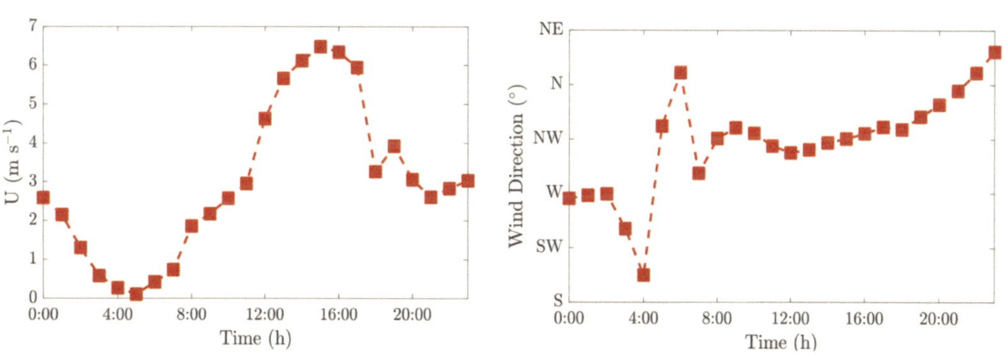

Figure 6. Hourly meteorological data, for 24th September 2010, simulated using the WRF model and used as inflow data in the CFD simulations: (a) wind speed and (b) wind direction.

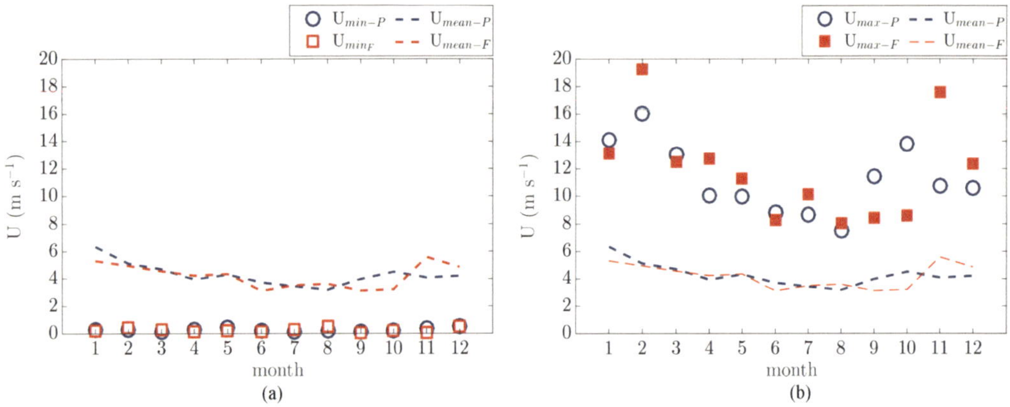

Figure 7. Extreme events recorded in the recent past and the future medium-term climate: (a) minimum and (b) maximum monthly values of wind speed, together with the monthly average values.

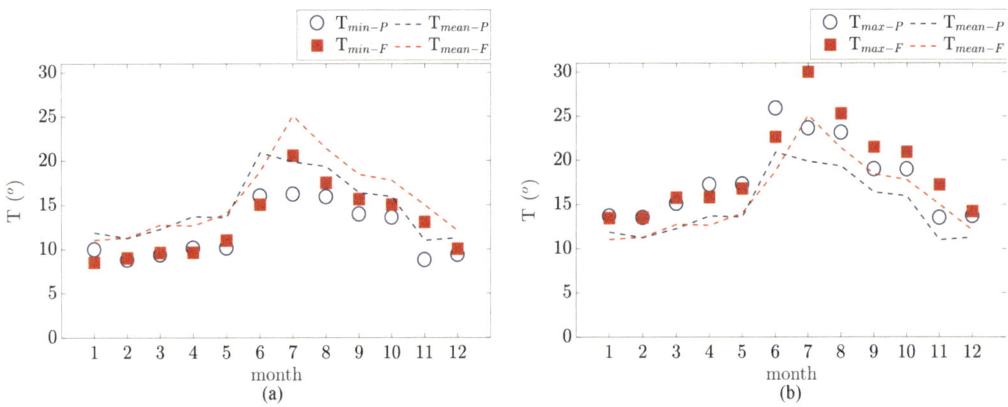

Figure 8. Extreme events recorded in the recent past and the future medium-term climate: (a) minimum and (b) maximum monthly values of temperature, together with the monthly averaged values.

4. Assessment of GI effects on flow dynamics using CFD and wind tunnel simulations

The effects of green infrastructures on flow dynamics are assessed by comparison between the baseline morphological scenario and the corresponding green scenario, in the first step of this study. Then, the accuracy of the numerical and physical results is evaluated through the comparison between both results and the estimation of statistical parameters.

4.1. Impact of GI on flow dynamics

Figure 9 shows the measured and simulated data for the baseline and the green scenarios and for an inflow wind blowing from North with wind speeds of 3 and 9 m s^{-1}, as example.

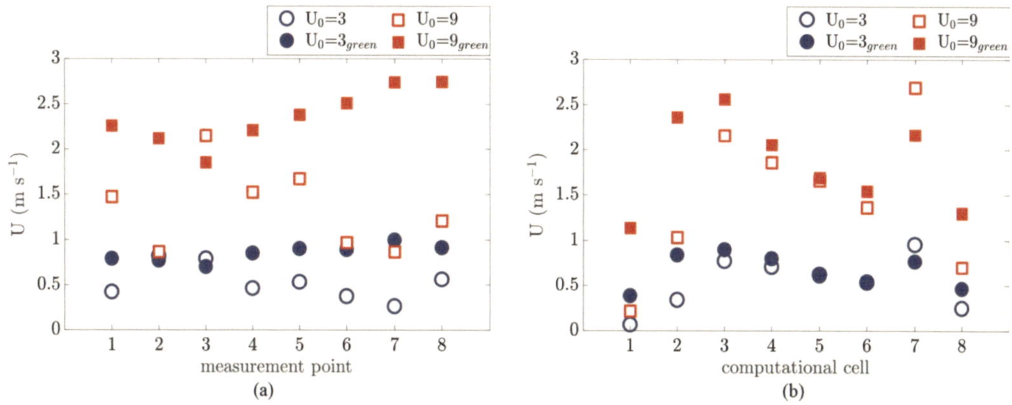

Figure 9. Comparison between the wind speed from the baseline and the green scenario: (a) measured in the wind tunnel and (b) simulated with the CFD model. These results are obtained from the numerical and physical simulations with an inflow wind blowing from North.

Hereafter, the effects of GI are studied in terms of increase or decrease of wind speed registered in the green scenario, when compared to the baseline. In the specific case of an inflow wind from North direction, point 8 is located immediately upstream from a barrier of trees, within one of the implemented green parks. At this location, both the CFD and wind tunnel results are in accordance, predicting an increase of wind speed in the green scenario. The increase of wind speed ranges between 0.4 and 1.5 m s^{-1} in the wind tunnel measurements, and between 0.3 and 0.9 m s^{-1}, in the CFD simulations, corresponding to an inflow wind speed of 3 and 9 m s^{-1}, respectively. Following in this section, the data analysis consistently correspond to an inflow wind speed of 3 and 9 m s^{-1}, respectively. Points 1 and 6 are located in the West and East boundaries of the street canyon, and in those points, both CFD and wind tunnel results point out an increase of wind speed. CFD results indicate an increase of wind speed, within the cell corresponding to the point 1 location, of 0.5 and 1.4 m s^{-1}, while the wind tunnel measurements denote an increase of 0.4 and 0.8 m s^{-1}. In point 6, the CFD model simulates a negligible increase of wind speed of 0.02 m s^{-1} and then an increase of 0.3 m s^{-1} (in the simulation with an inflow wind speed of 9 m s^{-1}). The wind tunnel results show an increase of wind speed of 0.5 and 1.5 m s^{-1}. Immediately downstream the newly implemented green parks are located points 2 and 7. CFD results show an increase of 0.4 and 1.4 m s^{-1}, in point 2, and a decrease of 0.3 and 0.5 m s^{-1} in point 7, whereas the wind tunnel measurements point out a negligible decrease of 0.1 m s^{-1} and an increase of 1.3 m s^{-1}, for inflow wind speeds of 3 and 9 m s^{-1}, in point 2, and an increase of 0.7 and 1.9 m s^{-1}, in point 7. Points 3–5 are located downstream far from the main avenue, but the results indicate some perturbations exerted by GI. CFD results show an increase of 0.2 and 0.6 m s^{-1}, in point 3, an increase of 0.1 and 0.3 m s^{-1}, in point 4, and a slight decrease of 0.03 m s^{-1} and a slight increase of 0.1 m s^{-1}, in point 5. The wind tunnel data show a decrease of 0.1 and 0.3 m s^{-1}, in point 3, and an increase of 0.4 and 0.7 m s^{-1}, for both points 4 and 5.

In conclusion, both numerical and physical results point out an overall increase of wind speed and a good agreement between CFD simulations and wind tunnel measurements to predict this trend. Exceptions are found in point 3, in the wind tunnel results, and in point 7, in CFD simulations, where a decrease of wind speed is registered.

Figure 10 presents the measured and simulated data for an inflow wind blowing from West. The effects of GI are over again studied in terms of increase or decrease of wind speed registered in the green scenario, when compared to the baseline.

In the specific case of an inflow wind from West direction, point 1 is located at the inlet of the domain and upstream the newly implemented green areas. At this location, the wind tunnel results present negligible differences of wind speed for the green scenario compared to the baseline. However, at the same location, the CFD results show a more significant impact of the green scenario pointing out a decrease of 0.4 and 1.4 m s^{-1}, in the simulations with inflow wind speeds of 3 and 9 m s^{-1}. Points 2 and 7 are located in the main avenue of the street canyon, near the adapted area, and are strongly affected by the presence of the new green areas. The wind tunnel results show an increase of 0.2 and 0.5 m s^{-1}, in point 2, and an increase of 0.5 and 1.5 m s^{-1}, in point 7. Thus, the location downstream in the street canyon is more affected by the GI. On the contrary, in CFD simulations, the effects of GI are more relevant in point 2, with an increase of wind speed of 1 and 3 m s^{-1}, while in point 7, an increase of 0.1 and 0.4 m s^{-1} is registered. Therefore, CFD and wind tunnel results are not in good agreement if analyzed in-depth locally. At the location of point 8 within the second green park, the wind tunnel results show an increase of 0.5 and 1.3 m s^{-1}, while the CFD results show a slight decrease of 0.3 and 0.6 m s^{-1}. Points 3 and 4 are located away from the intervention area, and an insignificant effect was theoretically expected. However, the wind tunnel results show an increase of wind speed of 0.8 and 2.1 m s^{-1}, in point 3, and an increase of 0.5 and 1.4 m s^{-1}, in point 4. CFD results point out an increase of wind speed of 0.5 and 1.4 m s^{-1}, in point 3, and a decrease of wind speed of 1 and 2.1 m s^{-1}, in point 4. At the locations of points 5 and 6, at the outlet of the domain, CFD results show negligible increases of wind speed, less than 0.1 m s^{-1}. Wind tunnel results point out significant increases of wind speed of around 1 m s^{-1}, for an inlet speed of 9 m s^{-1}, and of 0.7 and 0.8 m s^{-1}, at points 5 and 6, for an inflow wind speed of 3 m s^{-1}. The differences between points 5 and 6 are negligible, for both CFD and wind tunnel results, even if, theoretically, point 6 should be more affected by the green infrastructures, due to its location at the end of the street canyon.

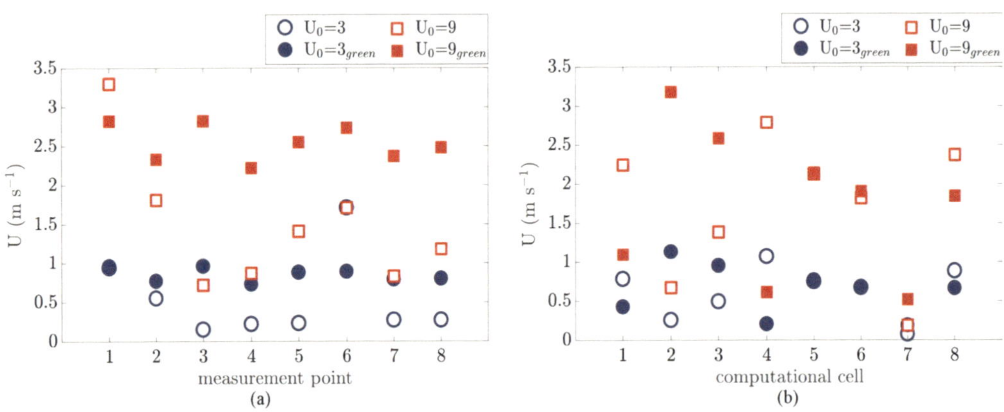

Figure 10. Comparison between the wind speed from the baseline and the green scenario: (a) measured in the wind tunnel and (b) simulated with the CFD model. These results are obtained from the numerical and physical simulations with an inflow wind blowing from West.

In conclusion, at a location nearby the implemented green areas the wind speed tends to increase, both in wind tunnel and CFD simulations. CFD and wind tunnel results do not agree at point 8, with relevant increase of wind speed predicted by the measurements, and a slight decrease of wind speed simulated by the CFD model.

4.2. Assessment of CFD performance

The CFD performance is evaluated by comparison with the wind tunnel measurements, using the validation metrics, such as the normalized mean square error (NMSE) and the fraction of simulated values within a factor of two of the measured values (FAC2), based on the metrics formula proposed by [58]. The normalized mean square error obtained for each set of wind speeds and directions ranges between 0.3 and 1 (inflow wind from Southeast and West, respectively) in the baseline scenario, while in the green scenario, the obtained NMSE ranges from 0.1 to 0.7 (inflow wind from North and Southeast, respectively). The factor FAC2 ranges between 0.9, for an inflow wind from Southeast, and 1.7, for an inflow wind from North, in the baseline scenario, and between 0.6 and 1.2 in the green scenario (over again for an inflow blowing from Southeast and North, respectively).

The acceptance criteria establish a value less than 1.5 for the NMSE. The fraction of the simulated values within a factor of two of the measured values in the wind tunnel should comprise between 0.5 and 2, following the acceptance criteria. Therefore, we can conclude that the CFD simulation results and the measured data in the wind tunnel are in good agreement, based on the acceptance criteria, for each set of wind speeds and directions, as well as for both the baseline and the green scenarios. Consequently, the obtained validation metrics confirm the ability of the CFD model to simulate the perturbation exerted by the green infrastructures on the turbulent flow dynamics.

Finally, both numerical and physical results denote the effects of green infrastructures on flow dynamics. Consequently, the demonstrated effects on flow dynamics should affect the air quality patterns.

5. Assessment of GI effects on particulate matter dispersion

Several CFD simulations were performed to assess the impact of green infrastructures on flow dynamics and, consequently, on PM10 dispersion, corresponding to **step 2** of this study. Furthermore, the comparison between the CFD simulation results and the PM10 concentrations measured at the air quality station will allow assessing the performance of the CFD model.

5.1. Assessment of CFD performance

Figure 11 presents the comparison between the hourly simulated and the measured PM10 concentrations at the AQS (in a 2 h time-basis average), on 24th September 2010. The daily averaged PM10 concentration value, from the measurements and the simulation results, is less than the established legal daily limit value of 50-μg m^{-3} (2008/50/EC Directive). **Figure 11**

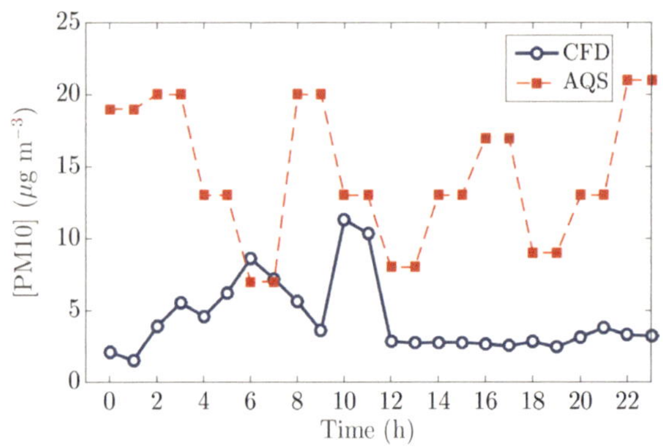

Figure 11. Comparison between hourly PM10 concentrations simulated by the CFD model and measured at the AQS.

points out a disagreement between the PM10 concentrations, simulated by the CFD model and measured at the AQS, and the traffic dynamics, mainly during night period. In addition, PM10 concentrations point out an overall underestimation by the CFD model.

The CFD performance is also evaluated using the validation metrics, i.e., the normalized mean square error and the fraction of simulated values within a factor of two of the measured values. The normalized mean square error is equal to 2.1, and the factor FAC2 is equal to 0.3. Thus, the NMSE is above the maximum value, defined equal to 1.5 as acceptance criteria, and the FAC2 is lower than the minimum accepted value of 0.5. Therefore, the CFD simulation results denote a weakness of the CFD model to simulate the impact of green infrastructures on particulate matter dispersion, when only considering the particulate matter emissions from road traffic.

5.2. Impact of GI

The impact of green infrastructures on PM10 dispersion is analyzed in an hourly basis on 24th September 2010. **Figures 12** and **13** present the differences of wind speed (**Figures 12a** and **13a**) and of PM10 concentrations (**Figures 12b** and **13b**), between the green and the baseline scenarios. These figures present the absolute differences at 1.5 m high. In addition, both **Figures 12** and **13** correspond to distinct inflow conditions in terms of emission rates; that is, **Figure 12** shows the differences at 4 am, during night and with low emission rates. **Figure 13** shows the differences at 8 am, in the morning and with high emission rates (the emission rates for each road segment are presented in **Figure 4** for these 2 h, as example).

Figure 12 shows the simulation results at 4 am initialized with a prevailing wind blowing from South-Southwest and a low wind speed of 0.3 m s^{-1}. The obtained maximum wind speed is equal to 0.79 m s^{-1}, in the baseline, and 0.84 m s^{-1}, in the green scenarios. In addition, the obtained maximum of PM10 concentration is equal to 13.6 and 29.6 μg m^{-3}, in the baseline and the green scenarios, respectively. The differences plotted in **Figure 12a** correspond to 38% of zero differences, 46% of positive differences, pointing out an overall increase of wind speed in the green scenario, and 16% of negative differences. In addition, we found 3% increases of wind speed of more than 0.1 m s^{-1} and 1% decreases of more than 0.1 m s^{-1}. **Figure 12b** denotes 69% of zero differences in PM10 concentrations, 15% of positive differences, and 16% of negative differences, indicating a similar number of occurrences of increases or decreases of PM10 concentrations. Furthermore, PM10 concentrations show 1% of increase above 0.1 μg m^{-3} and 0.5% of decrease below 0.1 μg m^{-3}.

http://dx.doi.org/10.5772/intechopen.72972

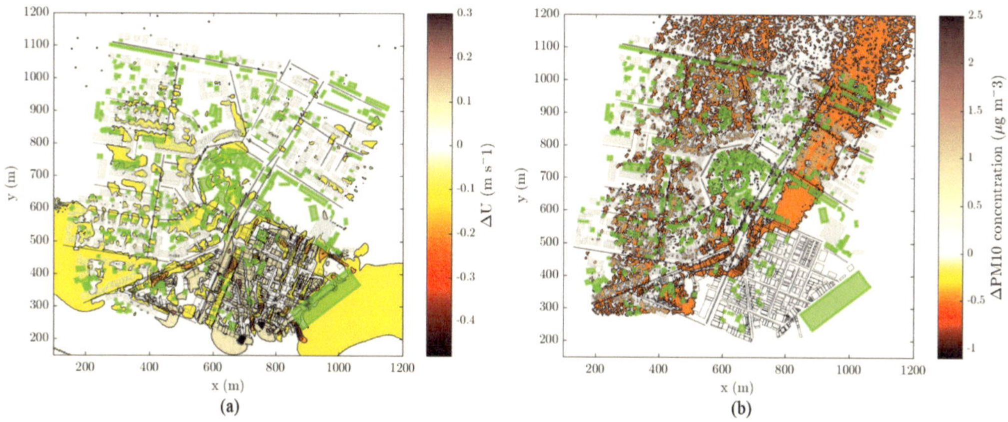

Figure 12. Horizontal iso-contour plots at 1.5 m high, at 4 am. (a) Differences of wind speed and (b) differences of PM10 concentrations between the green and the baseline scenario.

Figure 13 shows the simulation results at 8 am initialized with a prevailing wind blowing from Northwest and a wind speed of 2 m s^{-1}. The obtained maximum wind speed is equal to 4.7 m s^{-1}, in the baseline, and 4.5 m s^{-1}, in the green scenarios. In addition, the obtained maximum of PM10 concentration is equal to 16.9 and 60.3 μg m^{-3}, in the baseline and the green scenarios. The differences plotted in **Figure 13a** correspond to 39% of zero differences, 42% of positive differences, pointing out, over again, an overall increase of wind speed in the green scenario, and 19% of negative differences. Moreover, we found 4% increases of wind speed of more than 0.3 m s^{-1} and 3% decreases of more than 0.2 m s^{-1}. **Figure 13b** denotes 64% of zero differences in PM10 concentrations, 20% of positive differences and 16% of negative differences, indicating a similar number of occurrences of increases or decreases of PM10 concentrations. In addition, PM10 concentrations show 3% of increase above 0.1 μg m^{-3} and 0.8% of decrease below 0.1 μg m^{-3}.

Therefore, the implementation of green infrastructures promotes slight increases and decreases of wind speed. Specifically, the results denote a maximum increase of 0.34 m s^{-1} and a maximum decrease of 0.48 m s^{-1}, at 4 am, while at 8 am the variations of wind speed are found more

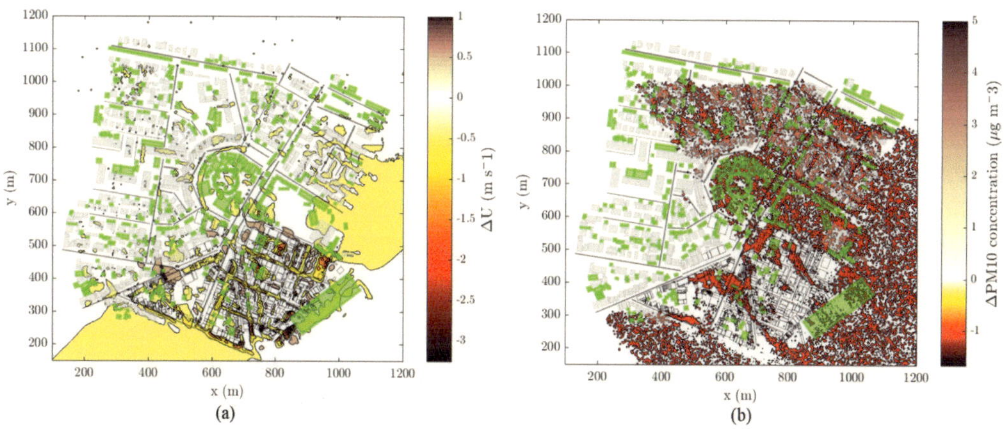

Figure 13. Horizontal iso-contour plots at 1.5 m high, at 8 am. (a) Differences of wind speed and (b) differences of PM10 concentrations between the green and the baseline scenario.

significant, with a maximum increase of 1.5 m s^{-1} and a maximum decrease of 3.3 m s^{-1}. These extreme variations of wind speed are recorded within the implemented green areas and in its surroundings. The perturbations exerted by GI on flow dynamics are more significant for higher inflow wind speeds. Consequently, these perturbations influence also the PM10 dispersion. Thus, the PM10 dispersion results in the green scenario point out an increase of PM10 concentrations of 3 μg m^{-3}, at 4 am, and of 6 μg m^{-3} at 8 am, and a maximum decrease in concentrations of 1.1 μg m^{-3}, at 4 am, and of 2 μg m^{-3}, at 8 am. The magnitude of the PM10 concentration variations is greater at 8 am, than at 4 am, mainly due to the distinct inflow conditions in terms of wind speed and emission rates.

Theoretically, increases of wind speed ($\Delta U > 0$) in a green scenario will led to enhanced dispersion of particulate matter, with lower concentrations in the green scenario ($\Delta C < 0$), compared to the baseline. On the contrary, a decrease of wind speed ($\Delta U < 0$) in a green scenario will promote the retention of pollutants, with an increase of PM10 concentrations ($\Delta C > 0$). However, for positive differences of wind speed, at 4 am, we have found 13% of positive and 10% of negative differences of PM10 concentrations (plus 19% of zero differences of concentrations), while for negative differences of wind speed, we have found 6% of positive and 5% of negative differences of PM10 concentrations (plus 8% of zero differences). Zero differences of wind speed mostly correspond to zero differences of concentrations (36%), with negligible positive and negative differences (~3%). At 8 am, positive differences of wind speed led to 7% of positive and 7% of negative differences of PM10 concentrations (plus 32% of zero differences of concentrations), while for negative differences of wind speed, we have found 2% of positive and 2% of negative differences of PM10 concentrations (plus 12% of zero differences). Zero differences of wind speed mostly correspond to zero differences of concentrations (25%), with a total of positive and negative differences equal to 14%. These results point out a nonlinear relationship between the wind speed and consequent pollutant dispersion patterns.

In conclusion, the overall effects of green infrastructures on air quality show that local air quality is strongly dependent on the linkages between meteorological conditions, the urban morphology and the emission rates.

A new set of CFD simulations were performed to assess the impact of green infrastructures on flow dynamics and, consequently, on PM10 dispersion, under recent past and medium-term future climate, corresponding to **step 3** of this study. The climate results presented in section 3.4 pointed out a decrease in the number of days with moderate to strong wind speed and an increase of low wind speed conditions, unfavorable conditions to air pollutant dispersion. Thus, CFD simulations under climate change were performed for the four cardinal directions, north, east, south and west, and the four intercardinal directions, northeast, southeast, southwest and northwest, for inflow wind speed representative of low wind speed conditions, i.e., 1 m s^{-1}, and for strong wind conditions, 6 m s^{-1}. The set of emission rates for each road segment obtained at 4 am, as example of low emission rates, and at 8 am, as example of high emission rates, was used as inflow conditions.

The effects of green infrastructures depend on inflow meteorological conditions and emission rates. Considering only the changes on the flow dynamics in medium-term climate, i.e., changes almost negligible in wind speed, the assessment of the effects of green infrastructures

http://dx.doi.org/10.5772/intechopen.72972

procedure is similar to the one performed previously to the baseline climate (in 2010). The obtained conclusions for the baseline climate are also valid for medium-term future climate. The advantages of GI found in **Figures 12** and **13**, as well as the disadvantages, can be linearly predicted to medium-term climate.

6. Conclusions

The increased occurrence of extreme weather events and air pollution episodes, because of climate change, can cause a wide range of impacts on society, economy and environment.

This chapter presents a CFD model as a valid tool to assess climate change effects at local scale, and the role of green infrastructures as adaptation measures to increase resilience of urban areas. The CFD model presents a good performance for the simulation of flow dynamics. However, the model presents some weakness to simulate particulate matter dispersion. Therefore, the understanding of the influence of turbulent flow dynamics and the distinct emission sources contributing to fine particulate matter pollution still present a set of uncertainties. Furthermore, the most relevant conclusion of this analysis is the lack of understanding of the overall effects of GI on flow dynamics and pollutant dispersion. Future efforts should focus on the improvement of our understanding of the overall perturbations exerted by urban vegetation on the urban boundary layer.

Climate-driven changes in meteorology may also modify the natural emission patterns. In addition, future climate will also affect human activities, leading to an impact over the anthropogenic emissions. These key parameters should be taken into account, and as ongoing work on future projections of emissions, scenarios are being considered at local-scale simulations.

The results of this study present an important contribution to develop a set of adaptation measures, supported by scientific-based knowledge, from urban to district and street level, considering the geographical, demographical, economic and environmental characteristics of each urban area.

Acknowledgements

The authors would like to acknowledge the financial support of CLICURB project (EXCL/AAG-MAA/0383/2012), supported in the scope of the European Funds through COMPETE and by National Funds through the Portuguese Science Foundation (FCT) within project PEst-C/MAR/LA0017/2013. The authors further acknowledge COST Action FP1204 "Green Infrastructures Approach: linking environmental with social aspects in studying and managing urban forests" (GreenInUrbs). The authors also acknowledge the Portuguese "Ministério da Ciência, Tecnologia e Ensino Superior" for the PhD grants of Sandra Sorte (SFRH/BD/117164/2016) and Sandra Rafael (SFRH/BD/103184/2014).

Author details

Vera Rodrigues[1]*, Sandra Rafael[1], Sandra Sorte[1], Sílvia Coelho[1], Hélder Relvas[1], Bruno Vicente[1], Joana Leitão[1,2], Myriam Lopes[1], Ana Isabel Miranda[1] and Carlos Borrego[1]

*Address all correspondence to: vera.rodrigues@ua.pt

1 CESAM & Department of Environment and Planning, University of Aveiro, Aveiro, Portugal

2 Institute for Advanced Sustainability Studies (IASS), Potsdam, Germany

References

[1] EEA. The European Environment—State and Outlook 2015: Synthesis and Report. Copenhagen: European Environment Agency; 2015

[2] Ciscar JC, Feyen L, Soria A, et al. Climate Impacts in Europe. The JRC PESETA II Project. Publications Office of the European Union: European Commission, Joint Research Centre, Institute for Prospective Technological Studies; 2014

[3] Field CB, Barros VR, Mach KJ, et al. Climate Change 2014: Impacts, Adaptation, and Vulnerability. Part A: Global and Sectoral Aspects. Contribution of Working Group II to the Fifth Assessment Report of the Intergovernmental Panel on Climate Change. Cambridge, United Kingdom and New York, NY, USA: Cambridge University Press; 2014

[4] UN-HABITAT/WHO. Hidden Cities: Unmasking and Overcoming Health Inequities in Urban Settings. World Health Organization: The WHO Centre for Health Development, Kobe, and United Nations Human Settlements Programme (UN-HABITAT); 2010

[5] United Nations (UN). World Urbanization Urban Prospects: The 2014 Revision, Highlights. United Nations: Department of Economic and Social Affairs, Population Division; 2014. DOI: Report ST/ESA/SER.A/352

[6] EEA. Urban adaptation to climate change in Europe 2016: Transforming cities in a changing climate. Copenhagen: European Environment Agency; 2016. DOI: Report no 12/2016

[7] Roy S, Byrne J, Pickering C. A systematic quantitative review of urban tree benefits, costs and assessment methods across cities in different climatic zones. Urban Forestry & Urban Greening. 2012;**11**:351-363

[8] Churkina G, Grote R, Butler TM, Lawrence M. Natural selection? Picking the right trees for urban greening. Environmental Science and Policy. 2015;**47**:12-17

[9] O'Brien L, De Vreese R, Kern M, Sievänen T, Stojanova B, Atmis E. Cultural ecosystem benefits of urban and peri-urban green infrastructure across different European countries. Urban Forestry & Urban Greening. 2017;**24**:236-248

[10] Grote R, Samson R, Alonso R, Amorim JH, Cariñanos P, Churkina G, Calfapietra C. Functional traits of urban trees: Air pollution mitigation potential. Frontiers in Ecology and the Environment. 2016;**14**(10):543-550

[11] Carrus G, Scopelliti M, Lafortezza R, Colangelo G, Ferrini F, Salbitano F, Agrimi M, Portoghesi L, Semenzato P, Sanesi G. Go greener, feel better? The positive effects of biodiversity on the well-being of individuals visiting urban and peri-urban green areas. Landscape and Urban Planning. 2015;**134**:221-228

[12] Zuvela-Aloise M, Koch R, Buchholz S, Früh B. Modelling the potential of green and blue infrastructure to reduce urban heat load in the city of Vienna. Climatic Change. 2016;**135**:425-438

[13] Steeneveld GJ, Koopmans S, Heusinkveld BG, Theeuwes NE. Refreshing the role of open water surfaces on mitigating the maximum urban heat island effect. Landscape and Urban Planning. 2014;**121**:92-96

[14] Theeuwes NE, Solcerova A, Steeneveld GJ. Modelling the influence of open water surfaces on the summertime temperature and thermal comfort in the city. Journal of Geophysical Research Atmospheres. 2013;**118**(16):8881-8896

[15] Roth M. Review of atmospheric turbulence over cities. Quarterly Journal of Royal Meteorological Society. 2000;**126**:941-990

[16] Oke TR. Initial Guidance to Obtain Representative Meteorological Observations at Urban Sites. Geneva: World Meteorological Organization; 2016. Reference Report: WMO/TD no 1250

[17] Blackman K, Perret L, Savory E, Piquet T. Field and wind tunnel modelling of an idealized street canyon flow. Atmospheric Environment. 2015;**106**:139-153

[18] Masson V, Gomes L, Pigeon G, Liousse C, Pont V, Lagouarde J-P, Voogt J, Salmond J, Oke TR, Hidalgo J, Legain D, Garrouste O, Lac C, Connan O, Briottet X, Lachérade S, Tulet P. The canopy and aerosol particles interactions in TOulouse urban layer (CAPITOUL) experiment. Meteorology and Atmospheric Physics. 2008;**102**:135-157

[19] Lateb M, Meroney RN, Yataghene M, Fellouah H, Saleh F, Boufadel MC. On the use of numerical modelling for near-field pollutant dispersion in urban environments—A review. Environmental Pollution. 2016;**208**(Part A):271-283

[20] Connan O, Laguionie P, Maro D, Hébert D, Mestayer P, Rodriguez F, Rodrigues V, Rosant J-M. Vertical and horizontal concentration profile from a tracer experiment in a heterogeneous urban area. Atmospheric Research. 2015;**154**:126-137

[21] Franzese P, Huq P. Urban dispersion modelling and experiments in the daytime and nighttime atmosphere. Boundary-Layer Meteorology. 2011;**139**:395-409

[22] Carpentieri M, Hayden P, Robins AG. Wind tunnel measurements of pollutant turbulent fluxes in urban intersections. Atmospheric Environment. 2012;**46**:669-674

[23] Chavez M, Hajra B, Stathopoulos T, Bahloul A. Near-field pollutant dispersion in the built environment by CFD and wind tunnel simulations. Journal of Wind Engineering and Industrial Aerodynamics. 2011;**99**:330-339

[24] Efthimiou GC, Berbekar E, Harms F, Bartzis JG, Leitl B. Prediction of high concentrations and concentration distribution of a continuous point source release in a semi-idealized urban canopy using CFD-RANS modelling. Atmospheric Environment. 2015;**100**:48-56

[25] Di Sabatino S, Buccolieri R, Pulvirenti B, Britter R. Simulations of pollutant dispersion within idealised urban-type geometries with CFD and integral models. Atmospheric Environment. 2007;**41**:8316-8329

[26] Blocken B, Janssen WD, van Hooff T. CFD simulations for pedestrian wind comfort and wind safety in urban areas: General decision framework and case study for the Eindhoven University campus. Environmental Modelling & Software. 2012;**30**:15-34

[27] Blocken B. 50 years of computational wind engineering: Past, present and future. Journal of Wind Engineering and Industrial Aerodynamics. 2014;**129**:69-102

[28] Blocken B, Tominaga Y, Stathopoulos T. CFD simulation of micro-scale pollutant dispersion in the built environment. Building and Environment. 2013;**64**:225-230

[29] Tominaga Y, Stathopoulos T. CFD simulation of near-field pollutant dispersion in the urban environment: A review of current modeling techniques. Atmospheric Environment. 2013;**79**:716-730

[30] Hofman J, Bartholomeus H, Janssem S, Calders K, Wuyts K, van Wittenberghe S, Samson R. Influence of tree crown characteristics on the local PM10 distribution inside an urban street canyon in Antwerp (Belgium): A model and experimental approach. Urban Forestry & Urban Greening. 2016;**20**:265-276

[31] Amorim JH, Rodrigues V, Tavares R, Valente J, Borrego C. CFD modelling of the aerodynamic effect of trees on urban air pollution dispersion. Science of the Total Environment. 2013;**461-462**:541-551

[32] Abhijth KV, Kumar P, Gallagher J, McNabola A, Baldauf R, Pilla F, Broderick B, Di Sabatino S, Pulvirenti B. Air pollution abatement performances of green infrastructures in open road and built-up street canyon environments—A review. Atmospheric Environment. 2017;**162**:71-86

[33] Vos P, Maiheu B, Vankerkom J, Janssen S. Improving local air quality in cities: To tree or not to tree? Environmental Pollution. 2013;**183**:113-122

[34] Gromke C, Blocken B. Influence of avenue-trees on air quality at th urban neighborhood scale: Part II: Traffic pollutant concentrations at pedestrian level. Environmental Pollution. 2015;**196**:176-184

[35] Buccolieri R, Salim S, Leo L, Di Sabatino S, Chan A, Ielpo P, de Gennaro G, Gromke C Analysis of local scale tree-atmosphere interaction on pollutant concentration in idealized street canyons and application to a real urban junction. Atmospheric Environment. 2011;**45**:1702-1713

[36] Jeanjean APR, Monks PS, Leigh RJ. Modelling the effectiveness of urban trees and grass on PM2.5 reduction via dispersion and deposition at city scale. Atmospheric Environment. 2016;**147**:1-10. DOI: 10.1016/j.atmosenv.2016.09.033

[37] Salmond JA, Williams DE, Laing G, Kingham S, Dirks K, Longley I, Henshaw GS. The influence of vegetattion on the horizontal and vertical distribution of pollutants in a street canyon. Science of the Total Environment. 2013;**443**:287-298

[38] Janhäll S. Review on urban vegetation and particle air pollution—Deposition and dispersion. Atmospheric Environment. 2015;**105**:130-137. DOI: 10.1016/j.atmosenv.2015.01.052

[39] Sá E, Martins H, Ferreira J, Marta-Almeida M, Rocha A, Carvalho A, Freitas S, Borrego C. Climate change and pollutant emissions impacts on air quality in 2050 over Portugal. Atmospheric Environment. 2016;**131**:209-224

[40] Markakis K, Valari M, Colette A, Sanchez O, Perrussel O, Honore C, Vautard R, Klimont Z, Rao S. Air quality in the mid-21st century for the city of Paris under two climate scenarios; from the regional to local scale. Atmospheric Chemistry and Physics. 2014;**14**:7323-7340

[41] Skamarock WC, Klemp JB, Dudhia J, Gill DO, Barker DM, Huang XY, Wang W, Powers JG. A description of the Advanced Research WRF version 3. NCAR/TN-475+STR. Boulder, Colorado, USA: National Center for Atmospheric Research; 2008. 113 pp

[42] IPCC. Climate Change 2013: The Physical Basis. In: Stocker TF, Qin D, Plattner G-K, Tignor M, Allen SK, Boschung J, Nauels A, Xia Y, Bex V, Midgley PM, editors. Contribution of Working Group I to the Fifth Assessment Report of the Intergovernmental Panel on Climate Change. Cambridge, United Kingdom and New York, NY, USA: Cambridge University Press; 2013. 1535 pp

[43] Giorgetta MA, Jungclaus J, Reick CH, Legutke S, Bader J, Böttinger M, et al. Climate and carbon cycle changes from 1850 to 2100 in MPI-ESM simulations for the coupled model Intercomparison project phase 5. Journal of Advances in Modeling Earth Systems. 2013;**5**(3):572-597

[44] Launder BE, Spalding DB. The numerical computation of turbulent flows. Computer Methods in Applied Mechanics and Engineering. 1974;**3**(2):269-289

[45] Green S. Modelling turbulent air flow in a stand of widely spaced trees. Journal of Computational Dynamics and its Applications. 1992;**5**(3):294-312

[46] Katul GG, Mahrt L, Poggi D, Sanz C. One- and two-equation models for canopy turbulence. Boundary-Layer Meteorology. 2004;**113**(1):81-109

[47] Kaimal JC, Finnigan JJ. Atmospheric Boundary Layer Flows: Their Structure and Measurement. New York: Oxford University Press; 1994. p. 4289

[48] Poggi D, Porporato A, Ridolfi L, Albertson JD, Katul GG. The effect of vegetation density on canopy sub-layer turbulence. Boundary-Layer Meteorology. 2004;**111**(3):565-587

[49] Raupach MR, Shaw RH. Averaging procedures for flow within vegetation canopies. Boundary-Layer Meteorology. 1982;**22**(1):79-90

[50] Borrego C, Tchepel O, Costa AM, Amorim JH, Miranda AI. Emission and dispersion modelling of Lisbon air quality at local scale. Atmospheric Environment. 2003;**37**:5197-5205

[51] Dimitrova R, Sini J-F, Richards K, Schatzmann M, Weeks M, Perez Garcia E, Borrego C. Influence of thermal effects on the wind field within the urban environment. Boundary-Layer Meteorology. 2009;**131**(2):223-243

[52] Vardoulakis S, Dimitrova R, Richards K, Hamlyn D, Camilleri G, Weeks M, Sini J-F, Britter R, Borrego C, Schatzmann M, Moussiopoulos N. Numerical model inter-comparison for

wind flow and turbulence around single-block buildings. Environment Modeling & Assessment. 2011;**16**:169-181

[53] INE. Censos 2011. Resultados Definitivos—Região Norte: XV recenseamento geral da população e V recenseamento geral da habitação. Lisboa: Instituto Nacional de Estatística. p. 2013

[54] Instituto Português do Mar e da Atmosfera (IPMA). IPMA [Internet]. Available from: https://www.ipma.pt/pt/educativa/tempo.clima/ [Accessed: 07 July 2017]

[55] EEA. EMEP/EEA air pollutant emission inventory guidebook 2009. Technical guidance to prepare national emission inventories. Technical report no 9/2009. Copenhagen, Denmark

[56] CENSUS, 2011. Statistical Data for Portugal [Internet]. 2011. Available from: http://censos.ine.pt

[57] ANSSFP. Autoridade Nacional de Supervisão de Seguros e Fundos de Pensões [Internet]. 2011. Available from: http://www.asf.com.pt

[58] Chang J, Hanna S. Air quality model performance evaluation. Meteorology and Atmospheric Physics. 2004;**87**:167-196

Chapter 8

Computational Fluid Dynamics (CFD) Applied to a Glass Vaporization Chamber for Introduction of Micro- or Nano-Size Samples into Lab-Based ICPs and to a CFD-Derived (and Rapidly Prototyped Via 3D Printing) Smaller-Size Chamber for Portable Microplasmas

Hamid R. Badiei, Gordon Stubley, Ryan Fitzgerald,
Melanie Saddler and Vassili Karanassios

Additional information is available at the end of the chapter

http://dx.doi.org/10.5772/intechopen.72650

Abstract

Computational fluid dynamics (CFD) is used extensively in many industries ranging from aerospace engineering to automobile design. We applied CFDs to simulate flows inside vaporization chambers designed for micro- or nano-sample introduction into conventional, lab-based inductively coupled plasmas (ICPs). Simulation results were confirmed using smoke visualization experiments (akin to those used in wind tunnels) and were verified experimentally using an ICP-optical emission spectrometry (ICP-OES) system with a fast-response photomultiplier tube (PMT) detector, an ICP-OES system with a slower-response charge injection device (CID) detector, and an ICP-mass spectrometry (ICP-MS) system. A pressure pulse (defined as a momentary decrease of the optical emission intensity of ICP background) was not observed when employing widely used ICPs either with a CID detector or with ICP-MS. Overall, the simulations proved to be highly beneficial, for example, detection limits improved by as much as five times. Using CFD simulations as a guide, a rapidly prototyped, 3D-printed and smaller-size vaporization chamber (a scaled-down version of that used with ICPs) is being evaluated for potential use with a portable, battery-operated microplasma. Details are provided in this chapter.

Keywords: computational fluid dynamics, CFD, near-torch vaporization, NTV, ICP-OES, ICP-MS, microplasma, 3D printing, rapid prototyping

INTECH
open science | open minds

1. Introduction

According to Collins English dictionary, computational fluid dynamics (CFD) is "the prediction of the behavior of fluids and other effects of fluid motion past objects by numerical methods rather than experiments." In general terms, CFD simulations use computations based on applied mathematics and (primarily) physics to compute mass transfer, heat transfer, or fluid flow (e.g., a liquid or a gas) constrained by surfaces. It then uses computer graphics and visualization software to display the result of the computations. This way a **simulation** (i.e., a replica (or imitation) of the process being simulated over time) is obtained. Simulations can be used as research tools to predict fluid flow or to obtain insights under defined conditions (e.g., flow of air around an airplanes' wing). They can also be used as design tools to reduce the number of candidate prototypes to be evaluated before a final, experimentally verified design is fabricated. Experimental verification of simulations is often done using smoke experiments (e.g., in a wind tunnel), and this is followed by validation of prototypes (e.g., a test flight).

We used CFD simulations for rational development of vaporization chambers intended for use in elemental analysis of micro- or nano-size samples. One chamber was developed for sample introduction into a lab-size inductively coupled plasma (ICP), which is formed on the top part of an ICP torch and a CFD-derived chamber, smaller version of it for use with a portable, battery-operated, and small-size microplasma.

2. Micro- or nano-sample introduction into ICPs

Why sample introduction? Introduction of an initially ambient temperature sample into a gas-phase plasma (**Figure 1**) is the "Achilles' heel" of ICP spectrometry. Liquid samples are typically introduced into an ICP using a nebulizer requiring ~2 mL/min of sample and with <5% efficiency. Due to poor sample introduction efficiency, detection limits are impaired, and waste disposal issues are created, and due to the requirement for relatively large volumes of sample, micro- or nano-amounts of sample cannot be used.

Why elemental analysis of micro- or nano-samples? In many analytical situations, there is little sample available for analysis, for example, samples of bio-origin (e.g., metalloenzymes, constituting over 30% of all enzymes in the human body). Other examples include samples of clinical origin (e.g., lead (Pb) in the blood, every child in the USA must have Pb concentrations in their blood measured), forensics (e.g., for criminal activity investigations), and samples of interest to nanoscience and nanotechnology (e.g., due to costs involved in making large amounts of nanomaterials). Primarily due to small sample size, introduction of such samples by pneumatic nebulization (**Figure 1**) cannot be used.

How to introduce micro- or nano-samples into lab-size plasma? To replace the nebulizer/spray-chamber combination (**Figure 1**) and to enable micro- or nano-sample analysis capabilities, we have been developing and characterizing an electrothermal, near-torch vaporization (NTV) sample introduction system. An illustration of the NTV system as used by an ICP is shown in **Figure 2**.

http://dx.doi.org/10.5772/intechopen.72650

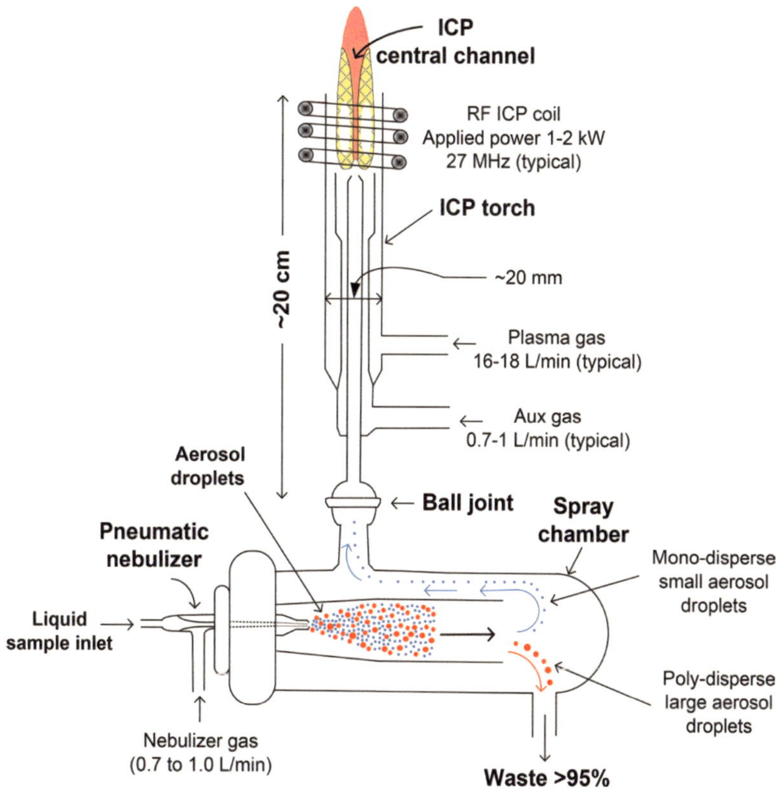

Figure 1. Nebulizer/spray-chamber combination for liquid sample introduction into an ICP torch.

Briefly, the NTV sample introduction system (**Figure 2a**) consists of a vaporization chamber that clips onto any ICP torch with a ball joint (**Figure 1**) and a coil filament made out of rhenium (Re) filament [1–5]. The coil filament is attached to a support rod. Power transfer cables running through the support connect the coiled filament to an external power supply. To deposit a liquid micro- or nano-size sample, the support rod with the coil secured to it is retracted from the vaporization chamber, an aqueous sample is pipetted onto the coil, and the support-rod coil combination with a liquid sample on the coil is reinserted into the chamber. Using an external power supply, low electrical power (e.g., <1 W) is applied to the coil, thus bringing its temperature to about 100°C, and as a consequence drying the liquid sample on the coil. Subsequently, higher electrical power is applied to the coil (e.g., ~50 W), thus raising the temperature of the coil to ~2000°C (or more, depending on applied power). At such temperatures, the dried sample residue that remained on the coil after drying is vaporized, and the vaporized sample is carried to an ICP by the carrier gas where it becomes gas-phase atoms; it gets excited (and/or ionized).

As illustrated in **Figure 2a**, when the support rod is inserted into the vaporization chamber, a seal is formed at the bottom of the chamber, and a vortex is formed inside the chamber. The vortex consists of a cylinder (constrained by the support rod and by the walls of the chamber) and of a cone (**Figure 2b**). In the center of the "cone," a lower-pressure zone is formed due to the vortex

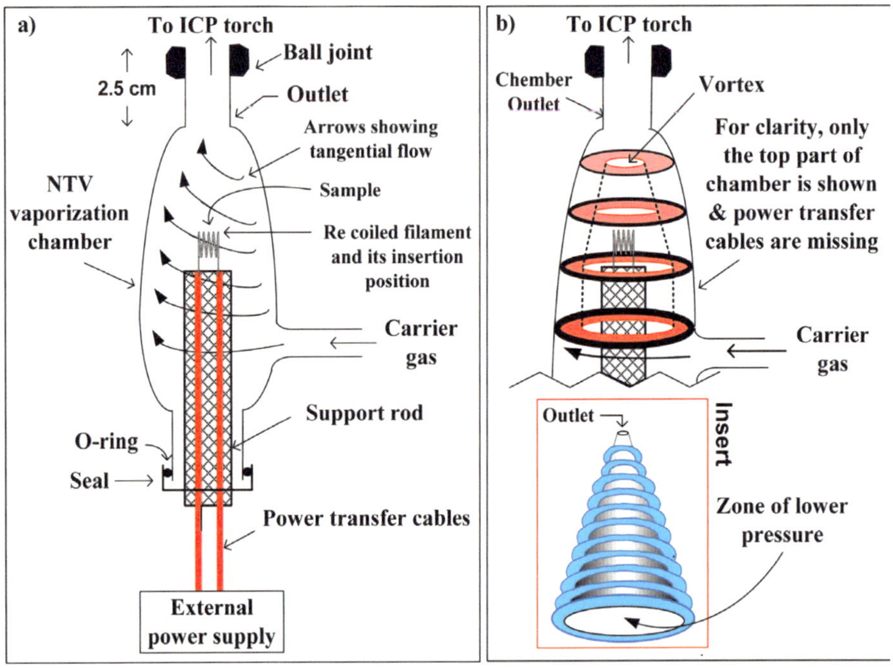

Figure 2. (a) Original, empirically designed vaporization chamber for micro- or nano-sample introduction. The ball joint allows connection to any ICP torch (**Figure 1**) with an appropriate ball joint. (b) Top part of the vaporization chamber (for clarity, only a few arrows—Representing hypothetical gas stream lines—Are shown). Insert: Hypothetical, engineered vortex-rings have been added for clarity.

(akin to an inverted vortex formed when draining a sink full of water). This way, the vaporized sample residue is kept in the center of the chamber and away from its walls (thus minimizing sample loss to the chamber walls).

Advantages of NTV (Figure 2) over a pneumatic nebulizer (Figure 1). Due to the use of relative large volumes of sample (e.g., in the mL range), a pneumatic nebulizer cannot be used for micro- or nano-sample introduction into an ICP. Also, due to its poor sample introduction efficiency (<5%), a nebulizer generates a significant amount of potentially hazardous waste (e.g., unused sample containing contaminants). NTV uses micro- or nano-amounts of sample, thus making waste disposal a nonissue. Furthermore, due to the high sample introduction efficiency of NTV (>80%), detection limits (defined as the minimum amount or concentration that can be detected with a stated statistical confidence) improve by a factor of 16 (or more) over those obtained using a nebulizer. Furthermore, although absolute-unit detection limits (pg or pictogram) do not change with volume, those expressed in relative concentration units (e.g., parts per billion or ppb) do. For instance, by changing sample volume from 5 μL to 50 μL, concentration detection limits improve by factor of 10. Experimental verification of this is provided in Section 8.3. Getting back to this ample, an overall improvement of detection limits of 160 (over those obtained with a nebulizer) can be realized. In chemical analysis, detection limits are a significant consideration and are considered by many as the key figure of merit.

Comparison of NTV with its main competitor. Electrothermal vaporization (ETV) from graphite supports is the main competitor to NTV for micro-sample introduction into ICPs. Absolute amount (in pg) detection limits are compared in **Table 1** (for ICP-optical emission spectrometry or ICP-OES). From these data, it can be concluded that NTV does equally as well as the best ever reported detection limits for ETV for Zn, Pb, and Cd and that it outperforms ETV for all other elements tested (e.g., Ca, Ba, Be, Mg, V). For Ca (with NTV-ICP-OES detection limits in the millions of atoms), NTV outperforms ETV by 10,000 times [3]. Clearly, NTV is worthy of further investigation, in this case, using CFD simulations for a rational (rather than empirical) design of a vaporization chamber.

Nature of emission signals generated by NTV sample introduction. An example transient signal obtained by pipetting a Pb-containing liquid sample (100 nL) onto the Re coil, by drying it (e.g., by applying 0.3 W for 2 min to the coil) and by rapidly vaporizing the dried sample residue that remained on the coil (by applying 25 W) and by monitoring the Pb 220 nm spectral line is shown in **Figure 3a**. The transient signal (**Figure 3b**) must be digitized using a relatively fast data acquisition rate (e.g., 100 Hz).

The pressure pulse is due to a momentary expansion of the carrier gas inside the sealed vaporization chamber (**Figure 2**) caused by the rapidly heated coiled filament (with a maximum heating rate of ~6000 °C per s). As the carrier gas expands, its flow rate increases. This momentary increase in flow rate is cooling the central channel of the ICP (**Figure 1**), thus decreasing plasma background emission intensity (and hence the dip in intensity shown in **Figure 3a**). The intensity depends on ICP power (e.g., ranging from 1 to 2 kW), on the wavelength monitored (as background intensity increases from 200 to 400 nm) and on the electrical power level applied to the coil. Electrical power applied to the coil translates to temperature of the coil, for example, from 25 W (~1800°C) to 60 W (~2750°C).

Would the pressure pulse complicate CFD simulations? To address this question, the pressure pulse was studied using experimental conditions that amplify significantly the intensity of the

Element	Wavelength (nm)	Detection limit (pg)	
		NTV (5 μL)	ETV (5 μL)
Zn	213.856	0.8	0.6–800
Pb	220.353	4	4–6500
Cd	228.802	0.8	1–600
Mg	279.553	0.03	0.1–5
V	309.311	0.09	5.9–2000
Be	313.042	0.09	5.9–2000
Ca	393.366	0.0003	15
Ba	455.403	0.07	0.3–0.5

Table 1. Comparison of detection limits between NTV-ICP-OES and ETV-ICP-OES [3].

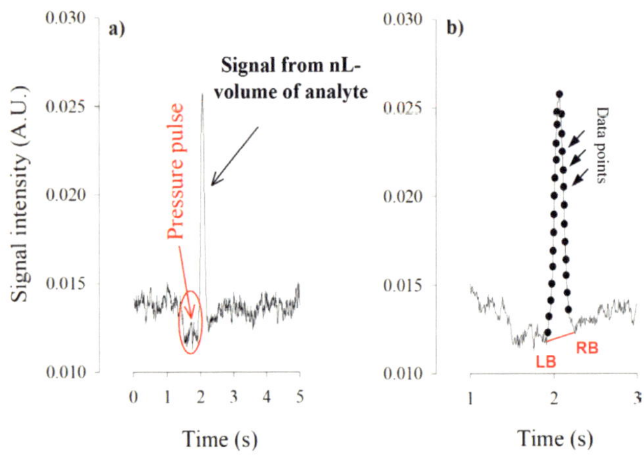

Figure 3. (a) Transient Pb signal: A momentary dip in plasma background intensity (a.k.a., a pressure pulse) is shown encircled. (b) Same as (a) but with the time axis expanded to show where the left background (LB) and right background (RB) correction points should be set for net peak height measurement or for net peak area integration. Filled circles show acquired data points (data were acquired for the entire duration of the signal; for clarity only a few points are shown).

pressure pulse (**Figure 4**). Lead (Pb) was monitored using the 220 nm spectral line, and it was chosen due to its high volatility (thus requiring a relatively low vaporization power of 25 W) and due to its low emission wavelength (where plasma background emission intensity is low).

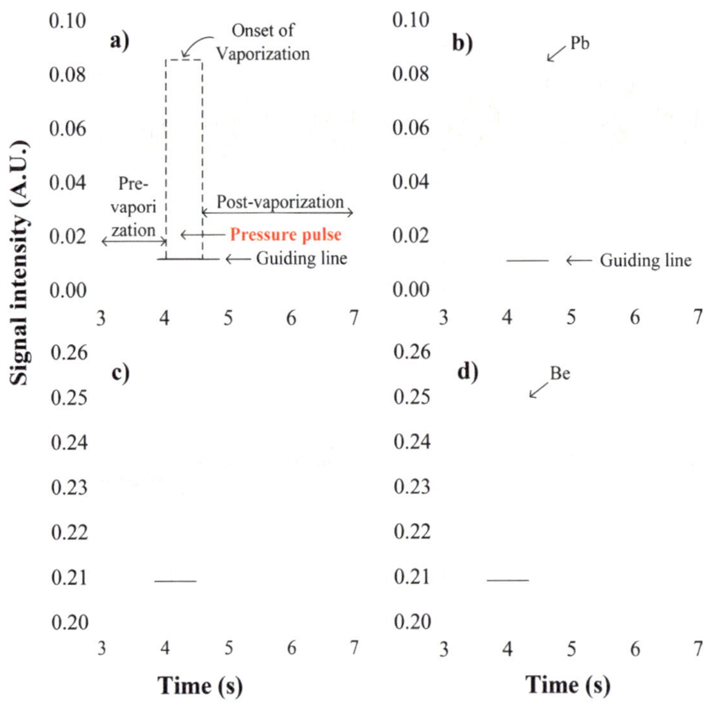

Figure 4. Transient signals obtained by running water blanks or Pb or Be (beryllium) analytes (i.e., the chemical species of interest). (a) Water blank at 220 nm and (b) a signal from a Pb (at 220 nm). And (c) signal obtained from a water blank at 313 nm and (d) from Be (at 313 nm).

Beryllium (Be) was selected due to its low volatility (thus requiring a relatively high vaporization power of 60 W) and its higher emission wavelength (at 313 nm, where plasma background emission intensity is higher than it is for Pb).

To facilitate discussion, the signal in **Figure 3a** is subdivided into three segments: a pre-vaporization event (with no electrical power applied to the coil), a vaporization event (with power applied to the coil), and a post-vaporization event (with continuous application of power for 10 s, the x-axis has been expanded for clarity). Thus, information about plasma emission is obtained before, during, and after vaporization.

For both Pb and Be (**Figure 4b** and **d**), the pre-vaporization plasma emission intensity has the same magnitude as the post-vaporization. However, for Be (**Figure 4c** and **d**), the post-vaporization background intensity did not return to its pre-vaporization level. There are two likely reasons for this. One, as the heated carrier gas reaches the ICP, some plasma energy is freed up (i.e., energy that would otherwise have been used to heat the carrier gas); thus background emission intensity increases. And two, some light emitted in the visible range of the spectrum by the glowing Re coil enters the spectrometer. However, background correction is not affected. As a sample starts to vaporize, the width of the pressure pulse decreases, but this is compensated for by setting the proper background correction points (**Figure 3b**). From these observations and from the observed linearity of calibration curves for many elements, it can be concluded that there is no need to take into consideration the pressure pulse in the CFD simulations.

3. Experimental: Using an ICP-OES system in a lab

An optical ICP spectrometer with a **fast-response p**hoto**m**ultiplier **t**ube (**PMT**) detector was mainly used (**Figure 5**) [2]. This spectrometer was selected due the sensitivity of the PMT and because transient signals can be acquired simultaneously from several PMT channels at 100 Hz, thus making it ideal for transient signals and for the study of a pressure pulse. It should be noted that faster heating rates and higher vaporization powers applied to the coil (corresponding to vaporization temperatures) generally translate to taller peak heights, to better **s**ignal-to-**n**oise **r**atios (**SNRs**) and to improved detection limits. They also translate to **a more intense pressure pulse**.

4. Fate of analytes in the chamber during vaporization

The phenomena taking place immediately after vaporization of a dried sample residue on a coil are influenced by the design of the vaporization chamber and by gas-flow dynamics. These can be grouped into two categories: the physical/chemical properties of the **analyte** (defined as chemical species of interest) and the sample's **matrix** (defined as whatever the analyte is in) and the processes that take place as the vaporized sample travels from the top of the coil to the outlet of the chamber.

To generalize [6–10] and unless an element (or a compound) of interest in the dried sample residue on the coil sublimes, to be vaporized, the solid residue must first become a liquid. As

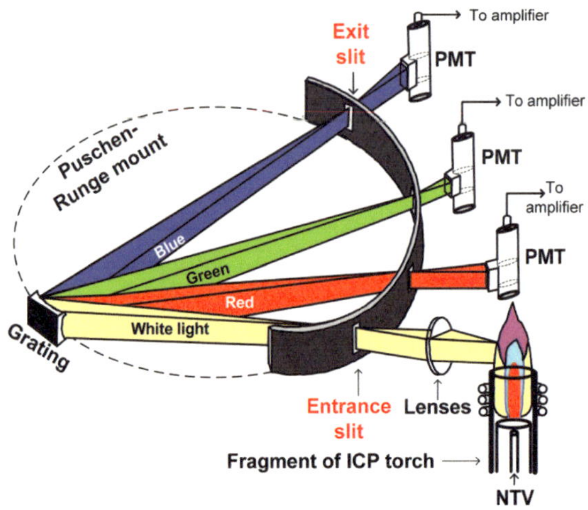

Figure 5. PMT-based, simultaneous optical spectrometer. See text for discussion.

the temperature of the coil increases, the residue first becomes a liquid, and then the liquid is vaporized. Nucleation takes place in the gas phase; the vapor condenses forming a particle-loaded aerosol with a critical particle diameter d_p. The value of d_p depends on parameters such as surface tension of the liquid droplet (σ), the molecular volume of the vapor species (V_m), the temperature (T, in Kelvin), and the saturation ratio (S). These parameters are related by the following equation (Eq. (1), where, k is the Boltzmann constant):

$$d_p = 4\sigma \frac{V_m}{k \cdot T \cdot \ln S} \quad (1)$$

The saturation ratio (S) is a measure of analyte supersaturation and is determined by dividing the partial vapor pressure p_{vap} (in atm) of the analyte of interest by the value of the equilibrium vapor pressure of a particular species at the temperature of nucleation (Eq. (2)):

$$S = \frac{p_{vap}}{p_{(T)}} \quad (2)$$

As the temperature of the surface of the Re coil increases and the analyte begins to vaporize, the partial pressure p_{vap} of an analyte in the carrier gas also increases. This can be estimated using the following equation (Eq. (3)):

$$p_{vap} = \frac{N_s \cdot T_g \cdot R}{V_g \cdot t_v} \quad (3)$$

where N_s is the number of moles of vapor from the evaporated sample, T_g is the initial temperature of the carrier gas, R is the gas constant, V_g is the flow rate of the carrier gas at T_g, and t_v is the mean evaporation time of the main portion of the sample.

From these equations it can be inferred that as the partial vapor pressure of the analyte (p_{vap}) increases (by increasing the temperature of the coil), the saturation ratio (S) also increases (Eq. (2)). Therefore, the critical diameter (d_p) of condensed particles in the aerosol shifts to smaller diameters (Eq. (3)), and as a result, the concentration of analyte particles (e.g., the number of particles per unit volume) increases.

Once an aerosol has been formed on top of the coil, a set of forces inside the chamber determine both particle size and fate of particles as they travel inside the chamber toward its outlet. For example, under the influence of a temperature gradient in the carrier gas (which is hotter closer to the coil and cooler on the chamber walls), particles in the aerosol tend to move toward the lower temperature region of the chamber. This phenomenon is known as *thermophoresis* (or *thermomigration*) [11–13]. Thermophoresis causes dispersion (i.e., causing a plug of aerosol to become wider), thus moving particles from the center of the chamber (ideally where they should be) toward the walls of the chamber (and may even be causing particle adhesion to the walls of the chamber thus possibly causing sample losses).

5. Toward an ideal vaporization chamber

From the foregoing it can be concluded that an **ideal** vaporization chamber prevents dilution (in the gas phase) of a vaporized sample inside the chamber by keeping the analyte (as much as possible) in the center of the chamber. This also reduces adhesion of vaporized particles on the walls to the chamber (thus reducing analyte loss). Narrower and shorter plugs of analyte (i.e., narrower spatially and shorter temporally) also minimize diffusion and thermomigration (both of which are time-dependent). In general, narrower and shorter plugs of vaporized sample generate sharper and more intense signals for the same amount of sample. Generally, more intense signals translate into improved detection limits.

From a practical point of view, geometrical simplicity of a vaporization chamber is an asset, at least from the point of view of its fabrication using a glassblower. For example, the original design was empirical (**Figure 2a**) and admittedly rather difficult to reproduce (from an exact geometrical shape and dimensions' point of view). Thus, an **ideal** chamber should have a well-defined and easy-to-reproduce geometry. An example of such a chamber is shown in **Figure 6**.

The "ideal" chamber (**Figure 6**) consists of a cone sitting on top of a cylindrical barrel. This design is akin to an inverted dust-sorting cyclone with well-defined dimensions. From the

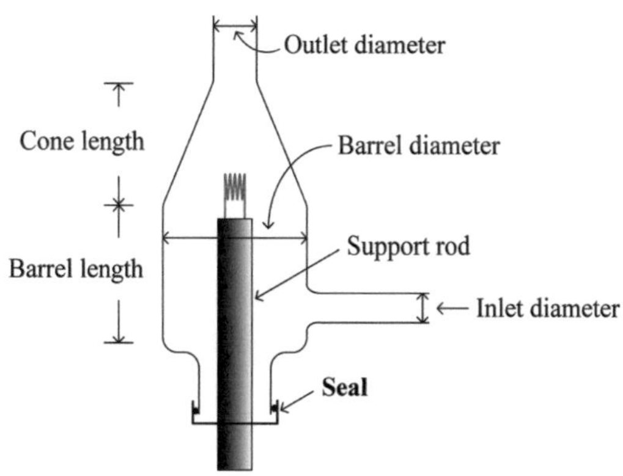

Figure 6. "Ideal" vaporization chamber. Dimensions are missing because they were decided based on the results of the simulations (as will be discussed in a later section). Power transfer cables running through the support rod and the external power supply have been omitted for simplicity.

practical point of view, glassblowing such an ideal chamber with reproducible and well-defined dimensions is easier to fabricate than an empirical one (**Figure 2**). Similar types of arguments apply to simulations.

6. Computational fluid dynamics for an ideal chamber

In simple terms, the key idea behind CFD is to use a computer to simulate fluid-flow, heat-transfer, and associated phenomena. At present, CFD simulations have found applicability in multibillion dollar-a-year industries, including automobile, aircraft, and aerospace. In this case, vaporization chambers can be "designed" and "tested" on a computer screen before being fabricated (typically by a manual, glassblowing process) and prior to being tested by an (expensive to purchase and operate) ICP.

The physical aspects of fluid flow are governed by three fundamental principles: conservation of mass (continuity equation), conservation of momentum (Navier–Stokes equations), and conservation of energy. These principles are described by partial differential equations and have been described elsewhere [14–20], so they will not be repeated. Computational fluid dynamics discretizes and replaces the differential equations by algebraic equations so that numerical solutions can be computed. The CFD software we used was originally developed in Waterloo, Canada, and it is now available from ANSYS Corp.

6.1. Steps required for simulation of an NTV chamber

There are three basic steps to a simulation: preprocessing, numerical solutions of equation (e.g., using a solver), and postprocessing. These will be discussed in conjunction with an NTV chamber.

6.2. Preprocessing

In preprocessing, the flow pattern to be simulated is transformed from a diagram into a form suitable for use by software. There are several steps taking place during preprocessing. Briefly:

(a) The target geometry of the fluid-flow domain is defined in computer terms.

(b) The physical phenomena (e.g., fluid flow, heat transfer) to be modeled are selected.

(c) The fluid properties (e.g., density, viscosity) and their values are entered into the software.

(d) Appropriate boundary conditions are specified on the flow domain boundaries (e.g., walls, inlets).

(e) A grid (or mesh) is generated; an example is shown in **Figure 7**. The target geometry is subdivided into small, nonoverlapping controlled volumes or elements or subdomains (also called cells).

Profiles of gas velocity, gas pressure, and gas temperature are calculated at the nodes of each cell. The accuracy of the calculations depends on the number of cells, and the larger the number

http://dx.doi.org/10.5772/intechopen.72650

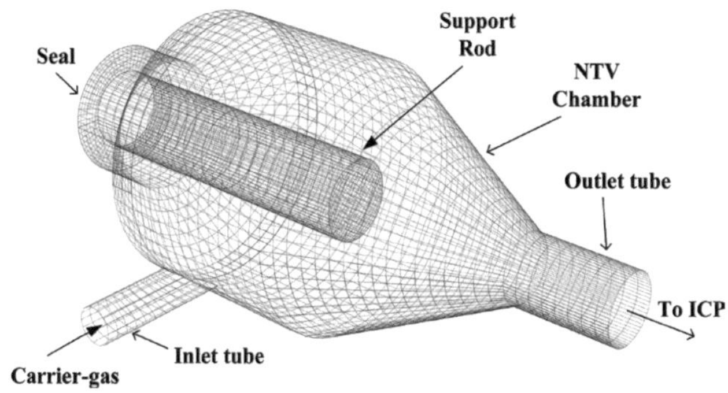

Figure 7. Meshed vaporization chamber with ~16,000 finite control volumes used for preprocessing.

of cells, the better the accuracy. But, there is a limit as to how many cells can be included, and this limit is set by the speed of the calculations and hence time and cost. A compromise number of cells were used in this project.

6.3. Numerical flow simulation using the "solver"

For the simulation, the algebraic equations are derived from the appropriate differential equations and are solved by employing an iterative method. Briefly, in the "solver" (as is called in the software used for this work), a finite volume method is used, and this involves the following steps:

(a) The equations that govern fluid flow are integrated over all finite control volumes (**Figure 7**).

(b) The algebraic equations are solved using an iterative method and an initial guess as a starting point.

(c) The iterations continue until an acceptable convergence is obtained.

In addition to the steps listed above, the operation of the solver requires the use of additional parameters. Although many of these parameters are employed using their default values, others must be explicitly set by the user. Included among them are the time step for the evolution of flow (i.e., each iteration is treated as a step forward in time), the choice of discretization scheme, and the selection of output fields. Although the focus is on steady-state simulations of fluid flow, a transient evolution is also used (as required to account for the rapidly heated Re coil). The choice of an appropriate time step is important because it dictates the rate of convergence. Good convergence was obtained when a time step was set to about 30% of the average residence time a parcel of fluid spends in the chamber. Also, the variation of gas-flow velocities and pressure inside the chamber (including flow fields between each node) were approximated to form discrete equations. These approximations are referred to as the "discretization scheme." There are different discretization schemes in the CFD software we used, the upwind differencing scheme was selected because it is suitable for highly convective flows and because it takes into consideration flow direction. In general, the solution of the algebraic equations is the most computationally intensive. In the version of the software we used, the operation of the solver is displayed using a graphical diagnostic tool in a separate window (called the solver monitor). At the end of each simulation, the results of the solver monitoring window can be saved to a file for future reference.

6.4. Postprocessing and visualization of simulations

The postprocessor provides graphical and quantitative information of the results calculated by the "solver." Examples of data visualization tools include grids, x-y plots, vector plots, animations, and fringe plots. A color fringe plot is similar to a contour plot with each color band representing a range of values, but unlike contour plots, control over the width of each color band is not allowed. To provide readable fringe plots when using black-and-white printing, only a couple of color fringe plots have been included in this chapter. As a replacement of color fringe plots, 2D plots at two different locations in the vaporization chamber are included instead. In addition, animations are a very useful visualization tool because they provide an overall progress (over time) of the dynamics of gas flow. For this chapter, individual frames were extracted from animations and were included. The results of the simulations of the NTV chamber will be presented next, aided by some of the data visualization tools mentioned above.

6.4.1. Pressure profile

A fringe plot of the pressure profile inside the chamber and on a plane cutting through the center of the chamber along its length is shown in **Figure 8a**. A region of higher pressure is shown at the bottom of the chamber and directly opposite to the carrier-gas inlet. The simulations

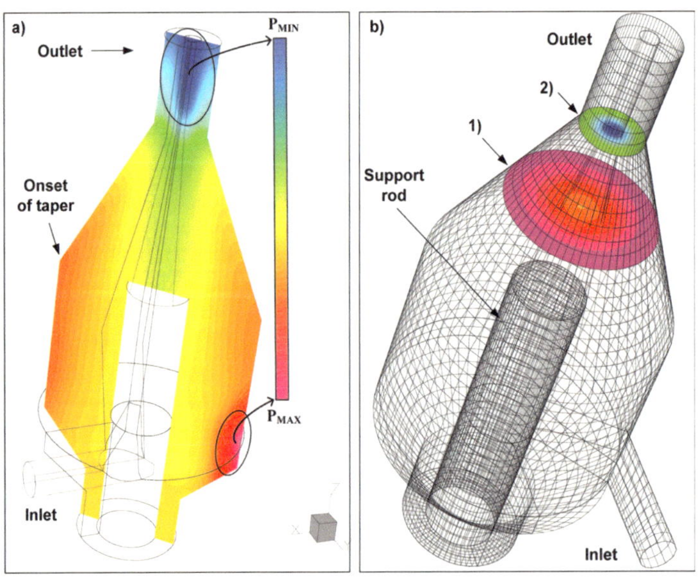

Figure 8. (a) Fringe plot of the pressure profile inside the chamber on a plane cutting through the chamber along its length (outline of chamber has been included). (b) Meshed vaporization chamber, identifying locations 1 and 2 that were used in subsequent figures.

show that there is (relatively) higher gas pressure on the walls of the chamber rather than in its center. As the chamber begins to taper (and it becomes narrower), the carrier gas generates a region of (relatively) lower pressure in the center of the chamber (as compared to the walls of the chamber). This was anticipated as shown in **Figure 2b**.

To illustrate pressure differences (important especially when using a black-and-white printed version of this work), fringe plots have been omitted, and 2D versions of pressure *versus* radial distance inside the chamber were selected for two locations (**Figure 8b**) inside the chamber. The results are shown in **Figure 9**.

The plots shown in **Figure 9** were purposely plotted using the same value for the y-axis to show the pressure drop as the chamber tapers and a vortex is formed. Using the dashed lines (**Figure 9**) as a guide, these plots reveal that pressure drops across the chamber (i.e., from the walls toward the center of the chamber) and that the pressure profiles are not ideally symmetrical. The slight asymmetry is likely due to the carrier gas being introduced only from one side of the chamber (**Figure 8**).

6.4.2. Tangential velocity profile

The 2D tangential velocity profiles are shown in **Figure 10** for the two positions identified in **Figure 8b**. As shown in **Figure 10a** (for position 1, **Figure 8b**), thc gas velocity at the wall is zero. The tangential velocity then steadily increases; it reaches a maximum, and it then drops to a minimum at the center of the chamber. There is a similar trend on the other side of the chamber but in the opposite direction. Similar trend (**Figure 10b**) was observed for position 2 (**Figure 8b**). In contrast to the data shown in **Figure 10a**, for the data shown in **Figure 10b**, there is an increase in the absolute magnitude of the tangential velocity as the carrier gas flows through the conical part of the chamber (**Figure 8**). In this case, to maintain a constant volumetric flow rate, the tangential gas velocity must increase as the diameter of the chamber decreases. The tangential velocity profiles for either side of the central axis of the chamber are not identical, likely due to the asymmetric introduction of carrier gas to the chamber through one inlet (**Figure 8**).

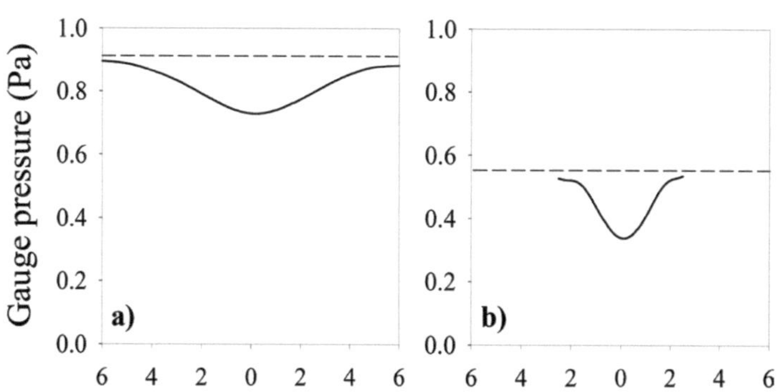

Figure 9. Pressure *versus* radial distance across the chamber's central axis at two cross sections. (a) At 20 mm from the carrier-gas inlet (1 in **Figure 8b**) and (b) at the base of the outlet (2 in **Figure 8b**).

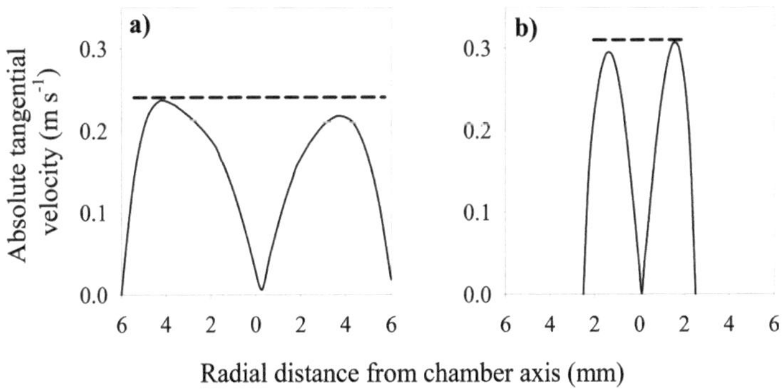

Figure 10. Tangential velocity *versus* radial distance from the chamber axis at two cross sections (**Figure 8b**). (a) At 20 mm above the carrier-gas inlet and (b) at the bottom of the chamber's outlet. The dash lines have been added to facilitate comparisons.

6.4.3. Radial velocity profile

Figure 11 shows radial velocity. This is a vector in the x direction (**Figure 8a**) and is a result of a pressure gradient; it is similar to **Figure 10**, and it is primarily responsible for keeping the analyte in the center of the chamber. As expected, the magnitude of the radial velocity (**Figure 11**) increased as the carrier gas reached the smaller diameter of the chamber. A max radial velocity was observed (at almost) the mid-distance between the wall and the center of the chamber. Imbalances in the magnitude of radial velocity on both sides of the chamber (**Figure 11**) have been observed, and these likely cause the vaporized analyte to be driven slightly away from the center of the chamber and thus somewhat disperse vaporized analytes.

6.4.4. Axial velocity profile

This velocity vector is in the z-direction (**Figure 8a**); it is specifically directed toward the outlet tube of the chamber, and it is responsible for carrying the vaporized analyte out of the chamber.

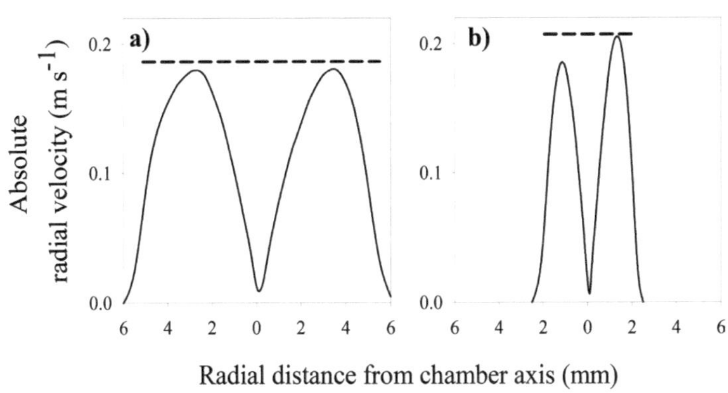

Figure 11. Radial velocity *versus* radial distance from the chamber axis at two cross sections (**Figure 8b**). (a) At 20 mm above the carrier-gas inlet and (b) at the bottom of the chamber's outlet. The dash lines have been added to facilitate comparisons.

http://dx.doi.org/10.5772/intechopen.72650

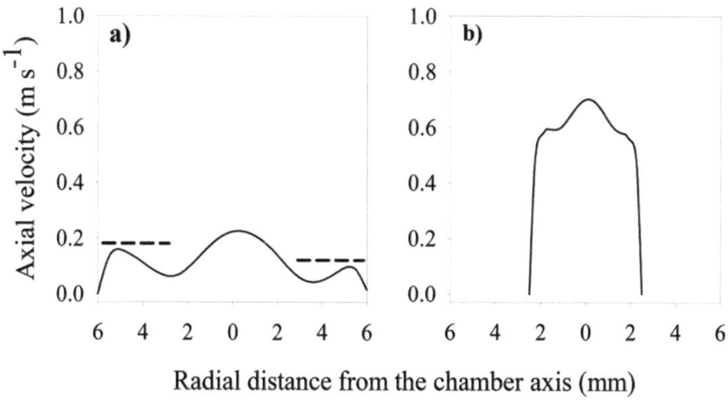

Figure 12. Axial velocity *versus* distance from the chamber axis at two cross sections. (a) At 20 mm above the carrier-gas inlet (**Figure 8b**) and (b) at the bottom of the outlet tube of the chamber. Dash lines have been included to facilitate comparisons.

As shown in **Figure 12**, axial velocity reaches a maximum at the center, and it increases as it reaches the bottom of the outlet of the chamber (**Figure 12b**). At 20 mm (**Figure 12a**), there are two distinct local minima. These are important because if a portion of vaporized analyte enters any of these regions, analyte loss could occur, and a longer (in the time domain) plug of vaporized analyte will be observed. These observations partially explain why carrier-gas-flow rate is an important parameter in NTV.

6.4.5. *Streak lines*

In streak lines, a fluid parcel can be tracked. Shown in **Figure 13** are two color-coded parcels of fluid (e.g., two streak lines). Streak lines can be coded to represent pressure, velocity, or time of arrival.

6.4.6. *Particle tracking, the effect of insertion position, and a dual-inlet chamber design*

Particle tracking permits the release (at a specific location) of a given number of particles (**Figure 14**). The properties of the particles can be set, e.g., their number, their size, their density, their temperature, and the direction of release. Particles follow the mean gas velocity, and by tracking particle position, the velocity and time of arrival at each node can also be followed. The data shown in **Figure 14** reveal the significance of insertion position, a proper insertion position (**Figure 14a**) in which particles are confined within the center of the chamber (thus producing sharp and more intense signals) and an improper insertion position (**Figure 14b**) showing particles dispersed throughout the chamber (thus producing wider signals). As mentioned, the sharper and more intense the analyte signal, the better the signal-to-noise ratio (SNR).

From the results shown in **Figure 15**, it can be concluded that by confining the analyte even more in the center of the chamber (e.g., by using a symmetrical design with a dual tangential inlet), narrower and sharper plugs of analyte would be produced at the outlet, and thus narrower and sharper signals would be measured at the detector. This has been confirmed experimentally, as will be discussed later.

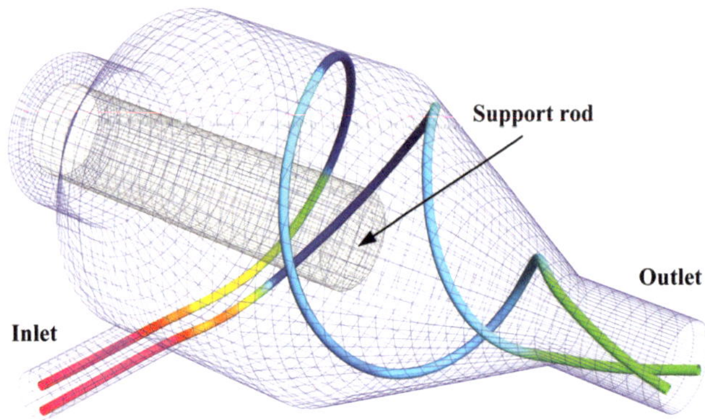

Figure 13. Two streak lines of a fluid parcel (e.g., carrier gas) are shown as they start from the inlet of the chamber, they swirl around inside the chamber, and they exit through its outlet.

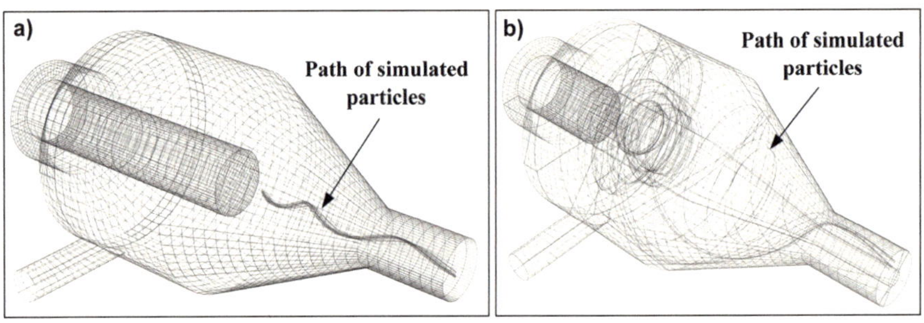

Figure 14. (a) Particles released at ~20 mm for the inlet and (b) particles released at 0 mm from the inlet.

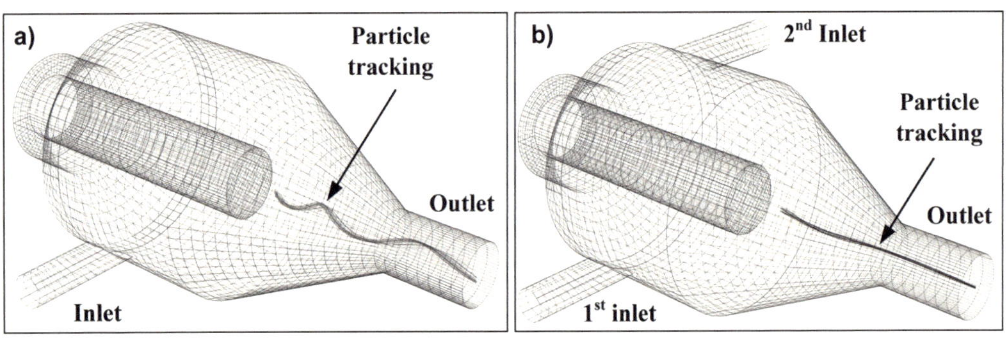

Figure 15. Comparison of two chamber designs: (a) a single-inlet chamber and (b) a dual-inlet chamber (two tangential inlets improve sample confinement within the center of the chamber).

In a separate simulation, the length of the outlet tube of a single-inlet chamber was extended from the typical ~2.5 cm (**Figure 2**) to ~17 cm, so that it would be of the same length as the inner tube of an ICP torch (**Figure 1**). This was done to examine how the extra length affects particle dispersion of vaporized plugs of analyte reaching the plasma. This simulation showed that the vortex formed inside the chamber is extinguished as the gas travels further into the (now) elongated outlet tube. Eventually, the flow becomes laminar (with a higher axial velocity at the center of this elongated tube). The bulk of the vaporized particles remains confined within

http://dx.doi.org/10.5772/intechopen.72650

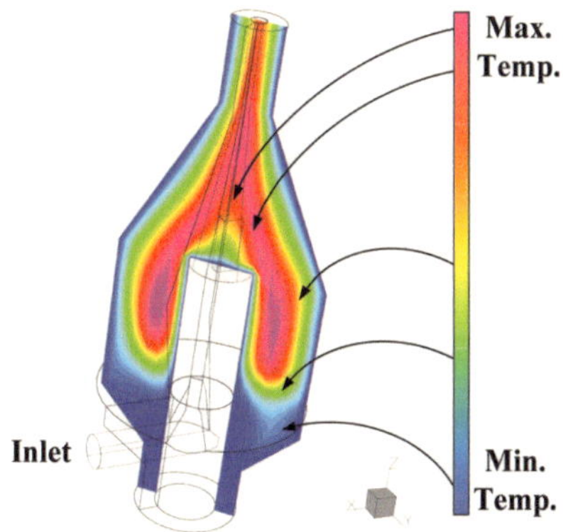

Figure 16. Fringe plot of the temperature profile on a plane cutting through the length of the chamber. An outline of the vaporization chamber has been included for guidance.

the center of the tube. However, the size of the vaporized plug increased by about 50%, thus broadening the peak measured by the detector. This simulation clearly shows that the length of the outlet tube should remain as is (**Figure 2**) and should not be elongated.

6.4.7. Video animations of streak lines or of particle tracking

Video animations are powerful means of visualizing simulations because they provide visual clues on how a gas or the vaporized particles propagate through the chamber in time. The results of a simulation are animated by repeating a simulation multiple times, with each repetition incrementing a key variable (e.g., time). At the end of each simulation, a snapshot is taken, and multiple snapshots are combined (e.g., stitched) together to make a video clip. Both streak lines and particle tracking can be animated. We generated video animations; for completeness, some examples are Internet accessible [21–23].

6.4.8. Simulation of a temperature profile

Heat transfer was also simulated, and a temperature profile inside the vaporization chamber was obtained by enabling the heat-transfer feature of the software used, by setting the vaporization temperature to 2500°C and the temperature of the wall and of the supporting rod to 25°C. Two mechanisms of heat transfer were considered, namely, thermal radiation and convection. An example of a temperature profile is shown in **Figure 16**. The temperature profile shows a relatively high-temperature region below the Re coil and around the support rod. It is likely that heat from the heated coil is radiatively transferred to this region.

7. Chambers designed based on simulation results

Based on the generic design of **Figure 6**, six chambers (**Figure 17**) with varying dimensions (**Table 2**) were simulated. And guided by the results of the simulations, they were fabricated. This was done to experimentally verify the effect of dual inlet, of barrel diameter and length, and of reduced inlet diameter.

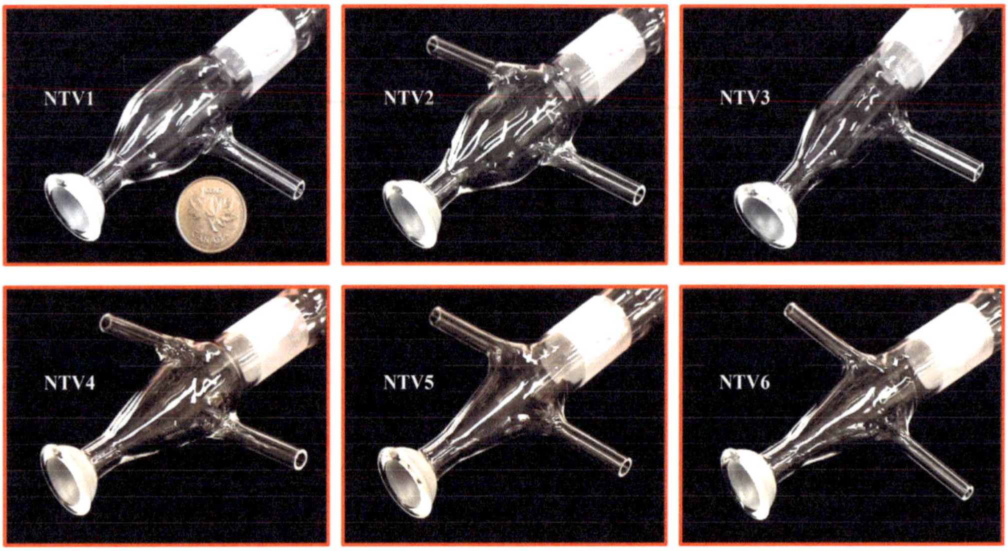

Figure 17. NTV vaporization chambers fabricated as a result of the CFD simulations. Dimensions listed in **Table 2**. A Canadian penny (a 1 cent coin) has been included for size.

From the standard deviations shown in **Table 2**, it can be concluded that the size of the particle plug has been reduced by a factor of ~4 (chambers NTV 1 *versus* NTV 6, **Figure 17**). In other words, chamber NTV6 is expected to produce narrower and sharper analyte signals, i.e., signals with an improved SNR.

Name	Barrel Dia./mm	Barrel Length/mm	Cone Length/mm	Inlet Dia./mm	No. of Inlets	Std. Dev. Time/s*
NTV1	20	15	15	3	1	4.81E-03
NTV2	20	15	15	3	2	4.11E-03
NTV3	15	15	15	3	1	3.52E-03
NTV4	20	7.5	22.5	3	2	3.68E-03
NTV5	15	7.5	22.5	3	2	1.70E-03
NTV6	15	7.5	22.5	2	2	1.15E-03

* The conditions used for the simulations and particle tracking are summarized below:

Fluid Properties
Density: 1.78 kg m^{-3}
Viscosity: 2.29E-5 Pa s
Specific heat (P): 520 J kg^{-1} °C^{-1}
Specific heat (V): 312 J kg^{-1} °C^{-1}

Boundary Conditions
- **Inflow** (steady)
Type: velocity (normal vector)
Flow rate: 0.7 L min^{-1}
- **Outflow** (steady)
Type: pressure (static, applied as face)
Pressure value: 0 Pa (gauge pressure)
- **Wall** (steady)
Type: stationary
Action: particles to reflect from walls

Solver Parameters
- Time step: 0.01 s
- Max. residual: 1.0E-5

Particle tracking
- Density: 4500 kg m^{-3}
- Average dia.: 1.0E-7 m
- Temperature: 1500°C
- Particle Emissivity: 1
- Speed: 1 m s^{-1}
- No. of particles: 200
- Release position: 20 mm from chamber inlet.

Table 2. Dimensions of the vaporization chambers designed and tested.

http://dx.doi.org/10.5772/intechopen.72650

The last column lists the standard deviation of the time of arrival of 200 particles, as determined by the simulations.

8. Experimental verification of CFD simulations

The results of the simulations were initially evaluated using smoke experiments. Subsequently, experimentally obtained results were obtained using three ICP systems: two of them configured for optical emission spectrometry (OES) measurements and one for mass spectrometry (MS) measurements.

8.1. Experimental verification using smoke visualization experiments

Initially, visualization using smoke was used to obtain a confirmation of the results of the simulations. Smoke was generated by pipetting a drop of oil onto the coil, by applying low electrical power to the coil (thus generating smoke) and by videotaping the resulting smoke streaks inside each of the vaporization chambers (**Figure 17**). To facilitate comparisons with the simulations, the chambers used for the smoke experiments were intentionally built the same size as those used for the simulations. Example still frames extracted from corresponding videos for a single-inlet and dual-inlet chambers are shown in **Figure 18**. There is a striking similarity between the simulations (**Figure 15**) and smoke visualization results (**Figure 18**).

For all chambers tested (**Figure 17**), the in situ generated smoke "streaks" were confined within the center of each chamber. Representative examples are shown in **Figure 18**. As shown in **Figure 18a** for a single-inlet chamber, smoke swirled (following a cork-screw-like trajectory) before exiting the chamber through its outlet. For a dual-inlet chamber (**Figure 18b**), smoke streaks roughly followed a straight line from the top of the coil toward the outlet tube of the chamber. It can thus be concluded that dual-chamber designs will produce shorter and sharper signals, therefore resulting in improved signal-to-noise ratios.

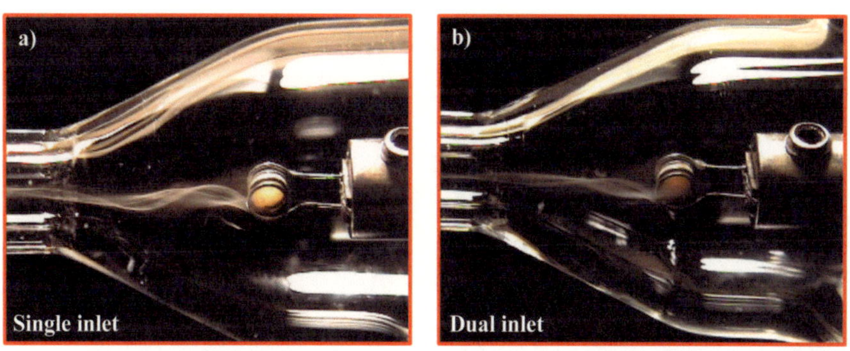

Figure 18. Example frames extracted from videos of smoke experiments. (a) Single-inlet chamber and (b) dual-inlet chamber. See text for discussion.

8.2. Experimental verification using NTV-ICP-OES with a fast-response PMT detector

An axially viewed ICP-AES system with multiple PMT detectors was used (**Figure 5**) [2]. The carrier-gas-flow rate, the coil insertion position, and the vaporization power were the same for all chambers tested (**Figure 17**). Although two elements were tested, for brevity only results for Zn are shown (**Figure 19**).

The effect of chamber design on analyte peak height and peak width is shown for Zn in **Figure 19a**. To facilitate comparisons, the same amount of analyte and the same operating conditions were used throughout (e.g., insertion position, flow rate, vaporization, and ICP power). A comparison of two chambers with otherwise similar dimensions (NTV1 and NTV 2, **Figure 17**) revealed that the chamber with a dual inlet (NTV2) showed sharper signals, thus also confirming the results of the simulations. From a comparison between the two single-inlet chambers (NTV1 and NTV3, **Figure 17**), it can be concluded that reduction of the barrel diameter (e.g., from 20 mm to 15 mm) offers an improvement in signal intensity, and it shows narrower and sharper signals. This was attributed to a higher gas velocity when using a smaller-volume chamber with the same volumetric flow rate. The last two chambers (both dual inlet, NTV5 and NTV6, **Figure 17**) showed significantly more intense signals and comparatively a smaller-intensity pressure pulse. Overall, chamber NTV6 outperformed all other chambers.

Background intensities between **Figure 19a** and **b** are different due to the use of different amplifier gains. The SNR computed using the average net intensity of the reproducibility signals (**Figure 19b**) was 156, thus making the detection limit (using the 3σ criterion) equal to an impressive 0.2 pg (or

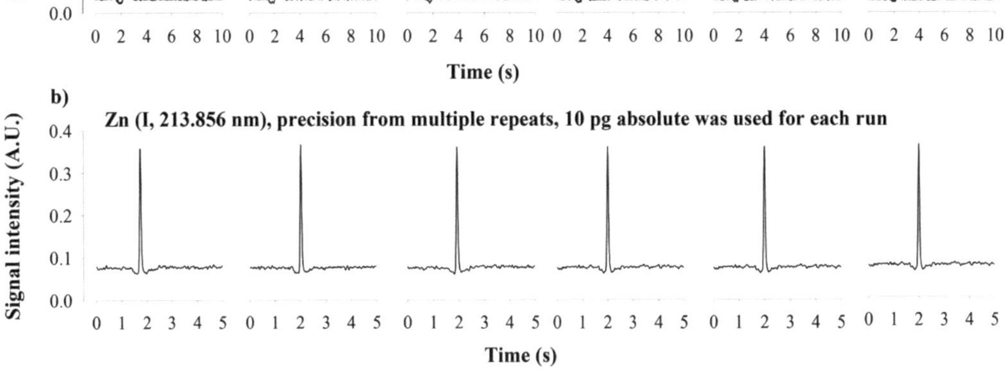

Figure 19. (a) Example signals obtained from Zn (150 pg absolute amount for each run) and for each chamber. (b) Example reproducibility using 10 pg (picogram or 10^{-12} g) of Zn (for each run) using chamber NTV6. For brevity, only the first 6 of 10 consecutive runs are shown.

http://dx.doi.org/10.5772/intechopen.72650

$0.2{\times}10^{-12}$ g) or 200 femtogram (fg, or $200{\times}10^{-15}$ g). Other detection limits were 0.8 pg for Pb and 0.4 pg for Cd. These improved over those listed in **Table 1** (obtained with an empirically designed chamber, **Figure 2**), for example, for Pb by ~5 times. Overall, the detection limits for Pb, Cd, and Zn are now all in the fg range (remarkable for ICP-OES). Precision was less than 2%, and this is similar to what has been reported for the empirically designed chamber. With the dual-inlet design, balancing two flows was challenging.

Overall, the results discussed above are in general agreement with the CFD simulations. The dual-inlet chamber-design-labeled NTV6 (**Figure 17**) incorporated improvements revealed during course of this work. For example, a smaller barrel diameter was used (thus reducing chamber volume and hence analyte dilution in the gas phase). The smaller diameter for the inlet tubes that was employed generated higher carrier-gas velocities; thus for the same absolute amount of analyte, plug was introduced into the ICP, and this generated higher analyte concentration per unit time. Thus taller and sharper signals were measured at the detector, and such signals generated improved SNRs and better detection limits.

Further confirmation of a potential broader utility and applicability of chamber NTV6 (**Figure 17**) was obtained by interfacing this chamber to two other ICP spectrometers: one with a charge injection device (CID) detector and the other an ICP-MS (Agilent model 7700).

8.3. Experimental verification using NTV-ICP-OES with a slow-response CID detector

To evaluate wider applicability of the NTV6 chamber (**Figure 17**), a spectrometer with a CID detector was used. At present, all currently commercially available ICP spectrometers are equipped with an integrating, slow-response detector, either a charge injection device (CID) or a charge coupled device (CCD). By design, integrating detectors cannot acquire data fast enough from transient signals and thus are not well suited for the study of a pressure pulse. The ICP spectrometer with a CID we used was a Thermo Fisher Jarrell Ash Iris (**Figure 20**). This spectrometer can acquire simultaneous data from a max of four wavelengths at a time, with a data acquisition rate of about 40 data points per second. To stretch out (in the time

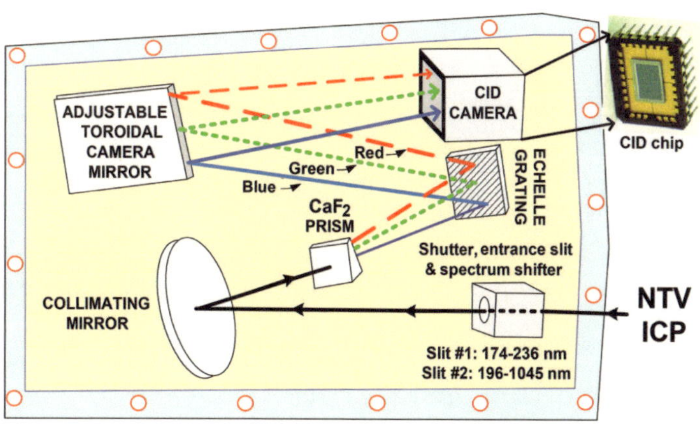

Figure 20. Instrumentation used for validation of chamber design using a spectrometer with a CID detector.

domain) the vaporized "plug" of analyte (and thus acquire signals with more data points), we used relatively lower vaporization powers; thus a measurable pressure pulse was not observed. An example involving Be (Beryllium) monitored using the 313 nm spectral line is shown in **Figure 21**; this is in stark contrast to the Be signal acquired with a PMT detector and shown in **Figure 4d**. Overall, for all elements tested thus far using this system, a pressure pulse was not observed.

8.4. Experimental verification using NTV-ICP-MS: Detection of ions rather than photons

Wider applicability was further demonstrated by interfacing NTV (Chamber NTV6) with an ICP-spectrometer (ICP-MS), in this case an Agilent model 7700, thus replacing detection of photons with detection of ions. By design, an ICP-MS of the type shown in **Figure 22a** with a quadrupole mass spectrometer (more accurately, a mass filter) is sequential rather than simultaneous, and it acquires mass-to-charge (m/z) data at a rate of about 10–100 data points per second (depending on manufacturer). Newer-generation ICP-MS systems can acquire thousands (or more) data points per second, and they can provide quasi-simultaneous measurement capabilities (e.g., PerkinElmer NexION 2000). A pressure pulse is not observed when using

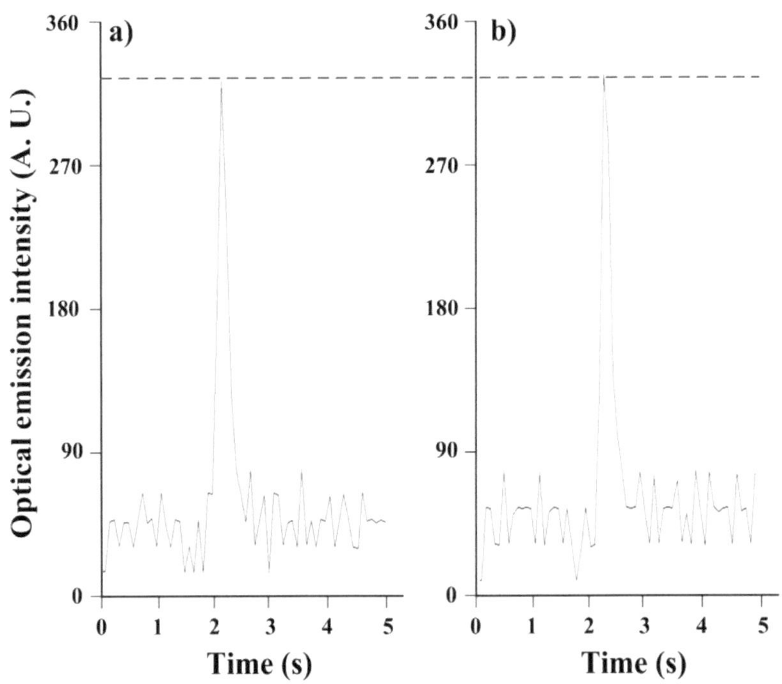

Figure 21. Example signals obtained using NTV and the ICP spectrometer with a CID detector (**Figure 20**). Lack of a pressure pulse at the higher wavelength for Be (at 313 nm) is noteworthy. Also shown is signal-intensity equivalency (per section 2.0 on advantages of NTV), for example, (a) signal obtained from Be by using 1 μL of 10 ppb (part per billion) solution (absolute amount = 10 pg) and (b) signal obtained from 100 μL of 0.1 ppb Be solution (absolute amount = 10 pg) and the same Be 313 nm spectral line. Integration time = 25 ms per data point.

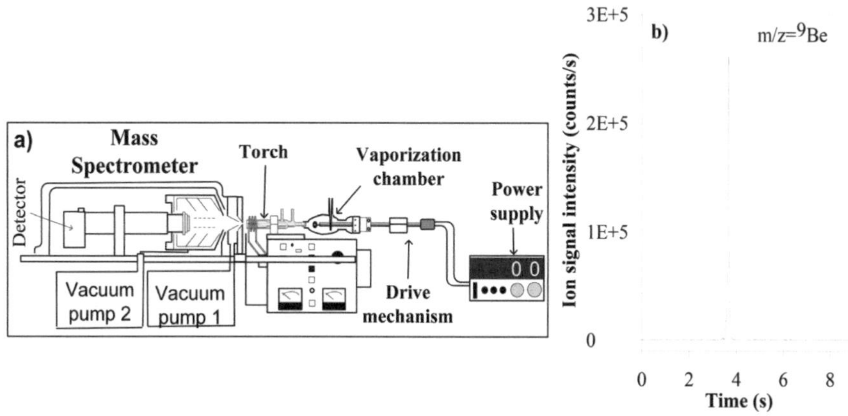

Figure 22. (a) Simplified diagram of ICP-MS. (b) Beryllium (Be) signal demonstrating that there is no pressure pulse when using NTV with ICP-MS.

NTV-ICP-MS because in ICP-MS ions are monitored at specific mass-to-charge ratios, thus making any contribution from plasma background nonexistent. For completeness, ICP-MS is about 1000–10,000 times more sensitive than ICP-OES (primarily due to the very low ICP background observed due to use of a MS). For comparison a signal obtained for Be is shown in **Figure 21b**, and lack of a pressure pulse is noteworthy (**Figure 22b** *versus* **Figure 4d** and **b**).

9. Conclusions drawn by employing ICP systems in a lab

Using smoke visualization experiments and experimentally obtained results by employing an ICP-OES system with a fast-response PMT detector, an ICP-OES system with an integrating (and relatively) slower-response CID detector, and an ICP-MS system, it has been demonstrated that computational fluid dynamics was particularly useful in improving analytical performance characteristics of ICPs. In particular, detection limit improved by a significant factor of ~4. Could similar improvements be obtained using a smaller version of an NTV chamber discussed thus far by coupling it to a portable, battery-operated, small-size microplasma? This question will be briefly addressed next using a rapidly prototyped chamber via 3D printing. 3D printing was selected to reduce costs and time delays when new chambers are needed to be made by the local glassblower.

10. A smaller chamber for microplasmas used in the field

Unlike ICPs discussed thus far that are tethered to a lab floor because they are bulky and heavy and because they require 1–2 kW of electrical power and consume about 20 L/min of expensive Ar gas (**Figure 1**), we have been developing battery-operated microplasmas we made using a variety of technologies ranging from semiconductor fabrication to 3D printing [24–35]. Microplasmas are those with one critical dimension in the micrometer (i.e., sub-mm) regime. We have been characterizing them [24–35], primarily for "taking part of the lab to the sample" types of applications, i.e., for analytical measurements *on-site*. Future microplasma-based spectrometers are envisioned to have wireless capability [36, 37] and (some) energy autonomy [38–42]. In contrast to ICPs, low gas consumption (e.g., 250 mL/min) and low-power requirements (e.g., ~10 W) are key characteristics of microplasmas. But although low-power operation enables microplasma portability, it also disables liquid sample introduction using a nebulizer (**Figure 1**). The reason is that when using a nebulizer, most of a liquid sample introduced into a microplasma is water. Plasma power required to vaporize the water solvent (introduced with the sample) is 10–30 W [24]. But microplasmas require ~10 W; thus using a nebulizer is not possible. One way of circumventing this is by using a smaller version of the NTV chamber (**Figure 6**). Since a liquid sample is dried prior to its introduction into a microplasma, plasma power is not consumed to vaporize the water solvent, thus enabling liquid micro- or nano-sample introduction into a low-power micoplasma. The instrumentation used is shown in **Figure 23**.

The vaporization chamber used with a microplasma (**Figure 23**) is a scaled-down version of the single-inlet NTV3 chamber (**Figure 17**). Scaling was done assuming that all dimensions (**Table 2**) scale linearly with the "optimum" carrier gas-flow rate of 250 mL/min determined experimentally. A single-inlet chamber was selected to avoid the use of dual mass flow controller (required to ensure balanced flow on both inlets), thus enhancing portability for use *on-site*. To confirm

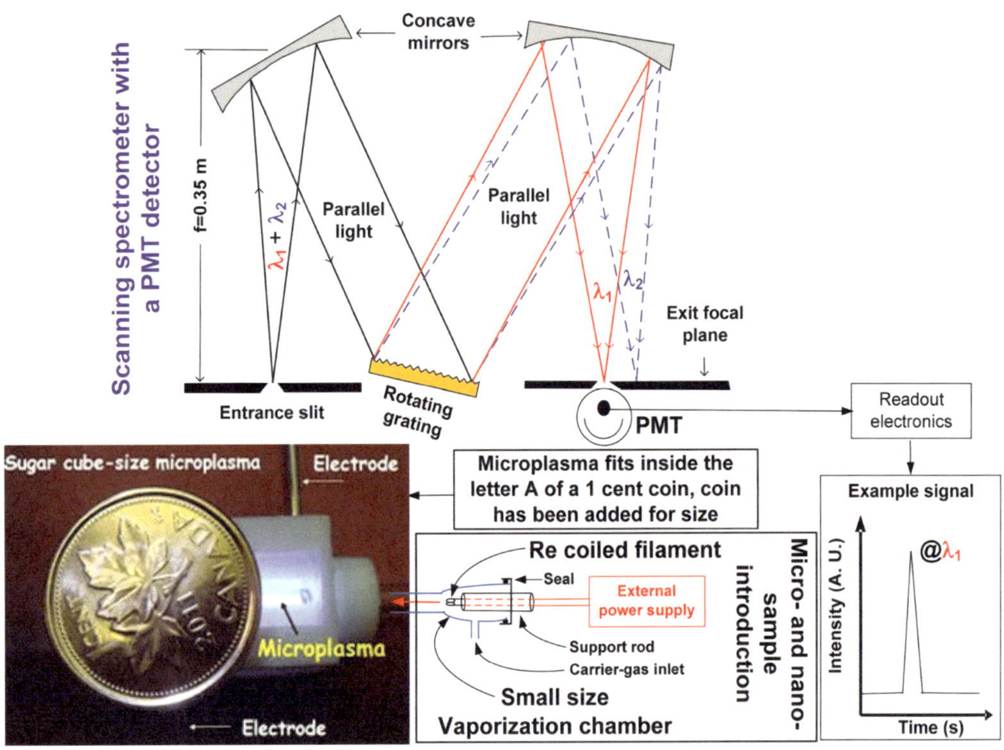

Figure 23. Instrumentation and micro- or nano-sample introduction into a 3D–printed microplasma.

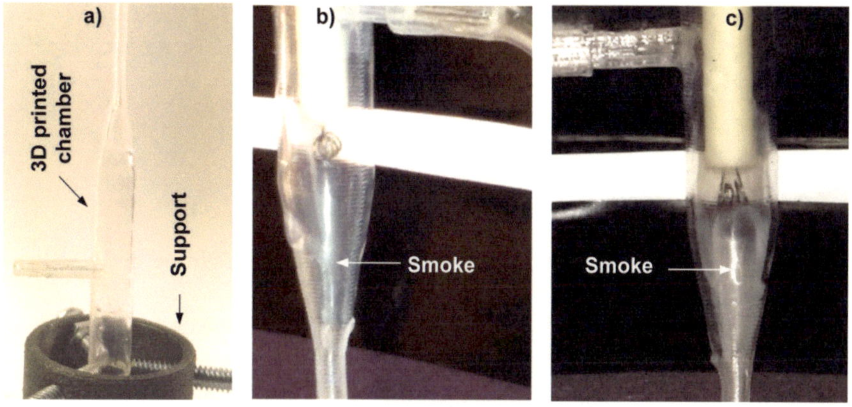

Figure 24. (a) 3D-printed vaporization chamber secured on its drying support. An XTC3D epoxy was used to enhance transparency through the chamber (as required to visually see and record smoke); the support was used to facilitate even drying of the epoxy. (b) Smoke confined to the center of the chamber. The smoke was generated from a drop of gasoline placed on the coil and by gently heating the coil using an external power supply—per **Figure 2a**. (c) Smoke diffused in the chamber (due to the use of an incorrect flow rate).

the scaling assumption and to evaluate flow-rate results, smoke visualization experiments were conducted using a 3D-printed vaporization chamber fabricated from polymeric (e.g., plastic) materials. 3D printing [27–29] was selected to avoid delays caused by the local glassblowing shop and to allow rapid prototyping of candidate chamber designs at a reduced cost. A single frame extracted from videos of smoke visualization experiments is shown in **Figure 24**. Based on these observations, a vaporization chamber has been fabricated using glass and has been used extensively with our microplasmas for measurements by optical emission (**Figure 23**).

11. Overall conclusions

Computational fluid dynamics simulations proved to be highly beneficial for the design of an improved-performance vaporization chamber that was tested with micro- or nano-samples and ICPs installed in a lab. For example, detection limits (a key figure of merit) improved by as much as five times. The best-performing and CFD-simulated chamber was tested with three different ICP spectrometers, thus demonstrating its wider applicability. A scaled-down version of a CFD-simulated NTV chamber has also been used with small-size, portable micro-plasmas, thus validating scaling-down assumptions and further demonstrating applicability and utility of CFD in plasma spectrometry. Microplasma-based spectrometers are expected to find future applicability for measurements in the field (i.e., *on-site*).

Acknowledgements

Financial assistance from the Natural Sciences and Engineering Research Council (NSERC) of Canada is gratefully acknowledged. A special thank you to Professor (now Emeritus) Cameron

McLeod and his research group at the Department of Chemistry, Sheffield University, UK, for use of their Agilent ICP-MS with our NTV system. A thank you to AEA/CFX of Waterloo, Canada, for a time-limited license to their software.

Author details

Hamid R. Badiei[1,2], Gordon Stubley[3], Ryan Fitzgerald[1], Melanie Saddler[1] and Vassili Karanassios[1]*

*Address all correspondence to: vkaranassios@uwaterloo.ca

1 Department of Chemistry and Waterloo Institute for Nanotechnology, University of Waterloo, Waterloo, Ontario, Canada

2 Perkin Elmer Inc., Ontario, Canada

3 Department of Mechanical and Mechatronics Engineering, University of Waterloo, Waterloo, Ontario, Canada

References

[1] Karanassios V, Grishko V, Reynolds GG. Elemental analysis of micro-samples of liquids or slurries by coiled-filament in-torch vaporization-inductively coupled plasma atomic emission spectrometry (ITV-ICP-AES). Journal of Analytical Atomic Spectrometry. 1999;**14**: 565-570. DOI: 10.1039/A807032F

[2] Badiei HR, Smith AT, Karanassios V. Rhenium-cup, in-torch vaporization (ITV) sample introduction for axially viewed ICP-AES and its application to the analysis of a microscopic, ng-weight solid sample. Journal of Analytical Atomic Spectrometry. 2002;**17**: 1007-1010. DOI: 10.1039/B001781G

[3] Badiei HR, Lai B, Karanassios V. Micro- and nano-volume samples by electrothermal, near-torch vaporization sample introduction using removable, interchangeable and portable rhenium coiled-filament assemblies and axially-viewed inductively coupled plasma-atomic emission spectrometry. Spectrochimica Acta Part B: Atomic Spectroscopy. 2012;**77**:19-30. DOI: 10.1016/j.sab.2012.07.025

[4] Badiei HR, McEnaney J, Karanassios V. Bringing part of the lab to the field: On-site chromium speciation in seawater by electrodeposition of Cr(III)/Cr(VI) on portable coiled-filament assemblies and measurement in the lab by electrothermal, near-torch vaporization sample introduction and inductively coupled plasma-atomic emission spectrometry. Spectrochimica Acta Part B: Atomic Spectroscopy. 2012;**78**:42-49. DOI: 10.1016/j.sab.2012.10.002

[5] Badiei HR, Liu C, Karanassios V. Taking part of the lab to the sample: On-site electrodeposition of Pb followed by measurement in a lab using electrothermal, near-torch vaporization (NTV) sample introduction and inductively coupled plasma-atomic emission spectrometry. Microchemical Journal. 2013;**108**:131-136. DOI: 10.1016/j.microc.2012.10.013

[6] Kantor T. Interpreting some analytical characteristics of thermal dispersion methods used for sample introduction in atomic spectrometry. Spectrochimica Acta Part B: Atomic Spectroscopy. 1988;**43**:1299-1320. DOI: 10.1016/0584-8547(88)80171-X

[7] Kantor T. Electrothermal vaporization and laser ablation sample introduction for flame and plasma spectrometric analysis of solid and solution samples. Spectrochimica Acta Part B: Atomic Spectroscopy. 2001;**56**:1523-1563. DOI: 10.1016/S0584-8547(01)00266-X

[8] Kantor T, Gucerb S. Efficiency of sample introduction into inductively coupled plasma by graphite furnace electrothermal vaporization. Spectrochimica Acta Part B: Atomic Spectroscopy. 1999;**54**:763-772. DOI: 10.1016/S0584-8547(99)00026-9

[9] Grégoire DC, Sturgeon RE. Analyte transport efficiency with electrothermal vaporization inductively coupled plasma mass spectrometry. Spectrochimica Acta Part B: Atomic Spectroscopy. 1999, 1999;**54**:773-786. DOI: 10.1016/S0584-8547(99)00008-7

[10] Ertas G, Holcombe JA. Determination of absolute transport efficiencies of be, cd, in, Pb and bi for electrothermal vaporization sample introduction into an inductively coupled plasma using an in-line electrostatic precipitator. Spectrochimica Acta Part B: Atomic Spectroscopy. 2003;**58**:1597-1612. DOI: 10.1016/S0584-8547(03)00134-4

[11] Piazza R. Thermophoresis: Moving particles with thermal gradients. Soft Matter. 2008; **4**:1740-1744. DOI: 10.1039/B805888C

[12] Braibanti M, Vigolo D, Piazza R. Does thermophoretic mobility depend on particle size? Physical Review Letters. 2008;**100**:108303. DOI: 10.1103/PhysRevLett.100.108303

[13] Zhao C, Cao Z, Fraser J, Oztekin A, Cheng X. Optimization of nanoparticle focusing by coupling thermophoresis and engineered vortex in a microfluidic channel. Journal of Applied Physics. 2017;**121**:024902. DOI: 10.1063/1.4973272

[14] Hoffmann AC, Stein LE. Computational fluid dynamics. In: Gas Cyclones and Swirl Tubes. Berlin: Springer; 2002. DOI: 10.1007/978-3-662-07377-3_7

[15] Ferziger JH, Peric M. Computational Methods for Fluid Dynamics. 3rd ed. Germany: Springer; 2002

[16] Wendt JF, editor. Computational Fluid Dynamics: An Introduction. Germany: Springer; 2008

[17] Chung TJ. Computational Fluid Dynamics. 2nd ed. Cambridge, UK: Cambridge University Press; 2010

[18] Pozrikidis Z. Introduction to Theoretical and Computational Fluid Dynamics. 2nd ed. Oxford, UK: Oxford University Press; 2011

[19] Blazek J. Computational Fluid Dynamics: Principles and Applications. Oxford, UK: Butterworth-Heinemann; 2015

[20] Aref H, Balachandar S. A First Course in Computational Fluid Dynamics. Cambridge, UK: Cambridge University Press; 2017

[21] Badiei HR, Stubley G, Karanassios V. CFD simulation, video clip of a simulation of a single-inlet NTV chamber. November 2017. https://youtu.be/YRooJG_EM4g

[22] Badiei HR, Stubley G, Karanassios V. CFD simulation, video clip of a simulation of a dual-inlet NTV chamber. November 2017. https://youtu.be/FmUawOjIZXM

[23] Badiei HR, Stubley G, Karanassios V. CFD Simulation, Video Clip of Streak-Lines inside a Single-Inlet NTV Chamber. November 2017. https://youtu.be/K4OK8JO3nu4

[24] Karanassios V. Microplasmas for chemical analysis: Analytical tools or research toys? Spectrochimica Acta Part B: Atomic Spectroscopy. 2004;**59**:909-928. DOI: 10.1016/j.sab.2004.04.005

[25] Karanassios V, Johnson K, Smith AT. Micromachined, planar-geometry, atmospheric-pressure, battery-operated microplasma devices (MPDs) on chips for microsamples of liquids, gases or solids by optical emission spectrometry. Analytical and Bioanalytical Chemistry. 2007;**388**:1595-1604. DOI: 10.1007/s00216-007-1273-4

[26] Weagent S, Karanassios V. Helium-hydrogen microplasma device (MPD) on postage-stamp-size plastic-quartz chips. Analytical and Bioanalytical Chemistry. 2009;**395**:577-589. DOI: 10.1007/s00216-009-2942-2

[27] Weagant S, Chen V, Karanassios V. Battery-operated, argon-hydrogen microplasma on hybrid, postage stamp-size plastic-quartz chips for elemental analysis of liquid microsamples using a portable optical emission spectrometer. Analytical and Bioanalytical Chemistry. 2011;**401**:2865-2880. DOI: 10.1007/s00216-011-5372-x

[28] Weagant S, Li L, Karanassios V. Rapid Prototyping of Hybrid, Plastic-Quartz 3D–Chips for Battery-Operated Microplasmas. London, UK: InTech Publishing; 2011. pp. 1-18 (Chapter 10)

[29] Shatford R, Karanassios V. Microplasma fabrication: from semiconductor technology for 2D–chips and microfluidic channels to rapid prototyping and 3D–printing of microplasma devices. Proceedings of the SPIE. 2014;**9106**:9106H1-9106H7. DOI: 10.11171/12.2050538

[30] Abbaszadeh S, Karim KS, Karanassios V. Measurement of UV from a microplasma by a microfabricated amorphous selenium detector. IEEE Transactions on Electron Devices. 2013;**60**(2):880-883. DOI: 10.1109/TED.2012.2231682

[31] Nguon O, Gauthier M, Karanassios V. Determination of the loading and stability of Pd in an arborescent copolymer in ethanol by microplasma-optical emission spectrometry. RSC Advances. 2014;**4**:8978-8984. DOI: 10.1039/C3RA46232C

[32] Nguon O, Huang S, Gauthier M, Karanassios V. Microplasmas: From applications to fundamentals. Proceedings of SPIE. 2014;**9105**:9101061-9101067. DOI: 10.1117/12.2050348

[33] Weagent S, Dulai G, Li L, Karanassios V. Characterization of rapidly-prototyped, battery-operated, Ar-H_2 microplasma on a chip for elemental analysis of microsamples by portable optical emission spectrometry. Spectrochimica Acta Part B: Atomic Spectroscopy. 2015;**106**:75-80. DOI: 10.1016/j.sab.2015.01.009

[34] Weagant S, Karanassios V. Battery-operated, planar-geometry microplasma on a postage-stamp size chips: Some fundamentals. Proceedings of SPIE. 2011;**8024**:80240L. DOI: 10.1117/12.884329

[35] Weagant S, Smith AT, Karanassios V. Mobile micro- and Nano-instruments: Small, cheap and under wireless control. ECS Transactions. 2010;**28**(14):1-6. DOI: 10.1149/1.3490180

[36] Trzcinski P, Weagent S, Karanassios V. Wireless data acquisition of transient signals for mobile spectrometry applications. Applied Spectroscopy. 2016;**70**:905-915. DOI: 10.1177/0003702816638304

[37] Trzcinski P, Karanassios V. How can wireless, mobile data acquisition be used for taking part of the lab to the sample, and how can it join the internet of things? Proceedings of SPIE. 2016;**9855**:985503. DOI: 10.1117/12.2224400

[38] Abbaszadeh S, Karim KS, Karanassios V. A microfabricated, low dark current a-se detector for measurement of microplasma optical emission in the UV for possible use on-site. Proceedings of SPIE. 2013;**8726**:87260S. DOI: 10.1109/TED.2012.2231682

[39] Zhang X, Karanassios V. Rapid prototyping of solar-powered, battery-operated, atmospheric-pressure, sugar-cube size microplasma on hybrid, 3D chips using a portable optical emission spectrometer. Proceedings of SPIE. 2012;**8366**:83660D. DOI: 10.1117/12.919550

[40] Shatford R, Karanassios V. 3D printing in chemistry: Past, present and future. Proceedings of SPIE. 2016;**9855**:98550B-998560. DOI: 10.1117/12.2224404

[41] Lee D, Dulai G, Karanassios V. Survey of energy harvesting and energy scavenging approaches for on-site powering of wireless sensor- and microinstrument-networks. Proceedings of SPIE. 2013;**8028**:8720S1. DOI: 10.1117/12.2016238

[42] Trizcinski P, Nathan A, Karanassios V. Approaches to energy harvesting and energy scavenging for energy autonomous sensors and microinstruments. Proceedings of SPIE. 2017;**10194**:10194A1-10194A9. DOI: 10.1117/12.2262957

Chapter 9

Analysis of Biomass Waste Cofiring into Existing Coal-Fired Power Plant Using Computational Fluid Dynamics

Arif Darmawan, Dwika Budianto,
Koji Tokimatsu and Muhammad Aziz

Additional information is available at the end of the chapter

http://dx.doi.org/10.5772/intechopen.70561

Abstract

Biomass utilization to generate electricity via combustion simply can be classified into firing and cofiring. Biomass cofiring into the pulverized coal boilers has some advantages compared to dedicated biomass firing in terms of capital cost and combustion efficiency. To understand the cofiring behavior of biomass and coal comprehensively, computational fluid dynamics (CFD) method can be used to analyze and solve problems involving fluid flows inside a combustor. A CFD modeling is significantly more effective from the perspectives of time and cost and safety and ease of scaling up; hence, it is usually performed before conducting a physical investigation through experiment. Moreover, the current state-of-the-art CFD modeling-based study is capable of solving the complexity of the interdependent processes such as turbulence, heat transfer via radiation, produced gas, and reactions in both the particle and gas phases during combustion. This chapter focuses on the study of cofiring of biomass, which is palm mill wastes, into the existing coal-fired power plant. Two palm mill wastes are evaluated: palm kernel shell and hydrothermally treated empty fruit bunch. Distributions of temperature and the produced are simulated to find the most optimum and applicable cofiring conditions.

Keywords: cofiring, computational fluid dynamics, modeling, waste biomass, coal, temperature distribution

1. Introduction

Biomass utilization through cofiring into existing coal-fired power plants or ones being constructed/planned becomes very important. Several European countries, Japan, and several coal-dependent countries such as China have implemented cofiring technology in their newly built coal-fired power plant with the biomass having a blending percentage of 10–20% in calorie basis [1]. Biomass cofiring with coal is believed to be able to enhance the domestic energy security through renewable energy utilization as well as improve the utilization of power plants that were initially designed for coal. To understand the cofiring behavior of biomass and coal inside the combustor, numerical method of computational fluid dynamics (CFD) can be used to analyze and solve problems involving fluid flows. This method is usually adopted before performing an experimental investigation.

To understand this issue comprehensively, this chapter is divided into three main parts:

- Scheme and technical aspects of biomass cofiring with coal
- Modeling approach to predict combustion behavior of cofiring biomass waste in existing coal-fired power plant
- Case study of palm oil waste cofiring (including result and discussion).

In Section 2, a brief knowledge about the technical aspects of biomass cofiring with coal is presented. In the next part (Section 3), CFD modeling for biomass cofiring with coal is reported. Furthermore, in Section 4, a case study of palm oil waste cofiring with coal will be discussed to evaluate the applicability of the CFD models. The palm oil waste reported in the Section 4 consists of palm kernel shell (PKS) and hydrothermally treated empty fruit bunch (HT-EFB) [2, 3].

Employing CFD to assist the cofiring behavior can give a deep discussion and a scientific knowledge to the reader. Scientists, engineers, and others who are interested in learning CFD and its current developments in biomass conversion technologies will find this chapter invaluable. Moreover, by understanding the CFD method, hopefully it can further be replicated into different biomass feedstocks and scales, depending on the research goal.

2. Retrofitting the existing coal power plants through cofiring for sustainable energy

In the future, biomass will play a significant role in many countries as energy source. The utilization of biomass using an appropriate technology is important to optimize its economic benefit and minimize the environmental impacts. The appropriate technology means applicable in small- and large-scales, energy-efficient, environmentally friendly, and decentralized. Some conversion techniques have been studied and applied in the recent years from small laboratory-scale up to large-scale, such as: pyrolysis, direct-combustion, gasification, and anaerobic digestion. In thermal conversion, direct-combustion is generally performed in the boilers or furnaces to produce steam that can be used for district heating or driving the turbines in power generation.

Utilization of biomass to generate electricity via direct-combustion can be technically classified into two types: firing and cofiring. Biomass cofiring to the existing power plants (as

http://dx.doi.org/10.5772/intechopen.70561

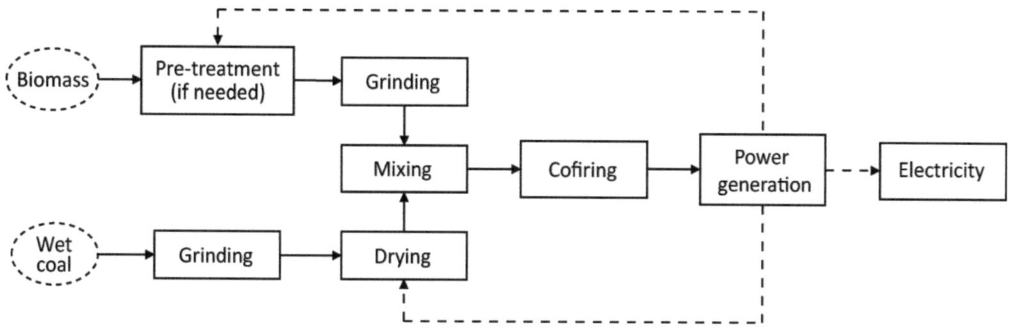

Figure 1. Basic schematic diagram of biomass and coal cofiring system.

shown in **Figure 1**), especially coal-fired power plants, has some advantages compared to dedicated biomass firing such as minimum capital cost and optimum combustion efficiency [2]. Other advantages of biomass cofiring into existing coal-fired power plant are that it can significantly reduce the emissions from the power plant and minimize the slagging inside combustor [3].

Biomass cofiring into coal-fired boilers can be performed in some different methods such as parallel cofiring, injection, pregasification, and comilling. Due to lower capital cost and high cofiring ratio, injection cofiring is the most feasible method applied in the industrial scale [4]. In this method, premilled biomass and pulverized coal are continuously mixed and cofed into the boiler.

Since developing countries are likely to put their future in the coal resources [5, 6], biomass cofiring seems to be a promising option for improving the energy sustainability and reducing the environmental impacts. Biomass can be classified into two categories: biomass waste and energy crops. In addition, properties such as moisture, nitrogen content are depending on their pretreatment [7]. For further discussion, it is also important to consider the biomass availability from the surrounding to avoid potential conflict, for example, with food production.

3. CFD modeling for coal and biomass cofiring inside a combustor

Once the fuel or mixed fuel is fed to the combustor, the following reactions occur continuously: preheating, evaporation or drying, devolatilization, gas-char combustion, pollutant generation, and radiation [8]. To understand this complex phenomenon, CFD is a powerful tool that can model and calculate fluid flows, heat and mass transfers, and chemical reactions as well as interactions of solids and fluids [9].

The general process for CFD-based combustion modeling is shown in **Figure 2**. CFD modeling method for the combustion of mixed biomass and coal particles is arguably a challenging

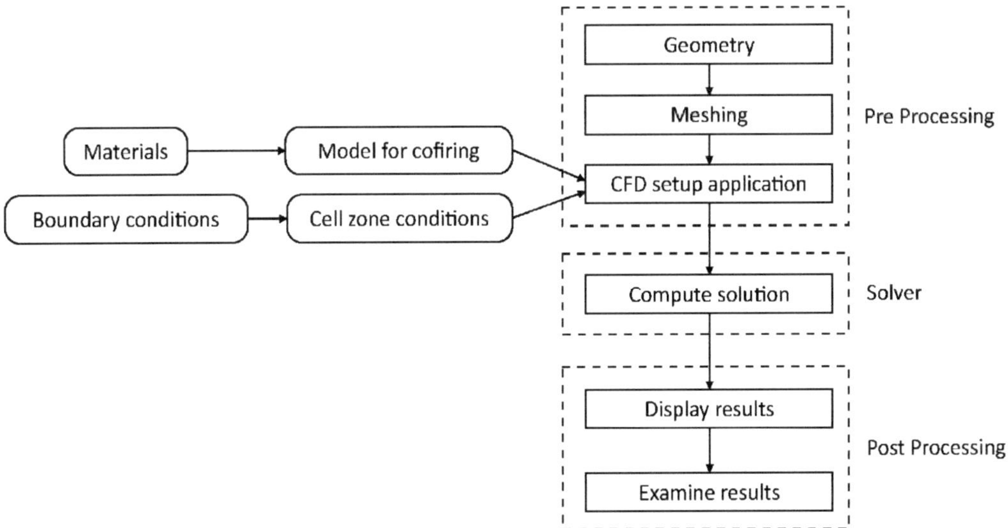

Figure 2. Summary of CFD process modeling.

work. However, compared to physical investigation through experiment, CFD modeling is considered more effective from both time and cost perspectives, as well as higher safety and easier scaling up. Hence, it is usually adopted before performing an experimental study. Related to cofiring using CFD analysis, it is expected that the combustion performance for all stages of the combustion including the combustion temperature, kinetic behavior, and concentration of the produced gases can be clarified. Cofiring simulation considers dynamical equations, conservation of mass (continuity), momentum and enthalpy, turbulence, radiation heat transfer, and reactions in both particle and gas phases [10].

3.1. Conservation equations

In the biomass cofiring, since combustion involves chemical reactions between mixed biomass-coal and an oxidant, the process is usually assumed and modeled as solid and gas or dilute two-phase flow which is approximated as Eulerian-Lagrangian equation. In this approach, the gas phase is modeled using Reynolds Averaged Navier-Stokes Equations (RANS) model. On the other hand, the solid phase is treated as a discrete phase. In addition, the trajectory of each particles is calculated using Newton's laws of motion in which the particles collision is considered using the sphere model [11]. Furthermore, both gas concentration and temperature distribution are approximated using the energy and mass transfer equations for the particles. The interactions of mass, momentum, and energy between the gas and solid particles are calculated using the particle-in-cell (PIC) approach with the consideration of particle state along the particle trajectories. The mathematical calculations are basically governed by the flow of fluid. In the conserved form, the continuity, momentum, and total energy conservations can be represented as Eqs. (1)–(5), respectively [12]:

http://dx.doi.org/10.5772/intechopen.70561

$$\frac{\partial \rho}{\partial t} + \nabla \cdot \left(\rho \vec{V} \right) = 0 \tag{1}$$

$$\frac{\partial (\rho u)}{\partial t} + \nabla \cdot \left(\rho u \vec{V} \right) = -\frac{\partial p}{\partial x} + \frac{\partial \tau_{xx}}{\partial x} + \frac{\partial \tau_{yx}}{\partial y} + \frac{\partial \tau_{zx}}{\partial z} + \rho f_x \tag{2}$$

$$\frac{\partial (\rho v)}{\partial t} + \nabla \cdot \left(\rho v \vec{V} \right) = -\frac{\partial p}{\partial y} + \frac{\partial \tau_{xy}}{\partial x} + \frac{\partial \tau_{yy}}{\partial y} + \frac{\partial \tau_{zy}}{\partial z} + \rho f_y \tag{3}$$

$$\frac{\partial (\rho w)}{\partial t} + \nabla \cdot \left(\rho w \vec{V} \right) = -\frac{\partial p}{\partial z} + \frac{\partial \tau_{xz}}{\partial x} + \frac{\partial \tau_{yz}}{\partial y} + \frac{\partial \tau_{zz}}{\partial z} + \rho f_z \tag{4}$$

$$\frac{\partial}{\partial t}\left[\rho\left(e + \frac{V^2}{2}\right)\right] + \nabla \cdot \left[\rho\left(e + \frac{V^2}{2}\vec{V}\right)\right] = \rho \dot{q} + \frac{\partial}{\partial x}\left(k\frac{\partial T}{\partial x}\right) + \frac{\partial}{\partial y}\left(k\frac{\partial T}{\partial y}\right)$$

$$+\frac{\partial}{\partial z}\left(k\frac{\partial T}{\partial z}\right) - \frac{\partial (up)}{\partial x} - \frac{\partial (vp)}{\partial y} - \frac{\partial (wp)}{\partial z} + \frac{\partial (u\tau_{xx})}{\partial x} + \frac{\partial (u\tau_{yx})}{\partial y} + \frac{\partial (u\tau_{zx})}{\partial z} + \frac{\partial (v\tau_{xy})}{\partial x} + \frac{\partial (v\tau_{yy})}{\partial y}$$

$$+\frac{\partial (v\tau_{zy})}{\partial z} + \frac{\partial (w\tau_{xz})}{\partial x} + \frac{\partial (w\tau_{yz})}{\partial y} + \frac{\partial (w\tau_{zz})}{\partial z} + \rho \vec{f} \cdot \vec{V} \tag{5}$$

where, ρ, V, p, f, τ, k, and $\dot{q}$ are density, velocity, pressure, body force per unit mass, shear force, thermal conductivity, and heat transferred through thermal conduction per unit time per unit area, respectively. u, v, and w are velocity components in each x, y, and z directions, respectively. In addition, e, $V^2/_2$, and $(e + V^2/_2)$ are internal, kinetic energy per unit mass, and total energy, respectively. We can say, Eqs. (1)–(3) represent each of mass (continuity equation in nonconservation form, momentum, enthalpy energy) conservations, respectively. Moreover, Eqs. (4) and (5) relate to the calculation of temperature and specific mass fraction, correspondingly.

3.2. Behavior of turbulence flows during combustion

The flow in the combustor, usually called as "turbulence," is very important to be considered in the combustion simulation. This physical phenomenon influences both heat and mass transfers inside the combustor. Turbulence occurs due to the inertia of the fluid covering time-dependent and convective acceleration, and which is characterized by the velocity fluctuations because of the complex geometry and high flow rates. Due to good solution and effective time during computation, k-ε (k-epsilon) turbulence model is widely adopted to calculate the RANS equations that are employed to model the cofiring. In addition, in CFD modeling, this k-ε turbulence model is generally employed to determine and solve the swirling combustion flows. There are two main equations involved in this model relating to each turbulent kinetic energy, k, and turbulent dissipation rate, ε. Both of them can be expressed in the following Eqs. (6) and (7), respectively:

$$\frac{\partial}{\partial t}(\rho k) + \frac{\partial}{\partial x_i}(\rho k u_i) = \frac{\partial}{\partial x_j}\left[\frac{\mu_t}{\sigma_k}\frac{\partial k}{\partial x_j}\right] + 2\mu_t E_{ij} E_{ij} - \rho\epsilon \tag{6}$$

$$\frac{\partial}{\partial t}(\rho\epsilon) + \frac{\partial}{\partial x_i}(\rho\epsilon u_i) = \frac{\partial}{\partial x_j}\left[\left(\mu + \frac{\mu_t}{\sigma_\epsilon}\right)\frac{\partial\epsilon}{\partial x_j}\right] + C_{1\epsilon}\frac{\epsilon}{k}2\mu_t E_{ij} E_{ij} - \rho C_{2\epsilon}\frac{\epsilon^2}{k} \tag{7}$$

where, k, ϵ, u_i, and E_{ij} are turbulent kinetic energy, turbulent dissipation, velocity component in corresponding direction, and deformation rate component, respectively. Furthermore, the turbulent viscosity, μ_t, is calculated using Eq. (8).

$$\mu_t = \rho C_\mu \frac{k^2}{\epsilon} \tag{8}$$

where $C_{1\epsilon}$, $C_{2\epsilon}$, C_μ, σ_k, and σ_ϵ are constants.

3.3. Development of radiation models for cofiring

Since the combustion temperature is relatively high, attention should be given for heat transfer through radiation. It controls both heat transfer and heat flux, especially during heating, drying, flame ignition, devolatilization, and char combustion. The suitable model for radiation can be selected from different radiation models such as:

- Discrete-ordinates model (DOM)
- P-1 model
- Discrete transfer radiation method (DTRM)

For certain cases, one radiation model may be more appropriate than another, depending on the boundaries and system conditions. Each model has advantages and limitations. P-1 model is widely used for specific application to pulverized coal-fired boilers. In addition, some researchers are also adopting P-1 radiation model for their research related to cofiring [2, 3, 13]. The DO model is more expensive but has an accurate process and is applicable for a large range of optic thickness. Furthermore, the DTRM model is suitable for a large range of optic thickness with less accuracy than DO model [14].

3.4. Particle phase reaction mechanisms

In cofiring process, we can consider the mixture of biomass waste and coal as a typical gas-solid flow with their chemical reactions. Furthermore, Eulerian-Lagrangian model can be adopted to figure the hydrodynamics of the mixture. Both particles are modeled separately as two discrete phase models. There are some reactions involved in the particle phase, especially the char combustion. It is assumed as char oxidation to produce CO that is released to the bulk gas in the combustor. It is important to note that, in general, char from biomass is more reactive and has higher heating rate than one from coal.

During devolatilization, the volatile matters exhausted from each biomass and coal are released to the bulk gas and then have reaction with O_2 (oxidation). The general reactions in both particle and gas phases for coal cofiring with biomass waste can be shown in the following reactions:

i. Char of coal

$$C + 0.5O_2 \rightarrow CO \tag{9}$$

ii. Char of biomass

$$C + 0.5O_2 \rightarrow CO \tag{10}$$

iii. Volatile matter of coal

$$CH_{\alpha1}O_{\alpha2}N_{\alpha3}S_{\alpha4}+_{\gamma1}O_2 \rightarrow CO+_{\gamma2}H_2O+_{\gamma3}O_2+_{\gamma4}N_2 \tag{11}$$

iv. Volatile matter of biomass waste

$$CH_{\alpha5}O_{\alpha6}N_{\alpha7}S_{\alpha8}+_{\gamma5}O_2 \rightarrow CO +_{\gamma6}H_2O +_{\gamma7}O_2+_{\gamma8}N_2 \tag{12}$$

and

$$CO + 0.5\,O_2 \rightarrow CO_2 \tag{13}$$

Composition and enthalpy formation for both biomass waste and coal are determined based on both proximate and ultimate analyses of each material. Therefore, the variables α and γ in the above reactions can be derived by proximate and ultimate analyses from each cofired material.

4. Case studies of biomass waste cofiring

4.1. Numerical analysis of cofiring of PKS into pulverized coal-fired boiler

4.1.1. Boiler dimensions and calculation conditions

The first step in the cofiring evaluation through CFD is determining the combustor or boiler dimensions and its layout of the meshing. The detailed part of the boiler is shown in **Figure 3**, including the feeding inlets in cross section. The boiler shape of this simulation referred to an existing coal-fired power plant with capacity 300 MWe. This boiler had a height, width, and breadth of 45, 12, and 15 m, correspondingly. To perform the simulation, a commercial CFD software was prepared. ANSYS DesignModeler was used to build the combustor model in 3D, and Fluent ver. 16.2 (ANSYS Inc.) is used to analyze the cofiring behavior. The cofiring simulation took account of governing equations (for mass, momentum, enthalpy, temperature, and specific mass fraction), turbulence, radiative heat transfer, and reactions for both the particle and gas phases.

The used biomass sample was PKS, which is one of solid wastes in palm milling to produce palm oil. The solid wastes in palm milling include empty fruit bunch (EFB), fiber, and PKS with ratios of about 23, 12, and 5%, respectively [15, 16]. Fiber is usually combusted inside the

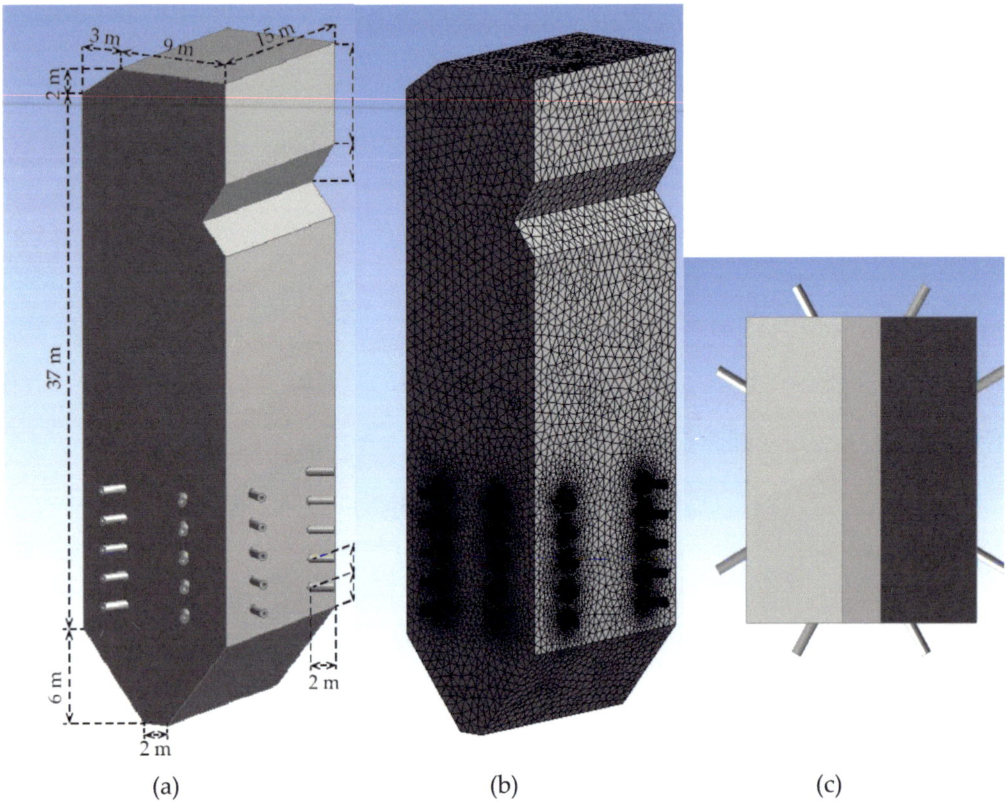

Figure 3. Schematic diagram of the boiler design: (a) boiler dimensions, (b) meshing layout, (c) inlet feed distribution (cross section).

mill to produce steam consumed for the milling, especially sterilization. In addition, an effective energy utilization of EFB has been proposed in previous studies [17, 18] for power generation. PKS has advantageous characteristics of low moisture content and higher calorific value, compared with those other solid wastes.

Both the coal and PKS characteristics are shown in **Table 1**. Since the case was designated to perform cofiring in Indonesia, the coal was collected from the country that is categorized as having low rank coal (LRC) with high moisture content. In addition, the PKS was obtained from a palm oil mill (POM) located in Sumatera Island. Due to high moisture content, initial drying was conducted in order to lower the moisture content up to 17.30%. Moreover, the PKS was used for cofiring with any initial pretreatment except grinding.

The fuel flow rates for coal and air under ambient condition were 73 and 630 kg s^{-1}, correspondingly. In addition, the air is approximated to contain N_2 and O_2 with concentrations of 79 mol% and 21 mol%, respectively. Each particle was regarded as to be a solid sphere, having particle sizes in the range of 60–200 mesh (74–250 μm). Furthermore, the bulk densities of the coal and PKS were considered to be 700 and 600 kg m^{-3}, respectively. The ambient temperature, combustor wall thickness, and external and internal emissivity coefficients were set at 300 K, 0.2 m, 0.9, and 0.6, respectively.

Component	Properties	Coal		PKS
		As-received	As-used	As-used
Proximate analysis (wt%)	Fixed carbon	24.93	40.23	24.35
	Volatile matter	25.76	41.57	66.77
	Moisture	48.76	17.30	3.86
	Ash	0.56	0.90	5.02
Ultimate analysis (wt%)	Carbon	35.30	56.98	43.77
	Hydrogen	2.29	3.69	5.85
	Oxygen	11.23	18.13	42.32
	Nitrogen	1.75	2.83	0.89
	Sulfur	0.11	0.17	0.00
LHV (MJ kg^{-1})		13.84	22.33	17.68

Table 1. Material composition of coal and PKS particles used in the study.

The simulation was performed using a Quad-core Intel Core i7 2.9 GHz CPU and 16 GB of RAM. The total mesh of the 3D model used to represent the combustor was an approximately 1,805,305 tetrahedral cell unstructured grid. In the CFD modeling, the temperature distribution and concentration of the produced gases (CO_2, CO, O_2, NO_x, and SO_x) were evaluated. In addition, five different PKS mass fractions were tested: 0% (100% coal), 10, 15, 25, and 50%.

4.1.2. Results and discussion

4.1.2.1. Temperature distribution

Temperature distribution for each PKS mass fraction is shown in **Figure 4**. Generally, higher PKS mass fraction leads to higher flame temperatures inside the boiler, since higher PKS mass fraction means larger amount of volatile matter emitted during cofiring. The average temperature in the upper part of boiler, especially at the freeboard, is lower than the lower part of boiler. It is considered as the result of heat loss across the boiler.

In **Table 1**, it can be observed that the used PKS has higher volatile matter and lower moisture content compared to the coal, since the used coal was LRC with relatively low calorific value. With this condition, the devolatilization of PKS particles would be faster and earlier than the devolatilization of the coal particles. It resulted in higher and more uniform combustion temperature at high PKS mass fraction. Because the water has a relatively high heat capacity, the increase of PKS mass fraction also leads to the decrease of the total moisture content of the mixed fuel, influencing the combustion temperature.

The average temperature at boiler outlet for PKS mass fractions of 0, 10, 15, 25, and 50% are 1390, 1414, 1422, 1513, and 1494 K, respectively. Although insignificant, cofiring with a PKS mass fraction of 25% resulted in higher combustion temperature compared to a mass fraction of 50%. In contrast to the moisture content, a higher PKS mass fraction decreased the total amount of fixed carbon (including char) in the mixed fuel. Therefore, the heat obtained from

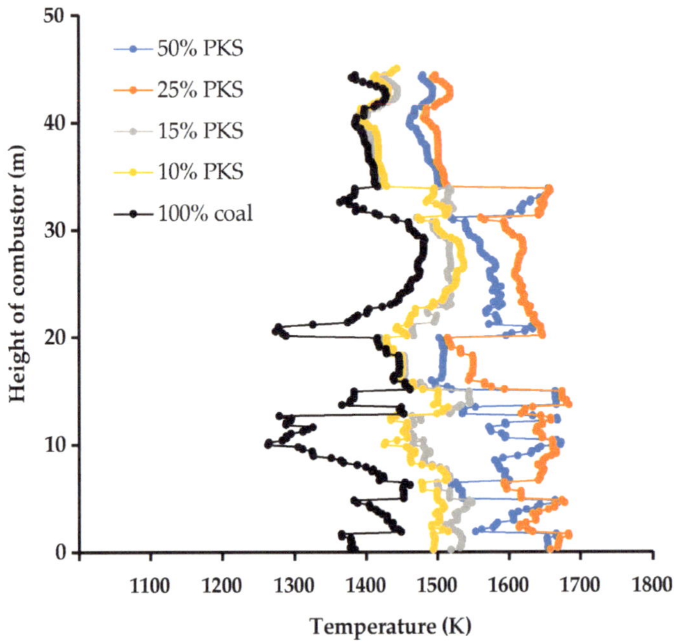

Figure 4. Temperature distribution at the center along the height of the boiler for each different PKS mass fraction.

the char combustion fell since the PKS mass fraction increased. The temperature distribution profile suggested that the optimum combustion performance of coal and PKS cofiring can be achieved at a PKS mass fraction of 25%.

4.1.2.2. Distribution of CO_2, CO, O_2, NO_x, and SO_x

Figures 5–7 [3] represent the CO_2, CO, and O_2 gases distribution inside the boiler, respectively. Generally, higher PKS mass fraction led to a lower CO_2 concentration, lower CO concentration, and higher CO_2, respectively. This is because PKS has a relatively high O_2 content, part of which persists and is exhausted together with the nitrogen and other flue gases.

Figures 8 and **9** [3] represent the cross-sectional NO_x and SO_x distribution at the center of the boiler. Higher PKS mass fraction leads to higher NO_x concentration and increased significantly as the PKS mass fraction increased to 25%. According to the Zeldovich mechanism [19], at above 1600 K, thermal NO_x generation can occur easily. The maximum combustion temperature at PKS mass fractions of 25 and 50% exceeded this value. This suggested that a lower PKS, of up to 15%, is the appropriate cofiring condition for limiting NO_x emissions.

4.2. Retrofitting existing coal power plants through cofiring with hydrothermally treated empty fruit bunch

4.2.1. Combustor dimensions and calculation conditions

In the second study case, detailed geometry of used small drop tube furnace (DTF) is shown in **Figure 10**. DTF can generate results in efficient time and cost, with similar results to those

http://dx.doi.org/10.5772/intechopen.70561

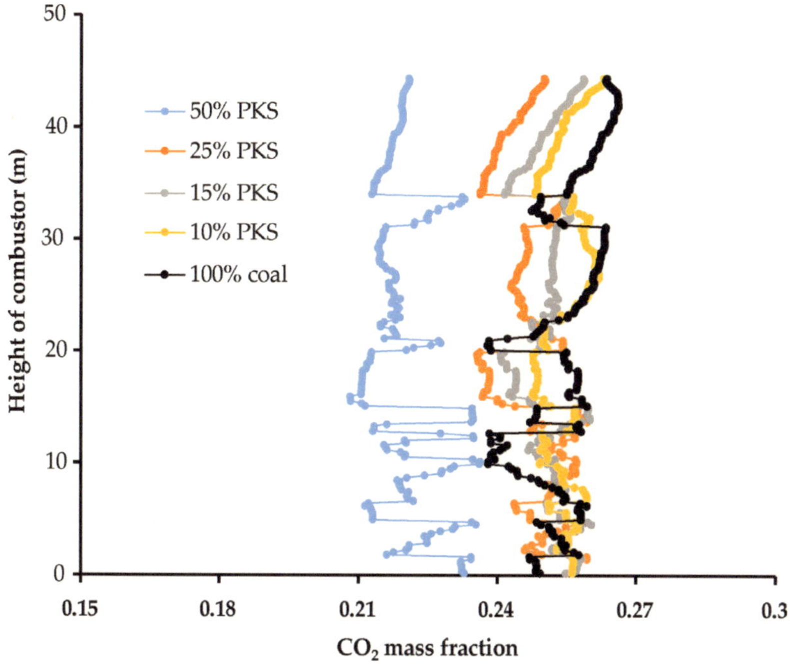

Figure 5. CO_2 distribution at the center along the height of the boiler at each different PKS mass fraction.

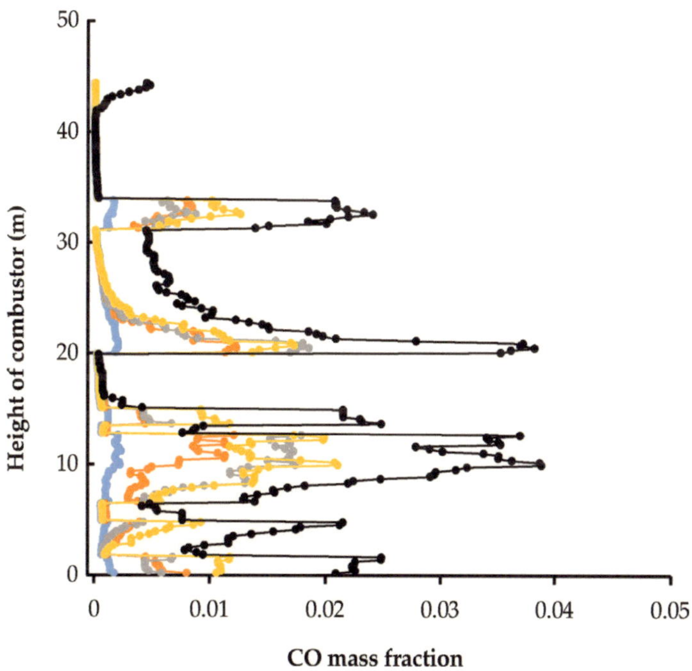

Figure 6. CO distribution at the center along the height of the boiler at each different PKS mass fraction.

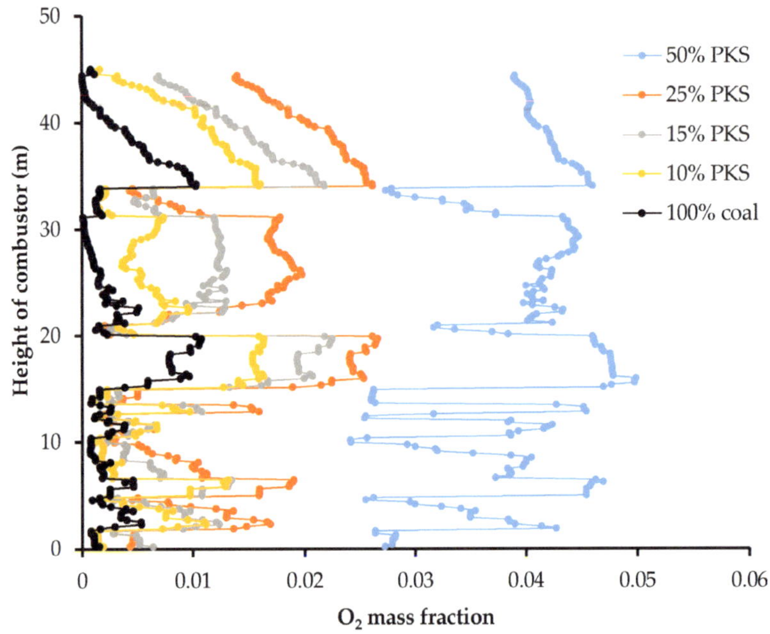

Figure 7. O_2 distribution at the center along the height of the boiler at each different PKS mass fraction.

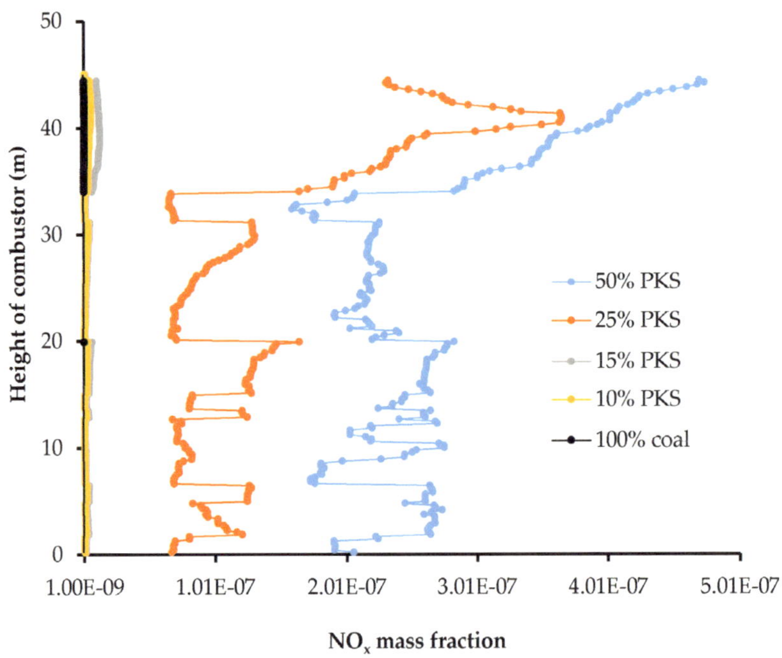

Figure 8. NO_x distribution at the center along the height of the boiler at each different PKS mass fraction.

http://dx.doi.org/10.5772/intechopen.70561

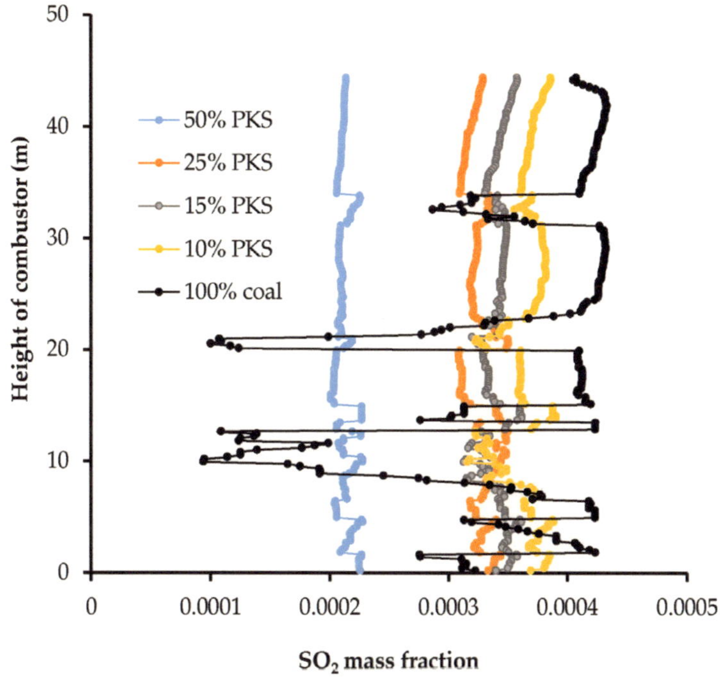

Figure 9. SO_2 distribution at the center along the height of the boiler at each different PKS mass fraction.

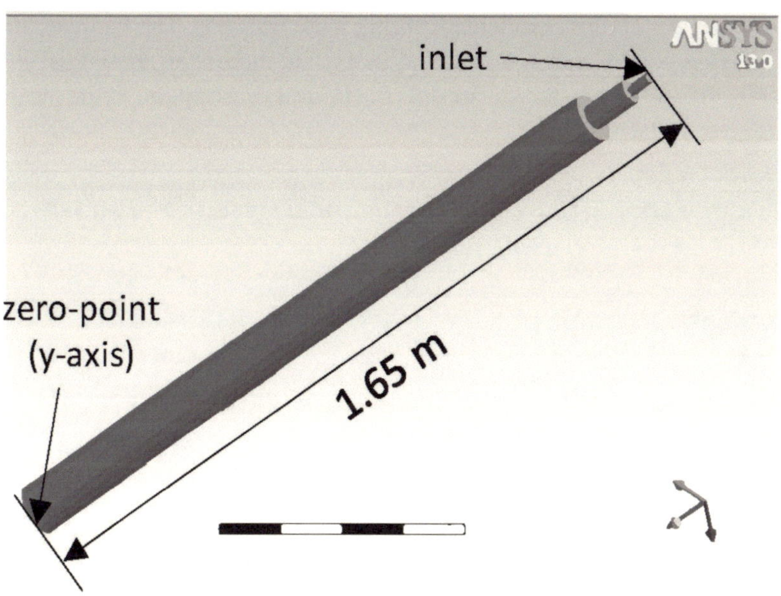

Figure 10. Geometry of DTF or combustor used in the simulation [2].

conducted in the real boiler. The combustion process takes place inside the tubular furnace and in the downward direction. The detailed report of this study can be read in the full paper written by Darmawan et al. [2].

The coal used in the simulation is originated from Kalimantan, Indonesia. This coal is classified as low rank coal having high moisture content and lower calorific value. On the other hand, the biomass, which is EFB, is hydrothermally treated in order to reduce the moisture content, increase the calorific value, and improve the mechanical properties [20, 21]. Hydrothermal treatment (HT) is also generally known as wet torrefaction [22]. **Table 2** shows the compositions of used coal and HT-EFB including proximate and ultimate analyses.

In the simulation, a commercial CFD software ANSYS DesignModeler and Fluent ver. 16.2 (ANSYS Inc.) are used to build 3D combustor model and analyze the cofiring behavior. As discussed earlier, cofiring simulation includes some considerations of dynamics equations, conservation of mass (continuity), momentum and enthalpy, turbulence (k-ε turbulence model), radiation heat transfer (P-1 model), and reactions in both particles (Eulerian-Lagrangian model) and gas (global two-steps reactions) phases. Some additional boundary conditions include (1) fuel and air inlet flow rates that are 1.38×10^{-5} kg s^{-1} and 1.6×10^{-4} kg s^{-1} at 300 K, (2) furnace wall temperature, wall roughness, and internal emissivity that are set to 1300 K (isothermal), 0.5, and 1, respectively, and (3) feeding wall is considered isothermal at 300 K.

4.2.2. Results and discussion

An HT-EFB after hydrothermal treatment is found to become more uniform and coal-like. Hydrothermal treatment also can improve the drying and dehydration performance, thus the moisture content of the HT-EFB decreases to approximately 3%. This characteristic is very important in the combustion system. **Figures 10** and **11** [3] show the temperature distribution along the axis of the DTF under different cofiring mass fractions. The figure excludes axis of the DTF at high temperatures of 0–0.6 m considering that there is no substantial change in the bottom of DTF and can be neglected. The dots in **Figure 11** correspond to the measured result

Components	**Raw coal [3]**	**Dried coal [3]**	**Raw EFB [23]**	**HT-EFB [24]**
Proximate analysis				
Fixed carbon (wt% wb)	24.93	40.23	3.71	28.62
Volatile matter (wt% wb)	25.76	41.57	34.84	62.57
Moisture (wt% wb)	48.76	17.30	60.00	3.00
Ash (wt% wb)	0.56	0.90	1.46	5.82
Ultimate analysis				
C (wt% wb)	35.30	56.98	17.97	52.92
H (wt% wb)	2.29	3.69	2.49	5.35
O (wt% wb)	11.23	18.13	17.60	32.06
N (wt% wb)	1.75	2.83	0.47	0.85
S (wt% wb)	0.11	0.17	0.01	0.00
Calorific value (MJ kg^{-1})	13.84	22.34	17.02	22.22

Table 2. Material composition.

obtained from experimental validation for coal. In general, higher HT-EFB mass fraction will increase the temperature inside the combustor. HT-EFB mass fractions of 50% result in the highest outlet temperature (maximum of 1536 K) (**Figure 12**).

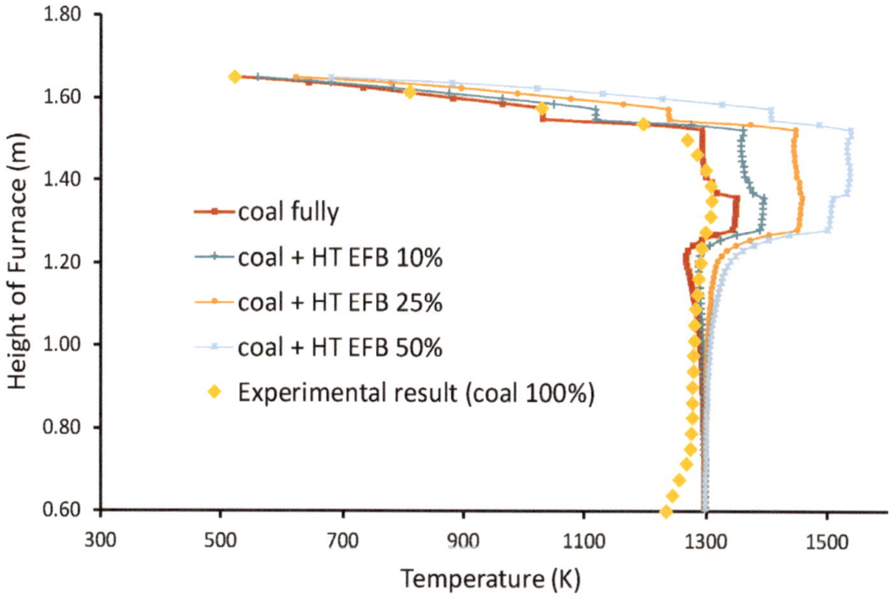

Figure 11. Temperature distribution inside the combustor of HT-EFB cofiring.

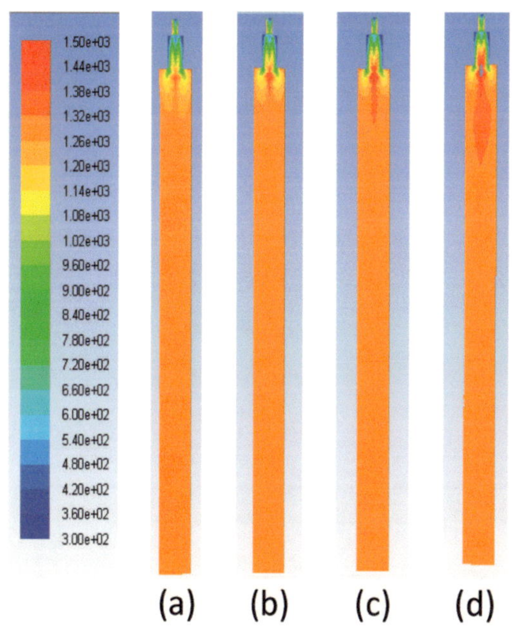

Figure 12. Temperature distribution of coal and HT-EFB cofiring across the combustor: (a) coal fully (b) HT-EFB 10% (c) HT-EFB 25% (d) HT-EFB 50%.

Fuel combustion process involves three basics stages as mentioned in Section 3: devolatilization, volatile combustion, and char oxidation. Compared to the main combustion area, a lower temperature is observed in the upper part of the combustor where the devolatilization process occurred. The mixture is pyrolyzed and then evolves as volatile matter. The devolatilization of HT-EFB particles occurs earlier and in a shorter time than coal because of lower moisture content of HT-EFB and higher volatile matter content. On the other hand, since coal has significantly higher moisture content, its particles require a longer time for drying and the devolatilization to occur. Therefore, in high HT-EFB mass fraction, the flame temperature remains high and distributed more uniformly although it is located in a lower part of the combustor. In addition, as HT-EFB has a lower moisture content than coal, high HT-EFB mass fraction leads to the lower total moisture content of the mixed fuel of HT-EFB and coal in the combustor system. Finally, this condition affects the flame temperature due to high heat capacity of water.

4.2.3. Distribution of produced CO and CO_2

In contrast to the fuel coal combustion, HT-EFB cofiring has increased carbon monoxide concentrations and nitrogen monoxide in the combustion. **Figures 13** and **14** [3] represent further information about the concentration of CO and CO_2 gases during cofiring.

Regarding the produced CO concentration, higher mass fraction of HT-EFB leads to the increase of CO mass fraction during initial reaction of combustion. The volatile matter, especially from

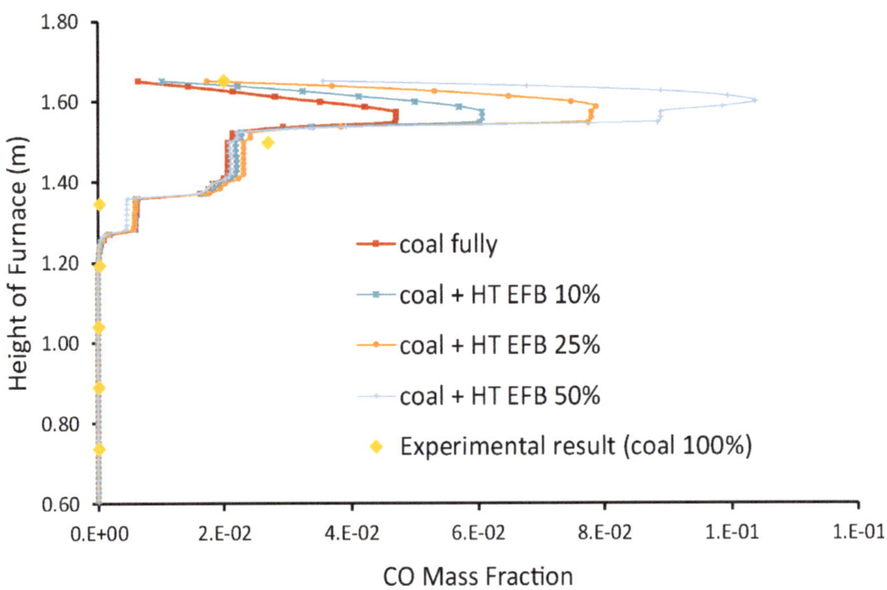

Figure 13. CO mass fraction along the combustor height under different HT-EFB mass fractions.

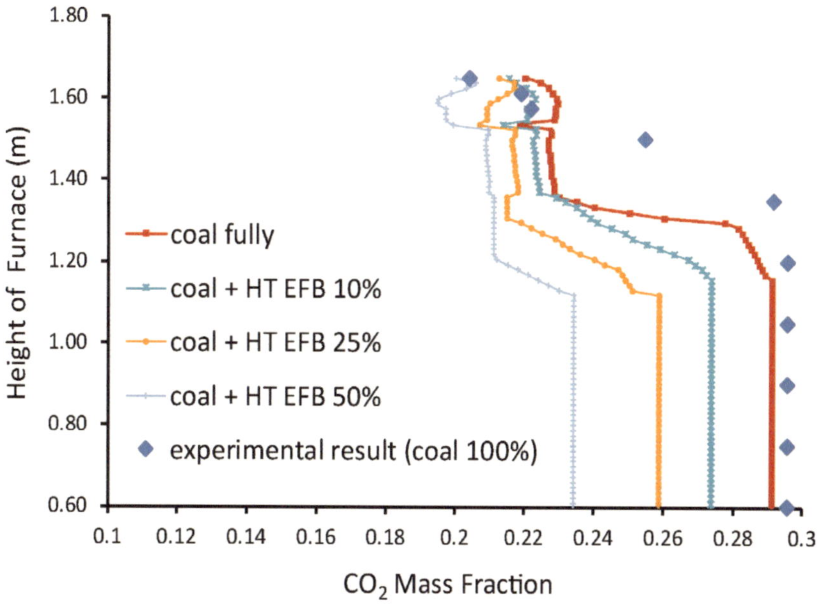

Figure 14. CO_2 mass fraction along the combustor height under different HT-EFB mass fraction.

HT-EFB, is oxidized under high combustion temperature forming CO. Afterward, CO reacts further with O_2 (air) along the combustor forming CO_2. In addition, coal cofiring with HT-EFB results in lower CO_2 concentration following the increase of both HT-EFB mass fraction (**Figure 9**). The dots in **Figure 10** show the CO_2 pollutant observed during the experimental study; meanwhile, the lines show CO_2 emission based on a simulation model.

5. Conclusion

Cofiring of biomass waste in a pulverized coal power plant was studied using CFD. This chapter has discussed performance for all stages of the combustion including the combustion temperatures, kinetics behavior, and concentration of the produced gases (CO_2, CO, O_2, NO_x, and SO_x). Moreover, the current state-of-the-art CFD modeling-based study is capable of solving the complexity of the interdependent processes such as turbulence, heat transfer via radiation, complex reactions in both the particle, and gas phases and the produced gas.

For further development, cofiring of biomass waste with coal can be clarified by a pilot experimental scale before being applied in full-scale power plants. This validation is necessary after conducting CFD simulation. To be remembered, it is also very important to take account of the biomass waste supply from the surrounding resources to avoid potential conflict with food production or prevent from potential shortage of sustainable biomass supply.

Acknowledgements

This work was partially supported by Indonesian government, which contributed to it through the program of the Indonesia Endowment Fund for Education (LPDP).

Author details

Arif Darmawan[1,2], Dwika Budianto[2], Koji Tokimatsu[1] and Muhammad Aziz[3]*

*Address all correspondence to: aziz.m.aa@m.titech.ac.jp

1 Department of Transdisciplinary Science and Engineering, Tokyo Institute of Technology, Yokohama, Kanagawa, Japan

2 Agency for the Assessment and Application of Technology, Serpong, Tangerang Selatan, Indonesia

3 Institute of Innovative Research, Tokyo Institute of Technology, Meguro, Tokyo, Japan

References

[1] Livingston WR Biomass ash and the mixed ashes from cofiring biomass with coal. In: Proceedings of the IEA Clean Coal Workshop, 25–26 January 2011, Drax Power Station, London, UK

[2] Darmawan A, Dwika D, Aziz M, Tokimatsu T. Retrofitting existing coal power plants through cofiring with hydrothermally treated empty fruit bunch and a novel integrated system. Applied Energy. 2017;**204**:1138-1147

[3] Aziz M, Dwika B, Oda T. Computational fluid dynamic analysis of cofiring of palm kernel shell into coal fired power plant. Energies. 2016;**9**:137. DOI: 10.3390/en9030137

[4] Xu W, Niu Y, Tan H, Wang D, Du W, Hui S. A new agro/forestry residues cofiring model in a large pulverized coal furnace: Technical and economic assessments. Energies. 2013;**6**:4377-4393

[5] IEA. Energy Technology Perspectives: Scenarios & Strategies to 2050. Paris: OECD/IEA; 2010

[6] IEA. World Energy Outlook 2010. Paris: OECD/IEA; 2010

[7] Williams A, Pourkashanian M, Jones JM. The combustion of coal and some other solid fuels. Symposium (International) on Combustion. 2000;**28**(2):2141-2162

[8] Tabet F, Gokalp I. Review on CFD based models for cofiring coal and biomass. Renewable and Sustainable Energy Reviews. 2015;**51**:1101-1114

[9] Ranade VV, Gupta DF. Computational Modeling of Pulverized Coal Fired Boilers. Boca Raton, USA: CRC Press; 2015

[10] Budianto D, Aziz M, Cahyadi, Oda T. Numerical investigation of cofiring of palm kernel shell into pulverized coal combustion. Journal of the Japan Institute of Energy. 2016;**95**: 605-614

[11] Oevermann M, Gerber S, Behrendt F. Euler-Lagrange/DEM simulation of wood gasification in a bubbling fluidized bed reactor. Particuology. 2009;**7**:307-316

[12] Anderson JD. Governing equations of fluid dynamics. In: Wendt JF, editor. Computational Fluid Dynamics. Berlin, Germany: Springer-Verlag; 2009. p. 15–51.

[13] Hu Z, Ma X, Chen Y, Liao Y, Wua J, Yu Z, et al. Co-combustion of coal with printing and dyeing sludge: Numerical simulation of the process and related NO_X emissions. Fuel. 2015;**139**:606-613

[14] Eaton AM, Smoot LD, Hill SC, Eatough CN. Components, formulations, solutions, evaluation, and application of comprehensive combustion models. Progress in Energy and Combustion Science. 1999;**25**:387-436

[15] Aziz M, Oda T, Kashiwagi T. Design and analysis of energy-efficient integrated crude palm oil and palm kernel oil processes. Journal of the Japan Institute of Energy. 2014;**94**:143-150

[16] Aziz M, Kurniawan T, Oda T, Kashiwagi T. Advanced power generation using biomass wastes from palm oil mills. Applied Thermal Engineering. 2017;**114**:1378-1386

[17] Aziz M, Prawisudha P, Prabowo B, Budiman BA. Integration of energy-efficient empty fruit bunch drying with gasification/combined cycle systems. Applied Energy. 2015;**139**: 188-195

[18] Aziz M, Kurniawan T. Enhanced utilization of palm oil mill wastes for power generation. Chemical Engineering Transactions. 2016;**52**:727-732

[19] Clean Air Technology Center (MD-12), Nitrogen Oxides (NOx), Why and How they are Controlled, Technical Bulletin of Environmental Protection Agency, EPA 456/F-99-006R, 1999, North Carolina, USA. Available from: http://www3.epa.gov/ttncatc1/cica/other7_e.html (accessed on Dec 2015)

[20] Zaini IN, Novianti S, Nurdiawati A, Irhamna AR, Aziz M, Yoshikawa K. Investigation of the physical characteristics of washed hydrochar pellets made from empty fruit bunch. Fuel Processing Technology. 2017;**160**:109-120

[21] Lokahita B, Aziz M, Yoshikawa K, Takahashi F. Energy and resource recovery from tetra Pak waste using hydrothermal treatment. Applied Energy. in press. DOI: 10.1016/j.apenergy.2017.05.141

[22] Mu'min GF, Prawisudha P, Zaini IN, Aziz M, Pasek AD. Municipal solid waste processing and separation employing wet torrefaction for alternative fuel production and aluminum reclamation.Waste Management. 2017;**67**:106-120

[23] Lam PS, Lam PY, Sokhansanj S, Lim CJ, Bi XT, Stephen JD, Pribowo A, Mabee WE. Steam explosion of oil palm residues for the production of durable pellets. Applied Energy. 2015;**141**:160-166

[24] Novianti S, Biddinika MK, Prawisudha P, Yoshikawa K. Upgrading of palm oil empty fruit bunch employing hydrothermal treatment in lab-scale and pilot scale. Procedia Environmental Sciences. 2014;**20**:46-54

Chapter 10

CFD Modelling of Coupled Multiphysics-Multiscale Engineering Cases

Mario E. Cordero, Sebastián Uribe, Luis G. Zárate,
Reyna Natividad Rangel,
Alejandro Regalado-Méndez and Ever Peralta Reyes

Additional information is available at the end of the chapter

http://dx.doi.org/10.5772/intechopen.70562

Abstract

Many of the engineering problems have multiphysics and multiscale nature. Non-isothermal flows, stirred reactors, turbulent mixing and membrane filtration, are prevalent cases in which the coupling of several physics phenomena is required for the adequate prediction of overall behaviors. Also, a multiscale analysis, where the same phenomenon is analyzed at different scales, can lead to better understanding of the phenomena, which can be used in optimization and to provide adequate scale-up methodologies. Studies incorporating both multiscale and multiphysics analysis are rarely addressed in literature; in fact, these kinds of problems will be the research challenge in the next years. Computer fluid dynamics (CFD) techniques have shown to be promising to deal with these kinds of systems. In this chapter, these are used to implement a multiscale analysis of the hydrodesulphurization (HDS) process for light gas-oil (LGO). The aforementioned is carried out by the analysis of mass an energy transport at: (1) microporous (MP) scale, (2) pseudo-homogeneous catalyst (PHC) scale, and by analysis of (3) momentum and mass transport at reactor scale (RS). In addition, a particular discussion is made regarding the proper establishment of the model, its validation, the use of different boundary conditions, its justification; and the dependence of solutions of parameters and initial and boundary conditions.

Keywords: multiphysics models, multiscale models, HDS process, effective transport coefficients, transport in porous media

1. Introduction

The multiscale phenomena are common issues for many applications in several processes and phenomena of interest overall engineering fields. From the design, implementation and optimization of processes and equipment, to the Process Safety Engineering, this multiscale nature represents a great challenge to overcome. An example of this is the study of industrial fires, in which the fire can reach over 50 m in height, and the produced smokes may have effects on the environment in lengths of tens or even hundredths of kilometers. Also, in these phenomena, the hydrodynamics of circulating air has a crucial effect in the behavior of the fires, which have a different characteristic length scale, of a few kilometers. Furthermore, it is known that there is also a turbulent transport of energy, which has a predominant contribution over the energy transport in these phenomena, and important parameters as the turbulent kinetic energy varies in the inertial subrange of 1×10^{-3} m; while the scale for the dissipation of kinetic energy (Kolmogorov scale) is about 1×10^{-4} m. An even smaller scale occurs in the molecular diffusion of the species involved in the phenomenon (Batchelor scale), which is in the range of $1 \times 10^{-5} - 1 \times 10^{-6}$ m.

Another example of this multiscale nature is present in multiphase catalytic chemical reactors, where three different length-scale analysis levels can be distinguished: (1) reactor level, (2) catalyst or catalyst's clusters level, and (3) catalyst microstructure level. Every level prior mentioned having physical and chemical phenomena taking place at different scales, and being of individual interest for different kinds of analysis. For example, at the last-mentioned level, there is an interest into investigating over the size and distribution of noble metal crystals, commonly named adsorbed islands, their interaction with the supporting material, and other key aspects that determine the catalyst activity. These phenomena take place at scales around $1 \times 10^{-9} - 1 \times 10^{-8}$ m; it is noteworthy that in the study of this low scale, even the continuum assumptions are not valid, and therefore there is a need to implement molecular analysis. At the catalyst cluster lever, the characteristic length can be set to the pellet radius, which are found commercially in the range of $1 \times 10^{-3} - 1 \times 10^{-2}$ m. In this scale, there is an interest in the phenomena taking place inside the porous microstructure of the catalyst and in the boundary layer, where coupled phenomena of mass and energy transport occur in lengths below 1×10^{-3} m, and phenomena of resistance to the transport between the phases occur below 1×10^{-4} m. In the large scale, the reactor length, the phenomena occur in length scales of around 1×10^{2} m. In this, there is an interest in the study of maldistribution, incomplete wetting, phases distribution, hot spot formation, among other issues, which can be caused by phenomena at lower scales. For both of the mentioned examples, a similar discussion can be made regarding the time scales. **Figure 1** depicts the length scale of the phenomena taking place in the study of catalytic reactor. This example will be further developed in order to give insight into the multiscale and multiphysic nature of engineering problems.

In addition, it is important to note that both examples also present a strong multiphysic nature; both involve chemical reactions of hundreds, up to thousands, of chemical species, multiphase transport of species, energy transport generated by the reaction nature, and momentum transport of fluid phases that interact with solids. Due to these complexities, mathematical methods have been developed in order to better understand these interactions and the phenomena that is hardly observable by experimental methods. In this context, CFD techniques have come into view as promising alternatives into the multiphysic-multiscale modelling. However, these approaches face the obstacle of the high nonlinearity and high grade of coupling between the phenomena, physics and scales. Furthermore, in the catalytic reactor study, further nonlinearities

http://dx.doi.org/10.5772/intechopen.70562

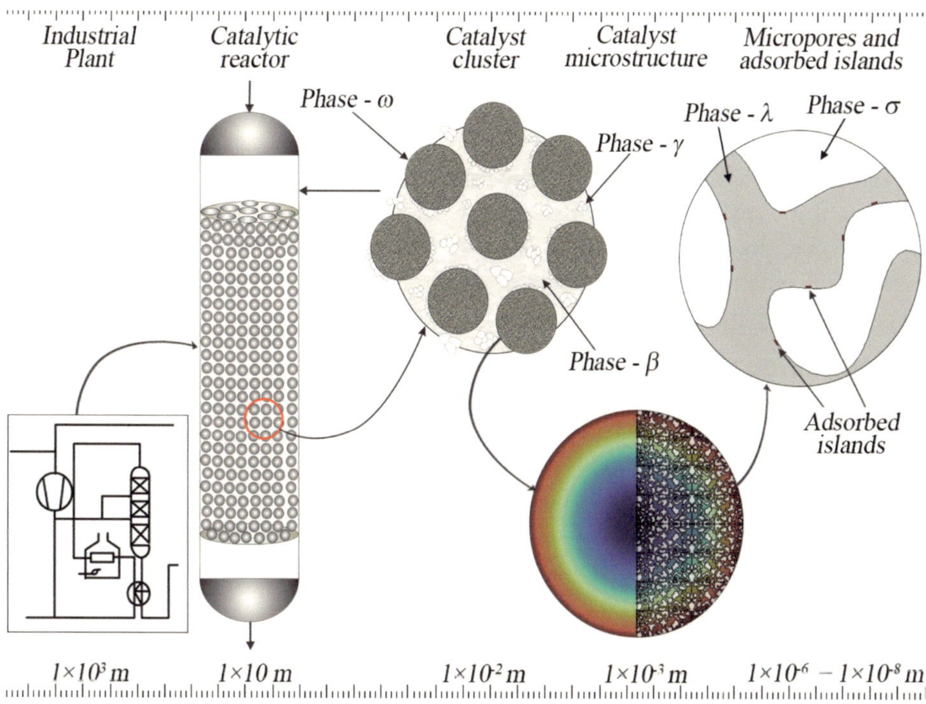

Figure 1. Schematic representation of the multiscale in catalytic reactors.

are present as a result of the nonlinear dependence of the concentrations and temperature fields to the chemical reactions. Additionally, in the reactor scale, more coupling nonlinearities are present [1] due to the extra phenomena, such as adsorption/desorption at solid-fluid interfaces, caused by heterogeneities of the porous media. Then, it is natural to think that a precise description of the effects and dependence between the scales must be taken into account to properly describe the phenomena.

In scientific community, it has been recognized that in complex systems, the dominant issue is the existence of multi spatial-temporal scales and its multiphysics nature; and it has identified that its comprehension is at the frontier of state of art of process engineering, as well as in science and technology of many fields and disciplines [2]. In spite of the above, the knowledge developed in engineering fields until the first years of the present century has been extending from understanding macro-scale field (mass, energy, velocity, etc.) distribution and individual phenomena, focusing on mechanisms at microscale, to the understanding of coupling between phenomena at different scales. To enable these studies, it has been necessary to make average assumptions over fields transport equations to studying heterogeneity both in time and in space. However, due to the limitation in the knowledge to deal with non-equilibrium and nonlinear phenomena, the quantification of chemical and physical processes at different scales is yet a major challenge. The use of average and linear approaches and simplification of heterogeneities is insufficient to deal with multiscale spatial-temporal structures and nonlinear phenomena, then the multiscale analysis have emerged as promising tool to improve models, theories, and knowledge about these systems. The development of computers and advances in numerical methods have allowed the development of software and advances in measurement at small and non-invasive scales, and have also favored the development of the multiscale analysis [3–7].

A critical step in the development of multiscale models is the establishment of *bridges* that allow the coupling of variables and parameters between the different scales, and the transfer of information between these scales [4]. Regarding this latter aspect, it is also important to determinate if the transferred information between the scales is required to be in two-ways (up to down, and down to up scales) or one-way (down to up scales) [8]. The consideration of these aspects is what will allow the analysis of complex systems moving from the reductionism of average simplifications to a holistic form of study.

Great efforts into the CFD analysis of multiscale systems have been developed in recent years. It is noteworthy the work of Ding and co-workers [7], who developed a multiscale methodology aided by CFD simulation, for a catalytic distillation with bale packings, considering micro and macroscales, focusing only in the hydrodynamics. In the microscale, a volume of fluids (VOF) method is implemented in a representative elementary unit (REU) to simulate the gas-liquid flow considering the packing geometry, in order to study the liquid split proportion. While in the macroscale, a unit network model is developed, where the liquid split proportion from the microscale model is taken as an input, in order to measure the liquid holdup and pressure drops. It is important to note that in this work, the two scales are communicated in only one way. This means that the information of the microscales phenomena scales up to the macroscale, but the effects from the macroscale to the microscales are neglected. Also, no multiphysic analysis in developed. Several works where multiscale analysis is carried out only in the hydrodynamics can be found in literature [9, 10]; however, works where coupled multiscale and multiphysic analyses are performed, are scarce.

As an example of the aforementioned, the works of Xie and Luo can be mentioned [11]. They developed an Euler-Euler two-phase model and a population balance model (PBM) to simulate a liquid-liquid suspension polymerization process. The model considers momentum, turbulence, mass and energy transport equations, while PBM considers a Breakage Kernel and Coalescence Kernel. It is important to highlight is that these differential equations have the same domain, implying solutions at the same time and length scales. The authors consider that as the polymerization process occurs in a lower length-scale, and the kinetics of this process occurs in an atomic scale, the multiscale is captured through the effects of these. These kinds of models have been recently developed, and there is still a need to clarify certain aspects regarding the multiscale-multiphysic nature, and how should it be addressed and incorporated to the models. Thus, further works that incorporate the multiscale-multiphysic analyses, and address the establishment of *bridges* that connect the scales and how these communicate the information, are yet desirable.

In this work, an effort to contribute to the knowledge of multiphysic-multiscale modelling is developed. The analysis of a hydrodesulphurization (HDS) process for a light gas-oil (LGO) through COMSOL Multiphysics CFD simulations is addressed and discussed, considering three different scales (i) micropores (MP) scale, (ii) pseudo-homogeneous catalyst (PHC) scale, and (iii) reactor scale (RS). The analysis takes into account the effect of the microstructure geometry on upper scales, and how is this information captured and communicated. In addition, the effect of the reactor scale over the lower scales is analyzed, by means of the observed differences when the catalyst model is solved without the effect of the reactor behavior. By the last, a discussion regarding the boundary conditions establishment, model validation, and dependence of solution of the model parameters, is presented.

2. HDS process and HDS reactor

The hydrodesulphurization (HDS) is part of catalytic hydrotreatment (HDT) process where the content of some crude oil contaminants containing sulfur is reduced using hydrogen over a catalyst of NiMo or CoMo supported on Al_2O_3. This is one of the most important processes in crude oil refining, because it allows reducing the emission of SO_x and NO_x, which are synthesized by fuel combustion. These emissions are strong environmental contaminants; in addition, they can prejudice the performance of the catalysts used in refining processes, as well as the catalysts used in catalytic converters of vehicles [12].

The most important equipment in a HDT unit is the three-phase HDS reactor, and thus this has been target of extensive investigation and modelling. In HDS reactors, gas and liquid phases (hydrogen and a fraction of hydrocarbons) are contacted with a solid phase (catalyst). The reactions occur between the dissolved gas reactant and the liquid-phase reactant at the surface of the catalyst. Depending on whether the main mass-transfer resistance is located, three-phase catalytic fixed-bed reactors can operate either, with a continuous gas and a distributed liquid phase (trickle operation), or with a distributed gas and a continuous liquid phase (bubble operation). Commercial HDS reactor usually operates in a trickle-bed regime, with concurrent downward flow of gas and liquid over a randomly fixed bed of catalyst particles where the reactions take place [13]. The HDS reactor operates at elevated pressures and temperatures because the solubility of gases in liquids increases with rising partial pressure and the reaction rate is favored with those temperature magnitudes.

Given the importance of the HDS process and the growing pressure exerted by the new environmental regulations reducing the maximum limits of sulfur content in fossil fuels, have led to the need for optimization of HDS reactors; which in turn requires deeper and more detailed knowledge of the phenomena that occur in the HDS reactor. To obtain the knowledge that allows the optimization of the HDS reactor, the CFD techniques are very promising, as they allow to obtain punctual and average values for the fields of concentration, temperature, etc.

In reactor modelling, a common approach is to make corrections to the intrinsic reaction rate (r_i) to take into account the effects of the mass and energy transport resistances inside and outside the catalyst, through a called effectiveness factor (η), defined by Eqs. (1) and (2).

$$(r_i)_{observed} = \eta (r_i)_{intrinsic} \tag{1}$$

$$\eta = \frac{\int_{V_{catalyst}} r_i(c_i' s, T) dV}{\int_{V_{catalyst}} r_i(c_i' s, T)|_{at\ surface\ condition}\, dV} \tag{2}$$

The correction is due to that *"it is not possible or it is hard"* to solve the exact heterogeneous mass and energy transport equations with superficial reaction, which are valid inside the pores and the solid matrix of catalyst; the aforementioned, is due to that the geometry of the equations domains is unknown or very complicated. Therefore, the mass and temperature fields necessary to evaluate the intrinsic reaction rate in Eq. (1), are evaluated through solving pseudo-homogeneous mass and energy transport equations with reaction taking place in all catalyst. In this pseudo-homogeneous model, the porous nature and its mass and energy transport characteristics, inherent of the real heterogeneous catalyst, are represented or incorporated through two effective transport coefficients, the effective diffusivity and conductivity coefficients ($\mathbf{D}_{eff}$, $\mathbf{K}_{eff}$). It is important to emphasize that in the described approach, there are two events where the transport of information from a small to a larger scale is carried out. In precise form, the first take place when the effective transport coefficient captures geometry characteristics and transport phenomena happening at porous microstructure scale; and the second takes place when mass and energy features, inside catalytic particle are incorporated to correct the reaction rate, which is used at reactor scale.

In this chapter, an example where the multiphysics and multiscale nature of trickle bed reactor's (TBR's) for HDS process are discussed is addressed. The CFD models are constituted by models at three different scales: (a) porous microstructure scale of catalyst, (b) catalyst particle scale, and (c) reactor scale. In **Figure 1**, the three scales and the geometric details of the implementing models here are shown.

3. Multiscale CFD models

3.1. Micropores CFD model

At MP scale, the heterogeneous mass and energy transport equations are solved, taking into account the transport phenomena occurring inside pores and solid matrix of a catalytic particle. In this system, the effective transport coefficients are evaluated.

3.1.1. Porous microstructure geometric model

To perform the mentioned above, a representative model of the geometry microstructure of a catalyst was constructed using a vectored model of a real porous media taken from a micrograph found in literature [14]. This was used and adapted in order to replicate parameters comparable with typical values of HDS systems such as pore diameter $d_p = 20 - 200$ nm [15] and porosity $0.3 \leq \varepsilon_\lambda \leq 0.6$ [16]. It is worth noticing that a real geometric model of pores distribution has been built for the catalytic particle of 0.35 mm of diameter, at scales of 4:1 and 2:1 of the real scale.

Figure 2 shows detail of geometric representation of catalytic particle incorporating an explicit porous microstructure, which is constituted by a solid matrix (*phase-σ*) and the fluid phase formed by the interstitial spaces left by the solid matrix (*phase-λ*). In addition, the solid-fluid interphase ($A_{\sigma\lambda}$) where the superficial reaction takes place, is illustrated.

http://dx.doi.org/10.5772/intechopen.70562

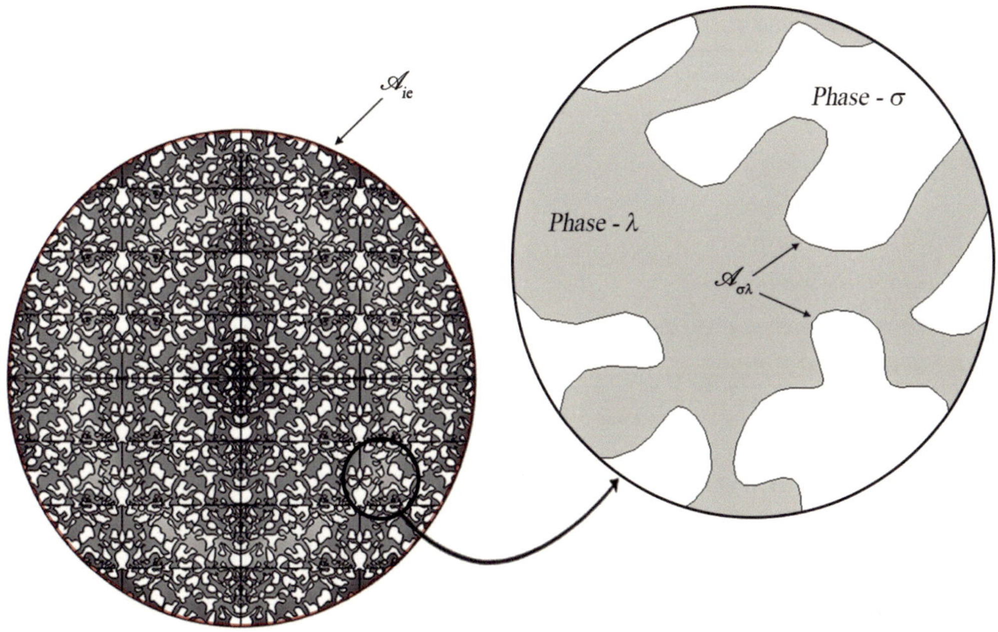

Figure 2. Representation of the heterogeneous catalyst micropores model.

3.1.2. Heterogeneous mass and energy transport model

The transport model for the MP model, is formed by local mass and energy transport equations. For the case of the mass transport, it is considered that there is only transport in the interstitial phase, because the porous matrix is considered to be impermeable; while for energy transport both phases carry energy, so there is an equation for each domain.

It is important to note that due to capillarity forces, the micropores are completely filled [12], consequently the fluid inside of catalyst's pores is stagnant, there are no convective contributions to the mass and energy transport, and there is no need for a momentum balance equation. Therefore, the mass and energy transport models are reduced to Eqs. (3) and (4), respectively [17]

$$\nabla \cdot \left(\mathrm{D}_i^{\lambda} \nabla C_i^{\lambda} \right) = 0; \qquad i = \{R - S, H_2, H_2S\}\ specie \tag{3}$$

$$-k_j \nabla^2 T^j = 0; \qquad j = \{\sigma, \lambda\}\ phase \tag{4}$$

It is important to note that in the transport Eqs. (3) and (4) there is no reaction term and heat source term, respectively, thus concentrations and temperature fields are due to the non-homogeneous boundary conditions. In fact, the superficial reaction, as well as the heat generation by reaction are considered as a no-homogeneous boundary condition (see **Table 1**).

When it is considered that the reaction takes place in all the fluid-solid interface within the pores of the catalyst, a simplification has been made because actual the reaction takes place in a lower scale on the active phase of the catalyst, which are nothing more than small cumulus of

Mass transfer $(i\text{-}specie = R\text{-}S, H_2, H_2S)$		
$-\mathbf{n}_{\sigma\lambda}\cdot D_i^{\lambda}\ \nabla C_i^{\lambda} = \nu_i\ a_v\ r_{HDS}$ *(superficial reaction)*	at $A_{\sigma\lambda}$	(5)
$C_i^{\lambda} = C_i\vert_{bulk}$ *(bulk phase concentration)*	at $A_{\lambda e}$	(6)
Heat transfer in liquid phase (phase-Λ)		
$-\mathbf{n}_{\sigma\lambda}\cdot k_{\Lambda}\nabla T_{\Lambda} = a_v(-\Delta H_{HDS})r_{HDS}$ *(energy generation at porous interphase)*	at $A_{\sigma\lambda}$	(7)
$T_{\Lambda} = T_0$ *(bulk phase temperature)*	at $A_{\Lambda e}$	(8)
Heat transfer in solid phase (phase-σ)		
$-\mathbf{n}_{\sigma\lambda}\cdot k_{\sigma}\nabla T_{\sigma} = a_v(-\Delta H_{HDS})r_{HDS}$ *(energy generation at porous interphase)*	at $A_{\sigma\lambda}$	(9)
$T_{\sigma} = T_0$ *(bulk phase temperature)*	at $A_{\sigma e}$	(10)

Table 1. Boundary conditions of heterogeneous transport CFD model.

crystals of metals or metal salts, which are deposited on the surface (so-called adsorbed islands). Moreover, on these adsorbed islands phenomena of adsorption and desorption of products and reagents take place.

The foregoing means that both reaction and adsorption/desorption phenomena occur at discrete locations on the surface of the catalyst and not on the entire surface. Fortunately, the experimentally determined kinetics expressions takes into account the proper considerations in order to express the reaction that takes place in punctual as a reaction occurring throughout the catalytic interfacial surface. Also, the predictions of the models considering surface reaction have proven to be accurate enough [18].

The boundary value problem specified by Eqs. (3) and (4) are set to satisfy the boundary conditions shown in **Table 1**.

Where $A_{\lambda e}$ and $A_{\sigma e}$ represent the external catalyst boundaries; $-\mathbf{n}_{\sigma\lambda}$ is the unitary normal vector that points from σ - phase to λ - phase; ν_i is the stoichiometric coefficient for each specie; and $C_i\vert_{bulk}$ is the concentration of the specie i at reactor bulk conditions.

Note that in the boundary conditions (5), (7), and (9), the reaction rate (r_{HDS}) is multiplied by the parameter a_v, which is defined as the ratio of interstitial volume to fluid-catalyst interfacial area ($a_v = V/A_{\sigma\lambda}$) [18]. This parameter appears by virtue of averaging process of mass transport equations and superficial reaction rate and allows us to relate the reaction rate obtained by experimental data $\langle r_i^{\omega}\rangle^{\omega}\left[mol/m^3s\right]$ with the superficial velocity $r_i[mol/m^2s]$.

$$r_i = a_v\langle r_i^{\omega}\rangle^{\omega} \tag{11}$$

3.2. Effective coefficients evaluation

A theoretical development to evaluate these coefficients has been established by Whitaker and co-workers, within the framework of the method of volume averaging [18]. The expressions that allow the evaluation of the effective diffusivity and effective conductivity coefficients are Eqs. (12) and (13), respectively. Note that these expressions are valid for any engineering case involving diffusion and conductive heat transfer through porous media where reaction takes place at interphase area.

$$\mathbf{D}_{eff,i} = \mathrm{D}_i^{\lambda}\left(\mathbf{I} + \frac{1}{V_{\lambda}}\int_{\mathrm{A}_{\lambda\sigma}} \mathbf{n}_{\sigma\lambda}\mathbf{b}_{\lambda} dA\right) \tag{12}$$

$$\frac{\mathbf{K}_{eff}}{k_{\lambda}} = (\varepsilon_{\lambda} + \varepsilon_{\sigma}\kappa)\mathbf{I} + \frac{(1-\kappa)}{\mathrm{V}}\int_{\mathrm{A}_{\lambda\sigma}} \mathbf{n}_{\lambda\sigma}\mathbf{b}_{\Lambda} dA \tag{13}$$

In the equations above, ε_i represent the volume fraction occupied by each *i-phase;* **I** is the identity tensor; and κ is the quotient of conductivities of the solid phase to fluid phase $\kappa = k_{\sigma}/k_{\lambda}$.

To evaluate the effective coefficients, the evaluation of so-called closure vectors $\mathbf{b}_{\lambda}$ and $\mathbf{b}_{\Lambda}$ are required, which is done through the solution of boundary value problems described by the following equations.

$$\nabla^2 \mathbf{b}_{\lambda} = 0 \tag{14}$$

$$\nabla^2 \mathbf{b}_i = 0; \qquad i - phase = \Lambda, \sigma \tag{15}$$

These boundary value problems are the result of the averaging process for the punctual mass and energy transport Eqs. (3) and (4), of a decomposition of scales, and of a proposal for a solution of the deviations field problem using the source terms boundary value problem for deviations for mass and energy average equation. For more details, the reader is invited to review the work of Whittaker [18] and extensive literature regarding Method of volume averaging [19–21].

On the other hand, in Eqs. (14) and (15), the subscripts Λ and λ, both refer to the fluid phase, however, it is important to differentiate them as they come from the solution of a different boundary value problem.

The boundary conditions set to both problems are shown in **Table 2**.

In these, **r** is the position vector that locates any points in the average volume, and l_i represent the three non-unique lattice vectors that are required to describe a spatially periodic porous medium [22]. Then, boundary conditions (17) and (20) are actually periodicity conditions, implying that these boundary value problems are usually solved in periodic domains inherent to periodic representative unitary cells (RUC).

It must be noted that the boundary value problem for the closure vectors are essentially geometrical, and that the vector field is generated by non-homogeneous boundary conditions; this means that the vector field is generated by the presence of solid-fluid interphases ($\mathrm{A}_{\sigma\lambda}$) inside of porous media. Also, it should be noted that information of the porous structure and its effects are captured by the closure vectors, and that the closure vectors for mass and energy are different. Implying that something else that the geometrical characteristics are captured

Mass transfer		
$-\mathbf{n}_{\lambda\sigma}\cdot\nabla\mathbf{b}_{\lambda}=\mathbf{n}_{\lambda\sigma}$	*at* $A_{\sigma\lambda}$	(16)
$\mathbf{b}_{\lambda}(\mathbf{r}+l_i)=\mathbf{b}_{\lambda}(\mathbf{r})$	*for* $i=1,2,3,\ldots$	(17)
Heat transfer		
$\mathbf{b}_{\Lambda}=\mathbf{b}_{\sigma}$	*at* $A_{\sigma\lambda}$	(18)
$-\mathbf{n}_{\Lambda\sigma}\cdot\nabla\mathbf{b}_{\Lambda}=-\mathbf{n}_{\Lambda\sigma}\cdot\kappa\nabla\mathbf{b}_{\sigma}+\mathbf{n}_{\Lambda\sigma}(1-\kappa)$	*at* $A_{\sigma\lambda}$	(19)
$\mathbf{b}_{\Lambda}(\mathbf{r}+l_i)=\mathbf{b}_{\Lambda}(\mathbf{r});\quad i-phase=\Lambda,\sigma$	*for* $i=1,2,3,\ldots$	(20)

Table 2. Boundary conditions for closure boundary value problems.

through them. This information passes to upper scales through the effective transport coefficients (Eqs. (12) and (13)), implying that the porous structure affects the mass and energy transport at pellet scale. Then, in can be seen that this development is setting a *bridge* between the different length-scales.

3.3. Pseudo-homogeneous CFD model

The mass and energy pseudo-homogeneous transport equations for a catalytic particle are well established in the literature [23], for the analyzed HDS reaction here, these take the form:

$$\nabla\cdot\left(\varepsilon_{\lambda}\mathbf{D}_{eff}\nabla\left\langle C_i^{\omega}\right\rangle^{\omega}\right)=\nu_i\,r_{HDS}\qquad i-species=R-S,H_2,H_2S \tag{21}$$

$$\nabla\cdot\left(\mathbf{K}_{eff}\cdot\nabla\langle T\rangle^{\omega}\right)=(-\Delta H)r_{HDS} \tag{22}$$

In these expressions, $\left\langle C_i^{\omega}\right\rangle^{\omega}$ and $\langle T\rangle^{\omega}$ represent the intrinsic average of concentration for the *i-specie* and temperature fields, which are quite different from the punctual concentration and temperature fields $\left(C_i^{\lambda},T^{j}\right)$ of the heterogeneous model described by Eqs. (3) and (4). To clarify the above it is important to remember that the average fields of concentration and temperature present changes in lengths of scale of order of $l_{pellet}<D_{pellet}$, whereas the point fields undergo changes in the length scale of the order of $l_{porous}<d_{pore}$.

On the other hand, the effective coefficients of transport ($\mathbf{D}_{eff,i}$, $\mathbf{K}_{eff}$) necessary to solve the model at catalyst scale can be obtained by experimental data or by theoretical approaches. In the present case, these were obtained by the solution of boundary value problem for closure vector (Eqs. (14)–(20)) in conjunction with Eqs. (12) and (13).

The appropriate boundary conditions for the transport of matter and energy in the catalyst are shown in **Table 3**.

As can be observed, temperature and concentration of each specie at the bulk fluid inside reactor are required; this implies that there is a need to transfer information between the phenomena that take place on the catalytic scale and on the reactor scale. The transfer of the information of the nature of the resistances on the transport at catalyst scale, toward reactor scale, can be carried out through the effectiveness factor, as described in Section 2.1.

Figure 3 shows the relationship and differences between heterogeneous and pseudo-homogeneous mass transport at catalytic particle.

3.4. Heterogeneous CFD reactor scale model

The CFD reactor model considers an Eulerian approach, where gas and liquid phases are considered as interpenetrating, implying that both fluid phases have been the same domain. In the case of the solid phase, an explicit geometry for a fixed bed was built considering spherical catalytic particles of 0.35 mm of diameter. **Figure 4** shows the geometrical details for both interstitial (γ, β - fluid phases) and catalytic (ω - phase) domains.

The complete CFD model for the three-phase reactor consists of two momentum transport equations, one for each fluid phase, eight mass transport equations, one per specie, and three closures for the interaction between the solid, gas, and liquid phases.

Mass transfer ($i-specie = R-S, H_2, H_2S$)		
$\nabla\langle C_i^\omega\rangle^\omega = 0$ (*concentration continuity*)	at $r=0$	(23)
$\langle C_i^\omega\rangle^\omega = C_i\|_B$ (*bulk phase concentration*)	at $r=R_p$	(24)
Heat transfer		
$\nabla\langle T\rangle = 0$ (*temperature continuity*)	at $r=0$	(25)
$\langle T\rangle = \langle T\rangle_B$ (*bulk phase temperature*)	at $r=R_p$	(26)

Table 3. Boundary conditions for pseudo-homogeneous transport model.

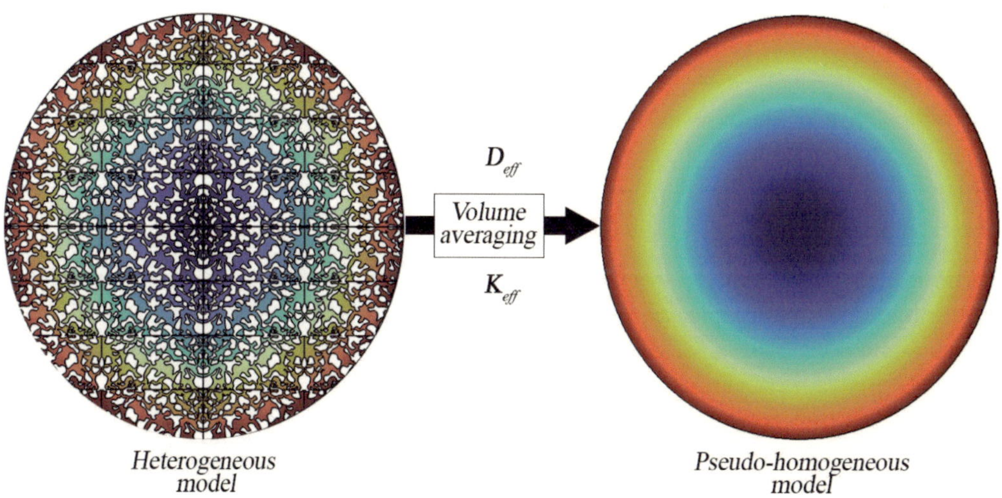

Figure 3. Concentration field for a catalytic particle obtained through the transport models at porous and catalyst scales.

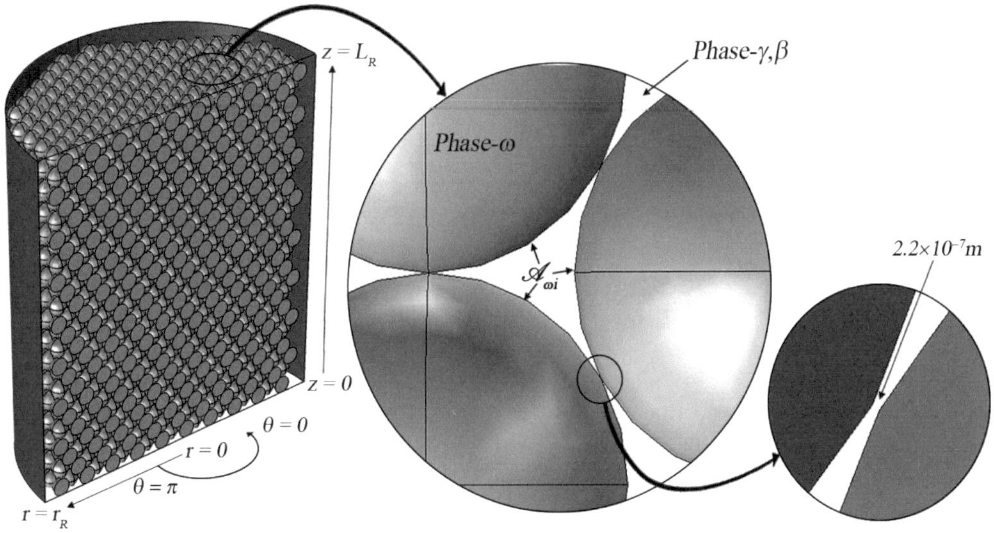

Figure 4. Geometrical details of the TBR model.

3.4.1. Hydrodynamic model for TBR

The hydrodynamic model at steady state is constituted by continuity and momentum transport equations:

$$\varepsilon_\gamma \rho_\gamma \nabla \cdot \mathbf{v}_\gamma = 0 \qquad \left(\rho_\gamma = cte\right) \tag{27}$$

$$\varepsilon_\beta \nabla \cdot \left(\rho_\beta \mathbf{v}_\beta\right) = 0 \tag{28}$$

$$\varepsilon_\gamma \rho_\gamma \left(\mathbf{v}_\gamma \cdot \nabla\right)\mathbf{v}_\gamma = \varepsilon_\gamma \nabla \cdot \left[-P\,\mathbf{I} + \mu_\gamma\left(\nabla \mathbf{v}_\gamma + \left(\nabla \mathbf{v}_\gamma\right)^T\right)\right] + \mathbf{F}_\gamma/\varepsilon_\gamma + \rho_\gamma \mathbf{g} \tag{29}$$

$$\varepsilon_\beta \rho_\beta \left(\mathbf{v}_\beta \cdot \nabla\right)\mathbf{v}_\beta = \varepsilon_\beta \nabla \cdot \left[-P\,\mathbf{I} + \mu_\beta\left(\nabla \mathbf{v}_\beta + \left(\nabla \mathbf{v}_\beta\right)^T\right) - \frac{2}{3}\mu_\beta\left(\nabla \cdot \mathbf{v}_\beta\right)\mathbf{I}\right] + \mathbf{F}_\beta/\varepsilon_\beta + \rho_\beta \mathbf{g} \tag{30}$$

In these, $\mathbf{v}_i$ and ε_i are the local interstitial velocity and volume fraction for both gas and liquid phase, respectively. In Eqs. (27) and (28), the gas phase is considering as compressible fluid.

The term ($\mathbf{F}_i/\varepsilon_i$) takes into account the momentum exchange between the phases through the momentum exchange coefficient K_{ij}, which has three contributions: liquid-gas, liquid-solid, and gas-solid interactions.

$$\mathbf{F}_i = \sum_{j=1}^{n} K_{ji}\left(\mathbf{v}_j - \mathbf{v}_i\right) \tag{31}$$

In the CFD model, the Attou momentum exchange model, which is actually a closure for the momentum transfer equations, was incorporated [24], which is considered adequate to take account of the interaction between phases in fixed bed three-phase reactors.

$$K_{\beta\gamma} = \varepsilon_\beta \left[\frac{E_1 \mu_\beta (1-\varepsilon_\beta)^2}{\varepsilon_\beta^2 d_p^2} \left(\frac{\varepsilon_\omega}{1-\varepsilon_\beta} \right)^{0.667} + \frac{E_2 \rho_\beta (\mathbf{v}_\beta - \mathbf{v}_\gamma)(1-\varepsilon_\beta)}{\varepsilon_\beta d_p} \left(\frac{\varepsilon_\omega}{1-\varepsilon_\beta} \right)^{0.333} \right] \tag{32}$$

$$K_{\beta\omega} = \varepsilon_\beta \left[\frac{E_1 \mu_\beta (1-\varepsilon_\beta)^2}{\varepsilon_\beta^2 d_p^2} \left(\frac{\varepsilon_\omega}{1-\varepsilon_\beta} \right)^{0.667} + \frac{E_2 \rho_\beta \mathbf{v}_\beta (1-\varepsilon_\beta)}{\varepsilon_\beta d_p} \left(\frac{\varepsilon_\omega}{1-\varepsilon_\beta} \right)^{0.333} \right] \tag{33}$$

$$K_{\gamma\omega} = \varepsilon_\gamma \left[\frac{E_1 \mu_\gamma \varepsilon_\omega^2}{\varepsilon_\gamma^2 d_p^2} + \frac{E_2 \rho_\gamma \mathbf{v}_\gamma \varepsilon_\omega}{\varepsilon_\gamma d_p} \right] \tag{34}$$

where E_1 and E_2 are de Ergun constants, and μ_i and ρ_i are i-phase viscosity and density, respectively.

3.4.2. *Mass transport model for i-specie at TBR*

The three-phase mass transport model is constituted by the following set of differential equations:

$$\nabla \cdot \left(-\mathrm{D}_i^\beta \nabla \left\langle C_i^\beta \right\rangle \right) + \mathbf{v}_\beta \cdot \nabla \left\langle C_i^\beta \right\rangle = N_i^{\beta\gamma} / \varepsilon_\beta \qquad i - specie = H_2, H_2S \tag{35}$$

$$\nabla \cdot \left(-\mathrm{D}_i^\gamma \nabla \langle C_i^\gamma \rangle \right) + \mathbf{v}_\gamma \cdot \nabla \langle C_i^\gamma \rangle = N_i^{\gamma\beta} / \varepsilon_\gamma \qquad i - specie = R - S, H_2, H_2S \tag{36}$$

$$\nabla \cdot \left(\varepsilon_\lambda \mathrm{D}_{eff,i} \nabla \langle C_i^\lambda \rangle^\lambda \right) = \nu_i \, r_{HDS} \qquad i - specie = R - S, H_2, H_2S \tag{37}$$

For case of fluid phases, the mass transport considers both the convective and diffusive contribution, and the chemical reaction does not take place in these phases. In addition, both fluid phases are coupled by a volumetric flux exchange term $\left(N_i^{\beta\gamma} / \varepsilon_\beta \right)$ defined by Eq. (38), in which $K_{g,i}^{\beta\gamma}$ is the gas-liquid mass transfer coefficient.

$$\mathbf{N}_i^{\beta\gamma} = K_{g,i}^{\beta\gamma} \left(\left\langle C_i^\beta \right\rangle R_g T / H_i - \langle C_i^\gamma \rangle \right) \tag{38}$$

For the catalytic phase, volumetric chemical reactions, and only the diffusive contribution to the mass transport are considered.

Table 4 shows the boundary conditions adequate for mass and momentum transport for the TBR model for the HDS process.

This rigorous model allows to access further than the local fields scale of concentration, velocity, and pressure, such as axial and radial reaction rates, interstitial fluxes for each individual specie, localization of channeling in the flows, and with further post-processing of the data, effectiveness factors for individual pellets, wall-effects analysis, and transfer resistances analysis, to name some examples.

Hydrodynamics $i-phase=\beta,\gamma$		
$\mathbf{v}_i=-\mathbf{n}\,v_i^0$ *(inlet velocity)*	*at* $z=L_R$	(39)
$P=-P^0;\ \mathbf{n}[\mu_i(\nabla\mathbf{v}_i+(\nabla\mathbf{v}_i)^T)]=0$ *(oulet pressure)*	*at* $z=0$	(40)
$\mathbf{v}_i=0$ *(no slip condition)*	*at* $r=r_R$ *and* $A_{\omega i}$	(41)
$\mathbf{n}\cdot\mathbf{v}=0;\ \ K_i-(K_i\cdot\mathbf{n})\mathbf{n}=0$ *(symmetry)*	*at plane in* $x=0$	(42)
$K_\gamma=\mu_\gamma\left(\nabla\mathbf{v}_\gamma+(\nabla\mathbf{v}_\gamma)^T\right)\mathbf{n};\ K_\beta=\left[\mu_\beta\left(\nabla\mathbf{v}_\beta+(\nabla\mathbf{v}_\beta)^T\right)-\frac{2}{3}\mu_\beta(\nabla\mathbf{v}_\beta)\mathbf{I}\right]\mathbf{n}$		
Mass transport in gas domain $(i-specie=H_2,H_2S)$		
$\left\langle C_{H_2}^\beta\right\rangle=C_{H_2}^0;\left\langle C_{H_2S}^\beta\right\rangle=C_{H2S}^0=0$ *(inlet concentration)*	*at* $z=L_R$	(43)
$-\mathbf{n}\cdot D_i^\beta\nabla\left\langle C_i^\beta\right\rangle=0$ *(outlet diffusive contribution)*	*at* $z=0$	(44)
$-\mathbf{n}\cdot\mathbf{N}_i^\beta=0$ *(impermeability)*	*at* $r=r_R$ *and* $A_{\omega\beta}$	(45)
$-\mathbf{n}\cdot\mathbf{N}_i^\beta=0$ *(symmetry)*	*at plane in* $x=0$	(46)
Mass transport in liquid domain $(i-specie=R-S,H_2,H_2S)$		
$\langle C_{R-S}^\gamma\rangle=C_{R-S}^0;\left\langle C_{H_2}^\gamma\right\rangle=\left\langle C_{H_2S}^\gamma\right\rangle=0$ *(inlet concentration)*	*at* $z=L_R$	(47)
$-\mathbf{n}\cdot D_i^\gamma\nabla\langle C_i^\gamma\rangle=0$ *(outlet diffusive contribution)*	*at* $z=0$	(48)
$-\mathbf{n}\cdot\mathbf{N}_i^\gamma=0$ *(impermeability)*	*at* $r=r_R$	(49)
$-\mathbf{n}\cdot\mathbf{N}_i^\gamma=K_{g,i}^{\beta\gamma}\left(\left\langle C_i^\beta\right\rangle R_gT/H_i-\langle C_i^\gamma\rangle\right)$ *(exchange flux)*	*at* $A_{\omega\gamma}$	(50)
$-\mathbf{n}\cdot\mathbf{N}_i^\gamma=0$ *(symmetry)*	*at plane in* $x=0$	(51)
Mass transport in solid domain $(i-specie=R-S,H_2,H_2S)$		
$\langle C_i^\omega\rangle^\omega=\langle C_i^\gamma\rangle$ *(not mass resistences)*	*at* $A_{\omega\gamma}$	(52)
$-\mathbf{n}\cdot\mathbf{N}_i^\omega=0$ *(concentration field continuity)*	*at catalyst centers*	(53)
$-\mathbf{n}\cdot\mathbf{N}_i^\omega=0$ *(symmetry)*	*at plane in* $x=0$	(54)

$\mathbf{N}_i^j$ is the total flux, given by $\mathbf{N}_i^j=-D_i^j\nabla\left\langle C_i^j\right\rangle+\mathbf{v}_j\left\langle C_i^j\right\rangle$.

Table 4. Boundary conditions for TBR model.

3.5. Kinetic model

In order to give insights into the communication of the information between length scales, a hydrodesulphurization (HDS) reaction for a light gas-oil (LGO) was implemented in both the heterogeneous micropores model and the TBR model. The reaction follows the stoichiometric expression.

$$R\text{-}S_{(liq)}+2H_{2(gas)}\rightarrow R\text{-}H_{2(liq)}+H_2S_{(gas)} \tag{55}$$

In this expression, R-S is the sulfurized specie and R-H_2 is the desulfurized specie.

Reaction follows a kinetic expression of type of Langmuir-Hinshelwood/Hougen-Watson [12], described by the following expression.

$$-r_{HDS} = \frac{k_{HDS}\left\langle C^{\theta}_{R-S}\right\rangle^{\theta}\left(\left\langle C^{\theta}_{H_2}\right\rangle^{\theta}\right)^{0.5}}{\left(1 + K_{H_2S}\left\langle C^{\theta}_{H_2S}\right\rangle^{\theta}\right)^{2}}; \qquad i - phase = \omega, \lambda \tag{56}$$

In this expression, $i = \omega$ for the TBR model that considers the catalyst as a pseudo-phase, and $i = \lambda$ for the heterogeneous micropores model. It should be remembered that it is also required to make the adjustment specified in Eq. (11).

3.6. CFD computation

To solve the CFD models at the three different scales previously described, COMSOL Multiphysics software simulations were implemented. Due to the multiphysic and multiscale nature, as well as to the highly non-linearity and the geometrical complexity of the models; great computational resources, as RAM memory, processing capacity and computational times were required [1]. Thus, the CFD models and representation to study these cases are, in a great extent, limited by computational resources, and therefore important simplification in geometries as symmetry assumptions have been implemented. In spite of the simplifications, great computational resources were necessary, as it can be seen in **Table 5**.

The models were solved in a workstation with a dual socket Intel® Xeon® E5-2603 v3 processor (15 M of Cache and 1.60 GHz) and 160 GB of RAM memory. It is important to note that a segregated solving method was used in computation with the purpose of obtaining sufficiency in installed RAM memory.

Also, it is important to note that several CFD commercial software have preloaded *templates* with the commonly used physics in most science and engineering areas. However, for the study and solution of the boundary values problems (BVPs) for the closure vectors there is no existing template, as it is a specific problem of mathematical nature. Then, it was proceeded to approach these problems aided by the "Coefficients Form Partial Differential Equation (PDE)" from COMSOL Multiphysics. The *user definitions and variables* were also used in order to incorporate the interfacial momentum exchange models that consider the interactions between the three phases, for the reactor model.

Model	**Mesh** $\left[\begin{matrix}\textit{Triangular} \\ \textit{Elements}\end{matrix}\right]$	**RAM memory [GB]**	**Virtual memory [GB]**	**Computing time [h]**
Micropores	6.15×10^6	13.6	41.1	0.4
Mass closure vector	2.5×10^6	13.4	33.13	0.3
Energy closure vector	6.15×10^6	90.84	110.9	0.82
Pseudo-homogeneous	5.6×10^4	1.26	1.48	0.004
Reactor model	6×10^6	80	110	3–1 week*

*Depending on the particular simulation/case tested.

Table 5. Details of the computing resources required in each CFD model.

3.7. Model assumptions

For the reactor scale model, the TBR is considered to operate in a Trickle regime where the gas and liquid flow descendant at co-current, and that the operation is isothermal. On another hand, the density and viscosity of gas and liquid phases are considered constant, that the catalyst activity do not change with time, and that vaporization and condensation of gasoil do not take place.

In addition, it is assumed that chemical reactions take place only in the solid catalyst, which is considered to be completely wet, for purposes of mass transport model. As for the selection of the value of $N_C = D_R/D_P$, in order to neglect the wall effects, a value of $N_C \approx 10$ is considered sufficient for an accurate prediction of both, pressure drop and holdup. A brief discussion about the results that support the N_C selection is presented within the results section. Also, it is considered that the ordered catalyst bed representation built for the model contains enough characteristics of a real catalytic bed, and that the symmetry assumption can be implemented. Further discussion in the results section support the validity of these assumptions.

For pellet scale model, it is considered that there is no resistance to heat transfer and mass on the surface of the catalyst.

4. Results

4.1. Mass and energy transport at micropores model scale

The solution of boundary value problem of mass and energy transport in porous scale allows the evaluation of concentration fields for $R\text{-}S$, H_2, and H_2S species in the liquid phase that fills the interstitial domain of the catalyst; as well as the temperature fields for the solid matrix and the interstitial fluid. **Figure 5** shows the details of the concentrations and temperature fields obtained from the micropores model, described by Eqs. (3)–(10). It is important to point out that the shown fields images were chosen due to the clarity of the scales.

It is noteworthy that the concentration fields are shown in the entirety of the fluid domain, which is consequence of the consideration that the interstitial fluid domain is completely filled due to capillarity forces. In addition, the model considers that the catalyst is completely wet, implying that the gas phase in the reactor do not contact the solid. Thus, there is no need to model the mass transport with the gas phase. Furthermore, due to these considerations, the gas phase, at this scale, cannot be modelled.

Also, the kinetic expression in Eq. (56) requires the H_2 concentration at the liquid phase; which must be determined by the equilibria between the H_2 concentrations in liquid and gas phases, as well by the mass transport resistances for the hydrogen between liquid and solid phase, Eq. (50). Thus, considering the prior, the H_2, H_2S and the temperature at the catalyst surface is set to be equal to those in the gas phase, Eqs. (6) and (10). These are clearly further simplifications in the modelling of the micropores model. These same simplifications are assumed in the pseudo-homogeneous pellet model.

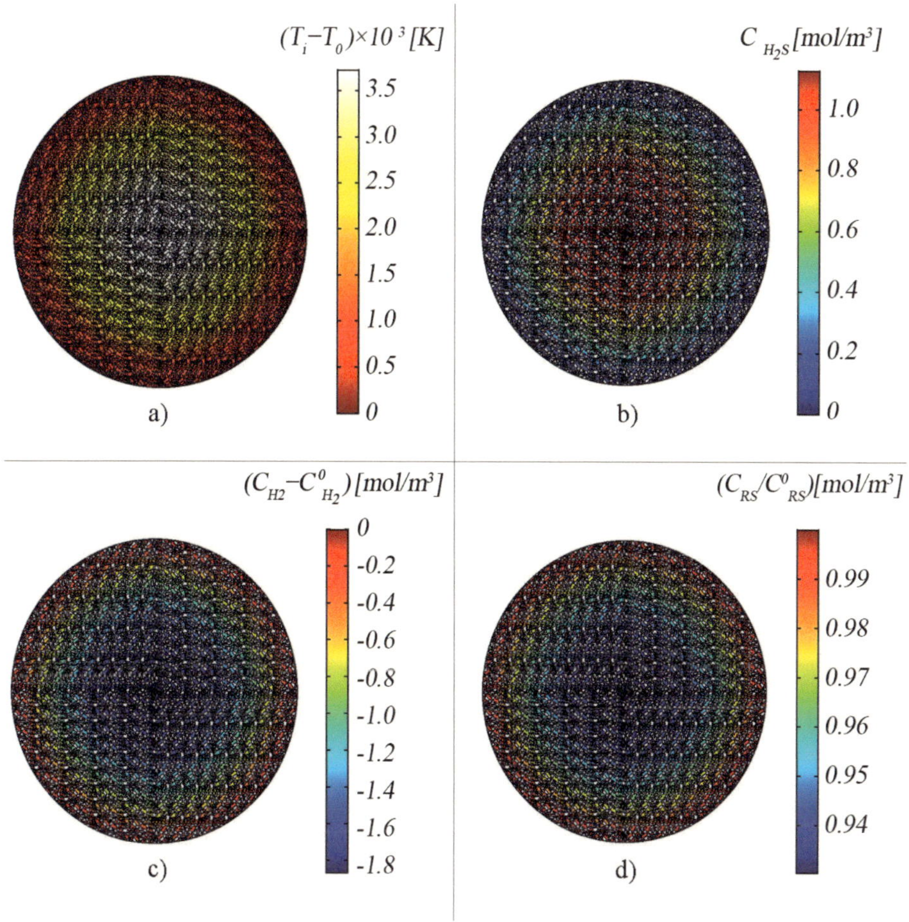

Figure 5. Concentration fields for the micropores model (a) temperature increase, (b) H_2S generation, (c) H_2 consumption, and (d) dimensionless sulfurated specie concentration.

Regarding the temperature increase field, it is noteworthy that the maximum temperature increase is lower than 4×10^{-3} K for a 0.35 mm diameter catalyst, which supports the assumption of an isothermal operation in the reactor model. Also, in the concentration fields, it can be seen that there is a generation of barely more than 1 mol/m^3 of H_2S, a consumption of 1.8 mol/m^3 of H_2, and a decrease of 6% of the sulfurized specie.

4.2. Mass and heat closure vectors, and effective transport coefficients

Figure 6 shows the closure vectors fields for the mass transfer and heat transfer problems, given by the solution of the boundary values problems of Eqs. (14)–(20). These results allow the evaluation of the effective transport coefficients ($\mathbf{D}_{eff}$, $\mathbf{K}_{eff}$), through Eqs. (12) and (13). Those evaluated coefficients are then used in the pseudo-homogeneous catalyst model and the reactor model. These are the *bridges* that up-scale the geometrical information and characteristics of the porous media in the catalyst microstructure to the upper scales. The tensor

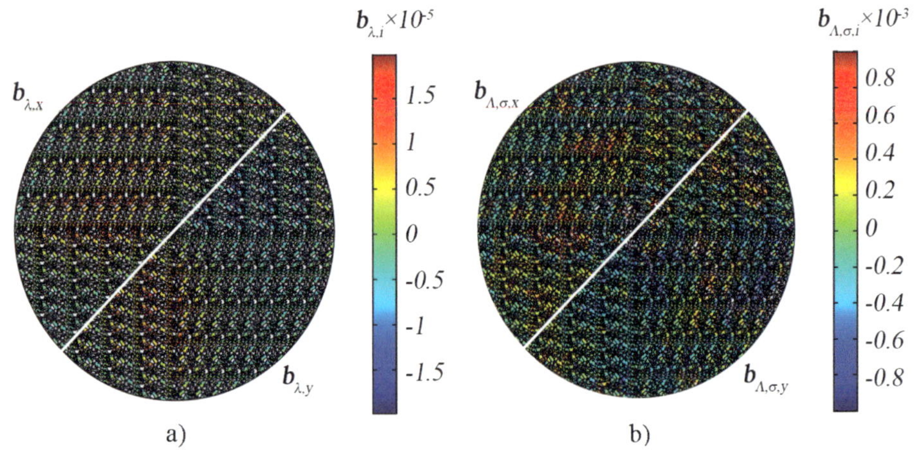

Figure 6. Closure vector fields (a) x and y components of the mass transfer closure vector and (b) x and y components of the heat transfer closure vector.

components evaluated values are $\left(\varepsilon_\lambda \mathrm{D}_{eff,xx}/\mathrm{D}_i^\lambda = \varepsilon_\lambda \mathrm{D}_{eff,yy}/\mathrm{D}_i^\lambda = 0.222848\right)$ and $(K_{eff,\,xx}/k_\Lambda = K_{eff,\,yy}/k_\Lambda = 3.84824)$, it can be seen that both tensors are symmetric.

4.3. Mass and energy transport at pseudo-homogeneous catalyst model scale

Figure 7 shows the solution for the boundary values problem specified by Eqs. (21)–(30); for comparison purposes, the selected shown fields are the same than those selected in **Figure 5**. In order to obtain these fields in the pseudo-homogeneous catalyst model, the evaluated effective transport coefficients shown in the last section were used in the coefficients of Eqs. (21) and (22).

As it can be seen, both models depict similar behaviors, although in the pseudo-homogeneous catalyst model the HDS reaction seems to be *slower* compared with the reaction in the micropores model. This difference conduces to an increase of temperature 28% lower, 10% less production of H_2S, 22% less consumption of the H_2, and 1% less decrease in the sulfurized specie concentration. The difference between both models can be attributed to that the geometric information captured by the effective coefficients is not enough, meaning that some information of the micropores structure is not scaling up.

4.4. Reactor model

4.4.1. Validation of the reactor model

It should be clear that, even though the models are theoretically suitable to describe and predict the transport phenomena in the systems, these needs to be validated in order to use their results in further applications with certainty. However, the validation is in many cases quite difficult as there are not enough available experimental data to compare or the experimental information is difficult to acquire, especially when microscales porous media models are intended to be validated, as the punctual microscales phenomena is hardly measurable or

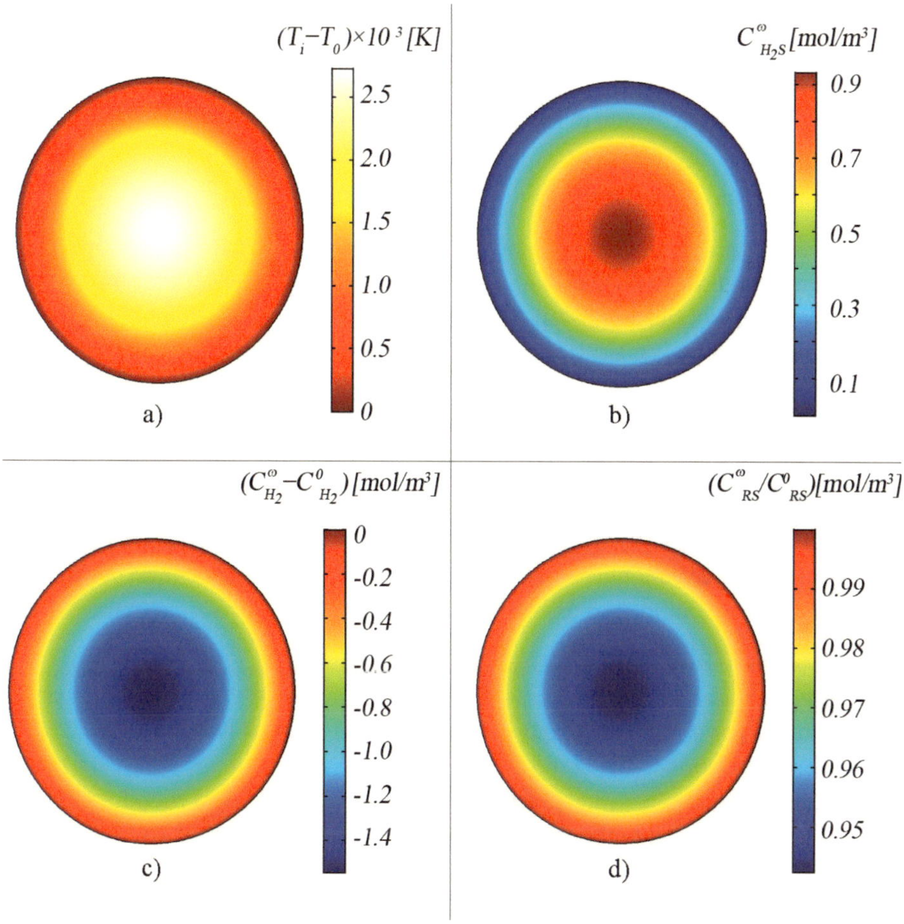

Figure 7. Concentration fields for the catalyst scale model (a) temperature increase, (b) H_2S generation, (c) H_2 consumption, and (d) dimensionless sulfurated specie concentration.

observable by experimental methods. Then, models with multiscale modelling approaches such as the presented in this chapter cannot be easily validated in the microscales.

For the micropores scale, the effective transport coefficients evaluated are in the range of the commonly found values in the literature, and thus the geometrical representation of porous structure can be considered as suitable. For the pseudo-homogeneous catalyst model, the mass and energy transport models have been extensively proved and validated in literature, then the model do not require more discussion about its validation.

In the case of the reactor model, the validation was carried out for the hydrodynamic and kinetic behavior. The hydrodynamics were validated against pressure drop and liquid holdup data found in literature [25], achieving mean absolute relative errors ($MARE = (\sum |Experimental - Predicted| / Experimental)/n$), below 5% in the pressure drop prediction and below 8% for liquid holdup. To validate the hydrodynamics, the geometrical characteristics of the bed, as the column and catalyst dimensions and bed porosity, were adapted to be similar to the experimental setup of

Al-Dahhan and co-worker [25]. For the kinetic behavior, the reactor geometrical model was adapted to have similar characteristics than reactor described in the theoretical work of Chacón and co-workers [12]. The model exhibits 5.12% difference in the prediction of the sulfurized conversion at 7 mm length (length of the reactor model discussed in this chapter).

4.4.2. Mass transport in the reactor model

In the reactor model scale, the velocities and pressure profiles in the fluid phases are obtained; as well as the concentration profiles for all species in the phases in which they are present. The sulfurized species do not undergo evaporation, and thus it can only be found in the liquid and solid phase; the gas phase is mainly constituted by the hydrogen, and contains a small amount of H_2S that is produced in the solid phase, and is able to transport through the fluid phase and solubilize in the gas phase; Also, the high pressures and temperatures enable the hydrogen to transport to the fluid phase and then to the solid, where the reaction takes place.

Figure 8 depicts concentration fields for the different species at the catalyst domain in the reactor model in a zx cut-plane, in a selected catalyst in the third layer of catalyst from the inlet: (a) dimensionless concentration of the sulfurized specie, (b) H_2S concentration produced by the reaction, (c) H_2 concentration, and (d) liquid to gas H_2 concentrations ratio in the fluid phases in several xy cut-planes in the reactor.

It is important to highlight that there are important resistances to the mass transfer of the hydrogen from the gas phase to the liquid phase; so that at most, only 25% of the hydrogen fed in the gas phase transports to the liquid phase. Thus, the hydrogen that reaches the catalysts is considerably less than the quantity considered for the micropores and pseudo-homogeneous models. In **Figure 8(d)**, it can also be seen that there is a wall-effect of around two catalyst diameters.

4.5. Comparison between scales

Figure 9 shows the H_2 concentration fields obtained in the different scales models: (a) micropores model, (b) pseudo-homogeneous model, (c) selected catalyst, in the third catalyst layer from the inlet, in the reactor model, and (d) shows the liquid to gas H_2 concentrations ratio, as well as the selected catalyst.

As it can be seen, in the micropores and the pseudo-homogeneous catalysts models, the H_2 concentration fields inside the catalyst particle domain are very similar, and show a symmetric distribution of the field, as previously discussed. However, this symmetrical behavior is not observed in the catalyst particle in the reactor model, and the H_2 concentration variations are in the range of 59.5–121.9 mol/m^3, which is a greater range that the one observed in the lower scales. And however, as seen by **Figures 5**, **7** and **8**, there is a lower consumption of the sulfurized specie in the selected catalyst in the reactor model. This is due to the interactions between the mass transport inside the catalysts, and the mass transport and hydrodynamics inside the reactor. Considering the prior observations, these exhibit that there is a need to stablish multiscale analyses and *bridges* that communicate the up-scales phenomena to the

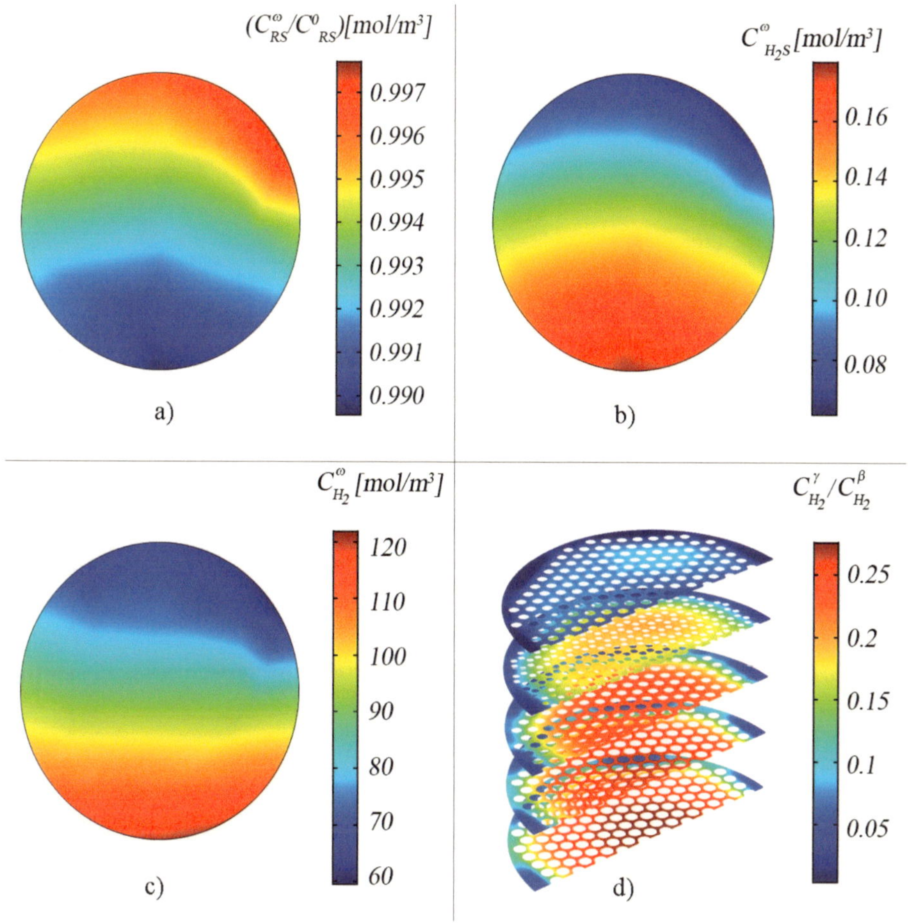

Figure 8. *zx* cut-plane in a selected catalyst in the reactor model (a) dimensionless sulfurized specie concentration, (b) H_2S concentration, (c) H_2 concentration, and (d) liquid/gas H_2 concentration ratio in the fluid phases.

down-scales in order to properly study the mass transport phenomena occurring in the micro-pores scales.

Another important aspect to highlight in **Figure 9(c)** is that a lower concentration can be seen at the top and higher concentration at the bottom of the catalyst. It is particularly noteworthy since the H_2 concentrations are expected to decrease when moving down in the reactor due to the reaction. The reason for this behavior can be found in **Figure 9(d)**, from which it can be deduced that much of the distribution/transport of the H_2 in the catalysts due to the distribution and transport of this specie in the liquid phase; which can be seen that increases when moving down in the reactor. In addition, it should be reminded that it was assumed that there are no resistances in the transport of the hydrogen from the liquid to the solid phase, which is specified by Eq. (56).

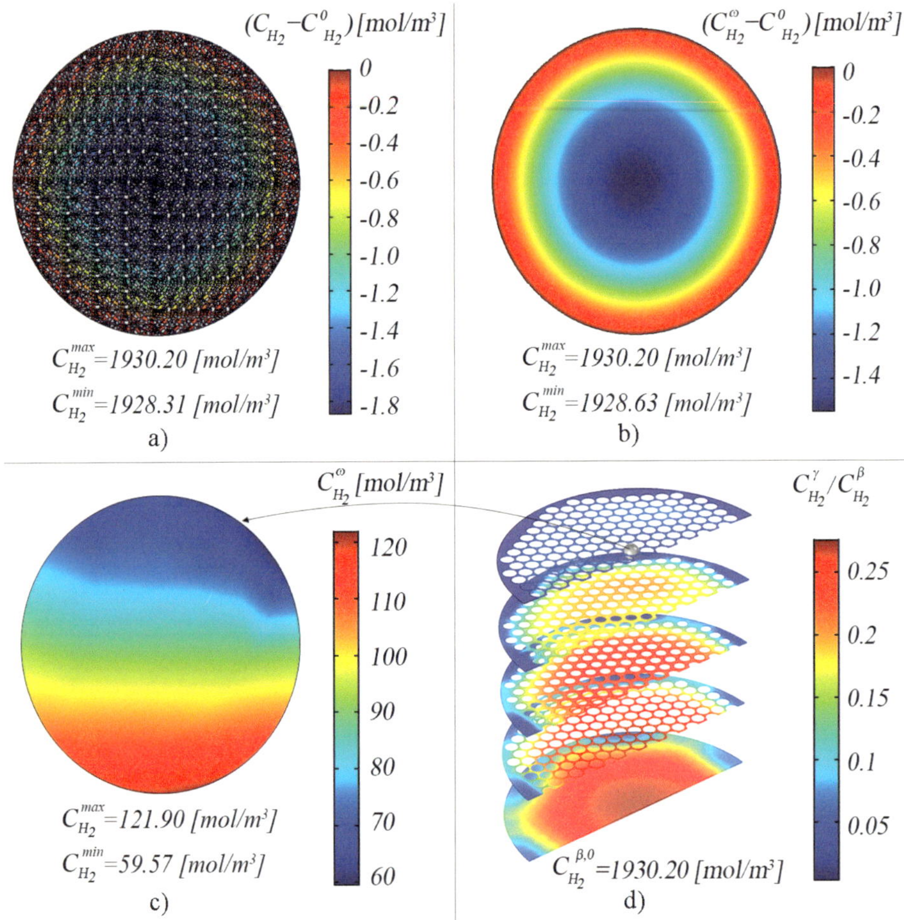

Figure 9. H_2 concentration fields at (a) micropores scale, (b) pseudo-homogeneous catalyst scale, (c) selected catalyst at reactor scale, and (d) selected catalyst particle with liquid/gas H_2 concentration ratio.

Further information on the H_2 concentration field behavior can be seen in **Figure 10**, where the total H_2 fluxes are shown inside the selected catalyst and in the surrounding interstitial fluid. These flux arrows are pointing the same direction in which the hydrogen is being dragged. In addition, it is observed that a great part of the H_2 behavior inside the catalyst is due to the concentration gradients inside the catalyst, which originate diffusive transport, and then it is not only due to the consumption for the HDS reaction. It can also be seen that there is an important influence of the surrounding fluid, which has diffusive and convective contributions to the mass transport, being the later greater than the diffusive.

It is important to note that this kind of analyses are possible as a result of the comparison of the information obtained from the solution of the different length scales models (multiscale analysis), as well as the establishment of detailed mathematical models for the phenomena involved (multiphysics analysis).

http://dx.doi.org/10.5772/intechopen.70562

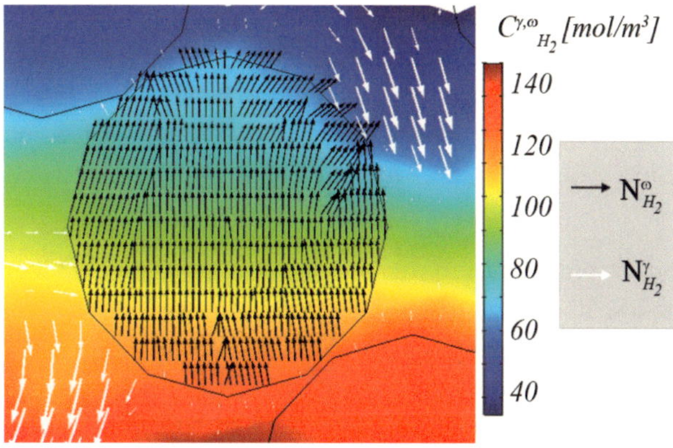

Figure 10. H_2 fluxes inside the selected catalyst and its surroundings fluid.

5. Conclusions

Simulation and analyses of an HDS process at different scales were carried out; the micropores and pseudo-homogeneous catalyst models included three mass transport equations for the consumed and generated species, two heat transfer equations for the micropores model, an one heat transfer equation for the pseudo-homogeneous catalysts model; at the reactor-scale, the model consisted of two momentum balance equations, and eight mass transport equations, for the consumed and produced species and their transport between phases. These models allow the multiphysics and multiscale analyses of the process, which is possible as the different length scales share information between them.

In the micropores representation model, with a 2:1 scale, the study and determination of the effective transport coefficients for the mass and heat transfer was carried out. The geometrical representation was developed from a vectorized micrograph of a real porous media obtained from literature. The evaluated coefficients are in the order of the ones found in literature, and can be thus considered as suitable.

In literature, it considered that the solution of the mass and heat transfer with superficial reaction at a micropores scale is hardly developed, and then *average* mass and heat transport equations are used (pseudo-homogeneous models). The proper equivalence between these two approaches is achieved through adequate values for effective transport coefficients. In the analyses shown here, it can be seen that similar tendencies in the concentration and temperature fields are achieved, but also differences that may be significant are shown.

The CFD reactor model for the HDS process has a good agreement with the experimental pressure drop and liquid holdup data, and with the theoretical conversion data. Thus, the model is considered as suitable for the prediction of hydrodynamics and kinetics behaviors, and can be used for further analyses.

The H_2 mass transport with reaction analysis in a catalytic particle at the different scales models allow to show that the upper scales phenomena, as the effect of the mass transport in the interstitial bed fluid, modifies in a great extent the behavior of the mass transport in the catalytic particle; that the micropores and the pseudo-homogeneous models are unable to represent that behavior; and that only a multiscale analysis allows to study and analyze these kinds of phenomena.

Also, regarding the implementation of the models in the CFD commercial software COMSOL Multiphysics, it was necessary to specify the boundary values problem (BVP) for the closure vector through the general COMSOL interphase for the "Coefficients Form PDE", suitable for many well-known PDEs systems; and for the reactor model, it was necessary to use the user definitions and variables to specify the interfacial momentum exchange models.

The three models at the different scales have been specified by commonly found boundary conditions for BVP with closed domains, this is Dirichlet, Neumann and Robinson boundary conditions. In order to specify that some information of the field, the field derivate or a combination of the field and its derivate, is known.

With the CFD reactor model, it is possible to analyze the wall effect, convective and diffusive fluxes for all species in every phase, reaction rate, and with further postprocessing, effectiveness factors, which allows to determine the effect of the T, P operation conditions, as well as the gas and liquid inflow velocities over the reactor conversion.

Nomenclatures

Abbreviations

MP micropores

PHC pseudo-homogeneous catalyst

RS reactor scale

HDS hydrodesulphurization

TBR trickle bed reactor

Symbols

d_p micropore diameter

D_p Pellet diameter

r_R reactor radius

L_R reactor length

A_{ij} interfacial area between phase i and j

D_i^j diffusion of specie i in the phase j

k_j specie j conductivity

N_c critical reactor to pellet diameters ratio

Sub-superscripts

0 at initial conditions

Greek letters

σ solid

β gas

γ liquid

λ catalyst micropores fluid

Λ catalyst micropores fluid

ω pseudo-homogeneous solid

ε_i volume fraction of phase i

Author details

Mario E. Cordero[1]*, Sebastián Uribe[1], Luis G. Zárate[1], Reyna Natividad Rangel[2], Alejandro Regalado-Méndez[3] and Ever Peralta Reyes[3]

*Address all correspondence to: marioedgar.cordero@upaep.mx

1 Universidad Popular Autónoma del Estado de Puebla, Puebla, México

2 Universidad Autónoma del Estado de México, Estado de México, México

3 Universidad del Mar, Oaxaca, México

References

[1] Zhang Q, Cen S. Multiphysics Modelling Numerical Methods and Engineering Applications. 1st ed. USA: Academic Press; 2016. 424 p

[2] Ge W, Chen F, Gao J, Gao S, Huang J, Liu X, Ren Y, Qichen S, Wang L, Wang W, Yang N, Zhang J, Zhao H, Zhou G, Li J. Analytical multi-scale method for multi-phase complex systems in process engineering—Bridging reductionism and holism. Chemical Engineering Science. 2007;**62**:3346-3377

[3] Lui W. Multi-scale catalyst design. Chemical Engineering Science. 2007;**62**:3502-3512

[4] Li J, Kuipers JAM. Effect of competition between particle-particle and gas-particle interactions on flow patterns in dense gas-fluidized bed. Chemical Engineering Science. 2007;**62**:3429-3442

[5] Koci P, Novák V, Stepánek F, Marek M, Kubícek M. Multi-scale modelling of reaction and transport in porous catalyst. Chemical Engineering Science. 2010;**65**:412-419

[6] Prasad V, Karim AM, Ulissi Z, Zagrobelny M, Vlachos DG. High throughput multiscale modeling for design of experimental catalyst and reactors: Applications to hydrogen production from ammonia. Chemical Engineering Science. 2010;**65**:240-246

[7] Ding H, xiang W, Lui C. A multiscale methodology for CFD simulation of catalytic distillation bale packings. Polish Journal of Chemical Engineering. 2016;**1**:24-32

[8] Chen Q, Zhai Z, Wang L. Computer modeling of multiscale fluid flow and heat and mass transfer in engineered spaces. Chemical Engineering Science. 2007;**62**:3580-3588

[9] Hu G, Li D. Multiscale phenomena in microfuidics and nanofluidics. Chemical Engineering Science. 2007;**62**:3443-3454

[10] Raynal L, Royon-Lebeaud A. A multi-scale approach for CFD calculations of gas-liquid flow within large size column equipped with structured packing. Chemical Engineering Science. 2007;**52**:7196-7204

[11] Xie L, Luo Z. Multiscale computational fluid dynamics-population balance model coupled system of atom transfer radical suspension polymerization in stirred tank rectors. Industrial and Engineering Chemistry Research. 2017;**56**:4690-4702

[12] Chacón R, Canale A, Bouze A, Sanchez Y. Modelling of a three-phase reactor for bitumen-derived gas oil hydrotreating. Brazilian Journal of Chemical Engineering. 2012;**29**:135-146

[13] Mederos FD, Ancheyta J. Mathematical modeling and simulation of hydrotreating reactors: Cocurrent versus countercurrent operations. Applied Catalysis A: General. 2007;**332**:8-21

[14] Auset M, Keller AA. Pore-scale processes that control dispersion of colloids in saturated porous media. Water Resources Research. 2004;**40**:1-11

[15] Rana MS, Ancheyta J, Maity SK, Rayo P. Support and porous diameter effect on the hydrodemetallization of Maya crude. Revista Mexicana de Ingeniería Química. 2006;**3**:227-235

[16] Gunjal P, Ranade VV. Modelling of laboratory and commercial scale hydro-processing reactors using CFD. Chemical Engineering Science. 2007;**66**:5512-5526

[17] Cordero ME, Natividad R, Zárate LG, Hernandez-Servin J-A, Salas JE. Estimation of effective diffusion coefficient and its effect on effectiveness factor for HDS catalytic process: A multi-scale approach. Catalyst Today. 2014;**220-222**:113-123

[18] Whitaker S. The method of Volume Averaging. 1st ed. Netherlands: Kluwer Academic Publisher; 1999. 220 p

[19] Varady MJ, Pearl TP, Bringuier SA, Mantooth BA. Vapor emission from porous materials with diffusive transport in the solid-phase. International Journal of Heat and Mass Transfer. 2017;**114**:758-768

[20] Benítez-Olivares G, Valdéz Parada FJ, Saucedo-Castañerda JG. Derivation of an upscaled model for mass transfer and reaction for non-food starch conversion to bioethanol. International Journal of Chemical Reactor Engineering. 2016:1-34

[21] Valdés-Parada F, Lasseux D, Bellet F. A new formulation of the dispersion tenson in homogeneous porous media. Advances in Water Resources. DOI: 10.1016/j.advwatres.2016.02.012

[22] Bensoussan A, Lions J-L, Papanicolaou G. Asymptopic Analysis for Periodic Structures. 1st ed. Amsterdam: North-Holland Publishing Company; 1978. 392 p

[23] Froment GF, Bischoff KB. Chemical Reactor Analysis and Design. 3rd ed. New York: John Wiley & Sons; 2010. 900 p

[24] Attou A, Boyer C, Ferschneider G. Modelling of the hydrodynamics of the cocurrent gas-liquid trickle flow through a trickle-bed reactor. Chemical Engineering Science. 1999;**54**: 785-802

[25] Al-Dahhan MH, Dudukovic MP. Pressure drop and liquid holdup in high pressure trickle-bed reactors. Chemical Engineering Science. 1994;**49**:5681-5698

Chapter 11

CFD Analysis of Turbulence Models to Achieve the Digester Mixing Process

Jorge Flores-Velazquez, Abraham Jesus Arzeta-Rios,
Waldo Ojeda Bustamante and
Teodoro Espinosa-Solares

Additional information is available at the end of the chapter

http://dx.doi.org/10.5772/intechopen.72171

Abstract

Mixing efficiency defines the features of physicochemical and biological reactions carried out in reactors or digesters. The reason for this influence is because it conditions the heat and mass transfer. That is why the mixing level and intensity become important aspects to study to know the effects they have on the processes. Furthermore, it should be noted that most of the mixing processes are carried out under turbulent conditions. Mixing enhancement evaluation is achieved in two ways, that is, experimentally and performing simulations. Simulations are based on numerical methods approximating solutions to results in line with reality. In this context, turbulence models applied in systems have great influence on the final numerical solution and, therefore, on the interpretation of improved mixing in reactors. It is also necessary to consider the influence of rheology in these simulations, since the working fluid does not always have a linear stress-strain relationship. In this way, an analysis of turbulence models and their applications in mixing characterization and the adequacy of these models to the reactor configuration and operating conditions is carried out. Mention is also made of the experiences around the study of turbulence in mixing tanks.

Keywords: turbulence models, mixing, digester, rheology, dead zones

1. Introduction

The use of biodigesters offers great advantages in energy production. The purpose of anaerobic digestion (AD) is the destruction of volatile solids by microorganisms in the absence of oxygen [1]. The AD is a common process to stabilize and reduce excesses or wastes of a different nature. For example, in a wastewater treatment plant and agricultural holdings, the AD allows a better treatment of animal or vegetable waste, by extracting much of the energy they contain. Besides, the use of biogas to generate electricity gives an additional value to the utilization of bioreactors in agricultural enterprises. The process of anaerobic digestion has several implications, and its effectiveness is based on aspects such as source, pH, temperature, reduction potential, hydraulic retention time (HRT) and mixing characteristics [2].

Mixing is one of the critical activities in the transformation process, a uniform mixture reduces the stratification, allows a better substrate dispersion, and if the mixture is not adequate, the digestion efficiency is reduced [3, 4]. When designing an anaerobic digestion system, the volume to be removed should be considered in relation to pump capacity, hydraulic retention time, sludge inflow rate, velocity gradient which relates the pump power, tank volume and sludge viscosity [1, 5].

Despite the technological advances in organic waste treatment, established mechanisms for design and operation require even more research. The AD is based on a combination of complex processes in which different residues are transformed mainly into a mixture composed of CH_4, CO_2 and H_2, which is called biogas [6].

Hydrodynamic performance of bioreactors is determined by the flow patterns inside. Consequently, biogas production is also conditioned by the reactor design, mainly referred to device dimensions and arrangement inside to favor the fluid movement and thereby generate the desired product [7]. Several models that allow relatively stable operation and provide desirable results have emerged. However, the punctual analysis of fluid movement inside the bioreactor is a complex issue mainly for the fluid characteristics, and of course by the geometry. This problem has been investigated using numerical methods, specifically computational fluid dynamics (CFD).

Digester design process involves several stages. A part is based on the calculation of organic loading rate as a function of temperature and input intensity. However, factors such as sedimentation, biogas, and sludge accumulation can influence on system hydrodynamic behavior and therefore on its removal efficiency. Generally, the predominance of mixed flows inside the reactor and its highly complex description is presumed, reason why a numerical discretization is attempted using CFD.

The evaluation and optimization of designs currently made with CFD allows to reduce the costs of prototype development [8]. Different studies have been conducted on improving hydrodynamic configurations using CFD [9, 10]. The use of CFD has allowed to understand that mixing is one of the most important activities for total solids reduction and biogas production. Despite the low speeds occurring inside a biodigester, it is advisable that the materials be completely mixed, so it is desirable to produce turbulence, which will be a function of rheological characteristics of fluid, flow rate, and dimensions and geometry of bioreactor.

Phenomena involving fluid movement at high velocities or in chaotic patterns can be inferred by turbulence models. Currently, robust turbulence models applicable to most physical processes have been developed. This is shown by the comparison of numerical solutions against experimental results.

With the addition of rheological properties of reaction materials, an appropriate turbulence model application for simulation becomes more complicated, since it is usual to find materials that do not present linear stress-strain behavior when flowing, that is, non-Newtonian fluids [11].

2. Factors affecting mixing

2.1. Geometric characteristics of containers

Flow dynamics of mixing process in anaerobic digesters has been analyzed from different standpoints. In waste degradation for energy generation, there are advances indicating the relevance of mixing process. Although good mixing can favor the material homogenization and exchange process between microorganisms and their environment, excessive mixing may also disrupt biological activities such as trophic processes [12, 13].

Studies on geometry influence in the mixing process include not only the container shape but also the shape of elements to generate movement inside the reactors. Agitation inside the anaerobic digestion containers is carried out mainly in the following three ways: (1) mechanical agitation with impellers, (2) pumped circulation and (3) gas recirculation [4].

The main type of reactor used in anaerobic digestion is the Continuous Stirred Tank Reactor (CSTR), from which various geometry investigations have been carried out, of flat bottom, conical, spherical or even egg-shaped reactors [14, 15]. The scale of the process is also a factor to be considered in the hydrodynamic performance of bioreactors, since there may be differences in performance when moving from a laboratory scale (**Figure 1**) to a full scale.

Large-scale agricultural waste treatment is commonly performed in covered lagoon digesters (**Figure 2**), which are reservoirs with a gas-tight cover mounted for biogas capture [10, 16]. Such reactors are used to exploit the methane production potential of animal waste. In these reactors, methane emission rates may vary depending on the covered lagoon area [17].

2.2. Fluid rheology

Total solids concentration in digestion fluids, besides having effects on degradation rate of organic matter, also has direct effects on rheological properties [14]. The study of fluid rheology entails the adjustment of CFD models to more real conditions [18, 19].

Figure 1. Laboratory-scale anaerobic reactor with pumped circulation.

Figure 2. Covered lagoon digesters for cow manure treatment.

Rheological behavior of fluids can be described by a basic diagram of shear rate against shear stress (**Figure 3**). The time-independent flow behavior is classified as Newtonian and non-Newtonian (shear thinning, shear thickening and yield stress) [11]. The rheological properties of non-Newtonian fluids greatly affect flow patterns, differing from those obtained with Newtonian fluids [19].

The description of nonlinear deformation of non-Newtonian fluids is characterized by generating rheological models, which must match experimental data that help obtain the value of model variables to be used. The rheological model application will depend on behavior and trend of experimental data, as well as the speed ranges achieved by the mixing equipment.

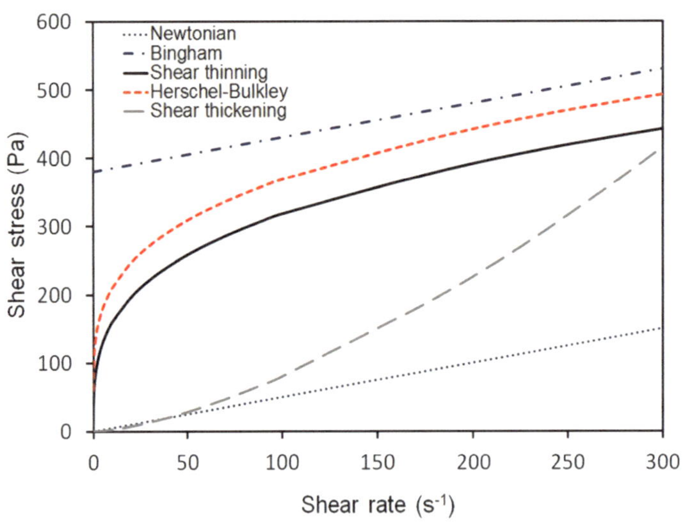

Figure 3. Shear rate versus shear stress for non-Newtonian fluids.

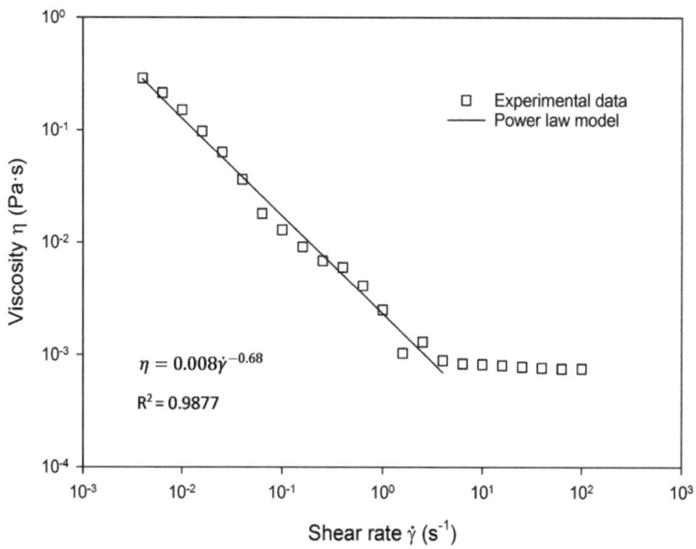

Figure 4. Flow curve of 4% cow manure and power law model fit to experimental data.

2.2.1. Power law model in rheology

The power law model (Eq. (1)) has been employed to adjust experimental data and to describe the rheological behavior of anaerobic digestion fluids [19].

$$\eta = k\dot{\gamma}^{n-1} \tag{1}$$

where η is viscosity, k is consistency coefficient, $\dot{\gamma}$ is shear rate and n is power law index.

Commercial CFD programs incorporate the power law model function for viscosity of non-Newtonian fluids. This model only fits to shear thinning region (**Figure 4**).

2.2.2. Herschel-Bulkley model

The capacities of the Herschel-Bulkley model (Eq. (2)) to show the sludge behavior before the flow occurs (very low shear stress) and when it begins to flow (shear stresses that exceed yield) make these yield stress models preferable in anaerobic digestion applications [20].

$$\tau = \tau_y + k\dot{\gamma}^n \tag{2}$$

where τ is shear stress, τ_y is yield stress, $\dot{\gamma}$ is shear rate, k and n are model factors.

2.2.3. Cross and Carreau viscosity models

The Cross (Eq. (3)) and Carreau (Eq. (4)) models are suitable to describe the shear dependence of aqueous dispersions [11].

$$\eta = \eta_\infty + \frac{\eta_0 - \eta_\infty}{1 + (K\dot{\gamma})^n} \tag{3}$$

$$\eta = \eta_\infty + \frac{\eta_0 - \eta_\infty}{\left[1 + (\lambda\dot{\gamma})^2\right]^N} \tag{4}$$

where η is non-Newtonian viscosity, η_∞ is viscosity in the lower Newtonian region, η_0 is viscosity in the upper Newtonian region, K and λ are time constants related to the relaxation times and n and N are dimensionless exponents.

These models have been employed to describe the flow curve of anaerobic sludge and model fluids with similar characteristics [21]. Although some commercial CFD packages have included rheological model functions, some authors have preferred to use user-defined functions (UDF) to incorporate them.

2.2.4. Use of model fluids

Fluid dynamics validations in anaerobic reactors usually use model fluids, which have rheological characteristics like digestion fluids, with the advantage of being translucent to allow the application of optical techniques for fluid movement visualization.

Xanthan gum solutions are non-Newtonian fluids that exhibit similar properties to various media used in anaerobic digestion [22]. The use of rheometers for determination of flow curves (**Figure 5**) is essential when determining the upper and lower Newtonian plateaus.

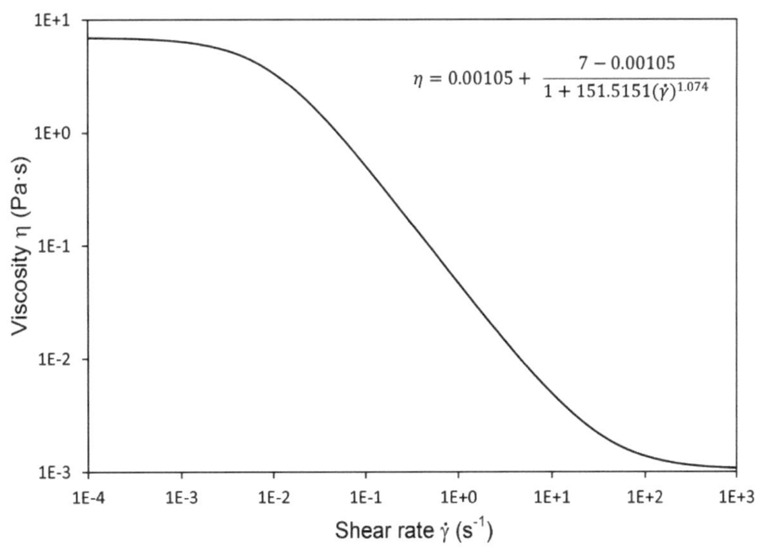

Figure 5. Flow curve of 0.05% xanthan gum solution and Cross viscosity model equation.

3. Turbulence models applied in characterization of mixing in bioreactors

Flow velocity, characteristic length and fluid properties are, among others, factors that define the flow type. Differences between the dynamic and kinematic viscosities can cause a turbulent flow, which in turn leads to the appearance of eddies whose description allows to infer mixing processes; however, due to the wide range of length and time scales that interact with each other, dynamic analysis is complex [23].

Turbulent flows are numerically simulated using methods such as Reynolds Average Navier-Stokes (RANS), Direct Numerical Simulation (DNS) and Large Eddy Simulation (LES). Although the most accurate method is DNS, it has the disadvantage of being computationally more expensive. The RANS simulation method is the most used in turbulent flow simulations in bioreactors; however, another method that could be appropriate to model the turbulent mixing in bioreactors is the embedded LES [4].

In CFD applications, the effectiveness of several turbulence models has been evaluated to mixing characterization of non-Newtonian fluids in anaerobic digesters, such as the standard k-ε model, RNG k-ε model, realizable k-ε model, standard k-ω model, SST k-ω model and the Reynolds Stress Model [8, 24].

3.1. k-ε turbulence models

The k-ε turbulence model is widely used in commercial CFD programs. This model has been tested under different flow conditions and is numerically robust and computationally less expensive [25]. Applications include studies on mixing performance improvement in CSTR used in anaerobic digestion [26, 27]. The transport equations of the model are shown as follows [28]:

$$\frac{\partial}{\partial t}(\rho k) + \frac{\partial}{\partial x_i}(\rho k u_i) = \frac{\partial}{\partial x_j}\left[\left(\mu + \frac{\mu_t}{\sigma_k}\right)\frac{\partial k}{\partial x_j}\right] + G_k + G_b - \rho\varepsilon \tag{5}$$

$$\frac{\partial}{\partial t}(\rho\varepsilon) + \frac{\partial}{\partial x_i}(\rho\varepsilon u_i) = \frac{\partial}{\partial x_j}\left[\left(\mu + \frac{\mu_t}{\sigma_\varepsilon}\right)\frac{\partial \varepsilon}{\partial x_j}\right] + C_{1\varepsilon}\frac{\varepsilon}{k}(G_k + C_{3\varepsilon}G_b) - C_{2\varepsilon}\rho\frac{\varepsilon^2}{k} \tag{6}$$

where ρ is liquid density, t is time, u is velocity, μ is viscosity, μ_t is turbulent viscosity, k and ε are turbulent kinetic energy and specific dissipation rate respectively, σ_k and σ_ε are turbulent Prandtl numbers, G_k represent the turbulent kinetic energy generation due to mean velocity gradients, G_b is turbulent kinetic energy generation due to buoyancy, $C_{1\varepsilon}$, $C_{2\varepsilon}$ and $C_{3\varepsilon}$ are constants.

3.2. k-ω turbulence models

The k-ω model has been applied to predict flow characteristics during the mixing of anaerobic sludge [8, 24]. This model is recommended when modeling the flow of non-Newtonian fluids to low Reynolds numbers [29]. The governing equations for turbulent kinetic energy and the specific rate of dissipation are as follows [30]:

$$\frac{\partial}{\partial t}(\rho k) + \frac{\partial}{\partial x_j}(\rho u_j k) = \rho \tau_{ij} \frac{\partial u_i}{\partial x_j} - \beta^* \rho k \omega + \frac{\partial}{\partial x_j}\left[\left(\mu + \sigma^* \frac{\rho k}{\omega}\right) \frac{\partial k}{\partial x_j}\right] \tag{7}$$

$$\frac{\partial}{\partial t}(\rho \omega) + \frac{\partial}{\partial x_j}(\rho u_j \omega) = \alpha \frac{\omega}{k} \rho \tau_{ij} \frac{\partial u_i}{\partial x_j} - \beta \rho \omega^2 + \sigma_d \frac{\rho}{\omega} \frac{\partial k}{\partial x_j} \frac{\partial \omega}{\partial x_j} + \frac{\partial}{\partial x_j}\left[\left(\mu + \sigma \frac{\rho k}{\omega}\right) \frac{\partial \omega}{\partial x_j}\right] \tag{8}$$

where p is static pressure, τ_{ij} is the Reynolds stress tensor, β and σ are body forces and k and ω are turbulent kinetic energy and specific dissipation rate, respectively.

4. Phenomenology of the CFD process applied in mixing of bioreactors

Mixing consists of making a uniform combination of two or more components, so it is present in many processes [31]. When analyzing air change rates of natural ventilation in buildings designated for agricultural or livestock production, the mixing is present.

In industrial processes where chemical reactions are carried out, mixing promotes contact between the reactants improving process efficiency. Particularly in bioreaction processes, mixing influences substrate and product transport toward and from the location of conversion by microorganisms [32].

The effect of different modes of mixing on biogas production has been studied [3]. The main modes of mixing in biodigesters are as follows: biogas recirculation, impeller mixing and pumped circulation [33]. The mixing methods have greater impact when dealing with higher solids content materials. Often, the increase in the concentration of total solids in digestate generates important rheological changes.

4.1. Temperature and density gradients in fluid modeling

Fluid motion can occur on a temperature gradient and, consequently, mass transport phenomena by convection. Two models are basic for the analysis of this phenomenon: flotation model for natural convection, which considers the variation of density as a function of temperature and the Boussinesq model (Eq. (9)) that has given adequate results [34].

$$\rho = \rho_i[1 - \beta(T - T_i)] \tag{9}$$

where ρ is density, β is the thermal expansion coefficient and T is temperature.

The fluid movement assumes a mixture of liquid, vapor and nonconsumable gases. The standard equation governing the mixing model and the mixing turbulence model describing the flow of the mass vapor fraction (f) can be written as follows [35]:

$$\frac{\partial}{\partial \varepsilon}(\rho f) + \nabla(\rho \vec{v}_V f) = \nabla(\gamma \nabla f) + R_e - R_c \tag{10}$$

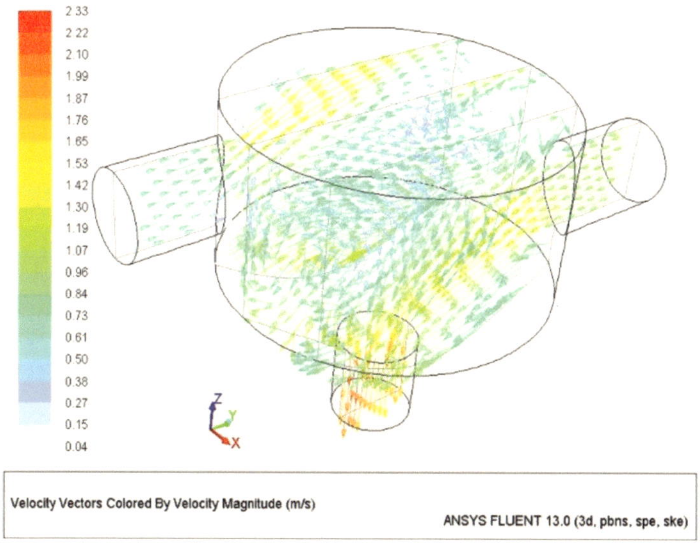

Figure 6. Detail of the velocity vectors in the container (m s^{-1}).

where v is velocity vector, γ is the effective exchange coefficient and R_e and R_c are terms included in the steam generation and condensation rate (rate of phase change).

Figure 6 shows the spatial distribution of velocity vectors, which leads to the entry of two solutions, under different fluid characteristics. According to the hypotheses presented, it is a turbulent flow whose centrifugal forces favor the separation of emulsions. Velocity increase at the exit of digester causes a change in mixture viscosity and consequently its ability to flow.

Because of the boundary conditions and flow characteristics, temperature distribution and corresponding density are shown in **Figures 7** and **8**, respectively. A parameter to qualify the process is the uniformity in the mixing, which in turn will be in function of the content of the solutions.

4.2. Flow patterns in single-phase models

To evaluate hydrodynamic performance of anaerobic reactors, single-phase CFD models have been used [14, 19]. In these models, it is assumed that multiphase effects such as sedimentation of solids, bubble formation and biogas flow in the aqueous phase are negligible.

4.2.1. Covered lagoon digester

The treatment of large-scale organic wastes is carried out in covered lagoon reactors (**Figure 9**). In these reactors, it is usual to find stagnant zones, where the flow velocity is very low and affects the anaerobic digestion process efficiency. Reduction of stagnant areas in covered lagoon reactors is a challenge that has been addressed through the CFD model generation.

The flow model consists of continuity (Eq. (11)) and Navier-Stokes equations for linear motion conservation (Eq. (12)) in its vector form at steady state, incompressible and isothermal flow [36].

$$\nabla \cdot \vec{v} = 0 \tag{11}$$

$$\rho[\nabla \cdot (\vec{v}\vec{v})] = -\nabla \cdot P + \nabla \cdot (\bar{\bar{\tau}}) + \bar{\bar{F}} \tag{12}$$

where $\bar{\bar{\tau}}$ is defined by Eq. (13).

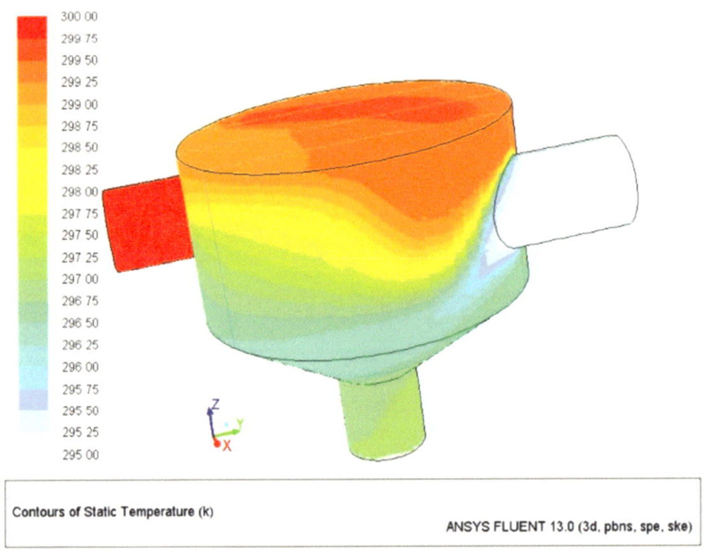

Figure 7. Temperature contours (K) in mixing reactor.

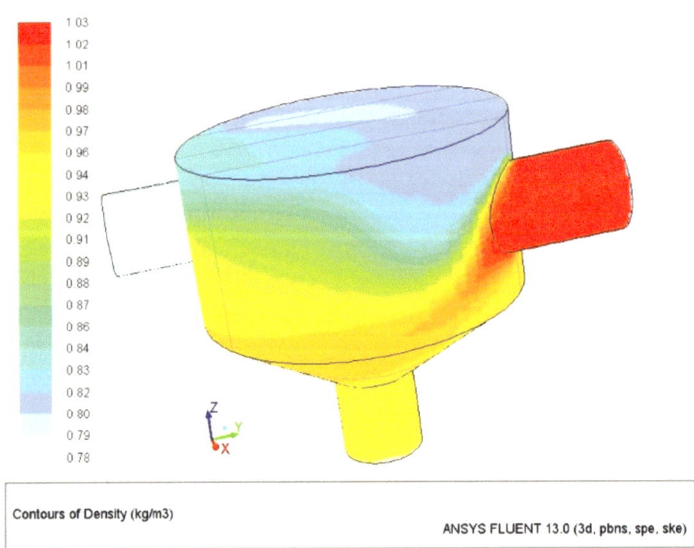

Figure 8. Density contours (kg m^{-3}) in mixing digester.

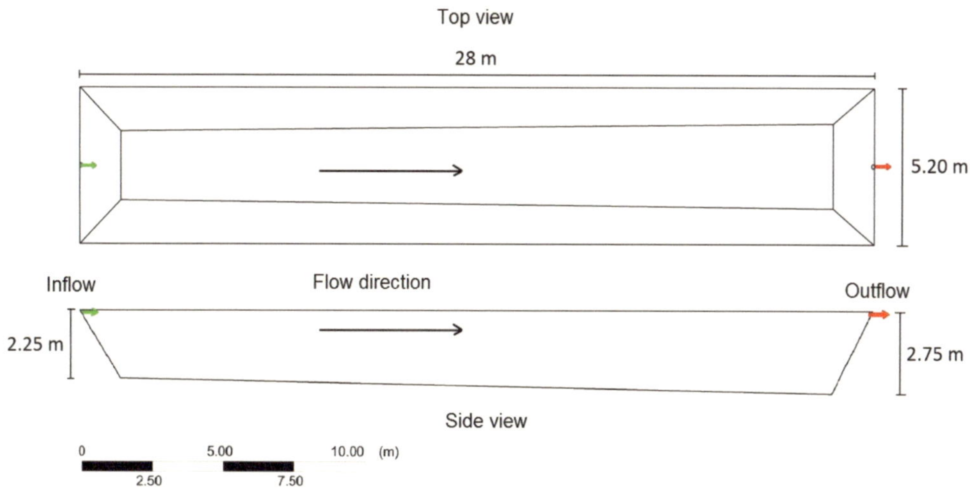

Figure 9. Covered lagoon digester model.

$$\bar{\bar{\tau}} = \mu \left[(\nabla \cdot \vec{v} + \nabla \cdot \vec{v}^{T}) - \frac{2}{3} \nabla \cdot \vec{v} I \right] \tag{13}$$

For the local turbulence calculations, transport equations for turbulent kinetic energy (k) and specific dissipation rate (ω) must be solved (Eqs. (7) and (8)). The incorporation of the Cross viscosity model to define the fluid rheology is done by programming and importing a user-defined function (UDF).

The hydrodynamic performance enhancement is achieved by recirculation incorporation in strategic sites. Streamlines (**Figure 10**) in the original configuration have two large swirls at the inflow; however, in most of the reactor, very low speeds are encountered. Vectors (**Figure 11**) show a velocity increase at the top and middle of the reactor when a recirculation is employed, which improves mixing and sludge digestion.

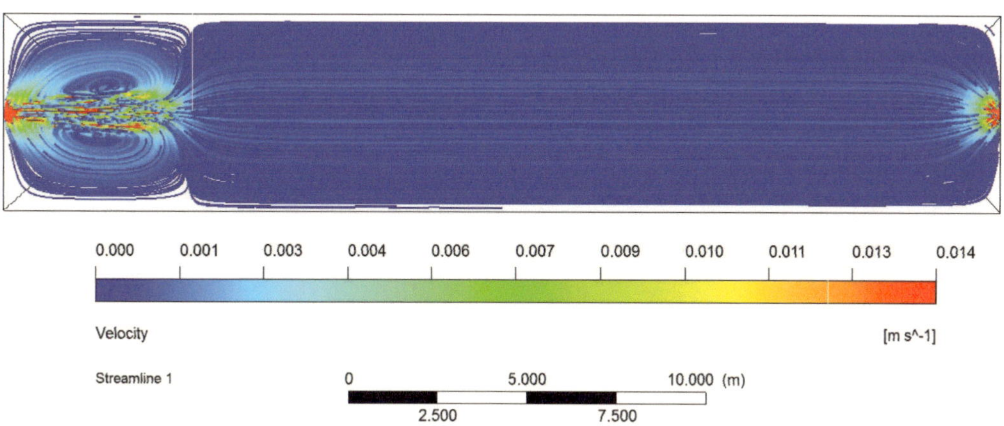

Figure 10. Streamlines in a top view of covered lagoon reactor.

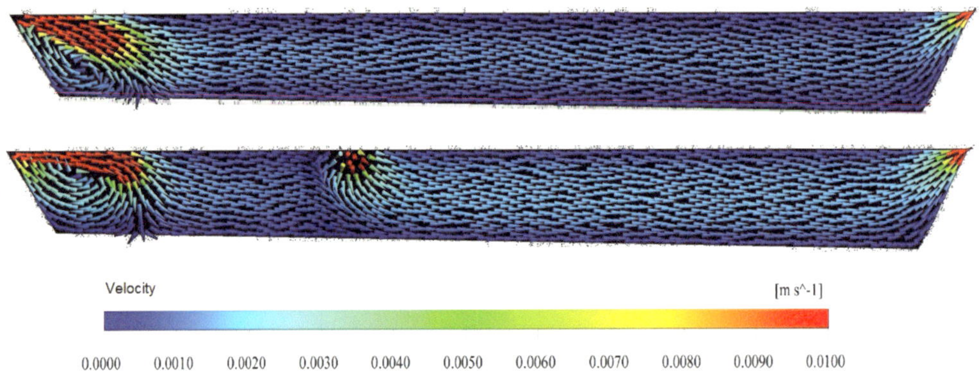

Figure 11. Velocity vectors in configuration A (without recirculation) and B (with recirculation).

4.2.2. Anaerobic reactor with recirculating jets

Currently, the mixing by recirculating jets (**Figure 12a**) is used in industrial digesters to treat organic wastes. Usually these are containers provided with submerged jets pointing downward and have the function of recirculating the digestion fluid by the action of a pump [15]. For single-phase CFD model development, the geometry is simplified by delimiting the part corresponding to the liquid (**Figure 12b** and **c**).

The inflow pipe length influences the velocity distribution within the container. **Figure 13** shows that higher velocity is at reactor bottom, whereby a better homogenization is achieved because the bottom sediments are entrained by the generated stream and are dispersed throughout the reactor.

4.3. Multiphase flow

Although mixing modeling has been approached considering that flow in reactor is a single phase, cases in which the multiphase effect is considerable have also been considered [37].

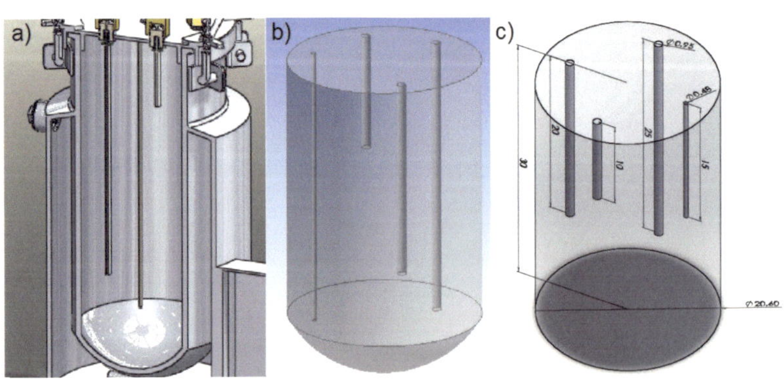

Figure 12. (a) The inside of a reactor with recirculating jets, (b) configuration of the jets in the liquid phase and (c) different jet configuration.

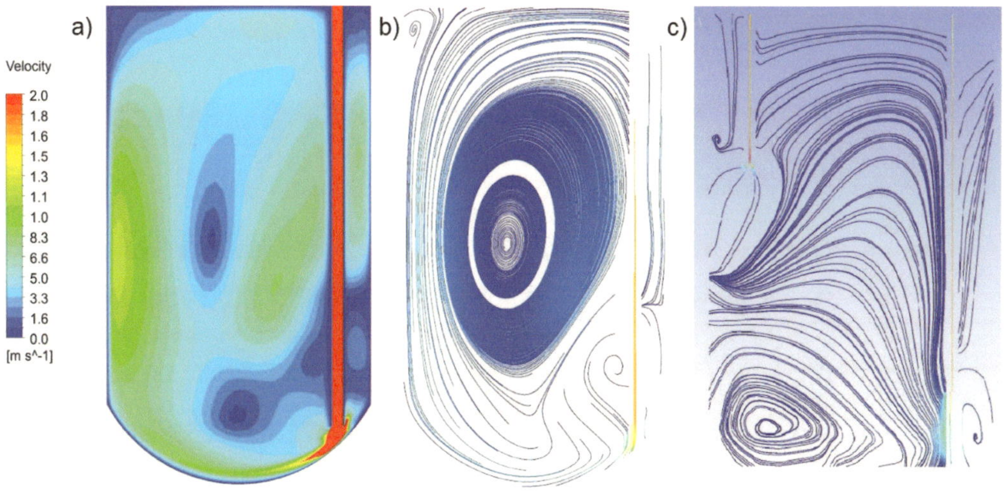

Figure 13. (a) Reactor velocity contours with recirculating jets, (b) streamlines generated by spherical bottom and (c) streamlines on changing reactor bottom and jets length.

Mixing modeling in anaerobic digestion processes should be approached considering the multiple phases involved in the process. The approaches used for multiphase flow description can be grouped into two types: the Eulerian approach and the Lagrangian approach [33].

4.4. Dead space in mixing vessels

Mixing dead zones detection is performed to improve mixing in digesters. Recirculation incorporation causes disturbances and material movement inside the digester and reduces dead spaces, increasing biogas production due to a better microorganism distribution in material.

To define a dead space (**Figure 14**), the concept of hydraulic retention time (HRT) has been used, that is, the time it takes the material to perform the path from inflow to outflow of digester [38]; mathematically, it is defined as follows:

$$HRT = \frac{V}{Q} \tag{14}$$

where V is total volume of digester and Q is volumetric flow at the digester inlet.

Volumetric flow (Q) causes the material to have a certain mean velocity within the digester, whose magnitude is a result of the velocity vector ($\vec{v}$), which has components in x, y, z (u, v, w). Therefore, to calculate the limit velocity to define a dead space, the following mathematical relationship is used.

$$v_{dead\ zone} \leq \frac{reactor\ lenght}{\sqrt{3}\ (HRT)} \tag{15}$$

Those regions where the velocity is less than or equal to the limit velocity ($\vec{v} \leq v_{dead\ zone}$) are considered as dead space.

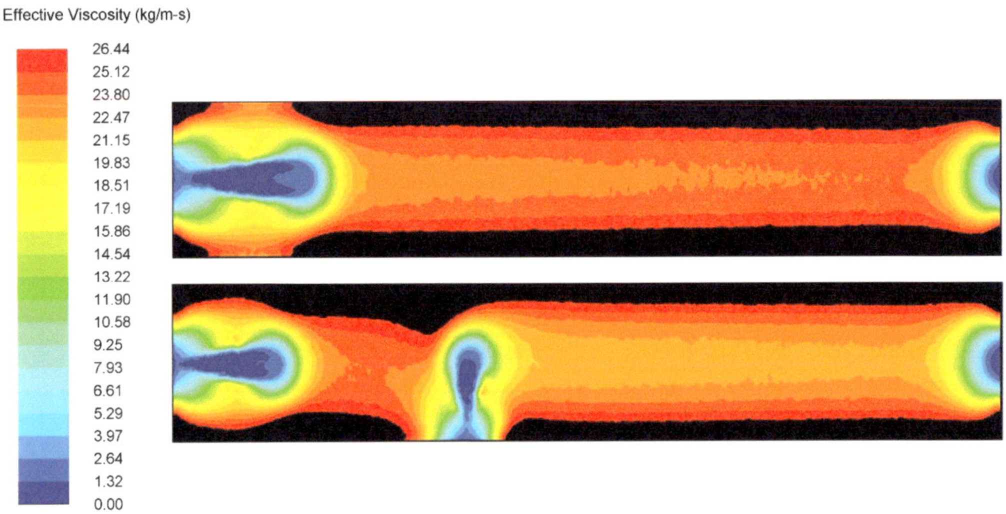

Figure 14. Dead space (black area) in different inflow configurations.

5. Conclusions

The mixing processes in anaerobic reactors are influenced not only by the inlet and outlet flows but also by the rheological properties of the fluid and the geometric characteristics of the reactor. There is an optimum mixing intensity that can maximize energy production with the lowest energy input possible for mixing. Beyond a point, there are no returns in terms of methane generation with increasing energy input. The variability of anaerobic digestion involves the application of different turbulence models of turbulence, which must be analyzed to determine the adjustment of results obtained with reality.

Author details

Jorge Flores-Velazquez[1]*, Abraham Jesus Arzeta-Rios[1], Waldo Ojeda Bustamante[1] and Teodoro Espinosa-Solares[2]

*Address all correspondence to: jorge_flores@tlaloc.imta.mx

1 Mexican Institute of Water Technology, Jiutepec, Morelos, Mexico

2 Chapingo Autonomous University, Texcoco, Mexico, Mexico

References

[1] Meroney RN, Colorado PE. CFD simulation of mechanical draft tube mixing in anaerobic digester tanks. Water Research. 2009;**43**(4):1040-1050

[2] Terashima M, Goel R, Komatsu K, Yasui H, Takahashi H, Li YY, et al. CFD simulation of mixing in anaerobic digesters. Bioresource Technology. 2009;**100**(7):2228-2233

[3] Karim K, Thomas Klasson K, Hoffmann R, Drescher SR, DePaoli DW, Al-Dahhan MH. Anaerobic digestion of animal waste: Effect of mixing. Bioresource Technology. 2005; **96**(14):1607-1612

[4] Wu B. Advances in the use of CFD to characterize, design and optimize bioenergy systems. Computers and Electronics in Agriculture. 2013;**93**:195-208

[5] Espinosa-Solares T, Morales-Contreras M, Robles-Martínez F, García-Nazariega M, Lobato-Calleros C. Hydrodynamic characterization of a column-type prototype bioreactor. Applied Biochemistry and Biotechnology. 2008;**147**(1-3):133-142

[6] Valle-Guadarrama S, Espinosa-Solares T, López-Cruz I, Domaschko M. Modeling temperature variations in a pilot plant thermophilic anaerobic digester. Bioprocess and Biosystems Engineering. 2011;**34**(4):459-470

[7] Vesvikar MS, Al-Dahhan M. Flow pattern visualization in a mimic anaerobic digester using CFD. Biotechnology and Bioengineering. 2005;**86**(6):719-732

[8] Bridgeman J. Computational fluid dynamics modelling of sewage sludge mixing in an anaerobic digester. Advances in Engineering Software. 2012;**44**(1):54-62

[9] Wu B. CFD simulation of mixing in egg-shaped anaerobic digesters. Water Research. 2010;**44**(5):1507-1519

[10] Wu B, Chen Z. An integrated physical and biological model for anaerobic lagoons. Bioresource Technology. 2011;**102**(8):5032-5038

[11] Rao M. Rheology of Fluid, Semisolid, and Solid Foods: Principles and Applications. 3rd ed. Springer US: Boston, MA; 2014. 461 p

[12] Sindall R, Bridgeman J, Carliell-Marquet C. Velocity gradient as a tool to characterise the link between mixing and biogas production in anaerobic waste digesters. Water Science & Technology. 2013;**67**(12):2800-2806

[13] Wu J, Bi L, Zhang JB, Poncin S, Cao ZP, Li HZ. Effects of increase modes of shear force on granule disruption in upflow anaerobic reactors. Water Research. 2012;**46**(10):3189-3196

[14] Wu B. CFD simulation of mixing for high-solids anaerobic digestion. Biotechnology and Bioengineering. 2012;**109**(8):2116-2126

[15] Sajjadi B, Raman AAA, Parthasarathy R. Fluid dynamic analysis of non-Newtonian flow behavior of municipal sludge simulant in anaerobic digesters using submerged, recirculating jets. Chemical Engineering Journal. 2016;**298**:259-270

[16] Wilkie AC. Anaerobic digestion of dairy manure: Design and process considerations. In: Dairy Manure Management: Treatment, Handling, and Community Relations. Ithaca, NY: Cornell University; 2005. pp. 301-312

[17] Sharpe R, Harper L. Methane emissions from an anaerobic swine lagoon. Atmospheric Environment. 1999;**33**(22):3627-3633

[18] Craig KJ, Nieuwoudt MN, Niemand LJ. CFD simulation of anaerobic digester with variable sewage sludge rheology. Water Research. 2013;**47**(13):4485-4497

[19] Wu B, Chen S. CFD simulation of non-Newtonian fluid flow in anaerobic digesters. Biotechnology and Bioengineering. 2008;**99**(3):700-711

[20] Baroutian S, Eshtiaghi N, Gapes DJ. Rheology of a primary and secondary sewage sludge mixture: Dependency on temperature and solid concentration. Bioresource Technology. 2013;**140**:227-233

[21] Eshtiaghi N, Yap SD, Markis F, Baudez J-C, Slatter P. Clear model fluids to emulate the rheological properties of thickened digested sludge. Water Research. 2012;**46**(9):3014-3022

[22] Espinosa-Solares T, Tecante A, Tanguy PA. Flow patterns in rheologically evolving model fluids produced by hybrid dual mixing systems. Chemical Engineering & Technology. 2001;**24**(9):913-918

[23] Versteeg HK, Malalasekera W. An Introduction to Computational Fluid Dynamics: The Finite Volume Method. 2nd ed. Pearson Education: Harlow, England; 2007. 503 p

[24] Wu B. CFD investigation of turbulence models for mechanical agitation of non-Newtonian fluids in anaerobic digesters. Water Research. 2011;**45**(5):2082-2094

[25] Alexopoulos A, Maggioris D, Kiparissides CCFD. Analysis of turbulence non-homogeneity in mixing vessels: A two-compartment model. Chemical Engineering Science. 2002;**57**(10):1735-1752

[26] Vakili M, Esfahany MN. CFD analysis of turbulence in a baffled stirred tank, a three-compartment model. Chemical Engineering Science. 2009;**64**(2):351-362

[27] Kasat G, Khopkar A, Ranade V, Pandit A. CFD simulation of liquid-phase mixing in solid–liquid stirred reactor. Chemical Engineering Science. 2008;**63**(15):3877-3885

[28] Launder BE, Spalding DB. The numerical computation of turbulent flows. Computer Methods in Applied Mechanics and Engineering. 1974;**3**(2):269-289

[29] Coughtrie AR, Borman DJ, Sleigh PA. Effects of turbulence modelling on prediction of flow characteristics in a bench-scale anaerobic gas-lift digester. Bioresource Technology. 2013;**138**:297-306

[30] Wilcox DC. Formulation of the k-w turbulence model revisited. AIAA Journal. 2008; **46**(11):2823-2838

[31] Brennan JG, editor. Food Processing Handbook. Weinheim, Germany: Wiley-VCH Verlag GmbH & Co. KGaA; 2006. 582 p

[32] Van't Riet K, Van der Lans R. Mixing in bioreactor vessels. In: Moo-Young M., editor. Comprehensive Biotechnology. 2nd ed. Elsevier; 2011. p. 63-80

[33] Wu B. CFD simulation of gas and non-Newtonian fluid two-phase flow in anaerobic digesters. Water Research. 2010;**44**(13):3861-3874

[34] Boulard T, Wang S. Radiactive and convective heterogeneity in a plastic tunnel: Consequences on crop transpiration. Plasticulture. 2002;**121**:22-35

[35] ANSYS-FLUENT. User's Guide. Lebanon: Ansys Inc.; 2009

[36] Çengel YA, Cimbala JM. Fluid Mechanics: Fundamentals and Applications. NY: McGraw Hill; 2006. 929 p

[37] Dapelo D, Alberini F, Bridgeman J. Euler-Lagrange CFD modelling of unconfined gas mixing in anaerobic digestion. Water Research. 2015;**85**:497-511

[38] Gerardi MH. The Microbiology of Anaerobic Digesters. New Jersey: John Wiley & Sons; 2003. 177 p

Chapter 12

CFD for the Design and Optimization of Slurry Bubble Column Reactors

Omar M. Basha and Badie I. Morsi

Additional information is available at the end of the chapter

http://dx.doi.org/10.5772/intechopen.71361

Abstract

Despite the notion that computational fluid dynamics (CFD) models are considered complicated, expensive, time-consuming and difficult to formulate, their implementation offers an advanced prospect to move beyond empirical models, which inherit severe limitations in terms of flexibility, scale-up, and optimization of slurry bubble column reactors (SBCRs). This is because complex hydrodynamics coupled with chemical reactions in such reactors increase the uncertainty in using empirical models, leading to significant startup delays and overruns. Recent work by Basha et al. has shown that properly validated CFD models provide an exceptional opportunity to gain detailed temporal and spatial information about the local hydrodynamics and overall behavior as well as performance of SBCRs. This chapter provides a comprehensive overview of different CFD frameworks which could be used to model SBCRs, namely the multi-Eulerian, direct numerical simulations (DNS) and large Eddy simulation (LES). The steps required in developing CFD models and the optimization of different sub-models, such as interphase interactions, solid-phase representation, bubble population balance, bubble-induced turbulence, mass transfer and reaction kinetics are highlighted. Different convergence criteria for meshing, solution stability and techniques for maximizing the CFD model scale without compromising accuracy are addressed. An example of using CFD multi-Eulerian frameworks to describe the local hydrodynamics in a pilot-scale SBCR (0.3-m ID, 3-m height) operating under the Fisher-Tropsch (F-T) synthesis process are also provided.

Keywords: CFD, slurry bubble column, multi-Eulerian simulation, direct numerical simulation, large Eddy simulation, sub-grid scale (SGS), Fischer-Tropsch, mass transfer, multiphase systems

1. Introduction

Slurry bubble column reactors (SBCRs) are multitubular columns, operating with gas-liquid-solid systems mostly under isothermal conditions as the heat of reaction is removed through carefully designed cooling tubes or pipes with a large surface area for heat transfer [1, 2]. The power needed for mixing and suspending the solid (catalyst) in SBCRs is primarily provided by the gas flowing upward at high superficial velocity within the churn-turbulent flow regime. The gas is often sparged from the bottom of the reactor through specially designed distributors, with controlled pressure drop and nozzle sizes.

SBCRs are used in numerous important industrial applications, such as: (1) catalytic hydrogenation of carbon monoxide to syncrude via Fischer-Tropsch (F-T) synthesis: The Oryx gas-to-liquid (GTL) process (34,000 bpd) built in Qatar by Sasol [3]; (2) hydrogenation of glucose to sugar alcohols (D-glucose, sorbitol, D-xylose, mannitol, etc.): 60,000 metric tons annual capacity plant built in China by Global Bio-Chem [4]; (3) slurry phase hydrocrackers [5]; (4) catalytic wet air oxidation treatment of wastewater [6]; (5) catalytic synthesis of organic chemicals and polyolefins [7]; (6) polymerization of ethylene in a slurry of cyclohexane and a solid catalyst (Chromium, Ziegler Natta), the Solvay process [8]; and (7) the ALFOL process for synthesis of fatty alcohols developed by Conoco [7, 9]. These reactors are often preferred over multitubular fixed-bed reactors due to their numerous advantages, including better temperature control, easier construction, ability of online catalyst addition and withdrawal, higher effectiveness factor, higher gas and liquid holdups, lower pressure drop and more reasonable interphase mass transfer rates with low energy input [1]. SBCRs, however, inherit some disadvantages, such as high degree of liquid back-mixing, strong catalyst attrition, increased side reactions, problematic catalyst separation from the molten products, complex hydrodynamics and ultimately difficult scale up.

In SBCRs, the reactants in the gas-phase have to travel from the gas-phase bulk through the gas-film, gas/liquid interface, liquid-film, liquid-phase bulk, liquid/solid film to reach the solid (catalyst) surface. The reactants then have to diffuse inside the catalyst pores until they reach its active sites, where the chemical reaction takes place. This series of events is illustrated in **Figure 1**. Once the reaction products are formed, they start diffusing all the way back from the active sites to the catalyst to the gas-phase bulk.

The overall reaction rate, Eq. (1), is shown in terms of the resistances encountered in the reaction process:

$$R_s = \frac{C_G - C_S}{\frac{1}{H_e k_G a} + \frac{1}{k_L a} + \frac{1}{k_S a_S} + \frac{1}{k_o a_P \eta}} \tag{1}$$

In this equation, C_G and C_S are the concentrations of the reactant in the bulk gas and inside the catalyst particle, respectively; k_L, k_G and k_S are the liquid-side, gas-side and liquid-solid mass transfer coefficients, respectively; *He* is the Henry's Law constant, a and a_S are the gas-liquid and liquid-particle interfacial areas; k_o is the pseudo-kinetic rate and η is the catalyst effectiveness.

Since the diameter of the catalyst particles frequently used in SBCRs is micron-sized, the interfacial area between the liquid and the catalyst surface is considerably large, and as such, the mass transfer resistance between the liquid and solid phases could be neglected. Moreover, since the vapor pressure of the products (wax) in the gas-phase is negligible, the resistance to mass transfer in the gas-film could be neglected. Thus, the two remaining resistances which have to be considered are the reaction kinetic and the volumetric liquid-side mass transfer. SBCRs typically operate in the churn-turbulent flow regime to guarantee complete suspension

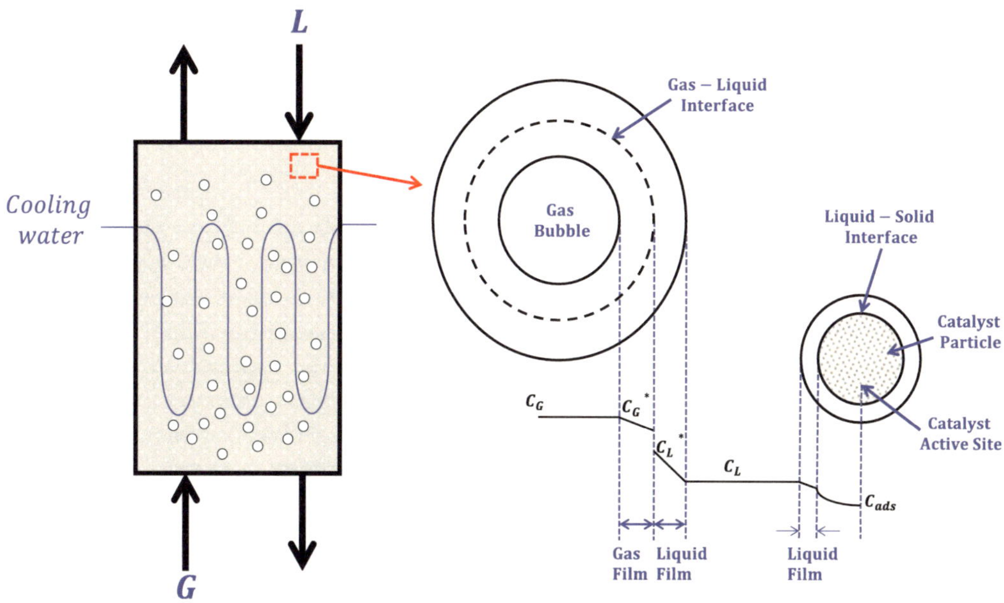

Figure 1. Schematic of slurry bubble column reactor and concentration profiles for mass transfer into a slurry with catalytic particles.

of the fine catalyst particles at high solid loading. The gas holdup in SBCRs could reach 50% by volume and consequently the mass transfer behavior is primarily controlled by the gas-liquid interfacial area (*a*).

Modeling of SBCRs is a complex task which requires, among others, detailed description of the hydrodynamics, reaction kinetics and mass as well as heat transfer parameters. Over the past century, extensive efforts have been made to accurately model the behavior and performance of SBCRs with the aim of enhancing the understanding of the complex hydrodynamics and their effects on the reactor performance in order to enable better design, operation and troubleshooting [10]. Earlier studies focused mainly on experimentally examining the macroscopic fluid dynamic behavior of three-phase fluidized beds and developing empirical correlation. Similarly, empirical one-dimensional (1-D) models have been proposed for SBCRs [11–13], such as the axial dispersion models and multiple cell circulation models, which provide valuable information and predictions of the overall reactor performance. Two-dimensional (2-D) models were also proposed to account for dispersion coefficients, which could be calculated from the first principles, but were empirically obtained. The flow structure and internal recirculation zones in SBCRs, however, were ignored in both 1-D and 2-D models.

With the advent of increasing computational power, the use of computational fluid dynamics (CFD) has gained considerable attention in modeling purposes. Over the past decade, significant advances have been made in numerical modeling of two-phase, gas-solid and gas-liquid flow systems. However, understanding the behavior of the three-phase flows is still limited because of the complex phenomena underlying interactions among the phases, including the particle-bubble interaction and the liquid interstitial effect during particle-particle collision. Recently, several CFD models have been reported to simulate three-phase systems, such as fluidized beds and SBCRs [14–17]. This chapter focuses mainly on the use of CFD modeling in the design of SBCRs.

2. CFD modeling of SBCRs

The presence of three (gas-liquid-solid) coexisting phases in SBCRs, exhibiting significant relative motions, where the exchange of mass, energy and momentum across their interfaces are a dynamic process, represent a challenging modeling task. In this situation, the two most commonly used CFD modeling strategies [18] are the Eulerian-Eulerian or multi-fluid Eulerian [19] and the Eulerian-Lagrangian frameworks [20]. The Eulerian-Eulerian approach assumes that the dispersed and continuous phases are separate interpenetrating quasi-continuous phases, which interact with each other within the computational domain in a fixed Eulerian frame, and a set of Navier-Stokes equations is solved for each of the phases. In this approach, the properties of fluid flow, momentum and heat transfer are represented at a macroscopic level rather than dealing with the individual constituents at a microscopic level. The coupling between the motion of the dispersed and continuous phases is achieved by implementing momentum exchange terms into the momentum balance equations of the respective phase. The Eulerian-Lagrangian approach, on the other hand, assumes that the dispersed phase consists of representative particles transported with the continuous phase and a set of Navier-Stokes equations, which include coupling between the continuous and dispersed phases, is solved only for the continuous phase, whereas the dispersed-phase particles are tracked by solving individual motion equations for each particle. It should be emphasized that when using CFD for modeling large-scale applications, it is critical to strike a balance between the model accuracy and usability and the computational time.

The preceding discussion indicates that the multi-fluid Eulerian modeling is the best suited for large-scale applications with multi-phase turbulent flows, such as SBCRs. Also, the Eulerian-Lagrangian modeling is best suited for fundamental studies, such as bubble-bubble and/or bubble-liquid interactions, and thus it is limited to small superficial gas velocities and phase holdups, unlike those in SBCRs. Therefore, the bulk of this chapter is dedicated to the multi-fluid Eulerian approach for modeling industrial-scale SBCRs.

Earlier, CFD works relied heavily on model simplifications to lower the computational cost, such as using a 2-D Cartesian geometry with axisymmetry and isothermal flow or lumping the gas and liquid phases into one pseudo-homogeneous phase. Recent modeling efforts [2, 17] have been more focused on accurately capturing the interphase interactions of the three phases in detailed 3-D geometries. Basha et al. [10] have comprehensively summarized CFD modeling efforts of three-phase reactors. They pointed out that one of the major drawbacks in these CFD modeling efforts of SBCRs is the lack of model validation. It is important to emphasize that careful and rigorous validation of CFD models is a critical step in the development process, which cannot be overlooked if the model is to be used for the design and optimization purposes. Moreover, validations need to be conducted keeping in mind that data obtained with air-water-solid systems in small-scale reactors at ambient pressures and temperatures cannot satisfactorily be used in the validation of SBCRs, which are designed for high-pressure, high-temperature and high superficial gas velocity applications. This is because such validation will bring into question the scaling up protocol to large-scale industrial SBCRs.

http://dx.doi.org/10.5772/intechopen.71361

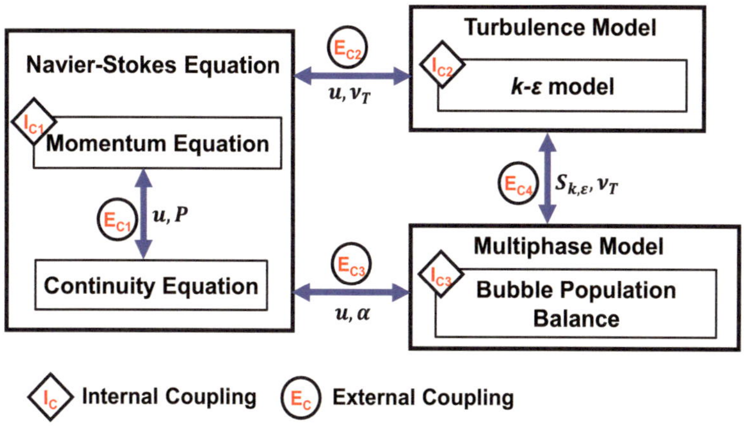

Figure 2. Schematic of the model components and their couplings.

2.1. Multi-fluid Eulerian modeling approach

A schematic of the CFD model components based on a multi-fluid Eulerian approach for modeling SBCRs is shown in **Figure 2**. It consists of three main components: (i) the core hydrodynamics model, consisting of the Navier-Stokes equations; (ii) the multiple-fluid model based on an analog of Boussinesq approximation to represent the natural convection and (iii) the population balance equations to describe the size distribution of the dispersed gas-phase.

The mass and momentum conservation equations are:

$$\frac{\partial(\rho_k \alpha_k)}{\partial t} + \nabla\left(\rho_k \alpha_k \vec{u}_k\right) = \dot{m}_{kn} \tag{2}$$

$$\frac{\partial\left(\rho_k \alpha_k \vec{u}_k\right)}{\partial t} + \nabla\left(\rho_k \alpha_k \vec{u}_k \vec{u}_k\right) = -\alpha_k \cdot \nabla p_f + \nabla\left(\alpha_k \vec{\tau}_k\right) + \alpha_k \rho_k g + \vec{u}_{kn} \dot{m}_{kn} + \vec{M}_k \tag{3}$$

where k indicates the phase (G for gas, L for liquid and S for solid); $\vec{u}_k$ = (u, v, w) is the velocity of phase k; $\dot{m}_{kn}$ is the mass transfer rate between phases k and n; $\vec{u}_{kn}$ is the relative velocity between phases k and n; α is the volume fraction of each phase; $\vec{M}_k$ is the overall interfacial momentum; p_f is the fluid pressure and τ is the stress tensors.

The stress tensor $\vec{\tau}_k$ is represented as:

$$\vec{\tau}_{k=G,L} = \alpha_k \mu_{k,eff}\left(\nabla \vec{u}_k + \left(\nabla \vec{u}_k\right)^T - \frac{2}{3}\vec{I}\left(\nabla \cdot \vec{u}_k\right)\right) \tag{4}$$

μ_{eff}, is the effective viscosity, which is typically the sum of the molecular and turbulent viscosities.

For the liquid-phase, the effective viscosity, accounting for the three contributions (1) molecular viscosity, $\mu_{L,M}$, (2) shear induced turbulence viscosity, $\mu_{L,T}$ and (3) additional term due to the bubble induced turbulence, $\mu_{L,B}$ is represented as:

$$\mu_{\text{eff}} = \mu_{\text{L,M}} + \mu_{\text{L,T}} + \mu_{\text{L,B}}. \tag{5}$$

The turbulent viscosity is expressed as:

$$\mu_{L,T} = C_{\mu,B}\rho_L\left(\frac{k^2}{\varepsilon}\right), \quad \text{with} \quad C_{\mu,B} = 0.6 \tag{6}$$

For the gas-phase, the effective viscosity is represented as the sum of the molecular viscosity $\mu_{G,M}$ and the turbulence-induced viscosity:

$$\mu_{\text{eff}} = \mu_{\text{G,M}} + \mu_{\text{G,T}}. \tag{7}$$

where the turbulence-induced viscosity for the gas-phase is represented as:

$$\mu_{G,T} = \frac{\rho_L}{\rho_G}\left(\mu_{L,T}\right) \tag{8}$$

2.1.1. Turbulence model

As the mass and momentum balances are obtained through the ensemble averaging formulations, the terms u_k and u_k' represent the mean and fluctuating components of the velocity, thus the unclosed terms in the stress tensor, Eq. (4), should be modeled in order to accurately account for mixing and turbulence effects. Generally, liquid mixing in SBCRs is a resultant of three major contributing mechanisms [21, 22]: (1) global convective circulation of the liquid-phase induced by the non-uniform radial gas holdup distribution; (2) turbulent diffusion due to the presence of large and small eddies generated by the rising gas bubbles and (3) molecular diffusion, which is negligible when compared with the other diffusion mechanisms. Thus, to predict the effects of turbulence, CFD models primarily concentrate on the methods which make use of turbulence models. These methods are typically based on scaling laws and are specifically developed to account for the effects of turbulence without recourse to a prohibitively fine mesh and direct numerical simulation (DNS). Most of the conclusions and observations regarding turbulence are based on the order-of-magnitude estimates, which follow from logical applications of scaling laws and dimensional analysis.

Generally, the turbulent length scale (eddy sizes) is a physical quantity related to the size of large eddies, containing the energy in the turbulent flow. A variety of length scales exists within the turbulent flow, where the largest eddies in the flow account for most of the momentum and energy transport, and their sizes are only constrained by the physical boundaries of the flow. The sizes of the smallest eddies, on the other hand, are determined by the viscosity. Therefore, the effect of viscosity increases with decreasing length scales. The smallest length scales are those where the kinetic energy is dissipated into heat. The turbulence eddies are visualized as molecules, constantly colliding, exchanging momentum and obeying laws similar to the kinetic theory of gases. Most models of Reynolds stress, using an eddy viscosity hypothesis, based on an analogy between the molecular and turbulent motions, are described as follows:

$$-\overline{\rho u_i u_j} = \mu_T\left(\frac{\partial u}{\partial x_i} + \frac{\partial u}{\partial x_j}\right) - \frac{2}{3}\delta_{ij}\left(\mu_T\frac{\partial u}{\partial x_k} + \rho k\right) \tag{9}$$

where μ_T is the turbulent or eddy viscosity, which unlike molecular viscosity, is not a fluid property, but depends on the local state of flow or turbulence; μ_T is a scalar quantity, which varies significantly within the flow domain; and k is the turbulent kinetic energy.

Although there are numerous turbulence models as outlined elsewhere [21, 22], the most widely used is the two-equation (k-ε) model in which the turbulent kinetic energy (k) and the turbulent energy dissipation (ε) are calculated based on the following governing equations, respectively:

$$\frac{\partial(\rho k)}{\partial t} + \nabla\left(\rho k \vec{u}\right) = \nabla\left(\mathrm{Pr}_{eff,k}^{-1}\mu_{eff}\nabla k\right) + G_k + G_b - \rho\varepsilon - Y_M + S_k \tag{10}$$

$$\frac{\partial(\rho\varepsilon)}{\partial t} + \nabla\left(\rho\varepsilon\vec{u}\right) = \nabla\left(\mathrm{Pr}_{eff,\varepsilon}^{-1}\mu_{eff}\nabla\varepsilon\right) + C_{\varepsilon 1}\frac{\varepsilon}{k}\left(G_k + C_{\varepsilon 3}G_b\right) - C_{\varepsilon 2}\rho\frac{\varepsilon^2}{k} - R_\varepsilon + S_\varepsilon \tag{11}$$

where G_k is the generation of turbulence kinetic energy due to the mean velocity gradients; G_b is the generation of turbulence kinetic energy due to buoyancy; Y_M is the contribution of the fluctuating dilation in compressible turbulence to the overall dissipation rate; $C_{\varepsilon 1}$, $C_{\varepsilon 2}$, $C_{\varepsilon 3}$ are constants which are varied based on the application. $\mathrm{Pr}_{eff,k}^{-1}$ and $\mathrm{Pr}_{eff,\varepsilon}^{-1}$ are the inverse effective Prandtl numbers for k and ε, respectively derived analytically using the Random-Number Generator (RNG) theory. In addition, S_k and S_ε are user-defined source term. The equations used to calculate some of the above parameters are:

$$G_k = \mu_t\left(\frac{\partial\vec{U}_i}{\partial x_j} + \frac{\partial\vec{U}_j}{\partial x_i}\right)\frac{\partial\vec{U}_i}{\partial x_j} - \frac{2}{3}\frac{\partial\vec{U}_k}{\partial x_k}\left(3\mu_t\left(\frac{\partial\vec{U}_k}{\partial x_k}\right) + \rho k\right) \tag{12}$$

$$G_b = \begin{cases} \dfrac{\mu_t}{\rho\sigma_p}g_i\dfrac{\partial p}{\partial x_i} & fullbouyancymodel \\[2ex] \dfrac{\mu_t}{\rho\sigma_p}\rho\beta g_i\dfrac{\partial T}{\partial x_i} & Boussinesqbouyancemodel \end{cases} \tag{13}$$

$$\left|\frac{\mathrm{Pr}_{eff}^{-1} - 1.3929}{\alpha_0 - 1.3929}\right|^{0.6321} \cdot \left|\frac{\mathrm{Pr}_{eff}^{-1} + 2.3929}{\alpha_0 + 2.3929}\right|^{0.3679} = \frac{\mu_{\mathrm{mol}}}{\mu_{\mathrm{eff}}},\ \alpha_0 = 1 \tag{14}$$

where $\alpha_0 = 1$, (μ_{mol}) is the molecular viscosity. In the high Reynolds number limit where $\left(\frac{\mu_{\mathrm{mol}}}{\mu_{\mathrm{eff}}} \ll 1\right)$, and $\mathrm{Pr}_{eff,\varepsilon}^{-1} = \mathrm{Pr}_{eff,k}^{-1} \approx 1.393$ [23].

It is important to note that the selection of the most appropriate turbulence model for SBCRs will depend on the reactor geometry and the superficial velocities of the gas and liquid phases. Also, different models have to be tested and validated to determine which is the most suitable for the given SBCR design and operating conditions [18, 24].

2.1.2. *Momentum exchange terms and interphase coefficient correlations*

In a SBCR, the solid particles are fluidized in the liquid-phase due to the momentum transfer to it from the gas-phase. Therefore, capturing accurately the interaction dynamics between the three phases is critical in developing the CFD model. The momentum exchange term in the momentum balance Eq. (3), which describes the interface forces between the phases is described as:

$$\vec{M}_k = \vec{M}_{Drag} + \vec{M}_{Lift} + \vec{M}_{Virtual\ Mass} + \vec{M}_{Wall\ lubrication} + \vec{M}_{Turbulence\ dispersion} \quad (15)$$

The right-hand side (RHS) terms of Eq. (15) represent the interphase drag, lift, virtual mass, wall force, and turbulence dispersion, respectively. The drag force is by far the most important force in describing the momentum transfer between phases, whereas other forces, such as lift, buoyancy virtual mass and turbulent dispersion have more a tuning effect, which can be optimized during the validation process.

Significant efforts have been reported investigating each of these momentum terms separately, and numerous terms have been summarized elsewhere [10]. While there is extensive work on two-phase flow systems, studies investigating three-phase hydrodynamics are rather limited. Moreover, the gas-liquid and liquid-solid drag models available were obtained mostly using air-water or air-water-glass beads under ambient conditions, which will bring into question about their applicability for modeling large-scale industrial SBCRs, operating with organic media under high pressures and temperatures. Several investigators [18, 25] have underscored the need for better and more representative drag correlations for CFD modeling of the hydrodynamics in three-phase reactors. Therefore, the selection of the appropriate terms and coefficients not only highly dependent on the system conditions, but also require extensive validation to determine the best combination that most accurately capture the behavior of the SBCR. Basha et al. [24] have recently identified the momentum interphase terms (**Table 1**) as well and the interphase coefficient expressions (**Table 2**) to represent SBCRs operating in the churn-turbulent flow regime for the Fischer-Tropsch synthesis process.

Term	Expression
Drag [26]	$\vec{M}_{D,G} = \vec{M}_{D,G-L} + \vec{M}_{D,G-S}$, $\vec{M}_{D,L} = \vec{M}_{D,L-G} + \vec{M}_{D,L-S}$, $\vec{M}_{D,S} = \vec{M}_{D,S-G} + \vec{M}_{D,S-L}$ $G-L: \vec{M}_{D,G-L} = \frac{3}{4}\frac{C_{D,G-L}}{d_b}\alpha_G\alpha_L\rho_L\left\|\vec{u}_G - \vec{u}_L\right\|\left(\vec{u}_G - \vec{u}_L\right)$ $S-L: \vec{M}_{D,S-L} = \frac{3}{4}\frac{C_{D,S-L}}{d_p}\alpha_S\alpha_L\rho_L\left\|\vec{u}_S - \vec{u}_L\right\|\left(\vec{u}_S - \vec{u}_L\right)$ $S-G: \vec{M}_{D,G-S} = \frac{3}{4}\frac{C_{D,S-G}}{d_p}\alpha_S\rho_G\left\|\vec{u}_S - \vec{u}_G\right\|\left(\vec{u}_S - \vec{u}_G\right)$
Lift [27]	$\vec{M}_{L,L} = \alpha_G\rho_L C_L\left(\vec{u}_G - \vec{u}_L\right) \times \left(\nabla \times \vec{u}_L\right)$
Virtual Mass [28]	$\vec{M}_{VM} = \alpha_G\rho_L 0.5\left(\frac{D\vec{u}_G}{Dt} - \frac{D\vec{u}_L}{Dt}\right)$
Lateral [29]	$\vec{M}_W = \begin{cases} \frac{\alpha_G\rho_L\left(\vec{u}_G - \vec{u}_L\right)}{D_S}\max\left(0, -0.0064 + 0.0166\frac{D_S}{y_w}\right)n_w & y_w < \left(\frac{C_{w2}}{C_{w1}}\right)D_S \\ 0 & y_w > \left(\frac{C_{w2}}{C_{w1}}\right)D_S \end{cases}$ y_w : *distancefromwall*, n_w = *vectornormaltowall*
Turbulence dispersion [30]	$M_{TD} = 0.2\rho_L k\nabla\alpha_G$

Table 1. Momentum interphase terms used by Basha et al. [24].

Term	Model
Gas-liquid drag [31]	$C_{D,G-L} = \begin{cases} \left(\frac{24}{\mathrm{Re}_b}\right)\left(1+0.1\mathrm{Re}_b^{0.75}\right) & N_\mu < 36\sqrt{2}\frac{\left(1+0.1\mathrm{Re}_b^{0.75}\right)}{\mathrm{Re}_b^2} \\ \frac{2}{3}\sqrt{\mathrm{E\ddot{o}}_b} & N_\mu \geq 36\sqrt{2}\frac{\left(1+0.1\mathrm{Re}_b^{0.75}\right)}{\mathrm{Re}_b^2} \end{cases}$
Gas-solid drag [32]	$C_{D,G-S} = \begin{cases} \left(\frac{24}{\mathrm{Re}_p}\right)\left(1+0.15\mathrm{Re}_p^{0.687}\right) & \mathrm{Re}_p < 1000 \\ 0.44 & \mathrm{Re}_p \geq 1000 \end{cases}$
Liquid–solid drag [33]	$C_{D,L-S} = \alpha_s^{-1.65}\max\left(\frac{24}{\alpha_s \mathrm{Re}_{S-L}}\left(1+0.15(\alpha_s \mathrm{Re}_{S-L})^{0.687}\right), 0.44\right), \; \mathrm{Re}_{S-L} = \frac{\rho_L \lvert u_S - u_L \rvert d_p}{\mu_L}$
Liquid-gas lift [34]	$C_{L,L-G} = \begin{cases} \min[0.288\tanh(0.12\mathrm{Re}), f(Eo_d)] & E\ddot{o}_d < 4 \\ f(E\ddot{o}_d) = 0.00105E\ddot{o}^3 - 0.0159E\ddot{o}_d^2 - 0.0204E\ddot{o}_d + 0.474 & 4 \leq E\ddot{o}_d \leq 10 \\ -0.29 & E\ddot{o}_d > 10 \end{cases}$ $E\ddot{o} = \frac{g\Delta\rho d_B^2}{\sigma}, \; E\ddot{o}_d = E\ddot{o}\left(1+0.163E\ddot{o}^{0.757}\right)^{2/3}$

Table 2. Interphase coefficient expressions used by Basha et al. [24].

2.1.3. *Bubbles representation*

At low superficial gas velocities, bubble interaction can be neglected and the bubble diameter is not significantly influenced by coalescence and breakup processes. However, when modeling SBCRs, which typically operate in the churn-turbulent flow regime, the effect of bubbles interaction becomes significant and the effects of coalescence and breakup must be taken into account. This will allow accurate representation of the range of bubble sizes, which exists within the flow, and better description of the local interfacial area concentration, which is a critical parameter in the determination of the inter-phase mass, momentum and heat transfer.

Moreover, bubble size variation is intimately related to bubble-particle collisions, since the presence of solids was reported to significantly affect the bubble sizes within the SBCR. Similarly, the presence of bubbles is critical in the suspension of solid particles, which can be transported in the wake of rising bubbles or their settling velocity can be reduced due to bubbles holding up the solid particles. Furthermore, the presence of both solid particles and gas bubbles has a significant effect on the turbulent velocity fluctuations within the liquid-phase, where solid particles and large gas bubbles greater than the eddy length scale tend to enhance the turbulent velocity fluctuations, whereas solid particles and gas bubbles smaller than the eddy length scale will dampen the velocity fluctuations.

Generally, bubble-particle collisions can yield two different consequences: the particle is ejected from the bubble surface, or the particle penetrates the bubble leading to either bubble breakage or non-breakage. Bubble-particle collisions generate perturbations on the bubble surface. After the bubble-particle collision, three factors become crucial in determining the coalescence or breakage of the bubble [26]: (1) shear stress, which depends on the liquid velocity gradient and the relative bubble-particle impact speed, and tends to break the gas bubble; (2) surface tension force, which tends to stabilize the gas bubble and drive it to recover its original shape; and (3) viscous force, which slows the growth rate of the surface perturbation, and tends to stabilize the bubble. Accordingly, the gas bubble coalescence and breakage models are classified into four main categories [35]: (1) turbulent fluctuation and collision; (2) viscous shear stress; (3) shearing-off process and (4) interfacial stability. The bubbles induced turbulence and bubble population balance are discussed below.

2.1.3.1. Bubble-induced turbulence model

The bubble-induced turbulence is represented by introducing two source terms, S_k and S_ε, into the *k*-*ε* Eq. [36, 37] as:

$$S_k = \left(\frac{\rho_G}{\rho_G + C_{VM}\rho_G}\right)\alpha_G\left(\frac{3\,C_D}{4\,d_B}\right)\left|\vec{u_G} - \vec{u_L}\right|\left(q_{LG} - 2k_L + \vec{u_d}\cdot\vec{u_r}\right); \quad S_\varepsilon = C_{\varepsilon 3}\frac{\varepsilon}{k}S_k \tag{16}$$

where q_{LG} is the covariance of the liquid-phase and the dispersed gas-phase velocities; u_r and u_d are the relative and drift velocities, respectively; and $C_{\varepsilon 3} = 1.2$.

This model is rigorously derived by writing the equation of motion for a single bubble and rearranging it in terms of the fluid velocity, where the drag and mass coefficients (C_D and C_{VM}) appear in the formulation. The equations for the relative and drift velocities are:

$$\vec{u_r} = \left[\vec{uG} - \vec{u_L}\right] - \vec{u_d}\,, \quad \vec{u_d} = -\vec{D}^{\,t}_{12}\left[\frac{\Delta\alpha_2}{\alpha_2} - \frac{\Delta\alpha_1}{\alpha_1}\right] \tag{17}$$

The drift velocity ($\vec{u}_d$) is a statistical quantity due to the conditional averaging. It may not be negligible as it accounts for the dispersion effects due to the bubbles transport by the turbulent fluid motion. $\vec{D}^{\,t}_{12}$ is the fluid-bubble dispersion tensor, which is expressed in terms of the fluid-bubble velocity covariance [q_{LG}] and the fluid-bubble turbulent interaction time scale $\left[\tau^t_{12}\right]$. For the purpose of practical computations [38], the dispersion tensor is simplified to its diagonal form [37, 39–41] as:

$$\vec{D}^{\,t}_{12} = \frac{1}{3}\vec{\tau}^{\,t}_{12}q_{LG}\cdot I \tag{18}$$

where I is a 3 × 3 identity matrix

2.1.3.2. Bubble population balance

It is necessary to take into account the bubble breakup and coalescence phenomenon in the CFD model when a bubble column or a slurry bubble column operates in the heterogeneous flow regime. The typical approach is to use population balance models, which describe the variation in a given population property over the space and time within a velocity field. Assuming that each bubble class travels at the same mean algebraic velocity, the individual number density of a bubble class *i* can be expressed as [42]:

$$\frac{\partial n_i}{\partial t} + \nabla(u_G n_i) = \left(\sum_J R_J\right)_i = B_C + B_B - D_C - D_B \tag{19}$$

where $\left(\sum_J R_J\right)_i$ represents the net change in the number density distribution due to the coalescence and breakup of bubbles; B_C and B_B represent the birth rate due to coalescence and breakage of bubbles; and D_C and D_B represent the death rate due to coalescence and breakage of bubbles, respectively.

There are numerous breakup and coalescence models reported in the literature, and available in commercial CFD packages. For modeling an F-T SBCR, the model proposed by Lou and Svendsen [43] for the breakup rate of bubbles was determined to be the most suitable. Their model was developed based on the assumption of bubble binary breakup (each bubble breaks up into two distinctly smaller bubbles) under isotropic turbulence. The "daughter" bubble sizes were accounted for using a dimensionless variable (f_{BV}):

$$f_{BV} = \frac{d_I^3}{d_I^3 + d_{II}^3} \tag{20}$$

where d_I and d_{II} represent the diameters of the daughter bubbles in the binary breakage of a parent bubble of diameter d and volume v. The breakup rate of the bubbles can be represented as:

$$\Omega_B(v : vf_{BV}) = 0.923(1-\alpha_G)n\left(\frac{\varepsilon}{d^2}\right)^{1/3} \int_{\xi_{min}}^{1} \frac{(1+\xi)^2}{\xi^{11/3}} \exp\left(-\frac{12c_f\sigma}{\beta\rho_L\varepsilon^{2/3}d^{5/3}\xi^{11/3}}\right)d\xi \tag{21}$$

where $\xi_{min} = \lambda_{min}/d$ and $\xi = \lambda/d$, represent the size ratio between an eddy and a bubble in the inertial subrange and β is a constant derived from fundamental consideration and it equals 2. Subsequently, the birth and death rates due to breakup are represented as:

$$B_B = \sum \Omega_B(v_j : v_i)n_i, \tag{22}$$

$$D_B = \Omega_i n_i \qquad \text{where } \Omega_i = \sum_{m=1}^{N} \Omega_{mi} \tag{23}$$

On the other hand, the bubble coalescence occurring due to bubble collision is caused by three major forces: (1) wake entrainment, (2) buoyancy and (3) random turbulence. Wake entrainment has been widely accepted to be negligible [44]; and the effect of buoyancy is eliminated since all bubbles of the same class are assumed to travel at the same mean velocity. Therefore, the only remaining driving force is the random turbulence. The coalescence rate due to random turbulent collision from Prince and Blanch [45] was determined to be the most suitable for F-T SBCR modeling, as:

$$\chi_{ij} = \frac{\pi}{4}\left[d_i + d_j\right]^2\left(u_{Ti}^2 + u_{Tj}^2\right)^{0.5} \exp\left(-\frac{t_{ij}}{\tau_{ij}}\right) \tag{24}$$

u_T is the turbulent velocity in the inertial subrange of isotropic turbulence and can be estimated as: [46]

$$u_T = \frac{r_{ij}^{2/3}}{\varepsilon^{1/3}} \tag{25}$$

The contact time between two colliding bubbles with radii ri and rj is:

$$\tau_{ij} = \frac{r_{ij}^{2/3}}{\varepsilon^{1/3}} \tag{26}$$

The time for two bubbles with radii ri and rj to coalesce is:

$$t_{ij} = \left(\frac{r_{ij}^3 \rho_l}{16\sigma}\right)^{0.5} \ln\left(\frac{h_o}{h_f}\right) \tag{27}$$

where h_o and h_f represent the initial bubble film thickness and the critical film thickness. Their values were reported to be 10^{-4} and 10^{-8} m, respectively. rij is the equivalent radius which can be expressed as:

$$r_{ij} = \frac{2r_i r_j}{\left(r_i + r_j\right)} \tag{28}$$

Then, the number density for individual bubble groups governed by birth and death due coalescence can be represented as:

$$B_C = \frac{1}{2}\sum_{k=1}^{i}\sum_{j=1}^{i} \eta_{jki} \chi_{ij} n_i n_j$$

$$\text{where } \eta_{jki} = \begin{cases} \left(v_j + v_k\right) - v_{i-1}/\left(v_i - v_{i-1}\right) & if\ v_{i-1} < v_j + v_k < v_i \\ v_{i+1} - \left(v_j + v_k\right)/\left(v_{i+1} - v_i\right) & if\ v_i < v_j + v_k < v_{i+1} \\ 0 & ifneither \end{cases} \tag{29}$$

$$D_C = \sum_{m=1}^{N} \chi_{ij} n_i n_j \tag{30}$$

where χ_{ij} is coalescence rate of bubbles ($m^{-3}\ s^{-1}$), (Eq. (24)).

It is important to note that this bubble population balance model will be developed for a SBCR operating under typical pressures and temperatures of F-T synthesis; and it might be possible that other correlations/parameters could provide a better fit under different conditions.

2.1.3.3. Solid-phase representation

For the solid-phase, the effect of particle-particle interactions can be accounted for by introducing additional terms into the stress tensor. The kinetic theory of granular flow (KTGF) is used to represent the solids behavior. The stress tensor for the solid-phase is represented as:

http://dx.doi.org/10.5772/intechopen.71361

$$\tau_S = \alpha_S\mu_S\left(\nabla\vec{u_S} + \left(\nabla\vec{u_S}\right)^T\right) - P_s\,\vec{I} + \alpha_S\mu_S\left(\lambda_S - \frac{2}{3}\right)\vec{I}\left(\nabla\cdot\vec{u_S}\right) \tag{31}$$

λ_S is the solids bulk viscosity, which describes the resistance of the particle suspension against compression and is written as:

$$\lambda_S = \frac{4}{3}\alpha_S^2 P_S d_p g_0 \left(1 + e_p\right)\sqrt{\frac{\Theta}{\pi}} \tag{32}$$

P_s is the solids pressure, which represents the normal solid-phase forces due to particle-particle interaction and is expressed [47] as:

$$P_s = \rho_S\alpha_S\Theta + 2g_0\rho_s\alpha_S^2\Theta\left(1 + e_p\right) \tag{33}$$

The first term in the RHS of the solid pressure equation is the kinetic contribution, which accounts for the momentum transferred through the system by particles moving across the imaginary shear layers in the flow. The second term in the RHS is the collisional contribution, which represents the momentum transferred by direct collisions.

ep is the restitution coefficient, representing the ratio of normal relative velocity after and before the collision. It equals 0.9 as proposed by Ding and Gidaspow [48].

g_0 is the radial distribution function, accounting for the increase in the probability of collisions when the particle density increases; and can be expressed as [26, 48]:

$$g_0 = 0.6\left[1 - \left(\frac{\alpha_S}{\alpha_{S,\max}}\right)^{1/3}\right]^{-1} \tag{34}$$

where $\alpha_{S,\max} = 0.62$, and beyond this value, the radial distribution function goes to infinity.

Θ is the granular temperature, which is a measure of the kinetic energy contained in the fluctuating velocity for the solid particles and it is defined using the algebraic model by Ding and Gidaspow [48], which helps minimize the computational load by avoiding to solve an additional differential equation along with its closure models:

$$\Theta = \frac{d_p^2}{30\left(1 - e_p\right)}\left(\nabla u_S + \left(\nabla u_S\right)^T\right) \tag{35}$$

μ_S is the solid-phase shear viscosity, which is an elastic force, arising from the solids in response to shear, compression and extension stresses exerted on it by the continuous liquid-phase. It should not be confused with the viscous forces, which arise during the fluid flow. The fluid viscosity is proportional to the rate of deformation over time, whereas, the solid viscosity is proportional to the amount of shear deformation. The following model by Gidaspow [14] is used to describe the solid-phase viscosity:

$$\mu_S = \frac{4}{5}\alpha_s^2 \rho_s d_p g_0 (1+e_p)\sqrt{\frac{\Theta}{\pi}} + \frac{2\frac{5\sqrt{\pi}}{96}\rho_s d_p \sqrt{\Theta}}{g_0(1+e_p)} \cdot \left[1 + \frac{4}{5}\alpha_s g_0 (1+e_p)\right]^2 \tag{36}$$

2.1.3.4. Kinetics and mass transfer

In cases of absorption and boiling processes occurring in a large-scale flow system, significant heat and mass exchanges that occur across the interfaces separating the gas and liquid phases must be appropriately accounted for within the three-fluid model. The interphase mass-transfer rate depends on the mass-transfer coefficient, the interfacial area, concentration and the rate of chemical reaction. The mass-transfer coefficient is a function of the local hydrodynamics, which are influenced, on one hand, by the bubble shrinkage due to physical or chemical absorption and, on the other hand, by the change of the physical properties due to the heterogeneous distributions of the chemical species.

In calculating the gas-liquid mass transfer in the transient CFD simulation, it is not possible to obtain the mass transfer coefficients from the hydrodynamic data generated using multi-Eulerian simulation. This is primarily due to the limitations at the interface in the jump boundary conditions from the gas to liquid, which ideally require empirical mass transfer data or correlations to be incorporated in the CFD model.

Using CFD to model mass transfer and interfacial phenomena from the first principles is feasible at a very small scale, such a single droplet, using a Lagrangian or a volume of fluid (VOF) scheme. However, it should be noted that Gidaspow et al. [14, 48] used the granular temperature approach to derive the mass transfer coefficients in multiphase systems. Nonetheless, this approach would not be possible for a large-scale SBCR. Actually, attempting multi-fluid Eulerian to perform multiphase-multicomponent mass transfer would result in numerically unstable sources and sinks.

Therefore, the species mass transfer rate from the dispersed phase to the continuous phase per unit volume, which appeared in Eqs. (2) and (3), is defined as:

$$\dot{m}_{kn} = k_L a \cdot (C^* - C_L) \tag{37}$$

where $k_L a$ is the volumetric liquid-side mass transfer coefficient, which is represented using an empirical correlation, Eq. (38), developed using numerous experimental data for different three-phase F-T systems obtained under elevated pressures and temperatures in a pilot-scale SBCR (0.3-m ID and 3-m height).

$$\begin{aligned} k_L a = 7.99 \times 10^{-9} \frac{\rho_L^{1.82} \rho_G^{0.27} u_G^{0.387} \Gamma^{0.173}}{\mu_L^{0.25} \sigma_L^{0.976} Mw_g^{0.02}} \left(\frac{P}{P - P_V}\right)^{0.242} \left(\frac{d_C}{d_C + 0.3}\right)^{0.1} \\ \times exp\left[-1.3C_p + 0.8C_p^2 - C_p^3 - 1675.7d_p + 0.176X_W\right] \end{aligned} \tag{38}$$

Moreover, when accounting for chemical reactions, an additional species conservation equation has to be considered as follows:

$$\frac{\partial(\rho_k \alpha_k y_k^i)}{\partial t} + \nabla(\rho_k \alpha_k u_k u_k y_k^i) = \nabla(\alpha_k \rho_k D_k^i \nabla y_k^i) + r_k^i - r_{kn}^{ij} \tag{39}$$

where y_k^i represents the mass fraction of species i in phase k. Also, r_k^i and r_{kn}^{ij} represent the F-T reaction kinetics rate and the rate of chemical absorption, respectively.

2.2. Direct numerical simulation (DNS) approach

In the case of DNS approach, the governing equations for the mass and momentum balances of each phase would be identical to Eqs. (1) and (2). However, the viscous shear stress (Eq. (3)) would not be resolved using turbulence models, but is resolved by tracking the evolution, position and flow structure near the interphase interfaces with no ensemble averaging. Typically, interface tracking or capturing algorithms are divided into three categories, front tracking, level set method and volume of fluid method. A brief outline of these methods is given below and more details can be found elsewhere [49–52]:

2.2.1. *Front tracking method*

In this method, a surface mesh within a control volume is used to track the interface front within the computational domain. The discretization of the balance equations, shown in **Figure 3**, is carried out on two separate sets of meshes to describe the solution: (1) a 3-D stage-structured non-adaptive Eulerian mesh and (2) a 2-D unstructured, adaptive and triangular Lagrangian front mesh. The Lagrangian coordinate of each marker on the interface is derived by integration

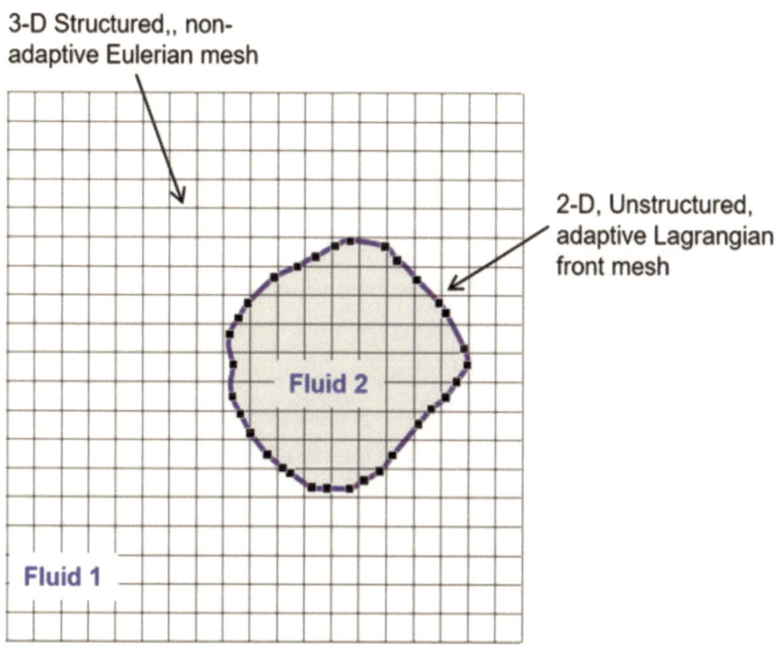

Figure 3. Front tracking method.

from the initial position at time t = 0, as shown in Eq. (40), where the interface velocity is determined using Eq. (41).

$$x_f^n = x_f^0 + \int_0^t u_f dt \tag{40}$$

$$u_f = \sum D(x - x_f)U(x) \tag{41}$$

where

$$D(x - x_f) = \begin{cases} (4\Delta)^{-\alpha} \prod_{i=1}^{\alpha} \left(1 + \cos\left(\frac{\pi}{2\Delta}|x - x_f|\right)\right) & for\ |x - x_f| < 2\Delta \\ 0 & for\ |x - x_f| \geq 2\Delta \end{cases} \tag{42}$$

Δ is the mesh spacing and $\alpha = 2, 3$ for 2 and 3 dimensions.

2.2.2. Level set method

In this method, a continuous function which is zero at the interface, positive on one side and negative on the other, is defined over the computational domain. The function ($\phi(\boldsymbol{x}, t)$) is the related to the liquid volume fraction field function as shown in Eq. (43):

$$F = \lim_{V \to \infty} \frac{1}{V} \iiint H_c(\phi(\boldsymbol{x}, t)) dV \tag{43}$$

where $H_c(\phi)$ is referred to as the Heaviside function, is represented as [52]:

$$H_c(\phi) = \begin{cases} 0 & for\ \phi < -\varepsilon \\ \frac{1}{2} + \frac{\phi}{2\varepsilon} + \frac{1}{2\pi} \sin\left(\frac{\pi\phi}{\varepsilon}\right) & for\ |\phi| \leq \varepsilon \\ 1 & for\ \phi > \varepsilon \end{cases} \tag{44}$$

where, ε is a parameter in the order of the mesh size (typically 1.5Δ). It is important to note that a re-distancing algorithm is required to regularize the function, as the numerical errors accumulate. Also, an extra re-distancing function, preserving $|\nabla\phi| = 1$ around the zero level of ϕ, is required.

2.2.3. Volume of fluid (VOF) method

The VOF method is an Eulerian treatment of the interface that requires accurate algorithms for the advection of the volume fraction function to preserve the mass conservation, which cannot be achieved by conventional differencing schemes due to numerical diffusion. The composition field must be advected by either the high-resolution interface capturing scheme to approximate the fluxes of volume fraction or the geometric reconstruction of the interface based on the simple line interface construction (SLIC). In this method, an indictor function, Eq. (45), is introduced to track the presence of one of the phases in the whole computational domain; and then it is used to evaluate the mixture physical properties. The advantage of this method is that it is easier to implement when compared with the other two methods and requires less computational effort. Moreover, the interface positions are not stored for each time-step, which allows for easier representation of large surface deformations and surface breakup and merging. However, the main disadvantage is that it is highly resolution dependent.

$$\mathrm{F} = \lim_{V\to\infty} \frac{1}{V} \iiint \chi^{l}(x, y, z, t) dV \tag{45}$$

2.2.4. *Large Eddy simulation (LES) approach*

In the large Eddy simulation (LES) approach, only large eddies are computed directly and thus a low-pass spatial filter is applied to the instantaneous Navier-Stokes conservation equations to formulate the 3-D unsteady governing equations for large-scale motions. This filtering method, also referred to as explicit filtering, allows for mesh independent results to be achieved since the truncation errors at the smallest resolved scales are not large. Different filtering methods can be found elsewhere [53]. Within the LES approach, the volume-averaging procedure can be derived by applying a spatial filter function, among others, available in the literature [54]. Also, in the LES approach, the filtering operation can be done according to Eq. (46), where $\mathrm{G}(|\mathbf{x} - \mathbf{x}'|)$ is an appropriate spatial filter function:

$$\overline{\varphi(\boldsymbol{x}', t)} = \int_{\Delta} \varphi(\boldsymbol{x}', t) G(|\boldsymbol{x} - \boldsymbol{x}'|) d\boldsymbol{x}' \tag{46}$$

The different phases are then identified by defining a quantity reflecting the average volumetric fraction of each phase inside the computational mesh volume. Eq. (47) shows the average volumetric fraction of the *k*-th phase. A component weighted volume averaging process can further be derived [55] as shown in Eq. (48). The instantaneous property $\varphi(\mathbf{x}', t)$ can thus be described using Eq. (49), where $\widetilde{\varphi(\mathbf{x}', t)}$ is the filtered resolvable component and $\varphi(\mathbf{x}', t)$ is the sub-grid scale (SGS) component, which accounts for the unresolved spatial variations at lengths smaller than the filter width.

$$\alpha^{k}(\boldsymbol{x}', t) = \overline{\chi^{k}(\boldsymbol{x}', t)} = \int_{\Delta} \chi^{k}(\boldsymbol{x}', t) G(|\boldsymbol{x} - \boldsymbol{x}'|) d\boldsymbol{x}' \tag{47}$$

$$\widetilde{\varphi(\boldsymbol{x}', t)} = \frac{\overline{\chi^{k}(\boldsymbol{x}', t)\varphi(\boldsymbol{x}', t)}}{\overline{\chi^{k}(\boldsymbol{x}', t)}} = \frac{\int_{\Delta} \chi^{k}(\boldsymbol{x}', t)\varphi(\boldsymbol{x}', t) G(|\boldsymbol{x} - \boldsymbol{x}'|) d\boldsymbol{x}'}{\int_{\Delta} \chi^{k}(\boldsymbol{x}', t) G(|\boldsymbol{x} - \boldsymbol{x}'|) d\boldsymbol{x}'} \tag{48}$$

$$\varphi(\boldsymbol{x}', t) = \widetilde{\varphi(\boldsymbol{x}', t)} + \varphi''(\boldsymbol{x}', t) \tag{49}$$

After filtering, the mass and momentum equations, the unsteady multi-fluid flows can be expressed using Eqs. (50) and (51), respectively.

$$\frac{\partial(\alpha^{k}\rho^{k})}{\partial t} + \nabla \cdot \left(\alpha^{k}\rho^{k}\widetilde{U^{k}}\right) = 0 \tag{50}$$

$$\frac{\partial\left(\alpha^{k}\rho^{k}\widetilde{U^{k}}\right)}{\partial t} + \nabla \cdot \left(\alpha^{k}\rho^{k}\widetilde{U^{k}}\otimes\widetilde{U^{k}}\right) = -\nabla\left(\alpha^{k}\widetilde{p^{k}}\right) + \nabla \cdot \left(\alpha^{k}\widetilde{\tau^{k}}\right) - \nabla \cdot \left(\alpha^{k}\tau^{k''}\right) + \alpha^{k}\rho^{k}g + \widetilde{M^{k}} \tag{51}$$

The filtered-averaged viscous shear stress component can be represented using Eq. (52).

$$\breve{\tau}^k = \mu^k \left[\nabla \breve{U}^k + \left(\nabla \breve{U}^k \right)^T \right] \tag{52}$$

The SGS stress tensor $\tau^{k''}$ is decomposed into both resolved and SGS components as shown in Eq. (53).

$$\tau^{k''} = \rho^k \left(\widetilde{U^k \otimes U^k} - \breve{U}^k \otimes \breve{U}^k \right) \Rightarrow \tau_{ij}^{k''} = \rho^k \left(\widetilde{U^k U^k} - \breve{U}_i^k \breve{U}_j^k \right) \tag{53}$$

The parameter $\tau_{ij}^{k''}$ is an unknown SGS tensor, representing the effects of SGS motion on the resolved fields of the LES simulation, and has to be represented using an SGS model. The prime objective of the SGS models is to accurately capture small dissipative scales by representing kinetic energy losses due to the viscous forces by accounting for their effect in a statistical manner. Numerous SGS models were developed and most of them are based on the Boussinesq hypothesis [56–59]. A brief description of the basic and dynamic SGS models is given in the following section.

2.2.4.1. Basic SGS model

In this model, the unresolved stress tensor ($\tau_{ij}^{k''}$), can be expressed according to the single-phase counterpart described in Eq. (54).

$$\tau_{ij}^{k''} = -2\mu_{SGS}\check{S}_{ij} + \frac{\delta_{ij}\tau_{kk''}}{3} \tag{54}$$

where μ_{SGS} is the SGS eddy viscosity and $\check{S}_{ij}$ is the strain rate of the large-scale resolved field expressed using Eq. (55).

$$\check{S}_{ij} = \frac{1}{2}\left(\frac{\partial \check{U}_i^k}{\partial x_j} + \frac{\partial \check{U}_j^k}{\partial x_i} \right) \tag{55}$$

The basic model of Smagorinsky [59] assumes that the SGS eddy viscosity can be described using a length and velocity scale, as shown in Eq. (56).

$$\mu_{SGS} = \rho C_1 \Delta^2 |\check{S}|; \quad \textit{Where } |S| = \left(2\check{S}_{ij}\check{S}_{ij}\right)^{0.5} \tag{56}$$

where C_1 is an empirical constant (Smagorinsky constant), which depends on the type of flow. It equals 0.18 for isotropic turbulence and 0.10 for flow near solid walls. For the multi-fluid approach, the value of the Smagorinsky constant for the continuous phase typically equals $(C_1)^{0.5}$. In some cases, a viscosity dampening function is used to accurately capture turbulent viscosity near solid surfaces. Details of this model are available elsewhere [54, 60–62].

2.2.4.2. Dynamic SGS model

The dynamic SGS model is based on the self-adaptive procedure developed by Germano et al. [63], which applies two different filters, a grid filter as described above $G(|\mathbf{x}-\mathbf{x}'|)$ and a test filter $\breve{G}(|\mathbf{x}-\mathbf{x}'|)$, where the latter has a larger width than the former. The component-weighted volume-averaging for the multi-fluid approach using the test filter can be defined using Eq. (57) for the continuous phase. When this test filter is applied to the instantaneous momentum equation, it results in Eq. (58).

$$\overline{\varphi(x',t)} = \frac{\overline{\overline{\chi^k}\widetilde{\varphi(x',t)}}}{\overline{\overline{\chi^k}}} \tag{57}$$

$$\frac{\partial\left(\overline{\alpha^k}\rho^k\breve{\widetilde{U^k}}\right)}{\partial t} + \nabla\cdot\left(\overline{\alpha^k}\rho^k\breve{\widetilde{U^k}}\otimes\breve{\widetilde{U^k}}\right) = -\nabla\left(\overline{\alpha^k}\breve{p^k}\right) + \nabla\cdot\left(\overline{\alpha^k}\breve{\tau^k}\right) - \nabla\cdot\left(\overline{\alpha^k}L^{k''}\right) + \overline{\alpha^k}\rho^k g + \overline{\widetilde{M^k}} \tag{58}$$

where L is difference between the grid and test level stress tensors represented by Eq. (59):

$$L^{k''} = T^{k''} - \breve{\tau^k} \Rightarrow L_{ij}^{k''} = T_{ij}^{k''} - \widehat{\tau_{ij}^{k''}} \tag{59}$$

The test filter stress ($T^{k''}$) is expressed using Eq. (60)

$$T^{k''} = \rho^k\left(\overline{\breve{U^k}\otimes U^k} - \breve{U^k}\otimes\breve{U^k}\right) \Rightarrow T_{ij}^{k''} = \rho^k\left(\overline{\breve{U_i^k}U_j^k} - \breve{U_i^k}\,\breve{U_j^k}\right) \tag{60}$$

Consequently, the filtered and sub-test stresses are represented using Eqs. (61) and (62).

$$\tau_{ij}^{k''} = \frac{\delta_{ij}\tau_{kk''}}{3} - 2C_d\Delta^2\left|\tilde{S^c}\right|\tilde{S_{ij}^c} \tag{61}$$

$$\tau_{ij}^{k''} = \frac{\delta_{ij}T_{kk''}}{3} - 2C_d\widehat{\Delta}^2\left|\widehat{\tilde{S^c}}\right|\widehat{\tilde{S_{ij}^c}} \tag{62}$$

The value of C_d is a case-specific constant. The value and derivation of C_d can be found elsewhere [64–66].

3. Advantages, limitations and prospects of DNS and LES

When modeling turbulence, it is important to realize that there is a wide spectrum of turbulent scales coexisting within the flow, which must be resolved. The larger eddies contain most of the turbulent kinetic energy, whereas the smaller eddies dissipate the energy that they receive from the larger eddies. Thus, the primary challenge in representing turbulence lies in accurately computing (as well as measuring) the contributions of all the scales within the spectrum.

Typically, the size of the computational domain must be at least an order of magnitude larger than the scales characterizing the turbulence energy, while the computational mesh must be fine enough to resolve the smallest dynamically significant length-scale (the Kolmogorov micro-scale) for accurate simulation.

The advances of CFD modeling of turbulent multiphase flows have been primarily focused on the development and application of models to accurately capture flow behavior at higher spatial and temporal resolutions. However, in modeling of SBCRs for design and optimization purposes, the grid size should be significantly larger than the gas bubbles and solid particles. Therefore, there is a significant dependence on having accurate interphase closure relationships to ensure model validity, especially in the churn-turbulent flow regime. Nonetheless, higher resolution models, such as DNS and LES, which resolve the turbulences at significantly smaller length scales without being dependent on interphase closure relationships, present a promising prospect for future modeling of SBCRs.

In the DNS approach, the Navier-Stokes equations are numerically solved without any turbulence models or closure relationships. The conservation equations are derived by considering the microscopic instantaneous equations governing each phase. The smallest possible lengths and timescales, which are compatible with continuum formulation are considered and all the scales of motion in addition to interfacial configurations are captured or fully resolved. This approach requires model resolution on the scale of the largest as well as the smallest turbulent eddies. Also, the exact location of the interfaces separating the different phases that co-exist within the flow are determined using suitable micro-level evolutionary tracking methods (Front tracking, level-set, VOF). Therefore, the DNS approach is computationally very expensive and at present it can be applied only to low Reynolds number flows over simple geometries. In general, it has been recognized that the computational effort required for DNS simulations are proportional to Re_L^3.

In the LES approach, the structure of the turbulent flow is viewed as the distinct transport of large- and small-scale motions. The large-scale motion is directly simulated on the scale of the underlying computational mesh; whereas the small-scale motion is represented using sub-grid scale (SGS) models. Since the large-scale motion is generally much more energetic and by far the most effective transporter of the conserved properties than the small-scale one, such an approach, which treats the large eddies as approximates of the small eddies makes perfect sense to be adopted for large-scale design and optimization scenarios. However, in comparison with the multi-fluid Eulerian approach, which has been developed to simulate large-scale macroscopic flow behavior with modeled microscopic behavior, the required computational resources for LES is comparatively very large, which currently prevents their wide scale application beyond laminar multi-phase systems. Additional details on the various numerical methods and approaches are discussed elsewhere [54, 67].

4. CFD modeling of a pilot-scale SBCR using the multi-fluid Eulerian approach

The multi-fluid Eulerian CFD formulation described above was used to model the local hydrodynamics (local phase holdups, phase velocity profiles and liquid turbulence intensity) in a pilot-scale SBCR (0.3-m ID, 3-m height), operating under the typical Fisher-Tropsch (F-T) process conditions. The multi-fluid Eulerian approach was implemented into ANSYS Fluent v 14.5, where the governing equations are solved using an Eulerian-multiphase segregated solver algorithm. The 3-D time-dependent simulations are conducted, both due to the nature of the geometry investigated and the bubble plume oscillations, which are characteristic of the churn-turbulent flow regime [68]. The RNG k-ε turbulence model was used, as it provides the best validation results as previously demonstrated elsewhere [69]. At the bottom of the reactor, Dirichlet velocity and volume fraction conditions for all phases were set, and a second-order spatially accurate QUICK scheme [70, 71] was employed to discretize all equations.

$$u_k(z = 0, t) = \beta, \tag{63}$$

where β is a constant.

Moreover, a multiphase variant of the SIMPLE scheme was used for pressure-velocity coupling [72]. The first order implicit time stepping was then used to advance the solution in time. Before each simulation, mesh and time independence studies were carried out in order to optimize the solution and computational time. In all simulations, quasi-steady state numerical solutions were obtained. This means that at the end of the calculations, all variables exhibit small oscillations around steady-state values, indicating that the statistical averages were reached for all variables.

Although the inlet volumetric flow rates are known, the velocity distribution is not specified. The most widely used practice is to use the knowledge of fully developed flow in pipes to specify the inlet velocity distribution. Therefore, for laminar flow through a cylindrical inlet pipe, one can specify a parabolic velocity profile as an inlet boundary condition; however, if the feed pipes have complex shapes, which is typical in SBCRs, it is necessary to develop an additional model, which include appropriate boundary conditions.

The outlet boundary conditions were implemented taking into account the following [73, 74]: (1) F-T SBCRs are typically operated in a semi-batch mode where the liquid level may reach the top of the reactor [75] and (2) Due to the F-T reaction, the liquid (mainly hydrocarbon products) formed inside the reactor is continuously removed using appropriate filtration devices located inside the reactor. Therefore, the following outlet boundary conditions were executed to account for the two aforementioned considerations:

1. The real computation domain is selected to be taller than the initial height of the reactor, similar to the work by Troshko and Zdravistch [73].
2. The initial liquid height is set by initializing the liquid volume fraction to 1 in the zone up to a known initial liquid height, while the gas volume fraction is set to 1 in the region above that.
3. The ambient media in the computational zone above the reactor is set to be stagnant CO, such that the values for the pressure, backflow gas volume fraction, backflow CO gas species concentration and backflow turbulent parameters, are 1 atmosphere, 1, 1, and 0, respectively [73].

The implementation of these outlet boundary conditions allowed for modeling of the slurry-phase height expansion due to the gas holdup and heterogeneous reactions without being affected by the gas-phase backflow. Moreover, due to the strong non-linear characteristics of the model, relaxation coefficients (Patankar [67]) are introduced in the momentum conservation equations. The convergence criterion adopted from Patankar [67], based on the pressure, is given by:

$$\left| \sum_{j=2}^{N} \sum_{i=2}^{N} P_{ij}^{(n+1)} - \sum_{j=2}^{N} \sum_{i=2}^{N} P_{ij}^{(n)} \right| < 10^{-9} \tag{64}$$

where N is the mesh size

A picture of the SBCR is shown in **Figure 4**, and additional details can be found elsewhere [76]. The gas-phase used was N_2, the liquid-phase was an F-T reactor wax and the solid-phase used was an iron-based catalyst, and details of the physical properties of the system are available elsewhere [76]. The SBCR is provided with a spider-type gas sparger containing six arms, where each arm has 6 orifices of 0.005 m ID on each side and on the bottom, totalling 108 orifices on the gas sparger. It should be emphasized that there are no orifices at the top of the arms so that solid particles could not plug them and the generated gas jets should be able to lift any solid particles which might settle at the bottom flange of the reactor. A picture of the gas sparger described above is given in **Figure 5 (a)**. The gas sparger is screwed onto a 0.0254 m ID

(a) (b)

Figure 4. (a) Photograph of the SBCR used in this study, (b) CFD geometry and mesh of the SBCR.

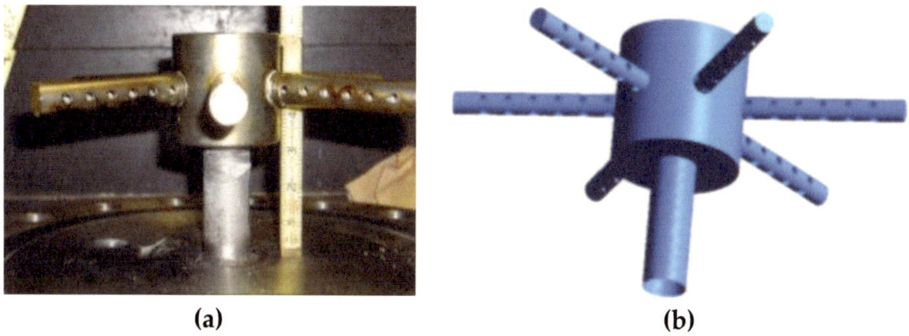

Figure 5. (a) Picture and (b) constructed geometry of the sparger used in this study.

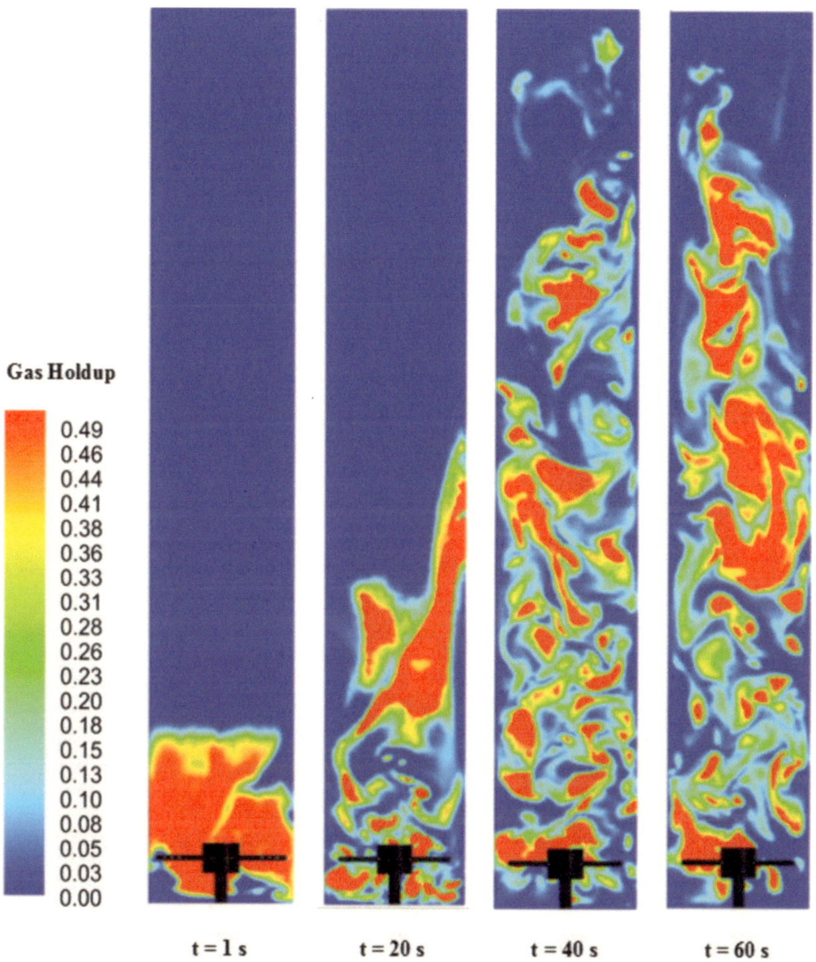

Figure 6. Snapshots of gas holdup contours at different times [2].

pipe to a height of 0.102 m from the bottom flange of the reactor. Also, its maximum height from the bottom of the reactor is about 0.152 m. The constructed geometry of this gas sparger is shown in **Figure 5 (b)**.

4.1. CFD prediction of the local gas holdup in the pilot-scale SBCR

The local gas-holdup is a critical parameter as it governs local pressure variations, liquid recirculation, overall mixing and heat and mass transfer within the SBCR. **Figure 6** shows the CFD model predictions as snapshots of gas holdup contours at different times of 0, 20, 40 and 60 s at an inlet superficial gas velocity = 0.20 m/s, temperature = 443 K and catalyst concentration = 11 vol%. It is clear from the figure that (1) there are significant axial and radial variations of the gas holdup within the reactor, (2) such variations are nonlinear and time-dependent and (3) the maximum gas holdup exhibited are located at the center of the reactor.

4.2. CFD prediction of the local liquid recirculation in the pilot-scale SBCR

Figure 7 shows the CFD model predictions in a form of different snapshots of liquid velocity vectors in the SBCR. As can be seen in these shots smaller and faster liquid recirculation cells are

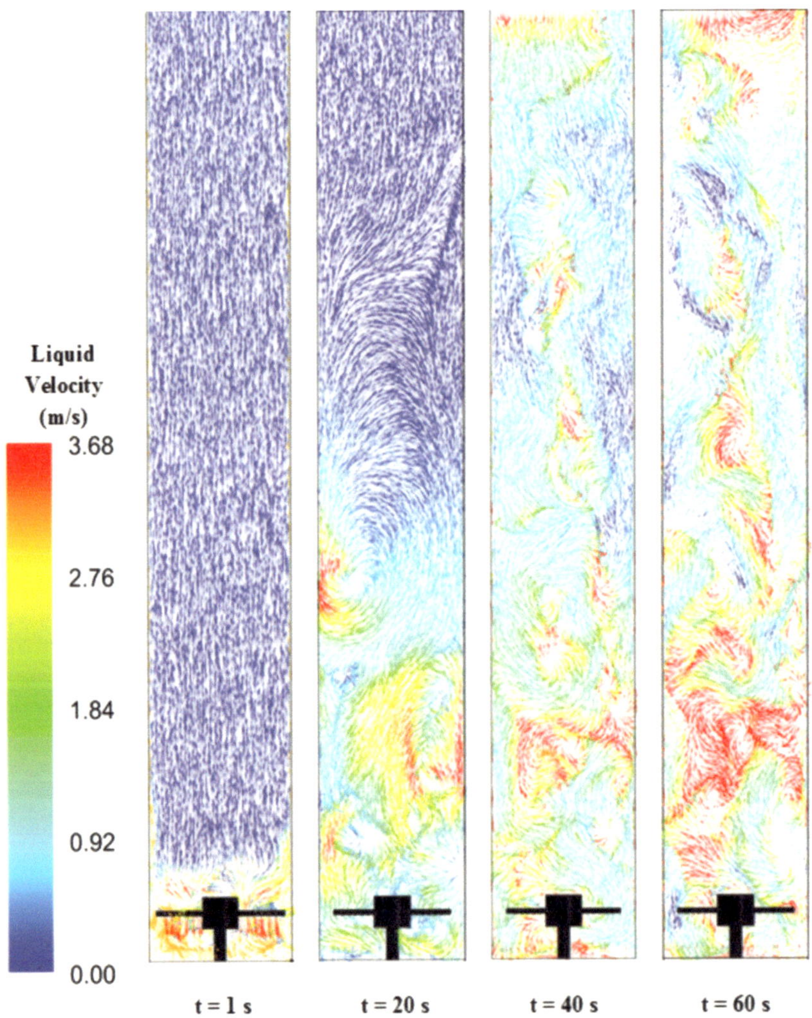

Figure 7. Snapshots of liquid velocity vectors at different times [2].

present in the vicinity of the sparger from the startup until it reaches a steady-state. These smaller and faster liquid recirculations are primarily due to the geometry of the spider-type sparger used in this simulation, where all gas sparging orifices were located on the sides and bottom and none the top of each sparger arm. Moreover, only large and slow liquid recirculation cells appear to develop above the gas sparger region (around 1.2 diameter from the bottom flange). Furthermore, stronger liquid recirculations and backmixing are present near the walls, as the liquid rises upward with the gas bubbles at the center of the reactor and then flows downward near the wall. Thus, the maximum liquid velocity occurs at the center of the reactor.

4.3. CFD prediction of the turbulence intensity in the pilot-scale SBCR

The CFD model was also used to generate different snapshots of the local turbulence intensity contours at different times in the SBCR, as shown in **Figure 8**. The turbulence intensity is defined as the root-mean-square of the velocity fluctuations to the mean flow velocity, Eq. (65). Generally, a turbulence intensity of ≤1% is considered low and that of ≥10% is considered high [77].

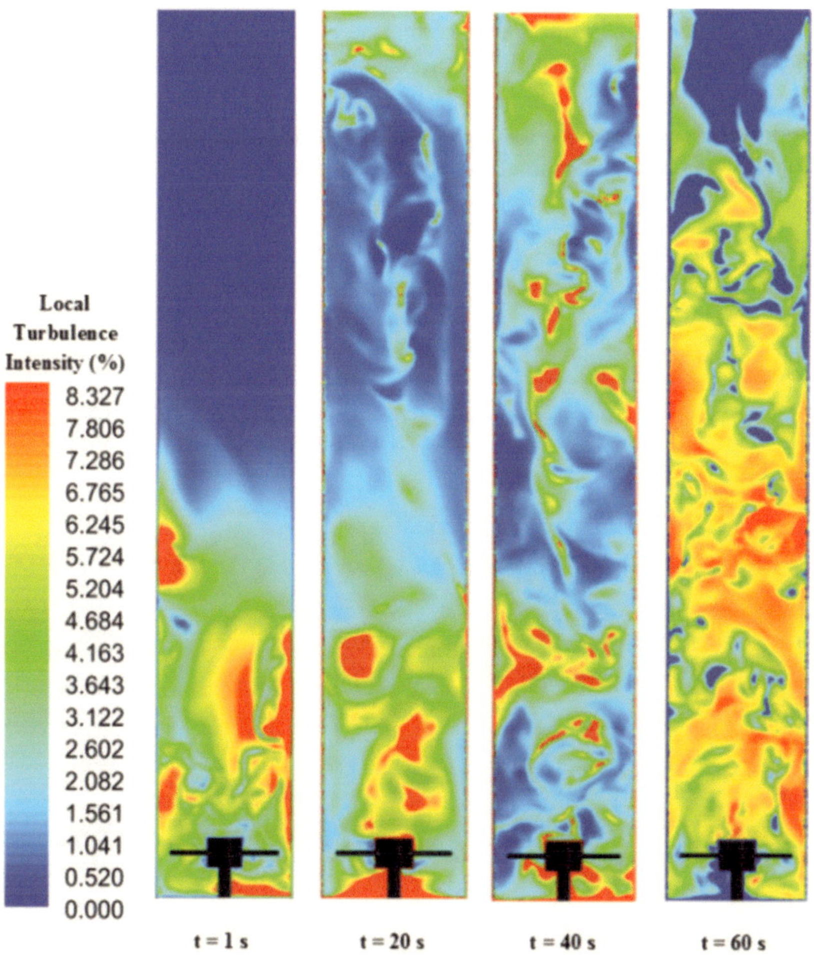

Figure 8. Snapshots of local turbulence intensity contours at different times [2].

As shown in **Figure 8**, higher liquid turbulence intensities are observed in the vicinity of the sparger up to 20 s, after that the turbulence intensity becomes more evenly distributed throughout the reactor, with higher turbulence intensities near the center of the reactor.

$$I = \frac{u'}{U} = \frac{\sqrt{\frac{1}{3}\left(u_x'^2 + u_y'^2 + u_z'^2\right)}}{\sqrt{U_x^2 + U_y^2 + U_z^2}} \tag{65}$$

4.4. Sensitivity of CFD model predictions to its sub-models and parameters

When developing CFD models for the design and optimization purposes, it is critical on one hand to identify the relative importance of each of the incorporated sub-models and parameters, and on the other hand to eliminate any unnecessary terms that needlessly increase the computational time without an acceptable increase in the prediction accuracy. For SBCRs, Basha et al. [2], demonstrated that the interphase drag is the most dominant exchange term, whereas, the other terms could be eliminated without significant effect on model predications, as long as the model was carefully validated. In addition, eliminating the bubble population balance was found to significantly reduce the accuracy of the CFD model predictions and increase errors by up to 9%, despite decreasing computational time by up to 23%. Thus, the degree of complexity employed in CFD modeling is dependent on the required prediction accuracy. Obviously, increased accuracy significantly increases the required computational time.

Nomenclature

a	Interfacial area
C^*	Equilibrium concentration (solubility) in the liquid phase (mol/m^3)
C_D	Drag coefficient
C_L	Concentration in the liquid phase (mol/m^3)
C_V	Volumetric concentration of solid particles in the slurry phase (vol.%)
d_C	Column diameter (m)
d_o	Sparger orifice diameter (m)
d_p	Particle diameter (m)
d_{32}	Sauter mean bubble diameter (m)
$Eö$	Eötvös number
f	Friction factor
F_C	Particle collision force (N)

http://dx.doi.org/10.5772/intechopen.71361

F_D	Drag force (N)
$F_{I,m}$	Suspension inertial force (N)
F_L	Lift force (N)
F_p	Continuous phase pressure gradient (N)
Fr	Froude number
F_{VM}	Virtual mass force (N)
g	Gravitational acceleration, m/s^2
G	Mass flow rate ($kg/m^2 \cdot s$)
Ga	Gallileo number
h	Reactor height (m)
h_{tot}	Mean total enthalpy (kJ/mol)
ΔH	Enthalpy (kJ/mol)
k	Turbulent kinetic energy (J/mol)
$k_L a$	Volumetric liquid side mass transfer coefficient (1/s)
K_L	Thermal conductivity (W/m·K)
l_e	Characteristic length scale of the eddies
MW	Molecular weight (kg/kmol)
PS	Saturation vapor pressure (Pa)
Pe	Peclet number
Pr	Prandtl number
P_V	Liquid-phase vapor pressure (bar)
r	Reaction rate (mol/kg catalyst·s)
R	Reaction term ($mol/m^3 \cdot s$)
Re	Reynolds number
P	Pressure (Pa)
S	Particle surface area per unit volume (m^2/m^3)
Sc	Schmidt number
Sh	Sherwood number
t	Time (s)

T	Temperature (K)
u_b	Gas bubble rise velocity (m/s)
u_G	Superficial gas velocity (m/s)
U	Overall heat transfer coefficient (kJ/m^2·s·°C)
v	Linear flow velocity (m/s)
$\widetilde{v}_{eff,\,rad}$	Radial momentum transfer coefficient (m^2/s)
ν_{sl}	Kinematic slurry viscosity (m^2/s)
y	Mole fraction of gas component

Greek Letters.

α_k	Phase volume fraction
ε	Turbulence dissipation (J/kg·s)
ε_g	Gas holdup
ε_L	Liquid holdup
η	Kinematic viscosity (m^2/s)
κ	Coefficient of bulk viscosity
μ	Viscosity (kg/m·s)
μ_b	Relative apparent bed viscosity
μ_T	Turbulent or eddy viscosity
υ	Local velocity of the dispersed phase
π	3.14
ρ	Density (kg/m^3)
σ	Surface tension (N/m)
τ	Viscous stress tensor (Pa)
τ_{rz}	Reynolds shear stress
$\vec{\phi}$	Body source per unit mass

Subscripts.

g or G	Gas
k	Phase
l	Liquid

http://dx.doi.org/10.5772/intechopen.71361

s	Solid
w	Wall

Author details

Omar M. Basha and Badie I. Morsi*

*Address all correspondence to: morsi@pitt.edu

Department of Chemical and Petroleum Engineering, University of Pittsburgh, Pittsburgh, PA, USA

References

[1] de Klerk A. Fischer-Tropsch Refining. Weinheim: Wiley-VCH Verlag & Co. KGaA; 2012

[2] Basha Omar M, Weng L, Men Z, Morsi Badie I. CFD modeling with experimental validation of the internal hydrodynamics in a pilot-scale slurry bubble column reactor. International Journal of Chemical Reactor Engineering. 2016;**14**:599

[3] Wood DA, Nwaoha C, Towler BF. Gas-to-liquids (GTL): A review of an industry offering several routes for monetizing natural gas. Journal of Natural Gas Science and Engineering. 2012;**9**:196-208

[4] Salmi TO, Mikkola JP, Warna JP. Chemical Reaction Engineering and Reactor Technology. Florida: Taylor & Francis; 2011

[5] Motaghi M, Ulrich B, Subramanian A. Slurry-Phase Hydrocracking - Possible Solution to Refining Margins. KBR;2011

[6] Schluter S, Steiff A, Weinspach PM. Modeling and simulation of bubble column reactors. Chemical Engineering and Processing Process Intensification. 1992;**31**:97-117

[7] L'Homme GA. Chemical Engineering of Gas-liquid-solid Catalyst Reactions: Proceedings of an International Symposium: CEBEDOC; 1978

[8] Smith JM. Chemical Engineering Kinetics. New York: McGraw-Hill; 1981

[9] Weissermel K, Arpe HJ. Industrial Organic Chemistry. Weinheim: Wiley-VCH Verlag GmbH & Co. KGaA; 2008

[10] Basha OM, Sehabiague L, Abdel-Wahab A, Morsi BI. Fischer-Tropsch synthesis in slurry bubble column reactors: Experimental investigations and modeling–A review. International Journal of Chemical Reactor Engineering. 2015;**13**:201-288

[11] Rados N, Al-Dahhan MH, Dudukovic MP. Modeling of the Fischer-Tropsch synthesis in slurry bubble column reactors. Catalysis Today. 2003;**79-80**:211-218

[12] Maretto C, Krishna R. Modelling of a bubble column slurry reactor for Fischer–Tropsch synthesis. Catalysis Today. 1999;**52**:279-289

[13] Sehabiague L, Morsi BI. Modeling and simulation of a Fischer–Tropsch slurry bubble column reactor using different kinetic rate expressions for iron and cobalt catalysts. International Journal of Chemical Reactor Engineering. 2013;**11**:309-330

[14] Gidaspow D. Multiphase Flow and Fluidization: Continuum and Kinetic Theory Descriptions. San Diego: Academic Press; 1994

[15] Grevskott S, Sannæs BH, Duduković MP, Hjarbo KW, Svendsen HF. Liquid circulation, bubble size distributions, and solids movement in two- and three-phase bubble columns. Chemical Engineering Science. 1996;**51**:1703-1713

[16] Mitra-Majumdar D, Farouk B, Shah YT. Hydrodynamic modeling of three-phase flows through a vertical column. Chemical Engineering Science. 1997;**52**:4485-4497

[17] Bakshi A, Altantzis C, Bates RB, Ghoniem AF. Study of the effect of reactor scale on fluidization hydrodynamics using fine-grid CFD simulations based on the two-fluid model. Powder Technology. 2016;**299**:185-198

[18] Hamidipour M, Chen J, Larachi F. CFD study on hydrodynamics in three-phase fluidized beds—Application of turbulence models and experimental validation. Chemical Engineering Science. 2012;**78**:167-180

[19] Panneerselvam R, Savithri S, Surender GD. CFD simulation of hydrodynamics of gas-liquid-solid fluidised bed reactor. Chemical Engineering Science. 2009;**64**:1119-1135

[20] Li Y, Zhang J, Fan L-S. Numerical simulation of gas-liquid-solid fluidization systems using a combined CFD-VOF-DPM method: Bubble wake behavior. Chemical Engineering Science. 1999;**54**:5101-5107

[21] Ranade VV. Computational Flow Modeling for Chemical Reactor Engineering. San Diego: Academic Press; 2002

[22] Jakobsen HA. Chemical Reactor Modeling: Multiphase Reactive Flows. Berlin, Heidelberg: Springer; 2008

[23] Ansys AF. 14.0 Theory Guide. Canonsburg, PA: ANSYS Inc.; 2011. pp. 218-221

[24] Basha OM, Weng L, Men Z, Morsi BI. CFD modeling with experimental validation of the internal hydrodynamics in a pilot-scale slurry bubble column reactor. International Journal of Chemical Reactor Engineering, AOP. 2016;**14**:599 p

[25] Zhang X, Ahmadi G. Eulerian-Lagrangian simulations of liquid-gas-solid flows in three-phase slurry reactors. Chemical Engineering Science. 2005;**60**:5089-5104

[26] Clift R, Grace JR, Weber ME. Bubbles, Drops, and Particles. New York: Academic Press; 1978

[27] Drew D, Cheng L, Lahey Jr RT. The analysis of virtual mass effects in two-phase flow. International Journal of Multiphase Flow. 1979;**5**:233-242

[28] Auton TR, Hunt JCR, Prud'homme M. Force exerted on a body in inviscid unsteady non-uniform rotational flow. Journal of Fluid Mechanics. 1988;**197**:241-257

[29] Antal SP, Lahey Jr RT, Flaherty JE. Analysis of phase distribution in fully developed laminar bubbly two-phase flow. International Journal of Multiphase Flow. 1991;**17**:635-652

[30] Burns AD, Frank T, Hamill I, and Shi JM. The favre averaged drag model for turbulent dispersion in Eulerian multi-phase flows. In: 5th International Conference on Multiphase Flow, ICMF; 2004

[31] Ishii M, Zuber N. Drag coefficient and relative velocity in bubbly, droplet or particulate flows. AICHE Journal. 1979;**25**:843-855

[32] Schiller L, Naumann Z. A drag coefficient correlation. Zeitschrift des Vereins Deutscher Ingenieure. 1935;**77**:318-320

[33] Wen CY, Yu YH. Mechanics of fluidization. Chemical Engineering Progress Symposium Series. 1966;**62**:100-111

[34] Tomiyama A, Tamai H, Zun I, Hosokawa S. Transverse migration of single bubbles in simple shear flows. Chemical Engineering Science. 2002;**57**:1849-1858

[35] Liao Y, Lucas D. A literature review of theoretical models for drop and bubble breakup in turbulent dispersions. Chemical Engineering Science. 2009;**64**:3389-3406

[36] Elghobashi SE, Abou-Arab TW. A two-equation turbulence model for two-phase flows. Physics of Fluids (1958-1988). 1983;**26**:931-938

[37] Oey RS, Mudde RF, van den Akker HEA. Sensitivity study on interfacial closure laws in two-fluid bubbly flow simulations. AICHE Journal. 2003;**49**:1621-1636

[38] De S, Ghosh S, Parichha R, De P. Gas hold-up in two-phase system with internals. Indian Chemical Engineer. 1999;**41**:112-116

[39] Lahey RT Jr, Drew DA. The three-dimensional time and volume averaged conservation equations of two-phase flow. In: Lewins J, Becker M, editors, Advances in Nuclear Science and Technology. Boston, MA: Springer US; 1988;**20**:1-69

[40] Issa R, Oliveira P. Modelling of turbulent dispersion in two phase flow jets. Engineering Turbulence Modeling and Experiments. 1993;**2**:947-957

[41] Wells MR, Stock DE. The effects of crossing trajectories on the dispersion of particles in a turbulent flow. Journal of Fluid Mechanics. 1983;**136**:31-62

[42] Kumar S, Ramkrishna D. On the solution of population balance equations by discretization—I. A fixed pivot technique. Chemical Engineering Science. 1996;**51**:1311-1332

[43] Luo H, Svendsen HF. Theoretical model for drop and bubble breakup in turbulent dispersions. AICHE Journal. 1996;**42**:1225-1233

[44] Li G, Yang X, Dai G. CFD simulation of effects of the configuration of gas distributors on gas-liquid flow and mixing in a bubble column. Chemical Engineering Science. 2009;**64**:5104-5116

[45] Prince MJ, Blanch HW. Bubble coalescence and break-up in air-sparged bubble columns. AICHE Journal. 1990;**36**:1485-1499

[46] Rotta JC. Turbulente Strömungen: eine Einführung in die Theorie und ihre Anwendung. Vol. 8. Göttingen, Germany: Universitätsverlag Göttingen; 2010

[47] Lun CKK, Savage SB. The effects of an impact velocity dependent coefficient of restitution on stresses developed by sheared granular materials. Acta Mechanica. 1986;**63**:15-44

[48] Ding J, Gidaspow D. A bubbling fluidization model using kinetic theory of granular flow. AICHE Journal. 1990;**36**:523-538

[49] van Sint Annaland M, Deen NG, Kuipers JAM. Numerical simulation of gas-liquid-solid flows using a combined front tracking and discrete particle method. Chemical Engineering Science. 2005;**60**:6188-6198

[50] Unverdi SO, Tryggvason G. A front-tracking method for viscous, incompressible, multi-fluid flows. Journal of Computational Physics. 1992;**100**:25-37

[51] Cartland Glover GM, Generalis SC. Gas-liquid-solid flow modelling in a bubble column. Chemical Engineering and Processing: Process Intensification. 2004;**43**:117-126

[52] Sussman M, Smereka P, Osher S. A level set approach for computing solutions to incompressible two-phase flow. Journal of Computational Physics. 1994;**114**:146-159

[53] Zhiyin Y. Large-eddy simulation: Past, present and the future. Chinese Journal of Aeronautics. 2015;**28**:11-24

[54] Yeoh GH, Tu J. Computational Techniques for Multiphase Flows. Oxford, UK: Elsevier Science; 2010

[55] Lakehal D, Smith BL, Milelli M. Large-eddy simulation of bubbly turbulent shear flows. Journal of Turbulence. 2002;**3**:1-21

[56] Lesieur M, Metais O. New trends in large-eddy simulations of turbulence. Annual Review of Fluid Mechanics. 1996;**28**:45-82

[57] Kajishima T, Nomachi T. One-equation subgrid scale model using dynamic procedure for the energy production. Journal of Applied Mechanics. 2006;**73**:368-373

[58] Veloudis I, Yang Z, McGuirk J. LES of wall-bounded flows using a new subgrid scale model based on energy spectrum dissipation. Journal of Applied Mechanics. 2008;**75**:021005

[59] Smagorinsky J. General circulation experiments with the primitive equations: I. The basic experiment. Monthly Weather Review. 1963;**91**:99-164

[60] Piomelli U. Models for Large Eddy Simulations of Turbulent Channel Flows Including Transpiration; 1989

[61] Fulgosi M, Lakehal D, Banerjee S, De Angelis V. Direct numerical simulation of turbulence in a sheared air-water flow with a deformable interface. Journal of Fluid Mechanics. 2003;**482**:319-345

[62] Van Driest ER. On turbulent flow near a wall. Journal of the Aeronautical Sciences. 1956; **23**:1007-1011

[63] Germano M, Piomelli U, Moin P, Cabot WH. A dynamic subgrid-scale eddy viscosity model. Physics of Fluids A: Fluid Dynamics. 1991;**3**:1760-1765

[64] Lilly DK. A proposed modification of the Germano subgrid-scale closure method. Physics of Fluids A: Fluid Dynamics. 1992;**4**:633-635

[65] Piomelli U, Liu J. Large-eddy simulation of rotating channel flows using a localized dynamic model. Physics of Fluids. 1995;**7**:839-848

[66] Ghosal S, Lund TS, Moin P, Akselvoll K. A dynamic localization model for large-eddy simulation of turbulent flows. Journal of Fluid Mechanics. 1995;**286**:229-255

[67] Patankar S. Numerical Heat Transfer and Fluid Flow. New York: McGraw-Hill Book Company; 1980

[68] Chen P, Sanyal J, Duduković MP. Numerical simulation of bubble columns flows: Effect of different breakup and coalescence closures. Chemical Engineering Science. 2005;**60**:1085-1101

[69] Basha O, Sehabiague L, Shi Z, Jia H, Weng L, Men Z, et al. Computational fluid dynamics modeling of complex spatio temporal phenomena in slurry bubble columns for Fischer tropsch synthesis. In: Presented at the Proceedings of 31st Annual International Pittsburgh Coal Conference, Pittsburgh, PA; 2014

[70] Leonard BP. Order of accuracy of QUICK and related convection-diffusion schemes. Applied Mathematical Modelling. 1995;**19**:640-653

[71] ANSYS I. Ansys CFX-solver theory guide. ANSYS CFX Release. 2010;**11**:69-118

[72] Vasquez SA, Ivanov VA. A phase coupled method for solving multiphase problems in unstructured meshes. In: Presented at the Proceedings of ASME FEDSM'00: ASME 2000 Fluids Engineering Division Summer Meeting, Boston; 2000

[73] Troshko AA, Zdravistch F. CFD modeling of slurry bubble column reactors for fisher-Tropsch synthesis. Chemical Engineering Science. 2009;**64**:892-903

[74] Matos EM, Guirardello R, Mori M, Nunhez JR. Modeling and simulation of a pseudo-three-phase slurry bubble column reactor applied to the process of petroleum hydrodesulfurization. Computers & Chemical Engineering. 2009;**33**:1115-1122

[75] Saxena SC, Chen ZD. Hydrodynamics and heat transfer of baffled and unbaffled slurry bubble column. Reviews in Chemical Engineering. 1994;**10**:195-400

[76] Sehabiague L, Basha OM, Hong Y, Morsi B, Shi Z, Jia H, et al. Assessing the performance of an industrial SBCR for Fischer-Tropsch synthesis: Experimental and modeling. AICHE Journal. 2015;**61**:3838-3857

[77] Millikan CB, Klein AL. The effect of turbulence. Aircraft Engineering and Aerospace Technology. 1933;**5**:169-174

Section 3

CFD in Numerical Modeling Approach of Experimental Cases

Two Different Formulations for Solving the Navier-Stokes Equations with Moderate and High Reynolds Numbers

Blanca Bermúdez, Alejandro Rangel-Huerta,
Wuiyevaldo Fermín Guerrero-Sánchez and
José David Alanís

Additional information is available at the end of the chapter

http://dx.doi.org/10.5772/intechopen.71921

Abstract

In this work, we discuss the numerical solution of the Taylor vortex and the lid-driven cavity problems. Both problems are solved using the Stream function-vorticity formulation of the Navier-Stokes equations in 2D. Results are obtained using a fixed point iterative method and working with matrixes A and B resulting from the discretization of the Laplacian and the advective term, respectively. We solved both problems with Reynolds numbers in the range of $3200 \leq Re \leq 7500$. Results are also obtained using the velocity-vorticity formulation of the Navier-Stokes equations. In this case, we are using only the fixed point iterative method. We present results for the lid-driven cavity problem and for the Stream function-vorticity formulation with Reynolds numbers in the range of $3200 \leq Re \leq 7500$. As the Reynolds number increases, the time and the space step size have to be refined. We show results for $3200 \leq Re \leq 20{,}000$. The numerical scheme with the velocity-vorticity formulation uses a smaller step size for both time and space. Results are not as good as with the Stream function-vorticity formulation, although the way the scheme behaves gives us another point of view on the behavior of fluids under different numerical schemes and different formulation.

Keywords: Navier-Stokes equations, velocity-vorticity formulation, Stream function-vorticity formulation, Reynolds number, fixed point iterative process

1. Introduction

The fixed point iterative method has already been used for solving the Navier-Stokes equations and the Boussinesq system under different formulations, see [1–4].

The idea behind this iterative method was to work with a symmetric and positive definite matrix. The scheme worked very well, as shown in [1–4], but the processing time was, in general, very large especially for high Reynolds numbers. Working with matrixes A and B, we are dealing with a non-symetric matrix, but it can be proved that it is strictly diagonally dominant for Δt sufficiently small. The processing time with the second method was reduced in approximately 30 or 35%.

Additionally, in order to show that the fixed point iterative method works well for moderate and high Reynolds numbers, we report results for the lid-driven cavity problem and Reynolds numbers in the range of $3200 \le Re \le 100{,}000$ using the Stream function-vorticity formulation and also the velocity-vorticity formulation, but in the case of the velocity-vorticity formulation, we just arrive to $Re = 20{,}000$, because of computing time and memory requirements.

Results, in both formulations, are obtained using the fixed point iterative method reported in [5], which is applied to a non-linear elliptic system resulting after time discretization. The method has shown to be robust enough to handle moderate and high Reynolds numbers, which is not an easy task, see [1, 2].

As the Reynolds number increases, the mesh has to be refined and a smaller time step has to be used, in order to capture the fast dynamics of the flow and, numerically, because of stability reasons, as mentioned in [6], although, with the velocity-vorticity formulation [7, 8], a finer mesh has to be used, both in time and in space.

The computing time is, in general, very large with this numerical scheme and for both formulations, so that is why we are looking forward to reduce computing time working with both matrixes A and B resulting from the discretization of the Laplacian and the advective term, respectively, instead of working just with matrix A, which is symmetric and positive definite.

With the Stream function-vorticity formulation, and for moderate and high Reynolds numbers, the second scheme was faster than the fixed point iterative method (see [9, 10]). With respect to the velocity-vorticity formulation, we are just showing results using the fixed point iterative method, and for lower Reynolds numbers, but we are looking forward to modify the scheme also in order to reduce computing time.

2. Mathematical model

Let $\Omega \subset R^N$ $(N = 2, 3)$ be the region of a viscous, incompressible, non-stationary flow and Γ is its boundary

$$\begin{cases} u_t - \dfrac{1}{\mathrm{Re}}\Delta u + \nabla p + (u \cdot \nabla)u = f, & \text{(a)} \\ \nabla \cdot u = 0 & \text{(b)} \end{cases} \tag{1}$$

These are the Navier-Stokes equations in primitive variables. This system must be provided with appropriate initial conditions $\mathbf{u}(x, 0) = \mathbf{u}_0(x)$ in Ω and boundary conditions $\mathbf{u} = \mathbf{g}$ on Γ.

When working in a two-dimensional region Ω, taking the curl in both sides of (Eq. (1a)) and taking into account that

http://dx.doi.org/10.5772/intechopen.71921

$$u_1 = \frac{\partial\psi}{\partial y}, u_2 = -\frac{\partial\psi}{\partial x}, \tag{2}$$

followed by (Eq. (1b)), with ψ the Stream function, u_1 and u_2 the two components of the velocity, we arrive to the Stream function-vorticity formulation of the Navier-Stokes equations.

The following system of equations is then obtained:

$$\begin{cases} \Delta\psi = -\omega & \text{(a)} \\ \omega_t - v\Delta\omega + \boldsymbol{u}\cdot\nabla\omega = f_\omega, & \text{(b)} \end{cases} \tag{3}$$

where ω is the vorticity given by $\omega = \frac{\partial u_2}{\partial x} - \frac{\partial u_1}{\partial y}$, and $v = \frac{1}{Re}$.

This system represents the Navier-Stokes equations in the Stream function-vorticity formulation. The incompressibility condition (Eq. (1b)), because of (Eq. (2)), is automatically satisfied and the pressure does not appear any more.

3. The velocity-vorticity formulation

Taking the curl in

$$\omega = -\nabla \times \boldsymbol{u}, \tag{4}$$

and using the identity $\nabla \times \nabla \times a = -\nabla^2 a + \nabla(\nabla \cdot a)$ and (Eq. (1b)), we obtain the following Poisson type equation for the velocity:

$$\Delta\boldsymbol{u} = -\nabla \times \omega \tag{5}$$

Two Poisson type equations for the velocity are obtained, which together with the equation for the vorticity give us:

$$\begin{cases} \Delta u_1 = -\frac{\partial\omega}{\partial y} & \text{(a)} \\ \Delta u_2 = \frac{\partial\omega}{\partial x} & \text{(b)} \\ \omega_t - v\Delta\omega + \boldsymbol{u}\cdot\nabla\omega = f_\omega & \text{(c)} \end{cases} \tag{6}$$

These are the Navier-Stokes equations in the velocity-vorticity formulation.

4. Numerical method for the Stream function-vorticity formulation

The following second-order approximation for the time derivative is used:

$$\omega_t(x, (n+1)\Delta t) \approx \frac{3\omega^{n+1} - 4\omega^n + \omega^{n-1}}{2\Delta t}, \tag{7}$$

where $n \geq 1, x \in \Omega$ and $\Delta t > 0$ is the time step.

The resulting discretization system reads:

$$\begin{cases} \Delta\psi^{n+1} = -\omega, \quad \psi|\Gamma = \psi_{bc} & \text{(a)} \\ \alpha\omega^{n+1} - v\Delta\omega^{n+1} + \boldsymbol{u}^{n+1}\cdot\nabla\omega^{n+1} = f_{\omega}, \quad \omega|\Gamma = \omega_{bc}, & \text{(b)} \end{cases} \tag{8}$$

where $\alpha = \frac{3}{2\Delta t}$ and $f_{\omega} = \frac{4\omega^n - \omega^{n-1}}{2\Delta t}$.

At each time level, the following non-linear system has to be solved.

$$\begin{cases} \Delta\psi = -\omega, \quad \psi|\Gamma = \psi_{bc} & \text{(a)} \\ \alpha\omega - v\Delta\omega + \boldsymbol{u}\cdot\nabla\omega = f_{\omega}, \quad \omega|\Gamma = \omega_{bc}, & \text{(b)} \end{cases} \tag{9}$$

To obtain $(\psi^1, \ \omega^1)$ in (Eq. (8)), any second-order strategy using a combination of one step can be applied and steady systems of the form (Eq. (9)) are also obtained.

For solving this system of equations, two strategies were used in this work: First, we used the fixed point iterative method described in [5]:

Denoting $R_{\omega}(\omega, \psi)$ by

$$R_{\omega}(\omega, \psi) = \alpha\omega - v\Delta\omega + \boldsymbol{u}\cdot\nabla\omega - f_{\omega} \text{ in } \Omega, \tag{10}$$

our system is equivalent to

$$\begin{cases} \Delta\psi = -\omega, \quad \psi|\Gamma = \psi_{bc} & \text{(a)} \\ R(\omega, \psi) = 0, \quad \omega|\Gamma = \omega_{bc} & \text{(b)} \end{cases} \tag{11}$$

Then, at each time level, the following the fixed point iterative process (see [5]) is used:

Given $\omega^{n,0} = \omega^n$ and $\psi^{n,0} = \psi^n$ solve until convergence in ω and ψ

$$\begin{cases} \Delta\psi^{n,m+1} = -\omega^{n,m} \ \ in \ \Omega, \\ \psi^{n,m+1} = \psi_{bc} \ on \ \Gamma \\ \omega^{n,m+1} = \omega^{n,m} - \rho_{\omega}(\alpha I - v\Delta)^{-1} R_{\omega}\left(\omega^{n,m}, \psi^{n,m+1}\right) \ in \ \Omega, \\ \omega^{n,m+1} = \omega_{bc}^{n,m+1} \ on \ \Gamma, \rho_{\omega} > 0; \end{cases} \tag{12}$$

and then take $\left(\omega^{n+1}, \psi^{n+1}\right) = \left(\omega^{n,m+1}, \psi^{n,m+1}\right)$.

To reduce the computing time, we worked in solving the system by the following method at each time step:

$$\begin{cases} \Delta\psi^{n+1} = -\omega^n, \quad \psi^{n+1}|\Gamma = \psi_{bc} & \text{(a)} \\ \left(\alpha I - \frac{v}{h^2}A\right)\omega^{n+1} + \frac{1}{2h}B\omega^{n+1} = f_{\omega}, \quad \omega^{n+1}|\Gamma = \omega_{bc}, & \text{(b)} \end{cases} \tag{13}$$

where A and B are the matrixes resulting from the discretization of the Laplacian and the advective term respectively, and (Eq. (13b)) is solved using Gauss-Seidel method.

5. Numerical method for the velocity-vorticity formulation

The second-order approximation (Eq. (7)) for the time derivative is used and the following non-linear system is obtained in Ω

$$\begin{cases} \Delta u_1 = -\dfrac{\partial \omega}{\partial y} \\ \Delta u_2 = \dfrac{\partial \omega}{\partial x}, \quad \boldsymbol{u}|\Gamma = \boldsymbol{u}_{bc} \\ R_\omega(\omega, \boldsymbol{u}) = 0, \quad \omega|\Gamma = \omega_{bc}, \end{cases} \tag{14}$$

where

$$R_\omega(\omega, \boldsymbol{u}) \equiv \alpha\omega - v\Delta\omega + \boldsymbol{u}\cdot\nabla\omega - f_\omega. \tag{15}$$

Using again the fixed point iterative method previously described, we have:

Given $\omega^{n,0} = \omega^n, u_1^{n,0} = u_1^n, u_2^{n,0} = u_2^n$ solve until convergence in ω, u_1 and u_2

$$\begin{cases} \Delta u_1^{n,m+1} = -\dfrac{\partial \omega^{n,m}}{\partial y} \\ \Delta u_2^{n,m+1} = \dfrac{\partial \omega^{n,m}}{\partial x}, \quad \boldsymbol{u}^{n,m+1}|\Gamma = \boldsymbol{u}_{b,c}^{n,m+1} \\ (\alpha I - v\Delta)\omega^{n,m+1} = (\alpha I - v\Delta)\omega^m - \rho_\omega > 0, \quad \omega^{n,m+1}|\Gamma = \omega_{bc}^{n,m} \end{cases} \tag{16}$$

and then take $\left(\omega^{n+1}, u_1^{n+1}, u_2^{n+1}\right) = \left(\omega^{n,m+1}, u_1^{n,m+1}, u_2^{n,m+1}\right)$.

6. Numerical experiments

With respect to the lid-driven cavity problem and using the Stream function-vorticity formulation $\Omega = [0,1] \times [0,1]$, the top wall is moving with a velocity given by (1, 0) and for the other walls, the velocity is given by (0, 0). Ψ is over-determined at the boundary ($\frac{\partial \psi}{\partial n}|\Gamma$ is also known) and there is no boundary condition for ω. In our case, we have followed the alternative proposed by Goyon [11]. $\Psi = 0$ is chosen over Γ. A translation of the boundary condition in terms of the velocity (primitive variable) has to be used. By Taylor series expansion of (Eq. (3a)), we obtained:

$$\begin{cases} \omega(0,y,t) = -\frac{1}{2h_x^2}\left[8\psi(h_x,y,t) - \psi(2h_x,y,t)\right] \\ \omega(a,y,t) = -\frac{1}{2h_x^2}\left[8\psi(a-h_x,y,t) - \psi(a-2h_x,y,t)\right] \\ \omega(x,0,t) = -\frac{1}{2h_y^2}\left[8\psi(x,h_y,t) - \psi(x,2h_y,t)\right] \\ \omega(x,b,t) = -\frac{1}{2h_y^2}\left[8\psi(x,b-h_y,t) - \psi(x,b-2h_x,t)\right] \end{cases} \quad (17)$$

where h_x, h_y denote the spatial step size in the directions of x and y, respectively.

In **Figures 1** and **2**, we show results for the lid-driven cavity problem with $Re = 5000$ and $Re = 7500$, with $h_x = h_y = 1/64$.

For the Taylor vortex problem, results are shown in **Figures 3** and **4** for $Re = 5000$ and $Re = 7500$, with $h_x = h_y = 2\pi/64$ and $t = 10$.

The exact Stream function and the vorticity are also shown in **Figure 5**, for $Re = 5000$. For this problem, $\Omega = [0, 2\pi] \times [0, 2\pi]$ the exact solution is known and is given by:

$$\begin{aligned} u_1(\mathrm{x},\mathrm{y},\mathrm{t}) &= -\cos(x)\sin(y)e^{\frac{2t}{Re}} \\ u_2(\mathrm{x},\mathrm{y},\mathrm{t}) &= \sin(x)\cos(y)e^{\frac{2\pi}{Re}} \end{aligned} \quad (18)$$

In the primitive variables formulation, we have as initial conditions:

$$\begin{aligned} u_1(x,y,t) &= -\cos(x)\sin(y) \\ u_2(x,y,t) &= \sin(x)\cos(y) \end{aligned} \quad (19)$$

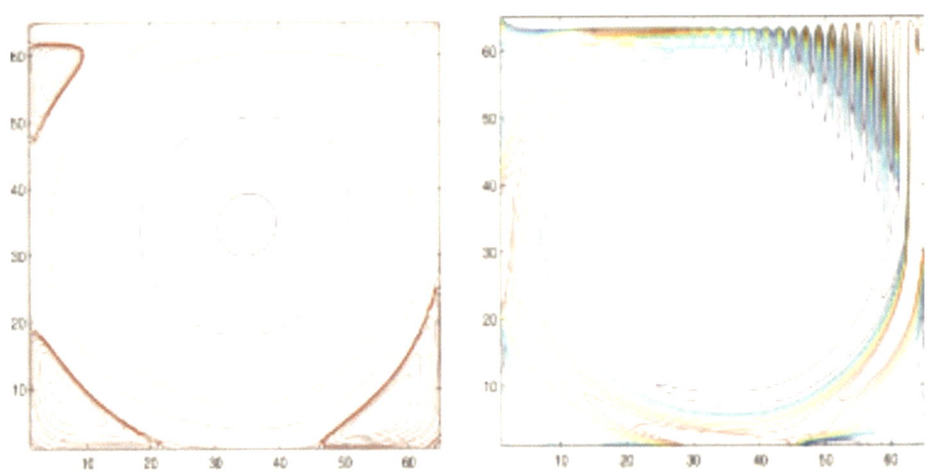

Figure 1. Streamlines (left) and isovorticity contours (right) for $Re = 5000$, $h_x = h_y = 1/64$.

http://dx.doi.org/10.5772/intechopen.71921

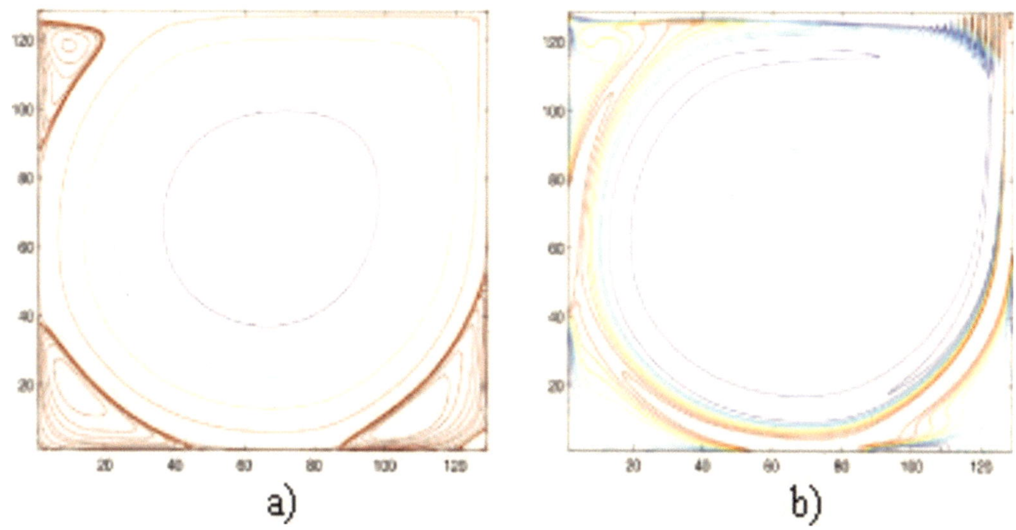

Figure 2. Streamlines (left) and isovorticity contours (right) for $Re = 7500$, $h_x = h_y = 1/64$.

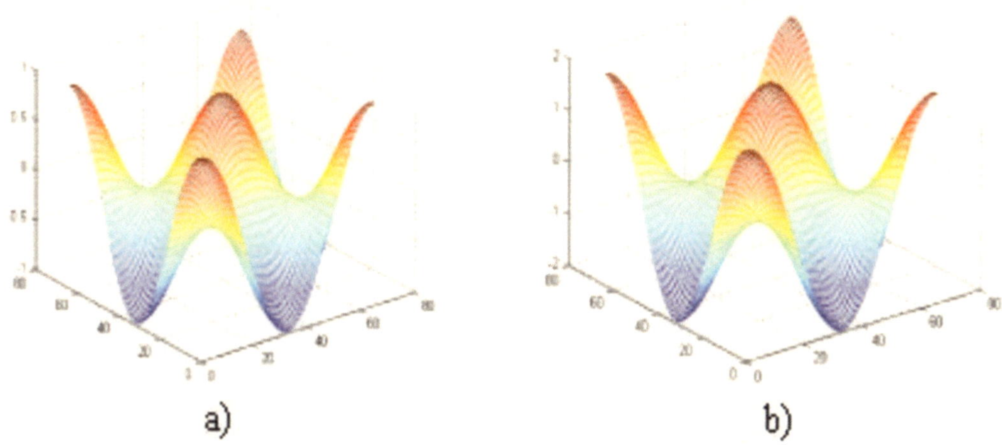

Figure 3. Stream function and vorticity for $Re = 5000$ $h_x = h_y = 2\pi/64$ and $t = 10$.

For the Stream function, the boundary conditions are:

$$\begin{aligned} \psi(x,0,t) = \psi(x,\pi,t) = \cos(x)e^{\frac{2t}{Re}} \\ \psi(2\pi,y,t) = \cos(y)e^{\frac{2t}{Re}} \end{aligned} \tag{20}$$

For the vorticity, the boundary conditions are:

$$\begin{aligned} \omega(x,0,t) = \omega(x,2\pi,t) = 2\cos(x)e^{\frac{2t}{Re}} \\ \omega(0,y,t) = \omega(2\pi,y,t) = 2\cos(y)e^{\frac{2t}{Re}} \end{aligned} \tag{21}$$

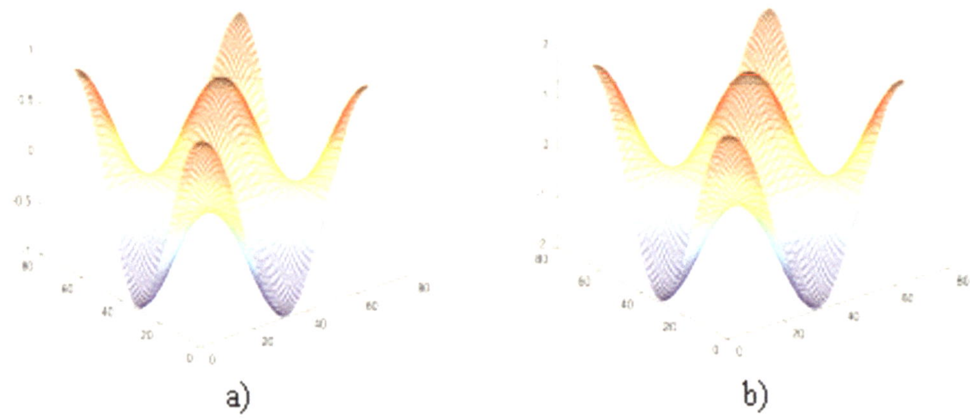

Figure 4. Exact stream function and vorticity for $Re = 5000$ $h_x = h_y = 2\pi/64$ y $t = 10$.

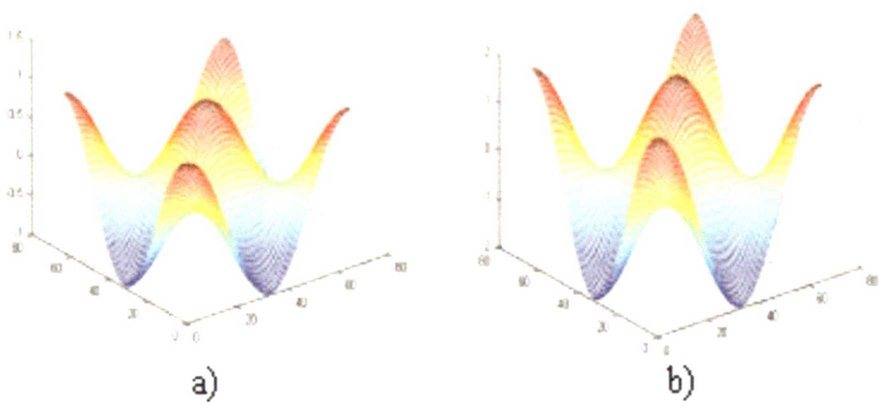

Figure 5. Stream function and vorticity for $Re = 7500$ $h_x = h_y = 2\pi/64$ y $t = 10$.

In **Tables 1** and **2**, we show computing times for the above-mentioned problems with both the methods; the Fixed Point Iterative Method and working with matrixes A and B.

In **Figure 6**, we show the streamlines and isovorticity contours for $Re = 25,000$, with $h = h_y = 1/728$. In **Figure 7**, we show results for $Re = 50,000$, with $h = h_x = h_y = 1/1024$. For these values of the Reynolds number, since there is no steady state, we show results for $T_{final} = 5$.

Re	Fixed point iterative method (s)	Working with A and B (s)
5000	153	120
7500	801	610.25

Table 1. Time in seconds, for both Reynolds numbers and the two methods described for the lid-driven cavity problem.

Re	Fixed point iterative method (s)	Working with A and B (s)
5000	15.5	12.75
7500	15.5	12.75

Table 2. Time in seconds, for both Reynolds numbers and the two methods for the Taylor vortex problem.

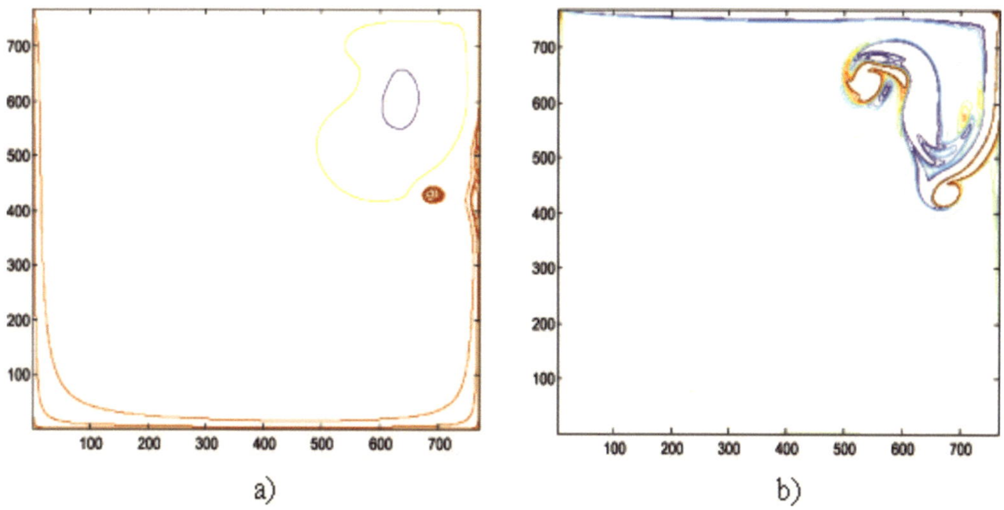

Figure 6. Streamlines (left) and isovorticity contours (right) for $Re = 25{,}000$, $h = h_x = h_y = 1/728$ y $dt = 0.00025$, $T_{final} = 5$.

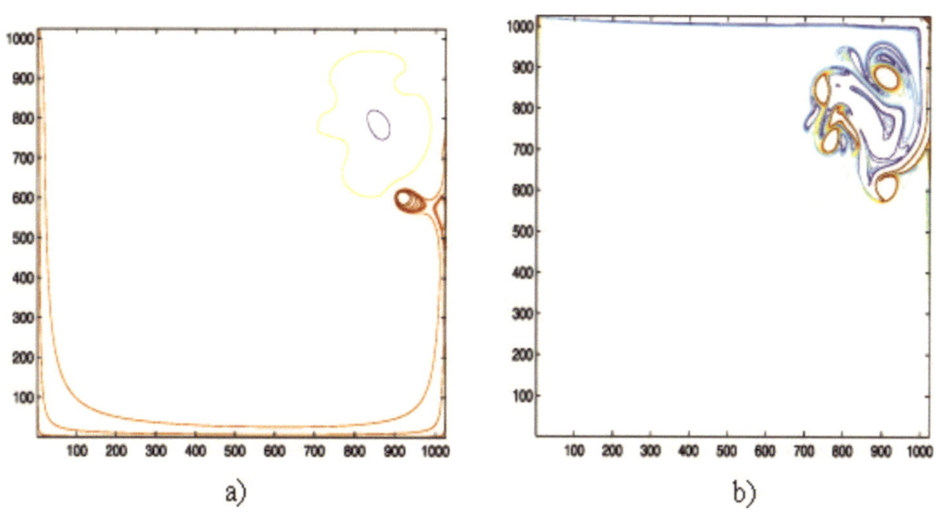

Figure 7. Streamlines (left) and isovorticity contours (right) for $Re = 50{,}000$, $h = h_x = h_y = 1/1024$ y $dt = 0.00025$, $T_{final} = 5$.

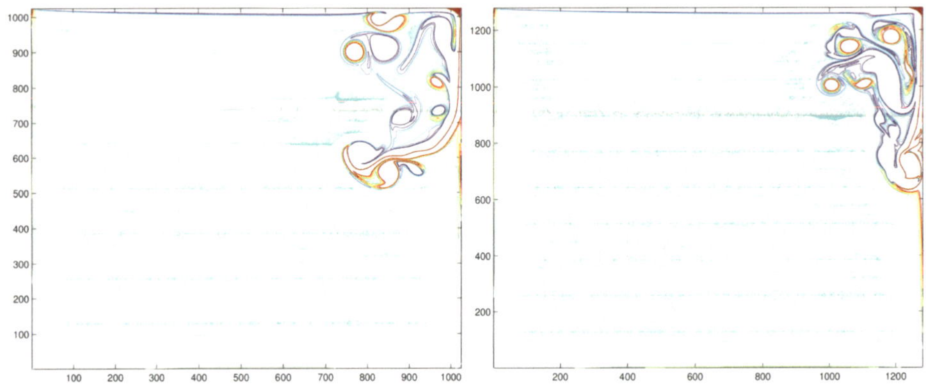

Figure 8. Isovorticity contours (left) for $Re = 75{,}000$, $h = h_x = h_y = 1/1024$ y $dt = 0.00025$, $T_{final} = 5$, isovorticity contours (right) for $Re = 100{,}000$, $h = h_x = h_y = 1/1280$ y $dt = 0.00025$, $T_{final} = 5$.

Then, in **Figure 8**, we show just the isovorticity contours for $Re = 75,000,$ with $h = h_x = h_y = 1/1024$ and for $Re = 100,000,$ with $h = h_x = h_y = \frac{1}{1280}$ and $T_{final} = 5$.

In the case of the velocity-vorticity formulation and the lid-driven cavity problem, the boundary condition for u is given by **u** = (1, 0) in the moving boundary y = b and **u** = (0, 0) anywhere else at the boundary.

Not all the results were obtained using the second-order discretization. In some cases, a fourth-order discretization has to be used, using the fourth-order option of Fishpack [12] (used in this work for solving the elliptic problems appearing).

In **Figure 9**, we show the streamlines and the isovorticity contours for $Re = 3200,\ h = h_x = h_y = 1/512,\ T_{final} = 50$.

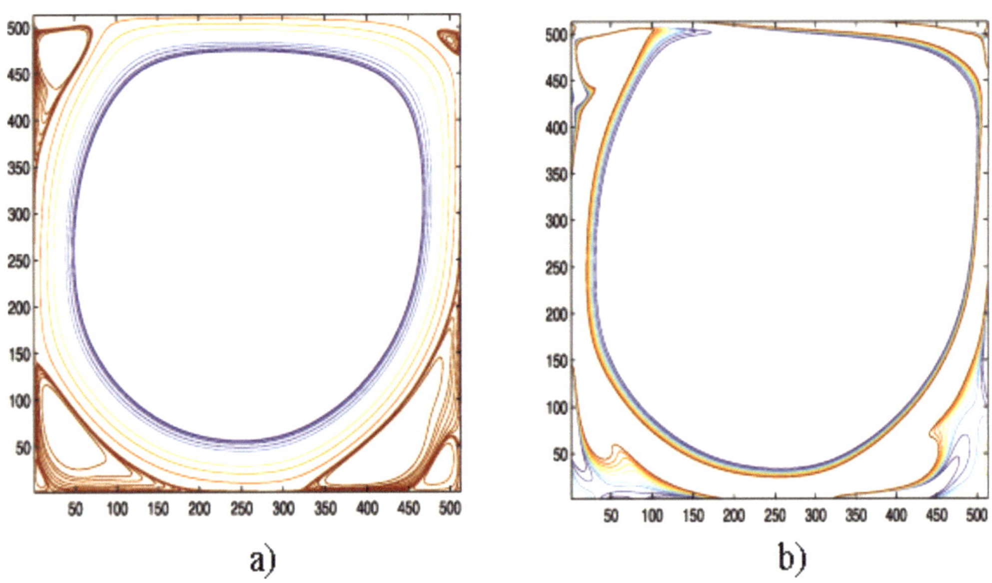

Figure 9. Streamlines (left) and isovorticity contours (right) for $Re = 3200$, $h = h_x = h_y = 1/512$ y $dt = 0.0001$, $T_{final} = 50$.

http://dx.doi.org/10.5772/intechopen.71921

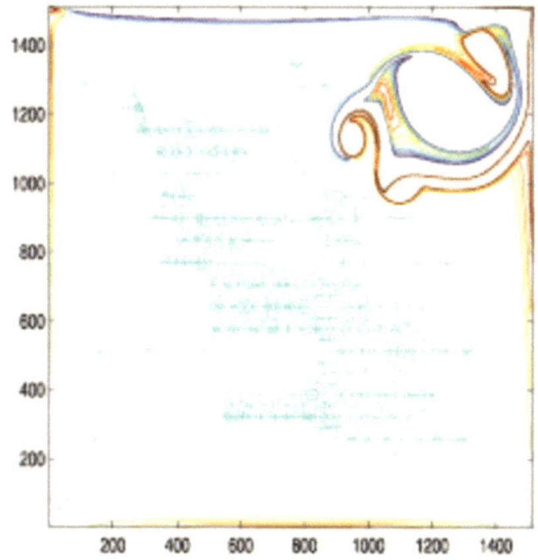

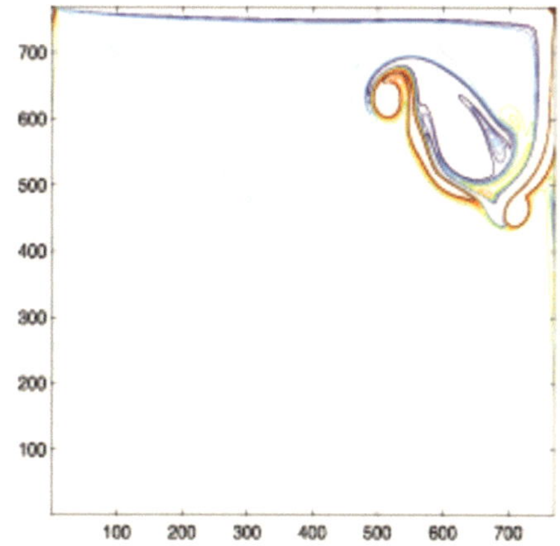

Figure 10. Isocontours for the vorticity for Re = 20,000, (a) velocity-vorticity formulation with $h = h_x = hy = 1/1512$, $dt = 0.0001$, $T_{final} = 5$, (b) Stream function-vorticity formulation with $h = h_x = hy = 1/768$, $dt = 0.0001$, $T_{final} = 5$.

In **Figure 10**, we show the isovorticity contours for $Re = 20,000$ with (a) $h = h_x = h_y = 1/1512$, $T_{final} = 5$, obtained using the velocity-vorticity formulation and (b) with the Stream function-vorticity formulation with $h = h_x = h_y = 1/768$, $T_{final} = 5$.

As can be noticed with the Stream function-vorticity formulation, we are using a value of h half of the size of the one used with the velocity-vorticity formulation. We assume the results obtained with the first-mentioned formulation are more reliable. Computing time for the velocity-vorticity formulation was much larger. We think there are still some numerical problems with this formulation and for very high Reynolds numbers.

7. Conclusions

For the lid-driven cavity problem results agree very well with those reported in the literature [1–4, 13, 14], and by working with matrixes A and B it was possible to reduce computing time between a 30 and 35%.

As can be seen in **Figures 1** and **2**, numerical oscillations occurred, given the high Reynolds numbers used in such a way that it is necessary to use smaller values of h [6], numerically because of stability of the method and physically in order to capture the fast dynamics of the flow.

For high Reynolds numbers and small values of h the computational work takes a lot of time, so reducing computing time becomes a very important fact. For the Taylor Vortex Problem [8, 15], processing time was also reduced between 30 and 35%.

With the velocity-vorticity formulation, as already mentioned, we only show results using the Fixed Point Iterative Method, and we are looking forward working with both matrixes A and B, in order to reduce computing time also with this formulation. This is the reason why we only show results till Re = 20,000 and not for higher Reynolds numbers.

In conclusion, the numerical scheme applied with the stream function-vorticity formulation is not as good with the velocity-vorticity formulation, although, the way it behaves with some values of the parameters and the order of discretization, gives us another point of view about the behavior of the fluids under different numerical methods and different formulations.

We must also say that our code has not been parallelized since it is difficult to do this. It must be taken into account that the equations, in both formulations, are coupled. We are looking forward to use a solver for the system of linear equations that can be parallelized. This can be viewed as a future work.

Acknowledgements

The authors would like to acknowledge the support received by the National Laboratory of Supercomputing from of the southeast of Mexico BUAP-INAOE-UDLAP (Laboratorio Nacional de Supercómputo del Sureste de México).

Author details

Blanca Bermúdez[1]*, Alejandro Rangel-Huerta[1], Wuiyevaldo Fermín Guerrero-Sánchez[2] and José David Alanís[3]

*Address all correspondence to: bbj@cs.buap.mx

1 Computer Science Faculty, Autonomous University of Puebla, Ciudad Universitaria, Puebla, Pue., México

2 Physics-Mathematics' Faculty, Autonomous University of Puebla, Ciudad Universitaria, Puebla, Pue., México

3 Division of Information Technologies and Communication, Technological University of Puebla, Puebla, Pue., México

References

[1] Bermúdez B, Nicolás A, Sánchez FJ, Buendía E. Operator splitting and upwinding for the Navier–Stokes equations. Computational Mechanics. 1997;**20**(5):474-477

[2] Nicolás A, Bermúdez B. 2D incompressible viscous flows at moderate and high Reynolds numbers. CMES. 2004;**6**(5):441-451

[3] Nicolás A, Bermúdez B. 2D thermal/isothermal incompressible viscous flows. International Journal for Numerical Methods in Fluids. 2005;**48**:349-366

[4] Bermúdez B, Nicolás A. Isothermal/thermal incompressible viscous fluid flows with the velocity–vorticity formulation. Información Tecnológica. 2010;**21**(3):39-49

[5] Nicolás A. A finite element approach to the Kuramoto Sivashinski equation. In: Advances in Numerical Equations and Optimization. SIAM; 1991

[6] Nicolás Carrizosa A, Bermúdez Juárez B. Onset of two dimensional turbulence with high Reynolds numbers in the Navier-Stokes equations. Computational Methods for Coupled Problems in Science and Engineering IV M. Papadrakakis, E. Oñate and B. Schrefler (Eds.) First edition, June 2011:996-1006

[7] Nicolás A, Bermúdez B. Viscous incompressible flows by the velocity–vorticity Navier–Stokes equation. CMES. 2007;**20**(2):73-83

[8] Bermúdez B, Nicolás A. The Taylor vortex and the driven cavity problems by the velocity–vorticity formulation. In: Proceedings of the 7th International Conference on Heat Transfer, Fluid Mechanics and Thermodynamics; 2010. pp. 629-632

[9] Bermúdez B, Juárez L. Numerical solution of an advection-diffusion equation. Información Tecnológica. 2014;**25**(1):151-160

[10] Bermúdez B, Posadas R. The Taylor vortex and the driven cavity problems in the stream functions-vorticity formulation. In: Proceedings of the 11th World Congress on Computational Mechanics (WCCM XI); 5th European Congress on Computational Mechanics (ECCM V); 6th European Congress on Computational Fluid Dynamics (ECDF VI). A Publication of CIMNE; 2014. pp. 3746-3755

[11] Goyon O. High Reynolds number solutions of Navier–Stokes equations using incremental unknowns. Computer Methods in Applied Mechanics and Engineering. 1996;**130**:319-335

[12] Adams J, Swarztrauber P, Sweet R. FISHPACK: A Package of FORTRAN Subprograms for the Solutions Elliptic PDE's. Boulder, Colorado, USA: The National Center for Atmospheric Research; 1980

[13] Glowinski R. Finite element methods for the numerical simulations of incompressible viscous flow. In: Introduction to the Control of the Navier-Stokes Equations, Handbook of Numerical Analysis, Vol. II, North-Holland, Amsterdam, 1991, 17-351

[14] Ghia U, Guia KN, Shin CT. High-re solutions for incompressible flow using the Navier–Stokes equations and a multigrid method. Journal of Computational Physics. 1982;**48**:387-411

[15] Anson DK, Mullin T, Cliffe KA. A numerical and experimental investigation of a new solution in the Taylor vortex problem. Journal of Fluid Mechanics. 1988:475-487

Chapter 14

Vibration Characteristics of Fluid-Filled Functionally Graded Cylindrical Material with Ring Supports

Muzamal Hussain, Aamir Shahzad,
Muhammad Nawaz Naeem and Maogang He

Additional information is available at the end of the chapter

http://dx.doi.org/10.5772/intechopen.72172

Abstract

Vibration analysis of fluid-filled functionally graded material (FGM) cylindrical shells (CSs) is investigated with ring supports. The shell problem is formulated by deriving strain and kinetic energies of a vibrating cylindrical shell (CS). The method of variations of Hamiltonian principle is utilized to change the shell integral problem into the differential equation (DE) expression. Three differential equations (DE) in three unknown for displacement functions form a system of partial differential equations (PDEs). The shells are restricted along the thickness direction by ring supports. The polynomial functions describe the influence of the ring supports and have the degree equal to the number of ring supports. Fluid loaded terms (FLT) are affixed with the shell motion equations. The acoustic wave equation states the fluid pressure designated by the Bessel functions of first kind. Axial modal deformation functions are specified by characteristic beam functions which meet end conditions imposed on two ends of the shell. The Galerkin method is employed to get the shell frequency equation. Natural frequency of FGM cylindrical shell is investigated by placing the ring support at different position with fluid for a number of physical parameters. For validity and accuracy, results are obtained and compared with the data in open literature. A good agreement is achieved between two sets of numerical results.

Keywords: functionally graded material (FGM), ring supports, cylindrical material, Galerkin technique (GT), Hamiltonian principle

1. Introduction

All over the word, applications of fluid-filled cylindrical shells have grown in engineering and science. Amendments in shell physical quantities are inducted to enhance strength and stability of cylindrical shells (CSs) [1, 2]. Additional burden due to fluid factor on a physical system may cause damage to it. In the recent times, this feature has appealed to scientists doing research on dynamical properties of materials to explore more about specific strength, stiffness and super corrosion resistance [3–7]. It has been acquired by highly developed complex materials. Study of vibratory response of cylindrical shells (CSs) containing fluids is very beneficial to study dynamic behavior for their applications. This presents a direct contact between a solid composition and a liquid material [8]. In a lot of fields of engineering and technology (mechanical, civil, aeronautics), its useful implications can be seen. Thin-walled cylindrical shells (CSs) have extensive applications in engineering and industry. They are found in chimney design, pipe flow, nuclear reactors and submarines.

For theoretical point of view, study of cylindrical shell vibrations is done to investigate analytical results and their closeness with experimental ones. Here the Galerkin procedure is employed to solve the shell governing equations. For the present cylindrical shells, functionally graded materials are utilized for their structure construction. In the radial thickness direction, material distribution is handled by the exponential volume fraction law. Due to this law, special types of integrals are evolved and are approximated numerically or analytically to evaluate material stiffness modulus. These integrals involve the material parameters of thickness variable by assuming the Poisson ratios of functionally graded constituent materials. For simplifying the integrals, these are presumed to be nearly equal to each other. This assumption simplifies the material stiffness integrals. Shell dynamical equations are framed by applying the Hamilton's variational principle to the Lagrangian functional that is obtained from the shell strain and kinetic energy expressions. These equations govern the shell vibration behavior. For this problem, a suitable and effective method is employed to achieve the shell frequency equation in the eigenvalue problem expression. Normally energy variational approaches are used to solve cylindrical shells problem. They consist of the Raleigh - Ritz method and the Galerkin method. The axial deformation functions are estimated by characteristic beam functions. They are achieved from the solutions of beam differential equation.

Pioneering research work on vibrations of cylindrical shells (CSs) has performed by Arnold and Warburton [8]. The consequence of end conditions on vibration characteristics of a circular cylindrical shell (CS) was considered by Fosberg in 1964 by using shell equation.

Najafizadeh and Isvandzibaei [5] analyzed vibration characteristics of functionally graded cylindrical shells with ring supports. They based their analysis higher order shear deformation theory of shells. It was perceived that the influence of ring supports and fluid terms was very significant on shell frequencies. Vibration characteristics of cylindrical shells containing fluid were studied experimentally and theoretically by Chung et al. [9]. Goncalves and Batista [10] presented a theoretical vibration study of cylindrical shells (CSs) partially filled and submerged in a fluid. Simply supported end conditions were imposed on both edges. Goncalves et al. [11] investigated the transient stability of empty and fluid-filled cylindrical shells and used to study the non-linear dynamic behavior of shallow cylindrical shells under axial loading. Gasser [12] studied the frequency spectra of bi-layered cylindrical shells by taking different materials in both layers such as isotropic as well as functionally graded material (FGM) and by taking two different FGM at the inner and outer layers of the CSs respectively. Sharma and Johns [13] explored the vibrations of CSs with clamped-free and clamped-ring-stiffeners conditions by applying the Raleigh-Ritz method and estimated the axial displacement deformation with the help of beam functions. Xi et al. [14] have studied vibrations of cross-ply plastic-coated circular fluid-filled CSs by applying a semi-analytical method based on Reissner-Mindline theory. Zhang et al. [4] studied vibrations of CSs and applied the wave propagation approach (WPA) to solve shell dynamical equations. This method depended on the eigenvalue of characteristic beam functions. Axial wave number was designated to a boundary condition (BC) by a simple formula. They compared the results determined by this method to ones found by a FEM to check the efficiency, robustness and accuracy of the procedure. It was seen by making these comparisons that their approach is more victorious and exact for shell vibration difficulties. It was concluded that the proposed approach could be useful for a problem with compound end states and also for fluid-filled cylindrical shells.

Zhang et al. [15] examined vibrations of CSs containing fluid by applying WPA. After that a similarity evaluation was conducted between uncoupled frequencies with the numerical outcome obtained in the literature. They also put side by side the coupled frequencies estimated by the WPA with those attained by FEM. Xiang et al. [16] accessed exact solution for the vibration characteristics of CS placed at intermediate position and used the domain decomposition technique for the sake of ordering in the segment of the shells. Zhao et al. [17] investigated the effects of vibration with ring stiffeners and stringer for the laminated cross-ply rotating CS and two methods: variational method and averaging approach are used for these effects. They determined that averaging method produced the inexact values and was sensitive whereas the fast and better results were deduced with variational method. Xiang et al. [18] accessed the vibration characteristics of CS placed at intermediate position with axially dense ring supports and used Flügge shell theory and the Timoshenko thin shell theory to analyze the buckling shells as composite materials. Due to FGM their composition vary constantly and smoothly through thickness.

Vibration characteristic of FGM shell with ring supports has investigated by Isvandzibaei and Awasare [19] and they used third order deformation shear theory and Hamilton's principle for free-free end. Lee and Chang [20] gave a numerical study of coupled problems of fluid conveying dual walled carbon annotates and examined the effects of characteristic ratio and Van der Waals forces on basic frequencies. Silva et al. [21] investigated the nonlinear vibrant behavior and instabilities of partially fluid-filled CS constrained to axial load and resulting in a distinct low-dimensional model for the analysis of the vibrations to observe the shell vibration. Shah et al. [22] gave a vibration analysis of a functionally graded CS containing a fluid. The shells were rested on elastic foundations. They analyzed effects of Winkler and Pasternak moduli on shell vibration characteristics. Xiong et al. [23] investigated the free vibration analysis of fluid-filled elliptical cylindrical shells and explained the sensitivity of frequency parameters to the elliptical parameter with length of CS. The cylinder is filled with a compressible non-viscous fluid and may be subjected to arbitrary time-harmonic on-surface mechanical drives is investigated by Hasheminejad and Alaei-Varnosfadrani [24]. The free vibration of fluid-filled CS covered partially in elastic foundation is investigated by Kim [25] and the elastic foundation of partial axial and angular dimensions is represented by the Pasternak model. The variation of the frequency parameters with respect to the layer thickness, the length-to-radius ratio, the length-to-thickness ratio, and circumferential node number are analyzed by Izyan et al. [26]. Soutis et al. [27] investigated influence of ring supports on free vibration of FGM which is placed on the middle layer and Study is carried out for placing ring support in different position of FGM's, to find the natural frequencies by Rayleigh–Ritz approach.

In the present paper, vibration frequency characteristics of fluid-filled CSs are investigated. The shells are constrained in the radial direction by ring supports. The present problem is formulated in integral form and is converted into a system of three partial differential equations (PDEs) with the unknown displacement functions. Modal forms for the three unknown functions are assumed such that the special and temporal variables are separated. Energy variation approach is used to solve PDEs so that an eigenvalue problem is cropped up. Axial modal dependence is roughly estimated by trigonometric functions for a simply supported CSs. For other end conditions, characteristic beam functions are taken. The radial constraints are presumed by the polynomial functions having degree equal to number of ring supports. Fluid pressure is stated by the acoustic wave equation and Bessel's functions of first kind. Axial modal displacement deformations are measured by beam characteristic functions which ensure to meet boundary conditions. The Galerkin technique is implemented to form the shell frequency equation which is solved by using MATLAB coding. The radial deflection is restrained by ring supports. This factor is expressed by the polynomial functions which carry the degree equal to the number of ring supports.

2. Formation of shell problem

2.1. Functionally graded shells

In practice a CS is constructed from a FGM which consists of two constituent materials. Two constituent materials having material parameters: E_1, E_2, ν_1, ν_2, and ρ_1, ρ_2. Then the effective material quantities: E_{fgm}, v_{fgm} and ρ_{fgm} are given as:

$$E_{fgm} = [E_1 - E_2]\left[\frac{z}{h}+\frac{1}{2}\right]^p + E_2, \nu_{fgm} = [\nu_1 - \nu_2]\left[\frac{z}{h}+\frac{1}{2}\right]^p + \nu_2, \rho_{fgm} = [\rho_1 - \rho_2]\left[\frac{z}{h}+\frac{1}{2}\right]^p + \rho_2 \quad (1)$$

The value of z lies as $0 < z < \infty$ in the radial direction. The volume fraction V_r for a functionally graded constituent material can be defined by the following function:

$$V_r = \left[\frac{z}{h}+\frac{1}{2}\right]^p \quad (2)$$

where p is the power law exponent which indicates the material variation profile through the shell thickness and keeps its real between zero and infinity.

2.2. Theoretical investigation

Consider **Figure 1** in which a geometrical sketch of a CS is given. L, R, and h are termed as shell geometrical parameters. Other shell basic quantities are material parameters and are designate by E, v and ρ.

where the forces and moments are designated by N and M have the directions along the longitudinal, tangential and shear directions correspondingly.

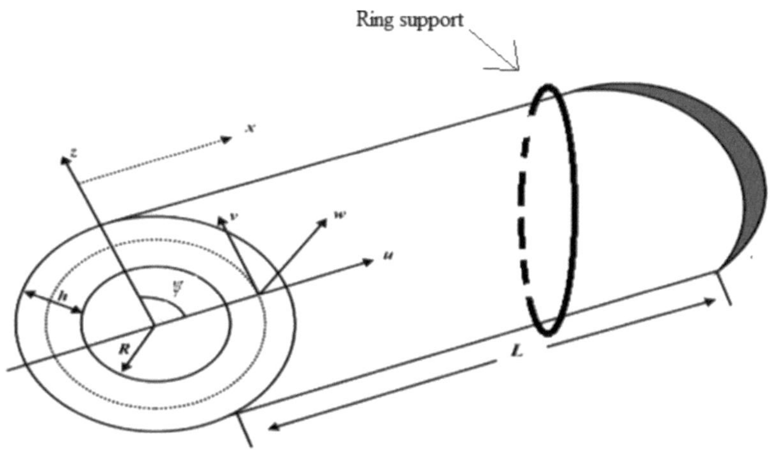

Figure 1. Geometrical sketch of a FG cylindrical shell with ring support.

$$(N_x, N_\Psi, N_{x\Psi}) = \int_{\frac{-h}{2}}^{\frac{h}{2}} (\sigma_x, \sigma_\Psi, \sigma_{x\Psi}) dz, \quad (M_x, M_\Psi, M_{x\Psi}) = \int_{\frac{-h}{2}}^{\frac{h}{2}} (\sigma_x, \sigma_\Psi, \sigma_{x\Psi}) z dz \tag{3}$$

where σ_x, σ_Ψ are the linear stresses along x and Ψ-directions respectively and $\sigma_{x\Psi}$ represents the shear stress along $x\Psi$-direction. For a cylindrical shell, the stresses defined in Eq. (3) are defined by the two dimensional Hook's law.

$$\begin{bmatrix} \sigma_x \\ \sigma_\Psi \\ \sigma_{x\Psi} \end{bmatrix} = \begin{bmatrix} Q_{11} & Q_{12} & 0 \\ Q_{12} & Q_{22} & 0 \\ 0 & 0 & Q_{66} \end{bmatrix} \begin{bmatrix} e_x \\ e_\Psi \\ e_{x\Psi} \end{bmatrix} \tag{4}$$

where the strains along x and Ψ directions are labeled by e_x and e_Ψ respectively and the shear strain is denoted by $e_{x\Psi}$ in the $x\Psi$ - direction. The first thin shell theory was developed by Love [7] which is based on Kirchhoff's perception for plates. Various thin shell theories have been deduced from this theory by modifying the geometrical and physical parameters. The members of the strain vector $[e]$ in Eq. (4) have been defined as linear functions of thickness coordinate z which taken from Love's [32] theory are stated as:

$$e_x = e_1 + z\kappa_1, e_\Psi = e_2 + z\kappa_2, e_{x\Psi} = \gamma + 2z\tau \tag{5}$$

here e_1, e_2 and γ denote strains with regard to the shell middle reference surface. κ_1, κ_2 and τ stand for the surface curvatures. The expressions for strain and curvature displacement relationship are written as:

$$\{e_1, e_2, \gamma\} = \left\{ \frac{\partial u}{\partial x}, \frac{1}{R}\left(\frac{\partial v}{\partial \Psi} + w\right), \left(\frac{\partial v}{\partial x} + \frac{1}{R}\frac{\partial u}{\partial \Psi}\right) \right\}$$

$$\{\kappa_1, \kappa_2, \tau\} = \left\{ -\frac{\partial^2 w}{\partial x^2}, -\frac{1}{R^2}\left(\frac{\partial^2 w}{\partial \Psi^2} - \frac{\partial v}{\partial \Psi}\right), -\frac{1}{R}\left(\frac{\partial^2 w}{\partial x \partial \Psi} - \frac{\partial v}{\partial x}\right) \right\} \tag{6}$$

By substituting Eqs. (5) and (6) into Eq. (4) and then substituting the resulting equation into Eq. (3). The force and moment results can be written as:

$$\begin{bmatrix} N_x \\ N_\Psi \\ N_{x\Psi} \\ M_x \\ M_\Psi \\ M_{x\Psi} \end{bmatrix} = \begin{bmatrix} A_{11} & A_{12} & 0 & B_{11} & B_{12} & 0 \\ A_{12} & A_{22} & 0 & B_{12} & B_{22} & 0 \\ 0 & 0 & A_{66} & 0 & 0 & B_{66} \\ B_{11} & B_{12} & 0 & D_{11} & D_{12} & 0 \\ B_{12} & B_{22} & 0 & D_{12} & D_{22} & 0 \\ 0 & 0 & B_{66} & 0 & 0 & D_{66} \end{bmatrix} \begin{bmatrix} e_1 \\ e_2 \\ \gamma \\ \kappa_1 \\ \kappa_2 \\ 2\tau \end{bmatrix} \tag{7}$$

where A_{ij}, B_{ij} and D_{ij} (i, j = 1, 2 and 6) are the extentional, coupling and bending stiffness defined respectively, as:

$$(A_{ij}, B_{ij}, D_{ij}) = \int_{\frac{-h}{2}}^{\frac{h}{2}} Q_{ij}(1, z, z^2)dz, \tag{8}$$

where coupling stiffness, B_{ij}'s vanish for a CS structured from isotropic materials where they exist for heterogeneous and an isotropic materials such as laminated FGM. For an isotropic material, Q_{ij} (i, j = 1, 2 and 6) are expressed as

$$Q_{11} = Q_{22} = \frac{E}{1-v^2}, Q_{12} = \frac{vE}{1-v^2}, Q_{66} = \frac{E}{2(1+v)} \tag{9}$$

where E and v are the Young's modulus and Poisson's ratio for the shell's material. In this study, the cylindrical shell is considered thin and valid with thickness-to- radius ratio is less than 0.05. For vibrating thin cylindrical shell, the strain energy expressed as

$$S = \frac{R}{2}\int_0^L\int_0^{2\pi} [A_{11}{e_1}^2 + A_{22}{e_2}^2 + 2A_{12}e_1e_2 + A_{66}\gamma^2 + 2B_{11}e_1k_1 + 2B_{12}e_1k_2 + 2B_{12}e_2k_1$$

$$+2B_{22}e_2k_2 + 4B_{66}\gamma\tau + D_{11}{k_1}^2 + D_{22}{k_2}^2 + 2D_{12}k_1k_2 + 4D_{66}\tau^2]d\Psi dx \tag{10}$$

Substituting the expression for the surface strains and the curvatures from the relationships (6)

$$S = \frac{R}{2}\int_0^L\int_0^{2\pi} \left[A_{11}\left(\frac{\partial u}{\partial x}\right) + \frac{A_{22}}{R^2}\left(\frac{\partial v}{\partial \Psi} + w\right)^2 + \frac{2A_{12}}{R}\left(\frac{\partial u}{\partial x}\right)\left(\frac{\partial v}{\partial \Psi} + w\right) + A_{66}\left(\frac{\partial v}{\partial x} + \frac{1}{R}\frac{\partial u}{\partial \Psi}\right)^2\right.$$

$$-2B_{11}\left(\frac{\partial u}{\partial x}\right)\left(\frac{\partial^2 w}{\partial x^2}\right) - \frac{2B_{12}}{R}\left(\frac{\partial u}{\partial x}\right)\left(\frac{\partial^2 w}{\partial x \partial \Psi} - \frac{\partial v}{\partial x}\right) - \frac{2B_{12}}{R}\left(\frac{\partial v}{\partial \Psi} + w\right)\left(\frac{\partial^2 w}{\partial x^2}\right)$$

$$-\frac{2B_{22}}{R^3}\left(\frac{\partial v}{\partial \Psi}+w\right)\left(\frac{\partial^2 w}{\partial \Psi^2}-\frac{\partial v}{\partial \Psi}\right)-\frac{8B_{66}}{R}\left(\frac{\partial v}{\partial x}+\frac{1}{R}\frac{\partial u}{\partial \Psi}\right)\left(\frac{\partial^2 w}{\partial x\partial \Psi}-\frac{\partial v}{\partial x}\right)$$

$$+D_{11}\left(\frac{\partial^2 w}{\partial x^2}\right)^2+\frac{D_{22}}{R^4}\left(\frac{\partial^2 w}{\partial \Psi^2}-\frac{\partial v}{\partial \Psi}\right)^2+\frac{2D_{12}}{R^2}\left(\frac{\partial^2 w}{\partial x^2}\right)\left(\frac{\partial^2 w}{\partial \Psi^2}-\frac{\partial v}{\partial \Psi}\right)$$

$$+\frac{4D_{66}}{R^2}\left(\frac{\partial^2 w}{\partial x\partial \Psi}-\frac{\partial v}{\partial x}\right)^2 d\Psi dx \tag{11}$$

Also for a cylindrical shell, its kinetic energy expression represented by T, is given as:

$$T=\frac{R}{2}\int_0^L\int_0^{2\pi}\rho_T\left[\left(\frac{\partial u}{\partial t}\right)^2+\left(\frac{\partial v}{\partial t}\right)^2+\left(\frac{\partial w}{\partial t}\right)^2\right]d\Psi dx \tag{12}$$

where ρ_T is expressed as:

$$\rho_T=\int_{\frac{-h}{2}}^{\frac{h}{2}}\rho dz \tag{13}$$

Now the shell problem is framed by the Lagrangian energy functional which is the difference between the shell kinetic and strain energies and is given as:

$$\prod = T - S \tag{14}$$

where $\prod$ denotes the Lagrangian functional. Substituting the expressions for strains and kinetic energies of the shell from Eqs. (11) and (12) respectively into Eq. (14). Calculus of variations process is applied to the integral terms to derive the Euler-Lagrange equations. Hamilton's variational principle is a process in which the variations in the variables are assumed to be zero. Implementation this principle to the Lagrangian functional which is an integral expression. The subsequent dynamical equations are obtained in the following system of PDEs:

$$A_{11}\frac{\partial^2 u}{\partial x^2}+\frac{A_{66}}{R^2}\frac{\partial^2 u}{\partial \Psi^2}+\left(\frac{A_{12}+A_{66}}{R}+\frac{B_{12}+2B_{66}}{R^2}\right)\frac{\partial^2 v}{\partial x\partial \Psi}+\frac{A_{12}}{R}\frac{\partial w}{\partial x}-B_{11}\frac{\partial^3 w}{\partial x^3}-\frac{B_{12}+2B_{66}}{R^2}\frac{\partial^3 w}{\partial x\partial \Psi^2}=\rho_T\frac{\partial^2 u}{\partial t^2}$$

$$\left(\frac{A_{12}+A_{66}}{R}+\frac{B_{12}+B_{66}}{R^2}\right)\frac{\partial^2 u}{\partial x\partial \Psi}+\left(A_{66}+\frac{3B_{66}}{R}+\frac{3D_{66}}{R^2}\right)\frac{\partial^2 v}{\partial x^2}+\left(\frac{A_{22}}{R^2}+\frac{2B_{22}}{R^3}+\frac{D_{22}}{R^4}\right)\frac{\partial^2 v}{\partial \Psi^2}$$
$$-\left(\frac{B_{12}+2B_{66}}{R}+\frac{D_{12}+2D_{66}}{R^2}\right)\frac{\partial^3 w}{\partial x^2\partial \Psi}+\left(\frac{A_{22}}{R^2}+\frac{B_{22}}{R^3}\right)\frac{\partial w}{\partial \Psi}-\left(\frac{B_{22}}{R^3}+\frac{D_{22}}{R^4}\right)\frac{\partial^3 w}{\partial^3 \Psi}=\rho_T\frac{\partial^2 v}{\partial t^2}$$

$$B_{11}\frac{\partial^3 u}{\partial x^3}-\frac{A_{12}}{R}\frac{\partial u}{\partial x}+\frac{B_{12}+2B_{66}}{R^2}\frac{\partial^3 u}{\partial x\partial \Psi^2}+\left(\frac{B_{12}+2B_{66}}{R}+\frac{D_{12}+4D_{66}}{R^2}\right)\frac{\partial^3 v}{\partial x^2\partial \Psi}+\left(\frac{B_{22}}{R^3}+\frac{D_{22}}{R^4}\right)\frac{\partial^3 v}{\partial \Psi^3}$$
$$-\left(\frac{A_{22}}{R^2}+\frac{B_{22}}{R^3}\right)\frac{\partial v}{\partial \Psi}-D_{11}\frac{\partial^4 w}{\partial x^4}-\frac{2(D_{12}+2D_{66})}{R^2}\frac{\partial^4 w}{\partial x^2\partial \Psi^2}-\frac{D_{22}}{R^4}\frac{\partial^4 w}{\partial \Psi^4}+\frac{2B_{12}}{R}\frac{\partial^2 w}{\partial x^2}$$
$$+\frac{2B_{22}}{R^3}\frac{\partial^2 w}{\partial \Psi^2}-\frac{A_{22}}{R^2}w=\rho_T\frac{\partial^2 w}{\partial t^2} \tag{15}$$

3. Application of Galerkin technique

Two energy variational techniques namely viz., the Rayleigh-Ritz method and the Galerkin technique (GT) are exploited to solve shell motion equations because these methods yield results fast with enough accuracy. The present CS is analyzed by applying the Galerkin technique (GT) for their vibrations. This approach is very expedient, simple and convenient to use to find vibration frequencies and has been widely engaged by numerous mathematicians [25, 28, 29]. Modal displacement forms are designated by x, Ψ and t. The following modal deformation displacement functions for u, v and w are adopted as:

$$u(x,\Psi,t)=p_m\frac{d\varphi}{dx}\sin n\Psi\cos\omega t$$

$$v(x,\Psi,t)=q_m\varphi(x)\cos n\Psi\cos\omega t$$

$$w(x,\Psi,t)=r_m\varphi(x)\sum_{i=1}^{k}(x-a_i)^{z_i}\sin n\Psi\cos\omega t \tag{16}$$

Here the parameters p_m, q_m and r_m present vibration amplitudes in the x, Ψ and z directions respectively. The position of ith ring support with the circular direction of the shell is denoted by a_i and z_i has value, 1 when a ring support exists and is 0, when no rings hold up. For this purpose the modal displacement forms for u, v and w given in the relation (12) respectively and their corresponding partial derivatives are substituted into Eq. (15) by taking, $z_i=1$ for a single ring support, the resulting equations are integrated with respect to x from 0 to L, the following equations are got:

$$\left(A_{11}I_1-n^2\frac{A_{66}}{R^2}I_2\right)p_m-n\left(\frac{A_{12}+A_{66}}{R}+\frac{B_{12}+2B_{66}}{R^2}\right)I_2q_m+\begin{bmatrix}\frac{A_{12}}{R}(I_6+I_7)-B_{11}(I_8+3I_9)\\+n^2\frac{B_{12}+2B_{66}}{R^2}(I_6+I_7)\end{bmatrix}r_m=-\omega^2\rho_T I_2 p_m$$

$$n\left(\frac{A_{12}+A_{66}}{R}+\frac{B_{12}+2B_{66}}{R^2}\right)I_3p_m+\left[\left(A_{66}+\frac{3B_{66}}{R}+\frac{4D_{66}}{R^2}\right)I_3-n^2\left(\frac{A_{22}}{R^2}+\frac{2B_{22}}{R^3}+\frac{D_{22}}{R^4}\right)I_4\right]q_m$$
$$+\left[n\left(\frac{A_{22}}{R^2}+\frac{B_{22}}{R^3}\right)I_{10}+n^3\left(\frac{B_{22}}{R^3}+\frac{D_{22}}{R^4}\right)I_{10}-n\left(\frac{B_{12}+2B_{66}}{R}+\frac{D_{12}+4D_{66}}{R^2}\right)(I_{11}+2I_{12})\right]r_m=-\omega^2\rho_T I_4 p_m$$

$$\left(-\frac{A_{12}}{R}I_{18}+B_{11}I_{19}-n^2\frac{B_{12}+2B_{66}}{R^2}I_{18}\right)p_m+\left[n\left(\frac{A_{22}}{R^2}+\frac{B_{22}}{R^3}\right)I_{10}+n^3\left(\frac{B_{22}}{R^3}+\frac{D_{22}}{R^4}\right)I_{10}\right.$$

$$\left.-n\left(\frac{B_{12}+2B_{66}}{R}+\frac{D_{12}+4D_{66}}{R^2}\right)I_{18}\right]q_m+\left[-\frac{A_{22}}{R^2}I_3+\frac{2B_{12}}{R}(I_{14}+2I_{15})-2n^2\frac{B_{22}}{R^3}I_{13}\right.$$

$$\left.-D_{11}(I_{16}+4I_{17})+2n^2\frac{D_{12}+2D_{66}}{R^2}(I_{14}+2I_{15})-\frac{D_{22}}{R^4}I_{13}\right]r_m=-\omega^2\rho_T I_{13}r_m \tag{17}$$

where the integral terms are listed in Appendix-I. Terms in Eq. (17) are arranged to form the homogeneous algebraic linear equations (HALEs) in p_m, q_m and r_m. This leads to the formation of the shell frequency equation the eigenvalue shape as:

$$\begin{aligned} d_{11}p_m+d_{12}q_m+d_{13}r_m&=-\omega^2\rho_T p_m I_2\\ d_{21}p_m+d_{22}q_m+d_{23}r_m&=-\omega^2\rho_T q_m I_4\\ d_{31}p_m+d_{32}q_m+d_{33}r_m&=-\omega^2\rho_T r_m I_{13}\end{aligned} \tag{18}$$

So the above equations are written in the eigenvalue problem notation as:

$$\begin{pmatrix} d_{11} & d_{12} & d_{13}\\ d_{21} & d_{22} & d_{23}\\ d_{31} & d_{32} & d_{33}\end{pmatrix}\begin{pmatrix} p_m\\ q_m\\ r_m\end{pmatrix}=-\omega^2\rho_T\begin{pmatrix} I_2 & 0 & 0\\ 0 & I_4 & 0\\ 0 & 0 & I_{13}\end{pmatrix}\begin{pmatrix} p_m\\ q_m\\ r_m\end{pmatrix} \tag{19}$$

3.1. Annexation of fluid terms

The acoustic pressure generated by a fluid is described by the wave equation in cylindrical coordinate system (x,Ψ,r) and is presented as:

$$\frac{1}{r}\frac{\partial}{\partial r}\left(r\frac{\partial q}{\partial r}\right)+\frac{1}{r^2}\frac{\partial^2 q}{\partial\Psi^2}+\frac{\partial^2 q}{\partial x^2}=\frac{1}{c^2}\frac{\partial^2 q}{\partial t^2} \tag{20}$$

where t, q, c represents respectively the time, acoustic pressure and speed of sound in the fluid. The acoustic pressure produced in the fluid meets the equation of motion Eq. (20) and is articulated by the following modal function expression:

$$q=q_m\sin n\theta J_n(k_r r)\Psi(x)\cos(\omega t) \tag{21}$$

Here $J_n(k_r r)$ represents the Bessel's function of first kind with order n. It is the same number as the circumferential wave number. ω denotes the natural frequency for the CS, k_r stands for the radial wave number and axial wave number k_m is designated by for a number of boundary conditions that has been indicates in Ref. [10]. There exists a relation between k_m and k_r is written as:

$$(k_r R)^2=\Omega^2\left(\frac{c_L}{c_f}\right)^2-(k_m R)^2 \tag{22}$$

where c_L and c_f denote the speeds of the sound in the empty and fluid-filled cylindrical shells respectively. Ω is the non-dimensional frequency parameter. An assumption is made that the fluid and the shell radial displacement must be the same at the borderline of the interior wall of the shell and it is made sure that the fluid is kept with the interaction between the fluid and the shell wall. A coupling condition relation of a fluid with the shell wall exists and is defined by the following expression:

$$\left\{\frac{1}{i\omega\rho_f}\right\}\left(\frac{\partial q}{\partial r}\right) = \frac{\partial w}{\partial t} \tag{23}$$

By applying this condition at $r = R$, the fluid loading term (*FLT*) owing to the existence of the fluid pressure is given by

$$FLT = \left(\frac{\omega^2 \rho_f J_n(k_r R)}{k_r J'_n(k_r R)}\right) r_m \tag{24}$$

$J'_n(K_r r)$ denotes the differentiation of the Bessel's function with respect to the argument $(k_r R)$. The fluid loaded term (*FLT*), which represents the fluid pressure, is annexed with the frequency Eq. (18) for an empty CS. Ultimately the shell frequency equation for fluid-filled functionally graded CS is articulated in the following forms:

$$\begin{pmatrix} d_{11} & d_{12} & d_{13} \\ d_{21} & d_{22} & d_{23} \\ d_{31} & d_{32} & d_{33} \end{pmatrix} \begin{pmatrix} p_m \\ q_m \\ r_m \end{pmatrix} = -\omega^2 \rho_T \begin{pmatrix} I_2 & 0 & 0 \\ 0 & I_4 & 0 \\ 0 & 0 & I_{13} + \dfrac{\rho_f J_n(k_r R)}{k_r J'_n(k_r R)} \end{pmatrix} \begin{pmatrix} p_m \\ q_m \\ r_m \end{pmatrix} \tag{25}$$

The expressions for the terms $d_{ij}{}^{'}s$, I_2, I_4 and I_{13} are given in Appendix-I. This is an eigenvalue problem involving the shell frequency. Presently, the MATLAB is generally used to calculate the physical problems in engineering and science. In our case, MATLAB computer software has been used to compute the shell frequencies through eigenvalues and eigenvectors. A single command 'eig' furnishes shell frequencies and mode shapes by calculating eigenvalues and eigenvectors respectively. It is significant that MATLAB can compute integrals that fairly easy to apply the Galerkin method with polynomial basis functions. The exact solution of integral equation is known and presents a sample of MATLAB code to illustrate the success of the method. In this way the Galerkin method is implemented to form the shell frequency equation that is solved by employing MATLAB software.

3.2. Effective material

Materials of cylindrical shells have a paramount role in analyzing shell vibrations. They impress their stability. In practice isotropic, laminated and functionally graded materials are used to manufacture them. Here functionally graded materials are benefitted to form the shells. These materials are advanced and useful in a highly environs. Their material properties are temperature - dependents. One of their material properties C is stated by the following relation:

$$C = C_0\left(C_{-1}T^{-1} + C_1T + C_2T^2 + C_3T^3\right) \quad (26)$$

where C_{-1}, C_0, C_1, C_2 and C_3 designate the temperature dependent constants. T is calculated in the Kelvin scale. These constants differ from material to material. Formula (26) is due to Toulokian [38]. A functionally graded cylindrical shell comprising of two constituent materials can be classified into two categories. This depends upon the arrangement of the two materials forming the shell. It is known that the stainless steel and nickel are used for structuring such types of shells. Stainless steel and nickel are used in its external and internal surfaces respectively for Category- I *(C-I)* CS structure, while for Category-II *(C-II)* cylindrical shell, stainless steel and nickel are taken for constituting its internal and external surfaces respectively. At temperature 300 K, the material properties for stainless steel and nickel of functionally graded cylindrical shell are: E, v, ρ for nickel are $2.05098 \times 10^{11}\,\text{N/m}^2$, 0.31, 8900 kg/m^3 and stainless steel are $2.07788 \times 10^{11}\,\text{N/m}^2$, 0.317756 and $81,666\,\text{N/m}^3$. These values have been taken from Ref. [3].

4. Numerical results

In this section, to check the validity and accuracy, for the determination of the natural frequencies with present methodology, empty and fluid-filled cylindrical shells with ring supports are analyzed and the results are compared with experimental and other numerical values found in literature. The stainless steel and nickel are used for structuring such types of shells. Stainless steel and nickel are used in its external and internal surfaces respectively for Category- I *(C-I)* CS structure, while for Category-II *(C-II)* cylindrical shell, stainless steel and nickel are taken for constituting its internal and external surfaces respectively. At temperature 300 K, the material properties for stainless steel and nickel of functionally graded cylindrical shell are: E, v , ρ for nickel are $2.05098 \times 10^{11}\,\text{N/m}^2$, 0.31, 8900 kg/m^3 and stainless steel are $2.07788 \times 10^{11}\,\text{N/m}^2$, 0.317756 and $81,666\,\text{N/m}^3$.

A few comparisons of analytical frequencies for isotropic cylindrical shells are exhibited to validate the present Galerkin technique. As a first example, the lowest dimensionless frequency $\Omega = \omega R\sqrt{(1-\nu^2)\rho/E}$ of a simply supported empty cylinder are compared with the solution derived using generalized differential quadrature method (DQM) by Loy et al. [2] as shown in **Table 1**. They are varied with circumferential wave mode, n for axial wave number $m = 1$. There is an excellent agreement is seen between two sets of frequency parameters results as the percentage difference is negligible.

As another example, the natural frequency of a simply supported empty cylinder is compared with Loy et al. [3], Ansari et al. [30] and Warburton [35] as shown in **Figure 2(a)**. They are varied with axial wave number, m for circumferential wave mode, n = 2, 3. For the same shell, the present results for a fluid-filled shell are compared with those numerical results obtained by Gonçalves and Batista [10], Gonçalves et al. [11] and obtained experimentally by Gasser [12] in **Figure 2(b)**. They are varied with circumferential wave mode, n for axial wave number, m = 1. There is an excellent agreement is seen between two sets of frequency parameters results.

n	Loy et al. [2]	Present	Difference %
1	0.016101	0.016102	0.006
2	0.009382	0.009383	0.010
3	0.022105	0.022106	0.004
4	0.042095	0.042097	0.004
5	0.068008	0.068009	0.001
6	0.099730	0.099732	0.002
7	0.137239	0.137241	0.001
8	0.180527	0.180528	0.000
9	0.229594	0.229596	0.000
10	0.284435	0.284436	0.000

Table 1. Comparison of frequency parameter $\Omega = \omega R\sqrt{(1-v^2)\rho/E}$ for a simply supported CS ($m = 1$, $L/R = 20$, $h/R = 0.01$, $\nu = 0.3$).

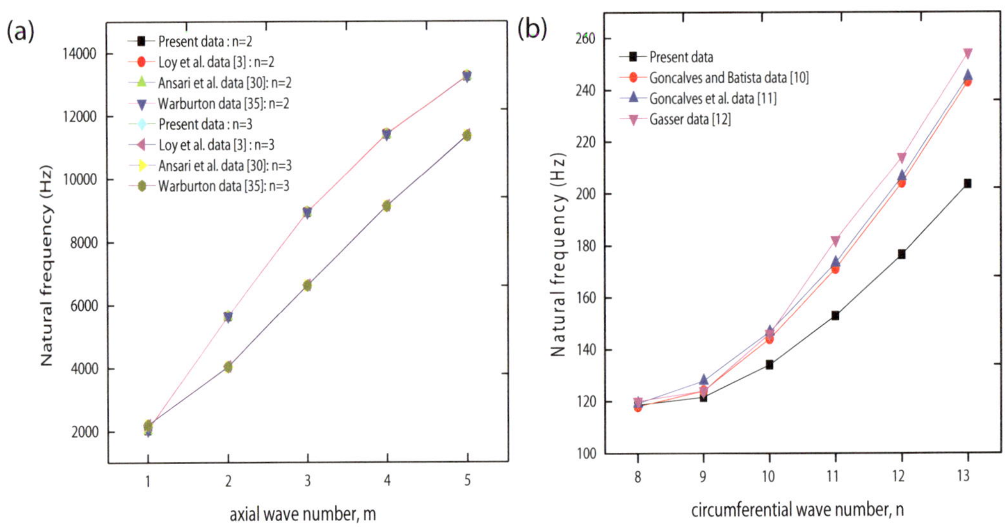

Figure 2. **(a)** Comparison of natural frequencies (Hz) for a simply supported CS ($L = 8$ in, $h = 0.1$ in, $R = 2$ in, $E = 30 \times 10^6$ lbf in^{-2}, $\nu = 0.3$, $\rho = 7.35 \times 10^{-4}$ lbf s^2 in^{-4}). **(b)** Comparison of natural frequencies (Hz) for a fluid-filled CS ($m = 1$, $L = 0.41$ m, $h = 0.001$ m, $R = 0.3015$ m, $E = 2.1 \times 10^{11}$ N/m^2, $v = 0.3$, $\rho = 7850$ kg/m^3).

When $n = 2, 3$, $m = 1$, the present values are 2046.4, 2199.0 and the values of Loy et al. [3] are 2050.7, 2204.0 which is good agreement between each other. **Figure 2(b)** exhibits a good coincidence between respective counters of the frequencies. The values at $n = 8, 9$ are less significant and on enhancing the value of n, the present numerical values are smaller than those of Gonçalves and Batista [10] and Gonçalves et al. [11] and Gasser [12]. This difference is the result of two separate analytical techniques.

4.1. Frequency analysis of fluid-filled cylindrical shell

Figure 3(a) reveals variations of natural frequencies (Hz) for a CS including fluid against L/R for circumferential wave modes $n = 1, 2, 3, 4, 5$ and the longitudinal wave mode, $m = 1$.

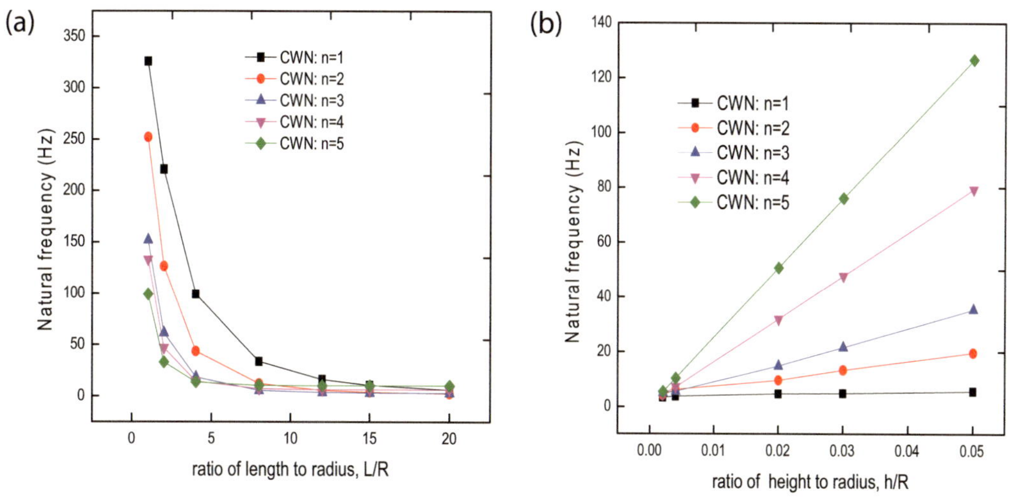

Figure 3. Variations of natural frequency **(a)** for fluid-filled CS against L/R. ($m = 1$, $h = 0.004$ m, $R = 1$ m, $E = 2.1 \times 10^{11}$ N/m^2, $v = 0.3$, $\rho = 7850$ kg/m^3, $\rho_f = 1000$ kg/m^3) **(b)** for fluid-filled CS with h/R ($m = 1$, $L = 8$ m, $R = 1$ m, $E = 2.1 \times 10^{11}$ N/m^2, $v = 0.3$, $\rho = 7850$ kg/m^3, $\rho_f = 1000$ kg/m^3).

The value of length-to-radius ratio is composed as $1 \le L/R \le 20$, the values of $L/R = 1$, at CWN: $n = 1, 2, 3, 4, 5$ are 325.625, 252.019, 151.816, 132.818, 99.128 and $L/R = 20$ are 6.2054, 2.3505, 2.8798, 6.3196, 10.0948. For the wave mode, $n = 1, 2, 3, 4, 5$ as L/R is made to grow i.e., the shell becomes longer and longer, the frequency reduces for each tangential wave mode.

Now the values of length-to-radius ratio $1 \le L/R \le 20$, at CWN: $n = 1$, the frequencies are 325.675, 220.745, 99.005, 33.693, 16.348, 10.770, 6.2054 and at CWN: $n = 5$ are 99.128, 33.017, 13.756, 10.3603, 10.1506, 10.1148, 10.0948 respectively. These results show that, on increasing the values of L/R the frequencies reduce to each CWN mode [36]. **Figure 3(b)** demonstrates variations of natural frequencies (Hz) for a CS enclosing fluid versus the h/R for the tangential wave modes, $n = 1, 2, 3, 4, 5$ and the longitudinal wave mode, $m = 1$. The value of height-to-radius ratio is composed as $0.002 \le h/R \le 0.05$, the values of $h/R = 0.002$, at CWN: $n = 1, 2, 3, 4, 5$ are 3.36929, 4.1911, 5.0052, 4.5812, 5.4979 and $h/R = 0.05$, are 5.6977, 19.6873, 35.4274, 79.3621, 126.739 respectively. As h/R is made to increase i.e., the shell gets thicker and thicker, the frequency increases. Now the values of height-to-radius ratio $0.002 \le h/R \le 0.05$, at CWN: $n = 1$, the frequencies are 3.36929, 3.7929, 4.6937, 4.9046, 5.6977 and at CWN: $n = 5$ are 5.4979, 10.3603, 50.7402, 76.0671, 126.7139. As h/R is made to increase i.e., these results shows that the frequency increases very slowly for $n = 1$ but for higher values of n, there is seen an appreciable increments in frequency values with each tangential wave mode. Previous study reveals that when the value of h/R increases then frequencies also increases [37].

4.2. Frequency analysis of fluid-filled cylindrical shells with ring support

In this section, frequency analysis for an isotropic CS enclosing fluid is performed by attaching some ring supports. These rings are located at some distance from one end of a cylindrical shell as shown in **Figure 4**.

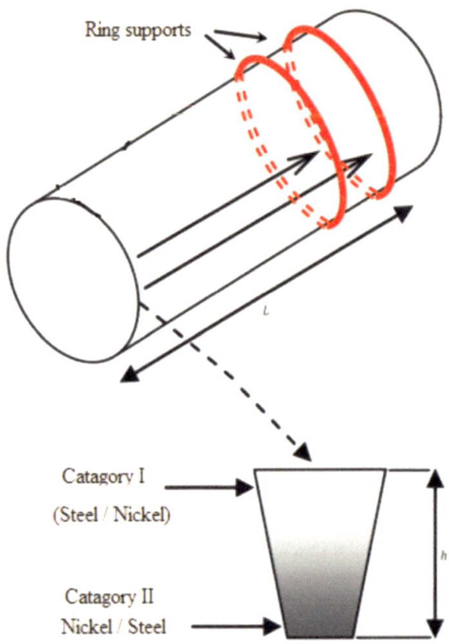

Figure 4. FGM shell with two ring supports (Ansari et al. [30]).

In **Figure 5(a)** variations of natural frequencies (Hz) for a CS containing fluid with ring supports versus L/R are demonstrated for three positions of the ring supports at $a = 0.3L$, $0.5L$, L. The value of L/R is taken as $1 \le L/R \le 20$, when L/R at ring support $a = 0.3L$, $0.5L$, L without fluid, the frequencies are 790.31, 863.378, 745.085 and $L/R = 20$ the values are 420.639, 516.775, 208.819 and now with fluid at $L/R = 1$ the values are 352.975, 362.764, 314.385 and $L/R = 20$, the values are 187.549, 217.132, 86.109 respectively. There is a substantial decrease in frequency values as the shell length gets higher [36]. Influence of fluid on vibration frequency is seen significantly visible that reduced them approximately to (40~50%). In **Figure 5(b)** natural frequencies (Hz) for a CS containing fluid without and with ring supports are exhibited with h/R. The value of h/R is taken as: $0.002 \le h/R \le 0.05$, when $h/R = 0.002$ at ring support $a = 0.3L$, $0.5L$, L without fluid are 413.2180, 548.4688, 215.4291 and $h/R = 0.05$ the values are 413.3080, 548.4888, 215.5019 respectively. Now with fluid at $h/R = 0.002$ the values are 273.6543, 365.6459, 144.5833 and $h/R = 0.05$, the values are 273.7139, 365.6592, 144.6321 respectively. The ring supports are located at $a = 0.3L$, $0.5L$, L. It is observed that frequencies enhance minutely for the thicker CSs [37]. Again the frequency has been considerably reduced when the fluid is added. From **Figure 5(a)** and **(b)**, it is observed that in both the cases, without fluid and with fluid for L/R and h/R, the value of ring support $a = 0.3L$ which is sandwich between $a = 0.5L$, L. It is seen that the influences of ring supports and fluid terms are converse to each other. The ring supports increase the frequencies whereas the fluid loaded terms lower them [32–34].

4.3. Frequency analysis of empty and fluid-filled cylindrical shells with ring supports

It is noted that the natural frequencies of the shells have varied by the location of ring support in the shell and this change also varies WOF and WF as shown in **Figure 6(a)–(d)**. It is evident

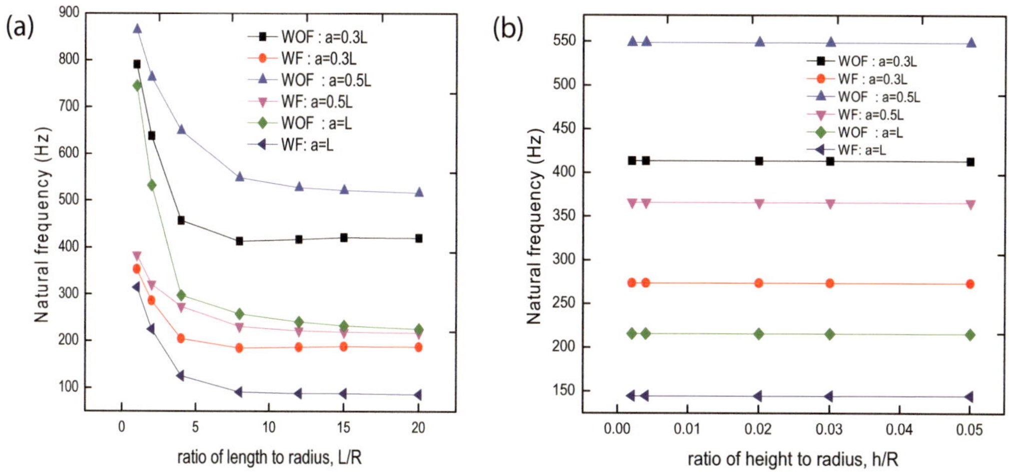

Figure 5. Variations of natural frequencies (Hz) for a WOF and WF cylindrical shell with ring support against (a) L/R (b) h/R ($n = 1$, $m = 1$, $L = 8$ m, $h = 0.004$ m, $R = 1$ m, $E = 2.1 \times 10^{11}$ N/m^2, $\upsilon = 0.3$, $\rho = 7850$ kg/m^3, $\rho_f = 1000$ kg/m^3).

from these figures that when the values of a $(0 < a < 0.5)$ increases then the natural frequencies also increases and $a = 0.5L$, it reaches its peak value but for $0.5L < a < 0.1L$, on increasing the value of a, it begins to decrease and rust itself as bell shape symmetric curve. It is clear seen that when the ring support is positioned at the center of the fluid-filled cylindrical shell, the natural frequency attains its extreme value; it is observed that the natural frequency decreases as the ring supports shifts from center toward right/left side of the fluid-filled cylindrical shell. Thus, when different exponent is adopted, the frequency curve is also symmetrical about the center of fluid-filled cylindrical shell for simply supported symmetric end condition imposed on the both shell ends.

In **Figure 6(a)**, variations of natural frequencies (Hz) with locations of the ring supports are listed with ring supports for WOF and WF. The ring support is composed as $0 \leq a \leq L$ and for the values at $a = 0$ for WOF and WF are 215.429, 140.665 and at $a = L$ the values are 215.429, 146.095 respectively. At $0.4L < a < 0.6L$ means $a = 0.5L$ for WOF and WF have a peak value 548.468, 548.358 but for $a = 0.4L$ the values are 518.609, 496.419 and $a = 0.6L$ are 518.609, 504.140 very closed to each other. In each case the shell frequencies goes up with the position of the ring supports to the highest values at the mid of the shell and then start to lower down to gain their initial values. It is noticed that the fluid addition has made frequency to decrease. From the previous data, the shell frequencies are affected highly as the fluid quantities [11, 31–35] and ring supports are appended [2, 5, 27, 36]. A beam type vibration of CSs crops up when the addition of ring supports are made.

Figure 6(b) and **(c)** display the comparisons of variations of natural frequencies (Hz) with ring supports for WOF and WF for *C-I* and *C-II* respectively. The ring support is composed as $0 \leq a \leq L$ and for volume fraction law, the exponent $p = 0.5$, 1, 15 is adopted, the values at $a = 0$ for WOF and WF are 207.058, 135.199 ($p = 0.5$), 205.346, 134.082 ($p = 1$), 201.012, 131.252 ($p = 15$) and at $a = L$ the values are 207.058, 140.46 ($p = 0.5$), 205.346, 139.255 ($p = 1$), 201.012, 136.316 ($p = 15$) for *C-I* and for *C-II*: 204.048, 133.234 ($p = 0.5$), 205.729, 134.332 ($p = 1$), 210.311, 137.324 ($p = 15$) and at $a = L$ the values are 204.048, 138.375 ($p = 0.5$), 205.729, 139.515 ($p = 1$), 210.311,

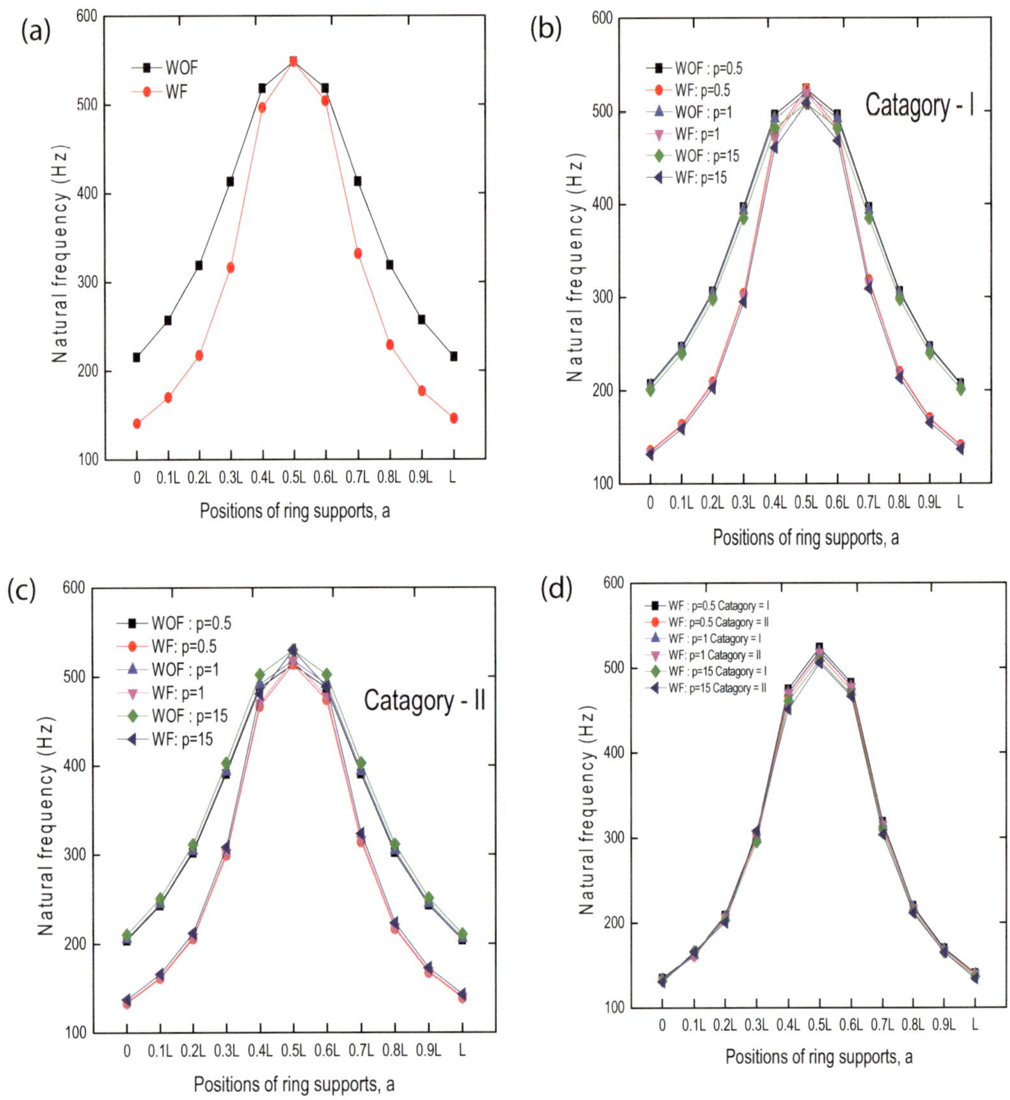

Figure 6. Variation of natural frequencies (Hz) (a) against the positions of the ring supports for WOF and WF cylindrical shell. ($n = 1$, $m = 1$, $L = 8$ m, $h = 0.004$ m, $R = 1$ m, $E = 2.1 \times 10^{11}$ N/m^2, $v = 0.3$, $\rho = 7850$ kg/m^3, $\rho_f = 1000$ kg/m^3) (b) versus the positions of ring supports for WOF and WF cylindrical shell with ring support: Category-I ($n = 1$, $m = 1$, $L = 8$ m, $h = 0.004$ m, $R = 1$ m) (c) Category-II (d) Category-I and II.

142.622 ($p = 15$) respectively. For *C-I*, at $0.4L < a < 0.6L$ means $a = 0.5L$ have a extreme value of frequency 523.924, 523.819 ($p = 0.5$), 519.591, 519.487 ($p = 1$), 508.626, 508.524) ($p = 15$), for both WOF and WF but for $a = 0.4L$ the values of frequencies are 496.188, 474.957 ($p = 0.5$), 492.085, 471.030 ($p = 1$), 481.699, 461.088 ($p = 15$) and $a = 0.6L$ are 496.188, 482.345 ($p = 0.5$), 492.085, 478.356 ($p = 1$), 481.699, 468.260 ($p = 15$) very closed to each other for both WOF and WF. For *C-II*: at $0.4L < a < 0.6L$ means $a = 0.5L$ have a maximum frequency value 513.823, 513.720 ($p = 0.5$), 518.059, 517.955 ($p = 1$), 529.595, 488.154 ($p = 15$) for both WOF and WF but for $a = 0.4L$ the values are 487.212, 466.366, 491.226, 470.208 ($p = 1$), 502.164, 480.678 ($p = 15$) and

$a = 0.6L$ are 487.212, 473.619, 491.226, 477.521 (p = 1) 502.164, 488.154 (p = 15) very closed to each other for both WOF and WF. In both cases, the frequencies first rise, attain their maximum at the mid position and then fall down to original values at the other shell end. There is observed a reduction in frequency values owing to fluid term induction [11, 32–34]. It is concluded that the maximum point and other relative value of *C-II* are bit smaller than that of corresponding value of *C-I*. This conclusion is also shown in **Figure 6(d)** where *C-I* and *C-II* are illustrated in one graph. In **Figure 6(d)** variations of frequencies for two categories with ring supports for fluid-filled for *C-I* and *C-II* are cataloged with the locations of the ring supports. The ring support is composed for fluid-filled as $0 \le a \le L$, for volume fraction law, the exponent p = 0.5, 1, 15 is adopted, the values at $a = 0$ are 135.99, 133.234 (p = 0.5), 134.082, 132.332 (p = 1) 131.252, 130.324 (p = 15) and at $a = L$ for category-I and for category-II, the values are 140.416, 138.375 (p = 0.5), 139.255, 139.515 (p = 1), 136.316, 133.622 (p = 15). For *C-I*, *C-II* at $0.4L < a < 0.6L$ means $a = 0.5$ have a maximum value 513.819, 513.720 (p = 0.5), 519.487, 517.955 (p = 1), 508.524, 505.489 (p = 15) but for $a = 0.4L$ the values are 474.957, 466.366 (p = 0.5), 471.030, 470.208 (p = 1), 461.088, 450.678 (p = 15) and $a = 0.6$ are 482.342, 473.342 (p = 0.5), 478.356, 477.521 (p = 1), 468.260, 466.154 (p = 15) respectively. Here for *C-I* cylindrical shells, frequencies are some bit higher for those of *C-II* ones [32–34]. The effects of fluid-filled cylindrical shell with ring supports are perceived to be very conspicuous in the variation of natural frequencies.

5. Summary

Theoretical vibration analysis of cylindrical shells (CSs) has a significant importance in applied mathematics and mechanics in view of their practical uses. Here the shell problem has been associated with investigation vibrations of cylindrical shells with ring supports. They shells have been supposed to be constructed from functionally graded materials. They materials are advanced and smart for their physical properties. Moreover these shells have been assumed to contain fluid. Here the Galerkin technique is employed to obtain the shell frequency equation. Effect of ring supports on shell vibration is inducted by a polynomial function which has degree equal to the number of ring supports. From the study of results, it is observed that vibration frequencies of cylindrical shells decrease significantly when the fluid loaded terms are appended. However their variations are alike to that behavior which is noticed for the cylindrical shells not containing fluid and attachment of ring supports boost much the vibration frequencies. For functionally graded material cylindrical shells, variations of frequencies with the circumferential wave modes for length-to-radius ratio, height-to-radius ratio for fluid-filled cylindrical shell and also for fluid-filled cylindrical shell with ring supports has been analyzed. It is seen that the influences of ring supports and fluid terms are converse to each other. The ring supports increase the frequencies whereas the fluid loaded terms lower them. However, the increments and decrements in the shell frequency depend upon the order of functionally graded material constituents forming a cylindrical shell. The induction of fluid-filled with ring support on the cylindrical shell has a prominent effect on the natural frequency as compared to the shell frequency without fluid attached with ring support. Different position of ring supports with and without fluid with various exponent law for category-I, II or both are analyzed. It is concluded that in both cases, the frequencies first rise, attain their maximum values at the mid position and then fall down to original values at the other shell end.

Moreover, there is observed a reduction in frequency values owing to fluid term induction. It is also concluded that the maximum point and other relative value of category-II are bit smaller than that of corresponding value of category-I An extension of this analysis procedure can be performed to investigate vibrations of rotating fluid isotropic and functionally graded cylindrical shells with ring supports.

List of symbols

A_{ij}	Extensional stiffness
B_{ij}	Coupling stiffness
D_{ij}	Bending stiffness
E	Young's modulus
h	Shell thickness
L	Shell length
v	Poisson's ratio
ω	Natural angular frequency
$d_{ij}(i,j=1,2,3)$	Shell parameters
q	Acoustic pressure
c	Speed of sound in the fluid
$J_n(k_r r)$	Bessel's function of first kind
c_f	Speeds of the sound in fluid – filled cylindrical shell
Ω	Non-dimensional frequency parameter
E_1, E_2	Young's moduli
ν_1, ν_2	Poisson's ratios.
ρ_1, ρ_2	Mass densities
$E_{fgm}, v_{fgm}, \rho_{fgm}$	Effective material quantities
T	Kelvin scale
C_r	Material properties
V_r	Volume fractions
k	Number of ring supports
R_0, R_1	Outer and inner radii of the shell
h/R	Thickness to radius ratio

http://dx.doi.org/10.5772/intechopen.72172

L/R	Length to radius ratio
n	Circumferential wave number
m	Half- axial wave number
C	Material property
$C_0, C_{-1}, C_1, C_2, C_3$	Coefficients of temperature
p	Volume fraction law or Power law exponent
Q_{ij}	Reduced stiffness
R	Shell radius
T(K)	Temperature function of Kelvin
x	Axial coordinate
Ψ	Circumferential coordinate
z	Radial coordinate or thickness variable
$u(x, \Psi, t)$	Deformation displacement functions in x direction
$v(x, \Psi, t)$	Deformation displacement functions in Ψ direction
$w(x, \Psi, t)$	Deformation displacement functions in z direction
V_{fi}	Volume fraction
ρ	Mass density of shell material
ρ_t	Mass density per unit length
S_{11}, S_{22}, S_{12}	Surface curvatures
k_r	Radial wave number
k_m	Axial wave number
c_L	Speeds of the sound in the empty cylindrical shell
ρ_f	Indicates the density of the fluid density
p_m, q_m and r_m	Vibration amplitudes in the x, Ψ and z directions

Abbreviations

CSs	Cylindrical shells
FGM	Functionally graded material
WF	With fluid

FLT	Fluid loading term
C-I	Category-I
WPA	Wave propagation approach
ODEs	Ordinary differential equations
PDEs	Partial differential equations
FFCS	Fluid-filled cylindrical shell
WOF	Without fluid
CWN	Circumferential wave number
C-II	Category-II
FEM	Finite element method

A. Appendix-I

$$d_{11} = \left(A_{11}I_1 - n^2\frac{A_{66}}{R^2}I_2\right)$$

$$d_{12} = -n\left(\frac{A_{12}+A_{66}}{R} + \frac{B_{12}+2B_{66}}{R^2}\right)I_2$$

$$d_{13} = \left[\frac{A_{12}}{R}(I_6+I_7) - B_{11}(I_8+3I_9) + n^2\frac{B_{12}+2B_{66}}{R^2}(I_6+I_7)\right]$$

$$d_{21} = n\left(\frac{A_{12}+A_{66}}{R} + \frac{B_{12}+2B_{66}}{R^2}\right)I_3$$

$$d_{22} = \left[\left(A_{66} + \frac{3B_{66}}{R} + \frac{4D_{66}}{R^2}\right)I_3 - n^2\left(\frac{A_{22}}{R^2} + \frac{2B_{22}}{R^3} + \frac{D_{22}}{R^4}\right)I_4\right]$$

$$d_{23} = \left[n\left(\frac{A_{22}}{R^2} + \frac{B_{22}}{R^3}\right)I_{10} + n^3\left(\frac{B_{22}}{R^3} + \frac{D_{22}}{R^4}\right)I_{10} - n\left(\frac{B_{12}+2B_{66}}{R} + \frac{D_{12}+4D_{66}}{R^2}\right)(I_{11}+2I_{12})\right]$$

$$d_{31} = \left(-\frac{A_{12}}{R}I_{18} + B_{11}I_{19} - n^2\frac{B_{12}+2B_{66}}{R^2}I_{18}\right)$$

$$d_{23} = \left[n\left(\frac{A_{22}}{R^2} + \frac{B_{22}}{R^3}\right)I_{10} + n^3\left(\frac{B_{22}}{R^3} + \frac{D_{22}}{R^4}\right)I_{10} - n\left(\frac{B_{12}+2B_{66}}{R} + \frac{D_{12}+4D_{66}}{R^2}\right)I_{18}\right]$$

$$d_{33} = \left[-\frac{A_{22}}{R^2}I_3 + \frac{2B_{12}}{R}(I_{14}+2I_{15}) - 2n^2\frac{B_{22}}{R^3}I_{13} - D_{11}(I_{16}+4I_{17}) + 2n^2\frac{D_{12}+2D_{66}}{R^2}(I_{14}+2I_{15}) - \frac{D_{22}}{R^4}I_{13}\right]$$

where

$I_1 = \int_0^L \frac{d^3\varphi}{dx^3}\frac{d\varphi}{dx}dx$	$I_2 = \int_0^L \frac{d\varphi}{dx}\frac{d\varphi}{dx}dx$	$I_3 = \int_0^L \frac{d^2\varphi}{dx^2}\varphi(x)dx$
$I_4 = \int_0^L \varphi(x)\varphi(x)dx$	$I_5 = \int_0^L \frac{d^4\varphi}{dx^4}\varphi(x)dx$	$I_6 = \int_0^L (x-a)\frac{d\varphi}{dx}\frac{d\varphi}{dx}dx$
$I_7 = \int_0^L \varphi(x)\frac{d\varphi}{dx}dx$	$I_8 = \int_0^L (x-a)\frac{d^3\varphi}{dx^3}\frac{d\varphi}{dx}dx$	$I_9 = \int_0^L \frac{d^2\varphi}{dx^2}\frac{d\varphi}{dx}dx$
$I_{10} = \int_0^L (x-a)\varphi(x)\varphi(x)dx$	$I_{11} = \int_0^L \frac{d^2\varphi}{dx^2}(x-a)\varphi(x)dx$	$I_{12} = I_7$
$I_{13} = \int_0^L \varphi^2(x)(x-a)^2dx$	$I_{14} = \int_0^L \frac{d^2\varphi}{dx^2}\varphi(x)(x-a)^2dx$	$I_{15} = \int_0^L \frac{d\varphi}{dx}\varphi(x)(x-a)dx$
$I_{16} = \int_0^L \frac{d^4\varphi}{dx^4}\varphi(x)(x-a)^2dx$	$I_{17} = \int_0^L \frac{d^3\varphi}{dx^3}\varphi(x)(x-a)dx$	$I_{18} = \int_0^L \frac{d^2\varphi}{dx^2}\varphi(x)(x-a)dx$
$I_{19} = \int_0^L \frac{d^4\varphi}{dx^4}\varphi(x)(x-a)dx$		

Author details

Muzamal Hussain[1], Aamir Shahzad[2,3]*, Muhammad Nawaz Naeem[1] and Maogang He[3]

*Address all correspondence to: aamirshahzad_8@hotmail.com

1 Department of Mathematics, Government College University Faisalabad (GCUF), Faisalabad, Pakistan

2 Molecular Modeling and Simulation Laboratory, Department of Physics, Government College University Faisalabad (GCUF), Faisalabad, Pakistan

3 Key Laboratory of Thermo-Fluid Science and Engineering, Ministry of Education (MOE), Xi'an Jiaotong University, Xi'an, P. R. China

References

[1] Greif R, Chung H. Vibrations of constrained cylindrical shells. AIAA Journal. 1975;**13**(9):1190

[2] Loy CT, Lam KY, Shu C. Analysis of cylindrical shells using generalized differential quadrature method. Shock and Vibrations. 1997;**4**:193-198

[3] Loy CT, Lam KY, Reddy JN. Vibration of functionally graded cylindrical shells. International Journal of Mechanical Sciences. 1999;**41**:309-324

[4] Zhang XM, Liu GR, Lam KY. Vibration analysis of thin cylindrical shells using wave propagation approach. Journal of Sound and Vibration. 2001a;**239**(3):397-403

[5] Najafizadeh MM, Isvandzibaei MR. Vibration of functionally graded cylindrical shells based on higher order shear deformation plate theory with ring support. Acta Mechanica. 2007;**191**(1–2):75-91

[6] Rayliegh JWS. Theory of Sound. London: Macmillan; 1884

[7] Love AEH. On the small free vibrations and deformation of thin elastic shell. Philosophical Transactions. Royal Society of London. 1888;**A179**:491-549

[8] Arnold RN, Warburton GB. The flexural vibrations of thin cylinders. Proceedings of the Institution of Mechanical Engineers A. 1953;**167**:62-80

[9] Chung H, Turula P, Mulcahy TM, Jendrzejczyk JA. Analysis of cylindrical shell vibrating in a cylindrical fluid region. Nuclear Engineering and Design. 1981;**63**(1):109-1012

[10] Goncalves PB, Batista RC. Frequency response of cylindrical shells partially submerged or filled with liquid. Journal of Sound and Vibration. 1987;**113**(1):59-70

[11] Goncalves PB, da Silva Frederico MA, del Prado Zenon JGN. Transient stability of empty and fluid-filled cylindrical shells. J. of the Braz. Soc. of Mech. Sci. & Eng. 2006;**XXVIII**(3/331): 1-8

[12] Gasser LFF. Free vibrations on thin cylindrical shells containing liquid [M.S. thesis]. Rio de Janeiro: Federal Univ. of Rio de Janeiro, peccoppe-ufrj; 1987 (in Portuguese)

[13] Sharma CB, Johns DJ. Vibrations characteristics of clamped-free and clamped-ring-stiffened circular cylindrical shells. Journal of Sound and Vibration. 1971;**14**:459-474

[14] Xi ZC, Yam LH, Leung TP. Free vibration of a partially fluid-filled cross-ply laminated composite circular cylindrical shells. The Journal of the Acoustical Society of America. 1997;**101**(2):909-917

[15] Zhang XM, Liu GR, Lam KY. Coupled vibration of fluid-filled cylindrical shells using the wave propagation approach. Applied Acoustics. 2001b;**62**:229-243

[16] Xiang Y, Ma YF, Kitipornchal S, Lim CW, Lau CWH. Exact solutions for vibration of cylindrical shells with intermediate ring supports. International Journal of Mechanical Sciences. 2002;**44**:1907-1924

[17] Zhao X, Liew KM, Ng TY. Vibrations of rotating cross-ply laminated circular cylindrical shells with strings and ring stiffeners. International Journal of Solids and Structures. 2002;**39**:529-545

[18] Xiang Y, Wang CM, Lim CW, Kitipornchai S. Buckling of intermediate ring supported cylindrical shells under axial compression. Thin-Walled Structures. 2005;**43**(3):427-443

[19] Isvandzibaei MR, Awasare PJ. Effects edge and free-free boundary conditions for analysis, free vibration of functionally graded cylindrical shell with ring based on third order shear deformation theory using Hamilton's principle. World Academy of Science, Engineering and Technology. 2010;**61**:219-225

[20] Lee HL, Chang WJ. Vibration analysis of fluid-conveying double-walled carbon nanotubes based on nonlocal elastic theory. Journal of Physics: Condensed Matter. 2009;**21**:115302, 1-5

[21] Silva FMA, Goncalves PB, Del Prado ZJGN. Nonlinear vibrations of axially loaded cylindrical shells partially filled with fluid. In: Proceedings of DINCON'10 9th Brazilian Conference on Dynamics, Control and their Applications, June 07–11; 2010. pp. 643-663

[22] Shah AG, Mahmood T, Naeem MN, Arshad SH. Characteristics of fluid-filled cylindrical shells based on elastic foundations. Acta Mechanica. 2011;**216**:17-28

[23] Xiong L, Li TY, Zhu X, Zhu XM. Free vibration analysis of fluid-filled elliptical cylindrical shells. Applied Mechanics and Materials. 2013;**437**:102-109

[24] Hasheminejad SM, Alaei-Varnosfadrani M. Active radiation control of a submerged piezocomposite hollow sphere. Journal of Intelligent Material System and Structure. 2015;**26**:2073-2091

[25] Kim Y. Effect of partial elastic foundation on free vibration of fluid-filled functionally graded cylindrical shells. Acta Mechanica Sinica. 2015;**31**:920

[26] Izyan N, Viswaanathan MD, Aziz KK, Prabaker K. Free vibration of layered cylindrical shell filled with fluid. Applied Mathematics and Mechanics (English Edition). 2016;**37**:803

[27] Soutis C, Shahid HA, Naeem MN. Influence of ring support on free vibration of sandwich functionally graded cylindrical shell with middle layer of isotropic material. Journal of Engineering Research. 2016;**4**(1):159-186

[28] Amabili M, Pellicano F, Paidoussis MP. Nonlinear vibrations of simply supported, circular cylindrical shells, coupled to quiescent fluid. Journal of Fluids and Structure. 1998; **12**(7):883-918

[29] Goncalves PB, Batista. Non-linear vibration analysis of fluid-filled cylindrical shells. Journal Sound and Vibration. 1988;**127**(1):133-143

[30] Ansari R, Rahimi GH, Hemmatnezhada M. Vibration of functionally graded cylindrical shells with ring support. Scientia Iranica B. 2011;**18**(6):1313-1320

[31] Gonacalves PB, Del Prado ZJGN. Low-dimensional Galerkin models for nonlinear and instability analysis of cylindrical shell. Nonlinear Dynamics. 2005;**41**(1):129-145

[32] Weiqiu C, Ding HJ, Guo YM, Yang QD. Free vibrations of fluid-filled orthotropic cylin-25 drical shells. Journal of Engineering Mechanics. 1997;**123**(11):1130

[33] Shah SA. Axially symmetric vibrations of fluid-filled poroelastic circular cylindrical shells. Journal of Sound and Vibration. 2008;**318**:389-405

[34] Pellicano F, Amabili M. Stability and vibration of empty and fluid-filled cylindrical shells under static and period axial loads. International Journal of Solids and Structures. 2003; **40**(13–14):3229-3251

[35] Warburton GB. Vibration of thin cylindrical shells. Journal of Mechanical Engineering Science. 1965;**7**:399-407

[36] Zhang L, Xiang Y. Vibration of open circular cylindrical shells with intermediate ring supports. International Journal of Solids and Structures. 2006;**43**:3705-3722

[37] Liu Y, Chu F. Nonlinear vibrations of rotating thin circular cylindrical shell. Nonlinear Dynamics. 2012;**67**:1467-1479

[38] Toulokian YS. Thermophysical Properties of High Temperature Solid Materials. New York: Macmillan; 1967

Chapter 15

CFD Simulations of Crude Oil Fouling on Heat Transfer Surfaces

Ramasamy Marappa Gounder and Sampath Emani

Additional information is available at the end of the chapter

http://dx.doi.org/10.5772/intechopen.71886

Abstract

Advancements in the computational techniques have led to the development of various numerical models and methods to predict the occurrence of crude oil fouling in heat exchangers. Computational fluid dynamics has been employed in the field of crude oil fouling research in the recent past, which led to the concept of investigating the effects of various operating conditions on deposit formations on heat transfer surfaces. Various processes associated with crude oil fouling, such as asphaltenes precipitation and chemical reactions, have been studied through CFD simulations. This chapter provides state-of-the-art review on various CFD approaches and describes the discrete-phase CFD modeling of crude oil fouling through asphaltenes deposition on heat transfer surfaces.

Keywords: crude oil, fouling, discrete phase, CFD, heat transfer

1. Introduction

Crude oil is one of the major fossil fuels/energy resources in today's world. Crude oil consists of a complex mixture of hydrocarbons with various molecular weights which are distilled into various fractions in refineries. The crude oil is normally preheated by recovering heat in a battery of preheat exchangers from the separated fractions and pump-around flows from crude distillation unit. Efficient recovery of heat from the product streams is very essential to minimize the specific energy requirement of processing the crude oil as nearly 6% of the total energy content of each barrel of crude oil is used in the refinery itself.

The deposition of unwanted materials on heat transfer surfaces is termed as fouling. The heat exchangers in the crude preheat trains are highly prone to fouling due to the presence of solid particles and components that precipitate as solid particles upon heating the crude oils. Fouling in the crude preheat train leads to several consequences in the refineries. Efficient recovery of heat in the heat exchangers and the delicate balance of heat integration suffer a major blow due to the fouling in heat exchangers. The foulant deposits, with much lower thermal conductivities than that of the tube metal, reduce the heat transfer coefficients and eventually result in decreased energy recovery. When the extent of fouling reaches the limits of operation either in the furnace that provides the additional heat necessary or in the pumping capacity due to the increased pressure drops, a plant shutdown becomes necessary for cleaning the heat exchangers and restoring their heat transfer efficiencies. Furthermore, crude oil fouling has also a high impact on the environment. It has been observed that about 2.5% of the worldwide environmental pollution emissions are caused due to fouling [1]. Crude oil fouling involves production losses during planned and unplanned shutdowns for cleaning and high costs for cleaning and associated activities. The total cost of fouling in various refineries has been estimated to be approximately $1.5 billion per year globally [2].

Fouling process is a physicochemical phenomenon and its mechanisms have been classified into the following five types: particulate (sedimentation) fouling; chemical reaction fouling; corrosion fouling; crystallization fouling; and biological fouling. Particulate fouling is described as the deposition of dirt, clay, or rust suspended in the fluid onto the heat transfer surface [3]. The deposition resulting from one or more chemical reactions between the components contained in the fluid is termed as chemical reaction fouling [4, 5]. When the deposition is the result of a chemical reaction that involves a component in the fluid and the metal surface, it is called as corrosion fouling [6]. Corrosion fouling usually results in a rough surface and creates new sites for fouling. The precipitation of dissolved salts in the saturated solutions due to their solubility changes with temperature and deposition on the heat transfer surfaces is known as crystallization fouling [6]. Biological fouling is the formation of organic films consisting of microorganisms that promote attachment of microorganisms, such as mussels, algae, etc., [7]. Crude oil fouling in refineries can occur by any of the mechanisms described above except the biological fouling. Irrespective of the fouling mechanism, the last steps of the fouling process, in general, are the transportation and/or deposition of solid particles on the heat transfer surfaces.

The crude oil fouling mitigation techniques, generally in practice, are frequent cleaning of heat exchangers, use of chemical additives, i.e., anti-foulants, operation under threshold fouling conditions and use of physical methods such as modified tube bundles with helical baffles, coated tubes, twisted tubes, and tube inserts. Operations at or under the threshold fouling conditions will ensure zero or minimum fouling. Threshold fouling conditions are normally specified by operating regimes of high flow velocities and low film temperatures. The uncertainties involved in establishing the effectiveness of fouling mitigation techniques in refineries have led to the development of various fouling simulation and predictive models.

Various empirical, semi-empirical, and fundamental fouling models have been proposed to study the crude oil fouling phenomenon [8–12]. Most of the fouling models in literature predict fouling rates based on the operating conditions and fluid properties and the models do not include the mathematical descriptions of fluid flow and heat transfer processes. Computational fluid dynamics, on the other hand, provides an opportunity to model fluid flow and heat transfer behaviors along with the fouling phenomenon simultaneously. Even though, the physical and chemical phenomena involved in fouling processes are highly complex, the overall understanding of the fouling behavior and its mechanisms were enhanced from the past few decades with various CFD models [13–16].

In general, shell and tube heat exchanger design assumes that fluid flow through the bundle of tubes is evenly distributed. Practical experience has shown that this is not always true and the consequences of maldistribution in terms of poor performance and increased fouling are often severe [17]. Uneven distribution of fluid flow means areas of low velocity and vortex formation within the tube bundle leading to areas of ineffective heat transfer and increased risk of tube side fouling. Computational fluid dynamics has not often been used to investigate the crude oil fouling phenomena in shell and tube heat exchangers. Studies on shell-side crude oil fouling in shell and tube heat exchangers have been reported in literature, which neglected the tube side fluid flow [18–20]. An arbitrary fixed linear temperature profile on the tube wall was assumed to investigate the shell side fouling which neglects the thermal interactions between tube and shell-side fluids. These studies have demonstrated that fouling is more prone to happen near the inlet and baffle openings due to low velocity zones.

In this chapter, an attempt has been made to review the various CFD models for predicting the crude oil fouling phenomena. Section 2 presents the fouling studies using CFD modeling and effects of operating conditions on fouling. Section 3 presents the CFD simulations of asphaltenes deposition in a heat exchanger tube through Discrete Phase Model (DPM). A summary of present trend in employing CFD to crude oil fouling and future developments will be discussed in Section 4.

2. Computational fluid dynamics and fouling modeling

2.1. Introduction to CFD

Computational fluid dynamics is one of the branches of fluid dynamics that uses numerical methods and algorithms to solve and analyze various fluid flow problems [21]. It gives an insight into flow patterns that are difficult, expensive, or impossible to study using experimental techniques. Its applications in a wide variety of disciplines in process industries have led to a reduction in the need for physical experimentations.

Being time-dependent in nature, fouling is a process that should be monitored continuously in time. As such, fouling experiments are time-consuming and often difficult to perform. In view of the above, CFD has been used as one of the predominant approaches to investigate crude oil fouling phenomena. The crude oil fouling process involves momentum transfer, mass transfer, heat transfer, flow turbulence, and chemical reactions. Detailed CFD models describing the fouling processes are often very complex to solve numerically and requires simplifications for reducing the computational load. The fluid-flow is generally governed by incompressible Navier-Stokes equations for mass, momentum and energy as given in Eqs. (1)–(3).

Continuity equation:

$$\frac{\partial \rho}{\partial t} + \nabla.(\overline{\rho v}) = 0 \tag{1}$$

Momentum equation:

$$\frac{\partial(\overline{\rho v})}{\partial t} + \nabla.(\overline{\rho v v}) = -\nabla p + \nabla.(\overline{\tau}) + \rho\overline{g} \tag{2}$$

Energy equation:

$$\frac{\partial(\rho C_P T)}{\partial t} + \nabla.\left(\rho C_P\ \vec{v}\ T\right) = \nabla.(k\Delta T) + H \tag{3}$$

Fouling mechanisms are generally associated with turbulent flows, mainly due to the higher fluid velocities and complex geometry of heat exchangers. The turbulent flow condition is the chaotic and random state of fluid motion, associated with disturbances in the fluid streamlines of laminar flows [22]. Turbulent flow plays a significant role in various fluid dynamic applications and its modeling has undergone intensive research. The simulation of turbulent flow using Navier-Stokes equations is possible through direct numerical simulations (DNS) model, which requires a huge amount of computational time and memory. Due to the limitations in the computational capabilities, the basic conservative equations such as mass, momentum and energy are unable to resolve the fluid motion associated with turbulent flow regimes [23]. Therefore, most of the cases involving turbulent flows are solved through Reynolds-averaged Navier Stokes (RANS) equations which are developed by adapting suitable time-averaging techniques on Navier-Stokes equations. Several turbulence models such as *k*-ε, *k*-ω, Reynolds Stress Model (RSM), etc., are available within the RANS equations to approximate the influence of turbulent fluctuations in the flow domain. In *k*-ε turbulence model, the energy in the turbulence is computed from the turbulent kinetic energy (*k*) and the rate of dissipation of the turbulent kinetic energy is computed from the turbulent dissipation (ε). The *k*-ω turbulence model predicts turbulence with turbulence kinetic energy (*k*) with a specific rate of dissipation (ω). Reynolds Stress Model is a higher-level turbulence model which is considered for predicting the complex interactions in the turbulence flow fields. The most common turbulence model considered in the field of crude oil fouling is *k*-ε model [13, 24–28], which assumes that the turbulence is isotropic and requires less computational time for simulation.

The turbulent kinetic energy, *k* is described by:

$$\frac{\partial k}{\partial t} + (v_i \cdot \nabla)k - \nabla \cdot \left(\frac{\mu_t}{\sigma_k}\nabla \cdot k\right) = P^k - \varepsilon + S_k \tag{4}$$

and dissipation rate, ε (epsilon) is given by:

$$\frac{\partial \varepsilon}{\partial t} + (v_i \cdot \nabla)\varepsilon - \nabla \cdot \left(\frac{\mu_t}{\sigma_\varepsilon}\nabla\varepsilon\right) = \frac{\varepsilon}{k}\left(C_1 P^k - C_2\varepsilon\right) + S_\varepsilon \tag{5}$$

The *k*-ω turbulence model was also considered in a few crude oil fouling CFD studies [14, 16, 29]. It is found to be numerically stable and is reported to achieve precise simulation results in comparison with other models [16, 30].

Specific dissipation rate, ω (omega) used in the k-ω turbulence model is given by:

$$(\overline{v}.\nabla)\omega = \nabla \cdot \left[\left(\mu + \mu_T \sigma_\omega \right) \nabla \omega \right] + \alpha \frac{\omega}{k} P_k - \beta_0 \omega^2 \tag{6}$$

2.2. Fouling modeling

Fouling can occur either through a series of reactions and/or without any reactions. The deposition process associated with fouling is studied through CFD simulations by two routes, viz.: (i) asphaltenes deposition fouling and (ii) chemical reaction fouling [13, 31, 32].

2.2.1. Asphaltenes deposition fouling

Asphaltenes constituents are categorized as the most polar and highest molecular weight fraction of petroleum [26, 33] and are considered as the heaviest component in the crude oil [34]. Asphaltenes tend to precipitate and deposit on heat transfer surfaces [35] under changes in pressure and temperature conditions. The probability of the precipitated asphaltene particles ending up as foulant deposits on the heat transfer surface depends on various forces acting on the particles such as inertial, gravity, drag, Saffman lift, buoyancy, thermophoretic, etc. Particles in high fluid velocity regions have higher inertial forces and the probabilities of particles reaching the heat transfer surface and rebound or splash are high and, therefore, cause less fouling. At high temperature gradients near the surface, the thermophoretic forces predominate the other forces acting on the particles and favor the particles to stick to the surface as foulant particles.

Several CFD models that capture some or all the above forces were developed to understand the fouling phenomena associated with asphaltene particles in the crude oil [13, 15, 16, 29, 31, 32, 36–38]. The CFD models employed were classified into Eulerian-Eulerian and Eulerian-Lagrangian models based on how the solids phase is treated. The Eulerian-Eulerian model treats the particles as a continuum and applies the governing equations in a similar approach as that for the fluid phase [39], while the Eulerian-Lagrangian method treats the particles as a discrete phase and the pathway of individual particles are tracked [39, 40].

2.2.1.1. Eulerian-Eulerian model

Multiphase fluids are modeled in CFD by three different Eulerian-Eulerian multiphase models, viz.: (i) Volume-of-Fluid (VOF) model, (ii) mixture model, and (iii) Eulerian model. Volume-of-Fluid model is desirable for the studies in which the interface between two or more immiscible fluids is of interest [26]. Mixture model is mostly considered for simulating the particle-laden flows, bubbly flow regimes, etc. The basic assumption in the mixture model is that all the phases share the same turbulence field [41]. Eulerian model is the most complex model compared with VoF and mixture models and is used for simulating bubble columns, particle suspension and fluidized beds.

In Eulerian-Eulerian models, the components of the crude oils are categorized into two phases, viz.: (i) non-asphaltenes and (ii) asphaltenes. The non-asphaltenes phase of the crude oil is assumed as the primary phase, while the asphaltenes are considered as the secondary phase

[13, 32]. In order to understand the fluid flow behavior and asphaltenes deposition in the system, one of the Eulerian-Eulerian multiphase models can be chosen. Volume-of-Fluid multiphase model is highly used for predicting the asphaltenes deposition on the heat transfer surfaces [13, 26, 31]. The deposition profile of asphaltenes is predicted from the volume fraction contours. The interface tracking between the phases is governed by the solution of a continuity equation for the volume fraction of multiphases. For q^{th} phase, interface tracking is computed as:

$$\frac{\partial}{\partial t}(\rho \Upsilon_i) + \nabla \cdot (\rho \Upsilon_i \overline{v}) = -\nabla \cdot \overline{j_i} + R_i + S_i \tag{7}$$

2.2.1.2. Eulerian-Lagrangian approach

The Eulerian-Lagrangian model treats the asphaltene particles as a discrete phase, in which, the model tracks the trajectory of the individual particles. The crude oil, which is the primary phase, is considered as a continuum on which the governing equations are computed. Asphaltene particles present in the crude oil are partly in the colloidal form and partly in dissolved form. The asphaltene particles precipitated from the crude oil might be carried forward with the flow without causing any fouling [42] while some of the asphaltene particles may get deposited on heat transfer surface due to various attractive/repulsive forces [43]. Several forces, such as gravity, drag, Saffman lift, buoyancy, Brownian diffusion, and thermophoretic, act on the asphaltene particles [37].

The trajectory of the asphaltene particles inside the heat exchanger tube is calculated by:

$$\frac{dv_p}{dt} = F_D\left(v - v_p\right) + \frac{g_i\left(\rho_p - \rho\right)}{\rho_p} + F_i \tag{8}$$

The particles drag force is estimated as:

$$F_D = \frac{18\mu}{\rho_p d_p^2} \frac{C_D \mathrm{Re}}{24} \tag{9}$$

where

$$C_D = \frac{24}{\mathrm{Re}}\left(1 + b_1 \mathrm{Re}^{b_2}\right) + \frac{b^3 \mathrm{Re}}{b_4 + \mathrm{Re}} \tag{10}$$

$$\mathrm{Re} = \frac{\rho d_p \left|v_p - v\right|}{\mu} \tag{11}$$

The thermophoretic force is computed by [44]:

$$F_{th} = -D_{T,p} \frac{1}{m_p T} \frac{\partial T}{\partial x} \tag{12}$$

where the thermophoretic force coefficient, $D_{T,p}$ is given by:

$$D_{T,p} = \frac{\mu^2 C_s\left(\left(\frac{k}{k_p}\right) + C_t Kn\right)}{\rho(1 + 3C_m Kn)\left(1 + 2\left(\frac{k}{k_p}\right) + 2C_t Kn\right)} \tag{13}$$

The magnitude of the shear-induced lift force on particles is computed using Saffman equation [45]:

$$\vec{F} = \frac{2Kv^{1/2}\rho d_{ij}}{\rho_p d_p (d_{lk} d_{kl})^{1/4}}\left(\vec{v} - \vec{v}_p\right) \tag{14}$$

2.2.2. Chemical reaction fouling

Chemical reaction fouling has been identified as the main cause of crude oil fouling on the heat transfer surfaces. A highly complex chemical kinetic scheme is involved in chemical reaction fouling route, in which, the intermediate species are formed via various elementary reactions. Various CFD studies investigated the coke formation due to the chemical reactions in the bulk and/or surface through species transport model [13, 14, 16, 25, 26, 46]. The components of crude oil such as, asphaltenes, salt, resins, etc., were added as species to bulk flow (crude oil). The basic assumption considered in the current chemical reaction models is that the chemical reaction fouling route involves a two-step reaction process [32], namely, initial generation of soluble precursors and formation of insoluble foulant particles, as

$$\underset{\text{(Soluble)}}{\text{Reactants}} \xrightarrow{r_1} \underset{\text{(Sparingly soluble)}}{\text{Precursor}} \xrightarrow{r_2} \underset{\text{(Insoluble)}}{\text{Foulant}}$$

where r_1 and r_2 are the reaction rates given by:

$$r_1 = k_1 c_{r,1}^m c_{r,2}^n \tag{15}$$

$$r_2 = k_2 c_p^l \tag{16}$$

and k_1 and k_2 are the reaction rate constants specified by the Arrhenius equation:

$$k_i = A\exp\left(\frac{-E}{RT}\right) \tag{17}$$

The CFD methodology involved in predicting the foulant mass through chemical reaction fouling route involves a three-step process. Initially, crude oil fluid flow without the foulant species is simulated in the heat exchanger. Subsequently, the foulant species are introduced in the fully developed fluid flow. The reactions of the species are defined on the tube surface to observe the formation of fouling layer. Petroleum is considered as the bulk fluid and the coke content is specified at the inlet as zero [13, 14].

2.3. Effect of operating conditions

2.3.1. *Flow velocity*

The flow velocity has a high significance on the deposition rate of fouling precursors from the crude oil. Asphaltene particles suspended from the crude oil will deposit on the heat transfer surface under low-velocity conditions. An increase in the flow velocity is expected to promote the dislodging of asphaltene particles deposited on the surface through increased shear stress [13, 16]. The inertial forces on the particles in high fluid velocity regions will be high. Thus, the probabilities of particles reaching the heat transfer surface and causing rebound or splash events are high and, therefore, cause less fouling. The irregular flow profiles, reverse flow paths, and low-velocity regions in the domain can be visualized through CFD study. Various CFD studies reported that fouling rate reduces with an increase in flow velocity [16, 29, 32]. The mass depositions of asphaltenes and coke on the heat transfer surface were observed to reduce gradually with increase in the Reynolds number [24, 25, 32]. Fouling resistance on the heat transfer surface was predicted at different flow velocities ranging from 0.05 to 0.2 m/s and observed that at higher velocities the fouling resistance decreases [47].

2.3.2. *Temperature difference between the bulk-fluid and wall*

Crude oil fouling is highly dependent on the temperature difference, ΔT, between the bulk-fluid and wall. Various CFD studies reported that with the decrease in temperature difference, the deposit formation reduces [13, 16, 27]. The reason behind the reduced deposition is because of the thermophoretic effect acting on the fouling precursors. Even though, a few experimental studies observed an increased deposit formation with a decrease in temperature difference, CFD studies have always shown a decrease in the crude oil fouling with lower temperature difference between the bulk-fluid and the wall. The effect of bulk temperature at constant wall temperature on coke deposition in a horizontal tube has been studied and observed that the coke deposition on the heat transfer surfaces decreases with an increase in the bulk temperature [24].

Computational fluid dynamics studies offered cost-effective investigations for understanding the crude oil fouling phenomena of crude oils on the heat transfer surfaces. The effects of operating conditions such as flow velocity, temperature difference, etc., have received relatively high attention in the literature. The susceptible locations of deposit formations and the transportation behavior of asphaltene particles in the heat exchanger have received less attention which led to the lack of understanding of non-uniform fouling in the heat exchangers.

3. CFD modeling of asphaltenes deposition in a heat exchanger tube

The behavior of the asphaltene particles is studied in a three-dimensional heat exchanger tube, the geometry, and mesh of which are shown in **Figure 1**. The heat exchanger tube CFD model is developed with a tube length and diameter of 500 and 25 mm, respectively. The asphaltene

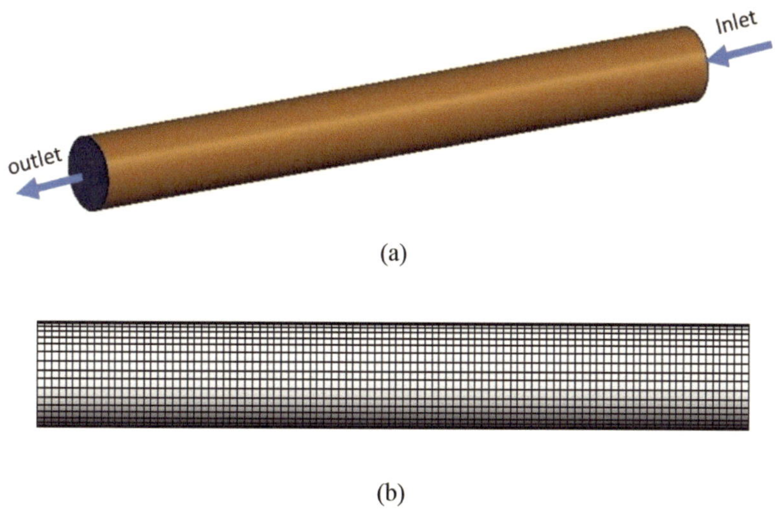

Figure 1: Heat exchanger tube (a) Geometry and (b) grid.

particles' behavior in the heat exchanger tube is studied through a Lagrangian-based DPM mathematical tool available in the commercial CFD software ANSYS FLUENT™ [48]. Discrete phase models are highly used in calculating the trajectories and velocities of particles inside the domain. The effects of various particle sizes on the particle flow paths and the effects of several attractive and repulsive forces on the particles can be predicted through DPM. The particles are considered as discrete phase which interacts with the primary phase. Over the past decades, DPM has been widely used in simulating dilute particle flows, particle deposition analysis, particle dispersion analysis, and vaporization and boiling of particles [49–52]. The influence of the particles on the primary phase is evaluated by momentum exchange fields which are based on the increase or decrease in the particle momentum. These models are generally applicable in situations where the particle volume fraction is less than 12%. Based on the primary phase, the individual particles are traced through various forces acting on it. The particle distribution profiles obtained through DPM and Eulerian-Eulerian simulations are compared and observed that, the DPM simulations provides a better understanding than the Eulerian approach [39].

The described governing equations (Eqs. (1)–(5)) and the appropriate forces (Eqs. (8)–(14)) are considered on the asphaltene particles. Discrete phase-CFD simulation requires a high computational power to expound the particles behavior. Therefore, simulations were performed by activating the enhanced wall treatment effects with k-ε turbulence model. The domain is discretized with 0.15 million quadrilateral cells and mesh independence test was performed to validate the consistency and accuracy of the simulation results.

Crude oil has been described as the bulk fluid and asphaltenes are described as discrete phase particles. As asphaltenes have the tendency to aggregate in an irreversible fashion with different particle diameters, the transportation of asphaltenes is modeled with various particles sizes. The asphaltene particles are injected from inlet surface in the heat exchanger. The properties of the asphaltene particles, boundaries, and operating conditions are given in **Table 1**. The correlations of crude oil properties used in this study are as follows:

Density:

$$\rho = 998.2 \times \left[\frac{((T_b \times 0.154) - 519.11)^{0.5}}{1070.19}\right] \tag{18}$$

Specific heat:

$$C_p = 3980.5 \times [0.4372 + (T_b \times 0.001011)] \tag{19}$$

Thermal conductivity:

$$k = 0.145 - 0.0001T_b \tag{20}$$

In the present simulation, discrete phase particle tracking method has been considered with forces such as gravity, drag, Saffman lift, thermophoretic, and stochastic collision acting on the particles. Initially, a dynamic simulation was performed without activation of the discrete phase models. Once the fully developed flow is observed in the domain, DPM was activated to study the stick, rebound, and splash events of the asphaltene particles as shown in **Figure 2**.

Once the heat exchanger geometry and mesh are developed, the operating and boundary conditions are specified for mesh dependence study. The chosen mesh was used to perform the non-asphaltenes flow simulation with crude oil as medium. The simulation is iterated till the desired convergence with an error tolerance of 1×10^{-6} is achieved. Then, the asphaltene

Description	Value
Density	1200 kg·m^{-3}
Thermal conductivity	0.756 W·m^{-1}·K^{-1}
Heat capacity	1500 J·kg^{-1}·K^{-1}
Particle diameter	0.005–0.1 mm
Inlet	Velocity inlet
Wall	Wall with no-slip condition
Outlet	Outflow
Flow velocity	0.5–1.5 m/s
Bulk temperature	333 K
Wall temperature	375 K

Table 1. Asphaltene particles' properties, boundaries, and operating conditions.

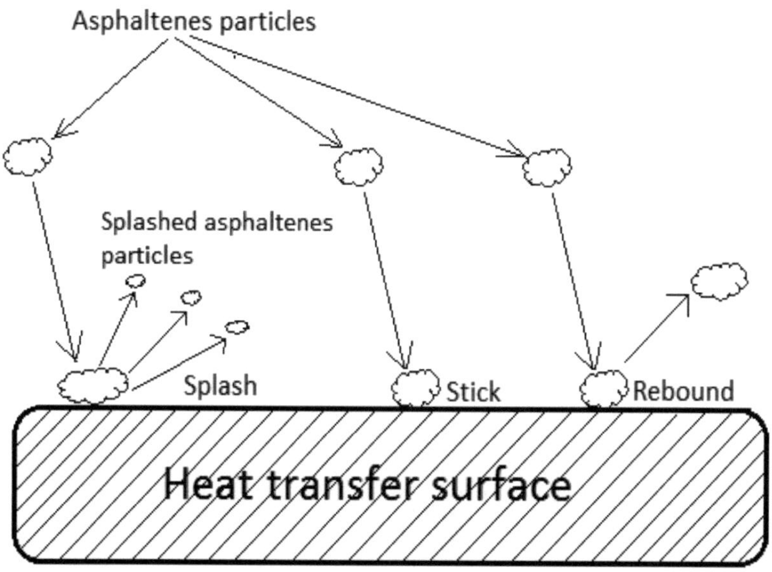

Figure 2. Particle events on the heat transfer surface.

particles are injected into the domain from inlet and their trajectories are investigated with the DPM. As asphaltene particles are physically adhered to the heat transfer surface, a particle based Lagrangian frame approach is employed to understand the transportation and adhesion behavior of asphaltene particles in the heat exchanger. The simulation methodology followed in this study is shown in flow chart in **Figure 3**.

The CFD simulations investigated the transportation and adhesion behavior of asphaltene particles in the heat exchanger tube. The stick, rebound and splash behavior of the asphaltene particles were studied from the discrete phase CFD simulations. From the results obtained, asphaltenes mass deposition and deposition film thickness are estimated, which are shown in **Figures 4–6**.

The foulant layer spreading of deposited asphaltene particles is observed from **Figure 4**. Due to the force of gravity, asphaltene particles are deposited on the bottom portion of the tube. **Figures 5** and **6** shows the graphical representation of asphaltenes mass deposition and deposition film thickness at various crude oil velocities. It is observed that, at low fluid velocity conditions, asphaltene particles will have a higher mass deposition and deposition film thickness compared with the high fluid velocity conditions.

A three-dimensional CFD study was performed to predict the asphaltenes mass deposition from crude oil on the heat transfer surface. From the results obtained, fluid velocity is observed to have a high impact on mitigation of fouling. The discrete phase CFD simulation results clearly forecasts the asphaltene particles deposition locations in the tube, deposition mass, and

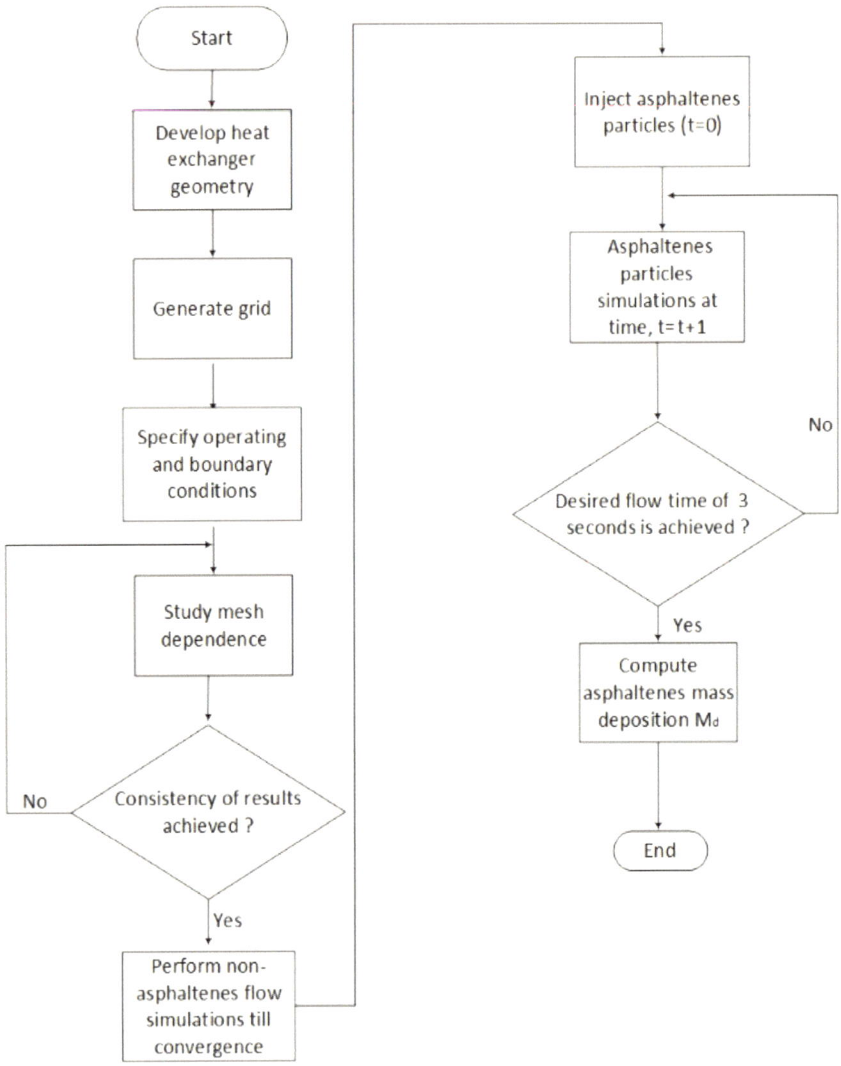

Figure 3. Flow chart—simulation methodology.

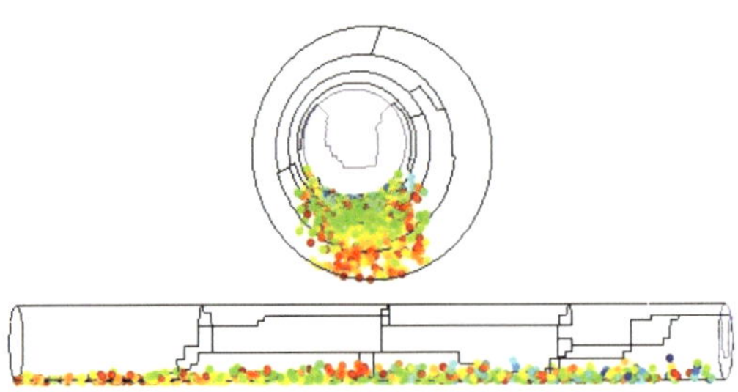

Figure 4. Asphaltene particles' deposition.

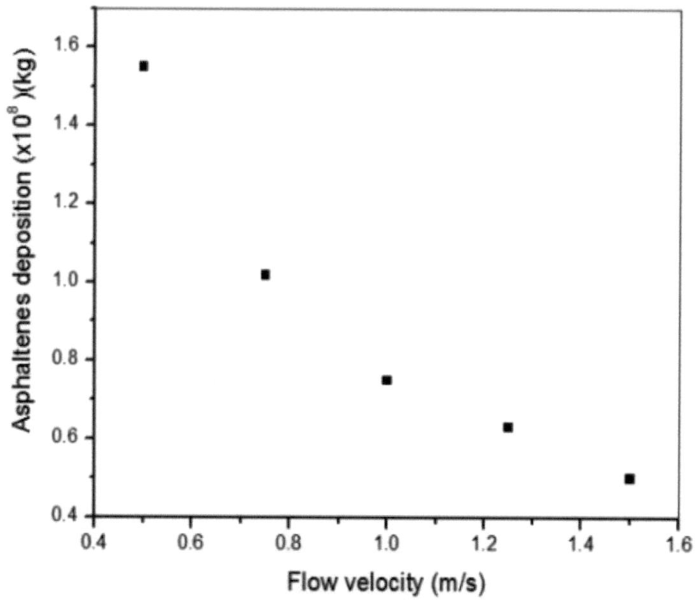

Figure 5. Asphaltene particles' mass deposition vs. flow velocity.

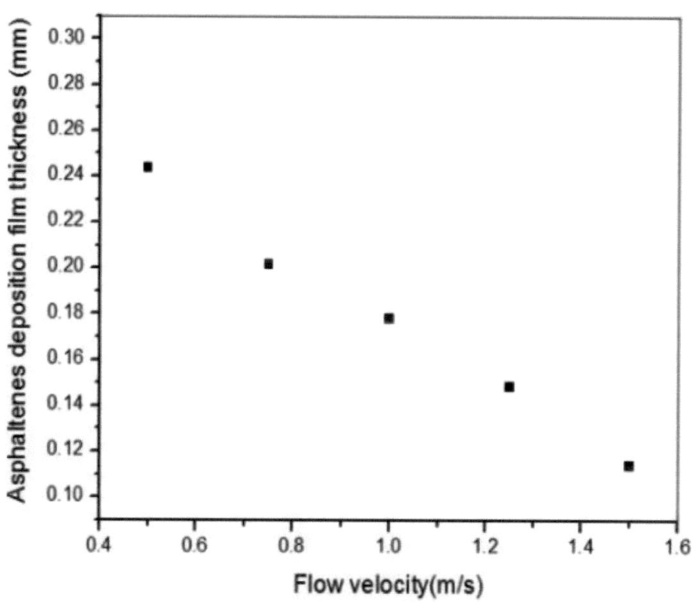

Figure 6. Asphaltene particles' deposition film thickness vs. flow velocity.

deposition film thickness. Therefore, the non-symmetric fouling behavior of crude oil can be modeled using the available CFD techniques, through which the susceptible regions of concern can be predicted in the shell and tube heat exchangers.

4. Conclusions

Although, the fouling phenomena of crude oils are highly complex, the application of CFD simulations offered a high understanding of the fouling process on the heat transfer surfaces. The discrete phase CFD simulation results clearly forecasts the asphaltene particles deposition locations in the tube, deposition mass, and deposition film thickness. The fluid velocity is observed to have a high impact on mitigation of fouling. More research is required to understand the fluid flow behavior of crude oil in the shell and tube heat exchangers. Therefore, the future of CFD in crude oil fouling research is to investigate the flow paths and susceptible regions of crude oil fouling in the heat exchangers.

Nomenclature

A	pre-exponent factor (1·s)
C_1	empirical constant, 1.44
C_2	empirical constant, 1.92
C_A	asphaltenes concentration, kg·m^{-3}
$C_A C_D$	drag coefficient
C_p	concentration of the precursor, kg·m^{-3}
C_{r1}, C_{r2}	concentration of the reactants, kg·m^{-3}
C_A	diffusion coefficient, m^2·s
$C_A d_{ij}$	deformation tensors
$D_{T,p}$	thermophoretic force coefficient
E	activation energy, J·mol^{-1}
C_A	drag force, N
$C_A F_i$	additional force acting on the particle
F_{th}	thermophoretic force
$C_A \overline{g}$	gravitational force, m·s^{-2}
H	energy source term
J	mass flux from the oil-phase to fouling phase, mol·m^{-2}·s^{-1}
K	equilibrium constant
k	thermal conductivity, W·m^{-1}·K^{-1} in Eq. (3), turbulent kinetic energy, J·kg^{-1} in Eq. (4)
C_A	reaction rate constant
Kn	Knudsen number

L_x	number of moles present for each phase
m, n	orders of reactants and precursors
m_p	particle mass, kg
m_d	mass deposition rate, kg·m^{-2}·s^{-1}
n	the normal vector on the tube walls
P	shear production of turbulence, Pa·s
R	rate of production of species in Eq. (7), universal gas constant, J·mol^{-1}·K^{-1} in Eq. (17)R
Re	Reynolds number
S	rate of creation
T	temperature, K
v	fluid velocity, m·s^{-1}

Greek letters

τ	shear stress, Pa
θ	parameter that depends on L_x
ρ	density, kg·m^{-3}
Υ	mass fraction of species
η	dimensionless function
ΔH	precipitation enthalpy
μ	fluid viscosity, kg·m^{-1}·s^{-1}
ω	specific turbulence dissipation rate, J·kg^{-1}·s^{-1}
ε	turbulence dissipation rate, J·kg^{-1}·s^{-1}
σ_k	empirical constant, 1.00
σ_ε	empirical constant, 1.30

Subscripts

A	asphaltenes
b	bulk
w	wall

s surface

p particle

p, q phase

Author details

Ramasamy Marappa Gounder* and Sampath Emani

*Address all correspondence to: marappagounder@utp.edu.my

Department of Chemical Engineering, Universiti Teknologi PETRONAS, Seri Iskandar, Perak D.R., Malaysia

References

[1] Müller-Steinhagen H, Malayeri M, Watkinson A. Heat exchanger fouling: Environmental impacts. Heat Transfer Engineering. 2009;**30**:773-776

[2] Wiehe I. Petroleum fouling: Causes, tools and mitigation methods. In: Proceedings of the 9th Topical Conference on Refinery Processing; 2006

[3] Hasson D. Precipitation Fouling. New York: Hemisphere Publishing Corp; 1981. pp. 527-568

[4] Watkinson AP, Panchal C. A Critical Review of Organic Fluid Fouling. IL, USA: Argonne National Lab; 1990

[5] Watkinson A, Wilson D. Chemical reaction fouling: A review. Experimental Thermal and Fluid Science. 1997;**14**:361-374

[6] Awad M. Fouling of Heat Transfer Surfaces, Heat Transfer—Theoretical Analysis, Experimental Investigations and Industrial Systems. Croatia: InTech; 2011: 506-542. ISBN: 978-953-307-226-5

[7] Kent C. Biological fouling: Basic science and models. In: Fouling Science and Technology. Dordrecht: Springer; 1988. pp. 207-222

[8] Shetty N, Deshannavar UB, Marappagounder R, Pendyala R. Improved threshold fouling models for crude oils. Energy. 2016;**111**:453-467

[9] Knudsen J, Lin D, Ebert W. The determination of the threshold fouling curve for a crude oil. In: Understanding Heat Exchanger Fouling and Its Mitigation. Proceedings of an International Conference on Understanding Heat Exchanger Fouling and Its Mitigation, Begell House, New York, 1999. pp: 265-272. ISBN: 156700136X 9781567001365

[10] Polley GT, Wilson D, Yeap B, Pugh S. Evaluation of laboratory crude oil threshold fouling data for application to refinery pre-heat trains. Applied Thermal Engineering. 2002;**22**: 777-788

[11] Panchal C, Kuru W, Liao C, Ebert W, Palen J. Threshold conditions for crude oil fouling. In: Understanding Heat Exchanger Fouling and Its Mitigation. Proceedings of an International Conference on Understanding Heat Exchanger Fouling and Its Mitigation, Begell House, New York, 1999. pp: 273-282. ISBN: 156700136X 9781567001365

[12] Kern D, Seaton R. A theoretical analysis of thermal surface fouling. British Chemical Engineering. 1959;**4**:258-262

[13] Emani S, Ramasamy M, Shaari KZBK. Effect of shear stress on crude oil fouling in a heat exchanger tube through CFD simulations. Procedia Engineering. 2016;**148**:1058-1065

[14] Bayat M, Aminian J, Bazmi M, Shahhosseini S, Sharifi K. CFD modeling of fouling in crude oil pre-heaters. Energy Conversion and Management. 2012;**64**:344-350

[15] Sileri D, Sahu K, Ding H, Matar O. Mathematical modelling of asphaltenes deposition and removal in crude distillation units. In: International Conference on Heat Exchanger Fouling and Cleaning VIII. Schladming Austria; 2009. pp. 245-251

[16] Haghshenasfard M, Hooman K. CFD modeling of asphaltene deposition rate from crude oil. Journal of Petroleum Science and Engineering. 2015;**128**:24-32

[17] Mukherjee R. Effectively design shell-and-tube heat exchangers. Chemical Engineering Progress. 1998;**94**:21-37

[18] Jatale A, Srinivasa M. CFD Modeling of Fouling in Crude Oil Refinery Heat Exchangers. Spring Meeting and 11th Global Congress on Process Safety-AIChE, Austin, 2015

[19] Wang Y, Lu Q, Zheng Y, Yuan B, Tao H. A CFD-based analysis on trends of heat exchanger fouling. In: 2012 Asia-Pacific Power and Energy Engineering Conference. IEEE; 2012. pp. 1-4

[20] Clarke R, Nicolas F. CFD investigation of maldistribution effects on crude oil fouling in shell and tube exchangers. In: Second International Conference on Petroleum and Gas Phase Behaviour and Fouling. Copenhagen, Denmark; 2000

[21] Anderson JD, Wendt J. Computational Fluid Dynamics. Heidelberg: Springer; 1995

[22] Tu J, Yeoh GH, Liu C. Computational Fluid Dynamics: A Practical Approach. Oxford: Butterworth-Heinemann; 2012

[23] Sun D-W. Computational Fluid Dynamics in Food Processing. Boka Raton: CRC Press; 2007. ISBN: 9780849392863

[24] Li X-G, Zhang L-H, Zhang R-Y, Sun Y-L, Jiang B, Luo M-F, Li X-G. CFD modeling of phase change and coke formation in petroleum refining heaters. Fuel Processing Technology. 2015;**134**:18-25

[25] Nazar S, Ali R, Banisharifdehkordi F, Ahmadzadeh S. Mathematical modeling of coke formation and deposition due to thermal cracking of petroleum fluids. Chemical Engineering & Technology. 2016;**39**:311-321

[26] Fontoura D, Matos E, Nunhez J. A three-dimensional two-phase flow model with phase change inside a tube of petrochemical pre-heaters. Fuel. 2013;**110**:196-203

[27] Souza B, Matos E, Guirardello R, Nunhez J. Predicting coke formation due to thermal cracking inside tubes of petrochemical fired heaters using a fast CFD formulation. Journal of Petroleum Science and Engineering. 2006;**51**:138-148

[28] Fouzia D, Park TS. Effect of inlet velocity on the crude oil coking and gas phase formation in a straight pipe. Journal of Applied Mathematics and Physics. 2016;**5**:17

[29] Seyyedbagheri H, Mirzayi B. CFD modeling of high inertia asphaltene aggregates deposition in 3D turbulent oil production wells. Journal of Petroleum Science and Engineering; **2016**

[30] Wilcox DC. Turbulence Modeling for CFD. 3rd ed. LA: D.C.W. Industries, Inc.; 2006

[31] Yang J, Serratos MGJ, Fari-Arole DS, Müller EA, Matar OK. Crude oil fouling: Fluid dynamics, reactions and phase change. Procedia IUTAM. 2015;**15**:186-193

[32] Coletti F, Hewitt G. Crude Oil Fouling. Elsevier, USA: Gulf Professional Publishing; 2015

[33] Jamialahmadi M, Soltani B, Müller-Steinhagen H, Rashtchian D. Measurement and prediction of the rate of deposition of flocculated asphaltene particles from oil. International Journal of Heat and Mass Transfer. 2009;**52**:4624-4634

[34] Daaou M, Larbi A, Martínez-Haya B, Rogalski M. A comparative study of the chemical structure of asphaltenes from Algerian petroleum collected at different stages of extraction and processing. Journal of Petroleum Science and Engineering. 2016;**138**:50-56

[35] Ge Q, Yap Y, Vargas F, Zhang M, Chai J. Numerical modeling of asphaltene deposition. Computational Thermal Sciences. 2013;**5**:153-163

[36] Miri R, Zendehboudi S, Kord S, Vargas F, Lohi A, Elkamel A, Chatzis I. Experimental and numerical modeling study of gravity drainage considering asphaltene deposition. Industrial & Engineering Chemistry Research. 2014;**53**:11512-11526

[37] Mirzayi B, Mousavi Dehghani SA, Chakan MB. Modeling of asphaltene deposition in pipelines. Journal of Petroleum Science and Technology. 2013;**3**:15-23

[38] Zhu H, Jing J, Li Q, Yu X, Junwen C. Simulations of asphaltene deposition in submarine pipelines by CFD. In: International Oil and Gas Conference and Exhibition in China. Society of Petroleum Engineers; 2010

[39] Zhang Z, Chen Q. Comparison of the Eulerian and Lagrangian methods for predicting particle transport in enclosed spaces. Atmospheric Environment. 2007;**41**:5236-5248

[40] Al-Fulaij H, Cipollina A, Micale G, Ettouney H, Bogle D. Eulerian–Lagrangian modeling and computational fluid dynamics simulation of wire mesh demisters in MSF plants. Desalination. 2016;**385**:148-157

[41] Cokljat D, Slack M, Vasquez S, Bakker A, Montante G. Reynolds-stress model for Eulerian multiphase. Progress in Computational Fluid Dynamics, An International Journal. 2006; **6**:168-178

[42] Kohse BF, Nghiem LX. Modelling asphaltene precipitation and deposition in a compositional reservoir simulator. In: SPE/DOE Symposium on Improved Oil Recovery. Society of Petroleum Engineers; 2004

[43] Behbahani TJ, Behbahani ZJ. A new study on asphaltene adsorption in porous media. Petroleum and Coal. 2014;**56**:459-466

[44] Talbot L, Cheng R, Schefer R, Willis D. Thermophoresis of particles in a heated boundary layer. Journal of Fluid Mechanics. 1980;**101**:737-758

[45] Saffman P. The lift on a small sphere in a slow shear flow. Journal of Fluid Mechanics. 1965;**22**:385-400

[46] Mahulkar AV, Heynderickx GJ, Marin GB, Varbanov P, Lam H, Klemes J, Pierucci S. Simulation of coking in convection section of steam cracker. Chemical Engineering. 2012;**29**

[47] Brahim F, Augustin W, Bohnet M. Numerical simulation of the fouling process. International Journal of Thermal Sciences. 2003;**42**:323-334

[48] http://www.ansys.com/Products/Fluids/ANSYS-Fluent

[49] Emani S, Ramasamy M, Ki Zilati KS. CFD modelling of shell-side asphaltenes deposition in a shell and tube heat exchanger. American Institute of Physics. 2017;**1859**:020118-1-020118-7

[50] Emani S, Ramasamy M, Ki Zilati KS. Transportation and adhesion of asphaltenes in a heat exchanger tube through CFD siumulations. American Institute of Physics. 2017;**1859**: 020119-1-020117-7

[51] Pirker S, Kahrimanovic D, Goniva C. Improving the applicability of discrete phase simulations by smoothening their exchange fields. Applied Mathematical Modelling. 2011;**35**: 2479-2488

[52] Subhasish M, Mayur JS, Elham D, Geoffrey ME. Investigation of droplet evaporation in a bubbling fluidized bed. In: Ninth International Conference on CFD in the Minerals and Process Industries. CSIRO; Melbourne, Australia; 2012

Chapter 16

Surrogate Model Applied for Analysis of Uncertain Parameters in Turbulent Mixing Flows

Boštjan Končar, Andrej Prošek and Matjaž Leskovar

Additional information is available at the end of the chapter

http://dx.doi.org/10.5772/intechopen.70564

Abstract

The water mixing experiment in the Generic Mixing Experiment (GEMIX) facility performed at the Paul Scherrer Institute is used as a benchmark case to investigate the influence of the main uncertain parameters on the turbulent mixing under isokinetic flow conditions. The benchmark experiment features two horizontal water streams with the same inlet velocity that merge together to form a mixing flow inside the larger horizontal square channel. The turbulence intensity and the velocity profile at the inlet were used as the main uncertain input parameters. The selected set of computational fluid dynamics (CFD) simulations based on different combinations of values for uncertain parameters has been performed with the code NEPTUNE_CFD that solves the Reynolds Averaged Navier Stokes (RANS) equations with the k-ε turbulence model. To investigate the influence of the uncertain parameters over a wide range of values, the surrogate model called optimal statistical estimator (OSE) was used to generate the response surface of the results. It has been demonstrated that the OSE method can be successfully applied to build the response surface from a limited set of simulation points. For the two-parameter problem of the current study, only a few CFD simulation points are found sufficient to construct the quality response surface.

Keywords: turbulent mixing, surrogate model, optimal statistical estimator, CFD simulation, response surface

1. Introduction

Computational fluid dynamics (CFD) simulations are affected by uncertainties, due in large part to the increasing complexity of physical models and the inherent introduction of random model data. The identification of the main uncertain parameters and the evaluation of their influence on the simulation results are crucial steps in estimating the simulation accuracy. For turbulent flows, not only that the uncertainty in the choice of the turbulent model parameters has to be considered, but also the physical properties of the fluid and the experimentally provided boundary conditions can be largely affected by uncertainties. The choice of single values for these "input" parameters often leads to considerable differences between the simulation and experimental results. The sensitivity of the simulation results to the range of different combinations of input parameters can be evaluated by hundreds of CFD simulations. However, even a simple steady-state simulation of a turbulent flow can take several hours to complete. One way to alleviate this burden is the construction of a surrogate model that mimics the behaviour of the CFD simulation as closely as possible while being computationally much cheaper. Such models are based on a complex mathematical response function that is constructed on a limited number of intelligently selected data (CFD) points. Several methods that deal with the sensitivity or uncertainty of CFD computations can be found in the literature [1–4].

The uncertain parameters affecting the turbulent flow presented in this study are investigated on a typical CFD case. The benchmark experiment featuring the mixing of two turbulent flows performed at the Paul Scherrer Institute (PSI) [4] has been used in the analysis. To analyse the effect of the sensitivity parameters, a series of CFD simulations is performed with the code NEPTUNE_CFD that solves the Reynolds Averaged Navier Stokes (RANS) equations with the k-eps turbulence model [5]. The optimal statistical estimator (OSE) method [6] is used for the response surface generation.

2. Turbulent mixing benchmark

To investigate the main turbulent mixing mechanisms, the experimental data of the water mixing experiment Generic Mixing Experiment (GEMIX) were used [4]. The GEMIX facility, located at the Paul Scherrer Institute (PSI), features the horizontal test section where the two horizontal water streams with different temperatures or densities can be mixed.

The selected benchmark case considers the mixing of two isothermal flows with the same density and mass flow rate. The schematic representation of the test section is shown in **Figure 1**. The inflow section consists of two slightly inclined rectangular channels separated by the splitter plate that merge into the larger square channel with the cross section of 50 mm by 50 mm. The water with a mass flow rate of 1 kg/s flows through the upper and lower channel into the mixing section, where the two water streams mix together to form a turbulent mixing layer. The profiles of velocity and turbulent quantities were measured at two axial locations, 70 mm and 450 mm behind the splitter plate, as shown in **Figure 1**. A detailed description of the experiment and the measurement techniques are given in [7].

2.1. Uncertain parameters at the inlet

The complete information about the flow conditions in the experiment requires the measurement of velocity and turbulent quantities at several locations along the flow. In the considered

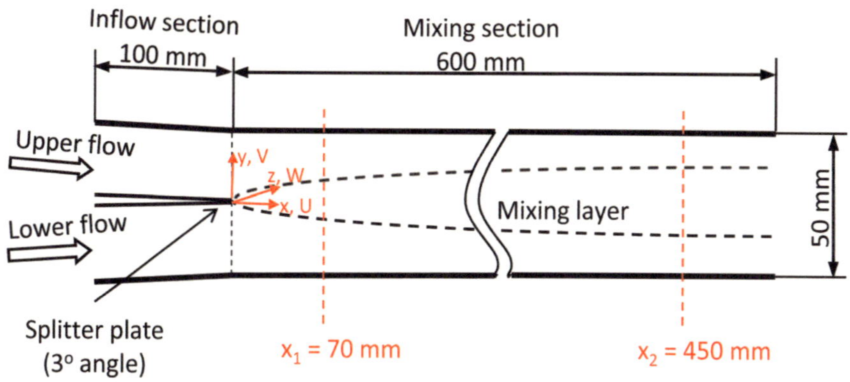

Figure 1. Setup of the GEMIX experiment.

experiment, these data are provided in the mixing section, but the velocity and turbulence profiles have not been measured in the region of the two inflow channels. Trying to impose a uniform flow with the low level of turbulence, a flow straightener followed by several grids of different densities was placed inside each of the inflow channels [4]. Nevertheless, at the known mass flow rate, the velocity profile and turbulence at the inlet can be treated as uncertain parameters with an estimated range of values.

One may assume that the profile inlet velocity can take the values between the uniform and the fully developed turbulent profile shape. This can be written in a parametrised form using the parameter α as

$$U(y,z) = \left(\frac{\alpha}{U_d(y,z)} + \frac{1-\alpha}{U_u}\right)^{-1} \quad (1)$$

where $U_d(y,z)$ stands for the fully developed velocity profile and U_u for the uniform velocity. The fully developed velocity profile was obtained from a separate simulation in a single long rectangular channel of the same cross section and was imposed for both inlet flows. For the purpose of the implementation into the CFD code, the velocity profiles between the uniform and fully developed profile shape were approximated by trigonometric mathematical functions that are exactly zero at the wall. The product of two series of cosine functions (Fourier series) is used:

$$U_d(y,z) = \left(\sum_{n=1}^{26}\left(a_n \cos\frac{n\pi y}{L_y}\right)\right)\left(\sum_{n=1}^{26}\left(b_n \cos\frac{n\pi z}{L_z}\right)\right) \quad (2)$$

where a_n and b_n are coefficients obtained with the least-squares method and L_y and L_z represent the dimensions of the channel. The parameter α in Eq. (1) is varied between 0 and 1 (0 represents uniform and 1 fully developed axial velocity profile) in steps of 0.2.

The second uncertain parameter is the turbulence intensity β at the inlet, which describes the ratio between the turbulent velocity fluctuations and the mean velocity. In the present work, it is assumed that the turbulence intensity β may vary between 0% and the high turbulence level of 25%.

3. CFD simulations

The simulations were carried out with the NEPTUNE_CFD 2.0.1 code [8] developed by Electricite de France (EDF) and Commissariat a l'Energie Atomique (CEA, France). NEPTUNE_CFD 2.0.1 is a dedicated code for modelling of transient flows in nuclear reactor systems. Phenomena that involve mixing of turbulent flows are of high interest in nuclear industry, especially from the perspective of hypothetical accident conditions [5].

The momentum and turbulence transport equations are solved using the Reynolds Averaged Navier Stokes (RANS) approach. The standard k-ε model with the logarithmic wall function near the walls was used for the turbulence modelling. The calculations were performed on a computational mesh with 475,000 hexahedral elements with mesh refinement near the channel walls and around the splitter plate. The simulation and mesh details are provided in [9].

The mass flow rate is the same at both inlets (1 kg/s), which corresponds to the average liquid velocity of 0.8 m/s. The shape of the inlet velocity profile is set by Eq. (1) and depends on the parameter α. The density of the water is 998 kg/m^3 at the temperature of 23°C. Besides the velocity, also the turbulence intensity β has to be prescribed at the inlet. No-slip boundary conditions are used on the wall, and a constant pressure is set at the outlet of the domain. All simulations were performed at constant turbulent Schmidt number Sc = 0.7. The constant time step of 0.02 s is used for the calculations. About 100 time steps are sufficient to reach the converged solution.

3.1. Matrix of CFD simulation points

The relevant output results are the profiles of the turbulence kinetic energy k and the downstream velocity component U (in x direction, see **Figure 1**) at two locations: 0.07 and 0.45 m downstream from the edge of the splitter plates. To evaluate the effect of random values of uncertain parameters on the results, a series of simulations was performed, independently combining different values of α and β. The matrix of CFD simulation points is presented in **Figure 2**. It can be seen that the calculation points are distributed much densely and in equidistant steps of 1% at lower values of β (between 0 and 4%), whereas their distribution is uneven and rather scarce at higher values. Overall 40 simulations have been carried out. But this is not nearly enough to cover the complete space of results for the range of α (0–1) and β (0–25%) values. In between, the surrogate (or response surface) model can be used.

http://dx.doi.org/10.5772/intechopen.70564

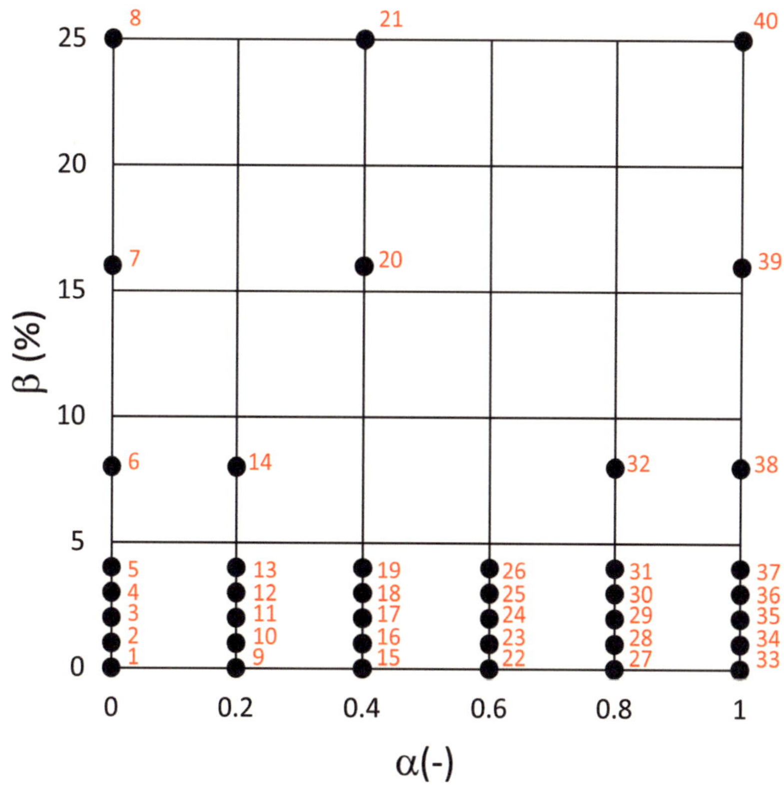

Figure 2. Matrix of CFD simulation points.

4. Optimal statistical estimator (OSE) method

Hundreds of time-consuming CFD simulations would be needed to cover the entire space of results for different combinations and values of input parameters. Instead, the surrogate model can be used to replace the numerous code simulations. Surrogate modelling is based on the construction of the mathematical response function from the limited number of selected data points aiming to estimate the system response or, in other words, to define the relationship between specific system inputs and outputs. In this way, the constructed response surface can be used for the sensitivity analysis of the impact of uncertain parameters.

In the work of [6], the response surface was generated by the optimal statistical estimator (OSE) method, which can be easily applied for multidimensional space. Basic equations for the response surface generation with OSE are provided in this section; details are described in [6]. The OSE method uses a linear combination of code-calculated output values (or their corrected values as explained later) and coefficients C_n, which represent the measure of similarity between a given vector of input data G and the vector G_n for the nth calculation. The optimal statistical estimator $\widehat{H}_o(G)$ and the coefficients C_n are defined as

$$\widehat{H}_o(G) = \sum_{n=1}^{N} C_n H_n \tag{3}$$

$$C_n \equiv \frac{\delta_a(G - G_n)}{\sum_{n=1}^{N} \delta_a(G - G_n)} \tag{4}$$

where $G = (x_1, x_2, \ldots, x_M)$ is a given input data vector, $G_n = (x_{n1}, x_{n2}, \ldots, x_{nM})$ and $H_n = (x_{n(M+1)}, x_{n(M+2)}, \ldots, x_{nI})$ are the input and output data vectors for the nth calculation, respectively; M is the number of input parameters; I the number of input and output parameters; and N is the number of calculated (or measured) values. Since the Dirac delta function δ appears in the denominator of Eq. (4) in the original derivation for the one-dimensional case, an approximation for δ was used to make the formula applicable [10]. Among various possible approximations, the Gaussian function was the most appropriate, and for the M-dimensional case, it was adapted to

$$\delta_a(G - G_n) = \left(\prod_{i=1}^{M} \frac{1}{\sqrt{2\pi}\cdot\sigma_i}\right) \exp\left(-\frac{1}{2}\sum_{i=1}^{M}\left(\frac{x_i - x_{ni}}{\sigma_i}\right)^2\right) \tag{5}$$

where σ_i is the width of the Gaussian curve determined by the user. The selection of the adequate width σ_i needs special attention. Widening of the Gaussian curve by selecting a larger width σ_i extends the influence area of the particular input data point to its surroundings, i.e. also to the neighbouring data points. To uniformly cover the volume with samples, the width σ_i for dimension i is defined as follows:

$$\sigma_i = \frac{S_i \cdot f_c}{N_i}, i = 1, 2, \ldots, I, \tag{6}$$

where S_i is the distance between the minimum and maximum value of the data points x_{ni} ($n = 1, 2, \ldots, N$) and N_i is the number of intervals between the data points. The corrective factor f_c should be selected by the user based on the desired and previously tested performance of OSE. The contribution of each data point to the estimation of the final result can then be adjusted by f_c. If f_c is equal to 1.0, the width σ_i is equal to the distance between two adjacent points, and the influence is thus extended approximately to its neighbour points. On the other hand, if f_c is close to 0, in the one-dimensional case, this would result in a stepwise function. With increasing f_c the OSE function becomes smoother between the data points but at the cost of less accurate predictions at the data points, which can be eliminated by appropriately shifting the data point values as performed in the present analysis. OSE is applied correctly if the OSE function between the calculated points is smooth and the calculated points are correctly predicted. More details about how the contribution of each calculated data point to the final output parameter estimation can be adjusted by the corrective factor f_c can be found in [6].

Using the derived optimal statistical estimator $\widehat{H}_o$, the complete estimated vector can be defined as a composition

$$Y = \left(G \bigoplus \widehat{H}_o\right) = Y(X) \tag{7}$$

The function $Y(X)$ is modelled by OSE. The vector Y is influenced by the input parameters, which are directly transferred to the output, while the optimal statistical estimator determines the complementary components $\widehat{H}_o(G)$ of the above composition representing the output values. One of the most important characteristics of this estimator is that it involves the highly nonlinear coefficients C_n; therefore the response surface for highly nonlinear functions can be efficiently generated.

For assessing the adequacy and predictive capability of OSE, the root mean square error and coefficient of determination for the mth input parameter are used:

$$RMS_m = \left(\frac{\sum_{n=1}^{N}\left(x_{nm} - x_{est,m}\right)^2}{N}\right)^{1/2} \tag{8}$$

$$R_m^2 = \frac{\sum_{n=1}^{N}\left(x_{est,m} - x_{avg,m}\right)^2}{\sum_{n=1}^{N}\left(x_{nm} - x_{est,m}\right)^2} \tag{9}$$

for $m = (M + 1), (M + 2), \ldots, I$, where M is the number of input uncertain parameters and I is the number of the input and output parameters. Here x_{nm} is the nth code-calculated value of the mth output parameter, $x_{est,m}$ is nth estimated value with the optimal statistical estimator (see Eq. (3)) and $x_{avg,m}$ is the mean of the N code-calculated values of the mth output parameter. The assessment of the predictive capability of the optimal statistical estimator with the two proposed statistics is perfect when $RMS_m = 0$ and $R_m^2 = 1$.

To produce the output results, the values of the input parameters ($x_1, x_2, \ldots, x_M$) are randomly sampled (e.g. by Monte Carlo method) each time, and then the corresponding unknown output values are estimated by the optimal statistical estimator using Eqs. (3)–(9). Each time the new coefficients C_n are calculated, while the values of H_n are the data points, determined in the phase of the response surface generation by OSE.

The values are based on computer code calculation values to achieve the desired predictive capability of OSE for the code-calculated values. If the statistics RMS_m and R_m^2 do not show the desired predictive capability of OSE, this means that the influence of the neighbour computer code calculation values is too large. This influence may be eliminated by appropriately shifting the computer code calculation values. Their shifting is performed in an iterative way till the results predicted by OSE do not agree with the originally non-shifted calculation values. Using this approach, a perfect agreement of the OSE results with the calculated data points can be obtained. If the estimated value $x_{est,m}$ initially exceeds the code-calculated value x_{nm}, the new value is decreased for the difference between the estimated and code-calculated value and vice versa. This is done in iterative steps until the desired accuracy of the estimated value is obtained in the points (i.e. values of input parameters) used in the N code calculations. Due to the highly non-linear functions, only a few iterations are normally needed to achieve a reasonable agreement. In this way the code-calculated values can always be matched.

5. Results and discussion

5.1. CFD simulation results

The results of the NEPTUNE_CFD sensitivity calculations are presented in **Figures 3–6**. In **Figure 3** the axial velocity profiles at two locations 0.07 and 0.45 m downstream the splitter

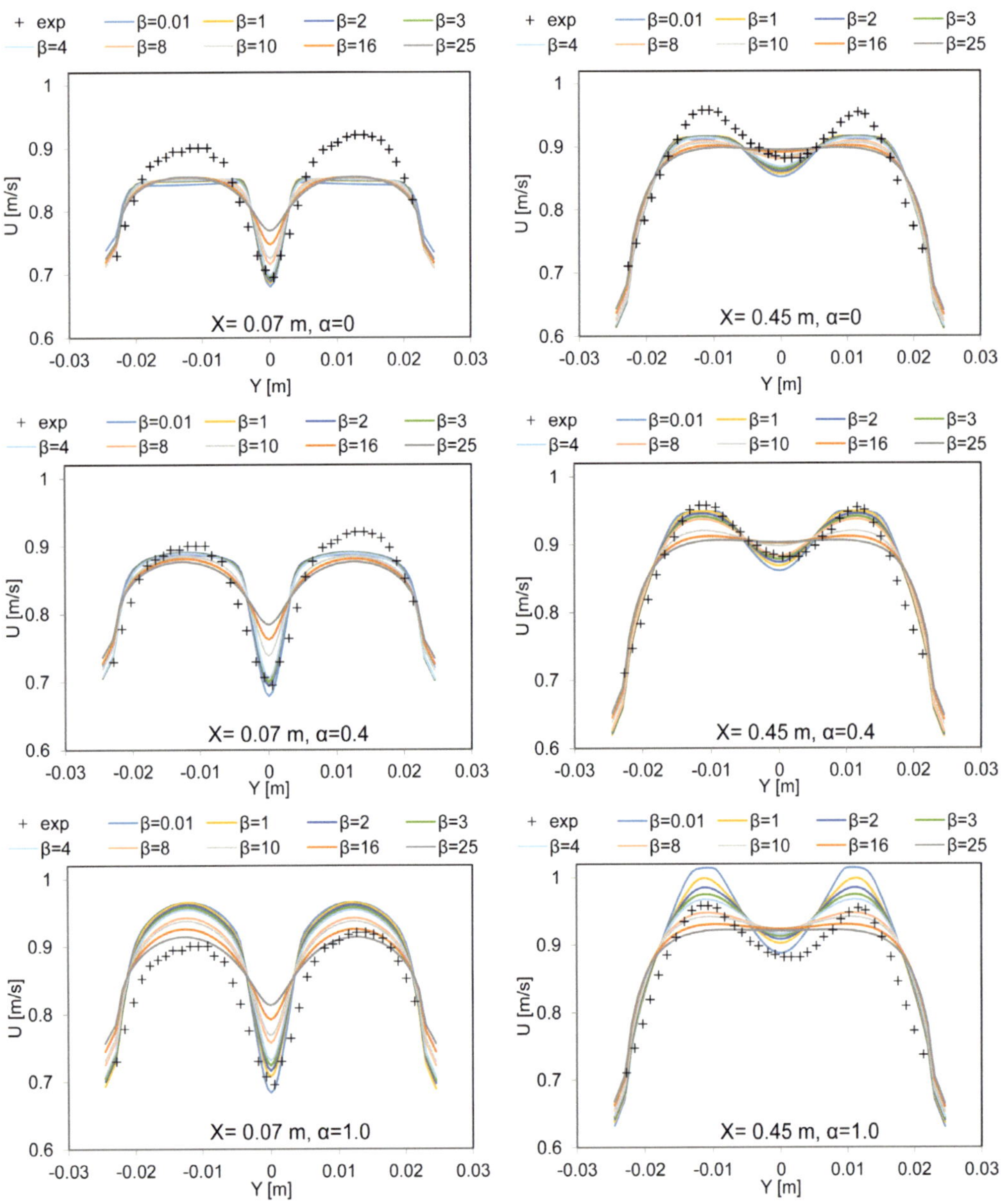

Figure 3. Downstream velocity U dependence on β for $\alpha = 0$, 0.4 and 1.0: (left) 0.07 m downstream of the splitter plate and (right) 0.45 m downstream of the splitter plate.

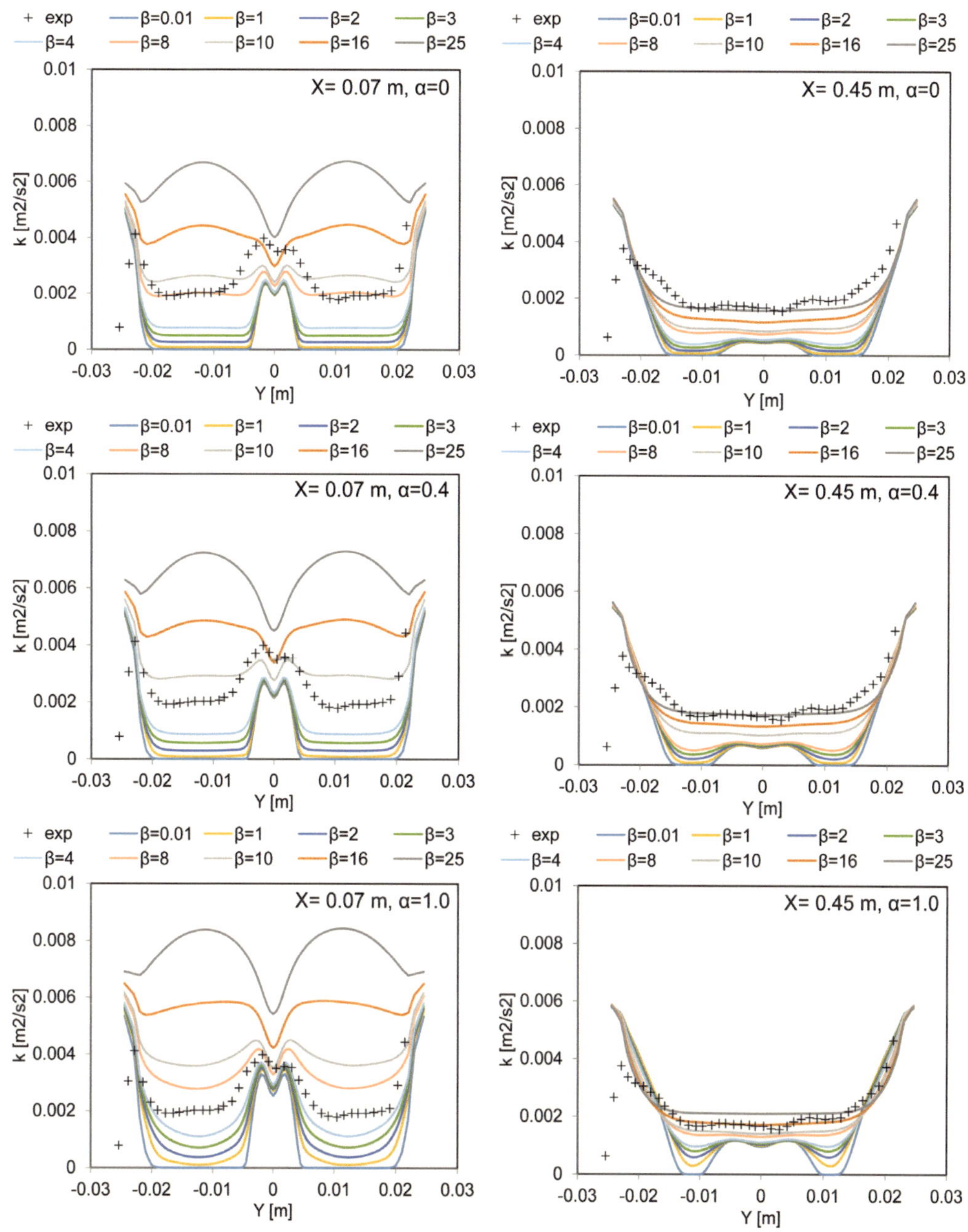

Figure 4. Turbulence kinetic energy k dependence on β for $\alpha = 0$, 0.4 and 1.0: (left) 0.07 m downstream of the splitter plate and (right) 0.45 m downstream of the splitter plate.

plate are shown. The sensitivity to the inlet turbulence intensity β is presented for three different values of inlet velocity profiles ($\alpha = 0$, 0.4 and 1). As shown, high values of β tend to smooth the velocity gradients. The smoothing effect at higher β values is more pronounced for the profiles with $\alpha = 0.4$ and 1. It can be seen that the highest turbulent intensities $\beta = 16$ and 25

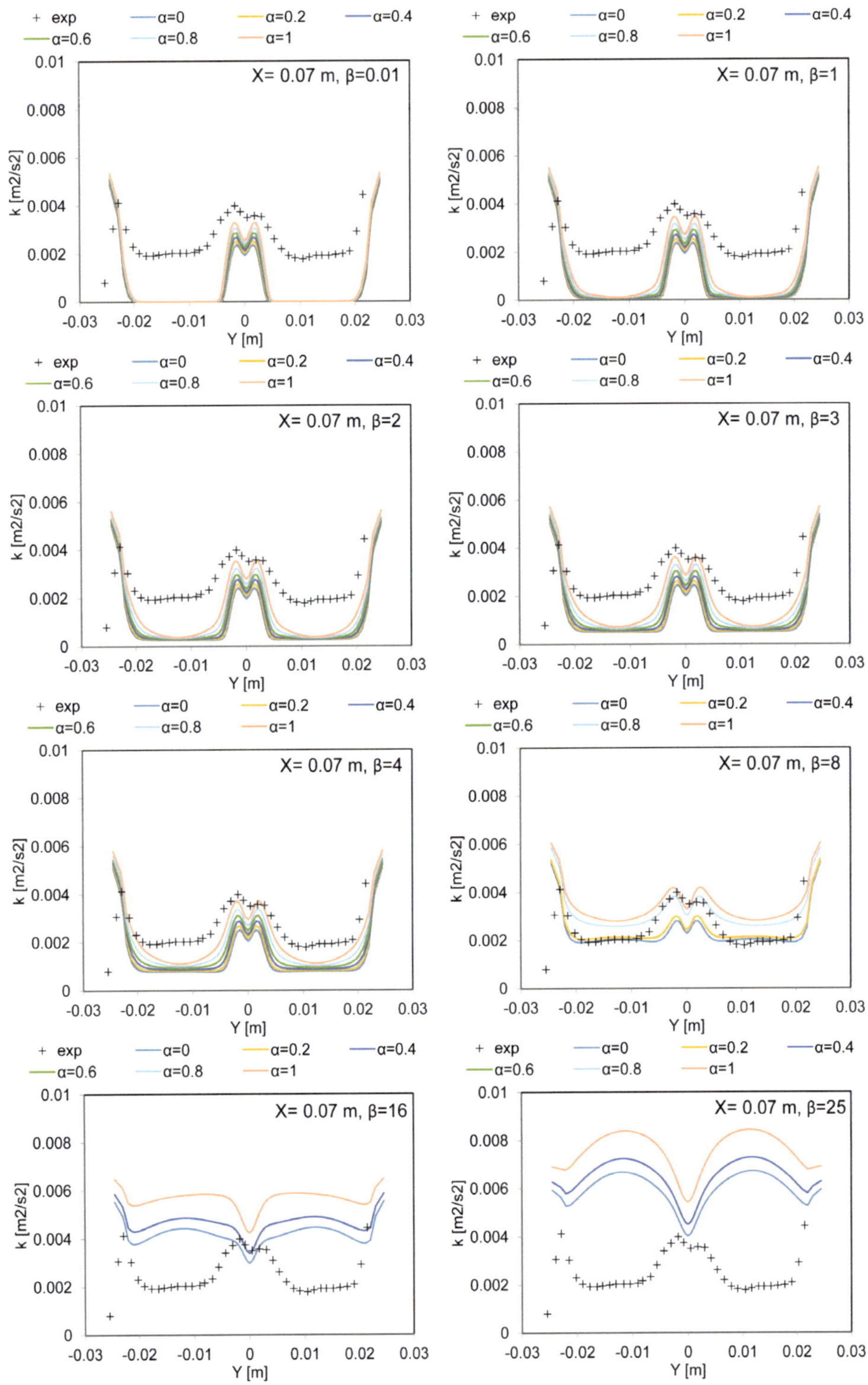

Figure 5. Turbulence kinetic energy k dependence on α for β = 0.01, 1, 2, 3, 4, 8, 16 and 25% at 0.07 m downstream of the splitter plate.

http://dx.doi.org/10.5772/intechopen.70564

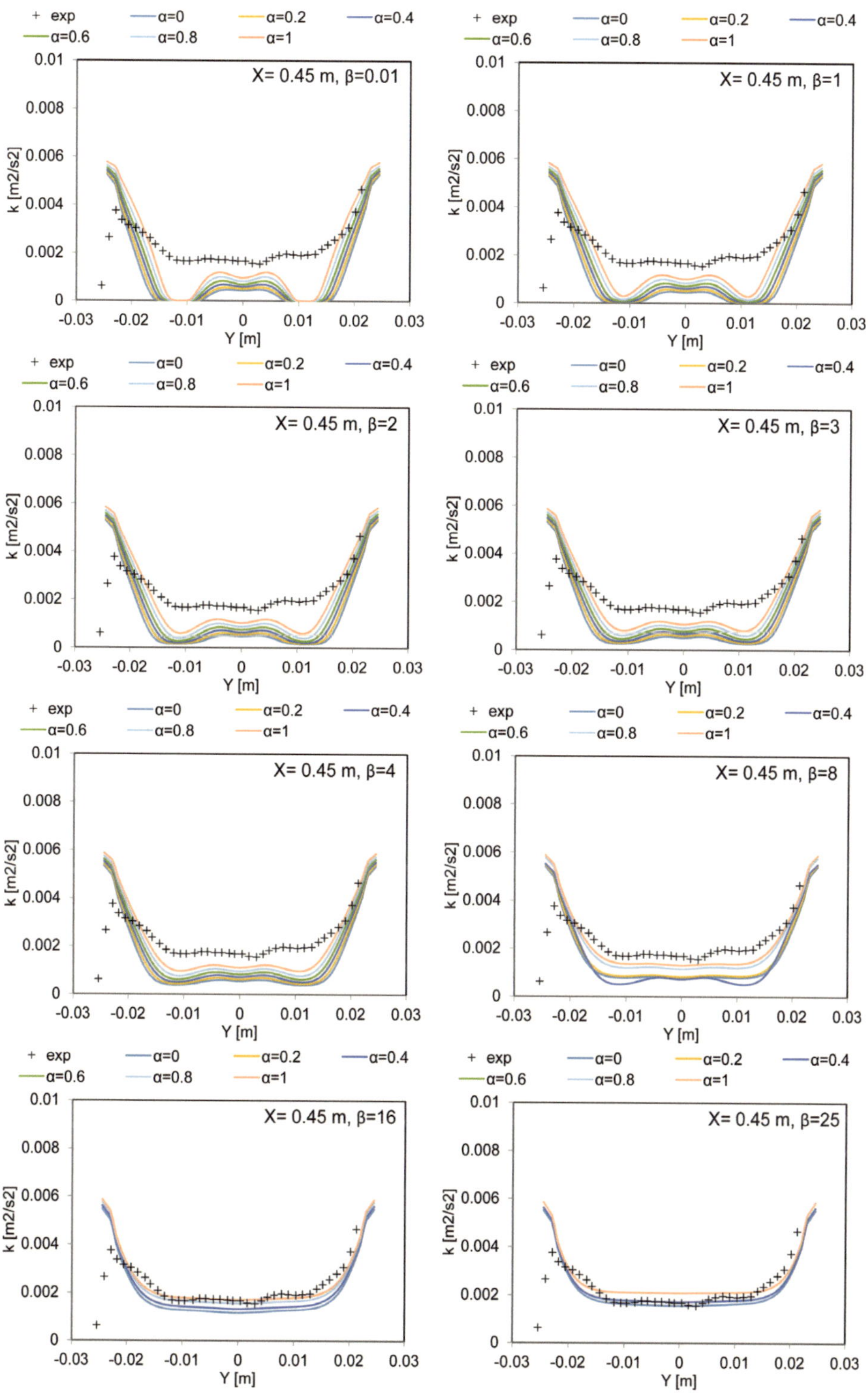

Figure 6. Turbulence kinetic energy k dependence on α for β = 0.01, 1, 2, 3, 4, 8, 16 and 25% at 0.45 m downstream of the splitter plate.

significantly flatten the velocity profile farther away from the splitter plate, at 0.45 m. However it is less likely that such high turbulence intensities would appear in this type of flow.

The simulated profiles of turbulence kinetic energy k at two downstream locations, 0.07 and 0.45 m, are shown in **Figure 4**. Different curves represent different values of β at three inlet velocity profiles α (0, 0.4 and 1). It can be observed that low values of the inlet turbulence intensity (β up to 4%) significantly underpredict the experimental values of k for both downstream locations. On the other hand, the results for high β (10–25%) clearly overestimate the experimental data at the closest measuring location, 0.07 m behind the splitter plate. Farther away, at 0.45 m, the predictions with the highest β values match the experiment in the central, mixing part of the flow channel. The influence of β is similar for the three α values, except that the simulated k profiles tend to be smoother for the uniform velocity inlet ($\alpha = 0$). In addition, the asymmetry in the measured data can be observed, resulting in different deviations between the measured and simulated turbulent kinetic energy at the lower and upper side of the channel (left and right side of the figures).

The influence of β on the turbulent kinetic energy k is additionally discussed in **Figures 5** and **6**, where the dependence on α is shown for several different β values. **Figure 5** presents the results just behind the splitter plate (at 0.07 m) and **Figure 6** the results farther in the mixing region (at 0.45 m). At 0.07 m, the best agreement between the simulation and experiment is obtained for $\beta = 8\%$ (**Figure 5**), whereas further downstream, at 0.45 m (**Figure 6**), the simulations with $\beta = 8\%$ underpredict the measured data. At this axial location, the profiles with β values of 16 and 25% match the experimental data. This result indicates that the dissipation of turbulence kinetic energy k in the existing k-ε turbulence model is higher than in the experiment.

5.2. Response surface generated by OSE method

For the reference OSE calculation, all 40 simulation points (see **Figure 2**) are used to generate the response surface (Case C0). It should be noted that for creating the 3D figures of the NEPTUNE_CFD-calculated data, the missing data in the calculational matrix at given α were obtained by interpolation in α direction as missing data would be otherwise set to 0 on the graph. Also, for the 3D graph to be proportional in β direction, the NEPTUNE_CFD-calculated data were linearly interpolated so that the distance between two points was set equal to 1% in β direction for comparison purposes with the response surface constructed by OSE.

The CFD-calculated results of the output parameters are available in the interval (−0.0245, 0.0245 m) with step size 0.0005 m. This means 99 discrete points. The results are given at two x axis positions: $x = 0.07$ m and 0.45 m. For each discrete point (at given value of x and y), there is a surface (function of α and β), which has to be generated by OSE. Considering two output parameters at two axial locations, this means that four times 99 response surfaces were automatically generated by OSE for each case and only some are shown.

Figures 7 and **8** show the comparison between the 3D plots of the NEPTUNE_CFD simulation points and the response surfaces generated by the OSE reference case C0. The dependency of the downstream velocity U and turbulence kinetic energy k on the parameters α and β, at different locations in the mixing region, is presented.

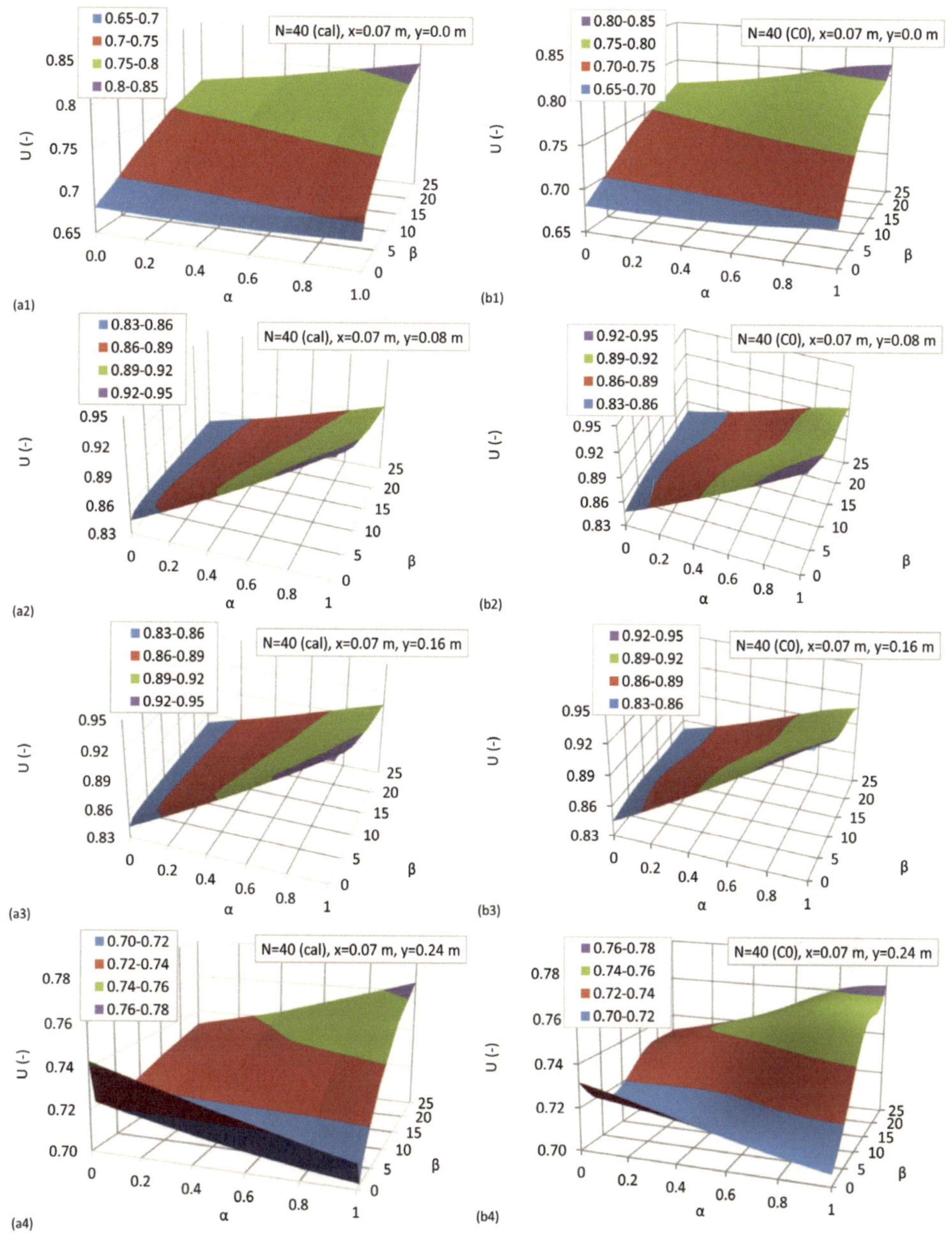

Figure 7. Downstream velocity U dependence on α and β at downstream location 0.07 m for four y axis positions: (a) NEPTUNE_CFD calculation and (b) response surface generated by OSE.

Although the construction points in the calculation matrix are scarcely distributed (see **Figure 2**) at higher β values, a good agreement between the NEPTUNE_CFD calculation and the OSE response surface can be observed. At the middle of the channel (y = 0 m), the velocity U increases with increasing β, while the dependence on α is smaller (see **Figure 7**(a1) and (b1)).

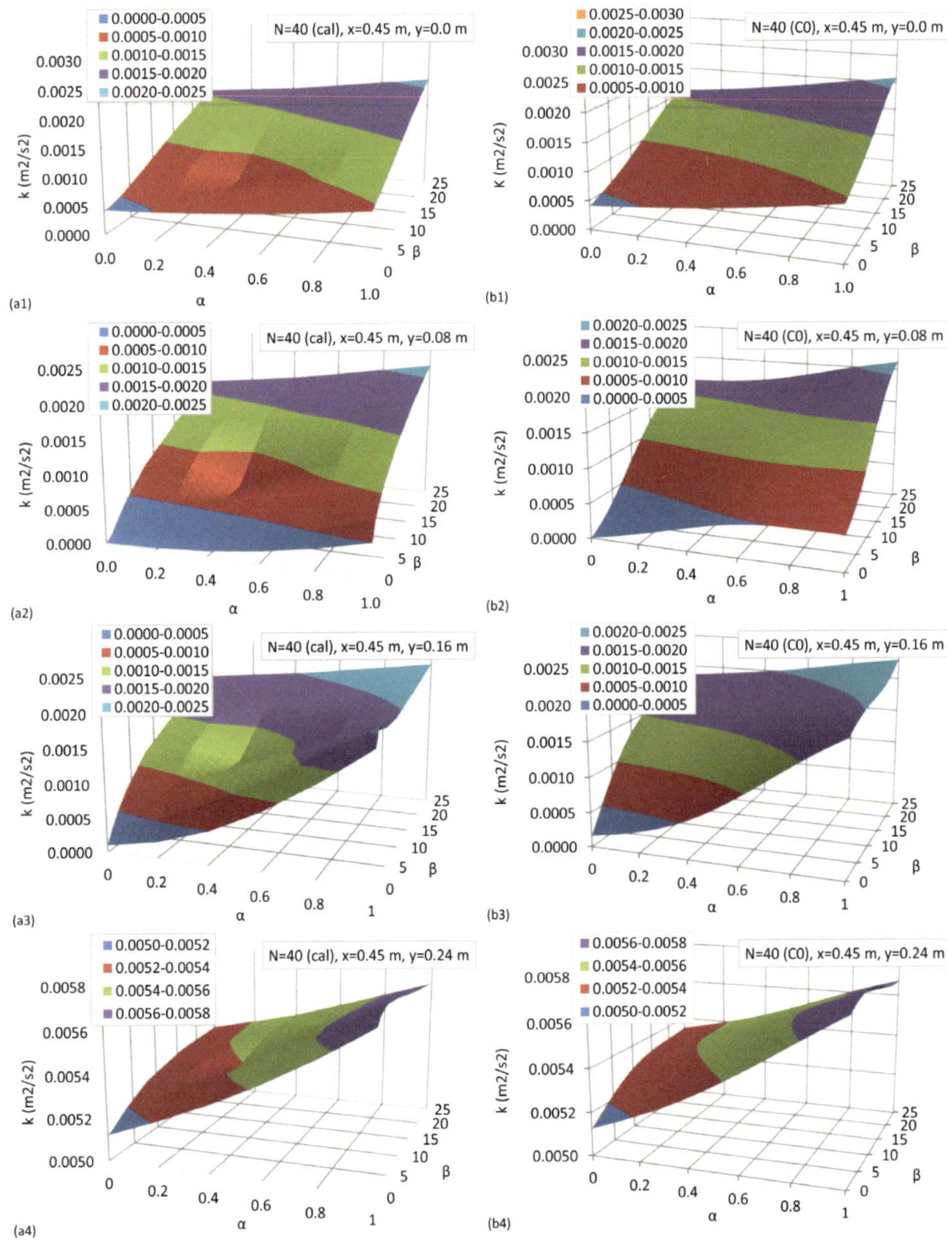

Figure 8. Turbulence kinetic energy k dependence on α and β at downstream location 0.45 m for four y axis positions: (a) NEPTUNE_CFD calculation and (b) response surface generated by OSE.

The response surface is smooth and in good agreement with the surface plotted from the calculated data points as the relations are rather linear. On the other hand, at location y = 0.08 m, the velocity U increases with α and decreases with β as shown in **Figure** 7(a2). More data in β direction would further improve the agreement for this more nonlinear relation.

Similar is true for the velocity U at $y = 0.16$ m. Finally, from **Figure 7**(b4) it can be seen that at $\alpha = 0$ the code-calculated value has not been matched for the highly nonlinear surface. **Figure 8** showing the turbulence kinetic energy shows that the highest values are obtained at the maximum α and β value. The code-calculated values were matched by OSE (R^2 always above 0.99). It should be noted that the graph plotted from the calculated data has many interpolated data (in one direction only); therefore visually the agreement does not seem to be so perfect.

As already mentioned, the selected number of points (i.e. 40 points) is relatively scarcely distributed across the calculation matrix. Nevertheless, the main strength of the OSE method is its capability to efficiently generate the response surface even with much fewer number of construction points [11], in particular for the two-parameter problems. To demonstrate this, the following cases with reduced number of calculation points are considered for the response surface generation:

- Case 1 (C1): 19 calculations (1, 5, 6, 7, 8, 11, 14, 15, 20, 21, 22, 26, 29, 32, 33, 37, 38, 39, 40)
- Case 2 (C2): 11 calculations (1, 7, 8, 14, 20, 21, 26, 32, 33, 39, 40)
- Case 3 (C3): 9 calculations (1, 7, 8, 20, 21, 26, 33, 39, 40)
- Case 4 (C4): 5 calculations (1, 8, 20, 33, 40)

Figures 9 and **10** show the influence of the number of calculated points on the response surface generation for the downstream velocity U and the turbulence kinetic energy k, respectively. In the case with 40 calculational points (C0 case) for the response surface generation by OSE, the value of the corrective factor f_c is set to $f_c = 1.5$ and the number of iterations to 90. The distances $S1$ and $S2$ are 1 and 25, respectively, and the number of the intervals $N1$ and $N2$ is 5. Finally, in the cases with less than 40 calculation points, f_c is changed to $f_c = 2.0$ to widen the influence of the neighbouring points. Generally, R^2 was above 0.97. The only exceptions are the points describing U at y values near the walls (less than −0.21 m and higher than 0.21 m), where R^2 was around 0.82 (see **Figure 7**(b4)). Closely observing **Figure 3**, the velocity U near the walls drops significantly.

Figure 9 clearly shows that the agreement with the calculated 3D graph decreases with lowering the number of calculated points used for the response surface generation. Nevertheless, the applied simulation points are perfectly predicted in all cases ($R^2 = 1$ even for case C4 with the lowest number of points). However, if the number of used points is low, the agreement in the region between these points is not perfect.

The comparison of k values in **Figure 10** shows that the response surfaces for the cases C0 and C1 are in good agreement with the calculated 3D graph, while some deviation can be observed at the surfaces with a lower number of points (cases C2, C3 and C4).

In addition to the qualitative comparison of the surfaces in **Figure 9**, in **Table 1** a quantitative comparison is shown between the CFD code simulations and the four OSE predictions generated either from all 40 code calculation values (C0 case; see also **Figure 9(b)**), from 19 code simulation values (C1 case; see also **Figure 9(c)**), from 11 code simulation values (C2 case; see also **Figure 9(d)**) and from 5 code simulation values (C4 case; see also **Figure 9(f)**). It can be

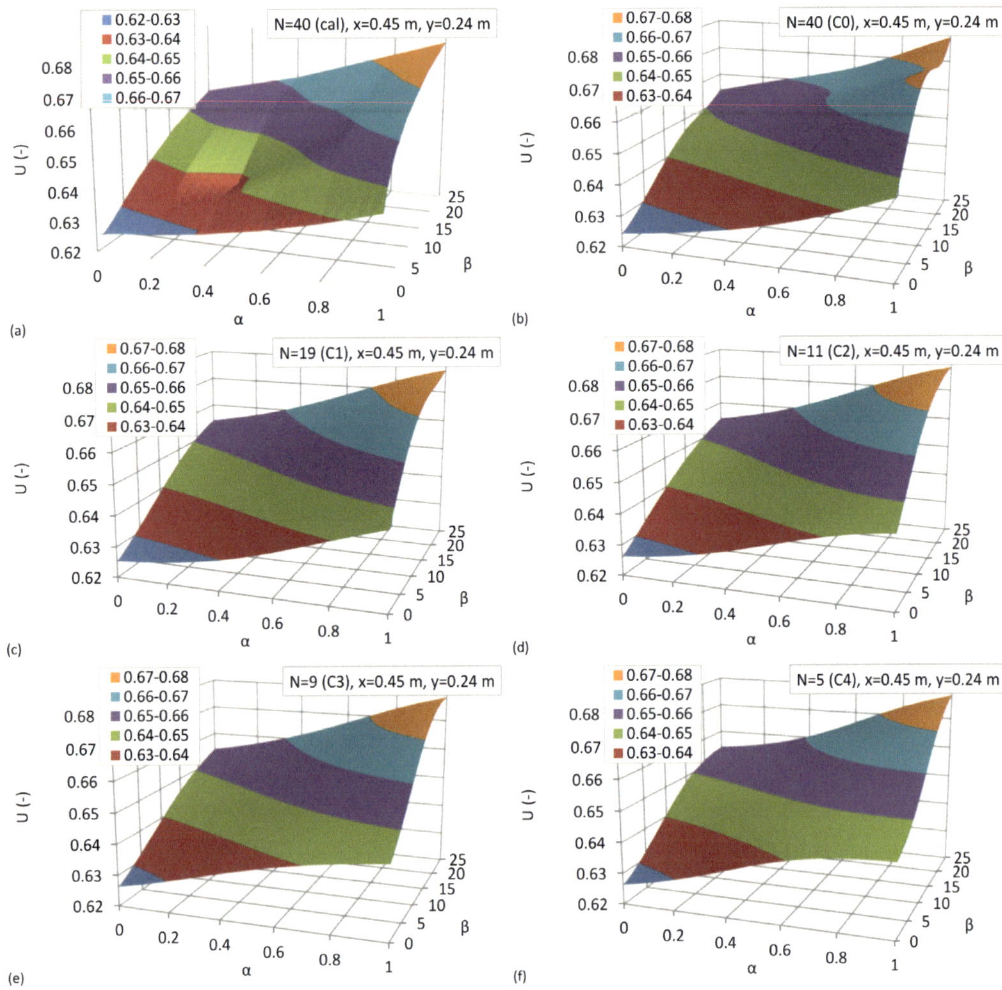

Figure 9. Downstream velocity U dependence on α and β at $x = 0.45$ m and $y = 0.24$ m: (a) NEPTUNE_CFD calculation, (b) C0 by OSE, (c) C1 by OSE, (d) C2 by OSE, (e) C3 by OSE and (f) C4 by OSE.

seen that in the base case, the difference in the downstream velocity is less than 0.4% (0.19% in average). For the C1, C2 and C4 cases, the maximum difference in the downstream velocity is 1.20% (0.23% in average), 1.44% (0.45% in average) and 2.73% (0.76% in average), respectively. Case C3 is not shown in **Table 1**, but the maximum difference is 1.94% (0.61% in average).

The obtained results suggest that in the case when thousands of complex computer code runs are needed for the Monte Carlo statistical analysis, the surrogate model can be used to replace the numerous CFD code simulations. In the case of a lower accuracy of response surface at a certain discrete value, a few additional calculations can be added in the vicinity of this point to better describe the space until a satisfactory agreement is obtained.

http://dx.doi.org/10.5772/intechopen.70564

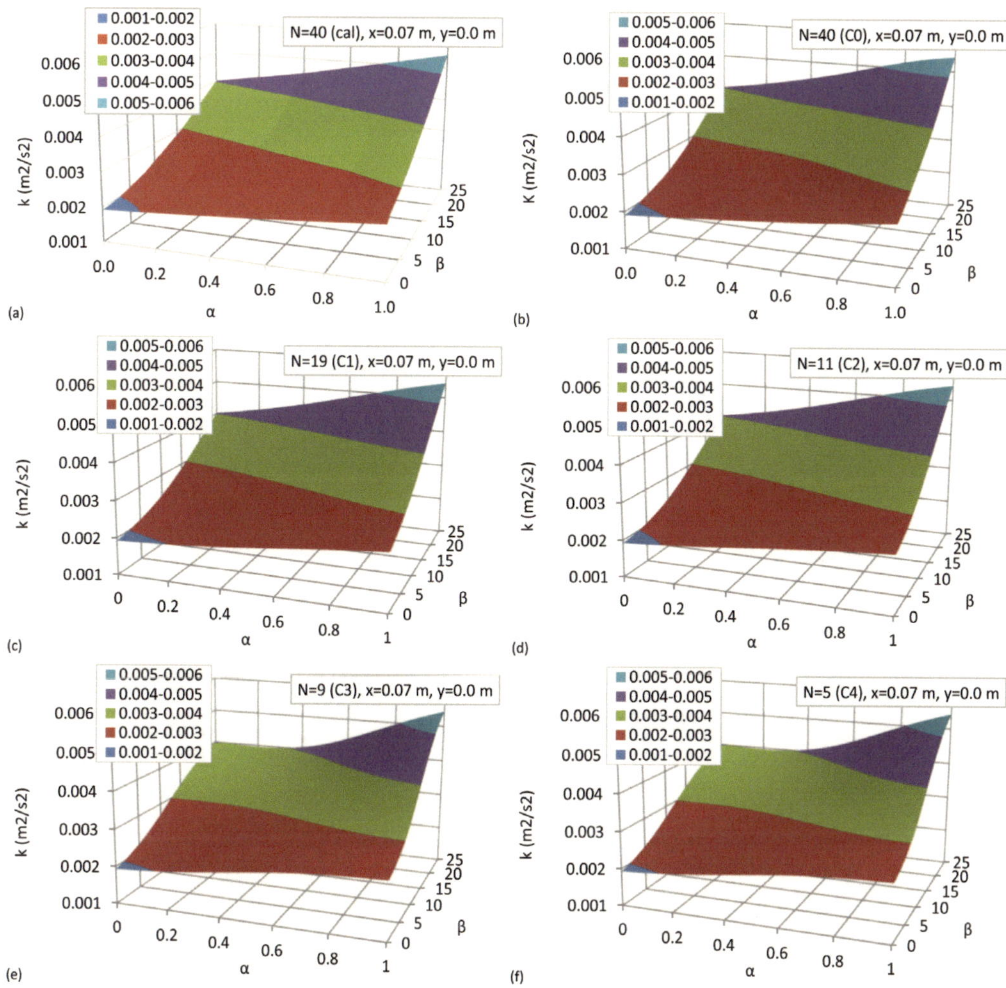

Figure 10. Turbulence kinetic energy k dependence on α and β at x = 0.07 m and y = 0.0 m: (a) NEPTUNE_CFD calculation, (b) C0 by OSE, (c) C1 by OSE, (d) C2 by OSE, (e) C3 by OSE and (f) C4 by OSE.

B(%)/α	**Discrepancy between code-calculated values and OSE values for downstream velocity W**					
	0	**0.2**	**0.4**	**0.6**	**0.8**	**1**
	(a) OSE: C0 case (maximal discrepancy 0.36%)					
0	−0.06%	−0.13%	−0.20%	−0.32%	−0.52%	−0.67%
1	0.06%	0.03%	0.04%	0.09%	0.14%	0.31%
2	0.02%	0.04%	0.08%	0.13%	0.18%	0.36%

B(%)/α	Discrepancy between code-calculated values and OSE values for downstream velocity W					
	0	0.2	0.4	0.6	0.8	1
3	0.03%	0.06%	0.08%	0.10%	0.12%	0.27%
4	0.04%	0.06%	0.05%	0.02%	0.00%	0.12%
8	−0.09%	−0.18%	−1.69%		−0.70%	−0.58%
16	0.10%		−0.04%		−0.03%	0.22%
25	−0.04%		0.03%			−0.06%
	(b) OSE: C1 case (maximal discrepancy −1.20%)					
0	−0.07%	−0.03%	−0.07%	−0.32%	−0.58%	−0.46%
1	0.01%	0.12%	0.19%	0.14%	0.15%	0.55%
2	−0.04%	0.13%	0.26%	0.24%	0.26%	0.65%
3	−0.03%	0.16%	0.30%	0.28%	0.27%	0.61%
4	−0.01%	0.19%	0.32%	0.27%	0.23%	0.51%
8	−0.03%	0.10%	−1.20%		−0.21%	−0.07%
16	−0.04%		−0.10%		−0.34%	−0.11%
25	0.02%		0.05%			0.08%
	(c) OSE: C2 case (maximal discrepancy 1.44%)					
0	−0.02%	−0.72%	−1.23%	−1.41%	−1.05%	−0.02%
1	0.11%	−0.46%	−0.79%	−0.74%	−0.13%	1.16%
2	0.08%	−0.35%	−0.56%	−0.46%	0.14%	1.38%
3	0.12%	−0.22%	−0.37%	−0.26%	0.29%	1.44%
4	0.16%	−0.10%	−0.21%	−0.12%	0.36%	1.41%
8	0.16%	0.09%	−1.31%		0.15%	0.84%
16	−0.03%		−0.06%		−0.38%	−0.08%
25	0.01%		0.02%			0.03%
	(d) OSE: C4 case (maximal discrepancy 2.73%)					
0	0.00%	−0.42%	−0.98%	−1.33%	−0.98%	0.00%
1	0.37%	0.03%	−0.37%	−0.43%	0.24%	1.53%
2	0.56%	0.28%	−0.01%	0.04%	0.78%	2.09%
3	0.76%	0.52%	0.29%	0.41%	1.17%	2.45%
4	0.93%	0.70%	0.52%	0.68%	1.45%	2.68%
8	1.03%	0.83%	−0.58%		1.67%	2.73%
16	0.09%		0.00%		0.54%	1.17%
25	0.00%		−0.24%			0.00%

Table 1 Discrepancy in percent between code-calculated values and OSE values for downstream velocity U at $x = 0.45$ m and $y = 0$ m: (a) C0 case, (b) C1 case, (c) C2 case and (d) C4 case.

6. Conclusions

The mixing of two horizontal turbulent flows was investigated on the GEMIX experimental case. Two sensitivity parameters were considered as uncertainty variables: inlet velocity profile and inlet turbulence intensity. Both variables were treated as the main uncertain parameters with a certain range of randomly distributed values. The NEPTUNE_CFD code was used to perform a series of parametric CFD calculations, combining different values of turbulence intensity and velocity profile at the inlet. The sensitivity analysis of the NEPTUNE_CFD results shows that the implemented turbulence model predicts a higher dissipation of turbulence kinetic energy than observed in the experiment.

A surrogate method called optimal statistical estimator (OSE) was used to generate the full response surface of the output results from the limited number of input CFD predictions. The output results featured downstream velocity and turbulence kinetic energy profiles at few locations in the mixing region. The study demonstrates the efficiency of the response surface generation by the OSE method. The method is especially convenient when few parameters are varied. In the case of a two-dimensional problem, OSE clearly shows its ability to generate a quality response surface even if only a few calculation points are available. This suggests that in the case when thousands of complex computer code runs are needed for the Monte Carlo statistical analysis, the surrogate model can be used to replace the numerous CFD code simulations.

Acknowledgements

The authors acknowledge the financial support from the Slovenian Research Agency (research core funding No. P2-0026 "Reactor engineering").

Author details

Boštjan Končar, Andrej Prošek* and Matjaž Leskovar

*Address all correspondence to: andrej.prosek@ijs.si

Jožef Stefan Institute, Ljubljana, Slovenia

References

[1] Knio OM, Le Maitre OP. Uncertainty propagation in CFD using polynomial chaos decomposition. Fluid Dynamics Research. 2006;**38**:616-640

[2] Barth T. On the propagation of statistical model parameter uncertainty in CFD calculations. Theoretical and Computational Fluid Dynamics. 2012;**26**:435-457

[3] Lacor C, Dinescu C, Hirsch C, Smirnov S. Implementation of intrusive polynomial chaos in CFD codes and application to 3D Navier-Stokes. Lecture Notes in Computer Science. 2013;**92**:193-223

[4] Badillo A, Kapulla R, Ničeno B. Uncertainty quantification in CFD simulations of isokinetic turbulent mixing layers. In: Proceedings of NURETH-15; Pisa, Italy; 2013. pp. 559.1-559.14

[5] EDF. NEPTUNE_CFD version 2-0-1 Theory Guide; 2013

[6] Prošek A, Mavko B. Evaluating code uncertainty—II: An optimal statistical estimator method to evaluate the uncertainties of calculated time trends. Nuclear Technology. 1999;**126**:186-195

[7] Fokken J, Kapulla R, Galgani G, Schieb O, Pawa K, Prasser HM. LIF-measurements and self-similarity considerations in a stably stratified isokinetic turbulent mixing layer. In: Proceedings of 18. GALA-Fachtagung: Lasermethoden in der Strömungsmesstechnik; Cottbus, Germany; September, 2010

[8] EDF. NEPTUNE_CFD version 2-0-1 User Guide; 2013

[9] Prošek A, Končar B, Leskovar M. Uncertainty analysis of CFD benchmark case using Optimal Statistical Estimator. Nuclear Engineering and Design. 2016; In press (https://doi.org/10.1016/j.nucengdes.2016.12.008)

[10] Grabec I, Sachse W. Automatic modeling of physical phenomena: Application to ultrasonic data. Journal of Applied Physics. 1991;**69**:6233-6244

[11] Prošek A, Končar B, Leskovar M. Uncertainty quantification of NEPTUNE_CFD calculation by optimal statistical estimator method. In: Proceedings of 24th International Conference Nuclear Energy for New Europe—NENE 2015; Portorož, Slovenia; 2015. pp. 202.201-202.208